Communications in Computer and Information Science 1902

Rationale

The CCIS series is devoted to the publication of proceedings of computer science conferences. Its aim is to efficiently disseminate original research results in informatics in printed and electronic form. While the focus is on publication of peer-reviewed full papers presenting mature work, inclusion of reviewed short papers reporting on work in progress is welcome, too. Besides globally relevant meetings with internationally representative program committees guaranteeing a strict peer-reviewing and paper selection process, conferences run by societies or of high regional or national relevance are also considered for publication.

Topics

The topical scope of CCIS spans the entire spectrum of informatics ranging from foundational topics in the theory of computing to information and communications science and technology and a broad variety of interdisciplinary application fields.

Information for Volume Editors and Authors

Publication in CCIS is free of charge. No royalties are paid, however, we offer registered conference participants temporary free access to the online version of the conference proceedings on SpringerLink (http://link.springer.com) by means of an http referrer from the conference website and/or a number of complimentary printed copies, as specified in the official acceptance email of the event.

CCIS proceedings can be published in time for distribution at conferences or as postproceedings, and delivered in the form of printed books and/or electronically as USBs and/or e-content licenses for accessing proceedings at SpringerLink. Furthermore, CCIS proceedings are included in the CCIS electronic book series hosted in the SpringerLink digital library at http://link.springer.com/bookseries/7899. Conferences publishing in CCIS are allowed to use Online Conference Service (OCS) for managing the whole proceedings lifecycle (from submission and reviewing to preparing for publication) free of charge.

Publication process

The language of publication is exclusively English. Authors publishing in CCIS have to sign the Springer CCIS copyright transfer form, however, they are free to use their material published in CCIS for substantially changed, more elaborate subsequent publications elsewhere. For the preparation of the camera-ready papers/files, authors have to strictly adhere to the Springer CCIS Authors' Instructions and are strongly encouraged to use the CCIS LaTeX style files or templates.

Abstracting/Indexing

CCIS is abstracted/indexed in DBLP, Google Scholar, EI-Compendex, Mathematical Reviews, SCImago, Scopus. CCIS volumes are also submitted for the inclusion in ISI Proceedings.

How to start

To start the evaluation of your proposal for inclusion in the CCIS series, please send an e-mail to ccis@springer.com.

Luca Longo
Editor

Explainable Artificial Intelligence

First World Conference, xAI 2023
Lisbon, Portugal, July 26–28, 2023
Proceedings, Part II

Springer

article received at least three reviews from scholars in academia and industry, with 99% of them holding a PhD in an area relevant to the topics of the conference. The general chair of the conference, along with the programme committee chairs, carefully selected the top contributions by ranking articles across several objective criteria and evaluating and triangulating the qualitative feedback left by the 188 international reviewers. The reviewing process was intensive, and it ensured that xAI 2023 adhered to the highest standards of quality. All accepted contributions are included in these proceedings and were invited to give oral presentations. Besides the main technical track, several special tracks were introduced, each proposed and chaired by one or more scholars, to allow the identification of highly innovative areas within the larger field of eXplainable Artificial Intelligence. Special track chairs were encouraged to be innovative in designing their topics to attract relevant scholars worldwide. Similarly, a parallel track was designed to give a chance to scholars to submit novel late-breaking pieces of work that are specific in-progress research studies relevant to xAI, and present them as posters during the main event. A demo track was also organised, providing a mechanism for scholars to demo software prototypes on explainability or real-world applications of explainable AI-based systems. A doctoral consortium was organised, with lectures delivered by renowned scientists to PhD scholars who submitted their doctoral proposals on future research related to eXplainable Artificial Intelligence. A separate programme committee was set up for the late-breaking work, demo and doctoral consortium tracks.

Finally, a panel discussion was held with renowned scholars in xAI and all in all, the 1st World Conference on eXplainable Artificial Intelligence offered a truly multi-disciplinary view while inspiring the attendees to come up with solid recommendations to tackle hot-topic challenges of current technologies built with Artificial Intelligence. As the Monument of the Discoveries, right outside the conference centre, celebrates the Portuguese Age of Discovery during the 15th and 16th centuries, xAI 2023 symbolises a new mechanism for exploring and presenting novel directions for the design of the explainable intelligent systems of the future that are transparent, sustainable and ethical and have a positive impact on humans.

Luca Longo

Organizing Committee

General Chair

Luca Longo   Technological University Dublin, Ireland

Programme Committee Chairs

Francisco Herrera   Granada University, Spain
Javier Del Ser   Tecnalia & University of the Basque Country,
                                      Spain
Luca Longo   Technological University Dublin, Ireland

Doctoral Consortium Chairs

Luis Paulo Reis   University of Porto, Portugal
Sarah Jane Delany   Technological University Dublin, Ireland

Inclusion and Accessibility Chair

Alessandra Sala   Shutterstock, Ireland

Student Support Chair

Federico Cabitza   University of Milano-Bicocca, Italy

Programme Committee

Arianna Agosto   University of Pavia, Italy
Jaumin Ajdari   South East European University, Rep. of
                                      Macedonia
Jose M. Alonso   University of Santiago de Compostela, Spain
Andrea Apicella   Federico II University, Italy
Annalisa Appice   University Aldo Moro of Bari, Italy

Corrado Mencar	University of Bari Aldo Moro, Italy
Fabio Mercorio	University of Milano-Bicocca, Italy
Luis Miralles	Technological University Dublin, Ireland
Sandra Mitrovic	University of Applied Sciences of Southern Switzerland, Switzerland
Rami Mochaourab	RISE Research Institutes of Sweden, Sweden
Jose M. Molina	Universidad Carlos III de Madrid, Spain
Maurizio Mongelli	Consiglio Nazionale delle Ricerche, IEIIT, Italy
Anna Monreale	University of Pisa
Antonio Moreno	Universitat Rovira i Virgili, Spain
Yazan Mualla	Université de Technologie de Belfort-Montbéliard, France
Cataldo Musto	University of Bari, Italy
Grzegorz J. Nalepa	Jagiellonian University, Poland
Axel-Cyrille Ngonga Ngomo	Paderborn University, Germany
Anh Nguyen	University of Wyoming, USA
Ruairi O'Reilly	Munster Technological University, Ireland
D. O'Sullivan	Trinity College Dublin, Ireland
Andrea Omicini	Alma Mater Studiorum, Università di Bologna, Italy
Jeroen Ooge	Katholieke Universiteit Leuven, Belgium
Chun Ouyang	Queensland University of Technology, Australia
Andres Paez	Universidad de los Andes, Colombia
Paolo Pagnottoni	University of Pavia, Italy
Enea Parimbelli	University of Pavia, Italy
Miguel Angel Patricio	Universidad Carlos III de Madrid, Spain
Andrea Pazienza	A3K Srl & NTT DATA SpA, Italy
Michael Pazzani	University of California, San Diego, USA
Felice Andrea Pellegrino	Università degli Studi di Trieste, Italy
Roberto Pellungrini	University of Pisa, Italy
Alan Perotti	CENTAI Institute, Italy
Tiago Pinto	Universidade de Trás-os-Montes e Alto Douro, INESC-TEC, Portugal
Roberto Prevete	University of Naples Federico II, Italy
Ricardo Prudencio	UFPE, Brazil
Santiago Quintana-Amate	Airbus, France
Antonio Rago	Imperial College London, UK
Wael Rashwan	Technological University Dublin, Ireland
Bujar Raufi	Technological University Dublin, Ireland
Oliver Ray	University of Bristol, UK
Luis Paulo Reis	APPIA, University of Porto/LIACC, Portugal
Alessandro Renda	Università degli Studi di Firenze, Italy

Lucas Rizzo   Technological University Dublin, Ireland
Marcel Robeer   Utrecht University, The Netherlands
Mohammad Rostami   University of Southern California, USA
Araceli Sanchis   Universidad Carlos III de Madrid, Spain
Carsten Schulte   University of Paderborn, Germany
Christin Seifert   University of Marburg, Germany
Pedro Sequeira   SRI International, USA
Edwin Simpson   University of Bristol, UK
Carlos Soares   University of Porto, Portugal
Timo Speith   Universität Bayreuth, Germany
Gregor Stiglic   University of Maribor, Slovenia
Gian Antonio Susto   Università degli Studi di Padova, Italy
Jacek Tabor   Jagiellonian University, Poland
Nava Tintarev   University of Maastricht, The Netherlands
Alberto Tonda   Université Paris-Saclay, France
Alicia Troncoso   Universidad Pablo de Olavide, Spain
Matias Valdenegro-Toro   University of Groningen, The Netherlands
Zita Vale   GECAD - ISEP/IPP, Portugal
Jan Vanthienen   Katholieke Universiteit Leuven, Belgium
Katrien Verbert   Katholieke Universiteit Leuven, Belgium
Gianni Vercelli   University of Genoa, Italy
Giulia Vilone   Technological University Dublin, Ireland
Fabio Vitali   University of Bologna, Italy
Marvin Wright   Leibniz Institute for Prevention Research and
                                         Epidemiology - BIPS & University of Bremen,
                                         Germany
Arjumand Younus   University of Galway, Ireland
Carlos Zednik   Eindhoven University of Technology,
                                         The Netherlands
Bartosz Zieliński   Jagiellonian University, Poland

Acknowledgements

A thank you goes to everyone who helped in the organising committee for the 1st World Conference on eXplainable Artificial Intelligence (xAI 2023). A special thank you goes to the PC chairs, the doctoral committee chairs, the inclusion & accessibility chair and the student support chair. Also special thanks to the keynote speaker, Peter Flach, who, with Paolo Giudici and Grégoire Montavon took part in the conference's interesting panel discussion and provided their lectures during the doctoral consortium. A word of appreciation goes to the organisers of the special tracks, and those who chaired them during the conference. We are grateful to the members of the organisation and the volunteers who helped sort out the logistics and last-minute challenges behind organising such a large conference with great enthusiasm, effort and professionalism. A special thank you goes to the researchers and practitioners who submitted their work and committed to attending the event and turning it into an opportunity to meet and share findings and new avenues of research.

Contents – Part II

Actionable eXplainable AI, Semantics and Explainability, and Explanations for Advice-Giving Systems

Surveys, Benchmarks, Visual Representations and Applications for xAI

Towards the Visualization of Aggregated Class Activation Maps to Analyse the Global Contribution of Class Features

Igor Cherepanov[1]([✉]) [iD], David Sessler[1] [iD], Alex Ulmer[1] [iD],
Hendrik Lücke-Tieke[1] [iD], and Jörn Kohlhammer[1,2] [iD]

[1] Fraunhofer IGD, 64283 Darmstadt, Germany
{igor.cherepanov,david.sessler,alex.ulmer,hendrik.luecke-tieke,
joern.kohlhammer}@igd.fraunhofer.de
[2] Technische Universität Darmstadt, 64289 Darmstadt, Germany

Abstract. Deep learning (DL) models achieve remarkable performance in classification tasks. However, models with high complexity can not be used in many risk-sensitive applications unless a comprehensible explanation is presented. Explainable artificial intelligence (xAI) focuses on the research to explain the decision-making of AI systems like DL. We extend a recent method of Class Activation Maps (CAMs) which visualizes the importance of each feature of a data sample contributing to the classification. In this paper, we aggregate CAMs from multiple samples to show a global explanation of the classification for semantically structured data. The aggregation allows the analyst to make sophisticated assumptions and analyze them with further drill-down visualizations. Our visual representation for the global CAM illustrates the impact of each feature with a square glyph containing two indicators. The color of the square indicates the classification impact of this feature. The size of the filled square describes the variability of the impact between single samples. For interesting features that require further analysis, a detailed view is necessary that provides the distribution of these values. We propose an interactive histogram to filter samples and refine the CAM to show relevant samples only. Our approach allows an analyst to detect important features of high-dimensional data and derive adjustments to the AI model based on our global explanation visualization.

Keywords: Explainable AI · Feature Importance · Visualization

1 Introduction

Machine learning has progressed from simple algorithms to highly complex models. While early approaches could be interpreted easily, new and more sophisticated models are difficult to explain. The architecture of simple models, e.g., decision trees, is comprehensible and its decision-making process can be explained by the decision path in the tree. More recent deep learning (DL) models based neural networks outperform simple models in many areas such as medicine, autonomous robots and vehicles, speech, audio and image processing. These DL models are constructed by many nested and interconnected neurons that are able to identify complex patterns in data. However, just the model performance is not sufficient for risk-sensitive applications. Transparency and trust in the models are considered very important not only for ML developers but also for the domain experts who use these models. Therefore, more attention is put into research on how to explain complex artificial intelligence (AI) approaches. Explainable artificial intelligence (xAI) focuses on techniques and algorithms to provide high-quality interpretable, human-understandable explanations of AI decisions. This builds trust in the models, helps to better understand the models, and allows to evaluate the models by domain experts. Based on this, a higher accuracy and correctness of models is achievable.

The decision explanations can be described locally, providing an explanation for a particular classified sample, as well as globally, describing the importance of the features as a whole. One of these techniques is called class activation map (CAM) and has its origin in image classification. The CAM approach is restricted to convolutional neural networks (CNN) with a global average pooling (GAP) layer after the last convolutional layer and has the advantage of a local explanation that is directly calculated from the trained CNN model. A CAM visualizes the impacting regions of an image that led to the specific classification by linearly combining activation maps (also called feature maps) on the last layer with the weights of the last fully connected layer corresponding to a target class neuron.

We transfer this approach to semantically structured data and extend it to aggregated CAMs with an interactive visualization approach. Semantically structured data has a predefined structure where the order or position of each information unit is fixed. For example, the header information for network packets has a defined structure. Because the data is semantically structured, an aggregation of CAMs is feasible and we can derive global information about the classification. Our approach scales well with high-dimensional data and provides an overview visualization and an interactive histogram to filter relevant parts to improve the analysis.

Our visualization design is based on the established visualization mantra by Shneiderman [49]: "Overview first, zoom and filter, details on demand". The goal is to provide an overview for a global explanation of the features that had a strong or weak impact on the classification for a particular class. This overview is calculated on the basis of the aggregated CAMs. Then, the analyst can select single features that are interesting and view the distribution of impacts for all samples for this feature in a histogram. Finally, the histogram can be interactively used as a filter to exclude or select parts of the CAM samples and show a refined aggregation visualization. The iterative approach of a drill-down can be leveraged to refine a CAM and the underlying patterns it reveals, enabling further examination and analysis. Overall, our contributions are:

1. An aggregation approach for CAMs as a global explanation technique for the classification of semantically structured data.
2. A visualization design to show two key indicators for a fast overview of the global explainability of a class.
3. An interactive approach to filter relevant samples to create a more detailed level of explainability.

2   Related Work

We group the work that is related. We first discuss xAI approaches, before we look at related work that proposes visual techniques.

2.1   Explainable AI

There is a wide range of different methods for xAI [5,37,53]. In this section, we will review the most common methods, that are also intended for a local explanation, and through the extensions can also be used for a global explanation.

One of the established methods is local interpretable model-agnostic explanations (LIME) [44]. This approach builds local surrogate models that are interpretable with the goal to approximate the individual predictions of the underlying complex model. In this approach, new data points are created consisting of perturbed samples and the corresponding predictions of the black box model. These newly generated samples are weighted based on the closeness to the corresponding point. Then LIME trains an interpretable model on this new dataset. Based on this interpretable model, the prediction of the black box model is explained. In this approach, an approximated model is built for the local explanations but it does not have to be a reliable global explanation. Furthermore, LIME indicates the instability of the explanations [4].

Another approach inspired by Shapley [48] applied in cooperative game theory and has been adapted for use in xAI to attribute the contribution of each feature to an individual prediction. The goal of Shapley values is to estimate the contributions to the final model outcome from each feature separately among all possible feature combinations while preserving the sum of contributions being equal to the final outcome. The calculation of Shapley values is only feasible for low-dimensional data. For multi-dimensional data KernelSHAP and TreeSHAP were presented by Lundberg et al. [34] to compute approximated Shapley values. The KernelSHAP is a kernel-based estimation approach for Shapley values inspired by local surrogate models from the aforementioned proposed LIME approach [44]. The TreeSHAP reduces the computational complexity but works only with tree-based ML models such as decision trees, random forests and gradient boosted trees. Based on the work of Lundberg et al. [34] some further modified KernelSHAP variants of this method were proposed [1] which considers feature dependencies in data. These approaches provide impact values for each feature for an individual sample prediction. The global impact is determined also by averaging the absolute Shapley values per feature in the data, similar to our approach. Then the resulting values can be plotted in a bar chart, sorted by decreasing impact. However, the variability among the absolute Shapley values is not considered. Furthermore, the Shapley values of all samples can be visualized in the so-called summary plot, which illustrates the distribution of the Shapley values per feature. In this plot, the y-axis is determined by feature name and the Shapley values of each sample are located on the x-axis. These visualizations are used only to explain the model decisions for one class.

Methods like LIME or SHAP are based on an explanation by learning an interpretable approximated model locally around the prediction. Our approach is based on a method that is extracted directly from the learned model which is applied to CNN models and is called Class Activation Map (CAM) [65]. CAM is an explanation technique used in computer vision to interpret and understand the decisions made by convolutional neural networks (CNNs) using global average pooling (GAP) for image classification tasks. CAM provides a saliency map of impacting regions of an image that contributed most to the prediction of a particular class. The GAP is performed on the convolutional feature maps from the last layer. These resulting values are used as features for a fully-connected layer that produces the desired output layer. We obtain the resulting CAM by summing convolutional feature maps multiplied by the back-projected weights of the output layer. The use of CAM was applied to the time series data [61] as well as to network data [16]. For this type of data, it is meaningful to leave one dimension of the kernels at 1 since the input data samples represent a vector. In work by Cherepanov et al. [16], the CAMs were already aggregated by averaging to analyze the global differences between the network application classes. In their work, network experts were interviewed. They said that a single CAM is simple and intuitive to understand and fits within the alignment of the hexadecimal representation of PCAPs. In this work, we extend the visualization of aggregation and also provide several methods for an analyst to build the resulting CAM for a global explanation.

2.2   Visualization

Information visualization plays a crucial role in assisting, controlling, refining, and comparing for various domain and ML experts at different stages of an ML pipeline [15,20,24,33,46]. From the beginning of this pipeline, these visualization approaches can be used to facilitate the understanding of complex raw data. Visualization of data [59], and data transformation [21], allow experts to gain insight, identify patterns, and uncover relationships [47]. For selecting a fitting algorithm, visualization methods provide a valuable means of comparison. Experts can interactively benchmark the performance of different algorithms, allowing them to make informed decisions based on their specific needs and goals [42,51]. In this way, experts can select the most appropriate algorithm for their tasks, promoting efficient and effective analysis. The information visualization and visual analytics research fields propose a number of approaches that cover these points [13,50]. Furthermore, visualization facilitates the fine-tuning of parameters for various methods. By visually evaluating the impact of different parameter settings on the results, ML experts can optimize the performance of their chosen algorithms [14]. This iterative process empowers users to refine and enhance their models, leading to improved accuracy and reliability. There are also some approaches that visually explain how some ML methods work [58,63,64]. Finally, visualization serves as a means to represent the results of analyses and predictions made by models. It enables domain experts to communicate and comprehend the outcomes and diagnose the model and identify problems effectively as proposed in work by Collaris et al. [17]. Additionally, the integration of xAI techniques into visualization empowers domain analysts to understand the predictions made by models in a transparent and interpretable manner [16,22,52]. This ensures that users can trust and comprehend the decision-making process of the model, enhancing their confidence in the results [13].

In the past heatmaps were mostly used for CAM visualization, hence, we highlight related work from the visualization and machine learning communities. First, we show visualizations for CAMs and then compare them to high-dimensional heatmap visualizations for other application domains. With that, we explain the advantages and shortcomings of these approaches and provide a design rationale based on the findings.

CAMs and their visualization originated from the image classification domain, where the goal is to show which pixels lead to the detection of an object in an image. Therefore, the image is overlaid with a semi-transparent heatmap using a rainbow color map [65]. Orange and red colors show a high recognition rate while purple and blue show no signal. Recent approaches show how these visualizations are used extensively to explain and improve the recognition models [29,39,62]. While this visualization method has its benefits, all of the approaches use a rainbow color map. Research in the visualization and cognition community showed that this color map has a lack of perceptual ordering, often misleading the interpretation [8]. The data domain for CAMs can be normalized to a range around zero, e.g. -1 to $+1$, where -1 is an indicator that this feature does not represent a class and $+1$ is a clear indicator for a class. Research has shown that for this diverging data domain, certain colors are more suitable for human perception [26]. One of these is for example the blue to red color map with a neutral white in the middle. Based on this we adapted our visualization of CAMs. This color map is also often used in high-dimensional heatmap visualization in other research domains [7]. For structured data, multiple approaches have shown a matrix-styled heatmap, highlighting the separation of single features [36]. For such high-dimensional visualizations interactive features like selecting, sorting and filtering are very important [23]. Other works from the visualization community extended the matrix heatmap visualization with additional visual indicators besides color [7,45] or extended it to hexagonal maps [55]. Based on these approaches we used the size of the filled rectangle in a matrix cell to visualize another quantitative value. This improves the fast overview of the data and is beneficial for our use case of aggregated global CAMs as we can also show the variability of the aggregation.

Finally, the interactivity of such an aggregated visualization is important [49]. The user has to be able to focus the analysis on relevant parts of the data and see the raw data to understand the aggregation. We designed the visual-interactive approach based on the established visualization mantra.

Based on the related work we extend the CAM visualization and add new interactive elements to improve the analysis workflow. According to the best of our knowledge, none of the recent approaches aggregate CAMs and visualize them the way we do in this paper.

3   Approach

3.1   Semantically Structured Data

Semantically structured data is a special form of structured data where the order or position of each information unit is fixed. Consequently, it becomes feasible to aggregate local explanations in the form of CAMs for each information unit or feature across multiple samples. One example of this is network traffic data that has a specific protocol header information with a fixed order of units. Images on the contrary are not semantically structured because an object can be at different parts of the image. A difference to structured high-dimensional data is that semantically structured data should not be resorted for the visualization because neighborhood information is lost. Our approach is applicable if the aggregated features with the same semantic have the same position among all samples.

3.2   Technical Background

The CAM technique originated from image classification in the field of computer vision. In the case of images, each pixel is considered as input. The goal of the method is to highlight regions of an image sample that had the highest impact on the classification of the predicted class. The CAMs are extracted from a CNN model. Our approach focuses on semantically structured data in general. Therefore, we process each unit of transformed data as an input to the model. For example, if a sample is represented in bytes, each byte is considered as input. The kernels are not suitable with the second dimension greater than 1. Because the input sample is considered as an 1D vector and not as an image, where the upper and lower neighboring pixels can be related to each other. In the case of an 1D vector, only the neighboring properties in the same axis might be related to each other. For this reason, 1D kernels are applied with different lengths for CNN in our approach. Global average pooling (GAP) is performed on the feature maps from the last convolutional layer. Then, the resulting values after GAP are connected to the final fully-connected layer that produces the desired classification output. This structure allows us to construct a CAM by projecting back the weights of the output layer on the convolutional feature maps. In this way, we calculate the resulting CAM as a sum of all convolutional feature maps of the last convolutional layer multiplied by the weights of the output layer. The calculation of CAM is illustrated in Fig. 1a.

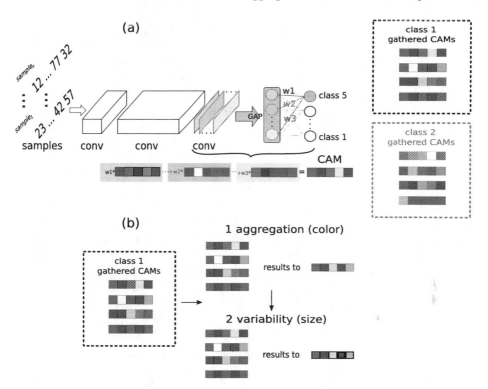

Fig. 1. (a) represents the calculation of a CAM for **the local explanation of a sample**. A CAM is obtained by taking the output of the last convolutional layer of the CNN and applying global average pooling (GAP) to reduce the spatial dimensions of the feature map to a single value per channel. This results in a feature vector that represents the importance of each channel in the final prediction. The feature vector is then passed through a softmax activation to obtain the class probabilities. The weighted sum of the feature maps, where the weights are the class probabilities, is then computed to obtain the final heatmap. (b) represents our approach to **aggregating the CAMs for a specific class**. The result of the aggregation is represented by two indicators. The first one aggregates the impact values for a feature, which is represented by the coloring. For the second the variability is calculated, which is represented by the size of a grid.

3.3 Aggregation of CAMs

The next step is to aggregate the CAMs of each predicted class. A number of CAMs of the same class are collected into an array. The result is a 2D array in which each row represents a CAM (horizontal axis) and each column represents the impact of the feature in a CAM (vertical axis). Our next task is to build an aggregated CAM that represents all these CAMs considering the values of the vertical axis as well as the variability among them. This procedure is shown in Fig. 1b.

We aggregate the values along the vertical axis to describe the importance of each feature with a single value, building the global CAM in the process. For this, we provide multiple methods for the aggregation. The result of these methods can represent different aspects of the impact distribution in the classification analysis. One of these methods is the calculation of the mean which can be used to assess the overall average of the distribution. An alternative method is the median of the CAM values. This serves a similar purpose but is less prone to be influenced by extreme values, that might be outliers. When two or more peaks in the density of the impact distribution exist, methods for calculating the global mode of a density are meaningful. For this, we apply the kernel density estimation method and take the most frequent value of the density [6].

In a potential application, it is reasonable to provide all these aggregation methods since they enable different types of analysis for users. Additionally, we calculate a second indicator that represents the variability of the feature impacts between all CAMs for the individual class. This value is used to assess if the range of the impact values is significantly predominant between all local CAMs of the considered class or the opposite, the values are highly spread out. As the indicator of variability, we implemented and tested variance, standard deviation, entropy, and the Gini coefficient. Before the calculation is applied, we normalize the values to [0, 1] to achieve comparability between the resulting variability values. After the calculation, in the case of variance and standard deviation, the results are normalized again to [0, 1] because the resulting value can be in the range of 0 to 0.25 or 0.5 respectively. This is done to ensure the same value domains for all variability indicators. After testing these four variability measures, we found that the values calculated through entropy spanned the value range more evenly and thus were best suited for our dataset. However, all these variability measures describe different characteristics of variability and therefore should all be included as a user parameter in a potential application.

3.4   Visualization

Getting a better global understanding of CNN model decisions in classification tasks is the main goal of this work. Visualizing numerical and statistical data has proven to enhance the capability of humans to understand complex subjects. This is the reason why visualizing the impact values and their distribution is an essential part of our approach. We utilize visualizations to provide an overview over large amounts of data points while simultaneously allowing the user to detect interesting patterns at a glance. For the visualization of distributions box plots or violin plots are commonly used [27]. However, while these plots work great to display and compare multiple distributions of values, they only work for the comparison of relatively few distributions. Since for our use case, a comparison of a hundred or more distributions is necessary we decided to propose a different solution. To make the visualization scale better for our needs we map the distributions to two indicators, it is aggregation and variability, before visualizing them. Further, we suggest interactive visualizations that reveal additional information about underlying data and its distributions on demand. This

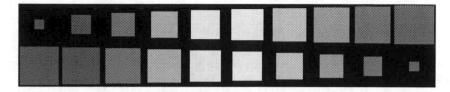

Fig. 2. Overview of visual mapping of the two indicators. The color represents the aggregated feature impact values while the size illustrates the variability of the impact distribution.

allows the analysts to drill-down and explore interesting regions of our explainability approach to gain a more robust understanding of the model behavior. In detail, we start with a visualization of the global aggregated CAMs including their variability values. For this, we transform the long one-dimensional vector of aggregated impact values into lines that we align on top of each other. This results in a structure similar to a text passage in a book where the features are ordered from left to right in a line and the vertical orientation of the lines is from top to bottom. Each grid cell in this visualization contains a square patch that represents two values, the aggregation and the variability, which we presented in the previous Sect. 3.2. We map the aggregated impact value for the feature importance to color. This way, it enables the analysts to efficiently detect patterns or regions in the long vector that are either contributing the most to the prediction of a class or are notable for other reasons. We choose a divergent color map as seen in Fig. 2 which maps features with the highest aggregated values to the color red, the features with the smallest aggregated value to blue, and the ones in the center of the value range to white. This coloring choice clearly indicates the most and least impactful features for the classification while also highlighting features where the model provides mixed results. We also considered classical color maps often used in the machine learning community like jet, viridis and turbo [8,31,43]. We discarded the former because of its issues regarding the brightness profile and the unsuitability for color-blind people. The latter two, while providing a higher distinguishability between values due to the use of a wider range of colors, could not satisfy our need to highlight the values directly in the center of the value range. Therefore, our choice was to implement a diverging color map, that keeps the colors familiar in the machine learning community at the start and the end of the spectrum. This design choice was also motivated by the work of Moreland [38] which reflects on the construction of diverging color maps. The white color in the center of the spectrum represents distributions where blue and red values in the features CAMs have a similar presence or mutually aggregate to a neutral value. Investigating the impact distributions of such mixed cells might yield insights into the prediction mechanisms of the model. The second parameter, the impact variability value, is mapped on the size of the square patch which is centered in each grid cell. An alternative visual representation that we considered for the representation of the impact variability was a bar plot. It supports the comparison of cells that are one-dimensionally orientated. However, we discarded this option because for the alignment of cells in 2D the benefits of a bar plot versus a square representation are mitigated. Further, the bar charts, starting at the bottom of each cell, created visual disorder, especially for the representation of a large amount of aggregated impact values. The centering of the square patches avoids this negative effect (see Fig. 2). It is important to define a minimum size for the squares, to still see the color of the aggregation values represented. This way analysts can inspect the impact values of the feature regardless of their variability. Further, we choose the size of the squares based on their area to accommodate the quadratic interdependency of the side length to area of the squares. This leads to a perceptually intuitive mapping of the numeric values to the visual representation. To display the actual values of the aggregation and variability, a tooltip should be provided, that can be accessed by hovering over one of the grid cells.

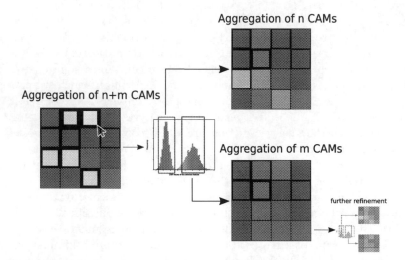

Fig. 3. Visual-interactive drill-down: Clicking on a colored cell in the grid shows the histogram of impact values in this cell. A range selection control allows filtering of the samples that then are used to display a CAM based on the aggregation of the selected subset. This interaction can be iteratively repeated.

Users can interactively select the aggregation and variability measures. This way, they can configure the visualization outputs to their analysis needs. To investigate distributions of interesting impact value aggregations the analysts can click on the corresponding cell. This interaction shows a histogram plot of the aggregated impact values as depicted in Fig. 3. Here, the analysts can explore the distribution characteristics and interactively select regions of the distribution with a range selector control. This interaction can be meaningful for features, where the histogram indicates multiple modes in the impact value distribution. Multiple modes suggest, that the same feature entails different impact indicators which is an interesting case worth analyzing. Selecting a range of the distribution provides a view of a sub-global CAM that has identical visual properties as the initially shown global CAM. This sub-global CAM is aggregated based on the samples that correspond to the selection in the histogram as shown in Fig. 3. Viewing such sub-global CAMs can help the analyst to understand if certain features in this class are not relevant for all samples or on the contrary relevant. The process of drilling down the aggregated CAMs can be iteratively repeated until the displayed CAM is only based on a single sample. Finally, interactive annotations of the inspected cells allow the analysts to mark cells during their exploration of the CAMs. This way, interesting cells can be highlighted, while cells that did not contribute to the understanding of the model could be discarded by marking them as not relevant for the prediction.

4   Usage Scenario

In this usage scenario, we describe how a network domain expert can exploit our proposed approach of aggregated CAMs for global explanations of predicted application classes by a CNN model. The classification of network data has received wide attention both in the scientific community and in the industry. Classifying network data is important for network security, network monitoring and management, traffic analysis, resource optimization, and cost management. Accurate classification of network data provides insights into the nature of network traffic, enabling organizations to ensure network security, optimize network performance, and effectively manage network resources. For this reason, there is a wide variety of approaches for network traffic classification, including solutions based on deep learning [11,40,41,57]. Since certain decisions based on these traffic classifications can be made, an explanation of the predictions is necessary. xAI enables transparency, interpretability, fairness, accountability, and security of AI systems, as well as increases trust from network experts [9,18,25]. Furthermore, through the explanations network experts can verify the correctness and robustness of the model. By incorporating their feedback ML experts can improve the model.

In our scenario, ML experts provide a model for network analysts. The model is based on a CNN architecture that performs best for network traffic data [2, 32]. The applied model has a similar structure as described in previous related work [16,32]. The CNN consists of the following feature map dimensions in the hidden layers: 16, 32, 64, 128, 128, 128 with stride size of 1 and 1D kernel size of 5, followed by GAP and a fully connected layer with the same number of outputs as application classes in the dataset. The CNN model was trained using the categorical cross entropy as loss function and Adam optimizer. The model is trained on the ISCX VPN-nonVPN dataset which is a widely used dataset in network classification research [10,28,60]. This dataset suffers from severe class imbalance, with the FTPS class having a significantly higher number of samples (7872K) compared to the AIM class (only 5K samples). To address this issue, we apply random undersampling to balance the classes [19], aiming to have approximately 5K samples per class, following a similar approach used in the work of Lotfollahi et al. [16,32]. In the data preprocessing phase, the Ethernet header is removed, source and destination IP addresses are masked to 0.0.0.0 and the shorter samples are padded to a fixed size of 1500 bytes [16,32]. We train the model until it achieves solid performance - on the training dataset: F1: 93.4 Recall: 93.5, Precision: 93.7, and on the test dataset F1: 92.8 Recall: 92.8, Precision: 93.0.

Pattern Observation. With the integration of the classification and its explanations in tools similar to Wireshark [12,56], the experts are able to see the impact of each byte for the prediction of an application class. A single CAM illustrates a local explanation of a classification. This explanation is useful for a closer examination of individual network packets. While local explanations provide a finer-grained understanding of the model predictions on individual samples, global explanations generalize to a broader overview of the model behavior. With our approach, we aim to explain a class globally by aggregating the CAMs for a particular class. The global representation allows the analyst to see the differences between the classes and deduce insight from them. The first indicator in our visualization is the color, which tells how many bytes in a PCAP contribute to a class prediction. The second indicator is the size of the square, that reflects the variability of the impact values in the distribution. The average of impact values for the first indicator and for the second entropy are the most representative on the dataset.

The resulting global CAM with our provided visualization allows analysts to easily detect the impact of each feature. The analysis of large red cells is the first step in the global CAM examination, as the analyst first confirms if the system is in line with his expert knowledge about network packets. The patterns represent the significant bytes of the packets of this class. The analyst examines distinct CAMs and starts to identify patterns among the application classes. She observes that certain bytes or byte ranges have different patterns of high-importance features (red cells). In Fig. 4b four patterns of four distinct classes are represented. Some application classes share similar patterns of byte importance, indicating potential similarities in their network traffic behaviors, such as the 10–12th bytes in three classes except the last one (Fig. 4b). These refer to the protocol and header checksum in the IP header. The first information can be quickly verified because specific applications use UDP, while others use TCP protocol. Every verification that an expert can confirm through his knowledge strengthens his confidence in the AI system. It is apparent that also other important bytes in the UDP or TCP header are significant for the classification. Next, the analyst examines the involved bytes in the header which represent the port number. Because they are also significant to the application class the analyst can confirm that the system is correct in this case, which again raises the trust in the system. Now more questionable impact values are analyzed. Certain bytes located at the beginning of payloads are significant for classification as seen in Fig. 4b in the third CAM visualization. This indicates information presenting the header of the corresponding application which is investigated further, by using the distribution histogram to reduce the data to relevant parts. The resulting patterns are analyzed by the expert and provide a comprehensive understanding of the data as well as the behavior of the model. Important features and consequently their data content can be identified and reviewed and specific decisions can be deployed for the network based on the findings.

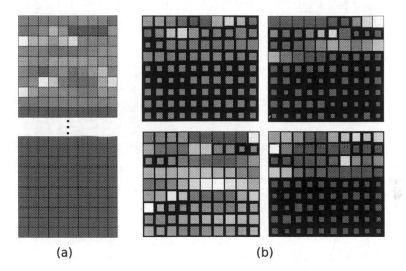

(a) (b)

Fig. 4. (a) A single CAM (10×150 dimensional) that represents a classified PCAP sample, the encrypted part of the CAM is cut out due to the size and irrelevance on classification. (b) Four aggregated CAMs represent distinct application classes of PCAPs. The aggregated CAMs are shortened to a smaller dimension since the encrypted part of PCAPs in the CAMs is always irrelevant for the predictions.

Drill-Down Exploration. For multi-peak impact value distributions, it is useful to refine the aggregated CAMs. Specific impact distributions within a class can potentially cancel out each other through aggregation. Cells that might contain such interference can be identified by the size of the squares. This is because smaller squares indicate a strong variability of impact values between the local CAMs. For example, if a feature of a class is significant in many samples, but, in others, this feature is not relevant for the classification. For instance, this can be information in the header that is not present in all network packages of a class. In this case, the network expert refines a global CAM for a class interactively based on a cell of interest with a smaller square. By selecting this cell it is useful to see the distribution of CAM impact values (see Fig. 5). If the visualization of the CAM values shows multiple modes in the distribution, it is meaningful to separate them from each other. The expert can filter the histogram by selecting a unique mode. The selection of the unique mode provides a uniform distribution of the impact values. In this way, the local explanations are selected where this feature was impacting. This allows the expert to filter out these packets with different impact features and investigate and compare their data content.

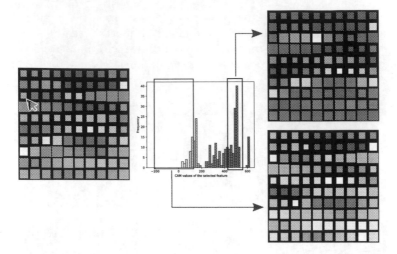

Fig. 5. An expert refines the global CAM for an application class (ICQ) by examining the distribution of impact values by eliminating particular CAMs.

Model Improvement. An individual CAM and aggregated CAMs are valuable in different contexts, and a combination of both provides a more comprehensive understanding of the model's behavior, strengths, and limitations. Using the local CAM as well as the global aggregated CAMs allows analysts to check the expectations of classifications through their expertise. In the process of using the model, its correctness and performance can be verified. In this way, the weaknesses of the classifications can be identified. There are potential weaknesses, such as the difficulty to distinguish certain classes from each other. Particular features of the input data could be misleading, such as the IP address, which is often eliminated from the input so as not to bias it [16,32]. This avoids overfitting, moreover, IP addresses have a high volatility, which would invalidate the model immediately. Furthermore, in the case of encrypted files, it is apparent that including the full 1500 bytes in the classification is not useful since the CAMs show that the encrypted part of the PCAPs is irrelevant for the classification of all PCAPs (see Fig. 4a). Thus, the analyst can keep the model much smaller in terms of the input data and consequently in terms of the total number of model parameters. The constant innovations and changes of the applications can also cause a change in the data characteristics of network traffic, called data drift [3]. When data drift occurs, the model performance may become less accurate or reliable. The explainability that clarifies classifications to an analyst helps to diagnose the reasons for model performance degradation and provides insight into the factors that contribute to data drift. In summary, aggregated CAMs help to diagnose, explain, and evaluate machine learning models, thereby enabling ML experts together with network analysts to maintain the reliability, correctness, and trustworthiness of a model.

5   Discussion and Future Work

Local CAMs provide an explanation of classification for one sample. With our approach, it is possible to aggregate CAMs generalizing a global explainability for each class. Our proposed visualization for the resulting CAM, the significant values are visualized taking into account also the variance among the CAM values for each feature. Our visualization allows a user to quickly discover impacting features in high-dimensional data. The resulting CAMs for each class represent the impacting values. Thus, it is possible to detect the most important features of a class and also to compare the patterns of these classes. However, our approach is limited to the CNN models trained on the semantically structured data, since the position of the features plays a significant role for the aggregation.

A future research direction might be to compare the CAMs with a distance measure. A resulting CAM is a two-dimensional vector, so by the distance measures also the similarities among the CAMs could be calculated. An investigation into which metric would be suitable for this is also interesting. The vectors of a CAM could also be weighted according to the importance of the impacting value or the variance between the values.

The patterns in a CAM may not always be easy to understand, which may prevent the extraction of simple patterns for each class. For example, Fig. 6 illustrates three classes from the UJIIndoorLoc dataset [54], in which the classes are distinguishable in terms of impacting features, however, the patterns appear to be too complex. The patterns have many impact features that are spread in an unstructured way in the aggregated CAM. Such patterns can possibly consist of different interferences in the aggregation caused by multiple modes in the impact distributions. Further, CAM refinement is suitable for this. The illustrated impact features in the global CAM reduce the possible starting points of selection for a CAM refinement. However, this remains as not a simple problem and does not guarantee the best result after a user's modification. It can also happen that the impacting properties are the same in distinct classes because they only show the position in the data and the content in this position must be examined by the user.

It would also be possible to sort the properties according to the feature impact value for further inspection if the data allows such a reordering. That way, correlating features would appear at similar locations, enhancing mental map building within the user, and therefore potentially ease the sense-making process. However, not all data can be sorted in this way. For network data such as PCAPs, each byte is an input into the CNN model and particular segments consist of multiple bytes [35].

There is also an option to use our visualization approach to illustrate the correlation between the impact values of gathered local CAMs. The collection of CAMs represents a matrix (number of impact values x number of CAMs), this collection can also be used to construct a correlation matrix that represents the correlation between the impact values. The correlation matrix would have the size number of impact values x number of impact values. In this way, the correlations between the impact values in the CAMs can be obtained. The correlations

Fig. 6. Aggregated CAMs for three distinct classes of the UJIIndoorLoc dataset [54].

matrix can also be visualized with our proposed visualization where the colors represent the positive or negative correlation value and the size represents the absolute correlation value. The correlation may possibly indicate which features have a synergetic effect on the model behavior.

In our ongoing research, we plan to further advance our proposed approach of aggregated CAMs by integrating it into a practical application that caters to the specific needs of domain experts. NetCapVis [16,56], an application from our previous work is especially suitable for this. There, we already evaluated the visualization of single CAMs for PCAP data with network experts. The results were overwhelmingly positive. We plan to integrate and evaluate our proposed approach with this application to confirm if experts can benefit from the global CAMs and their interactive refinement, allowing the classification to be interpreted and explained. We will seek their perspectives on the usefulness of the explanations in understanding network traffic patterns. Specific aspects that will be evaluated include:

- **Interpretability:** the extent to which the global explanations are understandable and interpretable by network experts, allowing them to gain insights into the underlying factors influencing the classification of different application classes.
- **Relevance:** the relevance of the explanations to the domain knowledge and expertise of the network experts, ensuring that the explanations align with their expectations and provide valuable insights specific to their field.
- **Actionability:** the practical utility of the explanations in enabling the network experts to take proactive actions, such as implementing targeted security measures, refining network configurations, or detecting and mitigating potential security threats effectively. This enables to validate and improve the resulting model by ML experts.
- **Usability:** including its interactivity, we aim to ensure that it provides a seamless and user-friendly experience for network experts.

We also plan to conduct evaluations to measure its potential for enhancing trust, transparency, and accountability in AI systems. For this purpose, we will conduct controlled experiments, field observation and interviews, and performance evaluations [30]. By gathering feedback from network experts, we aim to gain a better understanding of the strengths and weaknesses of our global explanation approach and identify areas for improvement. The insights gained from this evaluation will help us refine our approach to better meet the needs and expectations of domain experts and finally provide an intuitive user-friendly interactive end solution.

6   Conclusion

In this paper, we presented an aggregation approach for CAMs that serves as a global explanation technique for the classification of semantically structured data. Our visualization design provides two key indicators, namely feature impact and variability, allowing for a quick overview of the global explainability of a class. Furthermore, the interactive approach to filter relevant samples enables a more detailed and granular level of explainability, empowering users to delve deeper into the decision-making process of the model. We demonstrated the practical applicability of our approach by presenting a usage scenario with real data on a trained CNN model. Together, these advancements in aggregated CAMs offer a comprehensive and interpretable solution for the global explainability of predictions made by a CNN model, enhancing transparency and trust in its decision-making.

Acknowledgments. This research has been funded by the German Ministry of Education and Research and the Hessian State Ministry for Higher Education, Research, and the Arts as part of their support for the National Research Center for Applied Cybersecurity, ATHENE.

References

1. Aas, K., Jullum, M., Løland, A.: Explaining individual predictions when features are dependent: more accurate approximations to shapley values. Artif. Intell. **298**, 103502 (2021). https://doi.org/10.1016/j.artint.2021.103502
2. Aceto, G., Ciuonzo, D., Montieri, A., Pescapé, A.: Mobile encrypted traffic classification using deep learning: experimental evaluation, lessons learned, and challenges. IEEE Trans. Netw. Serv. Manage. **16**(2), 445–458 (2019). https://doi.org/10.1109/TNSM.2019.2899085
3. Ackerman, S., Raz, O., Zalmanovici, M., Zlotnick, A.: Automatically detecting data drift in machine learning classifiers (2021). https://doi.org/10.48550/arXiv.2111.05672
4. Alvarez-Melis, D., Jaakkola, T.S.: On the robustness of interpretability methods. CoRR abs/1806.08049 (2018). http://arxiv.org/abs/1806.08049
5. Angelov, P.P., Soares, E.A., Jiang, R., Arnold, N.I., Atkinson, P.M.: Explainable artificial intelligence: an analytical review. WIREs Data Min. Knowl. Discov. **11**(5), e1424 (2021). https://doi.org/10.1002/widm.1424
6. Arias-Castro, E., Qiao, W., Zheng, L.: Estimation of the global mode of a density: minimaxity, adaptation, and computational complexity. Electron. J. Stat. **16**(1), 2774–2795 (2022). https://doi.org/10.1214/21-EJS1972

7. Blumenschein, M., et al.: SmartExplore: simplifying high-dimensional data analysis through a table-based visual analytics approach. In: 2018 IEEE Conference on Visual Analytics Science and Technology (VAST), pp. 36–47. IEEE (2018). https://doi.org/10.1109/VAST.2018.8802486

8. Borland, D., Taylor Ii, R.M.: Rainbow color map (still) considered harmful. IEEE Comput. Graphics Appl. **27**(2), 14–17 (2007). https://doi.org/10.1109/MCG.2007.323435

9. Burkart, N., Huber, M.F.: A survey on the explainability of supervised machine learning. J. Artif. Intell. Res. **70**, 245–317 (2021). https://doi.org/10.1613/jair.1.12228

10. Canadian Institute for Cybersecurity: VPN-nonVPN dataset (2015). https://www.unb.ca/cic/datasets/vpn.html

11. Cao, Z., Xiong, G., Zhao, Y., Li, Z., Guo, L.: A survey on encrypted traffic classification. In: Batten, L., Li, G., Niu, W., Warren, M. (eds.) ATIS 2014. CCIS, vol. 490, pp. 73–81. Springer, Heidelberg (2014). https://doi.org/10.1007/978-3-662-45670-5_8

12. Chappell, L., Combs, G.: Wireshark network analysis: the official Wireshark certified network analyst study guide. Protocol Analysis Institute, Chappell University (2010)

13. Chatzimparmpas, A., Martins, R.M., Jusufi, I., Kucher, K., Rossi, F., Kerren, A.: The state of the art in enhancing trust in machine learning models with the use of visualizations. Comput. Graph. Forum **39**(3), 713–756 (2020). https://doi.org/10.1111/cgf.14034

14. Chatzimparmpas, A., Martins, R.M., Kucher, K., Kerren, A.: VisEvol: visual analytics to support hyperparameter search through evolutionary optimization. Comput. Graph. Forum **40**(3), 201–214 (2021). https://doi.org/10.1111/cgf.14300

15. Chatzimparmpas, A., Martins, R.M., Jusufi, I., Kerren, A.: A survey of surveys on the use of visualization for interpreting machine learning models. Inf. Vis. **19**(3), 207–233 (2020). https://doi.org/10.1177/1473871620904671

16. Cherepanov, I., Ulmer, A., Joewono, J.G., Kohlhammer, J.: Visualization of class activation maps to explain AI classification of network packet captures. In: 2022 IEEE Symposium on Visualization for Cyber Security (VizSec), pp. 1–11 (2022). https://doi.org/10.1109/VizSec56996.2022.9941392

17. Collaris, D., van Wijk, J.J.: ExplainExplore: visual exploration of machine learning explanations. In: 2020 IEEE Pacific Visualization Symposium (PacificVis), pp. 26–35 (2020). https://doi.org/10.1109/PacificVis48177.2020.7090

18. Das, A., Rad, P.: Opportunities and challenges in explainable artificial intelligence (XAI): a survey (2020). https://doi.org/10.48550/arXiv.2006.11371

19. Devi, D., Biswas, S.K., Purkayastha, B.: A review on solution to class imbalance problem: undersampling approaches. In: 2020 International Conference on Computational Performance Evaluation (ComPE), pp. 626–631 (2020). https://doi.org/10.1109/ComPE49325.2020.9200087

20. Endert, A., et al.: The state of the art in integrating machine learning into visual analytics. Comput. Graph. Forum **36**(8), 458–486 (2017). https://doi.org/10.1111/cgf.13092

21. Espadoto, M., Martins, R.M., Kerren, A., Hirata, N.S.T., Telea, A.C.: Toward a quantitative survey of dimension reduction techniques. IEEE Trans. Visual Comput. Graph. **27**(3), 2153–2173 (2021). https://doi.org/10.1109/TVCG.2019.2944182

22. Feng, S., Boyd-Graber, J.: What can AI do for me? Evaluating machine learning interpretations in cooperative play. In: Proceedings of the 24th International Conference on Intelligent User Interfaces, IUI 2019, pp. 229–239. Association for Computing Machinery, New York (2019). https://doi.org/10.1145/3301275.3302265

23. Fernandez, N.F., et al.: Clustergrammer, a web-based heatmap visualization and analysis tool for high-dimensional biological data. Sci. Data **4**(1), 1–12 (2017). https://doi.org/10.1038/sdata.2017.151

24. Gillies, M., et al.: Human-centred machine learning. In: Proceedings of the 2016 CHI Conference Extended Abstracts on Human Factors in Computing Systems, CHI EA 2016, pp. 3558–3565. Association for Computing Machinery, New York (2016). https://doi.org/10.1145/2851581.2856492

25. Gunning, D., Stefik, M., Choi, J., Miller, T., Stumpf, S., Yang, G.Z.: XAI-explainable artificial intelligence. Sci. Robot. **4**(37), eaay7120 (2019). https://doi.org/10.1126/scirobotics.aay7120

26. Harrower, M., Brewer, C.A.: ColorBrewer.org: an online tool for selecting colour schemes for maps. Cartogr. J. **40**(1), 27–37 (2003). https://doi.org/10.1179/000870403235002042

27. Hintze, J.L., Nelson, R.D.: Violin plots: a box plot-density trace synergism. Am. Stat. **52**(2), 181–184 (1998). https://doi.org/10.1080/00031305.1998.10480559

28. Iliyasu, A.S., Deng, H.: Semi-supervised encrypted traffic classification with deep convolutional generative adversarial networks. IEEE Access **8**, 118–126 (2020). https://doi.org/10.1109/ACCESS.2019.2962106

29. Jiang, P.T., Zhang, C.B., Hou, Q., Cheng, M.M., Wei, Y.: LayerCAM: exploring hierarchical class activation maps for localization. IEEE Trans. Image Process. **30**, 5875–5888 (2021). https://doi.org/10.1109/TIP.2021.3089943

30. Lam, H., Bertini, E., Isenberg, P., Plaisant, C., Carpendale, S.: Empirical studies in information visualization: seven scenarios. IEEE Trans. Visual Comput. Graph. **18**(9), 1520–1536 (2012). https://doi.org/10.1109/TVCG.2011.279

31. Liu, Y., Heer, J.: Somewhere over the rainbow: an empirical assessment of quantitative colormaps. In: Proceedings of the 2018 CHI Conference on Human Factors in Computing Systems, CHI 2018, pp. 1–12. Association for Computing Machinery, New York (2018). https://doi.org/10.1145/3173574.3174172

32. Lotfollahi, M., Jafari Siavoshani, M., Shirali Hossein Zade, R., Saberian, M.: Deep packet: a novel approach for encrypted traffic classification using deep learning. Soft. Comput. **24**(3), 1999–2012 (2019). https://doi.org/10.1007/s00500-019-04030-2

33. Lu, J., et al.: Recent progress and trends in predictive visual analytics. Front. Comp. Sci. **11**(2), 192–207 (2016). https://doi.org/10.1007/s11704-016-6028-y

34. Lundberg, S.M., Lee, S.I.: A unified approach to interpreting model predictions. In: Guyon, I., et al. (eds.) Advances in Neural Information Processing Systems. vol. 30. Curran Associates, Inc. (2017). https://proceedings.neurips.cc/paper_files/paper/2017/file/8a20a8621978632d76c43dfd28b67767-Paper.pdf

35. Mandl, P.: TCP und UDP Internals. Springer, Heidelberg (2018). https://doi.org/10.1007/978-3-658-20149-4

36. Metsalu, T., Vilo, J.: Clustvis: a web tool for visualizing clustering of multivariate data using principal component analysis and heatmap. Nucleic Acids Res. **43**(Webserver-Issue), W566–W570 (2015). https://doi.org/10.1093/nar/gkv468

37. Molnar, C.: Interpretable Machine Learning, 2 edn. (2022). https://christophm.github.io/interpretable-ml-book

38. Moreland, K.D.: Diverging color maps for scientific visualization (expanded). Technical report, Sandia National Lab. (SNL-NM), Albuquerque, NM, USA (2009)

39. Muhammad, M.B., Yeasin, M.: Eigen-CAM: class activation map using principal components. In: 2020 International Joint Conference on Neural Networks (IJCNN), pp. 1–7 (2020). https://doi.org/10.1109/IJCNN48605.2020.9206626
40. Nguyen, T.T., Armitage, G.: A survey of techniques for internet traffic classification using machine learning. IEEE Commun. Surv. Tutor. **10**(4), 56–76 (2008). https://doi.org/10.1109/SURV.2008.080406
41. Pacheco, F., Exposito, E., Gineste, M., Baudoin, C., Aguilar, J.: Towards the deployment of machine learning solutions in network traffic classification: a systematic survey. IEEE Commun. Surv. Tutor. **21**(2), 1988–2014 (2019). https://doi.org/10.1109/COMST.2018.2883147
42. Park, C., Lee, J., Han, H., Lee, K.: ComDia+: an interactive visual analytics system for comparing, diagnosing, and improving multiclass classifiers. In: 2019 IEEE Pacific Visualization Symposium (PacificVis), pp. 313–317 (2019). https://doi.org/10.1109/PacificVis.2019.00044
43. Reda, K., Szafir, D.A.: Rainbows revisited: modeling effective colormap design for graphical inference. IEEE Trans. Visual Comput. Graph. **27**(2), 1032–1042 (2021). https://doi.org/10.1109/TVCG.2020.3030439
44. Ribeiro, M.T., Singh, S., Guestrin, C.: "Why should i trust you?": explaining the predictions of any classifier. In: Proceedings of the 22nd ACM SIGKDD International Conference on Knowledge Discovery and Data Mining, KDD 2016, pp. 1135–1144. Association for Computing Machinery, New York (2016). https://doi.org/10.1145/2939672.2939778
45. Ruppert, T., Bernard, J., Ulmer, A., Lücke-Tieke, H., Kohlhammer, J.: Visual access to an agent-based simulation model to support political decision making. In: 14th International Conference on Knowledge Management and Data-driven Business, I-KNOW 2014, Graz, Austria, 16–19 September 2014, pp. 16:1–16:8 (2014). https://doi.org/10.1145/2637748.2638410
46. Sacha, D., et al.: What you see is what you can change: human-centered machine learning by interactive visualization. Neurocomputing **268**, 164–175 (2017). https://doi.org/10.1016/j.neucom.2017.01.105. Advances in artificial neural networks, machine learning and computational intelligence
47. Sacha, D., et al.: Visual interaction with dimensionality reduction: a structured literature analysis. IEEE Trans. Visual Comput. Graph. **23**(1), 241–250 (2017). https://doi.org/10.1109/TVCG.2016.2598495
48. Shapley, L.S.: Notes on the n-person game-II: the value of an N-person game. (1951). Lloyd S Shapley (1951)
49. Shneiderman, B.: The eyes have it: a task by data type taxonomy for information visualizations. In: Proceedings of the 1996 IEEE Symposium on Visual Languages, Boulder, Colorado, USA, 3–6 September 1996, pp. 336–343 (1996). https://doi.org/10.1109/VL.1996.545307
50. Sperrle, F., et al.: A survey of human-centered evaluations in human-centered machine learning. Comput. Graph. Forum **40**(3), 543–568 (2021). https://doi.org/10.1111/cgf.14329
51. Sperrle, F., Schäfer, H., Keim, D., El-Assady, M.: Learning contextualized user preferences for co-adaptive guidance in mixed-initiative topic model refinement. Comput. Graph. Forum **40**(3), 215–226 (2021). https://doi.org/10.1111/cgf.14301
52. Spinner, T., Schlegel, U., Schäfer, H., El-Assady, M.: explAIner: a visual analytics framework for interactive and explainable machine learning. IEEE Trans. Visual Comput. Graphics **26**(1), 1064–1074 (2020). https://doi.org/10.1109/TVCG.2019.2934629

53. Tjoa, E., Guan, C.: A survey on explainable artificial intelligence (XAI): toward medical XAI. IEEE Trans. Neural Netw. Learn. Syst. **32**(11), 4793–4813 (2021). https://doi.org/10.1109/TNNLS.2020.3027314
54. Torres-Sospedra, J., et al.: UJIIndoorLoc: a new multi-building and multi-floor database for WLAN fingerprint-based indoor localization problems. In: 2014 International Conference on Indoor Positioning and Indoor Navigation (IPIN), pp. 261–270 (2014). https://doi.org/10.1109/IPIN.2014.7275492
55. Trautner, T.B., Sbardellati, M., Stoppel, S., Bruckner, S.: Honeycomb plots: visual enhancements for hexagonal maps (2022)
56. Ulmer, A., Sessler, D., Kohlhammer, J.: NetCapVis: web-based progressive visual analytics for network packet captures. In: 2019 IEEE Symposium on Visualization for Cyber Security (VizSec), pp. 1–10 (2019). https://doi.org/10.1109/VizSec48167.2019.9161633
57. Velan, P., Čermák, M., Čeleda, P., Drašar, M.: A survey of methods for encrypted traffic classification and analysis. Int. J. Netw. Manage **25**(5), 355–374 (2015). https://doi.org/10.1002/nem.1901
58. Vig, J.: A multiscale visualization of attention in the transformer model. In: Proceedings of the 57th Annual Meeting of the Association for Computational Linguistics: System Demonstrations, pp. 37–42. Association for Computational Linguistics, Florence (2019). https://doi.org/10.18653/v1/P19-3007
59. Wang, J., Hazarika, S., Li, C., Shen, H.W.: Visualization and visual analysis of ensemble data: a survey. IEEE Trans. Visual Comput. Graph. **25**(9), 2853–2872 (2019). https://doi.org/10.1109/TVCG.2018.2853721
60. Wang, W., Zhu, M., Wang, J., Zeng, X., Yang, Z.: End-to-end encrypted traffic classification with one-dimensional convolution neural networks. In: 2017 IEEE International Conference on Intelligence and Security Informatics (ISI), pp. 43–48. IEEE (2017). https://doi.org/10.1109/ISI.2017.8004872
61. Wang, Z., Yan, W., Oates, T.: Time series classification from scratch with deep neural networks: a strong baseline. In: 2017 International Joint Conference on Neural Networks (IJCNN), pp. 1578–1585 (2017). https://doi.org/10.1109/IJCNN.2017.7966039
62. Yang, W., Huang, H., Zhang, Z., Chen, X., Huang, K., Zhang, S.: Towards rich feature discovery with class activation maps augmentation for person re-identification. In: Proceedings of the IEEE/CVF Conference on Computer Vision and Pattern Recognition, pp. 1389–1398 (2019)
63. Yu, R., Shi, L.: A user-based taxonomy for deep learning visualization. Visual Inform. **2**(3), 147–154 (2018). https://doi.org/10.1016/j.visinf.2018.09.001
64. Zhang, J., Wang, Y., Molino, P., Li, L., Ebert, D.S.: Manifold: a model-agnostic framework for interpretation and diagnosis of machine learning models. IEEE Trans. Visual Comput. Graph. **25**(1), 364–373 (2019). https://doi.org/10.1109/TVCG.2018.2864499
65. Zhou, B., Khosla, A., Lapedriza, À., Oliva, A., Torralba, A.: Learning deep features for discriminative localization. CoRR abs/1512.04150 (2015). http://arxiv.org/abs/1512.04150

Natural Example-Based Explainability:
A Survey

Antonin Poché[1,2]([✉]), Lucas Hervier[1,2], and Mohamed-Chafik Bakkay[1,2]

[1] IRT Saint Exupéry, Toulouse, France
{antonin.poche,lucas.hervier,mohamed-chafik.bakkay}@irt-saintexupery.com
[2] IRT SystemX, 2 boulevard Thomas Gobert, 91120 Palaiseau, France
{antonin.poche,lucas.hervier,mohamed-chafik.bakkay}@irt-systemx.fr

Abstract. Explainable Artificial Intelligence (XAI) has become increasingly significant for improving the interpretability and trustworthiness of machine learning models. While saliency maps have stolen the show for the last few years in the XAI field, their ability to reflect models' internal processes has been questioned. Although less in the spotlight, example-based XAI methods have continued to improve. It encompasses methods that use examples as explanations for a machine learning model's predictions. This aligns with the psychological mechanisms of human reasoning and makes example-based explanations natural and intuitive for users to understand. Indeed, humans learn and reason by forming mental representations of concepts based on examples.

This paper provides an overview of the state-of-the-art in natural example-based XAI, describing the pros and cons of each approach. A "natural" example simply means that it is directly drawn from the training data without involving any generative process. The exclusion of methods that require generating examples is justified by the need for plausibility which is in some regards required to gain a user's trust. Consequently, this paper will explore the following family of methods: similar examples, counterfactual and semi-factual, influential instances, prototypes, and concepts. In particular, it will compare their semantic definition, their cognitive impact, and added values. We hope it will encourage and facilitate future work on natural example-based XAI.

Keywords: Explainability · XAI · Survey · Example-based · Case-based · Counterfactuals · Semi-factuals · Influence Functions · Prototypes · Concepts

1 Introduction

With the ever-growing complexity of machine learning models and their large diffusion, understanding models' decisions and behavior became a necessity. Therefore, explainable artificial intelligence (XAI), the field that aims to understand

---

A. Poché and L. Hervier—These authors contributed equally to this work.

© The Author(s), under exclusive license to Springer Nature Switzerland AG 2023
L. Longo (Ed.): xAI 2023, CCIS 1902, pp. 24–47, 2023.
https://doi.org/10.1007/978-3-031-44067-0_2

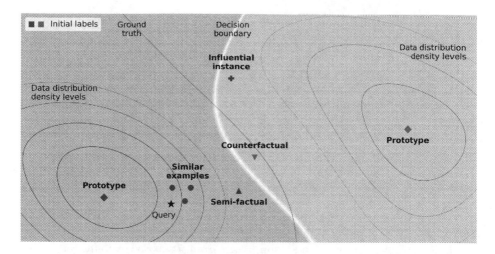

Fig. 1. Natural example-based explanation formats with respect to the query and the decision boundary. We can see similar examples are the closest elements to the query, while counterfactuals and semi-factuals are on either side of the point of the decision boundary the closest to the query. Prototypes are representative of each class in a dense zone of the dataset and the influential instance bends the decision boundary.

and clarify models, flourished with a huge diversity of methods. Several taxonomies have been proposed to differentiate between methods, with common components identified [2,4,50]: i) Local vs global: Local methods explain specific model decisions (in this case, the model's input is called the studied sample or query), while global methods provide insight into overall model behavior. ii) Post-hoc vs intrinsic vs explainable by-design: Post-hoc methods are applied to trained models, while by-design methods produce inherently explainable models. Intrinsic methods take into account model training without affecting the final state. iii) Black-box vs white-box: White-box methods require access to model weights/gradients. iv) Explanation formats which include: attribution methods [33,104], concepts [35,66], surrogate models [67,96], rule-based explanations [114], natural language explanations [19], dependencies [40,49], and example-based explanations [57,113].

Nonetheless, no matter the taxonomy of a method, its explanations are aimed at humans, hence, they should exploit the vast literature in philosophy, psychology, and cognitive science on how humans generate, understand, and react to explanations [79]. The psychology literature argued that, in everyday life, humans use examples as references to understand, explain something, or demonstrate their arguments [17,32,38,79,100]. Afterward, through user studies in the XAI field [35,51,61], researchers validated that example-based explainability provides better explanations over several other formats where example-based XAI corresponds to a family of methods where explanations are represented by or communicated through samples, or part of samples like crops.

However, previous surveying works on example-based XAI are either cursory as they survey XAI in general [2,4] or focus on a specific subset such as factual methods [26, 28, 102] or contrastive explanations [59, 84, 113]. In fact, example-based explainability can be divided into several sub-formats with many similarities. As such, covering them together allows conclusions from sub-fields of the literature to serve one another. Thus, we believe a single work thoroughly mapping, describing, and analyzing each example-based XAI sub-format will benefit the field. Besides, this survey will only cover natural example-based explainability methods – *i.e* methods where examples are training samples and are not generated. Indeed, to generate high-dimensional data points, methods essentially rely on deep neural networks [6, 62]. Nevertheless, for most high dimensional data, such approaches fail to ensure that generated examples are plausible and belong to the manifold (subspace of the input space where samples follow the data distribution), and examples need to be realistic for humans to interpret them [18]. Therefore, natural examples have two advantages, they do not use a model to explain another model which eases their acceptance, and natural examples are plausible by definition. In addition, apart from formats with only generative methods (such as feature visualizations [91]), we do not set aside any formats of example-based XAI as they may all bring new perspectives to others. Lastly, to navigate through the different formats we use the semantic definition of each format as it highlights the differences between formats. In some cases, examples from different formats may be the same sample, hence, clear semantic definitions are necessary to interpret examples.

Explanations in example-based explainability are all data points but there exist different semantic meanings to a given example. Depending on the relation between the example, the query, and the model, the information provided by the example will differ. The semantic definition of an example and the kind of insight it provides divide the example-based format into sub-groups, which are presented in Fig. 1. This overview is organized around those sub-groups (also called formats), this work will unfold as follows:

The first format is **similar examples** (or factuals) (Sect. 2), for the model, they are the closest elements to the query. Factuals give confidence in the prediction or explain misclassification, but they are limited to the close range of the considered sample. To provide insight into the model behavior on a larger zone around the query, **counterfactuals** and **semi-factuals** (Sects. 3.1 and 3.2) are more adapted. They are respectively the closest and the farthest samples on which the model makes a different and similar prediction. They are mainly used in classification, give insight into the decision boundary, and are complementary if paired. While they give an idea of the limit, they do not provide insights on how one could bend the decision boundaries of the model by altering the training data. This is addressed through **influential instances** (Sect. 4), the training samples with the highest impact on the model's state. In addition, contrary to previously listed example-based formats, influential instances are not limited to local explanations. Indeed, one can extract the most influential instances for the model in general. Another global explanation format is **Prototypes** (Sect. 5), which are a set of samples representative of either the dataset or a class. Most of the time they are selected without relying on the model and give an overview of the dataset, but some models are designed through prototypes, thus explainable by design. **Concepts** (Sect. 6), a closely-related format, is also investigated. A concept is the abstraction of the common elements between samples – e.g. for trees, the concepts could be trunk, branch, and leaf. To communicate such concepts, if they are not labeled, the easiest way is through examples of such concepts (often part of samples such as patches).

Thus we could summarize the contributions of this paper as follows: i) To the best of our knowledge, we are the first to compile natural example-based explainability literature in a survey. Previous works either covered the whole XAI literature with a superficial analysis of example-based XAI or focused on a given sub-format of example-based XAI. ii) For each format we provide simple definitions, semantic meaning, key methods, their comparison, their pros and cons, and examples, and pros and cons. We additionally ground formats into social sciences and depict their cognitive added values when possible. iii) We explore, classify, and describe available methods in each natural example-based XAI format. We highlight common points and divergences for the reader to understand each method easily, with a focus on key methods (see Table 1)

1.1 Notations

Throughout the paper, methods will explain a machine learning model $h : \mathcal{X} \to \mathcal{Y}$, with $\mathcal{X}$ and $\mathcal{Y}$ being respectively the input and output domain. Especially, this model is parameterized by the weights $\theta \in \Theta \subseteq \mathbb{R}^d$. If not specified otherwise, h is trained on a training dataset $\mathcal{D}_{train} \subset (\mathcal{X} \times \mathcal{Y})$ of size n with the help of a loss function $l : (\mathcal{X}, \mathcal{Y}, \Theta) \to \mathbb{R}$. We denote a sample by the tuple $z = (x, y)| \quad x \in \mathcal{X}, y \in \mathcal{Y}$. When an index subscript as i or j is added, e.g. z_i, it is assumed that z_i belongs to the training dataset. If the subscript "test" is added, z_{test}, the sample does not belong to the training data. When there is no subscript, the sample can either be or not in the training data. Finally, the empirical risk function is denoted as $\mathcal{L}(\theta) := \frac{1}{n} \sum_{(x,y) \in \mathcal{D}_{train}} l(x, y, \theta) = \frac{1}{n} \sum_{z_j \in \mathcal{D}_{train}} l(z_j, \theta)$, the parameters that minimized this empirical risk as $\theta^* := \arg\min_\theta \mathcal{L}(\theta)$ and an estimator of θ^* is denoted $\hat{\theta}$.

2 Similar Examples

In the XAI literature, similar examples, also referred to as factuals (see Fig. 2), are often used as a way to provide intuitive and interpretable explanations. The core idea is to retrieve the most similar, or the closest, elements in the training set to a sample under investigation z_{test} and to use them as a way to explain a model's output. Specifically, Case-Based Reasoning (CBR) is of particular interest as it mimics the way humans draw upon past experiences to navigate novel situations [38, 100]. For example, when learning to play a new video game, individuals do not typically begin from a complete novice level. Instead, they rely on their pre-existing knowledge and skills in manipulating game controllers and draw upon past experiences with similar video games to adapt and apply strategies that have been successful in the past. As described by Aamodt and Plaza [1], a typical CBR cycle can be delineated by four fundamental procedures: i) RETRIEVE: Searching for the most analogous case or cases, ii) REUSE: Employing the information and expertise extracted from that case to address the problem, iii) REVISE: Modifying the proposed solution as necessary, iv) RETAIN: Preserving the pertinent aspects of this encounter that could be beneficial for future problem-solving endeavors. In addition to being intuitive, the cases retrieved by a CBR system for a given prediction are natural explanations for this output.

While CBR systems are a must-know in the XAI literature, we will not review them as they have already been well analyzed, reviewed, motivated, and described many times [26,28,102]. Instead, the focus here is on case-based explanations (CBE) [102]. CBE are methods that use CBR to explain other systems, also referred to as twin systems [57,60]. In particular, explanations of the system under inspection are generally the outcomes of the RETRIEVE functionality of the twinned CBR system, which oftentimes relies on k-nearest neighbor (k-NN) retrieval [24]. The idea behind k-NN is to retrieve the k most similar training samples (cases) to a test sample z_{test}.

2.1   Factual Methods

One of the main challenges with CBE methods is to define similarity. Indeed, there are many ways of defining similarity measures, and different approaches are appropriate for different representations of a training sample [28]. Generally, CBR systems assume that similar input features are likely to produce similar outcomes. Thus, using a distance metric defined on those input features engenders a similarity measure: the closer the more similar they are. One of the simplest is the unweighted Euclidean distance:

$$dist(z, z') = ||x - x'||_2 \quad | \quad z = (x, y) \in (\mathcal{X} \times \mathcal{Y}) \tag{1}$$

However, **where** – *i.e.* in which space – the distance is computed does have major implications. As pointed out by Hanawa *et al.* [46], the input space does not seem to bring pieces of information on the internal working of the model under inspection but provides more of a data-centric analysis. Thus, recent methods rely instead on either computing the distance in a latent space or weighting features for the k-NN algorithm [31].

Computing distance in a latent space is one possibility to include the model in the similarity measure which is of utmost importance if we want to explain it, as pointed out by Caruana *et al.* [20]. Consequently, they suggested applying the Euclidean distance on the last hidden units h_{-1} of a trained Deep Neural Network (DNN) as a similarity that considers the model's predictions:

$$dist_{DNN}(z, z') = ||h_{-1}(x) - h_{-1}(x')||_2 \quad | \quad z = (x, y) \in (\mathcal{X} \times \mathcal{Y}) \tag{2}$$

Similarly, for convolutional DNN, Papernot and McDaniel [92], and Sani *et al.* [98] suggested conducting the k-NN search in the latent representation of the network and using the cosine similarity distance.

Weighting features is another popular paradigm in CBE. For instance, Shin *et al.* [106] proposed various **global weighting** schemes – *i.e.* methods in which the weights assigned to each input's feature remain constant across all samples as in Eq. (3) – where the weights are computed using the trained network to reveal the input features that were the most relevant for the network's prediction.

$$dist_{features\_weights}(z, z') = ||w(\hat{\theta})^T (x - x')||_2 \quad | \quad z = (x, y) \in (\mathcal{X} \times \mathcal{Y}) \quad (3)$$

Alternatively, Park *et al.* [93] examined **local weighting** by considering varying feature weights across the instance space. However, their approach is not *post-hoc* for DNN. Besides, Nugent *et al.* [89] also focused on local weighting and proposed a method that can be applied to any black-box model. However, their method involves generating multiple synthetic datasets around a specific sample, which may not be suitable for explaining a large number of samples or high-dimensional inputs. In the same line of work, Kenny and Keane [60,61] proposed COLE, by suggesting the direct k-NN search in the attribution space – *i.e* computing saliency maps [7,107,110] for all instances and performing a k-NN search in the resulting dataset of attributions. By denoting $c(\hat{\theta}, z)$ the attribution map of the sample z for the model parameterized by $\hat{\theta}$ gives:

$$dist_{COLE}(z, z') = ||c(\hat{\theta}, z) - c(\hat{\theta}, z')||_2 \quad (4)$$

They used three saliency map techniques [7,107,110] but nothing prevents one to leverage any other saliency map techniques. However, we should also point out that Fel *et al.* [34] questioned attribution methods' ability to truly capture the internal process of DNN. Additionally in [61], Kenny and Keane proposed to use the Hadamard product of the gradient times the input features as a contribution score in the case of DNN with non-linear outputs.

2.2   Conclusions on Similar Examples

Presenting similar examples to an end-user as an explanation for a model's outcomes has been shown through user studies [53,114] and psychology [32] to be generally more convincing than other approaches. However, the current limitations of similarity-based XAI are still significant. For instance, computing a relevant distance between z_{test} and every training data point becomes computationally prohibitive for large datasets. Thankfully, there are efficient search techniques available, as mentioned in the paper by Bhatia *et al.* [14].

Furthermore, **where** the distance is computed does have major implications [46]. Consequently, authors have suggested different feature spaces or weighting schemes to investigate, but their relevance to reflect the inner workings of a model remains questionable. In addition, it is still unclear in the literature if one approach prevails over others. In this regard, it is relevant to point out that psychological studies [32,78,88,112] underscore the importance of shared features, overall resemblance, context, and the interplay between perceptual and conceptual factors in similarity judgments. In fact, we can point out that none of the current factual methods leverage all those aspects at once.

Finally, considering the position of retrieved similar examples in relation to a model's decision boundaries is crucial for relevant explanations. Neglecting this can confuse users if factual examples contradict the model's prediction. Contrastive explanations address this issue and are discussed in Sect. 3.

3   Contrastive Explanations

Contrastive explanations are a class of explanation that provides the consequences of another plausible reality, the repercussion of changes in the model's input [17,113]. More simply, they are explanations where we modify the input and observe the reaction of the model's prediction, the modified input is returned as the explanation and its meaning depends on the model's prediction of it. Those methods are mainly *post-hoc* methods applied to classification models. This includes i) counterfactuals (CF): *an imagined alternative to reality about the past, sometimes expressed as "if only ..." or "what if ..."* [17], ii) semi-factuals (SF): *an imagined alternative that results in the same outcome as reality, sometimes expressed as "even if ..."* [17], and iii) adversarial examples (perturbations or attacks) (AP): *inputs formed by applying small but intentionally worst-case perturbations to examples from the dataset, such that the perturbed input results in the model outputting an incorrect answer with high confidence* [41]. Examples of those three formats are provided in Fig. 2 from Kenny and Keane [62].

AP and CF are both perturbations with an expected change in the prediction, they only differ in the goal as CF attempt to provide an explanation of the model's decision while AP are mainly used to evaluate robustness. In fact, AP can be considered CF [115], and for robust models, AP methods can generate interpretable CF [105]. Nonetheless, AP are hardly perceptible perturbations designed to fool the model [111], therefore, they are generative and those methods will not be further detailed in this work. Then, we can generalize SF and CF, with a given distance $dist$, and the examples conditioned space $\mathcal{X}_{cond(f,x)} \subset \mathcal{X}$:

$$CF(x_{test}) := \underset{x \in \mathcal{X}_{cond(f,x_{test})}|h(x) \neq h(x_{test})}{\arg\min} dist(x_{test}, x) \qquad (5)$$

$$SF(x_{test}) := \underset{x \in \mathcal{X}_{cond(f,x_{test})}|h(x) = h(x_{test})}{\arg\max} dist(x_{test}, x) \qquad (6)$$

For natural CF and SF, the input space is conditioned to the training set, $\mathcal{X}_{cond(f,x_{test})} = X_{train}$. While for AP, there is no condition on the input space, in Eq. (5), $\mathcal{X}_{cond(f,x_{test})} = \mathcal{X}$. The distance and the condition of the input space are the key differences between CF and SF methods.

This section discusses both counterfactuals and semi-factuals as they are often treated together in the literature [17,25,42,62]. The literature for both formats is large in social sciences and in XAI for generative methods, hence we will extract key findings before presenting natural example-based methods.

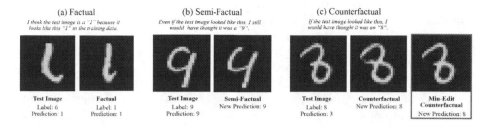

(a) Factual *I think the test image is a "1" because it looks like this "1" in the training data.* (b) Semi-Factual *Even if the test image looked like this, I still would have thought it was a "9".* (c) Counterfactual *If the test image looked like this, I would have thought it was an "8".*

Test Image	Factual	Test Image	Semi-Factual	Test Image	Counterfactual	Min-Edit Counterfactual
Label: 6	Label: 1	Label: 9	New Prediction: 9	Label: 8	New Prediction: 8	
Prediction: 1	Prediction: 1	Prediction: 9		Prediction: 3		New Prediction: 8

Fig. 2. Illustration of factuals, SF, and CF from Kenny and Keane [62]. The factual makes us understand the misclassification, while SF and CF show us how far or close the decision boundary is. Min-edit represents the AP, as differences are not visible.

3.1 Counterfactuals

The social science grounding of counterfactuals is deep, either in philosophy, or psychology. Indeed, the search for CF's semantic definition goes back a long time [13,44,72], and historically revolves around the notion of cause and effect, sometimes called facts and foils [75,79]. Then, Halpern and Pearl [44] argued that providing the cause of an event answers the question "Why?" and thus, provides a powerful explanation. Moreover, the philosophical literature argued that CF allow us to communicate and understand the causal relation between facts and foils [72,79]. Psychology also possesses a rich literature regarding CF [17,97], which has continued to evolve in recent years [18,59,80] thanks to the arrival of CF in XAI through Wachter *et al.* [115]. Humans' natural use of counterfactuals in many situations was highlighted by Byrne [17]: *From amusing fantasy to logical support, they explain the past, prepare the future, modulate emotional experience, and support moral judgments.* Furthermore, when people encounter CF they have both the counterfactual and the factual in mind [18]. The insights from philosophy and psychology [18,80] have shown the pertinence and potential of CF as well as SF for XAI. To match such promises, CF in XAI need to verify the definitions and properties of CF typically employed by humans.

Expected properties for natural CF can be extrapolated from conclusions and discovered properties in XAI for generated CF even though the literature on natural CF is slim. Such desirable properties for CF, derived from social sciences, could be summarized as follows: i) **plausibility** [58,59,113]: CF should be as realistic as possible; ii) **validity** [84]: if the model's prediction on CF differ from the prediction on the query (see the definition (5)); iii) **sparsity** [58, 84,113]: the number of features that were changed between CF and the query should be as little as possible; iv) **diversity** [54,84]: if several CF are proposed, they should be different from each other; v) **actionability** [58,113]: the method should allow the user to select features, to modify and specify immutable ones; vi) **proximity** [54,58,59,84]: CF should be as close as possible to the query.

Counterfactuals Methods: Keane *et al.* [59] argued that nearest unlike neighbors (NUN) [27] a derivative of nearest neighbors [24], are the ancestors of counterfactuals in XAI. NUN are the nearest element to the query that belongs to a different class. They are natural CF when the class is given by the model prediction. Natural counterfactuals and semi-factuals are faced with the same discussions around similarity as factuals section. However, here, the similarity should take into account sparsity.

NUN were first used in XAI by Doyle *et al.* [29,90] but not as an explanation, only to find SF. The only method to the best of our knowledge that uses NUN as explanations is KLEOR from Cummins and Bridge [25], they provided it as a complement to SF explanations to give intuition on the decision boundary. Nonetheless, they highlighted that the decision boundary might be much more complex than what the SF and CF pairs can reveal. Indeed, a line between SF and CF may intersect the decision boundary several times, which can lead to explanations that are not always faithful. Furthermore, Keane *et al.* [59] argued that "good natural counterfactuals are hard to find" as the dataset's low density may prevent sparse and proximal natural CF.

Counterfactuals as known in XAI were introduced by Wachter et al. [115], and flourished through generative methods as shown by the numerous surveys [54,84,113]. Two periods emerge: one focused on interpretable tabular data [113], and the other on complex data like images [6,62]. While generating plausible instances for the first period was not an issue it remains challenging for the second, even with diffusion models [6]. More research is needed to explore natural counterfactuals with their inherent plausibility [59,113]. Moreover, adversarial perturbations proved that for non-robust DNN, a generated example close to a natural instance is not necessarily plausible.

To conclude on counterfactuals, their large literature produced expected properties with deep social science grounding. Such desiderata highlight the pros and cons between generative and natural CF. Indeed, for high dimensional data, the reader is faced with the choice of simple and plausible natural CF or proximal and sparse generated CF through a model explaining another model.

3.2   Semi-factuals

SF literature is most of the time included in the CF literature be it in philosophy [42], psychology [17], or XAI [25,62]. In fact, SF, "even if ..." are semantically close to CF, "what if ..." [5,13,42], (see Eqs. (5) and (6)). However, psychology has demonstrated that human reactions differ between CF and SF. While CF strengthen the causal link between two elements, SF reduce it [18], CF increase fault and blame in a moral judgment while SF diminish it.

Expected properties for CF and SF were inspired by social science, hence, because of their close semantic definition, many properties are common between both: SF should also respect their definition in Eq. (6) (**validity**), then to make the comparison possible and relevant they should aim towards **plausibility** [5], **sparsity** [5], **diversity**, and **actionability**. Nonetheless, the psychological impact of CF and SF differ, hence there are also SF properties that contrast with CF properties. The difference between equations (5) and (6) – *i.e.* arg min vs arg max – suggests that to replace CF's proximity, SF should be the farthest from the studied sample, while not crossing the decision boundary [25]. As such, we propose the **decision boundary closeness** as a necessary property, and a metric to evaluate it could be the distance between SF and SF's NUN. Finally, SF should not go in any direction from the studied sample but aim toward the closest decision boundary. Therefore, it should be aligned with NUN [25, 29, 90], this property was not named, we suggest calling it **counterfactual alignment**.

Semi-factuals methods were first reviewed in XAI by a recent survey from Aryal and Keane [5]. They divided SF methods and history into four parts. The first three categories consist of one known method that will illustrate them:

- **SF based on feature-utility**, Doyle *et al.* [29] discovered that similar examples may not be the best explanations and suggested giving examples farther from the studied sample. To find the best explanation case, *dist* in Eq. (6) is a utility evaluation based on features difference.
- **NUN-related SF**, Cummins and Bridge [25] proposed KLEOR where Eq. (6)'s *dist* is based on NUN similarity. Then, they penalize this distance to make sure the SF are between the query and nearest unlike neighbors.
- **SF near local-region boundaries**, Nugent *et al.* [90] approximate the decision boundary of the model in the neighborhood of the studied sample through input perturbations (like LIME [96]). Then SF are given by the points that are the closest to the decision boundary.
- **The modern era: *post*-2020 methods**, inspired by CF methods, many generative methods emerged in recent years [55, 62].

To conclude, semi-factuals are a natural evolution of factuals. Moreover, their complementarity with counterfactuals was exposed through the literature, first to find and evaluate SF, then to provide a range to the decision boundary. Finally, generative and natural SF possess the same pros and cons as CF ones.

Even though contrastive explanations bring insights into a model's behavior, it has no impact on the current model situation, what led to this state, or how to change it. Contrastively, influential instances (see Sect. 4) extract the samples with the most influence on the model's training. Removing such samples from the training set will have a huge impact on the resulting model.

4   Influential Examples

Influential instances could be defined as instances more likely to change a model's outcome if they were not in the training dataset. Furthermore, such measures of influence provide one with information on "in which direction" the model decision would have been affected if that point was removed. Being able to trace back to the most influential training samples for a given test sample z_{test} has been a topic of interest mainly for example-based XAI.

4.1   Influential Instances Methods

Influence functions originated from robust statistics in the early 70s. In essence, they evaluate the change of a model's parameters as we up-weight a training sample by an infinitesimal amount [45]: $\hat{\theta}_{\epsilon, z_j} := \arg\min_\theta \mathcal{L}(\theta) + \epsilon l(z_j, \theta)$. One way to estimate the change in a model's parameters of a single training sample would be to perform *Leave-One-Out* (LOO) retraining, that is, to train the model again with the sample of interest being held out of the training dataset. However, repeatedly re-training the model to exactly retrieve the parameters' changes could be computationally prohibitive, especially when the dataset size and/or the number of parameters grows. As removing a sample z_j can be linearly approximated by up-weighting it by $\epsilon = -\frac{1}{n}$, computing influence helps to estimate the change of a model's parameters if a specific training point was removed. Thus, by making the assumption that the empirical risk $\mathcal{L}$ is twice-differentiable and strictly convex with respect to the model's parameters θ making the Hessian $H_{\hat{\theta}} := \frac{1}{n} \sum_{z_i \in \mathcal{D}_{train}} \nabla_\theta^2 l(z_i, \hat{\theta})$ positive definite, Cook and Weisberg [23] proposed to compute the influence of z_j on the parameters $\hat{\theta}$ as:

$$\mathcal{I}(z_j) := -H_{\hat{\theta}}^{-1} \nabla_\theta l(z_j, \hat{\theta}) \tag{7}$$

Later, Koh and Liang [68] popularized influence functions in the machine learning community as they took advantage of auto-differentiation frameworks to efficiently compute the hessian for DNN and derived Eq. (7) to formulate the influence of up-weighting a training sample z_j on the loss at a test point z_{test}:

$$\text{IF}(z_j, z_{test}) := -\nabla_\theta l(z_{test}, \hat{\theta})^T H_{\hat{\theta}}^{-1} \nabla_\theta l(z_j, \hat{\theta}) \tag{8}$$

This formulation opens its way into example-based XAI as it compares to the study of finding the nearest neighbors of z_{test} in the training dataset – *i.e.* the most similar examples (Sect. 2) – with two major differences though: i) points with high training loss are given more influence *revealing that outliers can dominate the model parameters* [68], and ii) $H_{\hat{\theta}}^{-1}$ measures what Koh and Liang called: *the resistance of the other training points to the removal of z_j* [68]. However, it should be noted that hessian computation remains a significant challenge, that could be alleviated with common techniques [3,77,101]. By normalizing Eq. (8), Barshan *et al.* [10] further added stability to the formulation.

Oftentimes, we are not only interested in individual instance influence but in the influence of a group of training samples (*e.g.* mini-batch effect, multi-source data, etc.). Koh *et al.* [69] suggested that using the sum of individual influences as the influence of the group constitutes a good proxy to rank those groups in terms of influence. Basu *et al.* [12] on their side suggested using a second-order approximation to capture possible cross-correlations but they specified it is most likely impracticable for DNN. In a later work, Basu *et al.* [11] concluded that influence function estimates for DNN are fragile as the assumptions on which they rely, being near optimality and convexity, do not hold in general for DNN.

LOO approximation is one of the previously mentioned motivations behind influence estimates as it avoids the prohibitive LOO retraining required for every sample in the training data. Thus, some authors proposed approaches that optimize the number of LOO retraining necessary to get a grasp on a sample's influence such as Feldman and Zhang [36]. Although this significantly reduces the number of retraining compared to naive LOO retraining, it still requires a significant amount of them. Recently, a new approach that relates to influence functions and involves training many models, was introduced with data models [52,99] which we do not review here.

As Basu *et al.* [11] pointed out, there is a discrepancy between LOO approximation and influence function estimates, especially for DNN. However, Bae *et al.* [9] claimed that this discrepancy is due to influence functions approaching what they call the proximal Bregman response function (PBRF), rather than approximating the LOO retraining, which does not interfere with their ability to perform the task they were thought for, especially XAI. Thus, they suggested evaluating the quality of influence estimates by comparing them to the PBRF rather than LOO retraining as it was done until now.

Influence computation that relies on kernels is another paradigm to find the training examples that are the most responsible for a given set of predictions. For instance, Khanna *et al.* [63] proposed an approach that relies on Fisher's kernels and they related it to the one from Koh and Liang [68] as a generalization of the latter under certain assumptions. Yeh *et al.* [117] also suggested an approach that leverages kernels but this time they relied on the representer theorem [103]. That allows them to focus on explaining only the *pre-activation prediction layer* of a DNN for classification tasks. In addition, their influence scores, called representer values, provide supplementary information, with positive representer values being excitatory and negative values being inhibitory. However, this approach requires introducing an $L2$ regularizer during optimization, which can prevent *post-hoc* analysis if not responsible for training. Additionally, Sui *et al.* [109] argued that this approach provides more of a *class-level* explanation rather than an *instance-level* explanation. To address this issue and the $L2$ regularizer problem, they proposed a method that involves hessian computation on the classification layer, with only the associated computational cost. However, the ability to retrieve relevant samples when investigating only the final prediction layer was questioned by Feldmann and Zhang [36], who found that memorization does not occur in the last layer.

Tracing the training process has been another research field to compute influence scores. It relies on the possibility to replay the training process by saving some checkpoints of our model parameters, or states, and reloading them in a post-hoc fashion [22,47,95]. In contrast to the previous approaches, they rely neither on being near optimality nor being strongly convex, which is more realistic when we consider the reality of DNN. However, they require handling the training procedure to save the different checkpoints, potentially numerous, hence they are intrinsic methods, which in practice is not always feasible.

4.2   Conclusions on Influential Instances

Influential techniques can provide both global and local explanations to enhance model performance. Global explanations allow for the identification of training samples that significantly shape decision boundaries or outliers (see Fig. 1), aiding in data curation. On the other hand, local explanations offer guidance for altering the model in a desired way (see Fig. 3). Although they have been compared to similar examples and have been shown to be more relevant to the model [46], they are more challenging to interpret and their effectiveness for trustworthiness is unclear. Further research, particularly user studies, is necessary to determine their ability to take advantage of human cognitive processes.

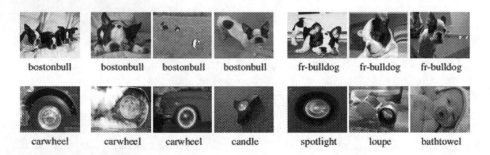

Fig. 3. Figure taken from F. Liu [95]: A tracing process for estimating influence, TracIn, applied on ImageNet. The first column is composed of the test sample, the next three columns display the training examples that have the most positive value of influence score while the last three columns point out the training examples with the most negative values of influence score. (fr-bulldog: french-bulldog)

5   Prototypes

Prototypes are a set of representative data instances from the dataset, while criticisms are data instances that are not well represented by those prototypes [64]. Figure 4 shows examples of prototypes and criticisms from Imagenet dataset.

Fig. 4. Figure taken from [64]: Learned prototypes and criticisms from Imagenet dataset (two types of dog breeds)

5.1   Prototype Methods

Prototypes and criticism can be used to add data-centric interpretability, *post-hoc* interpretability, or to build an interpretable model [83]. The data-centric approaches will be briefly introduced.

Prototypes for Data-Centric Interpretability: Clustering algorithms that return actual data points as cluster centers such as k-medoids methods [56,87] could be used to better understand the data distribution. We can consider the cluster centers as prototypes.

The abundance of large datasets has renewed the interest in the data summarization methods [8,73,74,82,108], which consist of finding a small subset of data points that covers a large dataset. The subset elements can be considered prototypes. Additionally, we found data summarization methods based on the Maximum Mean Discrepancy (MMD), such as MMD-critic [64] and Protodash [43], that learn both prototypes and criticisms.

Prototypes for *Post-hoc* Interpretability: Most prototype methods are data-centric that provide no information on the model. However, such methods can be computed in a meaningful search space for the model as done with similar examples Sect. 2.1 and give global explanations with the model vision of the dataset. Similarly, local explanations can be extracted by comparing studied samples to the closest prototypes in the search space. But to our knowledge, only one method explores such a possibility. Filho *et al.* [37] proposed M-PEER (Multiobjective Prototype-based Explanation for Regression) method that finds the prototypes using both the training data and the model output. It optimizes the error of the explainable model and the fidelity and interpretability metrics.

Prototype-Based Models Interpretable by Design: After data-centric and *post-hoc* methods, there are methods that construct prototype-based models. Those models are interpretable by design because they provide a set of prototypes that make sense for the model, those methods are mainly designed for classification. An interpretable classifier learns a set of prototypes $P_c \subseteq \{(x, y) \in$

$\mathcal{D}_{train}|y = c\}$. Each P_c captures the full variability of class c while avoiding confusion with other classes. The learned prototypes are then used by the model to classify the input. We identified three types of prototype-based classifiers:

- **Classifiers resolving set cover problems** select convex sets that cover each class with prototypes to represent it. Various types of convex sets such as boxes, balls, convex hulls, and ellipsoids can be used. Class Cover Catch Digraphs (CCCD) [76] and ProtoSelect [15] used balls where the centers were considered prototypes. Then, the nearest-prototype rule is used to classify the data points. CCCD finds, for each class c, a variable number of balls that cover all points of class c and no points of other classes. Its radius is chosen as large as possible. However, even within large classes, there can still be a lot of interesting within-class variability that should be taken into account when selecting the prototypes. To overcome this limitation, ProtoSelect used a fixed radius across all points, to allow the selection of multiple prototypes for large classes, and they also allow wrongly covered and non-covered points. They simultaneously minimize three elements: i) the number of prototypes; ii) the number of uncovered points; iii) the number of wrongly covered points.
- **Classifiers using Bayesian models for explanation**, Kim *et al.* [65] proposed the Bayesian Case Model (BCM) that extends Latent Dirichlet Allocation [16]. In BCM, the idea is to divide the data into s clusters. For each cluster, a prototype is defined as the sample that maximizes the subspace indicators that characterize the cluster. When a sample is given to BCM, this last one yield a vector of probability to belong to each of the s clusters which can be used for classification. Thus, the classifier uses as an input a vector of dimension s, which allows the use of simpler models due to dimensionality reduction. In addition, the prototype of the most likely cluster can then be used as an explanation.
- **Classifiers based on neural networks** learn to select prototypes defined in the latent space, which are used for the classification. This lead to a model that is more interpretable than a standard neural network since the reasoning process behind each prediction is "transparent". Learning Vector Quantization (LVQ) [70] is widely used for generating prototypes as weights in a neural network. However, the use of generated prototypes reduces their interpretability. ProtoPNet [21] also stocks prototypes as weights and trains them, but projects them to training samples patches representation during training. Given an input image, its patches are compared to each prototype, the resulting similarity scores are then multiplied by the learned class connections of each prototype. ProtoPNet has been extended to time series data via ProSeNet [81], or with a more interpretable structure with ProtoTree [86] and HPNet [48]. Instead of using linear bag-of-prototypes, ProtoTree and HPNet used hierarchically organized prototypes to classify images. ProtoTree improves upon ProtoPNet by using a decision tree which provides an easy-to-interpret global explanation and can be used to locally explain a single prediction. Each node in this tree contains a prototype (as defined by ProtoPNet) and the similarity scores between image patches and the prototypes

are used to determine the routing through the tree. Decision-making is therefore similar to human reasoning [86]. Nauta *et al.* [85] proposed a method called "This Looks Like That, Because" to understand prototypes similarities. This method allows checking why the model considered two examples as similar. For instance, it is possible that a human thinks that the common point between two examples is their color, while the model uses their shape. The method modifies some characteristics of the input image, such as hue, or shape, to observe how the similarity score changes. This allows us to measure the importance of each of these characteristics.

5.2 Conclusions on Prototypes

Most prototype methods are data-centric, but we have seen that applying such methods in a meaningful space for the model can bring *post-hoc* global and local explanations. Nonetheless, a second part of the literature constructs prototype-based classifiers explainable by design, those methods are promising and produce models with natural reasoning but adapting a new model to such architecture can be prohibitive.

6   Concept-Based XAI

Prototype-based models compare prototypical parts, *e.g.* patches, and the studied sample to make the classification. The idea of parts is not new to the literature, the part-based explanation field, developed for fine-grained classification, is able to detect semantically significant parts of images. The first part-based model required labeled parts for training and can be considered object detection with a semantic link between the detected objects. Afterward, unsupervised methods such as OPAM [94] or Particul [116] emerged, those methods still learned classification in a supervised fashion, but no labels were necessary for part identification. In fact, the explanation provided by this kind of method can be assimilated into concept-based explanations. A concept is an abstraction of common elements between samples, as an example Fig. 5 shows the visualization of six different concepts that the CRAFT method [35] associated with the given image. To understand parts or concepts, the method uses examples and supposes that with a few examples, humans are able to identify the concept.

6.1   Concepts Methods

Like in part-based XAI, the first concept-based method used labeled concepts. Kim et al. [66] introduced concept activation vectors (CAV) to represent concepts using a model latent space representation of images. Then, they design a post-hoc method, TCAV [66] based on CAV to evaluate an image correspondence to a given concept. Even though it seems promising, this method requires prior knowledge of the relevant concepts, along with a labeled dataset of the associated concepts, which is costly and prone to human biases.

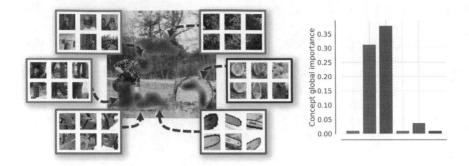

Fig. 5. Illustration from Fel *et al.* [35]. Natural examples in the colored boxes define a concept. **Purple box**: could define the concept of "**chainsaw**". **Blue box**: could define the concept of "**saw's motor**". **Red box**: could define the concept of "**jeans**". (Color figure online)

Fortunately, recent works have been conducted to automate the concept discovery in the training dataset without humans in the loop. For instance, ACE, proposed by Ghobarni et al. [39], employs a semantic segmentation technique on images belonging to a specific class of interest and use an Inception-V3 neural network to compute activations of an intermediate model layer for these segments. The resulting activations are then clustered to form a set of prototypes, which they refer to as "concepts". However, the presence of background segments in these concepts requires a post-processing clean-up step to remove irrelevant and outlier concepts. Zhang et al. [118] proposed an alternative approach to solving the unsupervised concept discovery problem through matrix factorizations [71] in the networks' latent spaces. However, such methods operate at the convolutional kernel level, which may lead to concepts based on shape and/or ignore more abstract concepts.

As an answer, Fel et al. [35] proposed CRAFT, which uses Non-Negative Matrix Factorization [71] for concept discovery. In addition to filling in the blank of previous approaches, their method provides an explicit link between the concepts' global and local explanations (Fig. 5). While their approach alleviates the previously mentioned issues, the retrieved concepts are not always interpretable. Nonetheless, their user study proved the pertinence of the method.

6.2 Conclusions on Concepts

Concept-based explanations allow *post-hoc* global and local explanations, by understanding the general concepts associated with a given class and the concepts used for a decision. We draw attention to methods that do not require expert knowledge to find out relevant concepts as they are prone to human bias. Even though automated concept discovery is making tremendous progress, the interpretation of such concepts and their ability to gain users' trust stay questionable as very few user studies have been conducted on the subject.

Table 1. Comparison table between the different natural example-based formats and methods. NA: Not applicable, FGCV: Fine-grained computer vision

SIMILAR EXAMPLES	Year	Global/Local	Post-hoc/Intrinsic	Model or data-type specificity	Distance	Weighting
Caruana et al. [20]	1999	Local	Post-hoc	DNN	Euclidean	None
Shin et al. [106]	2000	Local	Post-hoc	DNN	Euclidean	Global
Park et al. [93]	2004	Local	Intrinsic	DNN	Euclidean	Local
Nugent et al. [89]	2005	Local	Post-hoc	None	Euclidean	Local
Sani et al. [98]	2017	Local	Post-hoc	Deep CNN	Cosine similarity	Local
Papernot and McDaniel [92]	2018	Local	Post-hoc	Deep CNN	Cosine similarity	Local
Cole [60] [61]	2019	Local	Post-hoc	None	Euclidean	Local with attributions
CONTRASTIVE EXPLANATIONS	Year	Global/Local	Post-hoc/Intrinsic	Model or data-type specificity	Semi-factual group of method	
Doyle et al. [29,30]	2004	Local	Post-hoc	None	SF based on feature-utility	
NUN [25,27,29]	2006	Local	Post-hoc	None	Natural CF	
KLEOR [25]	2006	Local	Post-hoc	None	NUN-related SF	
Nugent et al. [90]	2009	Local	Post-hoc	None	Local-region boundaries	
INFLUENTIAL INSTANCES	Year	Global/Local	Post-hoc/Intrinsic	Model or data-type specificity	Requires model's gradients	
Koh and Liang [68]	2017	Both	Post-hoc	$\mathcal{L}$ twice-differentiable and strictly convex w.r.t. θ	Yes	
Khanna and al. [63]	2018	Local	Post-hoc	Requires an access to the function and gradient-oracles	Yes	
Yeh and al. [117]	2018	Local	Intrinsic	Work for classification neural networks with regularization	Yes	
Hara and al. [47]	2019	Local	Intrinsic	Models trained with SGD, saving intermediate checkpoints	Yes	
Koh and Liang [69]	2019	Both	Post-hoc	$\mathcal{L}$ twice-differentiable and strictly convex w.r.t. θ	Yes	
Basu and al. [12]	2019	Both	Post-hoc	$\mathcal{L}$ twice-differentiable and strictly convex w.r.t. θ	Yes	
Barshan and al. [10]	2020	Both	Post-hoc	$\mathcal{L}$ twice-differentiable and strictly convex w.r.t. θ	Yes	
Feldman and Zhang [36]	2020	Global	Intrinsic	Requires to train numerous models on subsampled datasets	No	
Pruthi and al. [95]	2020	Local	Intrinsic	Requires saving intermediate checkpoints	Yes	
Sui and al. [109]	2021	Local	Post-hoc	Work for classification neural networks	Yes	
Chan and al. [22]	2021	Both	Intrinsic	Requires saving intermediate checkpoints	Yes	
PROTOTYPES	Year	Global/Local	Post-hoc/Intrinsic	Model or data-type specificity	Task	Other
CCD [76]	2003	Both	NA	by-design	Classification	Set cover
ProtoSelect [15]	2011	Both	NA	by-design	Classification	Set cover
Kim et al. [65]	2019	Both	NA	by-design, tabular	Classification	Bayesian-based
ProtoPNet [21]	2019	Both	NA	by-design, FGCV	Classification	Neural network
ProSeNet [81]	2019	Both	NA	by-design, sequences	Classification	Neural network
ProtoTree [86]	2021	Both	NA	by-design, FGCV	Classification	Neural network
M-PEER [37]	2023	Both	Post-hoc	No	Regression	NA
CONCEPTS	Year	Global/Local	Post-hoc/Intrinsic	Model or data-type specificity	Need labeled concepts	Concepts format
OPAM [94]	2017	Global	NA	By-design, FGCV	Yes	part-based
TCAV [66]	2018	Global	Post-hoc	Neural network	Yes	same as input
ACE [39]	2019	Global	Post-hoc	Neural network	No	segmented parts
Zhang et al. [118]	2021	Global	Post-hoc	Neural network	No	segmented parts
CRAFT [35]	2022	Global	Post-hoc	Neural network	No	crops
Particul [116]	2017	Global	NA	By-design, FGCV	Yes	part-based

7 Conclusions and Discussions

This paper explored explainability literature about natural example-based explainability and provided a general social science justification for example-based XAI. We described each kind of explanation possible through samples. For each possibility, we reviewed what explanation they bring, then classified and presented the major methods. We summarize all explored methods in Table 1. We saw that all those methods are based on a notion of similarity. As such, for them to explain the model, the similarity between instances should take into account the model. There are two ways of doing it: project the instances in a meaningful space for the model and/or weight instances. Hence, similarity definitions from factuals (Sect. 2.1) can be ported to other formats and social science groundings could also be shared. However, if the training data is sparse in the search space, finding cases with good properties for a given format may be challenging.

Among the formats, contrastive explanations, prototypes, and concept examples can be generated, which brings competition to non-generative methods. We argue that both generative and natural examples have their pros and cons.

Indeed, natural examples are simple to compute and ensure plausibility while generated examples can be more proximal and sparse but require a model to explain another model (see Sect. 3.1 for properties definitions).

We have illustrated that the different example-based formats bring different kinds of explanations, and each one has its own advantages, Fig. 1 shows their diversity, have their scope of application, and complementarity. To summarize those advantages non-exhaustively: i) Factuals give confidence in the decisions of the model and are pertinent in AI-assisted decisions. ii) For classification, contrastive explanations give local insight into the decision boundary. iii) Influential instances explain how samples influenced the model training. iv) Prototypes and concepts give information on the whole model behavior, but may also be used to explain decisions. Nonetheless, like all explanations, we cannot be sure that humans will have a correct understanding of the model or the decision. Furthermore, there is no consensus on how to ensure a given method indeed explains the decisions or inner workings of the model. Moreover, for example-based explainability, the data is used as an explanation, hence, without profound knowledge of the dataset, humans will not be able to draw conclusions through such explanations. Therefore, the evaluation of example-based methods should always include a user study, which are scarce in this field and in XAI in general, especially with the lack of availability and consensus around quantitative metrics to evaluate example-based explanations. Finally, we hope our work will motivate, facilitate and help researchers to keep on developing the field of XAI and in particular, natural example-based XAI and to address the identified challenges.

Acknowledgments. This work has been supported by the French government under the "France 2030" program as part of the SystemX Technological Research Institute. This work was conducted as part of the Confiance.AI program, which aims to develop innovative solutions for enhancing the reliability and trustworthiness of AI-based systems. Additional funding was provided by ANR-3IA Artificial and Natural Intelligence Toulouse Institute (ANR-19-PI3A-0004).

We are also thankful to the DEEL's (https://www.deel.ai/) core team for their expertise and feedbacks. A.M. Picard, D. Vigouroux, C. Friedrich, V. Mussot, and Y. Prudent.

Finally, we are thankful to the authors who accepted our use of their figures. E.M Kenny and M.T. Keane [61,62], F. Liu [95], B. Kim [64], and T. Fel [35].

References

1. Aamodt, A., Plaza, E.: Case-based reasoning: foundational issues, methodological variations, and system approaches. AI Commun. **7**, 39–59 (1994)
2. Adadi, A., Berrada, M.: Peeking inside the black-box: a survey on explainable artificial intelligence (XAI). IEEE Access **6**, 52138–52160 (2018)
3. Agarwal, N., Bullins, B., Hazan, E.: Second-order stochastic optimization for machine learning in linear time. J. Mach. Learn. Res. **18**, 4148–4187 (2017)
4. Arrieta, A.B., et al.: Explainable artificial intelligence (XAI): concepts, taxonomies, opportunities and challenges toward responsible AI. Inf. Fusion **58**, 82–115 (2020)

5. Aryal, S., Keane, M.T.: Even if explanations: Prior work, desiderata & benchmarks for semi-factual XAI. arXiv preprint arXiv:2301.11970 (2023)
6. Augustin, M., Boreiko, V., Croce, F., Hein, M.: Diffusion visual counterfactual explanations. In: NeurIPS (2022)
7. Bach, S., Binder, A., Montavon, G., Klauschen, F., Müller, K.R., Samek, W.: On pixel-wise explanations for non-linear classifier decisions by layer-wise relevance propagation. PloS One **10**, e0130140 (2015)
8. Badanidiyuru, A., Mirzasoleiman, B., Karbasi, A., Krause, A.: Streaming submodular maximization: massive data summarization on the fly. In: KDD (2014)
9. Bae, J., Ng, N., Lo, A., Ghassemi, M., Grosse, R.B.: If influence functions are the answer, then what is the question? In: NeurIPS (2022)
10. Barshan, E., Brunet, M.E., Dziugaite, G.K.: RelatIF: identifying explanatory training samples via relative influence. In: AISTATS (2020)
11. Basu, S., Pope, P., Feizi, S.: Influence functions in deep learning are fragile. In: ICLR (2021)
12. Basu, S., You, X., Feizi, S.: On second-order group influence functions for black-box predictions. In: ICML (2020)
13. Bennett, J.: A Philosophical Guide to Conditionals. Clarendon Press (2003)
14. Bhatia, N., et al.: Survey of nearest neighbor techniques. arXiv preprint arXiv:1007.0085 (2010)
15. Bien, J., Tibshirani, R.: Prototype selection for interpretable classification. Ann. Appl. Stat. (2011)
16. Blei, D.M., Ng, A.Y., Jordan, M.I.: Latent Dirichlet allocation. JMLR **3**, 993–1022 (2003)
17. Byrne, R.M.: Counterfactual thought. Annu. Rev. Psychol. **67**, 135–157 (2016)
18. Byrne, R.M.: Counterfactuals in explainable artificial intelligence (XAI): evidence from human reasoning. In: IJCAI (2019)
19. Cambria, E., Malandri, L., Mercorio, F., Mezzanzanica, M., Nobani, N.: A survey on XAI and natural language explanations. IPM **60**, 103111 (2023)
20. Caruana, R., Kangarloo, H., Dionisio, J., Sinha, U., Johnson, D.: Case-based explanation of non-case-based learning methods. In: AMIA Symposium (1999)
21. Chen, C., Li, O., Tao, D., Barnett, A., Rudin, C., Su, J.K.: This looks like that: deep learning for interpretable image recognition. In: NeurIPS (2019)
22. Chen, Y., Li, B., Yu, H., Wu, P., Miao, C.: HYDRA: hypergradient data relevance analysis for interpreting deep neural networks. In: AAAI (2021)
23. Cook, R.D., Weisberg, S.: Residuals and Influence in Regression. Chapman and Hall, New York (1982)
24. Cover, T., Hart, P.: Nearest neighbor pattern classification. IEEE TIT **13**, 21–27 (1967)
25. Cummins, L., Bridge, D.: Kleor: a knowledge lite approach to explanation oriented retrieval. CAI **25**, 173–193 (2006)
26. Cunningham, P., Doyle, D., Loughrey, J.: An evaluation of the usefulness of case-based explanation. In: Ashley, K.D., Bridge, D.G. (eds.) ICCBR 2003. LNCS (LNAI), vol. 2689, pp. 122–130. Springer, Heidelberg (2003). https://doi.org/10.1007/3-540-45006-8_12
27. Dasarathy, B.V.: Nearest unlike neighbor (NUN): an aid to decision confidence estimation. Opt. Eng. **34**, 2785–2792 (1995)
28. De Mantaras, R.L., et al.: Retrieval, reuse, revision and retention in case-based reasoning. KER **20**, 215–240 (2005)

29. Doyle, D., Cunningham, P., Bridge, D., Rahman, Y.: Explanation oriented retrieval. In: Funk, P., González Calero, P.A. (eds.) ECCBR 2004. LNCS (LNAI), vol. 3155, pp. 157–168. Springer, Heidelberg (2004). https://doi.org/10.1007/978-3-540-28631-8_13

30. Doyle, D., Cunningham, P., Walsh, P.: An evaluation of the usefulness of explanation in a case-based reasoning system for decision support in bronchiolitis treatment. Comput. Intell. **22**, 269–281 (2006)

31. Dudani, S.A.: The distance-weighted k-nearest-neighbor rule. IEEE TSMC (1976)

32. Elgin, C.Z.: True Enough. Philosophical Issues (2004)

33. Fel, T., Cadène, R., Chalvidal, M., Cord, M., Vigouroux, D., Serre, T.: Look at the variance! Efficient black-box explanations with Sobol-based sensitivity analysis. In: NeurIPS (2021)

34. Fel, T., et al.: Don't lie to me! robust and efficient explainability with verified perturbation analysis. In: CVPR (2022)

35. Fel, T., et al.: CRAFT: concept recursive activation factorization for explainability. In: CVPR (2022)

36. Feldman, V., Zhang, C.: What neural networks memorize and why: discovering the long tail via influence estimation. In: NeurIPSs (2020)

37. Filho, R.M., Lacerda, A.M., Pappa, G.L.: Explainable regression via prototypes. ACM TELO **2**, 1–26 (2023)

38. Gentner, D.: Structure-mapping: a theoretical framework for analogy. Cogn. Sci. **7**, 155–170 (1983)

39. Ghorbani, A., Wexler, J., Zou, J.Y., Kim, B.: Towards automatic concept-based explanations. In: NeurIPS (2019)

40. Goldstein, A., Kapelner, A., Bleich, J., Pitkin, E.: Peeking inside the black box: visualizing statistical learning with plots of individual conditional expectation. JCGS **24**, 44–65 (2015)

41. Goodfellow, I.J., Shlens, J., Szegedy, C.: Explaining and harnessing adversarial examples. In: ICLR (2015)

42. Goodman, N.: The problem of counterfactual conditionals. J. Philos. (1947)

43. Gurumoorthy, K.S., Dhurandhar, A., Cecchi, G., Aggarwal, C.: Efficient data representation by selecting prototypes with importance weights. In: ICDM (2019)

44. Halpern, J.Y., Pearl, J.: Causes and explanations: a structural-model approach. Part II: explanations. BJPS (2005)

45. Hampel, F.R.: The influence curve and its role in robust estimation. JASA **69**, 383–393 (1974)

46. Hanawa, K., Yokoi, S., Hara, S., Inui, K.: Evaluation of similarity-based explanations. In: ICLR (2021)

47. Hara, S., Nitanda, A., Maehara, T.: Data cleansing for models trained with SGD. In: NeurIPS (2019)

48. Hase, P., Chen, C., Li, O., Rudin, C.: Interpretable image recognition with hierarchical prototypes. In: HCOMP (2019)

49. Hastie, T.: The Elements of Statistical Learning: Data Mining, Inference, and Prediction. Springer, Heidelberg (2009). https://doi.org/10.1007/978-0-387-84858-7

50. Holzinger, A., Saranti, A., Molnar, C., Biecek, P., Samek, W.: Explainable AI methods-a brief overview. In: Holzinger, A., Goebel, R., Fong, R., Moon, T., Müller, K.R., Samek, W. (eds.) xxAI 2020. LNCS, vol. 13200, pp. 13–38. Springer, Cham (2022). https://doi.org/10.1007/978-3-031-04083-2_2

51. Humer, C., Hinterreiter, A., Leichtmann, B., Mara, M., Streit, M.: Comparing effects of attribution-based, example-based, and feature-based explanation methods on AI-assisted decision-making. Preprint, Open Science Framework (2022)

52. Ilyas, A., Park, S.M., Engstrom, L., Leclerc, G., Madry, A.: Datamodels: predicting predictions from training data. In: ICML (2022)
53. Jeyakumar, J.V., Noor, J., Cheng, Y.H., Garcia, L., Srivastava, M.: How can i explain this to you? An empirical study of deep neural network explanation methods. In: NeurIPS (2020)
54. Karimi, A.H., Barthe, G., Balle, B., Valera, I.: Model-agnostic counterfactual explanations for consequential decisions. In: AISTATS (2020)
55. Karras, T., Laine, S., Aittala, M., Hellsten, J., Lehtinen, J., Aila, T.: Analyzing and improving the image quality of StyleGAN. In: CVPR (2020)
56. Kaufman, L., Rousseeuw, P.J.: Finding Groups in Data: An Introduction to Cluster Analysis. Wiley, Hoboken (2009)
57. Keane, M.T., Kenny, E.M.: The twin-system approach as one generic solution for XAI: an overview of ANN-CBR twins for explaining deep learning. In: IJCAI Workshop on XAI (2019)
58. Keane, M.T., Kenny, E.M., Delaney, E., Smyth, B.: If only we had better counterfactual explanations: five key deficits to rectify in the evaluation of counterfactual XAI techniques. arXiv preprint arXiv:2103.01035 (2021)
59. Keane, M.T., Smyth, B.: Good counterfactuals and where to find them: a case-based technique for generating counterfactuals for explainable AI (XAI). In: Watson, I., Weber, R. (eds.) ICCBR 2020. LNCS (LNAI), vol. 12311, pp. 163–178. Springer, Cham (2020). https://doi.org/10.1007/978-3-030-58342-2_11
60. Kenny, E.M., Keane, M.T.: Twin-systems to explain artificial neural networks using case-based reasoning: Comparative tests of feature-weighting methods in ANN-CBR twins for XAI. In: IJCAI (2019)
61. Kenny, E.M., Keane, M.T.: Explaining deep learning using examples: Optimal feature weighting methods for twin systems using post-hoc, explanation-by-example in XAI. KBS **233**, 107530 (2021)
62. Kenny, E.M., Keane, M.T.: On generating plausible counterfactual and semi-factual explanations for deep learning. In: AAAI (2021)
63. Khanna, R., Kim, B., Ghosh, J., Koyejo, S.: Interpreting black box predictions using fisher kernels. In: AISTATS (2019)
64. Kim, B., Khanna, R., Koyejo, O.O.: Examples are not enough, learn to criticize! Criticism for interpretability. In: NeurIPS (2016)
65. Kim, B., Rudin, C., Shah, J.A.: The Bayesian case model: a generative approach for case-based reasoning and prototype classification. In: NeurIPS (2014)
66. Kim, B., et al.: Interpretability beyond feature attribution: quantitative testing with concept activation vectors (TCAV). In: ICML (2018)
67. Kim, S., Jeong, M., Ko, B.C.: Lightweight surrogate random forest support for model simplification and feature relevance. Appl. Intell. **52**, 471–481 (2022)
68. Koh, P.W., Liang, P.: Understanding black-box predictions via influence functions. In: NeurIPS (2017)
69. Koh, P.W.W., Ang, K.S., Teo, H., Liang, P.S.: On the accuracy of influence functions for measuring group effects. In: NeurIPS (2019)
70. Kohonen, T.: The self-organizing map. IEEE (1990)
71. Lee, D.D., Seung, H.S.: Learning the parts of objects by non-negative matrix factorization. Nature **401**, 788–791 (1999)
72. Lewis, D.: Counterfactuals. Wiley, Hoboken (1973)
73. Lin, H., Bilmes, J.: Multi-document summarization via budgeted maximization of submodular functions. In: NAACL (2010)
74. Lin, H., Bilmes, J.: A class of submodular functions for document summarization. In: ACL HLT (2011)

75. Lipton, P.: Contrastive explanation. Roy. Inst. Philos. Supplements **27**, 247–266 (1990)
76. Marchette, C.E.P.D.J., Socolinsky, J.G.D.D.A.: Classification using class cover catch digraphs. J. Classif. **20**, 3-23 (2003)
77. Martens, J.: Deep learning via hessian-free optimization. In: ICML (2010)
78. Medin, D.L., Schaffer, M.M.: Context theory of classification learning. Psychol. Rev. **85**, 207 (1978)
79. Miller, T.: Explanation in artificial intelligence: insights from the social sciences. Artif. Intell. **267**, 1–38 (2019)
80. Miller, T.: Contrastive explanation: a structural-model approach. KER **36**, e14 (2021)
81. Ming, Y., Xu, P., Qu, H., Ren, L.: Interpretable and steerable sequence learning via prototypes. In: KDD (2019)
82. Mirzasoleiman, B., Karbasi, A., Badanidiyuru, A., Krause, A.: Distributed submodular cover: succinctly summarizing massive data. In: NeurIPS (2015)
83. Molnar, C.: Interpretable machine learning (2020). Lulu.com
84. Mothilal, R.K., Sharma, A., Tan, C.: Explaining machine learning classifiers through diverse counterfactual explanations. In: ACM FAccT (2020)
85. Nauta, M., Jutte, A., Provoost, J., Seifert, C.: This looks like that, because... explaining prototypes for interpretable image recognition. In: PKDD Workshop (2022)
86. Nauta, M., Van Bree, R., Seifert, C.: Neural prototype trees for interpretable fine-grained image recognition. In: CVPR (2021)
87. Ng, R.T., Han, J.: Efficient and effective clustering methods for spatial data mining. In: VLDB (1994)
88. Nosofsky, R.M.: Choice, similarity, and the context theory of classification. JEP LMC **10**, 104 (1984)
89. Nugent, C., Cunningham, P.: A case-based explanation system for black-box systems. Artif. Intell. Rev. **24**, 163–178 (2005)
90. Nugent, C., Doyle, D., Cunningham, P.: Gaining insight through case-based explanation. JIIS **32**, 267–295 (2009)
91. Olah, C., Mordvintsev, A., Schubert, L.: Feature visualization. Distill **2**, e7 (2017)
92. Papernot, N., McDaniel, P.: Deep k-nearest neighbors: towards confident, interpretable and robust deep learning. arXiv preprint arXiv:1803.04765 (2018)
93. Park, J.H., Im, K.H., Shin, C.K., Park, S.C.: MBNR: case-based reasoning with local feature weighting by neural network. Appl. Intell. **21**, 265–276 (2004)
94. Peng, Y., He, X., Zhao, J.: Object-part attention model for fine-grained image classification. IEEE TIP **27**, 1487–1500 (2017)
95. Pruthi, G., Liu, F., Kale, S., Sundararajan, M.: Estimating training data influence by tracing gradient descent. In: NeurIPS (2020)
96. Ribeiro, M.T., Singh, S., Guestrin, C.: Model-agnostic interpretability of machine learning. In: KDD (2016)
97. Roese, N.J., Olson, J.M.: Counterfactual thinking: a critical overview. What might have been: the social psychology of counterfactual thinking (1995)
98. Sani, S., Wiratunga, N., Massie, S.: Learning deep features for kNN-based human activity recognition. In: CEUR Workshop (2017)
99. Saunshi, N., Gupta, A., Braverman, M., Arora, S.: Understanding influence functions and datamodels via harmonic analysis. In: ICLR (2023)
100. Schank, R.C.: Dynamic Memory: A Theory of Reminding and Learning in Computers and People. Cambridge University Press, Cambridge (1983)

101. Schioppa, A., Zablotskaia, P., Vilar, D., Sokolov, A.: Scaling up influence functions. In: AAAI (2022)
102. Schoenborn, J.M., Weber, R.O., Aha, D.W., Cassens, J., Althoff, K.D.: Explainable case-based reasoning: a survey. In: AAAI Workshop (2021)
103. Schölkopf, B., Herbrich, R., Smola, A.J.: A generalized representer theorem. In: Helmbold, D., Williamson, B. (eds.) COLT 2001. LNCS (LNAI), vol. 2111, pp. 416–426. Springer, Heidelberg (2001). https://doi.org/10.1007/3-540-44581-1_27
104. Selvaraju, R.R., Cogswell, M., Das, A., Vedantam, R., Parikh, D., Batra, D.: Grad-CAM: visual explanations from deep networks via gradient-based localization. In: ICCV (2017)
105. Serrurier, M., Mamalet, F., Fel, T., Béthune, L., Boissin, T.: When adversarial attacks become interpretable counterfactual explanations. arXiv preprint arXiv:2206.06854 (2022)
106. Shin, C.K., Yun, U.T., Kim, H.K., Park, S.C.: A hybrid approach of neural network and memory-based learning to data mining. IEEE TNN **11**, 637–646 (2000)
107. Shrikumar, A., Greenside, P., Kundaje, A.: Learning important features through propagating activation differences. In: ICML (2017)
108. Simon, I., Snavely, N., Seitz, S.M.: Scene summarization for online image collections. In: ICCV (2007)
109. Sui, Y., Wu, G., Sanner, S.: Representer point selection via local Jacobian expansion for post-hoc classifier explanation of deep neural networks and ensemble models. In: NeurIPS (2021)
110. Sundararajan, M., Taly, A., Yan, Q.: Axiomatic attribution for deep networks. In: ICML (2017)
111. Szegedy, C., et al.: Intriguing properties of neural networks. arXiv preprint arXiv:1312.6199 (2013)
112. Tversky, A.: Features of similarity. Psychol. Rev. **84**, 327 (1977)
113. Verma, S., Boonsanong, V., Hoang, M., Hines, K.E., Dickerson, J.P., Shah, C.: Counterfactual explanations and algorithmic recourses for machine learning: a review. arXiv preprint arXiv:2010.10596 (2020)
114. van der Waa, J., Nieuwburg, E., Cremers, A., Neerincx, M.: Evaluating XAI: a comparison of rule-based and example-based explanations. Artif. Intell. **291**, 103404 (2021)
115. Wachter, S., Mittelstadt, B., Russell, C.: Counterfactual explanations without opening the black box: automated decisions and the GDPR. Harv. JOLT **31**, 841 (2017)
116. Xu-Darme, R., Quénot, G., Chihani, Z., Rousset, M.C.: PARTICUL: part identification with confidence measure using unsupervised learning. arXiv preprint arXiv:2206.13304 (2022)
117. Yeh, C.K., Kim, J., Yen, I.E.H., Ravikumar, P.K.: Representer point selection for explaining deep neural networks. In: NeurIPS (2018)
118. Zhang, R., Madumal, P., Miller, T., Ehinger, K.A., Rubinstein, B.I.: Invertible concept-based explanations for CNN models with non-negative concept activation vectors. In: AAAI (2021)

Explainable Artificial Intelligence in Education: A Comprehensive Review

Blerta Abazi Chaushi[1]([✉]), Besnik Selimi[2], Agron Chaushi[1], and Marika Apostolova[2]

[1] Faculty of Business and Economics, SEEU, Tetovo, North Macedonia
{b.abazi,a.caushi}@seeu.edu.mk
[2] Faculty of Contemporary Sciences and Technologies, SEEU, Tetovo, North Macedonia
{b.selimi,m.apostolova}@seeu.edu.mk

Abstract. Explainable artificial intelligence (AI) has drawn a lot of attention recently since AI systems are being employed more often across a variety of industries, including education. Building trust and increasing the efficacy of AI systems in educational settings requires the capacity to explain how they make decisions. This article provides a comprehensive review of the current level of explainable AI (XAI) research and its application to education. We begin with the challenges of XAI in education, the complexity of AI algorithms, and the necessity for transparency and interpretability. Furthermore, we discuss the obstacles involved with using AI in education, and explore several solutions, including human-AI collaboration, explainability techniques, and ethical and legal frameworks. Subsequently, we debate about the importance of developing new competencies and skills among students and educators to interact with AI effectively, as well as how XAI impacts politics and government. Finally, we provide recommendations for additional research in this field and suggest potential future directions for XAI in educational research and practice.

Keywords: Explainable AI · XAI · AI in education · Implications · Ethical considerations · Future directions

1 Introduction

Use of artificial intelligence (AI) in education is growing, from customized learning platforms to automated grading systems. As the use of AI increases in more sensitive areas, many questions arise regarding the openness and accountability of these systems (Samek & Müller, 2019). Making AI systems more visible and intelligible to humans is the goal of the burgeoning discipline of explainable AI, or XAI (Gunning et al., 2019). XAI is particularly important in areas where AI system decisions can have a big impact on students' learning results and educational prospects (Nagahisarchoghaei et al., 2023). Therefore, researchers have been investigating approaches to designing and implementing explainable AI systems in education (Holzinger et al., 2018; Laato et al., 2022) and exploring the ethical implications of their use (Laupichler et al., 2023). The research in XAI in education is vast and scattered around deferent themes and issues surrounding

L. Longo (Ed.): xAI 2023, CCIS 1902, pp. 48–71, 2023.
https://doi.org/10.1007/978-3-031-44067-0_3

the topic. Throughout the review, we analyzed more than 200 research papers on the topic and identified that most of the studies focus on one of the four identified areas of research: 1) Application of AI in education; 2) Issues with AI implementation in education; 3) AI tools for education; and 4) Ethical issues and regulatory frameworks with AI implementation in education. We developed a framework around these themes to steer this study, thus in we will follow the framework provided in Fig. 1 to address the issues and challenges associated with XAI in education.

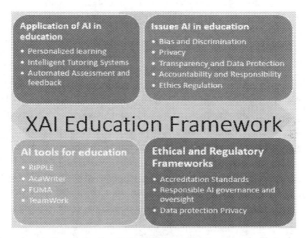

Fig. 1. Framework for analyzing XAI in Educational setting. (Authors' own work)

By definition, XAI is the ability of AI systems to provide explanations for their actions and decisions in a way that is understandable to humans. This is a significant field of research because conventional AI systems are frequently viewed as "black boxes" that make decisions using complicated mathematical models (Baum et al., 2022). Particularly in domains like education where decisions can have significant effects, this lack of transparency and interpretability can lead to suspicion and skepticism of AI systems. Therefore, by making AI systems more transparent, interpretable, and accountable, XAI aims to address these challenges (Nandi & Pal, 2022). There are various ways in which explainable AI (XAI) is relevant to education. Firstly, XAI can aid teachers in explaining to students how AI systems generate their recommendations or decisions, thereby enhancing the efficiency and personalization of learning experiences for individual students (J. Kim et al., 2022; Nandi & Pal, 2022). XAI can aid in the creation of efficient and personalized learning environments for students (Gunning, 2019). Secondly, XAI can assist in creating ethical and responsible AI educational systems by identifying and correcting any biases or unfairness in the decision-making process (Saeed & Omlin, 2023) and can contribute to the impartiality and fairness of AI-driven educational systems (Samek & Müller, 2019). Educators and policymakers can identify and rectify any biases or discriminatory behaviors in AI systems by making these systems more transparent and interpretable. Overall, XAI has the potential to transform education by enhancing the effectiveness, dependability, and ethics of AI systems (Holzinger et al., 2018; Laato et al., 2022; Laupichler et al., 2023; Nagahisarchoghaei et al., 2023).

2   Background and Context

2.1   Brief History of AI and its Application in Education

The application of artificial intelligence (AI) in education has a long history. According to a study conducted by Meacham, humans have started to search for ways to recreate our mental processes as early as 1763 when Thomas Bayes develops Bayesian inference. After more than 7 decades we have the next invention, "the analytical engine" developed by Charles Babbage to conduct mathematical computations. In 1955 for the first time the term AI is used in scientific conference held in Hanover, New Hampshire (Meacham, 2021). These are all events that have led to the development and adoption of AI in education. We can divide the adoption of AI into two phases, depending on the technology they use. Early research in the 1980s investigated the capabilities of AI for natural language processing (NLP), computer vision, and speech recognition. In the 1990s, the groundwork was laid for more sophisticated AI applications in education with the development of common foundational technologies, which paves the road for the beginning of the second phase. The second phase started with the expansion of AI application in education during the 2000s because of the adoption of machine learning and deep learning algorithms and continues to this date. With the potential to extend access to education, improve learning outcomes, and improve the overall quality and efficacy of educational systems, AI now is widely recognized as a key catalyst for educational innovation and transformation.

First Phase: Early research on AI was focused on using AI to develop adaptive learning platforms and intelligent tutoring systems. These systems were developed to offer students individualized feedback and support based on their unique needs and performance. The Intelligent Tutoring System (ITS), created in the 1970s by academics at the University of Illinois, was one of the first AI-driven educational systems. It used a rule-based expert system to give feedback and advice to students in algebra and computer programming (Woolf, 2010). The Cognitive Tutor and the ALEKS systems, which used machine learning algorithms to customize education to each student's learning preferences, were developed by researchers in the decades that followed (Baker & Inventado, 2014; Yakubu & Abubakar, 2022; Zhang, 2021).

Second Phase: With the advent of machine learning and deep learning algorithms in the 2000s, applications of AI in education expanded, encompassing anything from chatbots and virtual assistants to personalized learning platforms and automated grading schemes (Cavanagh et al., 2020). For instance, the renowned online learning site Khan Academy employs machine learning algorithms to customize its content and recommendations based on the interests and learning progress of its users (Khan Academy, n.d.). Similar to this, organizations like Coursera and Udacity employ AI-powered systems for automated grading and feedback, which can lessen teachers' workloads and increase the accuracy and speed of grading (Baker & Inventado, 2014). However, the application of AI in education also brings up significant issues about the accountability and transparency of these systems, as well as the requirement to guarantee their effectiveness, fairness, and morality. In response to these worries, the discipline of explainable AI (XAI) has arisen, with a focus on creating AI systems that are open, understandable, and answerable to people (Zeide, 2019).

The demand for AI in education is being driven by rising investments in AI and EdTech by both the public and private sectors, as well as by the growing use of edutainment. This is one of the reasons that global spending on artificial intelligence (AI), including software, hardware, and services for AI-centric systems, is expected to reach $154 billion in 2023, up 26.9% from the amount spent in 2022, according to a new forecast from the International Data Corporation (IDC) Worldwide Artificial Intelligence Spending Guide (Needham, Mass, 2023). The size of the global market for AI in education was estimated at USD 2.75 billion in 2023 and is projected to increase at a CAGR of 36.0% from 2022 to 2030 (Grand View Research, 2021).

2.2 Current State of AI Adoption in Education and the Challenges

Depending on the environment and educational level, the application of AI in education varies widely (Boyd-Graber et al., 2012). The extensive use of AI in higher education has made it possible for massive open online courses (MOOCs) to be given via platforms like Coursera, Udacity, and edX (Liyanagunawardena et al., 2013). While AI-powered systems have also been used to raise student engagement and retention, predictive analytics and early warning systems have been utilized to identify students who are at danger of dropping out or falling behind (Kizilcec et al., 2017). The use of AI in K–12 education, however, is still in its infancy, with the majority of applications concentrating on personalized learning and adaptive evaluation (Baker & Inventado, 2014). There are concerns about the effectiveness and scalability of these systems, as well as the potential unintended consequences, such as reduced human interaction and bias reinforcement (Holmes & Porayska-Pomsta, 2022).

The difficulties in implementing AI in education are numerous, ranging from technical problems like data security and privacy to ethical and social issues like algorithmic bias and interactions between humans and AI (Holmes & Porayska-Pomsta, 2022). Many AI systems lack interpretability and transparency, which can make it difficult for teachers and students to understand how these systems make decisions and respond (Walger et al., 2023). This can cause people to lose faith in technology and doubt its usefulness. Another issue is that many jobs, including assessment and grading, require human judgment and expertise, necessitating human monitoring and intervention in AI-powered educational systems (Liyanagunawardena et al., 2013). For AI to be used in education responsibly and ethically, educators, policymakers, researchers, and students must work together (Kizilcec et al., 2017).

The integration of artificial intelligence (AI) in education is expected to increase in the coming years due to advances in AI technology and the demand for flexible and personalized learning (Chen, 2022; Whalley et al., 2021). However, the implementation of AI in education requires a nuanced approach that considers the complexity and diversity of educational settings and emphasizes human-centered design (Blikstein, 2013; Vapnik & Izmailov, 2019). Effective integration of AI into education requires a multidisciplinary strategy that draws on expertise from computer science, education, psychology, and sociology (Raji et al., 2021; Xia & Li, 2022; Yadav et al., 2022). Understanding the effects of AI-powered educational systems on learning results, student engagement, and other crucial factors will require more investigation and evaluation (Kizilcec et al.,

2017; Zawacki-Richter et al., 2019). Ultimately, AI in education should complement rather than replace human intelligence (Dabbagh & Kitsantas, 2012).

A study conducted by HolonIQ, that surveys 464 institutions across both 2019 and 2022 Aug-Sep survey show that compared to 14% in 2019, 25% report successful AI investment and deployment in 2022. AI is slowly moving from being considered to being implemented with 44% of respondents having AI on their short to medium-term objectives. Similarly, the percentage of respondents who say AI is "on the radar" but aren't planning any actions has dropped from 24% in 2019 to 14% in 2022. The main three reasons for adopting AI for these institutions remain are improving learner outcomes (75% of respondents), cost savings due to automation (45% of respondents) and disrupting the market (43% of respondents) (HolonIQ, 2023). Moreover, the same report also highlights that more educational institutions are now claiming to have identified all of the potential AI prospects (40% in 2022 against 27% in 2019).This, on the other hand, leads to institutions not being prepared for the growing complexity and capabilities of the AI tools themselves, which demand new and different talent from both inside and outside the organization. Moreover, this complexity requires a shift in the mindset from only adopting AI to understanding it as well.

2.3   The Necessity of Explainable AI in the Educational Context

The goal of XAI is to create AI systems that can explain their decisions and behaviors clearly and understandable to people. As AI-powered systems are used for a range of functions, including personalized learning, evaluation, and student support, XAI is becoming more significant in the context of education (Manhiça et al., 2023; Zawacki-Richter et al., 2019). These systems frequently rely their judgments on intricate algorithms and models that are challenging for people to comprehend, which can breed mistrust and misunderstanding (Xu et al., 2021).

Several factors influence the need for XAI in the educational setting. As educational systems that utilize AI, particularly in areas such as student evaluation and grading, raise concerns about potential biases and ethical consequences, an increasing number of people are becoming anxious (Khosravi et al., 2022). It might be difficult to identify and reduce bias and guarantee justice and equity in educational outcomes if these systems are opaque and difficult to understand (4 Huang, Daumé III, & Boyd-Graber, 2017). By providing feedback and insights that can enlighten and direct human decision-making, XAI can help to enhance the efficacy of AI-driven educational systems, resulting in more effective and personalized learning opportunities for students (Liyanagunawardena et al., 2013).

Furthermore, XAI has the potential to support collaboration and interaction between humans and AI rather than displacing human judgment and knowledge. Educators and students can collaborate with AI systems to improve outcomes by making them more accessible and intelligible. For instance, XAI can assist teachers in determining how a particular AI-powered tutoring system is interacting with a student and provide recommendations for enhancing the learning process (Ouyang et al., 2022). Some of the main concepts commonly found in literature for XAI are summarized in Table 1 below.

Table 1. Summary of the key concepts and benefits of XAI in education

Concept of explainable AI in education	Reasons for its importance	Benefits	Authors
Develop AI systems that can explain their decisions and actions in a way that is understandable and transparent to humans	Growing concern about potential biases and ethical implications of AI-powered educational systems, and the need to improve their effectiveness	Promotes human-AI collaboration and interaction, helps to ensure transparency, fairness, and effectiveness of AI systems	(Doshi-Velez & Kim, 2017; Gilpin et al., 2018; Samek et al., 2017)
Usage of AI-powered systems for personalized learning, assessment, and student support	Lack of transparency and explainability in AI systems can lead to a lack of trust and understanding	Can help educators to understand how AI-powered systems are working with students and suggest adjustments to the learning process	(Brusilovsky et al., 2022; Holstein et al., 2019; Islam et al., 2022; Khosravi et al., 2022; Kolchenko, 2018)
Usage of XAI detect and mitigate bias and ensure fairness and equity in educational outcomes	XAI can provide feedback and insights that can inform and guide human decision-making	Leads to more personalized and effective learning experiences for students	(Buolamwini & Gebru, 2018; Lipton, 2018; Mittelstadt, 2019)

Source: Authors' own work

3   Key Themes and Issues

3.1   The Importance of Transparency and Accountability in AI-Powered Educational Systems

The significance of openness and responsibility in AI-driven educational systems is another major theme connected to explainable AI in education (Amer-Yahia, 2022; Zhai et al., 2021). For educators and students to understand how decisions are being made and make sure that these decisions are in line with educational aims and values, it is critical that AI systems used in education are transparent and easily understandable. In areas like student assessment and grading, where AI-powered systems can have major effects on students' academic performance and opportunities, transparency and accountability are especially essential. It can be challenging to identify prejudice, lessen it, and guarantee fair and equal educational outcomes in the absence of transparency and accountability (Dillenbourg & Jermann, 2010).

Making sure there is openness and accountability in educational systems powered by AI is not without its difficulties. The interpretation of AI models and algorithms can be difficult and sophisticated, even for subject-matter experts. Both educators and pupils may find it difficult to understand the decision-making process and to identify any potential biases or errors in the system as a result. Additionally, it can be challenging to ensure that AI-powered systems are open and accountable because there are sometimes no defined rules or criteria governing their usage in education. Finally, there is a need to strike a balance between the advantages of educational systems powered by AI and any associated hazards and moral ramifications.

3.2   Ensuring AI Models are Fair and Unbiased

The literature indicates that maintaining fairness and objectivity in AI-powered educational systems is a complicated problem. Bias can be introduced in AI models due to various factors, including prior discriminatory tendencies or a lack of consideration for the diversity of learners and their backgrounds. Biased AI models can result in unfair or unequal outcomes for learners, such as biased recommendations or unjust grading (Bojarski et al., 2016; Esteva et al., 2017; Holmes & Porayska-Pomsta, 2022). One issue is that biases could be unnoticeable and challenging to spot, particularly if they are present in the data used to train the model. Additionally, it could be challenging to decide what an AI model is expected to do in a particular circumstance due to different interpretations of fairness. Promoting diversity and inclusivity in AI development teams helps to ensure that models are developed with a knowledge of the various requirements and experiences of learners (Ouyang et al., 2022). Table 2 outlines some of the major obstacles to prove that AI models are impartial and fair, such as previous discriminatory trends in data, a lack of diversity and inclusivity in AI development teams, and conflicting notions of what constitutes justice. The table also identifies opportunities to address these issues.

Table 2. Key issues and challenges associated with ensuring that AI models used in education are fair and unbiased

Key Theme	Issues	Challenges	Opportunities	Authors
Need to ensure that AI models are fair and unbiased	- Historical patterns of discrimination in data	- Difficulty in detecting subtle biases	- Use of bias-detection tools and techniques	(Buolamwini & Gebru, 2018; Kelley et al., 2022)
	- Lack of diversity and inclusivity in AI development teams	- Determining what constitutes a fair AI model	- Ensuring diversity and inclusivity in AI development teams	(Erin Green et al., 2022; Veale et al., 2018)
	- Competing definitions of fairness	- Addressing ethical concerns and potential trade-offs of fairness	- Developing clear guidelines and standards for fairness in AI models	(Dwork et al., 2015; Kleinberg et al., 2018)

Source: Authors' own work

3.3   The Challenge of Balancing the Benefits of AI with the Risks and Limitations of the Technology

Another topic connected to XAI in education is the challenge of creating a balance between the benefits of AI and the risks and limitations of technology. By boosting student engagement, automating administrative duties, and personalizing learning experiences, AI can completely transform education. The use of AI in education is not without concerns, however, including the possibility of data breaches, the danger of over-reliance on technology, and the absence of transparency and accountability in some AI-driven educational systems. The risks and restrictions associated with AI in education must be addressed thoughtfully and proactively to fully reap their benefits. Table 3 below can be a helpful tool for organizing and presenting information about the challenges, risks, and limitations associated with using AI in education, as well as strategies for addressing them.

Table 3. Challenges, risks, and limitations associated with using AI in education

Challenge/Risk/Limitation	Strategies for Addressing
Data breaches and privacy concerns	- Adopting strong data protection policies and protocols - Regularly auditing and monitoring systems for potential vulnerabilities - Ensuring compliance with relevant data protection regulations
Over-reliance on technology	- Balancing the use of technology with other teaching methods and approaches - Encouraging critical thinking and creativity in students - Fostering a culture of digital literacy and responsible technology use
Lack of transparency and accountability in AI-powered systems	- Implementing explainable AI models that can provide clear explanations for their decisions and recommendations - Ensuring that AI models are regularly audited and tested for biases and fairness - Providing training and support to teachers and other stakeholders to understand and use AI-powered systems effectively

Source: (adapted from (Kumari et al., 2023) *and* (Vilone & Longo, 2020))

3.4   The Role of Human Oversight in Ensuring the Ethical and Responsible Use of AI in Education

The importance of human oversight in ensuring the ethical and responsible use of AI is another significant issue related to explainable AI in education. AI can improve learning outcomes and experiences, but it cannot take the place of human teachers and mentors. To make sure that all students' needs and interests are taken into consideration, human oversight is necessary. In order to prevent bias and discrimination, not only AI models must be ethical, accountable, and responsible, but also teachers should possess the knowledge and experience required to use AI-powered educational systems successfully and to give pupils the direction and assistance they need (*Artificial Intelligence - OECD*, n.d.; Herman, 2017; Kasneci et al., 2023). Table 4 highlights the important tasks and obligations of stakeholders involved in guaranteeing the moral and appropriate application of AI in education:

Table 4. Roles and responsibilities of parties involved in AI in education

Stakeholder	Roles and Responsibilities
AI developers	- Designing and developing AI models that are transparent, explainable, and free from bias and discrimination - Regularly testing and auditing AI models to ensure their fairness and accuracy
Educators	- Providing appropriate guidance and support to students using AI-powered educational systems - Ensuring that AI-powered systems are used in an ethical and responsible manner - Being aware of the limitations and risks of AI-powered systems and balancing their use with other teaching methods
Students	- Using AI-powered educational systems responsibly and ethically - Providing feedback on the effectiveness and appropriateness of AI-powered systems
Policymakers and regulators	- Developing policies and regulations that promote the ethical and responsible use of AI in education - Ensuring that AI-powered systems are transparent, accountable, and fair - Promoting transparency and accountability in the use of AI in education

Source: Authors' own work

3.5   Examples and Case Studies to Illustrate XAI in Education

Examples and case studies can assist in illuminating some of the problems and difficulties related to the application of explainable AI in education. AI-powered grading systems can raise concerns regarding accuracy and fairness. A study by ProPublica in 2019 showed that a well-known automated essay scoring system used in many US schools unfairly penalized Black students. Even when the essays were of comparable quality, the system was found to be biased toward white students compared to Black students (MacGillis, 2020). AI-powered individualized learning platforms that adjust to the unique requirements and preferences of pupils can suffer from the ability to reinforce prejudice and injustice. For instance, the AI model may make inaccurate assumptions and suggestions based on the student's color, gender, or socioeconomic position if it is trained on data that was not representative of the student community.

A case study of the use of AI in education featured IBM's "Project Debater" AI system, which was created to debate with human opponents. In 2019, a live debate took place between Project Debater and a top debater on the topic of whether preschool tuition should be subsidized. While the AI system was able to provide well-researched arguments and counterarguments, it was also criticized for its lack of emotional intelligence and originality compared to its human opponent (IBM Research, n.d.). Moreover, the focus of the majority of the research on automated essay grading is maximizing the agreement with the human rater, which considering that human judgments could be influenced, makes these fairly problematic (Amorim et al., 2018). Personalized learning systems have also issues especially moving from the traditional "one size fits all" to a personalize format of learning, and the question of inequality does not go away; on the contrary, it gets more obvious than ever (Bhutoria, 2022). On the other hand, through suggested tactics from the literature like the use of rubrics, exemplars, and peer review, the adaptive learning system RiPPLE can assist in developing evaluative judgment in large-class situations (Khosravi et al., 2020) as well as can be utilized to enhance the learner model's prediction ability in comparison to more conventional learner models (Abdi et al., 2020). Another tool such as AcaWriter (example) which is writing and learning analytics tool, can be very effective in an educational setting only if teachers are active participants in the co-design of a student-facing writing analytics tool (Shibani et al., 2020). FUMA, alternatively, is a case study in the promotion of global and local explanations in AI systems to understand the decision-making process of AI models and how the system works, but since the systems are overly complex, it is difficult for users to understand the explanations. Same with TeamWork Analytics, which emphasizes teamwork and collaboration while promoting accountability, trust, and sensemaking in AI-powered educational systems, can yield great success, however misunderstandings may result from incomplete explanations, making this a major drawback (Khosravi et al., 2022).

The topics and concerns surrounding explainable AI in education are complex and multifaceted (Bostrom & Yudkowsky, 2018). To build trust in AI-powered educational systems, transparency and accountability are essential, and creating equitable learning environments requires ensuring fairness and eliminating bias (Veale et al., 2018). Ethical decision-making and human oversight are necessary to ensure that AI is used in education to complement human instructors, rather than replace them (Tadepalli et al., 2017). Case studies and examples in Table 5 above illustrate these concepts and issues and provide insight into the best practices and potential challenges for implementing explainable AI in the classroom.

Table 5. Examples and Case Studies

Theme/Example/Case Study		Key Theme/Issue
Automated Essay-Scoring System Bias	Theme	Fairness and Accuracy, Bias in Training Data
Personalized Learning Systems	Theme	Bias and Inequality, Individualization vs. Standardization
Project Debater by IBM	Example/CaseStudy	Role of Human Oversight, Emotion and Originality vs. Well-Researched Arguments
RiPPLE	Example	Accountability and trust, AI literacy, Agency, Comparison, Local explanations, Content-based recommender systems, Elo rating system, Disengagement
AcaWriter	Example	Agency, Trust, AI literacy, Local explanations, Comparisons, Rule-based NLP, Narrowness of rules-based systems, Context sensitivity
FUMA	Case Study	Trust, Sensemaking, Global explanations, Local explanations, Clustering, Classification, User-centered design, Overly complexed models, May not benefit all students
TeamWork Analytics	Case Study	Accountability and Trust, Agency, Sensemaking, Rule-based learning, Co-design, Incomplete explanations, Dysfunctional behaviour

Source: Authors own work and extended list from (Khosravi et al., 2022)

4 Current Approaches to Explainable AI in Education

4.1 Algorithmic Transparency and Interpretability

The transparency and interpretability of the underlying algorithms are necessary for the explainability of AI models used in education (Bischl et al., 2017). Making interpretable models that produce outcomes that humans can easily understand and explain is one way to achieve algorithmic transparency (Doshi-Velez & Kim, 2017). No matter how sophisticated or intricate a model is, model-agnostic interpretability techniques allow it to be explained (Ribeiro et al., 2016). Some of these methods include SHapley Additive exPlanations (SHAP), feature importance ratings, and partial dependence plots (Lundberg & Lee, 2017).

To ensure transparency and trustworthiness of AI systems deployed in education, researchers and educators are exploring methods for making AI model training data more open and accountable, as well as creating transparent and interpretable models (Salloum et al., 2020). This requires ensuring that the data used in training the models is accurate, unbiased, and free from flaws or contradictions. To address these challenges, techniques such as bias detection and correction and data augmentation may be utilized (Farrow, 2023; B. Kim et al., 2020).

4.2 Human-AI Collaboration and Hybrid Models

The difficulty of explainable AI (XAI) in education is being addressed by hybrid models and human-AI collaboration. (Ehsan et al., 2022). These models enable a more effective and open learning environment by fusing the strengths of both AI and human intelligence.

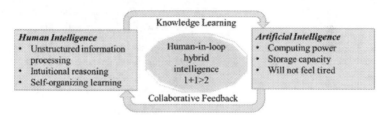

Fig. 2. Human-AI model. Adapted from (Zheng et al., 2017)

Students and teachers can have a better understanding of how AI systems make decisions and grow to trust their results through human-AI collaboration (Liu, 2021). In addition to providing educators with real-time feedback, hybrid models have the potential to provide adaptable learning experiences that are catered to each student's unique needs (Ratliff, 2019).

The development of systems that allow teachers to employ AI technologies to improve their teaching methods is one way to encourage human-AI collaboration in the educational setting (Bhutoria, 2022; Ehsan et al., 2022; Shibani et al., 2020). For example, AI-powered grading solutions can help educators save time and provide more personalized feedback to students (Aditomo et al., 2013). Another strategy is to create tutoring software driven by AI that can adjust to each student's specific learning preferences and needs while still providing feedback and explanations that are on par with those offered by human instructors. These initiatives could raise student interest, drive, and academic performance.

Interest in hybrid models that include both human and artificial intelligence is developing in educational settings (Akour et al., 2022). For instance, some academics are looking into the application of "human-in-the-loop" models (Fig. 2 above), in which initial decisions are made by AI systems and then assessed and changed by human experts. Other hybrid models blend artificial and human intelligence to provide predictions and explanations that are more accurate and reliable than those created using either approach alone. This approach enables a compromise between the speed and precision of AI and the complex decision-making skills of humans. Another kind of hybrid model combines the intelligence of humans and machines to give explanations and forecasts that are more reliable and accurate than those produced by either technique alone (Epstein et al., 2022) (Table 6).

Table 6. Examples of Human-AI Collaboration and Hybrid Models in Education

Approach	Description
AI-powered grading tools	Tools that use AI to assist teachers in grading and providing feedback to students
AI-powered tutoring systems	Systems that use AI to provide personalized and adaptive tutoring to students, while also providing human-like explanations and feedback
Human-in-the-loop models	Models where initial decisions made by AI systems are reviewed and adjusted by human experts
Hybrid models combining AI and human intelligence	Models that combine AI and human intelligence to generate more accurate and reliable explanations and predictions

Source: Authors' own work

In summary, these models are key strategies for achieving superior results in education. These approaches are aimed at improving teaching and learning outcomes by providing personalized and adaptive tutoring, accurate grading and feedback, and more reliable explanations and predictions.

4.3 Explainability Techniques and Tools

In the field of education, explainability techniques and tools are a collection of technologies that aim to shed light on the decision-making processes of AI systems. These tools make it possible for academics and researchers to go inside an AI system and find any biases or faults that might have been introduced during training. Partial dependence plots, feature importance ratings, and SHapley Additive exPlanations (SHAP) are some of the explainability techniques and tools that are most frequently used in education (Goodwin et al., 2022; Moon et al., 2022). The following are some of the explainability strategies and resources that are most frequently utilized in education:

1. Local Interpretable Model-Agnostic Explanations (LIME): This is a technique that allows users to generate explanations for individual predictions made by a model, making it easier to understand how the model arrived at its decisions.
2. Counterfactual Explanations: To explain the results of a model, this strategy entails creating alternative scenarios. Using this, one can determine what would have happened if certain factors had been changed.
3. SHAP (SHapley Additive exPlanations): This is a tool that assigns a value to each feature in a model, indicating how much that feature contributed to the final prediction.

4. Model Cards for Model Reporting: This is a standardized format for documenting the performance and behavior of an AI model, making it easier for users to understand its strengths and limitations.

The approaches and resources as depicted in Table 7 below, can be used by researchers and educators to improve the transparency and understanding of AI systems, as well as their general effectiveness in the educational setting.

Table 7. Overview of Explainability Techniques and Tools in Education

Technique/Tool	Description	Use	Examples	Limitations	Benefits
LIME	A local model-agnostic interpretability method that explains the predictions of any classifier by approximating it locally with an interpretable model	To explain individual predictions made by an AI model	Explaining why an AI system recommended a certain course of action to a student, or why it identified a specific error in a student's work	May not be effective in explaining complex models or large datasets	Provides simple and intuitive explanations for AI model predictions
SHAP	A method that quantifies the contribution of each feature to a prediction across the entire dataset	To determine the relative importance of different features in an AI model	Determining which features are most relevant in predicting a student's performance, or identifying which aspects of a course are most important for student success	Can be computationally expensive and may not always provide clear or actionable insights	Enables educators to understand how AI models are making predictions and identify areas for improvement
LRP	A layer-wise relevance propagation technique that identifies the contribution of each input feature to the final output of a neural network	To provide detailed information on how an AI model arrived at its output	Identifying which inputs were most relevant in making a decision, or understanding how a particular input affects the final output	Can be difficult to implement and may not work well with all types of neural networks	Provides a more granular level of explanation for AI models, enabling educators to identify potential biases or errors
Model Cards	A structured framework for documenting key information about an AI model, including its intended use, performance, and limitations	To provide a high-level overview of an AI model's capabilities and limitations	Sharing information about an AI model with stakeholders, such as educators, policymakers, and students	Requires manual input and may not capture all relevant information about a model	Enables greater transparency and accountability in AI models, and facilitates informed decision-making by stakeholders

Source: Authors own work (Adapted from (Aditya, 2022))

Table 7 provides an overview of four explainability techniques and tools used in education, including LIME, SHAP, LRP, and Model Cards. These tools are used to explain the predictions made by AI models, assess the relative weights of various model features, pinpoint the contributions of each input feature to a neural network's output, and offer a high-level overview of an AI model's strengths and weaknesses. Despite their limitations, these tools help educators understand how AI models are making predictions and spot potential biases or errors, which can increase AI model transparency and accountability and help stakeholders make well-informed decisions.

4.4   Ethical and Regulatory Frameworks for AI in Education

The growing use of AI in education has created a need for ethical and regulatory frameworks to ensure responsible and ethical implementation of the technology. A study conducted by Nguyen et.al. Provides a thematic analysis of ethical principles for artificial intelligence in education, including here governance and stewardship, transparency and accountability, sustainability, privacy, security and safety, inclusiveness and human centered AI in education (Nguyen et al., 2023). The use of AI in education raises questions about how this will affect key human rights concerns, therefore there is a need to develop further the ethical and legal frameworks that will handle these concerns (Fig. 3).

Fig. 3. Framework for Artificial Intelligence in Education. Adapted from (Hwang et al., 2020)

The ethical and legal frameworks for AI in education are summarized in Table 8 below. It emphasizes the significance of these frameworks in ensuring that AI-powered educational systems adhere to accepted moral and academic norms, safeguard students' and other stakeholders' rights to privacy and data protection, avoid bias and discrimination, and encourage responsible AI governance and supervision. Examples of pertinent restrictions, advantages, and regulations are provided in each framework. Gaining stakeholders' trust by comprehending and putting these concepts into practice can help to ensure that AI in education is employed in a safe, moral, and efficient manner. These frameworks are designed to address concerns about data security, fairness, bias, and transparency in AI-based educational systems (Nguyen et al., 2023). Strategies for achieving this goal include developing ethical guidelines and rules for the responsible use of AI in education, as well as organizations or other systems to regulate and supervise its usage. The initiatives to develop frameworks seek to increase public trust in AI-driven educational systems and ensure that the technology is used for the benefit of students and society as a whole (Sharma et al., 2022).

Table 8. Use, limitations, and benefits of regulatory and ethical frameworks

Ethical and Regulatory Frameworks for AI in Education	Use	Examples	Limitations	Benefits
Accreditation and Standards for AI in Education	Ensure that AI-powered educational systems meet established ethical and quality standards	IMS Global Learning Consortium, European Union's General Data Protection Regulation (GDPR)	Can be rigid and slow to adapt to new technology	Ensures that AI systems in education are safe, ethical, and effective
Data Protection and Privacy Regulations	Protect the privacy and data rights of students and other stakeholders	Family Educational Rights and Privacy Act (FERPA), Children's Online Privacy Protection Act (COPPA)	Can limit the amount and type of data that can be collected and used for AI models	Maintains trust and confidence in AI systems in education and protects sensitive information
Bias and Discrimination Prevention	Ensure that AI models are fair and unbiased towards all students, regardless of their race, gender, or other personal characteristics	Equity Literacy Institute's "Equity Audit" framework, Stanford's Fairness Indicators	Can be challenging to identify and eliminate all potential biases in AI models	Promotes equity and inclusivity in education, and helps to reduce the risk of harm or discrimination
Responsible AI Governance and Oversight	Ensure that AI systems in education are developed and deployed in an ethical and responsible manner	IEEE Global Initiative on Ethics of Autonomous and Intelligent Systems, Partnership on AI	Can be difficult to enforce and ensure compliance across different organizations and jurisdictions	Encourages transparency, accountability, and responsible use of AI in education, and helps to build trust with stakeholders

Source: Authors' own work

5 Implications and Future Directions

5.1 The Need for New Skills and Competencies for Educators and Learners

To effectively engage with AI and machine learning, educators and students must acquire new skills and competencies as these technologies continue to advance. Education professionals need to become familiar with the underlying algorithms and techniques utilized by these systems to fully harness the potential of explainable AI. They must also be able to critically assess the output of these systems and understand their limitations. In addition, students must be prepared to interact with AI in their educational experiences and have the necessary digital literacy skills to utilize and comprehend these tools (Laato et al., 2022). Even in the survey conducted by HolonIQ, the lack of talent with appropriate skill sets for AI work remain the highest barrier for adoption of AI in education, with 53% of respondents pointing that as major reason, accompanied by 50% of respondents saying that they are under-resources for AI (HolonIQ, 2023).

Table summarizing the skills and competencies needed to effectively interact with technologies in the educational context is provided in Table 9 below.

Table 9. Needed skills and competencies.

Skill/Competency	Description
Digital Literacy	The ability to effectively use digital technologies to locate, evaluate, create, and communicate information. This includes understanding how to use devices, software, and digital tools
Critical Thinking	The ability to analyze and evaluate information, arguments, and evidence in order to form well-reasoned conclusions and make informed decisions. This includes identifying biases and assumptions, evaluating sources, and drawing logical conclusions
Problem Solving	The ability to identify, analyze, and solve complex problems in a variety of contexts. This includes using critical thinking skills to identify the root cause of problems, generating and evaluating potential solutions, and selecting the best course of action
Collaboration	The ability to work effectively with others in a variety of contexts. This includes communicating clearly and respectfully, sharing knowledge and expertise, and working towards shared goals
Adaptability	The ability to be flexible and adapt to new situations and technologies. This includes being willing to learn new skills, embracing change, and being open to new ideas and ways of doing things

Source: Authors' own work

These abilities and skills are essential for both teachers and students to effectively connect with technologies in the educational context. As technology advances and becomes more prevalent in classrooms, people must have the skills and knowledge necessary to use these tools effectively and morally.

5.2 Potential Future Directions for Research and Practice in Explainable AI in Education

As the field of explainable AI in education continues to evolve, it is helpful to identify potential future research and practice directions (Minh et al., 2022). The development of more complex algorithms that can more accurately reflect the complexity of the learning process and offer thorough reasons for their judgments is one approach that is an option. The investigation of novel hybrid model approaches, in which human and AI systems work together more successfully and fluidly, is another direction. Ongoing studies are required on the ethical and legal frameworks to ensure that AI is used in education in ethical, transparent, and egalitarian (Holmes & Porayska-Pomsta, 2022). Finally, to provide them with the knowledge and skills necessary to navigate this fast-changing environment, educators, administrators, and policymakers must continue to pursue professional development. Based on the examination of more than 200 studies in this field, as well as analysis of reports and frameworks in XAI in education, we have recognized five areas of potential work to be conducted in this field as listed in Table 10 below.

Table 10. Future directions for research and practice in explainable AI in education

Potential Future Directions	Description what the research could involve
Integration of AI with social and emotional learning (SEL)	AI systems that can help students develop social and emotional skills, such as empathy and self-awareness
Personalized learning through adaptive AI	AI systems that can adapt to each student's learning style, pace, and interests, and provide personalized recommendations for learning materials and activities
Enhancing teacher professional development with AI	AI systems that provide personalized recommendations for training and resources based on the teacher's individual needs and performance. This could involve developing AI systems that can analyze teacher performance and provide feedback and support in real-time
Leveraging AI for educational assessment	Develop new forms of educational assessment: automated essay grading, adaptive testing, and predictive analytics. This could involve developing AI systems that can analyze student performance data to provide insights into their learning and suggest personalized interventions
Ensuring ethical and responsible use of AI in education	Future research and practice in explainable AI in education should continue to prioritize ethical and responsible use of AI in educational settings. This could involve developing frameworks for ethical and responsible use of AI in education, as well as tools for monitoring and regulating the use of AI in educational systems

Source: Authors' own work

The table outlines probable future directions for research and practice in explainable AI in education, such as the creation of more reliable and accurate models, the development of standards and best practices, the investigation of new AI applications in education, and the fusion of AI with other innovative technologies. The table also emphasizes the significance of cross-disciplinary cooperation, moral considerations, and continual assessment and monitoring of AI's effects on education. Some recommendations for future practice in explainable AI in education:

- Development of more user-friendly and accessible interfaces for educators and learners to understand and interpret AI-generated recommendations and decisions.
- Carrying out more empirical studies on the effectiveness of different explainability techniques and tools in improving the understanding and trust of AI in education.
- Designing and implementation of ethical and regulatory frameworks that address the unique challenges of AI in education, such as student privacy and data security.

The development and application of explainable AI in education can be advanced in a responsible, moral, and efficient manner by adhering to these suggestions.

6 Conclusion

In this review, we focused on the issues and problems relating to explainable AI in education. We discussed the challenges of implementing AI, the importance of explainability, and the need for human oversight. Moreover, we looked at current strategies for improving explainability, such as the interoperability and transparency of algorithms, human-AI collaboration, and ethical and regulatory frameworks. Likewise, we drew attention to the need for teachers and students to acquire new skills and knowledge as well as provided the implications for governance and policy. We concluded by highlighting the importance of continued research and development in explainable AI in education to warrant that XAI is utilized responsibly and ethically. We argue that future work should concentrate on interdisciplinary collaboration, user-centered and context-specific solution design, and transparency and ethical concerns promotion.

References

Abdi, S., Khosravi, H., Sadiq, S.: Modelling learners in crowdsourcing educational systems. In: Bittencourt, I.I., Cukurova, M., Muldner, K., Luckin, R., Millán, E. (eds.) AIED 2020. LNCS, vol. 12164, pp. 3–9. Springer, Cham (2020). https://doi.org/10.1007/978-3-030-52240-7_1

Aditomo, A., Goodyear, P., Bliuc, A.-M., Ellis, R.A.: Inquiry-based learning in higher education: principal forms, educational objectives, and disciplinary variations. Stud. High. Educ. **38**(9), 1239–1258 (2013)

Aditya, B.: Applied Machine Learning Explainability Techniques: Make ML Models Explainable and Trustworthy for Practical Applications Using LIME, SHAP, and More. Packt Publishing Ltd. (2022)

Akour, I.A., Al-Maroof, R.S., Alfaisal, R., Salloum, S.A.: A conceptual framework for determining metaverse adoption in higher institutions of gulf area: an empirical study using hybrid SEM-ANN approach. Comput. Educ.: Artif. Intell. **3**, 100052 (2022)

Amer-Yahia, S.: Towards AI-powered data-driven education. Proc. VLDB Endow. **15**(12), 3798–3806 (2022)

Amorim, E., Cançado, M., Veloso, A.: Automated essay scoring in the presence of biased ratings. In: Proceedings of the 2018 Conference of the North American Chapter of the Association for Computational Linguistics: Human Language Technologies, Volume 1 (Long Papers), pp. 229–237 (2018)

Artificial   intelligence—OECD.   (n.d.).   https://www.oecd.org/digital/artificial-intelligence/. Accessed 26 Apr 2023

Baker, R., Inventado, P.: Educational data mining and learning analytics, pp. 61–75 (2014). https://doi.org/10.1007/978-1-4614-3305-7_4

Baum, K., Mantel, S., Schmidt, E., Speith, T.: From responsibility to reason-giving explainable artificial intelligence. Philos. Technol. **35**(1), 12 (2022). https://doi.org/10.1007/s13347-022-00510-w

Bhutoria, A.: Personalized education and artificial intelligence in the united states, china, and India: a systematic review using a human-in-the-loop model. Comput. Educ.: Artif. Intell. **3**, 100068 (2022). https://doi.org/10.1016/j.caeai.2022.100068

Bischl, B., et al.: Openml benchmarking suites. ArXiv Preprint ArXiv:1708.03731 (2017)

Blikstein, P.: Gears of our childhood: constructionist toolkits, robotics, and physical computing, past and future. In: Proceedings of the 12th International Conference on Interaction Design and Children, pp. 173–182 (2013)

Bojarski, M., et al.: End to end learning for self-driving cars. ArXiv Preprint ArXiv:1604.07316 (2016)

Bostrom, N., Yudkowsky, E.: The Ethics of artificial intelligence, pp. 57–69 (2018). https://doi.org/10.1201/9781351251389-4

Boyd-Graber, J., Satinoff, B., He, H., Daumé, I.: Besting the quiz master: crowdsourcing incremental classification games, p. 1301 (2012)

Brusilovsky, P., Sosnovsky, S., Thaker, K.: The return of intelligent textbooks. AI Mag. **43**(3), 337–340 (2022)

Buolamwini, J., Gebru, T.: Gender shades: intersectional accuracy disparities in commercial gender classification. In: Conference on Fairness, Accountability and Transparency, pp. 77–91 (2018)

Cavanagh, T., Chen, B., Lahcen, R.A.M., Paradiso, J.R.: Constructing a design framework and pedagogical approach for adaptive learning in higher education: a practitioner's perspective. Int. Rev. Res. Open Distrib. Learn. **21**(1), 173–197 (2020)

Chen, Z.: Artificial intelligence-virtual trainer: innovative didactics aimed at personalized training needs. J. Knowl. Econ. 1–19 (2022)

Dabbagh, N., Kitsantas, A.: Personal learning environments, social media, and self-regulated learning: a natural formula for connecting formal and informal learning. Internet High. Educ. **15**(1), 3–8 (2012). https://doi.org/10.1016/j.iheduc.2011.06.002

Dillenbourg, P., Jermann, P.: Technology for classroom orchestration. New Sci. Learn.: Cogn. Comput. Collab. Educ. 525–552 (2010)

Doshi-Velez, F., Kim, B.: Towards a rigorous science of interpretable machine learning. arXiv: 1702.08608 (2017). https://doi.org/10.48550/arXiv.1702.08608

Dwork, C., Feldman, V., Hardt, M., Pitassi, T., Reingold, O., Roth, A.: The reusable holdout: preserving validity in adaptive data analysis. Science **349**(6248), 636–638 (2015)

Ehsan, U., et al.: Human-centered explainable AI (HCXAI): beyond opening the black-box of AI. In: CHI Conference on Human Factors in Computing Systems Extended Abstracts, pp. 1–7 (2022)

Epstein, Z., Foppiani, N., Hilgard, S., Sharma, S., Glassman, E., Rand, D.: Do explanations increase the effectiveness of AI-crowd generated fake news warnings? In: Proceedings of the International AAAI Conference on Web and Social Media, vol. 16, pp. 183–193 (2022)

Green, E., Chia, R., Singh, D.: AI ethics and higher education—good practice and guidance for educators, learners, and institutions. Globethics.net (2022)

Esteva, A., et al.: Dermatologist-level classification of skin cancer with deep neural networks. Nature **542**(7639), 115–118 (2017)

Farrow, R.: The possibilities and limits of XAI in education: a socio-technical perspective. Learn. Media Technol. 1–14 (2023)

Gilpin, L.H., Bau, D., Yuan, B.Z., Bajwa, A., Specter, M., Kagal, L.: Explaining explanations: an overview of interpretability of machine learning. In: 2018 IEEE 5th International Conference on Data Science and Advanced Analytics (DSAA), pp. 80–89 (2018)

Goodwin, N.L., Nilsson, S.R., Choong, J.J., Golden, S.A.: Toward the explainability, transparency, and universality of machine learning for behavioral classification in neuroscience. Curr. Opin. Neurobiol. **73**, 102544 (2022)

Grand View Research. AI In Education Market Size & Share Report, 2022–2030, p. 100 (2021). https://www.grandviewresearch.com/industry-analysis/artificial-intelligence-ai-education-market-report

Gunning, D., Stefik, M., Choi, J., Miller, T., Stumpf, S., Yang, G.-Z.: XAI—explainable artificial intelligence. Sci. Robot. **4**(37), eaay7120 (2019)

Herman, B.: The promise and peril of human evaluation for model interpretability. ArXiv Preprint ArXiv:1711.07414 (2017)

Holmes, W., Porayska-Pomsta, K.: The Ethics of Artificial Intelligence in Education: Practices, Challenges, and Debates. Taylor & Francis (2022)

HolonIQ. Artificial Intelligence in Education. 2023 Survey Insights (2023). https://www.holoniq.com/notes/artificial-intelligence-in-education-2023-survey-insights

Holstein, K., Wortman Vaughan, J., Daumé III, H., Dudik, M., Wallach, H.: Improving fairness in machine learning systems: what do industry practitioners need? In: Proceedings of the 2019 CHI Conference on Human Factors in Computing Systems, pp. 1–16 (2019)

Holzinger, A., Kieseberg, P., Weippl, E., Tjoa, A.M.: Current advances, trends and challenges of machine learning and knowledge extraction: from machine learning to explainable AI. In: Holzinger, A., Kieseberg, P., Tjoa, A.M., Weippl, E. (eds.) CD-MAKE 2018. LNCS, vol. 11015, pp. 1–8. Springer, Cham (2018). https://doi.org/10.1007/978-3-319-99740-7_1

Hwang, G.-J., Xie, H., Wah, B.W., Gašević, D.: Vision, challenges, roles and research issues of artificial intelligence in education. Comput. Educ.: Artif. Intell. **1**, 100001 (2020). https://doi.org/10.1016/j.caeai.2020.100001

IBM Research. Project Debater (n.d.). https://research.ibm.com/interactive/project-debater/. Accessed 26 Apr 2023

Islam, M.R., Ahmed, M.U., Barua, S., Begum, S.: A Systematic review of explainable artificial intelligence in terms of different application domains and tasks. Appl. Sci. **12**(3), Article 3 (2022). https://doi.org/10.3390/app12031353

Kasneci, E., et al.: ChatGPT for good? On opportunities and challenges of large language models for education. Learn. Individ. Differ. **103**, 102274 (2023)

Kelley, S., Ovchinnikov, A., Ramolete, G., Sureshbabu, K., Heinrich, A.: Tailoring explainable artificial intelligence: user preferences and profitability implications for firms. SSRN Scholarly Paper No. 4305480 (2022). https://doi.org/10.2139/ssrn.4305480

Khosravi, H., Gyamfi, G., Hanna, B.E., Lodge, J.: Fostering and supporting empirical research on evaluative judgement via a crowdsourced adaptive learning system. In: Proceedings of the Tenth International Conference on Learning Analytics & Knowledge, pp. 83–88 (2020). https://doi.org/10.1145/3375462.3375532

Khosravi, H., et al.: Explainable artificial intelligence in education. Comput. Educ.: Artif. Intell. **3**, 100074 (2022). https://doi.org/10.1016/j.caeai.2022.100074

Kim, B., Park, J., Suh, J.: Transparency and accountability in AI decision support: explaining and visualizing convolutional neural networks for text information. Decis. Support Syst. **134**, 113302 (2020)

Kim, J., Lee, H., Cho, Y.H.: Learning design to support student-AI collaboration: Perspectives of leading teachers for AI in education. Educ. Inf. Technol. **27**(5), 6069–6104 (2022). https://doi.org/10.1007/s10639-021-10831-6

Kizilcec, R.F., Pérez-Sanagustín, M., Maldonado, J.J.: Self-regulated learning strategies predict learner behavior and goal attainment in massive open online courses. Comput. Educ. **104**, 18–33 (2017)

Kleinberg, J., Lakkaraju, H., Leskovec, J., Ludwig, J., Mullainathan, S.: Human decisions and machine predictions. Q. J. Econ. **133**(1), 237–293 (2018)

Kolchenko, V.: Can modern AI replace teachers? Not so fast! Artificial intelligence and adaptive learning: personalized education in the AI age. HAPS Educator **22**(3), 249–252 (2018)

Kumari, M., Chaudhary, A., Narayan, Y.: Explainable AI (XAI): a survey of current and future opportunities. In: Hassanien, A.E., Gupta, D., Singh, A.K., Garg, A. (eds.) Explainable Edge AI: A Futuristic Computing Perspective. Studies in Computational Intelligence, vol. 1072, pp. 53–71. Springer, Cham (2023). https://doi.org/10.1007/978-3-031-18292-1_4

Laato, S., Tiainen, M., Najmul Islam, A.K.M., Mäntymäki, M.: How to explain AI systems to end users: a systematic literature review and research agenda. Internet Res. **32**(7), 1–31 (2022). https://doi.org/10.1108/INTR-08-2021-0600

Laupichler, M., Aster, A., Tobias, R.: Delphi study for the development and preliminary validation of an item set for the assessment of non-experts' AI literacy. Comput. Educ.: Artif. Intell. **4**, 100126 (2023). https://doi.org/10.1016/j.caeai.2023.100126

Lipton, Z.C.: The mythos of model interpretability: in machine learning, the concept of interpretability is both important and slippery. Queue **16**(3), 31–57 (2018)

Liu, B.: In AI we trust? Effects of agency locus and transparency on uncertainty reduction in human–AI interaction. J. Comput.-Mediat. Commun. **26**(6), 384–402 (2021)

Liyanagunawardena, T.R., Adams, A.A., Williams, S.A.: MOOCs: a systematic study of the published literature 2008–2012. Int. Rev. Res. Open Distrib. Learn. **14**(3), 202–227 (2013)

Lundberg, S.M., Lee, S.-I.: A unified approach to interpreting model predictions. In: Advances in Neural Information Processing Systems, vol. 30 (2017)

MacGillis, A.: The students left behind by remote learning. ProPublica (2020). https://www.propublica.org/article/the-students-left-behind-by-remote-learning

Manhiça, R., Santos, A., Cravino, J.: The impact of artificial intelligence on a learning management system in a higher education context: a position paper. In: Reis, A., Barroso, J., Martins, P., Jimoyiannis, A., Huang, R.Y.M., Henriques, R. (eds.) TECH-EDU 2022. CCIS, vol. 1720, pp. 454–460. Springer, Cham (2023). https://doi.org/10.1007/978-3-031-22918-3_36

Meacham, M.: A brief history of AI and education. Int. J. Adult Non Formal Educ. 1–2 (2021)

Minh, D., Wang, H.X., Li, Y.F., Nguyen, T.N.: Explainable artificial intelligence: a comprehensive review. Artif. Intell. Rev. **55**(5), 3503–3568 (2022). https://doi.org/10.1007/s10462-021-100 88-y

Mittelstadt, B.: Principles alone cannot guarantee ethical AI. Nat. Mach. Intell. **1**(11), 501–507 (2019)

Moon, J., Rho, S., Baik, S.W.: Toward explainable electrical load forecasting of buildings: a comparative study of tree-based ensemble methods with Shapley values. Sustain. Energy Technol. Assess **54**, 102888 (2022)

Nagahisarchoghaei, M., et al.: An empirical survey on explainable ai technologies: recent trends, use-cases, and categories from technical and application perspectives. Electronics **12**(5), Article 5 (2023). https://doi.org/10.3390/electronics12051092

Nandi, A., Pal, A.K.: Interpreting Machine Learning Models: Learn Model Interpretability and Explainability Methods. Springer, Heidelberg (2022)

Needham, Mass.: Worldwide spending on AI-centric systems forecast to reach $154 billion in 2023, according to IDC. IDC: The Premier Global Market Intelligence Company (2023). https://www.idc.com/getdoc.jsp?containerId=prUS50454123

Nguyen, A., Ngo, H.N., Hong, Y., Dang, B., Nguyen, B.-P.T.: Ethical principles for artificial intelligence in education. Educ. Inf. Technol. **28**(4), 4221–4241 (2023). https://doi.org/10.1007/s10639-022-11316-w

Ouyang, F., Zheng, L., Jiao, P.: Artificial intelligence in online higher education: a systematic review of empirical research from 2011 to 2020. Educ. Inf. Technol. **27**(6), 7893–7925 (2022)

Raji, I.D., Scheuerman, M.K., Amironesei, R.: You can't sit with us: exclusionary pedagogy in AI ethics education. In: Proceedings of the 2021 ACM Conference on Fairness, Accountability, and Transparency, pp. 515–525 (2021)

Ratliff, K.: Building rapport and creating a sense of community: are relationships important in the online classroom? J. Online Learn. Res. Pract. **7**(1) (2019)

Ribeiro, M.T., Singh, S., Guestrin, C.: "Why should i trust you?" Explaining the predictions of any classifier. In: Proceedings of the 22nd ACM SIGKDD International Conference on Knowledge Discovery and Data Mining, pp. 1135–1144 (2016)

Saeed, W., Omlin, C.: Explainable AI (XAI): a systematic meta-survey of current challenges and future opportunities. Knowl.-Based Syst. **263**, 110273 (2023). https://doi.org/10.1016/j.knosys.2023.110273

Salloum, S.A., Alshurideh, M., Elnagar, A., Shaalan, K.: Mining in educational data: review and future directions. In: Hassanien, A.-E., Azar, A.T., Gaber, T., Oliva, D., Tolba, F.M. (eds.) AICV 2020. AISC, vol. 1153, pp. 92–102. Springer, Cham (2020). https://doi.org/10.1007/978-3-030-44289-7_9

Samek, W., Müller, K.-R.: Towards explainable artificial intelligence. In: Samek, W., Montavon, G., Vedaldi, A., Hansen, L.K., Müller, K.-R. (eds.) Explainable AI: Interpreting, Explaining and Visualizing Deep Learning. LNCS (LNAI), vol. 11700, pp. 5–22. Springer, Cham (2019). https://doi.org/10.1007/978-3-030-28954-6_1

Samek, W., Wiegand, T., Müller, K.-R.: Explainable artificial intelligence: understanding, visualizing and interpreting deep learning models. ArXiv Preprint ArXiv:1708.08296 (2017)

Sharma, H., Soetan, T., Farinloye, T., Mogaji, E., Noite, M.D.F.: AI adoption in universities in emerging economies: prospects, challenges and recommendations. In: Mogaji, E., Jain, V., Maringe, F., Hinson, R.E. (eds.) Re-imagining Educational Futures in Developing Countries: Lessons from Global Health Crises, pp. 159–174. Springer, Cham (2022). https://doi.org/10.1007/978-3-030-88234-1_9

Shibani, A., Knight, S., Shum, S.B.: Educator perspectives on learning analytics in classroom practice. Internet High. Educ. **46**, 100730 (2020)

Tadepalli, P., Fern, X., Dietterich, T.: Deep reading and learning. OREGON STATE UNIV CORVALLIS CORVALLIS, USA (2017)

UNESCO. The promise of large-scale learning assessments: acknowledging limits to unlock opportunities. UNESCO (2019). https://unesdoc.unesco.org/ark:/48223/pf0000369697

Vapnik, V., Izmailov, R.: Rethinking statistical learning theory: learning using statistical invariants. Mach. Learn. **108**(3), 381–423 (2019)

Veale, M., Van Kleek, M., Binns, R.: Fairness and accountability design needs for algorithmic support in high-stakes public sector decision-making. In: Proceedings of the 2018 CHI Conference on Human Factors in Computing Systems, pp. 1–14 (2018)

Vilone, G., Longo, L.: Explainable artificial intelligence: a systematic review. ArXiv Preprint ArXiv:2006.00093 (2020)

Walger, L., et al.: Artificial intelligence for the detection of focal cortical dysplasia: challenges in translating algorithms into clinical practice. Epilepsia (2023)

Whalley, B., France, D., Park, J., Mauchline, A., Welsh, K.: Towards flexible personalized learning and the future educational system in the fourth industrial revolution in the wake of Covid-19. High. Educ. Pedag. **6**(1), 79–99 (2021)

Woolf, B.P.: Building Intelligent Interactive Tutors: Student-Centered Strategies for Revolutionizing e-Learning. Morgan Kaufmann (2010)

Xia, X., Li, X.: Artificial intelligence for higher education development and teaching skills. Wirel. Commun. Mob. Comput. **2022** (2022)

Xu, R., Baracaldo, N., Joshi, J.: Privacy-preserving machine learning: methods, challenges and directions. ArXiv Preprint ArXiv:2108.04417 (2021)

Yadav, A., et al.: A review of international models of computer science teacher education. In: Proceedings of the 2022 Working Group Reports on Innovation and Technology in Computer Science Education, pp. 65–93 (2022)

Yakubu, M.N., Abubakar, A.M.: Applying machine learning approach to predict students' performance in higher educational institutions. Kybernetes **51**(2), 916–934 (2022)

Zawacki-Richter, O., Marín, V.I., Bond, M., Gouverneur, F.: Systematic review of research on artificial intelligence applications in higher education–where are the educators? Int. J. Educ. Technol. High. Educ. **16**(1), 1–27 (2019)

Zeide, E.: Artificial intelligence in higher education: applications, promise and perils, and ethical questions. Educause Rev. **54**(3) (2019)

Zhai, X., et al.: A Review of artificial intelligence (AI) in education from 2010 to 2020. Complexity **2021**, e8812542 (2021). https://doi.org/10.1155/2021/8812542

Zhang, J.: Computer assisted instruction system under artificial intelligence technology. Int. J. Emerg. Technol. Learn. (IJET) **16**(5), 4–16 (2021)

Zheng, N., et al.: Hybrid-augmented intelligence: collaboration and cognition. Front. Inf. Technol. Electron. Eng. **18**(2), 153–179 (2017). https://doi.org/10.1631/FITEE.1700053

Contrastive Visual Explanations for Reinforcement Learning via Counterfactual Rewards

Xiaowei Liu[✉], Kevin McAreavey, and Weiru Liu

School of Engineering Mathematics and Technology, University of Bristol, Bristol, UK
{xiaowei.liu,kevin.mcareavey,weiru.liu}@bristol.ac.uk

Abstract. Causal attribution aided by counterfactual reasoning is recognised as a key feature of human explanation. In this paper we propose a post-hoc contrastive explanation framework for reinforcement learning (RL) based on comparing learned policies under actual environmental rewards vs. hypothetical (counterfactual) rewards. The framework provides policy-level explanations by accessing learned Q-functions and identifying intersecting critical states. Global explanations are generated to summarise policy behaviour through the visualisation of sub-trajectories based on these states, while local explanations are based on the action-values in states. We conduct experiments on several grid-world examples. Our results show that it is possible to explain the difference between learned policies based on Q-functions. This demonstrates the potential for more informed human decision-making when deploying policies and highlights the possibility of developing further XAI techniques in RL.

Keywords: Explainable reinforcement learning · Contrastive explanations · Counterfactuals · Visual explanations

1 Introduction

The aim of explainable AI planning (XAIP) and explainable reinforcement learning (XRL) is to help end-users better understand agent behaviour (e.g. learned policies) and how that behaviour relates to the environment (i.e. transition probabilities and rewards) [6,12,15]. Contrastive explanations are a particular approach to explainable AI (XAI) that seek to answer *contrastive why-questions*, with the aim of identifying the causes of one event (called the fact) relative to the causes of another (called the foil in the counterfactual case, meaning that the event did not occur in the actual world) [26]. Miller [31,32] emphasised the importance of contrastive explanations in explainable AI (XAI) based a survey of the relevant literature from philosophy and social science. Many recent studies have explored different aspects of contrastive explanations in XAIP and XRL [16,35,49].

© The Author(s), under exclusive license to Springer Nature Switzerland AG 2023
L. Longo (Ed.): xAI 2023, CCIS 1902, pp. 72–87, 2023.
https://doi.org/10.1007/978-3-031-44067-0_4

One possibility for contrastive explanations in XRL is to compare a learned policy under actual environmental rewards versus a learned policy under hypothetical (counterfactual) rewards. Such comparisons have analogies in several areas of RL. For example, preference-based RL [8,20,27] seeks to learn a policy that is optimal with respect to altered rewards that combine environmental rewards with human preferences. If a policy is learned under both kinds of rewards, then it opens the possibility of explaining one policy with respect to the other by way of contrast. An interesting research challenge then is how to generate contrastive explanations for RL to help humans better understand the impact of actual rewards on learned agent behaviour.

In this paper, we develop a framework for contrastive explanations in RL that compares the policy learned under actual rewards against policies learned under different counterfactual rewards. The actual reward configuration is just the actual rewards, while each counterfactual reward configuration is a partial alteration of the actual rewards. We assume that all policies are otherwise trained under the same conditions (e.g. same hyperparameters, same training steps). We adopt a post-hoc XAI paradigm to provide two types of contrastive explanation:

1. *Global explanation*: This type of explanation focuses on providing overall policy explanations about an agent's behaviour. It provides insights into how these policies behave in general by visualising (sub-)trajectories, and how decisions are made in some states among the configurations.
2. *Local explanation*: This type of explanation addresses the question, "Why was action a chosen in state s rather than action a'?" It provides more fine-grained information based on the action-value function in each configuration, allowing for a better understanding of agent behaviour.

The rest of this paper is organised as follows. Section 2 reviews related literature about explanation in XAIP and XRL. Section 3 formulates the main structure of contrastive explanation, and Sect. 4 offers illustrative explanation and further analysis on the cases. The last section offers conclusions, discussions and future works.

2 Related Work

Explainable AI (XAI) has obtained significant attention in recent years, driven by the advancement and wide application of machine learning and AI systems especially in decision making [23,40,44]. The systems pose challenges for trustworthiness if they simply employ more powerful and flexible models, albeit at the expense of model interpretability and transparency [12,30,33]. The complexity of the systems, as well as the difficulty explaining an agent's behaviour in planning and RL, have been acknowledged by many research papers [5,6,55] which further assessed the necessity of XAI for planning and RL. In this part, we review some literature that is closely related to the topics in XRL.

Policy Summarisation in RL. Policy summarisation has been a subject of much research in XAIP and XRL [24,45], which improves interpretability and provides an explanation regarding the agent's policy behaviour. One approach is the use of trajectory visualisation, which involves summarising the agent's policy by extracting important trajectories from simulations. For example, in [1], the authors discussed the design and implementation of the *HIGHLIGHTS* algorithm, which used state importance and the state diversity criteria for choosing the trajectories from the replay buffer. This approach was further extended in [18], which integrated saliency maps to local explanation through the visualisation of trajectories. In robotics and control, [17] utilises example trajectories to enable users to better anticipate the behaviours or goals of robots. Following this, [24] enhanced the example trajectories extraction by optimising an inverse reinforcement learning or imitation learning problem. Another approach to policy summarisation is generating an abstracted or hierarchical explanation through learned models or data about the policy. For instance, in [47], authors generated policy-level explanations for RL, which used a Markov chain to represent abstracted states and their transitions based on the training data. In [43], authors proposed a framework for learning hierarchical policies in multi-task RL that can learn human instructions and generate an explanation of its decisions by learned instructions back to humans. Similarly, in [54], authors proposed a policy abstraction method through an extended model of MDP for deep Q-networks. Besides, many prior studies have demonstrated effectiveness revealing an agent behaviour through trajectory visualisation and policy abstraction [3,19,34]. These works provide solid support for trajectory visualisation that serves as an effective approach to policy summarisation and explaining the agent's behaviour. Building upon this foundation, we extend these methods by incorporating contrastive explanations.

Critical States and Key Moments for Explanation in RL. [16] suggested that the essence of the policy relies on a few critical states or the corresponding agent's actions on those states, and proposed approaches for computing critical states based on the action-value function and the policy function. Similarly, [22] explored the importance of a state with the variance of its learning action-value function on states. Another study by [41] proposed a method which extracted key moments of the agent's decision with statistical information of the agents, delivered visual summaries and offered user studies of the performance. The authors further extracted key elements of interestingness from an agent's learning experience in [42], and presented a global and visual summarisation of agent behaviour based on elements including frequency and sequence. From another aspect, counterfactual state, which was proposed in [36] captured the key states that an agent chose a different action with minimal change to the input of the policy networks. Deep generative models were used to create counterfactual states and present visual counterfactual explanations to users on Atari games in this work. Recent research integrated generating counterfactuals in latent space with gradient-driven methods [53]. In the domain of robust RL, the detection of critical states against adversarial attacks adopted this metric [25]. Other studies [11,13,54] focused on the identification and visualisation of the salience of state features for Atari agents, which could be considered a metric of critical states.

Explanation via Rewards or Value Functions in RL. Notably, the contrasting descriptions were provided for users' queries related to predefined state transitions and expected reward outcomes of the agent [49]. This approach did not directly answer the contrastive questions on the agent's behaviour, but transformed the questions and provided answers by explaining the learned value functions instead. Similar to [14], the proposed method introduced contrastive explanations regarding the simulated outcomes of the rollouts based on two policies (the agent policy and the foil policy). The construction of the fact and foil in these papers, and the scheme for contrastive explanation are heuristics, which partially motivated the contrastive explanation for the difference in reward configurations in our work. The framework in [10] provided a policy evaluation method on the action-value function that identified the influence of state transitions by removing some transition data. According to [29], contrastive explanations were generated by action influence models which involved causal relationship of rewards and actions. [21] introduced an explanation framework based on reward decomposition, in which it is assumed that rewards can be decomposed into vector-like rewards with semantic meaning. It is extended in a user-study for real-time strategy games in [2], generated explanations for outcomes that agents intended to achieve in tabular RL approaches [52]. [28] further utilised reward decomposition to build a learnable framework for robotics.

From a boarder aspect of XRL, some works have considered aspects of user needs, such as personalised explanations [46] and the complexity of contrastiveness [35]. We refer readers to see systematic overview of topics in XRL [37,48,51,56].

3 Generating Contrastive Explanations for Two Policies

3.1 Preliminaries

In this work we consider infinite-horizon, discounted reward Markov Decision Processes (MDPs) [38,39]. An MDP is a tuple $\mathcal{M} = (S, A, P, R, \gamma)$ where S is a finite set of states, A is a finite set of actions, $P : S \times A \to \Delta(S)$ is a (stochastic) transition function where $\Delta(S)$ is the set of probability distributions over S, $R : S \times A \times S \to \mathbb{R}$ is a reward function, and $\gamma \in [0, 1)$ is a discount factor. The transition function P says if action a is executed in state s then the system will transition to state s' with probability $P(s, a, s')$, where $P(s, a, s')$ denotes the probability of reaching state s' according to distribution $P(s, a)$. The optimal value function $V^\star$ is defined for each $s \in S$ as:

$$V^\star(s) = \max_{a \in A} \sum_{s' \in S} P(s, a, s') \left[R(s, a, s') + \gamma V^\star(s') \right] \tag{1}$$

and the optimal action-value function $Q^\star$ is defined for each $a \in A$ as:

$$Q^\star(s, a) = \sum_{s' \in S} P(s, a, s') \left[R(s, a, s') + \gamma V^\star(s') \right] \tag{2}$$

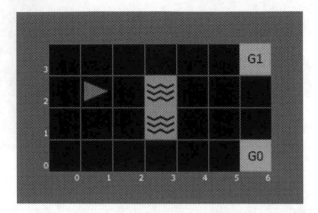

Fig. 1. A grid-world scenario.

A policy is a function $\pi : S \to A$. The optimal policy $\pi^\star$ can be extracted directly from the optimal action-value function, i.e. for each $s \in S$:

$$\pi^\star(s) = \text{argmax}_{a \in A} Q^\star(s, a) \qquad (3)$$

In planning (where P and R are known) a well-known approach to finding the optimal value function is value iteration [4]. In RL (where P and R are unknown) a well-known approach to finding the optimal action-value function is Q-learning [50]. In our proposed method, we assume access to both the learned policy and the learned action-value function as optimal functions defined in Eq. (2) and (3), which allows us to generate explanations from the decision-making processes of the agent. We consider MDPs with different reward functions R_i as $\mathcal{M}_i = (S, A, P, R_i, \gamma)$. The optimal policy, optimal value function and optimal action-value function on $\mathcal{M}_i$ are marked as $\pi_i^\star, V_i^\star(s)$ and $Q_i^\star(s, a)$.

Environment Description: A Demo of Grid-World. We consider a simple case with a 7×4 grid-world (Fig. 1). Four actions, *UP, DOWN, LEFT, RIGHT*, are available at each state with a random action rate with 0.1.[1] To reach the final destinations (*G0* and *G1* in green blocks) with the same positive reward, the agent (red triangle) has to avoid the absorbing states, the lava cells (orange), with a reward of 0. The agent initialises at one of the four cells on the far-left side of the lava, and every action taken receives a penalty of -0.01.

3.2 Identifying Critical States from Q-Functions

Critical states are defined as states where small changes can significantly affect the agent's behaviour, and they have been shown to be reliable indicators of an

---

[1] With 90% probability the agent moves one cell in the direction specified by the action (i.e. the action succeeds), or with 5% probability each the agent moves one cell either clockwise or anti-clockwise relative to the direction specified by the action (i.e. the action fails). This grid-world was implemented by Minigrid [7].

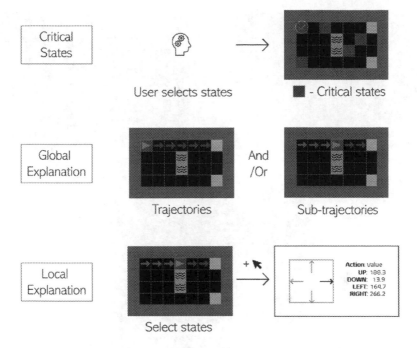

Fig. 2. An illustration of explanation process. Global explanation: agent (red triangle) starts at a state, an example (full) trajectory and/or sub-trajectory are visualised. Local explanation: local explanations are provided with a window on states of interest by interacting with the explainer, and with more information explained on the agent's state. (Color figure online)

agent's decision-making process [16]. One of the most commonly used metrics for defining critical states is the difference between the maximum and average action values of a state above a predetermined threshold. Let $\mathcal{C}_i$ denote the set of critical states under the optimal policy $\pi^\star$ for a given MDP. We refer this metric as *Max-mean* [16],

$$\mathcal{C}_i = \left\{ s \in S \mid \left(\max Q_i^\star(s, a) - \frac{1}{|A|} \sum_a Q_i^\star(s, a) \right) > \tau \right\}. \tag{4}$$

The number of critical states can vary depending on the reward function of the MDP. By changing the threshold τ according to the user's needs and the environmental reward function, the number of critical states can be adjusted accordingly. If there are K MDPs, we can denote the set of intersected states among these MDPs as $\mathcal{C}^{\mathrm{I}} = \cap_{i=1}^{K} \mathcal{C}_i$.

One of the commonly used metrics for the max-mean metric is the difference between the maximum and minimum action-values from the action-value function [1]. Another study by [22] explores the importance of a state by examining the variance of its action-value function at states during learning. We consider

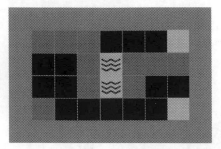 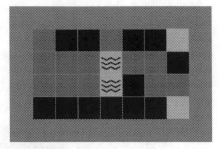

(a) Critical states (blue) with one re-ward function.

(b) Critical states (purple) with a different reward function.

(c) The intersected critical states (red) of two reward functions.

Fig. 3. Critical states from two different reward functions, and the intersected critical states which hint the important states in common of the two configurations.

these as variants of the Max-mean approach. We acknowledge that further evaluation of these methods through user studies is necessary to determine their efficacy in generating useful explanations of agents. A survey of related work on critical states and key moments is provided in Sect. 2, and we offered analysis in Sect. 5.3.

Before presenting more details, we provide an overview of how our methodology (referred to as the *explainer*) generates explanations for users (referred to as the *explainee*). The explainer initiates the process by generating critical states based on the specific questions of the explainee. Critical states are generated as a series of intersecting critical states if there are multiple policies. These critical states are then represented visually as contrastive trajectories. Each trajectory records the sequence of state-action pairs an agent takes, beginning from each critical state during simulations. Additionally, to provide further details to the user, the explainee can pause the visualisation and inquire about states of interest. In the event of such queries, the explainer presents contrastive explanations on different learned policies, including the feasible actions that can be executed, the relevant action values from those states, along with the optimal actions of each policy.

3.3   Global Explanation by Using Critical States

Firstly, the explainer presents a number of states based on a default threshold τ of the metric in Eq. (4). These states are then used as inputs to the explainer, and Monte Carlo simulations are initiated in parallel, recording the state-action pairs until termination states are reached (i.e., absorbing states or predefined maximum length of recording). We refer a *full trajectory* as a trajectory rollout history in which agent starts from the initial state of the environment and terminates until the agent reaches termination states. A *sub-trajectory* is a trajectory rollout history in which agent starts from the critical states and reaches termination states. To provide a comprehensive global explanation on states, we visualise full trajectories or partial trajectories rollouts (illustrated in Fig. 2). Finally, the corresponding trajectories with the maximal probability for the counterfactual reward function within the sample space are presented to the user either as videos or images with all the state-action pairs highlighted in contrast. These trajectories serve as contrastive global explanations, allowing the explainee to observe, comprehend the agent's behaviour and compare agents with respect to their reward functions in each configuration.

3.4   Local Explanation and Contrastive Explanation Based on Action-Values

If the users have further queries regarding how the policy acts on specific states, we visualise based on the states in question by displaying optimal actions and action-values of those states. We leverage the learned action-value function to generate local explanations for the agent's decision-making. For instance as shown in Fig. 5a and 5d, the action *RIGHT* is the optimal action as the explainee observe that it has the highest value. The explainer displays the relative importance of each action at a given state based on its action-value, and provides a more interpretable and informative explanation for the agent's decision.

We provide contrastive explanations on critical states in each reward configuration, highlighting the differences between the learned policies and their corresponding action-values. Specifically, we contrastively display the different critical states presented in the reward configuration based on the metric in Eq. (4). The intersected critical states are highlighted (for instance, in red in Fig. 3) to draw the attention of explainees to the potential significance of the states across multiple configurations. In our proposed framework, the explainee can choose specific states of interest, and the explainer will then display all the actions taken by agents and the action-values pairs from agents in a contrastive manner across different reward configurations. This allows the explainee to observe the different action-values pairs associated with the same action, and possible different optimal actions in a given state for better understanding of agents' behaviour. In addition, we can further enhance the local explanations by considering the uncertainty of the agent's action-value estimation.

4   Experiments

We consider two variants of this grid-world named GW$^+$ and GW$^-$ (see in Fig. 1) where the reward functions are set as:

- GW$^+$: The agent will receive a reward of $+1$ at *G0* (6,4) and a reward of $+3$ at *G1* (6,0).
- GW$^-$: The agent will receive a reward of $+3$ at *G0* (6,4) and a reward of $+1$ at *G1* (6,0).

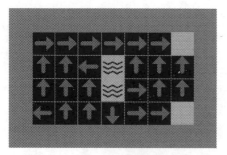 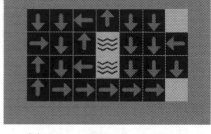

(a) A learned policy in GW$^+$.   (b) A learned policy in GW$^-$.

Fig. 4. Illustration of grid-world by Q-learning in GW$^+$ and GW$^-$ (blue and purple). (Color figure online)

The purpose of the setting is to give an illustrative example where reward functions are the only part vary and the transition functions in the MDPs remain the same. We designed such two intuitive reward functions under which Q-learning is used to learn policies. Specifically, we ran the algorithm on two grid-worlds denoted as GW$^+$ and GW$^-$, respectively, with a discount factor of 0.99 and learning rate of 0.01. The Q-tables are initialised with values $\mathcal{N}(0,1)$ and 14000 episodes. After the training process we output the Q-table as the learned action-value function.

We identify the critical states from each Q table and compute their intersection set $\mathcal{C}^I$, which provides a simple illustration of policy behaviour. To compute the critical states, we utilised the Max-mean method in Eq. (4) and set a predetermined parameter of $\tau = 80$ for better illustration. The resulting critical states for GW$^+$ and GW$^-$ are shown in Fig. 3. There were five intersected critical states, and we selected three of them for illustration: (0,3), (2,1), and (4,2).

To provide a global explanation, we report the learned policies for GW$^+$ and GW$^-$ in Fig. 4a and Fig. 4b, respectively, along with the optimal actions at each state indicated by arrows. We then present further global and contrastive explanations based on a sample of simulations shown in blue and purple colours in Fig. 5a, 5b, and 5c. The corresponding states are highlighted in the images. The explainees can observe that the agent's decisions starting from certain states

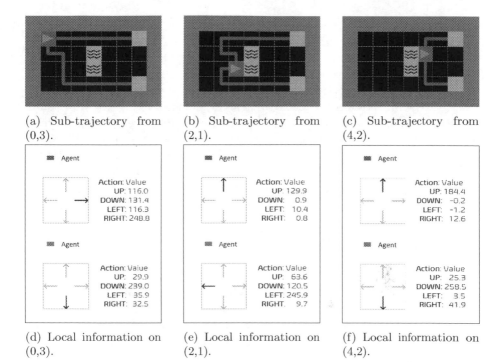

(a) Sub-trajectory from (0,3).

(b) Sub-trajectory from (2,1).

(c) Sub-trajectory from (4,2).

(d) Local information on (0,3).

(e) Local information on (2,1).

(f) Local information on (4,2).

Fig. 5. An example of contrastive explanation on three critical states. 5a–5c: Global contrastive explanation on agents in GW^+ (blue) and GW^- (purple). 5d–5f: Local contrastive explanation on actions in GW^+ and GW^-. (Color figure online)

can lead to completely different goal states which reveals the importance of understanding critical states and their impact on the overall policy behaviour. For example, in Fig. 5b, this figure illustrates two trajectories which are legible to the explainees in the presence of two possible goal states of the agent and the avoidance of lava states. If the agent starts at the left position next to the lava grid, with one policy, it takes the action *UP* and *LEFT*, then executed a series of action of *RIGHT* and eventually reaches the goal state on the top-right (*G1*). With a different policy, it takes the action *LEFT* and *DOWN*, and then provides another series of actions that reaches the goal state of bottom-right (*G0*). We observe at least two agent behaviours: the behaviour of reaching different goal states, and the behaviour of stepping away from the lava grid. From the perspective of the explainees' mental models, we wish they would attribute causes of the difference of reward configurations themselves from these behaviours, with possibly further observation on the local explanation of action-values. Though the visual explanation does not directly tell the explainees the actual factors on how and why the reward differs, it illustrates an explicable trajectory that help them comprehend the objectives of the agent's behaviours. Similar explanations apply to Fig. 5a and Fig. 5c.

Local and contrastive explanation are shown in Fig. 5d, 5e, and 5f. Providing action-values and optimal actions for each state in contrast contributes to a more comprehensive explanation of global contrastive explanation with trajectories. The explainee can observe differences among the action-values across actions, which could help explainees comprehend why the agent chose the learned action (highlighted in black) over the other three actions (shown in grey). For instance, in Fig. 5e, it has been demonstrated that the action *UP* is the optimal action for one agent, the blue agent, as it yields the highest action-value of 129.9. On the other hand, for the second agent, the purple agent, the optimal action is *LEFT*, with a corresponding optimal action-value of 245.9. The difference in optimal actions aid the explainees in attributing causal factors, e.g., why the agent ultimately reaches distinct goal states.

5   Conclusion and Discussion

In this study, we addressed the problem of explanation in RL by comparing policies based on their action-value functions where the policies are learned under different reward functions. Our proposed methods generating global and local explanations through trajectories based on intersected critical states. We further showed our explanation successfully demonstrating the contrastive behaviour by an example from Q-learning in a grid-world.

5.1   Discussion of Research Questions

In this subsection, we discuss our research questions and the knowledge contributed to the XAI community in this paper. The utilisation of counterfactual rewards within XRL is to address two broader and significant research questions:

Research Question 1: Casual attribution via counterfactual reasoning. Suppose that an action X has been learned by an agent and the explainees asked "why X?" as the action may look unexpected or weird. Humans are believed to answer such questions by identifying causes through counterfactual reasoning. In RL, the learned action in each state depends on characteristics of the underlying MDP, which consists of a transition function and a reward function. A reasonable cause in RL then might reference characteristics of the transition function and/or reward function that led to action X having been learned. An important question would be: what characteristics of the transition function and/or reward function are most relevant to the action X having been learned? In this paper, we limit our focus to the reward function. The objective of simulating hypothetical rewards is not to imply that X would not have been learned in the absence of the actual reward function. Instead, its purpose is to facilitate counterfactual reasoning in humans, enabling them to attribute characteristics of the actual reward function as causes for X having been learned. We focus on predefined hypothetical reward functions, but our objective remains the same: as an aid to understand the actual reward function and its impact on learned actions.

Research Question 2: Casual contrastive explanations. Suppose Research Question 1 has been answered and the explainees are able to attribute characteristics of the actual reward function as causes for X having been learned. Suppose again that the explainees proposed some other action Y which would have been normal/expected, and asked "why X rather than Y?" According to the question, action Y was not learned by the agent, so the explainees are not able to attribute characteristics of the actual reward function as causes for Y having been learned. Instead, we need a hypothetical reward function, and specifically one where Y would have been learned with all the settings being equal (i.e., the same transition function, hyper-parameters, and training steps etc.) However, if we have those causes, then we can answer the question by focusing on the aspects where the actual and hypothetical causes differ. In the paper we do not directly address Research Question 2, but we do lay some groundwork on how it could be addressed, mainly due to the need to construct hypothetical reward functions, but also in the need for visual comparisons. However, a major difference is that the hypothetical reward function is now significant; it must ensure that Y is learned, all else being equal. The same criteria may be reasonable for choosing hypothetical reward functions under Research Question 1.

5.2 Discussion of Findings

This paper contributions to the field of XRL in the sense that it addresses a previously unexplored question improving the users' comprehension of the agent behaviour through the construction of a hypothetical reward function. Specifically, we use the learned policies on both the hypothetical and actual reward functions to enable users to engage in counterfactual reasoning on the discrepancies existed between these reward functions. The proposed method offers a viable and natural means of addressing contrastive questions and limit the information scope to identification of critical states and trajectory visualisation. The metric used for critical states in this study builds upon a prior research. The visualisations presented in this paper leverage the established groundwork of trajectory visualisation methods, which have proven to be an effective approach to summarising policies and an agent's behaviour. We emphasise the importance of co-use for explaining the difference of reward functions: contrastive explanations visually based on trajectories and utilisation of action-values.

5.3 Limitations and Future Work

While this paper primarily focuses on computational methods rather than user studies, it is important to acknowledge the need for a user study to evaluate the effectiveness of the visual explanations provided and the validity under specific conditions. We recognise the significance of conducting a comprehensive user study as part of future work. We also provide possible future improvement on the following topics.

Critical States Identification. One limitation observed is the absence of user evaluation regarding the metrics employed for critical states identification. While the action-values can reveal the optimal action(s) that are preferred over alternative actions, future work should focus on providing explanations from the underlying reasons supporting such preferences, e.g., an epistemic perspective of certainty/uncertainty of the agent. Furthermore, in addition to computing critical states based on the action-value or value function, we posit that a similar metric can be applied to the policy function and potentially extended to continuous action spaces.

Textual Explanation and Interactive Interface. The proposed method primarily provide visual comparisons to facilitate casual attribution by humans, however, this could fail when the visualisation does not meet human's expectation. We recognise this limitation, and textual-based and question-based explanations could be used in enhancing the potential cognitive process by explainees in future work. The inclusion of an interactive interface is targeted to consider the needs and preferences in explanation for users [35, 46]. For instance, providing users with the capability to specify the desired number of critical states or certain type of metric they wish to view, particularly in situations where there may be an overwhelming number of states to consider. Moreover, particular attention would be given to prioritising the presentation of trajectory explanations that involve disagreement perceived by the explainees.

System Design. The proposed method exhibits limitations when applied to complex environments. The method heavily relies on an accurate model or simulator to generate trajectories supposing that the agent can be positioned in arbitrary states. Alternative solutions would be to compute critical states through pre-recording trajectories or employing episodic memory of an agent [9] in future work. While the computational cost increases when multiple policies need to be trained for real-world applications, the training of contrastive policies can be conducted in parallel. And in most scenarios, we believe that a limited form of contrastive explanations can be achieved sufficiently with only two policies. Furthermore, exploring the explanation of potential policy randomness and environmental uncertainty (e.g., random effects and transitions induced by the environment or random actions taken by the agent) is identified as a promising future direction.

Acknowledgement. The authors would thank anonymous reviewers for their valuable comments. This work is partially funded by the EPSRC CHAI project (EP/T026820/1).

References

1. Amir, D., Amir, O.: Highlights: summarizing agent behavior to people. In: AAMAS 2018, pp. 1168–1176 (2018)
2. Anderson, A., et al.: Explaining reinforcement learning to mere mortals: an empirical study. In: IJCAI 2019, pp. 1328–1334 (2019)
3. Annasamy, R., Sycara, K.: Towards better interpretability in deep q-networks. In: AAAI 2019, vol. 33, pp. 4561–4569 (2019)
4. Bellman, R.E.: Dynamic Programming. Princeton University Press (2010)

5. Chakraborti, T., Kulkarni, A., Sreedharan, S., Smith, D.E., Kambhampati, S.: Explicability? legibility? predictability? transparency? privacy? security? the emerging landscape of interpretable agent behavior. In: ICAPS 2019, vol. 29, pp. 86–96 (2019)
6. Chakraborti, T., Sreedharan, S., Kambhampati, S.: The emerging landscape of explainable automated planning & decision making. In: IJCAI 2020, pp. 4803–4811 (2020). Survey track
7. Chevalier-Boisvert, M., Willems, L., Pal, S.: Minimalistic gridworld environment for gymnasium (2018). https://github.com/Farama-Foundation/Minigrid
8. Christiano, P.F., Leike, J., Brown, T., Martic, M., Legg, S., Amodei, D.: Deep reinforcement learning from human preferences. In: NeurIPS 2017, vol. 30 (2017)
9. Cruz, F., Dazeley, R., Vamplew, P.: Memory-based explainable reinforcement learning. In: Liu, J., Bailey, J. (eds.) AI 2019. LNCS (LNAI), vol. 11919, pp. 66–77. Springer, Cham (2019). https://doi.org/10.1007/978-3-030-35288-2_6
10. Gottesman, O., et al.: Interpretable off-policy evaluation in reinforcement learning by highlighting influential transitions. In: ICML 2020, vol. 119, pp. 3658–3667 (2020)
11. Greydanus, S., Koul, A., Dodge, J., Fern, A.: Visualizing and understanding atari agents. In: ICML 2018, pp. 2877–2886 (2018)
12. Gunning, D.: Darpa's explainable artificial intelligence (XAI) program. In: Proceedings of the 24th International Conference on Intelligent User Interfaces, p. ii (2019)
13. Gupta, P., et al.: Explain your move: understanding agent actions using specific and relevant feature attribution. In: ICLR 2020 (2020)
14. Hayes, B., Shah, J.A.: Improving robot controller transparency through autonomous policy explanation. In: 2017 12th ACM/IEEE International Conference on Human-Robot Interaction (HRI), pp. 303–312 (2017)
15. Hoffmann, J., Magazzeni, D.: Explainable AI planning (XAIP): overview and the case of contrastive explanation (extended abstract). In: Krötzsch, M., Stepanova, D. (eds.) Reasoning Web. Explainable Artificial Intelligence. LNCS, vol. 11810, pp. 277–282. Springer, Cham (2019). https://doi.org/10.1007/978-3-030-31423-1_9
16. Huang, S.H., Bhatia, K., Abbeel, P., Dragan, A.D.: Establishing appropriate trust via critical states. In: 2018 IEEE/RSJ International Conference on Intelligent Robots and Systems (IROS), pp. 3929–3936. IEEE (2018)
17. Huang, S.H., Held, D., Abbeel, P., Dragan, A.D.: Enabling robots to communicate their objectives. Auton. Robot. **43**, 309–326 (2017)
18. Huber, T., Weitz, K., André, E., Amir, O.: Local and global explanations of agent behavior: integrating strategy summaries with saliency maps. Artif. Intell. **301**, 103571 (2021)
19. Hüyük, A., Jarrett, D., Tekin, C., van der Schaar, M.: Explaining by imitating: understanding decisions by interpretable policy learning. In: ICLR 2021 (2021)
20. Ibarz, B., Leike, J., Pohlen, T., Irving, G., Legg, S., Amodei, D.: Reward learning from human preferences and demonstrations in atari. In: NeurIPS 2018, vol. 31 (2018)
21. Juozapaitis, Z., Koul, A., Fern, A., Erwig, M., Doshi-Velez, F.: Explainable reinforcement learning via reward decomposition. arxiv (2019)
22. Karino, I., Ohmura, Y., Kuniyoshi, Y.: Identifying critical states by the action-based variance of expected return. In: Farkaš, I., Masulli, P., Wermter, S. (eds.) ICANN 2020. LNCS, vol. 12396, pp. 366–378. Springer, Cham (2020). https://doi.org/10.1007/978-3-030-61609-0_29

23. Kober, J., Bagnell, J.A., Peters, J.: Reinforcement learning in robotics: a survey. Int. J. Robot. Res. **32**, 1238–1274 (2013)
24. Lage, I., Lifschitz, D., Doshi-Velez, F., Amir, O.: Exploring computational user models for agent policy summarization. In: IJCAI 2019, pp. 1401–1407 (2019)
25. Lin, Y.C., Hong, Z.W., Liao, Y.H., Shih, M.L., Liu, M.Y., Sun, M.: Tactics of adversarial attack on deep reinforcement learning agents. In: IJCAI 2017, pp. 3756–3762 (2017)
26. Lipton, P., Knowles, D.: Contrastive Explanations, p. 247–266. Royal Institute of Philosophy Supplements, Cambridge University Press (1991)
27. Liu, R., Bai, F., Du, Y., Yang, Y.: Meta-reward-net: implicitly differentiable reward learning for preference-based reinforcement learning. In: NeurIPS 2022, vol. 35, pp. 22270–22284 (2022)
28. Lu, W., Magg, S., Zhao, X., Gromniak, M., Wermter, S.: A closer look at reward decomposition for high-level robotic explanations. arXiv abs/2304.12958 (2023)
29. Madumal, P., Miller, T., Sonenberg, L., Vetere, F.: Explainable reinforcement learning through a causal lens. In: AAAI 2020, pp. 2493–2500 (2020)
30. Marcus, G., Davis, E.: Rebooting AI: Building Artificial Intelligence We Can Trust. Pantheon Books, USA (2019)
31. Miller, T.: Explanation in artificial intelligence: insights from the social sciences. Artif. Intell. **267**, 1–38 (2019)
32. Miller, T.: Contrastive explanation: a structural-model approach. Knowl. Eng. Rev. **36**, e14 (2021)
33. Montavon, G., Samek, W., Müller, K.R.: Methods for interpreting and understanding deep neural networks. arXiv abs/1706.07979 (2017)
34. Mott, A., Zoran, D., Chrzanowski, M., Wierstra, D., Rezende, D.J.: Towards interpretable reinforcement learning using attention augmented agents. In: NeurIPS 2019, pp. 12360–12369 (2019)
35. Narayanan, S., Lage, I., Doshi-Velez, F.: (when) are contrastive explanations of reinforcement learning helpful? arXiv abs/2211.07719 (2022)
36. Olson, M.L., Khanna, R., Neal, L., Li, F., Wong, W.K.: Counterfactual state explanations for reinforcement learning agents via generative deep learning. Artif. Intell. **295**, 103455 (2021)
37. Puiutta, E., Veith, E.M.S.P.: Explainable reinforcement learning: a survey. arXiv abs/2005.06247 (2020)
38. Puterman, M.L.: Markov decision processes: discrete stochastic dynamic programming. In: Wiley Series in Probability and Statistics (1994)
39. Russell, S., Norvig, P.: Artificial Intelligence: A Modern Approach, 4th edn. Pearson (2020)
40. Schrittwieser, J., et al.: Mastering atari, go, chess and shogi by planning with a learned model. Nature **588**, 604–609 (2019)
41. Sequeira, P., Gervasio, M.: Interestingness elements for explainable reinforcement learning: understanding agents' capabilities and limitations. Artif. Intell. **288**, 103367 (2020)
42. Sequeira, P., Hostetler, J., Gervasio, M.T.: Global and local analysis of interestingness for competency-aware deep reinforcement learning. arXiv abs/2211.06376 (2022)
43. Shu, T., Xiong, C., Socher, R.: Hierarchical and interpretable skill acquisition in multi-task reinforcement learning. In: ICLR 2018 (2018)
44. Silver, D., et al.: Mastering the game of go without human knowledge. Nature **550**, 354–359 (2017)

45. Sreedharan, S., Srivastava, S., Kambhampati, S.: TLDR: policy summarization for factored SSP problems using temporal abstractions. In: ICAPS 2020, vol. 30, pp. 272–280 (2020)
46. Sreedharan, S., Srivastava, S., Kambhampati, S.: Using state abstractions to compute personalized contrastive explanations for AI agent behavior. Artif. Intell. **301**, 103570 (2021)
47. Topin, N., Veloso, M.: Generation of policy-level explanations for reinforcement learning. In: AAAI 2019, pp. 2514–2521 (2019)
48. Vouros, G.A.: Explainable deep reinforcement learning: state of the art and challenges. ACM Comput. Surv. **55**(5) (2022)
49. Waa, J., Diggelen, J., Bosch, K., Neerincx, M.: Contrastive explanations for reinforcement learning in terms of expected consequences. In: IJCAI 2018 - Explainable Artificial Intelligence (XAI) Workshop (2018)
50. Watkins, C.J., Dayan, P.: Q-learning. Mach. Learn. **8**, 279–292 (1992)
51. Wells, L., Bednarz, T.: Explainable AI and reinforcement learning-a systematic review of current approaches and trends. Front. Artif. Intell. **4** (2021)
52. Yau, H., Russell, C., Hadfield, S.: What did you think would happen? Explaining agent behaviour through intended outcomes. In: NeurIPS 2020, vol. 33, pp. 18375–18386 (2020)
53. Yeh, E., Sequeira, P., Hostetler, J., Gervasio, M.T.: Outcome-guided counterfactuals for reinforcement learning agents from a jointly trained generative latent space. arXiv abs/2207.07710 (2022)
54. Zahavy, T., Ben-Zrihem, N., Mannor, S.: Graying the black box: understanding DQNs. In: ICML 2016, pp. 1899–1908 (2016)
55. Zelvelder, A.E., Westberg, M., Främling, K.: Assessing explainability in reinforcement learning. In: Calvaresi, D., Najjar, A., Winikoff, M., Främling, K. (eds.) EXTRAAMAS 2021. LNCS (LNAI), vol. 12688, pp. 223–240. Springer, Cham (2021). https://doi.org/10.1007/978-3-030-82017-6_14
56. Čyras, K., Rago, A., Albini, E., Baroni, P., Toni, F.: Argumentative XAI: a survey. In: IJCAI 2021, pp. 4392–4399 (2021). Survey Track

Compare-xAI: Toward Unifying Functional Testing Methods for Post-hoc XAI Algorithms into a Multi-dimensional Benchmark

Mohamed Karim Belaid[1,2]([✉]) [iD], Richard Bornemann[1] [iD],
Maximilian Rabus[3] [iD], Ralf Krestel[4] [iD], and Eyke Hüllermeier[1,5] [iD]

[1] Ludwig-Maximilians-Universität, Munich, Germany
extern.karim.belaid@porsche.de, r.bornemann@campus.lmu.de, eyke@lmu.de
[2] IDIADA Fahrzeugtechnik GmbH, Munich, Germany
karim.belaid@idiada.com
[3] Dr. Ing. h.c. F. Porsche AG, Stuttgart, Germany
maximilian.rabus2@porsche.de
[4] ZBW - Leibniz Information Centre for Economics, Kiel University, Kiel, Germany
rkr@informatik.uni-kiel.de
[5] Munich Center for Machine Learning, Munich, Germany

Abstract. In recent years, Explainable AI (xAI) attracted a lot of attention as various countries turned explanations into a legal right. xAI algorithms enable humans to understand the underlying models and explain their behavior, leading to insights through which the models can be analyzed and improved beyond the accuracy metric by, e.g., debugging the learned pattern and reducing unwanted biases. However, the widespread use of xAI and the rapidly growing body of published research in xAI have brought new challenges. A large number of xAI algorithms can be overwhelming and make it difficult for practitioners to choose the correct xAI algorithm for their specific use case. This problem is further exacerbated by the different approaches used to assess novel xAI algorithms, making it difficult to compare them to existing methods. To address this problem, we introduce Compare-xAI, a benchmark that allows for a direct comparison of popular xAI algorithms with a variety of different use cases. We propose a scoring protocol employing a range of functional tests from the literature, each targeting a specific end-user requirement in explaining a model. To make the benchmark results easily accessible, we group the tests into four categories (fidelity, fragility, stability, and stress tests). We present results for 13 xAI algorithms based on 11 functional tests. After analyzing the findings, we derive potential solutions for data science practitioners as workarounds to the found practical limitations. Finally, Compare-xAI is a tentative to unify systematic evaluation and comparison methods for xAI algorithms with a focus on the end-user's requirements. The code is made available at:
https://karim-53.github.io/cxai/.

Supplementary Information The online version contains supplementary material available at https://doi.org/10.1007/978-3-031-44067-0_5.

Keywords: Explainable-AI · Feature Importance · Benchmark

1   Introduction

Explainable AI (xAI) algorithms are a set of approaches toward understanding black-box models. In recent years, xAI algorithms helped debug manifold issues in ML models, such as exposing underlying wrong patterns in classifying objects [1] or highlighting inequality and bias in decisions [2]. Moreover, given its essential impact on society, legislation in several countries now includes the "Right to explanation" [3] fulfilled by the various xAI tools available in the literature.

Different Implementations. It is difficult to define the best xAI solution given the number of known evaluation metrics. In addition, the long evolutionary history of specific xAI algorithms makes it even more difficult to evaluate each version. The Shapley values are an excellent example of this challenge. Sundararajan et al. stated that "...the functional forms of the Shapley value... are sufficiently complex as to prevent direct understanding..." [4]. Indeed, going through the theoretical background of Shapley values [5], its multiple approximations [6,7], generalizations [4,8] and final implementations [9,10] adapted to the AI field might mislead the end-user on the capability of the available tools.

Resulting Challenges. The variable requirements and implementations of the xAI algorithms might lead to data scientists facing considerable difficulties in accurately evaluating each xAI algorithm and remaining up-to-date on its evolution. This issue yields a clearly visible symptom known as the illusion of explanatory depth [11] in interpreting xAI results [12] as it has been confirmed that data scientists are prone to misuse interpretability tools [13].

Solutions and Recommendations. Many researchers did address this question by stressing the importance of structuring and documenting xAI algorithms [14,15], i.e., by highlighting the target end-users of the algorithm, its capabilities, limitations, and vulnerabilities. Finally, they recommend using quantitative metrics to make claims about explainability. Miller (2019) proposed a seminal paper on how to structure an explanation. He emphasized the importance of human-interpretable explanations and the use of natural language complemented by visualizations where appropriate. He also highlighted the need to consider the social and ethical implications of AI explanations. Miller's recommendations have been influential in shaping the field of Explainable AI and continue to guide researchers and practitioners toward developing more transparent and accountable AI systems. Overall, the solutions and recommendations put forward by researchers aim to increase the transparency, accountability, and trust in AI systems, particularly with regard to their decision-making processes [16].

Functional Testing as a Solution to Stated Recommendations. Functional testing aims to verify the end-user's requirement on the xAI algorithm by performing end-to-end tests in a black-box fashion. In other words, every functional test applies the xAI algorithm on a frozen AI model to verify if the output corresponds to the explanation expected by data scientists. A functional test could verify that the explanation accurately reflects the AI model (Fidelity), that it is not sensitive to adversarial attacks (Fragility), that it is stable to small variations in the model (Stability), or that it can effectively handle high dimensional data (Stress). Functional testing remains, unfortunately, sparsely used in literature and, thus, provides only a partial evaluation.

Research Questions. Given the unsolved burden of evaluating and correctly choosing xAI algorithms, we propose Compare-xAI that mitigates these two issues (non-unified benchmark for xAI algorithms and the illusion of explanatory depth during the interpretation of results) by addressing three research questions:

1. What are the dimensions to consider while testing an xAI algorithm from a data scientist practitioner's perspective?
2. How to score xAI algorithms despite the multitude of evaluation dimensions?
3. How to compare and choose between similar xAI algorithms?

The paper is structured as follows: First, we provide a comprehensive review of the existing literature on xAI evaluation methods, including functional tests and portability tests. We also discuss the challenges associated with navigating the vast array of available tests. Second, we present a benchmark for xAI algorithms and examine Miller's recommendations on how to present explanations. In the Methods and Findings section, we address three research questions concerning the dimensions to consider while testing an xAI algorithm, how to score xAI algorithms simply, and how to compare and choose between similar xAI algorithms. Finally, we discuss the limitations of our approach and suggest areas for future work, including design-related and implementation-related limitations.

2   Related Work

This section is a survey for xAI evaluation methods. It contains examples contrasting the difference between functional tests and portability tests. Following that, we examine some early attempts to regroup them into surveys or benchmarks.

2.1   xAI Evaluation Methods: Functional Tests vs Portability Tests

Researchers in the xAI field often propose a new method along with a set of functional or portability tests that outline the contrast between former work and their contribution.

Functional Tests. Functional testing is a popular testing technique for software engineers. The following definition is adapted from the software engineering field to our intended usage in machine learning [17]. Functional tests are created by testers without specific knowledge of the algorithm's internal modules, i.e., not the developers themselves. Therefore, the algorithm is considered a black-box and is executed from end to end. Each functional test is intended to verify an end-user requirement on the xAI algorithm rather than a specific internal module. Thus, functional tests share the advantage of being able to test different algorithms. On the other hand, failed tests do not inform about the location of the errors but rather attribute it to the entire algorithm. Functional tests for xAI algorithms usually exploit tabular synthetic data and few input features, e.g., considering a simple AND function. The xAI algorithm is expected to detect symmetry between the two binary features [9]. Simple examples showcase the undeniable limit of certain xAI algorithms. Nevertheless, specific tests could use real-world data. A good example is the MNIST dataset [18] which proved that certain xAI algorithms are attributing high importance to dummy pixels [19]: Since edge pixels are always black, a multi-layer perceptron will learn not to rely on these constant pixels. Consequently, the xAI algorithm should confirm that the AI model does not use these pixels. Papers proposing new xAI algorithms remain too short to list all known tests. In addition, some of the highlighted issues may be fixed without being subsequently noted in the respective publications.

Portability Tests. Portability tests for xAI algorithms evaluate real-world models and demonstrate the robustness of the xAI algorithm against multiple challenges at once (noise, correlated inputs, large inputs, etc.). They are used to claim the potential broad usage of one xAI algorithm rather than demonstrating the quality of the explanation. For example, Tsang et al. proved the portability of their proposed xAI across recommendation tasks by testing on that kind of AI model [20].

Navigating the Ocean of Tests Remains itself a Huge Challenge. First, many examples in the literature are portability tests which make the comparison between xAI algorithms complex. Second, tests could be redundant to emphasize the frequent occurrence of an issue, e.g., testing interaction detection with different transparent models [20]. Third, researchers could argue the correctness of specific functional tests' ground truth, e.g., causal explanation of the Shapley values [21] has been considered false in certain research [4].

Given the tremendous amount of xAI algorithms and dedicated metrics, surveys [22–27] have trouble providing an in-depth analysis of each algorithm and cannot cope with ongoing implementation updates. Nevertheless, Molnar's online book distinguishes itself with a continuously updated survey about xAI [28]. The initiative of a real-time survey faced great success and acceptance from the data science community.

2.2   Benchmarks for xAI Algorithms

There are specialized benchmarks in the literature, like the SVEA benchmark [29]. The latter focuses on computer vision tasks and proposes faster evaluations based on the small MNIST-1D dataset [30]. The ERASER benchmark [31] is centered on interpretability in NLP models using human-annotated rationales. Another benchmark utilizes exclusively human evaluation to assess xAI algorithms on real-world tasks [32]. On the one hand, benchmarking an xAI algorithm using computer vision and NLP models permits measuring the real success of an xAI tool in helping end-users even though human evaluation could be considered subjective and more costly to obtain. On the other hand, evaluation using real-world tasks does not allow debugging the xAI algorithm, i.e., two algorithms might fail to explain one black-box model for two different reasons.

xAI-Bench [33] evaluates each xAI algorithm on five metrics. Faithfulness measures the Pearson correlation between the feature importance and the approximate marginal contribution of each feature. Of course, one could argue that the ground truth explanation of a model could be slightly different from the marginal contribution of each feature on the observed dataset. The same argument holds for the monotonicity, infidelity, and GT-Shapley metrics. They define a ground truth output, which should be closely matched by the xAI algorithms. A specific xAI algorithm should be preferred over other xAI approaches, if its output better aligns with the ground truth. In contrast, functional tests discussed in previous paragraphs evaluate the correctness of the output using a pattern (not an exact ground truth). Therefore, Our paper focuses on functional tests using patterns as evaluation methods. The fifth metric used in xAI-Bench is remove-and-retrain (ROAR). It involves a re-evaluation of the model, which could alter the evaluation. Another critical factor affecting the algorithms' scores and ranking is the data distribution. The authors did circumvent the issue by testing on different distributions. However, it remains difficult to decide if the algorithm is failing this specific test or if it is generally sensitive to the data distribution. xAI-Bench is an excellent initiative to benchmark the correctness of an xAI algorithm, except that it does not allow for easy debugging and does not propose any final ranking of the xAI algorithm to help practitioners and laymen quickly pick the right tool. Property-based testing of black-box functions [34] provides an alternative to functional testing of xAI algorithms. Instead of applying the xAI algorithm to a synthetic scenario to observe its behavior, property-based testing approximates the dynamics of the method. This approximation can then be examined to find scenarios where the xAI algorithm deviates from the desired behavior. However, to get a good approximation of the tested methods, many different scenarios must be created to examine the method's behavior and obtain a reliable approximation, which is very time-consuming.

Altruist citemollas2022altruist presents a method for generating argumentative explanations through local interpretations of predictive models. Chrysostomou and Aletras [35] focus on improving the faithfulness of attention-based explanations for text classification tasks. Lastly, Hamamoto and Egi [36] propose a model-agnostic ensemble-based explanation correction method leveraging the Rashomon effect.

BASED-XAI [37] proposes one novel fidelity test that assesses the proposed ranking of the features. The test is adapted to five datasets and three xAI algorithms. Guidotti et al. [38] also primarily focus on fidelity tests on synthetic data and local feature importance. EvalXAI [39], on the other hand, focuses on

Fragility tests, i.e., adversarial attacks. The goal of Compare-xAI is to unify functional tests for xAI algorithms into an all-in-one multi-dimensional benchmark that encompasses fidelity, fragility, stability, and stress tests. This work allows data scientist practitioners to assess xAI algorithms on different test types but also with the same setup and parameters.

The Quantus toolkit [40] is an open-source library designed for evaluating the quality and reliability of neural network explanations, specifically. CLEVR-XAI [41] also focuses on evaluating neural networks, specifically. The work by Du et al. [42] is dedicated to the attribution of predictions in RNNs using additive decomposition. OpenXAI [43] is a broader benchmark which uses systematically logistic regression and neural networks models on each test. Compare-xAI tends to include various ML models like decision trees, neural networks, gradient boosting trees, and even user-defined black-box functions to reproduce specific pitfalls.

2.3   Miller's Recommendation on How to Present Explanations

In his seminal paper "Explanation in Artificial Intelligence: Insights from the Social Sciences", Miller (2019) advocates for the use of human-interpretable explanations in AI systems [16]. Miller argues that AI systems should provide explanations that are not only technically accurate but also understandable to human users. Miller recommends the use of natural language explanations, complemented by visualizations where appropriate, to increase the transparency and accountability of AI systems. He also highlights the importance of considering the social and ethical implications of AI explanations, including issues of fairness and bias. Miller's work has been influential in shaping the field of Explainable AI and his recommendations continue to be widely cited and adopted by researchers and practitioners.

Following the analysis of related work, Sect. 3 details how our proposed benchmark addresses the highlighted issues.

3   Methods and Findings

We compare various xAI algorithms through different functional tests to understand their respective advantage and pitfalls. The flowchart illustrated in Fig. 1 provides a concise summary of the research questions that will be analyzed in the subsequent sections.

3.1   RQ1: What are the Dimensions to Consider While Testing an xAI Algorithm from a Data Scientist Practitioner's Perspective?

The selection of tests to be used to analyze the performance of the xAI algorithm is not trivial. First, we need to determine which aspects of the xAI algorithm we want to test. Then, we need to find a set of tests that sufficiently cover the aspects of the xAI algorithm that we need to evaluate.

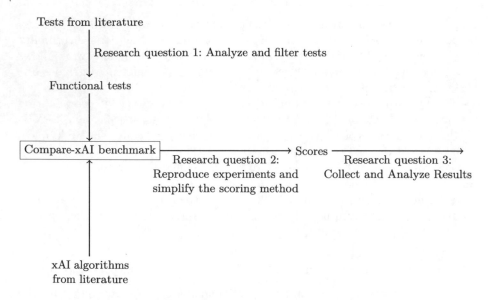

Fig. 1. The flowchart of the Compare-xAI Benchmark.

Method. We select the following research papers describing popular xAI algorithms [1,5,7,9,19,20,33,44–46], see Appendix B for more details about each algorithm. We select the functional tests in each of these papers. We broaden the range of selected tests by including additional ones from the related work [4,21,47–49], see Appendix A. Then, we apply the functional tests to all xAI-methods.

Findings. The significance of xAI algorithms has increased substantially through the incorporation of additional use cases and the generalization of each xAI algorithm to a wider range of machine learning models. This has been accompanied by an increase in expectations for xAI algorithms. However, this increase is not without problems. Indeed, it became more likely for xAI algorithms to not output the explanation expected by the data scientist practitioners. For this reason, a multitude of functional tests was created. We propose to categorize shortlisted functional tests into four common groups, sparsely adopted in literature [9,50–52] to ensure that the proposed benchmark covers a large variety of end-user requirements. In the following, we will introduce the four test categories using functional tests implemented in the Compare-xAI benchmark as concrete examples.

Fidelity answers the question of whether the xAI explanation faithfully reproduces the dynamics of the underlying model [51]. It is also named Faithfulness in certain related work [42,51,53]. The **Cough and Fever** [9] functional test examines the Fidelity by training a regression tree on a synthetic dataset, where the two input features are symmetric. The xAI algorithm should detect this symmetry and assign equal importance to the two features. Similarly, the **Cough and Fever 10 90** [9] functional test utilizes a regression tree trained on asymmetric features. Here the xAI algorithm should detect this asymmetry and assign the importance to the features accordingly. Fidelity is also named faithfulness [51], or consistency [9].

Fragility reflects how vulnerable the xAI algorithm is against adversarial attacks. For example, Attackers can exploit xAI algorithms based on feature perturbation by lowering the importance of certain features [52]. This vulnerability is exploited by the **Fooling Perturbation Algorithm**. We use a functional test based on the COMPAS dataset [54], where the xAI algorithm must correctly assign the highest importance to the feature *Race*, despite the attack by the Fooling Perturbation algorithm.

Stability evaluates whether the explanation provided by the xAI algorithm is too sensitive to minor variations in the underlying model or data. Common weaknesses of xAI algorithms with respect to stability are due to data distribution. Statistical dependencies [7], correlated features [13, 33], and random noise [4] can all lead to unstable xAI algorithm results. How susceptible an xAI algorithm is to instability can be tested, for example, with the test family **x0 plus x1** [48, 49]. In the first test case, the binary features of the synthetic dataset are statistically independent and have equal importance. We investigate how much changing the data distribution from uniform to non-uniform affects the result of the xAI algorithm. In the second test case, we again change the distribution from uniform to non-uniform, but this time the binary features are statistically dependent. In both test cases, the xAI algorithm should correctly assign equal importance to the two features despite the change in the underlying data distribution.

Stress examines whether the xAI algorithm scales gracefully with a higher number of parameters, for example, a higher number of input features [19], of tokens [7], of data points, etc. An example of an implemented stress test is using the **MNIST** dataset [19]. In this functional test, an MLP is trained on images of hand-drawn digits, each with 784 pixels (a high number of input features). A subset of these pixels are dummy pixels, i.e., they are not important for the prediction of the trained model. The xAI algorithm should correctly identify these dummy pixels. The final test result is the ratio between the correctly detected dummy pixels and the actual number of dummy pixels.

The functional tests presented here serve as an example for the reader to easily understand the four categories but are only a subset of the tests we employ in our benchmark. We refer the reader to Appendix A for an exhaustive list of all included tests, as well as their functionality and hyperparameters. Since fidelity is the most straightforward property to test, we note that most of the functional tests presented in the literature aim to test the xAI algorithms for their fidelity to the black-box model. Since we take the functional tests for this study from the literature, Compare-xAI reflects this imbalance, and most of the tests in our study fall into the fidelity category.

3.2   RQ2: How to Score xAI Algorithms in a Simple Way Despite the Multitude of Evaluation Dimensions?

Method. We propose to standardize the final score of each test to a range from zero to one. We obtain the benchmark results by applying the set of functional tests to each xAI algorithm, following the setup described in the answer to the first research question.

Table 1. Summary of the benchmark's results.

Score xAI algorithm	Fidelity [%]	Fragility [%]	Stability [%]	Stress [%]	Time per Test [Seconds]	Completed Tests
Random	48	06	11	50	0.0075	11
Permutation	73	56	99	55	9	11
Permutation_Partition	73	56	99	55	12	11
Partition	73	56	99	50	7	11
Tree_Shap_Approx	50	100	74		0.0057	8
Exact_Shapley_Values	73	56	99		1906	11
Tree_Shap	60	100	99		0.0004	8
Saabas	100	100	73		0.0012	8
Kernel_Shap	100	56	99	100	121	10
Sage	66	100	93	100	18	9
Lime	82	100	99	100	259	10
Maple	33	56	100	55	56	11
Joint_Shapley	42	48	98		1947	11

Findings. We present the average results obtained in each of the test categories by each xAI algorithm in our study in Table 1. Missing scores indicate that an explainer is either not able to complete any of the functional tests in that category or the time limit is exceeded. A failure in applying an explainer on a functional test is caused by mismatches between the family of AI models, a specific explainer is able to explain, or the dataset structure used by the functional test.

First, considering all implemented tests without filtering, none of the xAI algorithms did obtain the perfect score. Second, we can distinguish clusters of xAI algorithms by looking at their scores. This clustering reflects the original structure of these xAI algorithms. For example, the biggest cluster is formed by permutation-based algorithms. On average, an xAI algorithm is eligible for 10 tests (±1) depending on its portability.

Figure 2 visualizes the findings of Table 1 in an easy to understand manner. The spidergram is divided into the same four categories as the Table 1 of Fidelity, Fragility, Stability and Stress test, while also including the category of Portability. We define the Portability of an xAI algorithm as the number of test which it can successfully complete without encountering errors or exceeding

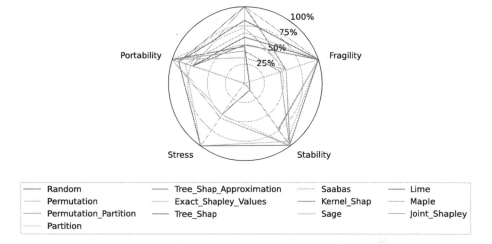

Fig. 2. Spidergram Performance Analysis of Indexed xAI Algorithms

the time limit. The Portability of an xAI algorithm is therefore a crucial aspect of its performance. This spidergram thus offers a multi-dimensional view of the performance and robustness of the xAI algorithms under consideration.

3.3 RQ3: How to Compare and Choose Between Similar xAI Algorithms?

The preliminary results of the Compare xAI benchmark confirm that there is no clear state of the art and that choosing the appropriate xAI algorithm requires additional effort. Therefore, the question arises: how data science practitioners should select an xAI algorithm according to their needs?

Method. We take the raw scores from the experiment we conducted according to the protocol we described in the first two research questions and analyze them for practical guidance for data science practitioners.

Findings

Different Portability. The literature presents a spectrum of xAI algorithms, each with varying degrees of specialization. Model-specific xAI algorithms, such as Tree SHAP [9], are tailored to specific AI models or explanation types. On the other hand, more versatile methods like Kernel SHAP [7] are designed to be compatible with a variety of AI models and can generate multiple types of explanations. This versatility stems from their model-agnostic nature, which allows them to elucidate the dynamics of a black box model solely based on its inputs and outputs. However, the expected format of input variables can differ among model-agnostic xAI algorithms, potentially limiting the number of tests they can perform and thus their overall portability.

Comparing Model-Specific and Model-Agnostic xAI Algorithms. One would expect model-specific xAI algorithms to have higher average scores and lower average time per test than model-agnostic xAI algorithms, but to be limited in the number of tests they can perform. This intuition is not supported by our study. We see that the two model-specific xAI algorithms, Tree SHAP and Approximated Tree SHAP, are among the fastest algorithms and can also perform the least number of tests. However, they do not perform the best in the tests they can perform. Model-agnostic xAI algorithms like Kernel SHAP are able to outperform various model-specific algorithms and can perform more tests. Still, Kernel SHAP takes an average of 121 s to run each test, which is six orders of magnitude slower than Tree SHAP. A data scientist should therefore choose a model-specific xAI algorithm for the black-box model under study if execution time is of great importance for their specific use case.

Divide and Conquer: Ensembles of xAI-Methods Perform Better. We find that different xAI-methods often have different strengths and weaknesses. However, these weaknesses cannot be reliably predicted before applying the xAI algorithm. Data scientists should therefore apply multiple xAI algorithms when seeking an explanation for the behavior of their models and derive their conclusions from the joint outputs of the xAI-methods. This can be seen with the xAI algorithms Kernel SHAP and Sage, as an example. Kernel SHAP outperforms Sage in the categories of Fidelity, Stability, and Stress tests. However, Sage strongly outperforms Kernel SHAP in the category of Fragility. A data science practitioner should therefore consult multiple xAI algorithms to gain a conclusive overview of the model's underlying behavior. The divide and conquer strategy can be achieved through one of the following strategies. Ensemble Techniques: This approach involves applying multiple xAI methods to the same model or data and combining their outputs. The rationale is that different xAI methods may excel in different areas, and by using an ensemble of methods, one can leverage their strengths and compensate for their weaknesses.

Aggregation Techniques: These techniques involve taking the outputs of multiple xAI methods (or multiple runs of the same method) and aggregating them to produce a single explanation. The aggregation can be done in various ways, such as by taking the average, the median, or by using more complex methods like weighted averaging or voting.

Meta-Explanation Techniques: These techniques involve using one xAI method to explain the outputs of another xAI method. For example, one could use a simpler, more interpretable model (like a decision tree or a linear model) to approximate the explanations produced by a more complex, less interpretable model (like a deep neural network). The simpler model's explanations then serve as a "meta-explanation" of the complex model's explanations.

More Compute Does Not Necessarily Imply Better Performance. Consistent with recent empirical findings in machine learning research, one would expect the performance of xAI algorithms to scale with their computational demands. However, we find no statistically significant correlation between the average time per test completion and the average score per test for the xAI algorithms. Nonetheless, the xAI algorithm that achieved the highest score for the functional tests, Kernel SHAP, takes an average of 121 s to complete each test, making it the fourth slowest xAI algorithm in our study.

Contrasting Findings of xAI Benchmarks. In comparing our results to existing benchmarks, it is evident that Compare-xAI takes a different approach from the related work. However, there are some xAI algorithms and metrics that we share in common with other studies.

For instance, both Compare-xAI and OpenXAI evaluated the performance of SHAP and LIME. Nevertheless, their findings diverged. OpenXAI concluded that LIME outperformed SHAP in the listed experiments, whereas Compare-xAI's results demonstrated that SHAP performed better on average in functional tests. These contrasting outcomes underscore the differences in approach and the challenge of defining a clear state-of-the-art in the xAI field.

Interestingly, both BasedXAI and Compare-xAI agree on SHAP's superior performance, despite employing different evaluation approaches. On the other hand, EvalXAI benchmarked the fragility of xAI algorithms through adversarial attacks. They revealed that LIME proved to be the most robust algorithm, particularly in image-related tasks. Confirming these findings, Compare-xAI also affirms the resilience of LIME against adversarial attacks based on its own set of tests.

Overall, the varying results and agreements among Compare-xAI, OpenXAI, BasedXAI, and EvalXAI shed light on the intricacies of the xAI field and the challenges inherent in establishing a definitive state-of-the-art.

4   Limitations and Future Work

Compare-xAI's weaknesses are classified into design-related and implementation-related limitations.

Design-Related Limitations. Compare-xAI is a benchmark made exclusively of quantitative metrics. It is objective as it does not include tests based on human evaluation. A common example of a necessary human evaluation is the study of the human mental model like the investigation of users' preferred explanation style [55]). Another example is the study of information overload, e.g., xAI's additional output information like the confidence interval [19]. Mainly, empirical studies are challenging to quantify [16] and integrate into an objective score. These and other non-quantifiable advantages/disadvantages will be included in the description we provide, of the xAI algorithm, in the future.

The second limitation is the study of hyper-parameters. Around half of the xAI algorithms used in this experiment have at least one binary parameter.

Only some of them have clear instructions on how to fine-tune their parameters. We, therefore, do not perform any manual hyperparameter tuning and leave it for future work. Nevertheless, certain xAI algorithms adapt their parameters internally given each task by relying on the model's structure, the dataset size, and the ML task.

Implementation-Related Limitations. The provided proof of concept includes, for now, 11 tests. Currently, none of them cover RL, GAN, unsupervised learning tasks, or rule-based explanations. The tested form of output is also limited to feature importance (local and global explanation). Testing feature interaction is still under development.

Despite the stated limitations, Compare-xAI should fulfill its primary objectives: first, assisting laymen in selecting the right xAI algorithm, and second, guiding researchers, practitioners, and laymen to avoid common mistakes in interpreting the output of the model by knowing in advance, the potential pitfalls of these popular xAI algorithms.

5   Conclusion

Explaining AI poses a delicate challenge, and the potential for misuse by end-users necessitates reliable and comprehensive evaluation tools [13]. In this context, Compare-xAI emerges as a unique and valuable benchmark. Its distinct contributions lie in its simplicity, scalability, ability to integrate any dataset and ML model, and, most importantly, its focus on the user's expected explanation. By addressing the pitfalls highlighted in surveys of xAI algorithms through concrete functional tests, Compare-xAI provides a robust evaluation framework.

With 13 post-hoc xAI algorithms, 11 tests, and 42 research papers currently indexed, Compare-xAI offers a unified benchmark that accurately reproduces experiments. Through a rigorous selection protocol, it effectively highlights the contrast between theoretical foundations and practical implementations, making the limitations of each method transparent. Additionally, Compare-xAI employs a simple and intuitive scoring method to absorb the vast quantity of xAI-related papers and mitigate human errors in interpreting xAI outputs. Its aim is to unify post-hoc xAI evaluation methods into a multi-dimensional benchmark while offering valuable insights into the strengths and weaknesses of different approaches.

Broader Impact

Compare-xAI holds tremendous potential across various use cases. It serves as an invaluable debugging tool for individual xAI algorithms and has the capacity to evolve into a global benchmark. While it may not provide a complete sorting of xAI algorithms, it successfully clusters comparable algorithms, enabling practitioners to efficiently filter and select the most suitable options while being fully aware of their limitations. This empowers end-users to avoid over-trusting algorithm outputs and steer clear of common mistakes in model explanations.

Furthermore, Compare-xAI facilitates detailed scoring and supports researchers in addressing specific questions regarding the performance and coverage of xAI algorithms. It assists in identifying failure cases, exploring alternative solutions, and highlighting areas where no xAI algorithm adequately addresses the problem. By continuously re-evaluating indexed xAI algorithms, Compare-xAI ensures an up-to-date benchmark of the state-of-the-art, fostering advancements and improvements in the field.

Beyond being a benchmark, Compare-xAI serves as a comprehensive and standardized analysis of related work. It also functions as an evaluation method for new research papers in xAI, promoting rigor and providing a framework for assessing novel contributions. Overall, Compare-xAI significantly enhances the evaluation and understanding of xAI algorithms, contributing to the advancement and responsible deployment of AI systems in various domains.

Acknowledgments and Disclosure of Funding. The authors gratefully acknowledge the support and funding provided by **IDIADA Fahrzeugtechnik GmbH**, Munich, Germany and **Dr. Ing. h.c. F. Porsche AG**, Stuttgart, Germany. Their generous contribution enabled the successful completion of this research project.

We thank Dorra El Mekki, Maximilian Muschalik, Patrick Kolpaczki and Michael Rapp for their thoughtful feedback on earlier iterations of this work.

A   Tests

For the proof-of-concept, the following list of tests is considered. Note that some tests count twice as they test both feature importance and feature attribution.

cough_and_fever answers the following question: *Can the xAI algorithm detect symmetric binary input features?*. The trained model's equation is [Cough AND Fever]*80. The test utilize **XGBRegressor** model trained on **a synthetic uniform distribution** dataset (total size: 20000). The test procedure is as follows: train a model such that its response to the two features is exactly the same. The xAI algorithm should detect symmetric features (equal values) and allocate them equal importance. The score is calculated as follows: 1 if the xAI detect the two features are symmetric. 0 if the difference in importance is above one unit. The test is classified in the **fidelity** category because it is a simple tree model that demonstrate inconsistencies in explanation [9].

cough_and_fever_10_90 answers the following question: *Can the xAI algorithm detect that 'Cough' feature is more important than 'Fever'?*. The trained model's equation is [Cough AND Fever]*80 + [Cough]*10. Cough should be more important than Fever globally. Locally for the case (Fever = yes, Cough = yes) the feature attribution of Cough should be more important. The test utilize **XGBRegressor** model trained on **a synthetic uniform distribution** dataset (total size: 20000). The test procedure is as follows: train a model with two features with unequal impact on the model. The feature with a higher influence on the output should be detected more important. The score is calculated as follows: Return 1 if Cough is more important otherwise 0. The test is classified in the **fidelity** category because it is a simple tree model that demonstrate inconsistencies in explanation due to the tree structure [9].

x0_plus_x1_distrib_non_uniform_stat_indep answers the following question: *Is the xAI able to explain the model correctly despite a non-uniform distribution of the data?*. The test demonstrate the effect of data distribution/causal inference. The test utilize **XGBRegressor** model trained on **a non-uniform and statistically independent** dataset (total size: 10000). The test procedure is as follows: Check if the explanation change when the distribution change. Check if non-uniform distributions affect the explanation. The score is calculated as follows: returns 1 if the two binary features obtain the same importance. The test is classified in the **stability** category because it assesses the impact of slightly changing the inputs [48].

x0_plus_x1_distrib_uniform_stat_dep answers the following question: *Is the xAI able to explain the model correctly despite a statistically-dependent distribution of the data?*. The test demonstrate the effect of data distribution/causal inference. The example was given in both [49] and [48]. The test utilize **XGBRegressor** model trained on **a uniform and statistically dependent** dataset (total size: 10000). The test procedure is as follows: Check if the explanation change when the distribution change. Check if statistically dependent distributions affect the explanation. The score is calculated as follows: returns 1 if the two binary features obtain the same importance. The test is classified in the **stability** category because To assess the impact of changing the inputs of f... This way, we are able to talk about a hypothetical scenario where the inputs are changed compared to the true features [48].

mnist answers the following question: *Is the xAI able to detect all dummy (constant and useless) pixels?*. The xAI algorithm should detect that important pixels are only in the center of the image. The test utilize **an MLP** model trained on **the** MNIST dataset (total size: 70000). The test procedure is as follows: simply train and explain the MLP model globally for every pixel. The score is calculated as follows: Return the ratio of constant pixels detected as dummy divided by the true number of constant pixels. The test is classified in the **stress** category because of the high number of input features. The test is adapted from [19].

fooling_perturbation_alg answers the following question: *Is the xAI affected by an adversarial attack against perturbation-based algorithms?*. Model-agnostic xAI algorithms that use feature perturbation methods might be vulnerable to this attack. The adversarial attack exploits a vulnerability to lower the feature importance of a specific feature. Setup: Let's begin by examining the COMPAS data set. This data set consists of defendant information from Broward County, Florida. Let's suppose that some adversary wants to mask biased or racist behavior on this data set. The test utilizes **a custom function** model trained on **the** COMPAS dataset (total size: 4629). The test procedure is as follows: The xAI algorithms need to explain the following corrupted model (custom function): if the input is from the dataset then the output is from a biased model. if not then the output is from a fair model. The score is calculated as follows: Return 1 if Race is the most important feature despite the adversarial attack. The score decreases while its rank decrease. The test is classified in the **fragility** category because fragility includes all adversarial attacks [47].

counterexample_dummy_axiom answers the following question: *Is the xAI able to detect unused input features?*. This is a counter-example used in literature to verify that SHAP CES do not satisfy the dummy axiom while BSHAP succeeds in this test. The test utilizes **a custom function** model trained on **a synthetic** dataset (total size: 20000). The test procedure is as follows: Train a model with one extra feature B that is dummy. The score is calculated as follows: returns 1 if the dummy feature B obtains a null importance. The test is classified in the **fidelity** category because assigning an importance of zero to a dummy feature reflects the model behavior (Fidelity) but also helps the data scientist to quickly understand the model.

a_and_b_or_c answers the following question: *Can the xAI algorithm detect that input feature 'A' is more important than 'B' or 'C'?*. This is a baseline test that the xAI should succeed in all cases. Model: A and (B or C). Goal: make sure that A is more important than B, C. Noise effect: even if the model output is not exactly equal to 1 still we expect the xai to give a correct answer. The test utilize **XGBRegressor** model trained on **a synthetic** dataset (total size: 20000). The test procedure is as follows: The model learns the following equation: A and (B or C). The explanation should prove that A is more important. The score is calculated as follows: If A is the most important feature then return 1. If A is the 2nd most important feature then return 0.5 i.e. 1- (1/nb of feature more important than A). If A is the last one: return 0 (completely wrong). The test is classified in the **fidelity** category because of the same reason as cough and fever 10–90: A's effect on the output is higher than B or C.

correlated_features answers the following question: *Can the xAI algorithm detect, that two of three input features are perfectly correlated?*. This is a fragility test, which attacks the xAI algorithm by introducing a third feature 'C' which is perfectly correlated with feature 'B'. The test utilizes a **XGBRegressor** model trained on **a synthetic** dataset with three input features (total size: 20000). The test procedure is as follows: The model is trained on a synthetic dataset with the three input features 'A', 'B' and 'C', of which 'B' and 'C' are perfectly correlated. The xAI algorithm should detect this correlation and only assign non-zero importance to one of the two correlated features. The score is calculated as follows: Since we do not care about which correlated feature is assigned the non zero importance value, we emply following scoring metric: 1-(min(B, C)/max(B, C)). This function assigns a value of zero if the assigned importance of the correlated features is equal, and 1 if one of the features is assigned an importance of zero. The test is classified in the **fragility** category because it tests the xAI algorithms ability to adjust to perfect correlation in the input features.

B xAI Algorithms

archipelago [20] separate the input features into sets. all features inside a set interact and there is no interaction outside a set. ArchAttribute is an interaction attribution method. ArchDetect is the corresponding interaction detector. The xAI algorithm is model agnostic i.e. it can explain any AI model. The xAI algorithm can output the following explanations: Feature interaction (local explanation).

baseline_random [33] Output a random explanation. It is not a real explainer. It helps measure the baseline score and processing time. The xAI algorithm is model agnostic i.e. it can explain any AI model. The xAI algorithm can output the following explanations: Feature attribution (local explanation), Feature importance (global explanation), Feature interaction (local explanation).

exact_shapley_values [5] is a permutation-based xAI algorithm following a game theory approach: Iteratively Order the features randomly, then add them to the input one at a time following this order, and calculate their expected marginal contribution [4]. The output is unique given a set of constrains defined in the original paper. The xAI algorithm is model agnostic i.e. it can explain any AI model. The xAI algorithm can output the following explanations: Feature importance (global explanation). The following information are required by the xAI algorithm:, A reference dataset (input only), The model's predict function

kernel_shap [7] it approximates the Shapley values with a constant noise [48]. The xAI algorithm is model agnostic i.e. it can explain any AI model. The xAI algorithm can output the following explanations: Feature attribution (local explanation), Feature importance (global explanation). The following information are required by the xAI algorithm:, A reference dataset (input only), The model's predict function

lime [1] it explains the model locally by generating an interpretable model approximating the original one. The xAI algorithm is model agnostic i.e. it can explain any AI model. The xAI algorithm can output the following explanations: Feature attribution (local explanation), Feature importance (global explanation). The following information are required by the xAI algorithm:, A reference dataset (input only), The model's predict probability function, Nature of the ML task (regression/classification), The model's predict function

maple [44] is a supervised neighborhood approach that combines ideas from local linear models and ensembles of decision trees [44]. The xAI algorithm is model agnostic i.e. it can explain any AI model. The xAI algorithm can output the following explanations: Feature attribution (local explanation), Feature importance (global explanation). The following information are required by the xAI algorithm:, AI model's structure, A reference dataset (input only), The train set, The model's predict function

partition [7] Partition SHAP approximates the Shapley values using a hierarchy of feature coalitions. The xAI algorithm is model agnostic i.e. it can explain any AI model. The xAI algorithm can output the following explanations: Feature attribution (local explanation), Feature importance (global explanation). The following information are required by the xAI algorithm:, A reference dataset (input only), The model's predict function

permutation is a shuffle-based feature importance. It permutes the input data and compares it to the normal prediction The xAI algorithm is model agnostic i.e. it can explain any AI model. The xAI algorithm can output the following explanations: Feature attribution (local explanation), Feature importance (global explanation). The following information are required by the xAI algorithm:, input features, A reference dataset (input only), The model's predict function

permutation_partition is a combination of permutation and partition algorithm from shap. The xAI algorithm is model agnostic i.e. it can explain any AI model. The xAI algorithm can output the following explanations: Feature attribution (local explanation), Feature importance (global explanation). The following information are required by the xAI algorithm:, input features, A reference dataset (input only), The model's predict function

saabas explain tree based models by decomposing each prediction into bias and feature contribution components The xAI algorithm can explain tree-based models. The xAI algorithm can output the following explanations: Feature attribution (local explanation), Feature importance (global explanation). The following information are required by the xAI algorithm:, AI model's structure

sage [19] Compute feature importance based on Shapley value but faster. The features that are most critical for the model to make good predictions will have large importance and only features that make the model's performance worse will have negative values.
Disadvantage: The convergence of the algorithm depends on 2 parameters: 'thres' and 'gap'. The algorithm can be trapped in a potential infinite loop if we do not fine tune them. The xAI algorithm is model agnostic i.e. it can explain any AI model. The xAI algorithm can output the following explanations: Feature importance (global explanation). The following information are required by the xAI algorithm:, True output of the data points to explain, A reference dataset (input only), The model's predict function

shap_interaction [45] SI: Shapley Interaction Index. The xAI algorithm is model agnostic i.e. it can explain any AI model. The xAI algorithm can output the following explanations: Feature interaction (local explanation).

shapley_taylor_interaction [46] STI: Shapley Taylor Interaction Index. The xAI algorithm is model agnostic i.e. it can explain any AI model. The xAI algorithm can output the following explanations: Feature interaction (local explanation).

tree_shap [9] accurately compute the shap values using the structure of the tree model. The xAI algorithm can explain tree-based models. The xAI algorithm can output the following explanations: Feature attribution (local explanation), Feature importance (global explanation). The following information are required by the xAI algorithm:, AI model's structure, A reference dataset (input only)

tree_shap_approximation is a faster implementation of shap reserved for tree based models. The xAI algorithm can explain tree-based models. The xAI algorithm can output the following explanations: Feature attribution (local explanation), Feature importance (global explanation). The following information are required by the xAI algorithm:, AI model's structure, A reference dataset (input only)

joint_shapley is an extension of the axioms and intuitions of Shapley values proposed by [56]. This xAI algorithm creates a powerset up to a user specified power k of all the input features and computes the average Shapley values for all different subsets. This leads to a more accurate attribution of importance for each input feature, but significantly increases the run-time.

C   Test Results

Table 2 contains test results without using any filter. **Tests** is the number of completed tests. **Time** is the average execution time per test. It informs the user about the relative difference in execution time between algorithms.

Table 2. Results for all Tests

Test	cough	cough_10_90	counter-example_or_c	a_and_b	non_uniform_dep	uniform_dep	non_uniform_indep	fooling_pertubation	corr. features	mnist	nb_features	Time per Test
Explainer	[%]	[%]	[%]	[%]	[%]	[%]	[%]	[%]	[%]	[%]	[%]	(Seconds)
Random	0	100	0	0	0	0	34	11	0	100	0	0.01
Permutation	20	100	100	100	100	100	100	11	11	100	100	9.90
Permutation_Partition	20	100	100	100	100	100	100	11	11	100	100	12.40
Partition	19	100	100	100	100	100	100	11	0	100	100	7.32
Tree_Shap_Approximation	0	100		100	65	59	100				100	0.01
Exact_Shapley_Values	19	100	100	100	100	100	100	11	0	0	100	1906.04
Tree_Shap	20	100		100	100	100	100				100	0.00
Saabas	100	100		100	62	60	100	0			100	0.00
Kernel_Shap	100	100	100	100	100	100	100	11		100	100	121.73
Sage	0	100	100		93	89	98			100	100	18.38
Lime	49	100	98	0	99	100	100	0		100	100	259.81
Maple	100	0	0	50	100	100	100	11	11	100	100	56.61
Joint_Shapley	61	0	67	100	98	98	99	0	0	0	96	1947.94

References

1. Ribeiro, M.T., Singh, S., Guestrin, C.: Why should I trust you? Explaining the predictions of any classifier. In: Proceedings of the 22nd ACM SIGKDD International Conference on Knowledge Discovery and Data Mining, pp. 1135–1144 (2016)
2. Dressel, J., Farid, H.: The accuracy, fairness, and limits of predicting recidivism. Sci. Advances **4**(1), eaao5580 (2018)
3. Goodman, B., Flaxman, S.: European union regulations on algorithmic decision-making and a "right to explanation". AI Mag. **38**(3), 50–57 (2017)
4. Sundararajan, M., Najmi, A.: The many Shapley values for model explanation. In: International Conference on Machine Learning, pp. 9269–9278. PMLR (2020)
5. Shapley, L.S.: Quota Solutions op N-person games1. Edited by Emil Artin and Marston Morse, p. 343 (1953)
6. Štrumbelj, E., Kononenko, I.: Explaining prediction models and individual predictions with feature contributions. Knowl. Inf. Syst. **41**(3), 647–665 (2014)

7. Lundberg, S.M., Lee, S.-I.: A unified approach to interpreting model predictions. In: Advances in Neural Information Processing Systems, vol. 30 (2017)

8. Sundararajan, M., Taly, A., Yan, Q.: Axiomatic attribution for deep networks. In: International Conference on Machine Learning, pp. 3319–3328. PMLR (2017)

9. Lundberg, S.M., Erion, G.G., Lee, S.-I.: Consistent individualized feature attribution for tree ensembles. arXiv preprint arXiv:1802.03888 (2018)

10. Staniak, M., Biecek, P.: Explanations of model predictions with live and breakdown packages. arXiv preprint arXiv:1804.01955 (2018)

11. Rozenblit, L., Keil, F.: The misunderstood limits of folk science: an illusion of explanatory depth. Cogn. Sci. **26**(5), 521–562 (2002)

12. Chromik, M., Eiband, M, Buchner, F., Krüger, A., Butz, A.: I think I get your point, AI! the illusion of explanatory depth in explainable AI. In: 26th International Conference on Intelligent User Interfaces, pp. 307–317 (2021)

13. Kaur, H., Nori, H., Jenkins, S., Caruana, R., Wallach, H., Vaughan, J.W.: Interpreting interpretability: understanding data scientists' use of interpretability tools for machine learning. In: Proceedings of the 2020 CHI Conference on Human Factors in Computing Systems, pp. 1–14 (2020)

14. Leavitt, M.L., Morcos, A.: Towards falsifiable interpretability research. arXiv preprint arXiv:2010.12016 (2020)

15. Kearns, M., Roth, A.: The Ethical Algorithm: The Science of Socially Aware Algorithm Design. Oxford University Press, Oxford (2019)

16. Miller, T.: Explanation in artificial intelligence: insights from the social sciences. Artif. Intell. **267**, 1–38 (2019)

17. Beizer, B.: Black-Box Testing: Techniques for Functional Testing of Software and Systems. Wiley, Hoboken (1995)

18. LeCun, Y., Cortes, C., Burges, C.J.: MNIST handwritten digit database. ATT Labs (2010). https://yann.lecun.com/exdb/mnist

19. Covert, I., Lundberg, S.M., Lee, S.-I.: Understanding global feature contributions with additive importance measures. In: Advances in Neural Information Processing Systems, vol. 33, pp. 17212–17223 (2020)

20. Tsang, M., Rambhatla, S., Liu, Y.: How does this interaction affect me? Interpretable attribution for feature interactions. In: Advances in Neural Information Processing Systems, vol. 33, pp. 6147–6159 (2020)

21. Elizabeth Kumar, I., Venkatasubramanian, S., Scheidegger, C., Friedler, S.: Problems with Shapley-value-based explanations as feature importance measures. In: International Conference on Machine Learning, pp. 5491–5500. PMLR (2020)

22. Mohseni, S., Zarei, N., Ragan, E.D.: A multidisciplinary survey and framework for design and evaluation of explainable AI systems. arXiv preprint arXiv:1811.11839 (2018)

23. Tsang, M., Enouen, J., Liu, Y.: Interpretable artificial intelligence through the lens of feature interaction. arXiv preprint arXiv:2103.03103 (2021)

24. Angelov, P.P., Soares, E.A., Jiang, R., Arnold, N.I., Atkinson, P.M.: Explainable artificial intelligence: an analytical review. Wiley Interdisc. Rev. Data Min. Knowl. Discov. **11**(5), e1424 (2021)

25. Zhou, J., Gandomi, A.H., Chen, F., Holzinger, A.: Evaluating the quality of machine learning explanations: a survey on methods and metrics. Electronics **10**(5), 593 (2021)

26. Rozemberczki, B., et al.: The Shapley value in machine learning. arXiv preprint arXiv:2202.05594 (2022)

27. Nauta, M., et al.: From anecdotal evidence to quantitative evaluation methods: a systematic review on evaluating explainable AI. arXiv preprint arXiv:2201.08164 (2022)

28. Molnar, C.: Interpretable machine learning. Lulu.com (2020)

29. Sattarzadeh, S., Sudhakar, M., Plataniotis, K.N.: SVEA: a small-scale benchmark for validating the usability of post-hoc explainable AI solutions in image and signal recognition. In: Proceedings of the IEEE/CVF International Conference on Computer Vision, pp. 4158–4167 (2021)

30. Greydanus, S.: Scaling down deep learning. arXiv preprint arXiv:2011.14439 (2020)

31. DeYoung, J., et al.: Eraser: a benchmark to evaluate rationalized NLP models. arXiv preprint arXiv:1911.03429 (2019)

32. Mohseni, S., Block, J.E., Ragan, E.D.: Quantitative evaluation of machine learning explanations: a human-grounded benchmark. arXiv preprint arXiv:1801.05075 (2020)

33. Liu, Y., Khandagale, S., White, C., Neiswanger, W.: Synthetic benchmarks for scientific research in explainable machine learning. arXiv preprint arXiv:2106.12543 (2021)

34. Sharma, A., Melnikov, V., Hüllermeier, E., Wehrheim, H.: Property-driven black-box testing of numeric functions. Softw. Eng. **2023** (2023)

35. Chrysostomou, G., Aletras, N.: Improving the faithfulness of attention-based explanations with task-specific information for text classification. arXiv preprint arXiv:2105.02657 (2021)

36. Hamamoto, M., Egi, M.: Model-agnostic ensemble-based explanation correction leveraging Rashomon effect. In: 2021 IEEE Symposium Series on Computational Intelligence (SSCI), pp. 01–08. IEEE (2021)

37. Hameed, I., et al.: Based-XAI: breaking ablation studies down for explainable artificial intelligence. arXiv preprint arXiv:2207.05566 (2022)

38. Guidotti, R.: Evaluating local explanation methods on ground truth. Artif. Intell. **291**, 103428 (2021)

39. Lin, Y.-S., Lee, W.-C., Berkay Celik, Z.: What do you see? Evaluation of explainable artificial intelligence (XAI) interpretability through neural backdoors. In: Proceedings of the 27th ACM SIGKDD Conference on Knowledge Discovery & Data Mining, pp. 1027–1035 (2021)

40. Hedström, A., et al.: An explainable AI toolkit for responsible evaluation of neural network explanations and beyond. J. Mach. Learn. Res. **24**(34), 1–11 (2023)

41. Arras, L., Osman, A., Samek, W.: CLEVR-XAI: a benchmark dataset for the ground truth evaluation of neural network explanations. Inf. Fusion **81**, 14–40 (2022)

42. Du, M., Liu, N., Yang, F., Ji, S., Hu, X.: On attribution of recurrent neural network predictions via additive decomposition. In: The World Wide Web Conference, pp. 383–393 (2019)

43. Agarwal, C., et al.: OpenXAI: towards a transparent evaluation of model explanations. In: Advances in Neural Information Processing Systems, vol. 35, pp. 15784–15799 (2022)

44. Plumb, G., Molitor, D., Talwalkar, A.S.: Model agnostic supervised local explanations. In: Advances in Neural Information Processing Systems, vol. 31 (2018)

45. Owen, G.: Multilinear extensions of games. Manag. Sci. **18**(5-part-2), 64–79 (1972)

46. Sundararajan, M., Dhamdhere, K., Agarwal, A.: The Shapley Taylor interaction index. In: International Conference on Machine Learning, pp. 9259–9268. PMLR (2020)

47. Ghorbani, A., Abid, A., Zou, J.: Interpretation of neural networks is fragile. In: Proceedings of the AAAI Conference on Artificial Intelligence, vol. 33, pp. 3681–3688 (2019)

48. Janzing, D., Minorics, L., Blöbaum, P.: Feature relevance quantification in explainable AI: a causal problem. In: International Conference on Artificial Intelligence and Statistics, pp. 2907–2916. PMLR (2020)

49. Hooker, G., Mentch, L., Zhou, S.: Unrestricted permutation forces extrapolation: variable importance requires at least one more model, or there is no free variable importance. Stat. Comput. **31**(6), 1–16 (2021)

50. Lakkaraju, H., Kamar, E, Caruana, R., Leskovec, J.: Faithful and customizable explanations of black box models. In: Proceedings of the 2019 AAAI/ACM Conference on AI, Ethics, and Society, pp. 131–138 (2019)

51. Melis, D.A., Jaakkola, T.: Towards robust interpretability with self-explaining neural networks. In: Advances in Neural Information Processing Systems, vol. 31 (2018)

52. Lakkaraju, H., Bastani, O.: "How do I fool you?" manipulating user trust via misleading black box explanations. In: Proceedings of the AAAI/ACM Conference on AI, Ethics, and Society, pp. 79–85 (2020)

53. Mollas, I., Bassiliades, N., Tsoumakas, G.: Altruist: argumentative explanations through local interpretations of predictive models. In: Proceedings of the 12th Hellenic Conference on Artificial Intelligence, pp. 1–10 (2022)

54. Larson, J., Mattu, S., Kirchner, L., Angwin, J.: How we analyzed the COMPAS recidivism algorithm. ProPublica **9**(1), 3 (2016)

55. Jeyakumar, J.V., Noor, J., Cheng, Y.-H., Garcia, L., Srivastava, M.: How can I explain this to you? An empirical study of deep neural network explanation methods. In: Advances in Neural Information Processing Systems, vol. 33, pp. 4211–4222 (2020)

56. Harris, C., Pymar, R., Rowat, C.: Joint Shapley values: a measure of joint feature importance. arXiv preprint arXiv:2107.11357 (2021)

Explainability in Practice: Estimating Electrification Rates from Mobile Phone Data in Senegal

Laura State[1,2]([envelope]) [ORCID], Hadrien Salat[3] [ORCID], Stefania Rubrichi[4] [ORCID],
and Zbigniew Smoreda[4] [ORCID]

[1] University of Pisa, Pisa, Italy
laura.state@di.unipi.it
[2] Scuola Normale Superiore, Pisa, Italy
[3] Alan Turing Institute, London, UK
[4] Orange Innovation, Châtillon, France

Abstract. Explainable artificial intelligence (XAI) provides explanations for not interpretable machine learning (ML) models. While many technical approaches exist, there is a lack of validation of these techniques on real-world datasets. In this work, we present a use-case of XAI: an ML model which is trained to estimate electrification rates based on mobile phone data in Senegal. The data originate from the Data for Development challenge by Orange in 2014/15. We apply two model-agnostic, local explanation techniques and find that while the model can be verified, it is biased with respect to the population density. We conclude our paper by pointing to the two main challenges we encountered during our work: data processing and model design that might be restricted by currently available XAI methods, and the importance of domain knowledge to interpret explanations.

Keywords: explainable AI · Use-case · Mobile Phone Data · Global South

1 Introduction

Explainable AI (XAI) provides techniques to better understand machine learning (ML) models. This is motivated by their lack of transparency, and an increased use of these models in resource allocation problems that critically affect individuals, such as hiring, credit rating, or in public administration.[1] While many XAI methods have been proposed, there is a certain lack of work that uses these methods on real-world data and thus confirms their relevance [20].

In this work, we present a use-case of XAI: we train an ML model to estimate electrification rates in Senegal, and evaluate it using two popular XAI techniques. The estimation of such socio-economic indicators can support policy planning

---

[1] https://algorithmwatch.org/en/automating-society-2020/.

© The Author(s), under exclusive license to Springer Nature Switzerland AG 2023
L. Longo (Ed.): xAI 2023, CCIS 1902, pp. 110–125, 2023.
https://doi.org/10.1007/978-3-031-44067-0_6

and is assumed to be a less costly and time-consuming alternative to traditional approaches such as collecting census or survey data. Policy planning involves considerable amounts of resources, thus, requires transparency and accountability. We draw on a dataset of mobile phone data, collected in 2013 and provided during the Data for Development challenge by Orange in 2014/15. We combine it with extracts from the 2013 census in Senegal, and estimate the electrification rate around single cell tower locations.

The contribution of our work is twofold: first, we show how XAI methods can be used to *verify* an ML model, and that our model is biased w.r.t. population densities. In our case, verifying means showing that the model indeed relies on features that relate to the predicted outcome, as given by domain knowledge. Thus, we confirm the relevance of XAI techniques. Second, we point towards two *challenges* of deploying XAI in practice that emerged during this work: pipeline design, and domain knowledge.

The paper is structured as follows: Sect. 2 provides the relevant background, Sect. 3 information on the dataset, followed by a description of the experiments in Sect. 4. Results are discussed in Sect. 5, followed by the limitations in Sect. 6. We conclude our paper in Sect. 7.[2]

2   Background and Related Work

2.1   Explainable AI

The field of explainable AI can be distinguished along three dimensions: black- vs white-box approaches, local vs global, and model-agnostic vs model-specific [11]. The term *white-box* refers to models that are interpretable, or explainable-by-design, while a *black-box* (BB) model is not interpretable, or accessible, e.g., due to intellectual property rights. The majority of used ML models belong to the latter, and it is exactly for those models that we have to design explanation techniques. These explanations can be distinguished by scale. *Local* techniques explain the prediction for a single data instance (often an individual, in our case a single cell phone tower). Here, prominent approaches are LIME [25] and SHAP [16]. Opposed to this, *global* approaches tackle a full explanation of the system, often by fitting an interpretable surrogate model. One example is the TREPAN algorithm [8], building a single decision tree over a neural network. Last, we differentiate between approaches that work on any (*model-agnostic*) or only one (*model-specific*) model. LIME [25] and SHAP [16] are considered model-agnostic, TREPAN [8] model-specific. A full survey of approaches can be found elsewhere, e.g., [2,11,18]. The latter includes a full chapter on interpretable (white-box) models.

LIME (Local Interpretable Model-Agnostic Explanations)   [25]. This method uses a randomly generated neighborhood, weighted according to a distance and

---

[2] The code of the project can be found here: https://github.com/lstate/explainabil ity-in-practice.git.

a kernel function, to fit a linear regression around the data instance in focus. This regression approximates the decision boundary, and its weights are interpreted as the *importance* of the features. A positive importance pushes the (here) classifier towards the predicted class, while a negative pulls it away and towards one of the other classes. Therefore, both the sign and magnitude of the importance matter.

SHAP (SHapley Additive exPlanations) [16]. Explanations are based on a game-theoretic approach, and provide for each feature its *contribution* towards the predicted outcome. Contributions are not only specific to an instance but also to the (here) class. If we sum over all contributions w.r.t. to a class C, and add this value on top of the expected value $E_C(f(x))$, we reach the predicted value of our model $f(x)$, which in turn determines the class (the highest value wins). Therefore, the sign and magnitude of a feature contribution matter as well.

Shortcomings LIME and SHAP. Both methods have some well-known shortcomings. We refer here to a few: regarding LIME, an open issue is the (mathematical) definition of a neighborhood as well as its robustness [4,18]. SHAP, on the other hand, has a well-defined mathematical background. Issues are its computational complexity and (for KernelSHAP) feature dependencies that are not considered.

2.2   Mobile Phone Data and Electrification

Mobile phones are a rich source of information, providing details about time, length and location of calls and other data. Combined with the fact that mobile phone penetration is generally high,[3] this opens possibilities for research, public policy, infrastructure planning, etc. Predicting socio-economic indicators from remotely accessible data is popular, and we observe an interest in using such data in countries of the Global South, where it might be a less costly and time-consuming alternative to traditional approaches such as collecting census or survey data. Different indicators can be predicted, and they vary based on available data and methods. Based on mobile phone data, examples are the estimation of socio-economic status and welfare indicators, literacy rate, population densities, and electric consumption [6,27,28]. For approaches using additional data sources, an example is the estimation of poverty measures [24,29]. In many cases, these studies are framed within the 17 SDGs.[4]

In this work, we focus on the estimation of electrification rates using mobile phone data. Relevant studies that investigate the relation of electricity and other indicators such as mobile connectivity or volume of visitors in Senegal are [13,26]. What is novel to our work is that we do not only estimate electrification rates, but we use XAI methods to understand these estimations and evaluate them. As such, we present a use-case of XAI, with a focus on the Global South. A recent survey on XAI projects centered around the Global South [22] showed that while

---

[3] https://ourworldindata.org/grapher/mobile-cellular-subscriptions-per-100-people.

[4] https://sdgs.un.org/goals.

the body of work in the field of XAI is growing rapidly, only 16 of the surveyed papers relate to the Global South (approx. 18,000 papers on the topic of XAI, in the same time span), with only one technical study that has similar focus and design as ours (focus on interpretable poverty mapping) [14].

3   Dataset

3.1   Mobile Phone Data

We use mobile phone data provided in the form of pre-aggregated call detail records (CDR), which were made available during the second Data for Development challenge launched by Orange in 2014/15. The original data were collected by Sonatel (*Société Nationale des Télécommunications du Sénégal*), which is the leading telecommunication company in Senegal (market share of 65% in 2013). CDRs are generated for billing purposes and are proprietary.

Senegal is a sub-Saharan country, located in the Northern Hemisphere near the Equator, on the West Coast of Africa. It covers 196,712 km². In 2013, the year when the data were collected, the population count approached 14M.[5] The original dataset contains more than 9 million individual mobile phone numbers, with an hourly resolution. Sonatel anonymized the data, Orange pre-aggregated and processed it further. The resulting dataset holds (cell) tower-to-tower activity, for calls (including call length) and text messages separately. Spatial coverage between call and text message data is different, text message data less available in the Eastern part of Senegal (see also appendix, Sect. A.1). These areas fall together with areas that are less electrified which might suggest a connection between access to electricity, poverty rate, literacy, and text message activity (see [13] for a study on the impact of access to electricity). All details on the dataset can be found here [19].

Table 1. Features and abbreviations. The type of an event (number of calls, call length or number of text messages) will be indicated by subscripts (CN, CL, SN, respectively).

te	number of events *within* Voronoi cell (synonymously used: total events)
out	number of outgoing events
in	number of incoming events
dc	degree centrality
cc	closeness centrality
out/in	ratio of outgoing over incoming events

We process this base data according to the following steps: 1) building one network per data type, amounting to three networks in total (number of calls, call length and number of text messages). Cell towers form the network nodes, and are labeled according to the electrification rate; 2) extracting each six features

---

[5] https://data.worldbank.org/country/senegal.

per network, amounting to a tabular dataset of a 1587 × 18; 3) binning the resulting dataset to create an ordered classification problem of 10 classes; 4) sub-sampling due to an imbalance of the dataset.

Regarding the network construction (step 1), we proceed as follows: we build a directed, weighted communication network from the data, based on the overall activity of 2013, i.e. with no resolution over time. While cell towers form the nodes, edges are created based on the activity in the network. Per cell tower (outgoing site in the original dataset) we aggregate over the receiving tower (incoming site in the original dataset) and sum over respective events, for example the number of calls between those two towers, and ignore thereby the time stamp. The total number of events per connection, and in the full year 2013, determines the weight of the edge. This will lead to a full matrix. It has elements on its main diagonal, as calls/messages appear also within a Voronoi cell. Also, it is not symmetric as the number of outgoing and incoming calls/messages between two cell towers is generally not the same. We repeat this network construction for all three types of data (call numbers, call length and message data). Cell tower locations are used to map the activity spatially, we rely on a Voronoi cell tessellation. The electrification rate of each of the Voronoi cells is assigned based on the 2013 census in Senegal.

Regarding the second step, the extracted features are listed in Table 1, they form the final tabular dataset. The number of events within a Voronoi cell, as well as outgoing and incoming events, are helpful for a general understanding of the activity in the network. Centrality measures are added as they are basic measures of communication networks. Further, centrality measures and the ratio between outgoing and incoming events are inspired by [27].

Steps 3 and 4 refer already to data preparation and are therefore discussed in Sect. 4.1.

3.2 Electrification Data

Electrification rate, population count, and population density originate from the 2013 census in Senegal [3]. Pre-processing is identical to Salat et al. [26]. The census contains questions about the source of lighting for each household and therefore informs us of stable access to electricity. In the context of this study, stable access means access either to the main power grid or to photo-voltaic systems that benefit from the year-round high solar irradiation in the country. The electrification rate of each census unit (*commune*) is given by the ratio between the total number of households with stable access and the total household count. We assume a homogeneous distribution of the population inside each commune, therefore the electrification rate of a Voronoi cell is given by the average electrification rate of all intersected communes weighted by the area of intersection. Salat et al. [26] report that the resulting electrification rates were in good agreement with the fine-grained nighttime lights intensity provided by NOAA [21]. The supporting shapefile containing the geographic boundaries and population counts at commune level was provided alongside another previous study [27].

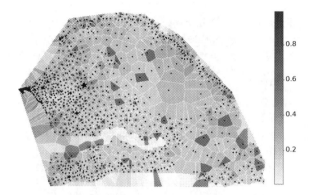

Fig. 1. Electrification rate as computed from census data, plotted over the Voronoi cell tessellation.

Figure 1 shows electrification rates in Senegal. Higher rates are observed around major cities: Dakar, the Capital, in the Western most part of the country, Saint-Louis in the North West, and the culturally significant city of Touba in the center. The electrification rates are also high along the more densely populated Northern/Eastern borders with Mauritania. This follows closely the electric grid of Senegal, discussed in [17]. We, therefore, observe a correlation between areas with a high electrification rate and a high density of cell towers.

4   Experiments

4.1   Preparation

Each row in the pre-processed tabular dataset (corresponding to a Voronoi cell/cell tower) is labeled by its electrification rate (for the pre-processing, see Sect. 3.1). We bin the data such that it holds 10 classes, ordered by electrification rate, and with a bin size of 0.1 ($[0, 0.1)$ electrification rate for class 0, $[0.1, 0.2)$ electrification rate for class 1, etc.). The resulting distribution is skewed towards higher values.[6] We subsample elements of class 9 (electrification rate $[0.9, 1]$), for the training sets only. We sample such that numbers in class 9 are reduced to the average count over all classes. Thus, we predict the electrification rate (as class), based on 18 features. We randomly split the dataset to create a training and a test set for the ML classifiers (ratio $7 : 3$), and split the test set to create a training and a test set for the explanations (ratio $7 : 3$).

4.2   Models

Classification. We train a set of different ML standard models to estimate electrification rates, the best-performing model will be the basis for all future experiments. This is based on the assumption that only this model would be used

---

[6] The ratio between instances in class 9 and the full dataset before subsampling is $imb = 33\%$.

in deployment. However, investigating the explanations for the remaining ML models could also provide valuable insights, and remains for future work.

First, we train a decision tree (DT), a random forest model (RF) containing 100 decision trees, and an extreme gradient boosting model (XGB) with default parameters. We use default parameters to ensure better reproducibility. Additionally, we run a simple test on the following ML models: a logistic regression (LOG), an AdaBoost classifier (ADA), a support vector machine (SVC), a multi-layer perceptron (MLP) and a Gaussian Naive Bayes model (BAY), all using default parameters. We compute the accuracy, the mean absolute error (MAE), and the ratio between the MAE and its maximum ($MAE_{max} = 9$).

Explanations. We compute local, model-agnostic explanations based on LIME and SHAP. A basic assumption of local XAI methods is that it is generally easier to approximate the decision boundary of a complex model locally and thus provide more faithful – i.e. better – explanations, than at the global level [25]. We particularly choose LIME and SHAP for the following reasons: both methods, including their shortcomings (see Sect. 2.1), are well known in the community.[7] Methods are also easily accessible and rely on interpretable features [18].

As LIME needs to compute some basic data features to generate explanations, it has to be initialized on the explanation training set. We use LIME tabular, retrieve the five most important features ($d = 5$), and use default parameters. Explanations are computed once over the given sets. Evaluations of explanations are computed over the explanation test set. For SHAP, we use the tree explainer, as we focus on the random forest model, and also default parameters.

4.3 Urban and Rural Areas

We hypothesize that the ML model predicts electrification rates with different accuracy for rural and urban areas, i.e. that the model is *biased* w.r.t to the population density. Therefore, we identify these regions in the test datasets and calculate the disaggregated accuracy values. Further, we compute the disaggregated explanations. We identify urban regions based on a population density $p > 1000/\text{km}^2$, as previously done in [26], otherwise as rural.

5 Results

5.1 Classification

Best performance is achieved by the random forest model ($acc = 0.516, MAE = 0.972$, see Table 2). However, excluding ADA and BAY, all models perform similarly well (extended results can be found in the appendix, Sect. A.2). As the classification is ordered, an MAE around one means that on average, the electrification rate is wrongly estimated by 0.1, which is acceptable. Note that while we need a sufficiently high performance of our models to proceed, the focus of this paper is not on model performance.

---

[7] 12.7M downloads of LIME python package, 63M downloads of SHAP python package, retrieved on 6th of April 2022 https://pepy.tech.

Table 2. Classification results. The higher the accuracy (*acc*) the better, the lower the *MAE* the better. Best values are underlined.

model	acc	MAE	MAE/MAE$_{max}$	acc$_{urban}$	acc$_{rural}$
DT	0.428	1.258	0.140	0.714	0.247
RF	<u>0.516</u>	<u>0.972</u>	<u>0.108</u>	0.854	0.301
XGB	0.491	1.027	0.114	0.789	0.301

5.2 Explanations

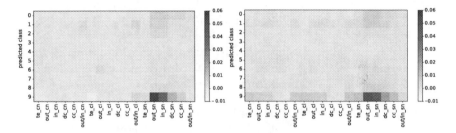

Fig. 2. Average importance (left, LIME) or contribution (right, SHAP) of a feature w.r.t. the predicted class. Both plots computed for RF classifier. Reminder of notation: Table 1.

We display results in Fig. 2, where we plotted the average *importance* (left, LIME) and the average *contribution* (right, SHAP) w.r.t. the *predicted* class. Both for LIME and SHAP, features based on text message data are highly relevant. This is especially prominent for outgoing and incoming events and the degree centrality and for class 9. Only in the case of LIME, we observe small negative values (e.g., total events based on call length, for class 9). The importance, *and* high contribution of text message data for the prediction is in line with the observation that text message activity could be correlated with the electrification rate (see also Sect. 3.1). As such, the information provided by this type of data is highly relevant for the model, providing cues to better discriminate.

For SHAP, we also computed the average over feature contributions w.r.t. *all possible* output classes (see Fig. 3). Why do we observe negative contributions for low classes? For a single data instance, features based on text message data generally push the model towards the predicted class (high positive contribution) but at the same time away from the other classes (high negative contribution), together they form the set of possible output classes. This effect is more prominent for data instances from higher classes. Positive contributions are particularly high for high classes, while negative contributions are high for low classes. Opposed, in Fig. 2, right, for better comparability with LIME, we only plotted contribution w.r.t. to the *predicted* class (and not all possible output classes), thus only positive contributions appear.

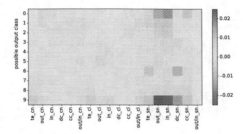

Fig. 3. Average contribution of a feature w.r.t. the possible output class.

Both methods confirm that the model relies on features that indeed relate to the predicted outcome. While a more in-depth analysis of the model and explanations is needed, this is a first good result.

We note that displayed values are only averages, thus positive and negative relevance values w.r.t. the same feature and class can cancel each other out. Nevertheless, they provide an informative summary of the model behavior.

Comparing LIME and SHAP. While both approaches produce some measure of *feature relevance*, the methods are different, thus the meaning of a feature relevance is not the same (see also Sect. 2.1). On one hand, if we study Fig. 2, we find only small differences. SHAP, on the other hand, can give us some additional information, if we consider the full output (see Fig. 3). However, in our particular case, it does entail no surprising insights. Therefore, while we acknowledge the mathematical basis of SHAP as an advantage, we cannot make a strong argument in favor of it, and against LIME.

5.3   Urban and Rural Areas

Disaggregated accuracy values are displayed in Table 2, and in the appendix in Sect. A.2. Excluding the AdaBoost model, the accuracy for rural areas is always lower than the accuracy as computed for the full test set, and the opposite is the case for urban areas. This difference in accuracy means that the model is *biased* w.r.t. to the population density.

We also computed disaggregated explanations, depicted in Fig. 4. They confirm the general relevance of features based on text message data for the prediction, as demonstrated already in the general case (previous section). Unsurprisingly, they show a different distribution of classes: while urban areas belong to class 6 or higher, rural areas span all classes. This is also reflected in the relevance of the features based on text message data, we observe the highest importance values, or contributions, as provided by LIME, or SHAP, respectively, for different classes, and depending on whether we look at urban or rural sub-populations. We further observe that the feature importance values, or feature contributions, are consistently higher in magnitude for the urban compared to rural sub-population. This supports our finding that the model is biased w.r.t. the population density.

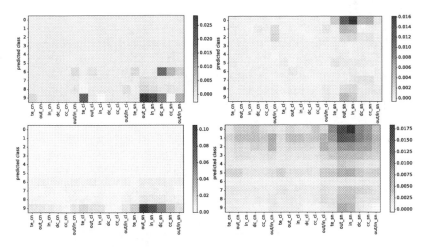

Fig. 4. Explanations by sub-population, w.r.t. predicted class: for urban regions (left) and rural regions (right), based on LIME (top row) or SHAP (lower row).

In Fig. 5, we show the explanations as provided by SHAP, w.r.t to *all possible* output classes, and disaggregated by sub-population. Similar to what we observed already in the previous section, we find in this case positive and negative values. As urban areas are tied to higher electrification classes, and rural areas to lower electrification classes, positive and negative values are correlated with opposing classes. Again, magnitudes are generally higher for urban compared to rural areas.

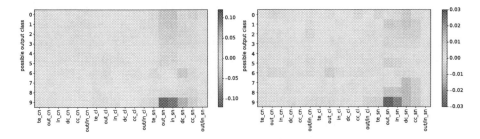

Fig. 5. Explanations by sub-population, w.r.t. possible output classes as provided by SHAP: for urban regions (left), and rural regions (right).

6 Limitations

Although the data come from a network provider who is the market leader (65% in 2013), they are not fully representative of the population. A good starting point to investigate this further is the work by Pestre et al. [23]. Salat et al. [26]

point towards other biases, for example, due to a shift from the mobile phone network to relying increasingly on internet platforms such as Facebook. Accounting for these biases, including further work on the bias w.r.t. population density is a next step. Also, we would like to apply other XAI methods such as LORE [10] to the ML model to understand whether we can extract some additional information. Another important extension is to run the explanations across all trained models and compare them with each other to understand better why there is a difference in performance.

Data used in this work are proprietary and private. It is connected to individuals (their mobile phones) and to be processed only under their consent. It was provided in an anonymized form and further aggregated to safeguard individuals. Being proprietary, the data cannot be shared beyond the project. An alternative could be relying on other open-source data, such as satellite imagery, which have already been proven useful for similar projects. While being fundamentally different from mobile phone data, extending the XAI use-case to these data is a valuable path to follow.

The data we used originate from Senegal, a country of the Global South. Being situated in Western Europe, we should critically reflect on how this might perpetuate power relationships [1]. While our focus is on providing a use-case of XAI, and to primarily verify a specific ML model that can estimate electrification rates in Senegal, we acknowledge the importance of local knowledge and domain expertise when evaluating data, and specifically when drawing policy implications [1,15].

7   Conclusion

In this work, after showing that electrification rates can be estimated from mobile phone data, we applied two local, model-agnostic explanation tools to verify our model. Both explanations perform well and agree with each other on stressing the relevance of text message data for the predicted outcome. They confirm the general validity of the model. We also showed that our model is biased w.r.t. to population densities. Thus, areas located in rural areas receive an unfair prediction, i.e. are more likely to be linked to a wrong electrification rate.

While the prediction of socio-economic indicators from remotely accessible data is not novel in itself, it is of high relevance, e.g., to support policy planning. Verifying such a model using XAI techniques is certainly important, and novel. This is complementary to the fact that there are generally few use-cases applying an XAI method on a real-world problem, most of them centered around the Global North [22].

Our analysis showed that XAI methods can be useful to verify an ML model in practice. However, we would like to caution against using these tools blindly, and summarize the challenges that emerged during our work as follows:

Pipeline Design. If the aim is to use an XAI method, data processing and choosing the model tasks are limited by the fact that most XAI methods focus on tabular, image or text data, and on classification problems. Adapting a problem to this could lead to a loss of information and lower prediction accuracy. Thus, efforts should be made to provide explanations for other task and data types (such as LASTS [12] for time series data, and beyond).

Domain Knowledge. While an isolated XAI method can be very useful for debugging purposes, domain knowledge is necessary to draw real-world connections, and eventually verify the model via the explanation. In our work, an example of such knowledge is the distribution of text message activity over Senegal. While domain knowledge needs to be available in the first place, it is usually external to the explanation. A direct integration into XAI methods via symbolic approaches could be therefore highly useful [5,7].

The work presented in this paper relies on a static network. We initially kept a second version of the dataset in the form of time series. Details on these experiments, including the trained ML model and explanations based on LASTS [12] can be found in the Appendix A.3. The time series data posed several challenges, among others, a high need of computing resources, few XAI approaches to use and compare, and a considerably higher amount of domain knowledge required for the interpretation of the data. For these reasons, we decided to continue working on the network data and leave the time series data for future work.

Acknowledgements. Thanks to Salvatore Ruggieri and Franco Turini. This work has received funding from the European Union's Horizon 2020 research and innovation programme under Marie Skłodowska-Curie Actions (grant agreement number 860630) for the project "NoBIAS - Artificial Intelligence without Bias" (https://nobias-project.eu/). This work reflects only the authors' views and the European Research Executive Agency (REA) is not responsible for any use that may be made of the information it contains.

Author contributions. *Laura State:* conceptualization, data processing and experiments, paper draft, writing and editing *Hadrien Salat:* data preparation, paper co-writing and editing *Stefania Rubrichi:* data curation, paper reviewing, co-supervision *Zbigniew Smoreda:* data curation, paper reviewing

A   Appendix

A.1   Data Distribution

Figure 6 shows the distribution of available call data (left panel) and text message data (right panel). While both data are more dense in the Western part of Senegal, text message data are specifically sparse in the Eastern part of the country.

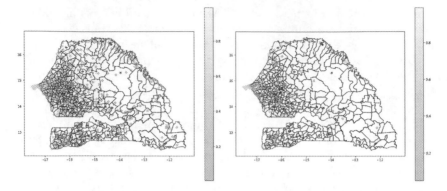

Fig. 6. Spatial distribution of available data. Left panel: call data, right panel: text message data. Colored points reference to cell tower locations. Call data based on CN. Plots based on time series data, outgoing.

A.2   Additional Results

Additional results for the prediction of the electrification rate are shown in Table 3. This second set of models is also trained with default parameters.

Further, we present a confusion matrix of the best performing model (RF, Fig. 7).

Table 3. Classification results. The higher the accuracy (acc) the better, the lower the MAE the better.

model	acc	MAE	MAE/MAE_{max}	acc_{urban}	acc_{rural}
LOG	0.463	1.331	0.148	0.778	0.264
ADA	0.195	1.463	0.162	0.119	0.243
SVC	0.465	1.296	0.144	0.784	0.264
MLP	0.455	1.138	0.126	0.741	0.274
BAY	0.294	1.604	0.178	0.384	0.236

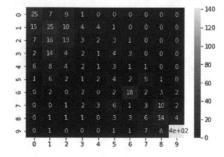

Fig. 7. Confusion matrix for the random forest model (accuracy of 0.516, MAE of 0.972, best performing model.

A.3   Time Series Data

In this section, we briefly describe the work on time series data.

Data Processing. A time series $S = s_1..s_T$ consists of $T = 24 \times 12$ ordered data points, each being the monthly average of the aggregated number of events per hour, such that $s_t, t \in 1..24$ represent the monthly average of the aggregated number of events per hour in January ("daily activity curve" for January), etc. Events are separated by direction (incoming or outgoing). Thus, per cell tower, we create *six* time series. We refer to the TS dataset based on number of calls as CN, based on length of calls as CL and based on number of text messages as SN, and use out/in for outgoing/incoming activity, respectively. We standardize each of the time series separately by applying the min-max scaler as provided by sklearn. Data labeling and subsampling applies as above. Data partitioning follows [12].

We find that text message data is heavily imbalanced, and that the dataset is smaller than the other datasets. Thus, we exclude this data from the time series analysis.

The variational autoencoder that is used in the explanation as displayed below, is trained for $k = 50$ dimensions and over $e = 500$ epochs. We used the "out CL" data and model for explanations as it provides the smallest MAE.

Classification. To classify based on time series data, we use ROCKET (RandOm Convolutional KErnel Transform) [9], a method based on random convolutional kernels for feature extraction and linear classification. Results are displayed in Table 4.

Explanations. Figure 8 shows a sample explanation by LASTS [12]. Explanations are provided in visual form and as rule, the latter can be read off the plot. The time series belongs to class 4, i.e. has an electrification rate between 0.4 and 0.5, and is correctly classified by the model. In the left panel, the factual rule is plotted against the original time series. The number above the shapelet indicates its index. The rule reads as follows: "If shapelet no. 12 is contained in the time series, then it is classified as class 4." This is mirrored by the rule

Table 4. Classification results. The higher the accuracy the better, the lower the MAE the better.

data	acc	MAE	MAE/MAE_{max}
out CN	0.605	0.758	0.084
out CL	0.600	0.637	0.071
in CN	0.601	0.761	0.085
in CL	0.532	0.814	0.090

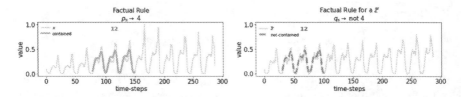

Fig. 8. Local explanation by LASTS, shapelet-based, out CL data. Explained time series belongs to class 4, correctly classified by ML model. Left: factual rule, plotted against original time series, right: rule of opposite class, plotted against synthetically generated time series. Time steps in hours.

for instances belonging to the opposite class (here: class 0..3, 5..9): 'If shapelet no. 12 is not contained in the time series, then it is not classified as class 4.", displayed in Fig. 8, right, plotted against a synthetically generated time series from a class different to class 4.

References

1. Abebe, R., et al.: Narratives and counternarratives on data sharing in Africa. In: FAccT, pp. 329–341. ACM (2021)
2. Adadi, A., Berrada, M.: Peeking inside the black-box: a survey on explainable artificial intelligence (XAI). IEEE Access **6**, 52138–52160 (2018)
3. Agence Nationale de la Statistique et de la Démographie: Census and gis data (2013).   https://www.ansd.sn/index.php?option=com_content&view=article&id=134&Itemid=262. Accessed Apr 2022
4. Alvarez-Melis, D., Jaakkola, T.S.: On the robustness of interpretability methods. CoRR abs/1806.08049 (2018)
5. Beckh, K., et al.: Explainable machine learning with prior knowledge: an overview. CoRR abs/2105.10172 (2021)
6. Blumenstock, J.E.: Calling for better measurement: estimating an individual's wealth and well-being from mobile phone transaction records. Center for Effective Global Action, UC Berkeley (2015). https://escholarship.org/uc/item/8zs63942
7. Calegari, R., Ciatto, G., Omicini, A.: On the integration of symbolic and sub-symbolic techniques for XAI: a survey. Intelligenza Artificiale **14**(1), 7–32 (2020)
8. Craven, M.W., Shavlik, J.W.: Extracting tree-structured representations of trained networks. In: NIPS, pp. 24–30. MIT Press (1995)
9. Dempster, A., Petitjean, F., Webb, G.I.: ROCKET: exceptionally fast and accurate time series classification using random convolutional kernels. Data Min. Knowl. Discov. **34**(5), 1454–1495 (2020)
10. Guidotti, R., Monreale, A., Ruggieri, S., Pedreschi, D., Turini, F., Giannotti, F.: Local rule-based explanations of black box decision systems. CoRR abs/1805.10820 (2018)
11. Guidotti, R., Monreale, A., Ruggieri, S., Turini, F., Giannotti, F., Pedreschi, D.: A survey of methods for explaining black box models. ACM Comput. Surv. **51**(5), 93:1–93:42 (2019)
12. Guidotti, R., Monreale, A., Spinnato, F., Pedreschi, D., Giannotti, F.: Explaining any time series classifier. In: CogMI, pp. 167–176. IEEE (2020)

13. Houngbonon, G.V., Quentrec, E.L., Rubrichi, S.: Access to electricity and digital inclusion: evidence from mobile call detail records. Hum. Soc. Sci. Commun. **8**(1) (2021). https://doi.org/10.1057/s41599-021-00848-0

14. Ledesma, C., Garonita, O.L., Flores, L.J., Tingzon, I., Dalisay, D.: Interpretable poverty mapping using social media data, satellite images, and geospatial information. CoRR abs/2011.13563 (2020)

15. Letouzé, E.: Applications and implications of big data for demo-economic analysis: the case of call-detail records. Ph.D. thesis, University of California, Berkeley, USA (2016)

16. Lundberg, S.M., Lee, S.: A unified approach to interpreting model predictions. In: NIPS 2017: Proceedings of the 31st International Conference on Neural Information Processing Systems, pp. 4765–4774 (2017)

17. Martinez-Cesena, E.A., Mancarella, P., Ndiaye, M., Schläpfer, M.: Using mobile phone data for electricity infrastructure planning. arXiv preprint (2015). https://arxiv.org/abs/1504.03899

18. Molnar, C.: Interpretable Machine Learning: A Guide for Making Black Box Models Explainable (2022). https://christophm.github.io/interpretable-ml-book/

19. de Montjoye, Y., Smoreda, Z., Trinquart, R., Ziemlicki, C., Blondel, V.D.: D4D-senegal: the second mobile phone data for development challenge. CoRR abs/1407.4885 (2014)

20. Murdoch, W.J., Singh, C., Kumbier, K., Abbasi-Asl, R., Yu, B.: Interpretable machine learning: definitions, methods, and applications. CoRR abs/1901.04592 (2019)

21. NOAA National Centers for Environmental Information (NCEI): Version 4 DMSP-OLS Nighttime Lights Time Series (2014). https://ngdc.noaa.gov/eog/dmsp/downloadV4composites.html. Accessed Apr 2022

22. Okolo, C.T., Dell, N., Vashistha, A.: Making AI explainable in the global south: a systematic review. In: COMPASS, pp. 439–452. ACM (2022)

23. Pestre, G., Letouzé, E., Zagheni, E.: The ABCDE of big data: assessing biases in call-detail records for development estimates. World Bank Econ. Rev. **34**(Supplement_1), S89–S97 (2019). https://doi.org/10.1093/wber/lhz039

24. Pokhriyal, N., Jacques, D.C.: Combining disparate data sources for improved poverty prediction and mapping. Proc. Natl. Acad. Sci. **114**(46), E9783–E9792 (2017). https://doi.org/10.1073/pnas.1700319114

25. Ribeiro, M.T., Singh, S., Guestrin, C.: "Why should I trust you?": explaining the predictions of any classifier. In: KDD, pp. 1135–1144. ACM (2016)

26. Salat, H., Schläpfer, M., Smoreda, Z., Rubrichi, S.: Analysing the impact of electrification on rural attractiveness in Senegal with mobile phone data. R. Soc. Open Sci. **8**(10) (2021). https://doi.org/10.1098/rsos.201898

27. Salat, H., Smoreda, Z., Schläpfer, M.: A method to estimate population densities and electricity consumption from mobile phone data in developing countries. PLOS ONE **15**(6) (2020). https://doi.org/10.1371/journal.pone.0235224

28. Schmid, T., Bruckschen, F., Salvati, N., Zbiranski, T.: Constructing socio-demographic indicators for national statistical institutes using mobile phone data: estimating literacy rates in Senegal. J. R. Stat. Soc. Series A (Statistics in Society) **180**(4), 1163–1190 (2017). https://www.jstor.org/stable/44682668

29. Steele, J.E., et al.: Mapping poverty using mobile phone and satellite data. J. R. Soc. Interface **14**(127), 20160690 (2017). https://doi.org/10.1098/rsif.2016.0690

A Novel Architecture for Robust Explainable AI Approaches in Critical Object Detection Scenarios Based on Bayesian Neural Networks

Daniel Gierse[✉], Felix Neubürger[iD], and Thomas Kopinski

South Westphalia University of Applied Sciences, Lindenstr. 53, 59872
Meschede, Germany
{gierse.daniel,neubuerger.felix,kopinski.thomas}@fh-swf.de

Abstract. Precise object detection algorithms are a mandatory requirement in safety critical applications such as autonomous driving or the analysis of safety critical situations. We provide a novel approach focusing on potential edge cases in order to address those specific situations which are often most the hardest part in bringing machine learning models into production within the aforementioned scenarios. We improve upon existing explainable artificial intelligence (XAI) methods by exploring both qualitative and quantitative approaches in the test setting of marker detection and develop novel techniques for quantifying the localization of explanations of the object detection models building upon class activation maps (CAMs). More specifically, we quantify CAMs via the shape of the pixel value sums across the CAMs axes. Building upon established object detection models our novel architecture is followed by the subsequent marker classification task via a reimplemented LeNet-like Bayesian CNN. Our presented results demonstrate that this approach to quantify the XAI techniques can improve the interpretability of both object detection and marker classification explanations by reducing their dimensionality. Moreover, the proposed method provides more clarity through increasingly interpretable explanations for the model's decisions, helping domain experts to better understand the model's behavior and improve the decision-making process. Our proposed approach can robustly be re-applied to other computer vision tasks focused on object detection and classification.

Keywords: Explainable AI · Object Detection · Object Classification · Uncertainty Quantisation

1 Introduction

Automatic video analysis algorithms in safety critical situations, e.g. in automotive crash tests, provide valuable insights into the safety of vehicles and help

We would like to thank the department for passive vehicle safety of BMW AG, Munich for the support of this research.

improve the design of novel variants. In order to analyze these tests, researchers typically use marker-based motion capture to track the movements of the vehicle and the occupants. However, this approach can be complicated by debris or other image artifacts and in this specific case confusion between different object (here: marker) types. In this paper, we propose a novel method for detecting different marker types in automotive crashtest videos. With this project we lay the groundwork with a use case for an end-to-end explainable AI pipeline that can be used across object detection and classification tasks. This end-to-end approach helps data scientists and decision makers to easier evaluate and interpret the results of the deep learning models. As a demonstration of the capabilities of this approach we evaluate the performance of several object detection models on this task, including Faster R-CNN, YOLOv5, and MobileNet. Our results show that YOLOv5 significantly outperforms the other models, achieving higher accuracy and faster processing times. Our innovative approach centers around tackling potential edge cases, specifically addressing the most challenging aspects of deploying machine learning models in production within the mentioned scenarios. To provide explanations for the object detection task, we use various XAI methods such as GradCAM, AblationCAM, and SHAP. These methods generate heatmaps that highlight the regions of the image that the model focuses on for detection. We compare the effectiveness of these methods across the different models. For the classification of the proposed markers, we use a Bayesian neural network as the classification head. We provide explanations for both the non-Bayesian and Bayesian approaches to classification. To further evaluate the robustness of our detection method, we use a VAE to generate "adversarial" images and analyze their impact on the explanations generated by the XAI methods. Finally, we use the Quantus framework [10] to provide quantitative metrics for evaluating the explainability of our models. This provides a more rigorous and statistically sound evaluation of the effectiveness of our XAI methods.

This article is structured as follows: In Sect. 2 we give an overview of the state of XAI in object detection. Section 3 describes the experimental setup and used data in more detail. The implemented pipelines and models are discussed in Sect. 4. In Sect. 5 we describe the combinations of methods we use to explain the object detection and classification networks. The experimental results are then shown and interpreted in Sect. 6 and finally discussed in Sect. 7.

2   Related Work

Explainable AI (XAI) has become an increasingly important research topic in recent years, especially in the domain of computer vision. In object detection and classification, there have been several studies that have explored XAI techniques to improve model interpretability and trustworthiness. One approach to achieving explainability in object detection is through the use of saliency maps which highlight the most important regions of an image contributing to the output of the model. In [1], the authors proposed a method for generating saliency maps for object detection using a Faster R-CNN model. Their approach involved computing the gradient of the output class scores with respect to the input image which is subsequently used to generate a saliency map. The authors demonstrated that their method could effectively identify the most important regions of an image for object detection and improve the interpretability of the model. Another approach within XAI in object detection is through the use of attention mechanisms which allow the model to focus on the most relevant regions of the image for making predictions. In [2], the authors proposed an attention-based approach for object detection using a YOLOv3 model. Their approach involved using a spatial attention mechanism to highlight the most important regions of the image for object detection. The authors demonstrated that their method could improve the accuracy of the model while also providing insights into how the model was making its predictions. Recently, there have been several studies that have explored the use of explainability techniques in YOLOv5 and Faster R-CNN models specifically. In [3], the authors proposed an approach for generating saliency maps for object detection using a YOLOv5 model. Their approach involved computing the gradient of the output class scores with respect to the input image and using this gradient to generate a saliency map. The authors demonstrated that their method could effectively identify the most important regions of an image for object detection and improve the interpretability of the YOLOv5 model. Another technique for XAI in object detection is Gradient-weighted Class Activation Mapping (GradCAM) [4], which generates class activation maps by computing the gradients of the output class scores with respect to the final convolutional layer of a model. In [5], the authors proposed a method for using GradCAM to generate heatmaps for object detection using a YOLOv3 model. Their approach involved computing the gradients of the output class scores with respect to the final convolutional layer of the model and using these gradients to generate heatmaps that highlighted the most important regions of the image for object detection. Another popular technique for XAI in machine learning is SHapley Additive exPlanations (SHAP) [6], which assigns a value to each input feature based on its contribution to the output of a model. In [7], the authors proposed a method for using SHAP to generate explanations for object detection using a Faster R-CNN model. Their approach involved computing the SHAP values for each input feature and using these values to identify the most important features for object detection. Ablation-CAM [8] is another recently proposed technique for XAI in object detection, which generates explanations by removing different parts of an image and analyzing the resulting changes in the model's output. In [9], the authors proposed a method for using AblationCAM to generate explanations for object detection using a YOLOv5 model. Their approach involved removing different regions of an image and analyzing the resulting changes in the model's output to identify the most important regions for object detection. Another approach to XAI is the use of quantitative methods, which provide a more rigorous and statistically sound evaluation of the explainability of deep learning models. One such framework is the Quantus framework proposed by Hedström et al. [10]. Quantus provides a systematic and comprehensive approach to evaluating the explainability of deep learning models using a set of metrics that measure different aspects of explainability, such as global versus local explanations, faithfulness, robustness and stability. Based on the quantitative approach to XAI to better evaluate the explanations for deep learning models we expand the methods from quantitative XAI to be implemented in currently not supported object detection models. Overall, these studies demonstrate the importance of XAI techniques in improving the interpretability and trustworthiness of object detection models such as YOLOv5 and Faster R-CNN and give insights in how these Models actually make their decisions. For the quantification of uncertainties in computer vision tasks Bayesian CNNs have been proposed. A Bayesian CNN is a type of deep learning model incorporating Bayesian principles for training and inference [11–13]. Unlike traditional CNNs that use point estimates to represent the model parameters, Bayesian CNNs treat the parameters as probability distributions. This allows for uncertainty quantification and model robustness. During training, Bayesian CNNs use a technique called Bayesian inference to estimate the posterior distribution of the model parameters given the training data [11]. This is done by updating the prior distribution of the parameters using the likelihood of the data and a regularization term [12]. The resulting posterior distribution is used to make predictions on new data points. Bayesian CNNs have been shown to outperform traditional CNNs in tasks where uncertainty quantification is important, such as image segmentation, medical imaging, and autonomous driving [13]. In this work we used the Bayesian CNN to quantify the uncertainty of the marker classification task as well es for the application of XAI Methods for specifically Bayesian computer vision tasks.

3   Experimental Setup and Data

The tracking of markers in automotive crash test videos is used for downstream kinematic analysis by safety engineers. In this work we detect and track different marker types (MXT, DOT and YQUAD) which are displayed in Fig. 1) and are commonly used by different safety agencies that carry out these crash tests. When detecting the markers the precision and reliability of the tracking is of utmost importance to fulfill the quality needed for further evaluations. In addition to the precise tracking of the markers the explainability of the predictions is highly relevant as consequences in decision making have great influence of the downstream analyses within human safety engineering. A blackbox model can not be properly audited since interpretation of the results is not quantitatively and qualitatively describable. To benchmark explainable AI methods for object detection on our dataset we implement a processing pipeline that detects, tracks and then provides explanations for these predictions. We do this for four different object detection architectures - MobileNet, Faster R-CNN50, Faster R-CNN50v2 and YOLOv5 to compare explanations that can be provided with these models. The Faster R-CNN model was chosen due to it being used in our previous projects on automotive crashtests, where we spotted some unexpected

Fig. 1. The three different marker types: Left: Crops of MXT (5 white circles) and DOT markers (one white circle). Right: Examples for the YQUAD marker type (black and yellow). (Color figure online)

problems that are described in more detail below, as well as it being implemented in PyTorch and supported by XAI frameworks. We then selected other networks from the same family for comparison. The YOLOv5 architecture was tested due to its performance in combination with XAI framework support and its implementation in PyTorch. While developing the marker detection we found that due to the highly dynamic environment of crashtests, debris can sometimes be falsely identified as the marker type we are looking for. These false positive detections should be understandable from the class activation maps provided by the XAI methods we use. In addition to the debris we found that sometimes the MXT and DOT marker types are mixed up by the Faster R-CNN classification head. This can be qualitatively explained by the DOT marker being a geometric subset of the MXT marker (cf. Fig. 1). To quantify the uncertainty of the MXT/DOT marker classification we employ a bayesian neural net as the quasi classification head of the object detectors in that use case. This bayesian neural net can then be analyzed with XAI methods developed for image classification. We did not implement additional classification networks for the YQUAD dataset since this is single-class and thus there was no further need for binary classification as no confusion between different marker types is possible in this case. In all videos that were gathered by us for the YQUAD dataset the marker always was the only type used by the crashtest engineers, and our project partner also requested a model specifically for this kind of targetmarker. Due to this we did not apply the Quantus framework to the YQUAD marker case.

The trained networks and their respective evaluation scores can be found in Table 1 for the object detection models and in Table 2 for the BNN and LeNet models. The images for both datasets were gathered from freely available 1080p Youtube videos of NCAP [31] or IIHS [32] crashtests, which had to be cut into smaller chunks as those are usually compilation videos containing multiple different views, where each chunk focuses on one specific crash test scenario from one camera perspective.

4   Object Detection Pipeline

We implemented two different pipelines in order to generate our results, the first one deals with the task of explaining the MXT/DOT marker detection

Table 1. Evaluation metrics for the different object detectors, evaluated on the labeled test datasets. The metric used for the accuracy evaluation is the Average Precision AP_{IoU} at different IoU thresholds to compare the label region with the predicted region. It can be seen that the YOLO architecture significantly outperforms the RCNN networks on our datasets. The MobileNet falls off quite a bit, especially when looking at the MXT/DOT dataset.

	backbone	MXT/DOT			YQUAD		
		AP	AP_{50}	AP_{75}	AP	AP_{50}	AP_{75}
Faster R-CNN	ResNet-50	72.9	95.1	92.7	76.1	98.2	94.8
Faster R-CNN	ResNet50v2	72.2	94.5	91.3	82.8	98.4	97.6
Faster R-CNN	MobileNetv3	57.1	87.6	66.2	66.2	96.0	81.4
YOLOv5	CSP-Darknet53	82.2	98.1	94.6	90.3	99.2	98.5

Table 2. Accuracy for the bayesian neural network and LeNet, both trained on the MXT/DOT dataset.

	Accuracy
BNN	94.6
LeNet	97.81

and classification process while the second focuses on the explanations for the YQUAD detections. Both are displayed in Figs. 2 and 3 respectively, where it also can be seen that the same methods are used to generate the class activation maps for the object detection part for each of them. We trained each of the four different object detection models mentioned above for both datasets (MXT/DOT and YQUAD), a selection of average precision scores [24] can be found in Table 1. In addition to the bayesian neural network for the MXT/DOT pipeline we also trained a LeNet to be able to compare the explanations between a deterministic and a probabilistic network (cf. Table 2).

In both pipelines we first run inference on crops from the input image (either taken from saved images or videos) for the object detection model which we want to evaluate in terms of explainability. These results are then further utilized to generate class activation maps for different, gradient-free explanation functions. Our implementation relies on the pytorch-gradcam library [14] which offers the functionality to use EigenCAM, ScoreCAM and AblationCAM methods to capture meaningful explanations. For these CAMs we furthermore calculate the normalized row and column sums to reduce the information down to one dimension per axis and also help to better visualize and quantize the actual activations.

In order to gain insight into the classification task in the MXT/DOT pipeline we utilize the Quantus framework [10] mentioned above to calculate activation maps for the Saliency, IntegratedGradients, GradientShap and FusionGrad explanation functions. Additionally we use it to quantize the capability of the

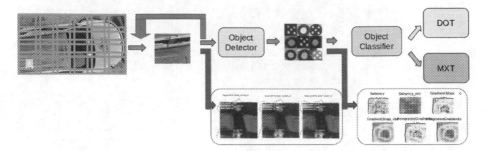

Fig. 2. This pipeline handles the MXT/DOT marker and segments the image into 15 different slices which get evaluated by the object detector. The detected regions of the slices are furthermore evaluated by the object classifier. We use the class activation maps displayed on the bottom to gain more insight into this process.

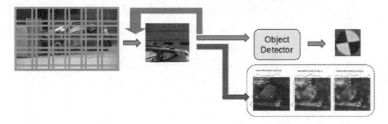

Fig. 3. Similar to the pipeline above, the input gets split into individual crops and then fed into the object detector. Activation maps assist in gathering more knowledge about the reasoning of the model.

individual explanations to capture the relevant features by testing and ranking their faithfulness against each other.

For the task of classifying MXT and DOT marker types we use a bayesian neural network to quantify the uncertainty in the predictions.

5   Methods of Explainable AI for Object Detection and Image Classification

In this section we will provide an overview and introduction on the explainability methods used in this paper. We first describe different approaches for the object detection and classification models before taking a look at the different metrics used to quantify these explanations.

5.1   Class Activation Maps for Object Detection Models

Methods to generate class activation maps can be divided into two distinct categories: gradient-based vs gradient-free methods. We chose to apply the Eigen-CAM [15], AblationCAM [16], and ScoreCAM [17] methods, which fall into the latter of the two. This choice was made due to the processing steps (NMS, argmax etc.) involved in object detection networks that follow after the feature extraction part (typically CNN), which leads to outputs typically not being differentiable, at least not in a generic way. The frameworks we used thus allowed only for classification models (Quantus) or restricted the usability for object detection models to the aforementioned gradient-free methods (pytorch-gradcam).

EigenCAM is a relatively simple approach to generate class activation maps by calculating the principal components of the projection $O_{L=k}$ of the input image onto the last convolutional layer. The class activation map L_{EigenCAM} is then obtained by further projecting $O_{L=k}$ onto the first eigenvector V_1 [15].

The second approach, **AblationCAM**, calculates activations by ablating each channel of the last convolutional layer of the network individually. The change in prediction from y^{class} to y_k^{class}, the class prediction value when channel k is ablated, gets weighted according to the following equation: [16]

$$w_k^c = \frac{y^{\text{class}} - y_k^{\text{class}}}{y^{\text{class}}}$$

These weights are then used to construct the final class activation map by taking the ReLU of the sum of all of the channels feature maps multiplied by their respective weight as stated here: [16]

$$L_{\text{AblationCAM}}^c = \text{ReLU}(\sum_k w_k^c \cdot A_k)$$

ScoreCAM takes the feature maps generated by the last convolutional layer, upsamples them and then uses each of them to mask one copy of the original input. Each of these copies is fed into the network, and the importance of the individual feature map is measured by the target score obtained. This score is used to weigh the contribution of the feature maps according to a factor α_k^c during the generation of the class activation map [17]:

$$L_{\text{ScoreCAM}}^c = \text{ReLU}(\sum_k \alpha_k^c \cdot A_k)$$

This equation shows that the sole difference between ScoreCAM and Ablation-CAM lies in the calculation of the weight attributions.

5.2   Saliency Maps for Object Classification Models

Quantus offers support for a variety of different methods to generate saliency maps for input images. We utilize four of those, namely Saliency (or Vanilla Gradients) [18,19], GradientShap [20], Integrated Gradients [21] and Fusion-Grad [22].

The first of these methods, **Saliency**, calculates the attribution of input features/pixels by propagating the output logits of the network back to the input layer. While this approach is quite intuitively simple, it suffers from various drawbacks like gradient vanishing effects plus possible insensitivity to changes due to activation functions like ReLU [21].

Integrated Gradients tries to solve these problems by defining a baseline x' which is then used to interpolate (in discrete steps) towards the original input image x, essentially an inverse fade-to-black in case of a black baseline. The contribution of a single pixel i is then calculated by taking the mean of the accumulated derivatives of network F with respect to i at each interpolation step $\frac{k}{m}$. This result is furthermore weighted by the difference between input and baseline to obtain the final contribution as can be seen in the following equation: [21]

$$\text{IntegratedGrads}_i^{\text{approx}} := (x_i - x_i') \cdot \sum_{k=1}^{m} \frac{\delta F(x' + \frac{k}{m} \cdot (x - x'))}{\delta x_i} \cdot \frac{1}{m}$$

The **FusionGrad** approach is a combination of SmoothGrad [23] and NoiseGrad [22]. The former adds noise to copies of the input and generates the resulting explanation map by taking the average of the individual maps of each noisy copy. NoiseGrad on the other hand adds noise to the models' weights, basically creating an ensemble of different networks to average out the result over. The goal of both of these methods is to enhance the important features, as these should (on average) stand out inbetween the noise, while simultaneously creating an inverse effect for less relevant ones. By combining both of these algorithms, FusionGrad is able to consider variations in the input data as well as the network itself [22].

GradientShap [20] is a method that behaves similarly to Integrated Gradients in that it tries to approximate the attribution values from a baseline to the original input image. It utilizes the models gradients to calculate Shapley values, which originally come from applications in cooperative game theory, and deliver further insights into the prediction process. Model features can be interpreted as players who generate the inference value by summing up their individual contributions (efficiency axiom [27]), delivering a result that is completely decomposable.

5.3   Quantitative Evaluation Metrics

All of the methods mentioned above try to deliver insights into the decision making process of the underlying network and can often be qualitatively interpreted by a human. In order to furthermore quantify the results of these methods, many different metrics have been derived, especially in recent years, which focus on different properties of the explanation functions. The authors behind the Quantus framework divide these metrics into six distinct categories Faithfulness, Robustness, Complexity, Randomisation, Localisation and Axiomatic, from which we chose the former four to conduct our tests by orienting ourselves on the choices made in another paper [26] written by some of the authors of the Quantus framework [10]. We also chose to ignore the Localisation metric as we did not utilise segmentation masks.

Faithfulness tries to quantify the impact of changing different features onto the model prediction, assuming that the perturbation of important features should have greater impact on the prediction outcome than the perturbation of features that are ranked lower in terms of importance by the individual explainability method. For this work we chose to utilize the FaithfulnessCorrelation [30] metric where the evaluation is performed by taking a random subset of fixed length of pixel indices and masking these pixels in the input with a baseline value. Then the network prediction for perturbed and unperturbed inputs are compared according to the following equation: [30]

$$\mu_F(f, g; x) = \operatorname*{corr}_{S \in \binom{|d|}{|S|}} \left(\sum_{i \in S} g(f, x)_i, f(x) - f(x_{[x_s = \bar{x}_s]}) \right)$$

where f is the predictor, g the explanation function, x the unperturbed input and $\binom{|d|}{|S|}$ the subset of random pixel indices to be perturbed.

The **robustness** metric takes a look at the resulting change in the explanation map when slightly changing the input image. This is taken under the assumption that this process should only lead to small differences in the map (and model prediction) when dealing with a robust explanation function. We utilize the AvgSensitivity [25] metric which is defined as following for input x, explanation map Φ and groundtruth class c: [26]

$$q_{\text{AverageSensitivity}} = \mathbf{E}_{x + \delta \in N_\epsilon(x) \le \epsilon} \left[\frac{||(\Phi(f, c, x) - \Phi(f, c, x + \delta))||}{||x||} \right]$$

This formula makes it clear that lower values suggest a higher robustness as the difference is measured.

Randomisation evaluates how random changes to the class label or network parameters lead to change in the explanation results, assuming that the latter should change given those factors. The RandomLogit [28] metric we use here measures the structural similarity between explanation maps of the original input and input with a random class label $\hat{c}$ as defined as follows for an explanation function Φ: [26]

$$q_{\text{RandomLogit}} = \text{SSIM}(\Phi(f, c, x), \Phi(f, \hat{c}, x))]$$

A lower SSIM score translates to a better explanation method performance as it represents a bigger change in the generated explanations given a wrong class label.

The final property we take into consideration in this work is called **complexity** and assesses the number of features that go into the explanation process, whereby fewer features are desired as they mean less complexity. The specific metric we choose in this category is called Sparseness where it is proposed [29] that only features that have a significant impact on the output decision should be reflected in the resulting explanations. The implementation in Quantus is defined by the following equation: [26]

$$q_{\text{Sparseness}} = \frac{\sum_{i=1}^{d}(2i - d - 1)\Phi(f, x)}{d\sum_{i=1}^{d}\Phi(f, x)},$$

and based on the Gini index, where a high Gini index represents a sparse contribution vector.

5.4   Bayesian Methods

When evaluating the bayesian classification head we do n forward passes of the input image to obtain n different samples of the Saliency, GradientSHAP, IntGrad and FusionGrad maps. These maps are then aggregated using the mean value for each input image pixel. In addition to the mean we also calculate the standard deviation of the pixel values to quantify the uncertainty of the activation maps. By doing this we can qualitatively see the learned posterior distributions of the BNN. The uncertainty of the activation maps provides a good qualitative image of the "confusion" of the BNN when its classification is uncertain.

6   Analysis Results

In this section we present our findings on the different aspects of the implemented pipelines.

6.1   Class Activation Maps for Object Detection

Here we show the resulting class activation maps for the trained object detection models for both marker datasets. The plots in Fig. 4 show the overlay of the input image with the corresponding class activation maps generated by the three different algorithms explained earlier. In this particular example it can be seen that the activation maps for the EigenCAM are more widely centered around the object but less noisy, while the ScoreCAM produces the more accurate results around the target regions. The AblationCAM picks up strong activations around the printed text on the car, but also localises the activations for the correct targets even better than the ScoreCAM algorithm. In this regard it has to be said that while the AblationCAM produces quite reliably good results across a variety of input images, the EigenCAM und ScoreCAM algorithms oftentimes fail

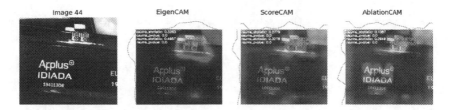

Fig. 4. Comparison of different class activation map algorithms.

to reliably and correctly capture the correct features on varying inputs or models. This makes sense as EigenCAM and ScoreCAM rely on the same underlying technique to capture activation maps as described above, based on which the ScoreCAM builds its masks for further calculations.

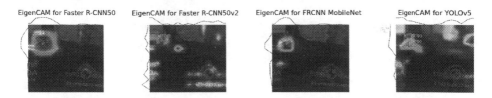

Fig. 5. Comparison of outputs of EigenCAM algorithm for all different network types on the MXT/DOT dataset.

By comparing the activations of the four different network architectures captured by EigenCAM (s. Fig. 5) we can see that the RCNN networks deliver similar explanations but tend to vary strongly in certain aspects. The FRCNN50 is the only one to capture high activations around all the target objects, but with some overshoot, while the EigenCAM representation of the FRCNN50v2 is way more noisy and fails to generate higher activations around the target regions when compared to those around the imprints on the car or the reflections in the door handle. The Mobilenet delivers the best results in term of target localisation but is slightly noisier than the FRCNN50, while the YOLOv5 network also captures strong activations at the side mirror and in the cockpit itself.

Taking a closer look at an example for the AblationCAM algorithm applied to images taken from the MXT/DOT dataset in Fig. 6 it can be seen how big the difference in outcomes for the same input image can be on slightly varying models. The Faster R-CNN50 does pick up high activations on the car imprints but fails to accurately capture those for the MXT markers, at least in their relative magnitude when compared to their surroundings. The explanations for the other two models resemble the expected results, even though it can be seen that the Mobilenet does pick up more activations around the imprinted text when compared to the FRCNN50v2 which mostly picks up the round shape of NCAP logo. The more distinct nature of the activations for the latter two models can also be seen in the histograms at the top and left side of the images where there are more distuingishable peaks when compared to the more uniform distribution of the Faster R-CNN50 model.

AblationCAM for Faster R-CNN50   AblationCAM for Faster R-CNN50v2   AblationCAM for Faster R-CNN MobileNet

Fig. 6. Comparison of the AblationCAM method for the three different Faster R-CNN models. While the results for the Faster R-CNN50v2 and the Mobilenet are quite localised and interpretable with distinct peaks at the expected positions, the outcome for the activation maps of the Faster R-CNN50 is way more uniform and seems to be inverted in certain parts of the image. It captures the relatively high activations for the imprints on the car and also picks up some activations on top of the MXT markers but does not weigh them accordingly.

When analyzing the explanations for the YQUAD dataset it became quickly apparent that the networks usually tend to have high activations around the marker objects itself, the imprints on the car as well as on the black and yellow scale tape that is attached at different position across the car. One example of this consistent behaviour can be found in Fig. 7 where this even leads to a misdetection for the FRCNN50 model while its two siblings also pick up relatively strong activations which do not lead to a false positive detection in their case.

Another interesting finding can be seen in Fig. 8 where it is shown that all of the networks correctly capture the YQUAD marker but with quite varying degrees of noise. The Mobilenet network does not pick up many activations apart from the correct one, while for the FRCNN50 these can also slightly be seen in the debris and on the background. The FRCNN50v2 model produces very high activations on multiple glas shards and the debris region in general, and while it did not lead to a wrongful detection in this case, this should make this model more prone to potential misdetection errors in these crashtest scenarios.

The Mobilenet in this case (and some others) seems to offer a built-in filter mechanism for smaller objects due to its lack of detection performance when compared to the bigger models, and thus produces the cleanest class activation map, but at the price of worse performance on smaller targets in general. The amount of activations on the smaller debris objects and background edges seem to correlate, at least in this particular case, with the evaluation results taken after the network training. Here it showed that the FRCNN50v2 network delivered the best performance when it comes to AP and AR on small images, while its predecessor came second and the Mobilenet dropped off quite a bit. It can be seen

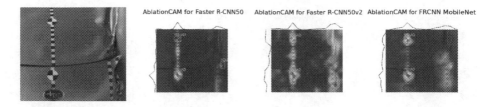

Fig. 7. This figure shows the results for the AblationCAM algorithm for three different RCNN networks. It can be seen that the models also capture activations on the stripes, in case of the Faster R-CNN50 this even leads to a wrong detection.

that similarities in the activations show in the experiments for the MXT/DOT and YQUAD datasets. For both types the underyling network captures strong activations when it comes to the imprints on the car itself and the NCAP logo.

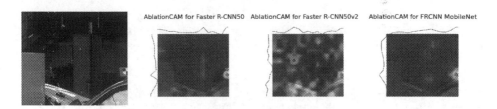

Fig. 8. AblationCAM results during crash and with debris flying around. All networks correctly pick up the activations around the targetmarker but have varying degrees of activations when it comes to the areas with debris.

6.2   Explanations for Object Classification Models

In this section we compare the results gathered by utilizing the Quantus framework [10] on the trained Bayesian neural network and LeNet.

We took the four different explanation functions Saliency (SAL), Integrated Gradients (IG), GradientShap (GS) and FusionGrad (FG) which were explained in a previous section (s. Sect. 5.2) and plotted the resulting outputs for various images on both network architectures. We used to evaluate the different explanation functions on 100 forward passes through the Bayesian classifier, finally taking the mean and standard deviation from the 100 generated explanation maps to try and capture uncertainties in the decision process. For the LeNet one forward pass through the network per explanation function and image is sufficient due to its non-probabilistic design, this also explains the lack of maps displaying the standard deviation. The produced maps are thus only comparable to the mean maps from the BNN. Red pixels represent highly positive activations, blue highly negative ones.

When comparing the explanation maps generated by both models (s. example in Fig. 9) it can be seen that they focus on the similar features and thus

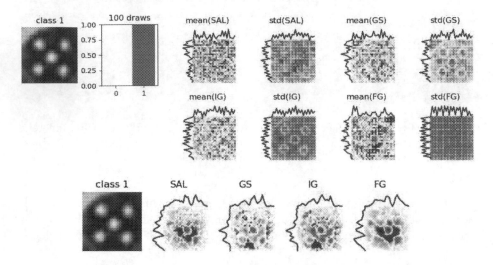

Fig. 9. Visualization of correct inference result (100% certainty for correct class) for the different explainability methods and two different network architectures. Top: Mean and standard deviation maps for the BNN. Bottom: Explanations for LeNet.

produce quite matching results. Both networks seem to clearly detect the different white circles of both marker types. These can be seen as red activations in both figures, especially when looking at the Integrated Gradients and GradientShap methods. Additionally there is a small border around these circles, independent of both networks, with neutral activation values. Interestingly there are also some negatively activated pixels in the inner circles, even though they are outweighed by the positive activations. Furthermore it seems as if the LeNet captures the individual circles with more consistent activations as there are less breakups inbetween positive pixel values. This is also reflected in the standard deviation maps for the BNN network where it can be seen that the highest deviations from the mean happen inside the circles themselves. On the left and top of each map we plotted the normalized distribution of the row- and columnwise accumulated pixel values. This should in theory lead to quite distinguishable peaks for the individual circles, meaning one peak for a DOT and three peaks for the MXT marker type per axis. While this does not provide any good results for the BNN, the distributions peaks for the LeNet clearly resemble the locations of the blobs in the input image, even though the result is a bit noisy.

In Fig. 10 we present another example, this time of a misclassification, which seems to confirm our initial findings. As mentioned above, we purposefully tried to generate images which are kind of in between both marker types to look at these specific scenarios. Even though the input image in this case is blurry with little contrast between the white inner circles, we as a human would most likely classify this as a MXT marker, both networks come to a different conclusion though. Looking at the explanation maps generated during this process it becomes clear why both models end up with the same, albeit wrong answer.

Both seem to only focus on the one big circle in the middle while the smaller circles seem to be too non-contrasting to be recognized as different, individual entities by the networks.

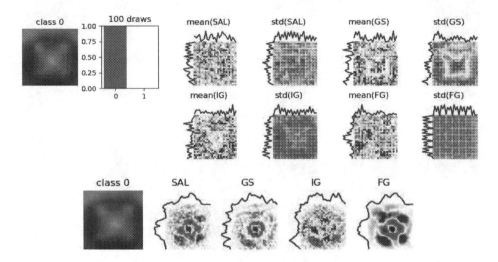

Fig. 10. Visualization of wrong inference result (100% certainty for wrong class) for the different explainability methods and two different network architectures. Top: Mean and standard deviation maps for the BNN. Bottom: Explanations for LeNet.

Furthermore it can be seen that the activation maps generated from the LeNet model are less blurry in the display of the activations when compared to its BNN counterpart. This makes intuitive sense due to the uncertainty inherent to the latter architecture.

One additional finding was the difference in the explanation maps of models trained on the same dataset but with different initial learning rates. Examples for the BNN can be found in graphic Fig. 11, where there is quite a significant difference between the explanation maps for the two models based on their learning rate. The maps generated from the model trained with the lower learning rate are more contrastive and more focused on the essential features, additionally they qualitatively deliver better explanations when it comes to the saliency maps. The same holds true when it comes to the LeNet (s. Fig. 12) where the lower learning rate also seems to have a positive impact on the contrastiveness of the resulting explanation map, but not as much as in the case of the BNN. Additionally we used the Quantus framework to evaluate which of the explanation functions delivers the best results when tested on the different metrics explained above. From taking a look at the visualization of the metrics for the different explanation algorithms in Fig. 13 it becomes obvious that there is no clear single winner for every input image and every category, and that the results also vary between LeNet and BNN architecture. Taking into consideration the results in Tables 3 and 4 it can be seen that, while the values for RandomLogit and Sparseness are

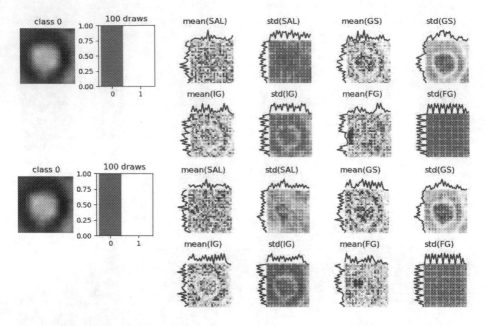

Fig. 11. Visualization of inference result as well as of mean and standard deviation maps for different explainability methods for the Bayesian neural network after training the model with different learning rates. Top: Learning rate 0.001. Bottom: Learning rate 0.0001.

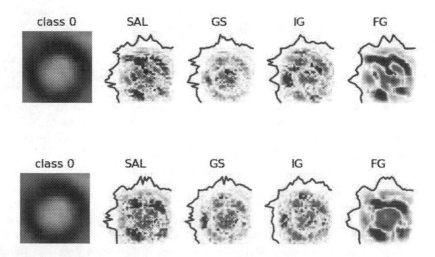

Fig. 12. Visualization of inference result as explanation maps for different explainability methods for the LeNet classifier after training the model with different learning rates. Top: Learning rate 0.001. Bottom: Learning rate 0.0001.

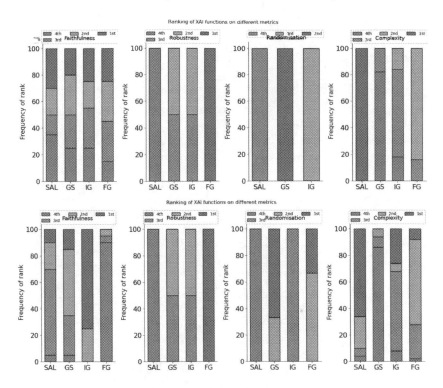

Fig. 13. Explainability functions ranked for the different evaluation metrics across multiple varying input parameters. It can be seen that there is not one singular, absolute approach that fits every circumstance best. Top: Rankings for the BNN model. Bottom: Rankings for LeNet.

in the same range and thus comparable to each other, the AvgSensitiviy and FaithfulnessCorrelation metrics seem to be broken for the BNN as the results seem to be unreasonably small or large when compared to the ones obtained for the LeNet. The Sparseness seems comparable across both models, as both times the GradientSHAP method delivers the highest score, followed by Integrated-Gradients and FusionGrad, while the least sparse explanations are generated by the Saliency method. Even though the order stays the same, the explanations generated for the LeNet classifier seem to be more sparse in general than the ones from the BNN. In case of the RandomLogit the results are again comparable in their resulting ranking order, but differ quite significantly in the absolute values for the individual properties. This method also fails to deliver results in case of the FusionGrad explanation function for this category as it always produces *NaN* values for the evaluated scores. The reason for this did not become clear to us as the values are calculated internally in the Quantus framework. Apart from that it shows that the SSIM is significantly lower on average in case of the BNN, meaning that the generated explanations tend to vary more heavily when trying to explain another class, which is the desired outcome. This might be explained due to the variance inherent to the BNN where even explanations on the same

Table 3. Scores for different evaluation metrics on the explanation functions for the Bayesian neural network classifier.

	BNN			
	Faithfulness Correlation	Sparseness	RandomLogit	AvgSensitivity
Saliency	−0.001	0.462	0.091	105.36
GradientSHAP	−0.011	0.553	0.198	59.11
IntegratedGrads	0.0029	0.526	0.171	61.98
FusionGrad	0.0001	0.500	–	16.63

Table 4. Scores for different evaluation metrics on the explanation functions for the LeNet classifier.

	LeNet			
	Faithfulness Correlation	Sparseness	RandomLogit	AvgSensitivity
Saliency	0.331	0.579	0.406	0.026
GradientSHAP	0.301	0.673	0.594	0.020
IntegratedGrads	0.239	0.616	0.447	0.018
FusionGrad	0.385	0.591	0.564	0.011

input target vary due to the probabilistic nature of the model. In general it can be seen that Saliency leads to the most change in explanation maps while GradientSHAP takes the last place in this category, followed by FusionGrad in case of the LeNet and IntegratedGradients in case of BNN. As FaithfulnessCorrelation and AvgSensitivity seem to be broken for the BNN classifier we only evaluate these metrics for the LeNet architecture, where FusionGrad shows to perform best, followed by Saliency, GradientSHAP and IntegratedGradients, respectively. These results interestingly differ from those in another paper [26] where it was found that FusionGrad scored significantly worse than Saliency and IntegratedGradients in terms of this property. At this time we can not explain the reason for this difference in results, but currently research is being conducted for the metaevaluation of XAI techniques [33] The explanations generated for the LeNet classifier seem to be quite robust according to the AvgSensitivity score in the table, where it can be seen that the FusionGrad approach takes the lead, followed by IntegratedGradients, GradientSHAP and Saliency. These results also interestingly differ from the findings in the aforementioned other paper [26] where FusionGrad came into last place in this category.

7   Discussion and Outlook

In this paper, we proposed a novel approach to improve the interpretability of object detection and marker classification in automotive crashtest videos using explainable artificial intelligence (XAI) techniques. Our results show that our XAI approach provides interpretable explanations for the model's decisions. Our approach is not limited to crashtest images, and can be transferred onto any object detection and classification problem. We used multiple class activation maps (CAMs) algorithms for different models. To make the object detection CAMs more interpretable in terms of the localization we calculated the row and column sums of the activation maps. This dimensionality reduction shows easier to interpret patterns for engineers. Even though there are some very defined and good results when it comes to the activation maps generated by the various CAM algorithms, it is important to note that there is a high variance in the quality of these findings. This goes as far as that the algorithms work fine on one image, yet fail to do so on another image from the same video, independent of position in the video etc. While there is no clear reason in the images why the algorithms should fail in these instances (blocked view, debris, obstruction etc.), it showed that the Eigen- and ScoreCAM seem to be more prone to this kind of variance when compared to the AblationCAM. This is most likely connected to the SVD which both of the former methods rely on to extract the activations from the underlying network. The results look inverted which is possibly due to the implementation of the SVD in numpy and scikit-learn which does deliver the correct magnitude of the activation, but not necessarily the right sign (+,-) for it. And while this also happens to the AblationCAM, albeit with a lower frequency, there is no clearcut explanation for this as the underlying method differs from the former two. The findings here show that the AblationCAM algorithm is mostly robust and reliable on a variety of inputs, so that in our opinion it is by far the best choice of the tested class activation map methods.

We also used quantitative XAI to evaluate the performance of our Bayesian CNN and LeNet models. The quantus scores and explanations provided additional insights into the model's behavior. The approach to combine methods of quantitative XAI with Bayesian Neural Networks yielded average explanations and standard deviations of these explanations that give additional insights. We found that not all metrics were viable for the Bayesian CNN, indicating that there is additional work to be done on other metrics. In addition, our results showed that the quantitative XAI for the LeNet model is comparable to the Bayesian CNN, suggesting that the XAI methods used in this paper can be applied to other deep learning architectures. Future work can be done to extend the proposed approach to other industrial domains that require object detection and classification, such as predictive maintenance, autonomous driving or medical imaging. In addition, further research can be done to investigate other metrics for evaluating the performance of Bayesian CNNs and to explore the applicability of our proposed approach to other deep learning architectures. Overall, our contribution demonstrates the effectiveness of using XAI techniques for improving object detection and marker classification interpretability in automotive crash test videos, and provides a promising direction for future research in the field of XAI.

References

1. Zhou, B., Khosla, A., Lapedriza, A., Oliva, A., Torralba, A.: Learning deep features for discriminative localization. In: Proceedings of the IEEE Conference on Computer Vision and Pattern Recognition, pp. 2921–2929 (2016)
2. Fu, C., Liu, W., Ranga, A., Tyagi, A., Berg, A.C.: DSSD: deconvolutional single shot detector. IEEE Trans. Pattern Anal. Mach. Intell. **42**(8), 2028–2041 (2019)
3. Bochkovskiy, A., Wang, C.Y., Liao, H.Y.M.: YOLOv5: improved real-time object detection. arXiv preprint arXiv:2011.08036 (2020)
4. Selvaraju, R.R., Cogswell, M., Das, A., Vedantam, R., Parikh, D., Batra, D.: Grad-CAM: visual explanations from deep networks via gradient-based localization. In: Proceedings of the IEEE International Conference on Computer Vision, pp. 618–626 (2017)
5. Siddiqui, S.A., Lee, J.: Object detection with grad-CAM generated heatmaps. arXiv preprint arXiv:2102.04042 (2021)
6. Lundberg, S.M., Lee, S.I.: A unified approach to interpreting model predictions. In: Advances in Neural Information Processing Systems, vol. pp. 4765–4774 (2017)
7. Zhang, C., Wu, J., Zhu, Q., Liu, Y.: A SHAP-based explanation method for object detection. Cogn. Comput. 1–13 (2021)
8. Zhang, B., Erhan, D., Wang, D., Resnick, C., Bengio, Y.: Ablation-CAM: visual explanations for deep convolutional networks. In: Proceedings of the IEEE/CVF Conference on Computer Vision and Pattern Recognition, pp. 7163–7172 (2020)
9. Liu, Y., Xu, D., Zhang, X., Wang, R., Yang, C.: YOLOv5 Model Interpretation using AblationCAM. arXiv preprint arXiv:2111.08521 (2021)
10. Anna, H., et al.: Quantus: an explainable AI toolkit for responsible evaluation of neural network explanations (2022). https://doi.org/10.48550/ARXIV.2202.06861
11. Gal, Y., Ghahramani, Z.: Bayesian convolutional neural networks with Bernoulli approximate variational inference. arXiv preprint arXiv:1506.02158 (2015)
12. Mandt, S., Hoffman, M., Blei, D.: Stochastic gradient descent as approximate Bayesian inference. In: Proceedings of the 32nd International Conference on Machine Learning (ICML), pp. 1538–1547 (2015)
13. Kendall, A., Gal, Y.: What uncertainties do we need in Bayesian deep learning for computer vision? arXiv preprint arXiv:1703.04977 (2017)
14. Gildenblat, J., Contributors: PyTorch library for CAM methods (2021). https://github.com/jacobgil/pytorch-grad-cam
15. Muhammad, M.B., Yeasin, M.: Eigen-CAM: class activation map using principal components (2020). https://doi.org/10.1109/IJCNN48605.2020.9206626
16. Desai, S., Ramaswamy, H.G.: Ablation-CAM: visual explanations for deep convolutional network via gradient-free localization. In: 2020 IEEE Winter Conference on Applications of Computer Vision (WACV), Snowmass, CO, USA, pp. 972–980 (2020). https://doi.org/10.1109/WACV45572.2020.9093360
17. Wang, H., et al.: Score-CAM: score-weighted visual explanations for convolutional neural networks. arXiv preprint arXiv:1910.01279 (2020)
18. Morch, N.J.S., et al.: Visualization of neural networks using saliency maps. In: Proceedings of ICNN 1995 - International Conference on Neural Networks, Perth, WA, Australia, vol. 4, pp. 2085–2090 (1995). https://doi.org/10.1109/ICNN.1995.488997
19. Baehrens, D., Schroeter, T., Harmeling, S., Kawanabe, M., Hansen, K., Müller, K.-R.: How to explain individual classification decisions. J. Mach. Learn. Res. **11**, 1803–1831 (2010)

20. Lundberg, S.M., Lee, S.-I.: A unified approach to interpreting model predictions. In: Proceedings of the 31st International Conference on Neural Information Processing Systems (NIPS 2017), pp. 4768–4777. Curran Associates Inc., Red Hook (2017)
21. Sundararajan, M., Taly, A., Yan, Q.: Axiomatic attribution for deep networks. In: Proceedings of the 34th International Conference on Machine Learning (ICML 2017), vol. 70, pp. 3319–3328. JMLR.org (2017)
22. Bykov, K., Hedström, A., Nakajima, S., Höhne, M.M.-C.: NoiseGrad - enhancing explanations by introducing stochasticity to model weights. In: Proceedings of the AAAI Conference on Artificial Intelligence, pp. 6132–6140 (2022)
23. Smilkov, D., Thorat, N., Kim, B., Viégas, F.B., Wattenberg, M.: SmoothGrad: removing noise by adding noise. arXiv, abs/1706.03825 (2017)
24. COCO - Common Objects in Context. https://cocodataset.org/#detection-eval. Accessed 17 Apr 2023
25. Yeh, C.-K., Hsieh, C.-Y., Suggala, A., Inouye, D.I., Ravikumar, P.K.: On the (in)fidelity and sensitivity of explanations. In: Advances in Neural Information Processing Systems, vol. 32. Curran Associates Inc. (2019). https://proceedings. neurips.cc/paper/2019/file/a7471fdc77b3435276507cc8f2dc2569-Paper.pdf
26. Bommer, P.L., Kretschmer, M., Hedström, A., Bareeva, D., Höhne, M.M.-C.: Finding the right XAI method - a guide for the evaluation and ranking of explainable AI methods in climate science. arXiv abs/2303.00652 (2023)
27. Rozemberczki, B., et al.: The Shapley value in machine learning. arXiv, abs/2202.05594 (2022)
28. Sixt, L., Granz, M., Landgraf, T.: When explanations lie: why many modified BP attributions fail. arXiv abs/1912.09818 (2020)
29. Chalasani, P., Chen, J., Chowdhury, A.R., Jha, S., Wu, X.: Concise explanations of neural networks using adversarial training. arXiv abs/1810.06583 (2020)
30. Bhatt, U., Weller, A., Moura, J.M.F.: Evaluating and aggregating feature-based model explanations. arXiv abs/2005.00631 (2020)
31. Euro NCAP. Euro NCAP - Youtube. Youtube. https://www.youtube.com/ @EuroNCAP_forsafercars
32. IIHS. IIHS-Youtube. Youtube. https://www.youtube.com/@iihs-hldi
33. Hedström, A., Bommer, P., Wickstrøm, K.K., Samek, W., Lapuschkin, S., Höhne, M.M.-C.: The meta-evaluation problem in explainable AI: identifying reliable estimators with MetaQuantus. arXiv:2302.07265 (2023)

xAI for Decision-Making and Human-AI Collaboration, for Machine Learning on Graphs with Ontologies and Graph Neural Networks

Explaining Black-Boxes in Federated Learning

Luca Corbucci[1]([⊠]) [iD], Riccardo Guidotti[1,2] [iD], and Anna Monreale[1] [iD]

[1] University of Pisa, Pisa, Italy
{luca.corbucci,anna.monreale}@phd.unipi.it
[2] ISTI-CNR, Pisa, Italy
riccardo.guidotti@isti.cnr.it

Abstract. Federated Learning has witnessed increasing popularity in the past few years for its ability to train Machine Learning models in critical contexts, using private data without moving them. Most of the work in the literature proposes algorithms and architectures for training neural networks, which although they present high performance in different predicting tasks and are easy to be learned with a cooperative mechanism, their predictive reasoning is obscure. Therefore, in this paper, we propose a variant of SHAP, one of the most widely used explanation methods, tailored to Horizontal server-based Federated Learning. The basic idea is having the possibility to explain an instance's prediction performed by the trained Machine Leaning model as an aggregation of the explanations provided by the clients participating in the cooperation. We empirically test our proposal on two different tabular datasets, and we observe interesting and encouraging preliminary results.

Keywords: Explainable AI · Federated Learning · Features Importance

1 Introduction

Federated Learning (FL) [14] has become a popular approach to training Machine Learning (ML) models on distributed data sources. This approach was originally proposed to preserve data privacy since the users involved do not have to share their training datasets with a central server. Usually, the models trained with FL are deep learning models and therefore their transparency remains a challenge [8,12]. Indeed, although the trained ML models present very excellent performance in different tasks, their drawback lies in their complexity, which makes them black-boxes and causes the non-interpretability of the internal decision process for humans [5]. However, when it comes to making high-stakes decisions, such as clinical diagnosis, the explanation aspect of the models used by Artificial Intelligence (AI) systems becomes a critical building block of a trustworthy interaction between the machine and human experts. Meaningful explanations [16] of predictive models would augment the cognitive ability of

L. Longo (Ed.): xAI 2023, CCIS 1902, pp. 151–163, 2023.
https://doi.org/10.1007/978-3-031-44067-0_8

domain experts, such as physicians, to make informed and accurate decisions and to better support responsibility in decision-making.

In the last years, the scientific community posed much attention to the design of explainable AI (XAI) techniques [1,4,8,12] but a relatively limited effort has been spent in the study of interpretability issues in FL [2,6,18,19]. Most of the studies of interpretability in FL are focused on the Vertical FL and exploit method based on feature importance.

In this paper, we address the problem of interpretability by proposing an alternative way to employ the explainer SHAP [13] in the context of FL. In particular, our proposal enables the explanation of an instance's prediction performed by the trained global ML model by aggregating the explanation of the clients participating in the federation. The proposed approach is based on the requirements that in order to produce the explanation of the global model is not necessary to access any information on the training data used by the clients. We propose an analytical methodology that enables a comparison to determine the approximation introduced by our approach with respect to a scenario where we simulate a server which can access the training data. Preliminary experiments conducted on two tabular datasets show that the approximation introduced by our proposal is negligible and that our SHAP explanation tends to agree with the explanation provided by the server in terms of the importance of each feature.

The remaining of the paper is organized as follows. Section 2 discusses the literature on XAI for FL. Section 3 provides an overview on FL and XAI and Sect. 4 presents our proposal and the analytical methodology adopted to validate it. In Sect. 5 we discuss the preliminary experimental results, while Sect. 6 discusses our findings and contributions to the field of XAI. Lastly, Sect. 7 concludes the paper and discusses future research directions.

2   Related Work

Machine learning has become more and more pervasive in our lives. ML models are used nowadays in many different contexts and can impact our lives. Alongside the development of novel ML techniques, there was a very active development of techniques to explain the reasoning of black box models [1,4,7,12]. Explainable Artificial Intelligence (XAI) is the research field that studies the interpretability of AI models [8]. This research field aims to develop methods that can be helpful to "open" these complex and not interpretable models and to explain their predictions. To this end, a lot of approaches have been developed in the past few years. Explanation methods can be categorized with respect to two aspects [8]. One contrasts *model-specific vs model-agnostic* approaches, depending on whether the explanation method exploits knowledge about the internals of the black-box or not. The other contrasts *local vs global* approaches, depending on whether the explanation is provided for any specific instance classified by the black-box or for the logic of the black-box as a whole. Finally, we can distinguish *post-hoc vs ante-hoc* methods if they are designed to explain a pre-trained approach or if they are interpretable by design. While the explanation of ML models has been widely addressed in recent years [1,4,8,12], quite surprisingly, the use of XAI in FL has not gained much attention. A review of the current approaches used to explain models trained with FL is presented in [2]. Most of the approaches provide post-hoc explanation by feature importance [6,18,19]. Wang et al. [19] exploits Shapley values to explain models trained with FL. In particular, they adopt SHAP [13] to compute the feature importance and measure the contributions of different parties in Vertical FL [20], where the users that participate in the training have the same sample space but different feature space. The choice to use Shapley values in FL is justified by the possible privacy risks that could arise from classical feature importance that may reveal some aspect of the private local data. Since cooperative learning explanations could reveal the underlined feature data from other users, it becomes essential to guarantee model privacy. Therefore, in [18], Wang proposes a method to explain models based on SHAP values able to balance interpretability with privacy. The main idea is to reveal detailed feature importance for owned features and a unified feature importance for the features from the other parties. In [6], Fiosina studies the interpretability issues in Horizontal FL [20]. In particular, they adopt a Federated deep learning model to predict taxi trip duration within the Brunswick region through the FedAvg algorithm [14]. In order to explain the trained model, the authors derive feature importance exploiting Integrated Gradients [10]. Explainable AI techniques have also been used to explain the misbehaviour of models trained using FL. Haffar et al. [9], focus on the wrong predictions of an FL model because these predictions could be signs of an attack. In order to observe changes in the model behaviour, the nodes involved during the computation explain the trained model at each epoch. An attacker's presence could be revealed by changes in feature importance between two consecutive epochs greater than a predetermined threshold. To the best of our knowledge, no previous work addressed the problem of interpretability in horizontal FL by designing a SHAP variant while adhering to participants' privacy.

3   Background

We keep this paper self-contained by summarizing the key concepts necessary to comprehend our proposal.

Federated Learning. FL [14] aims to train an ML model by exploiting the cooperation of different parties while protecting user data. The main idea is that participants in the federation do not have to share their data among themselves or with a server. Each participant first trains a *local* model using their own data. Then, it sends the gradient or weights of the model to a central server or to the other participants to the end of learning a *global* and common model[1].

   Depending on how many clients are involved in the training of the model and their nature, we can have two different types of FL: cross-silo and cross-

---

[1] We underline that the meaning of local and global in the context of FL is entirely different from the meaning in the context of XAI.

device [11]. In the cross-silo scenario, we only have a few clients (10–50) that should always be available during the training.

On the contrary, in the cross-device scenario, we can have millions of devices involved in the computation that can only train the model under certain conditions.

The most widely used architecture is the *server-based* one, where a central server orchestrates the communication between the clients and the server itself.

In this paper, we consider a cross-silos scenario with a server-based architecture. In particular, we adopt the *Federated Averaging (FedAvg)* aggregation algorithm [14]. In each round of this algorithm, the updated local models of the parties are transferred to the server, which then further aggregates the local models to update the global model. FedAvg works as follows. We suppose to have a central server S, which orchestrates the work of a federation of C clients. The goal is to train a neural network $\mathcal{N}$ by executing a given set of Federated rounds. The procedure starts with the server that randomly initializes the neural network parameters w_0 and then it executes the specified training rounds. We refer to them as *global iterations* to distinguish them from the training rounds executed on the client side, also called *local iterations*. A generic global iteration j can be split into four main phases: sending, local training, aggregation and evaluation phase. In the *sending* phase, the server samples a subset C_i of k clients and sends them w^j, that is the current global model's parameters, through the dedicated communication channels. Every client $c \in C_i$, after having received w^j, starts training it for E epochs on its private dataset, applying one classic optimizer, like SGD, Adam or RMSProp. The number of local epochs and the optimizer are user-defined parameters. Finally, the client c sends back to the server the updated model parameters w_c^{j+1}, ending the local training phase of the algorithm. When the server ends gathering all the results from the clients, it performs the *aggregation* phase, where it computes the new global model parameters, w^{j+1} as $w^{j+1} = w^j + \sum_{c \in C_i} \frac{n_c}{n} \Delta w_c^{j+1}$, where n_c is the number of records in the client c's training set and $n = \sum_{c \in C_i} n_c$. Therefore, in the last phase, the *evaluation* one, the server evaluates the new global model w^{j+1} according to the chosen metrics.

Feature Importance Explanations. Feature importance is one of the most popular types of explanation returned by local explanation methods [4,8]. For feature importance-based explanation methods, the explainer assigns to each feature an importance value which represents how much that particular feature is important for the prediction under analysis. Given a record x, an explainer $f(\cdot)$ models a feature importance explanation as a vector $e = \{e_1, e_2, \ldots, e_f\}$, in which the value $e_i \in e$ is the importance of the ith feature for the decision made by the black-box model $b(x)$. For understanding the contribution of each feature, the sign and the magnitude of each value e_i are considered. W.r.t. the sign, if $e_i < 0$, it means that the feature contributes negatively to the outcome y; otherwise, if $e_i > 0$, the feature contributes positively. The magnitude, instead, represents how great the contribution of the feature is to the final prediction y. In particular, the greater the value of $|e_i|$, the greater its contribution. Hence, when $e_i = 0$, it means that the ith feature is showing no contribution. An example of a feature based explanation is $e = \{(age, 0.8), (income, 0.0), (education, -0.2)\}, y = deny$. In this case, age is the most important feature for the decision $deny$, $income$ is not affecting the outcome, and $education$ has a small negative contribution.

In this paper, we adopted SHapley Additive exPlanations (SHAP) [13] a local post-hoc model-agnostic explanation method computing features importance by means of Shapley values[2], a concept from cooperative game theory. SHAP is one of the most widely used explanation methods returning explanations in terms of feature importance. The explanations returned by SHAP are *additive feature attributions* and respect the following definition: $g(z') = \phi_0 + \sum_{i=1}^{F} \phi_i z_i'$, where z' is a record similar to x obtained as a copy of x where some features and values are replaced with some real values observed from the training set or from a reference set X, while $\phi_i \in \mathbb{R}$ are effects assigned to each feature, and F is the number of simplified input features. SHAP retains three properties: *(i)* *local accuracy*, meaning that $g(x)$ matches $b(x)$; *(ii)* *missingness*, which allows for features $x_i = 0$ to have no attributed impact on the SHAP values; *(iii)* *stability*, meaning that if a model changes so that the marginal contribution of a feature value increases (or stays the same), the SHAP value also increases (or stays the same) [15]. The construction of the SHAP values allows us to employ them both *locally*, in which each observation gets its own set of SHAP values, and *globally*, by exploiting collective SHAP values. We highlight that SHAP can be realized through different explanation models that differ in how they approximate the computation of the SHAP values. In our experiments, we adopted *KernelExplainer*, i.e., the completely model-agnostic version.

4   SHAP Explanations in Horizontal FL

Our proposal is to exploit SHAP [13] to explain the ML model learned by the FedAvg algorithm [14], in the case of Horizontal FL architecture. We recall that SHAP requires access to the training set D_{tr}, or to a "reference set" which is similar to the training set used by the model to explain, to create records z' to study the impact of each feature value in the final prediction. Sometimes, to speed up the explanation process, a medoid of the dataset is used or a small set of centroids [17] describing D_{tr} with a few records capturing the main characteristics, i.e. feature-values [15]. As a consequence, in server-based FL, in order to explain the learned global model, it is necessary that the server may gain access to the complete set of training data of its clients or has the possibility of computing the centroids of the dataset resulting from the union of the training sets of all the clients. Since the basic idea of FL is to avoid data sharing, in this setting we propose to have an explanation of the global model as the result of the aggregation of local (client-side) explanations.

Let $C = \{c_1, \ldots, c_m\}$ the set of m clients participating to the cooperation. After the FL algorithm, each client $c_i \in C$ has its ML model M_i received by

---

[2] We refer the interested reader to: https://christophm.github.io/interpretable-ml-book/shapley.html.

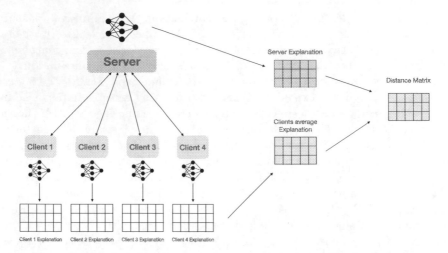

Fig. 1. Overview of our methodology. The server and all clients explain the model obtaining a matrix of SHAP values. The clients compute the mean of these matrices. To understand the difference between the explanations, we subtract the client's average explanation from the server explanation matrix.

the server. We denote with M_S the model on the server side resulting from the weights averaging. Each client c_i can derive a SHAP explainer ψ_i of its own model M_i which strongly depends on its training data. We propose to exploit the additive property of the SHAP values to generate explanations of the model M_S as an aggregation of explanations of the models belonging to M. More formally, given an instance x to be explained, the explanation of the prediction performed by the model M_S is obtained by $\psi_S(x) = \frac{1}{|C|} \sum_{c_i \in C} \psi_{c_i}(x)$. Specifically, the server's explanation $\psi_S(x)$ is composed by $|x|$ values resulting from the average of SHAP values of m clients, meaning that for each x_j we have $v_j = \frac{1}{|C|} \sum_{c_i \in C} \psi_{c_i}(x_j)$, where we assume that $\psi_{c_i}(x_j)$ returns the SHAP value associated by the client c_i to the feature x_j (Fig. 1).

Thus, according to our proposal, any client can derive its explanation for the instance x exploiting its own training data without the need to share them with the server, while the server only needs to receive the clients' explanations.

Analytical Methodology. In our experiments, we aim at comparing the proposed variant of SHAP explanations tailored for FL with the explanations obtained by the server. Hence, we propose an analytical methodology for validating our proposal based on the comparison of two settings: *(i)* the server gains access to training data of its clients i.e., $D_{tr} = \cup_{c_i \in C} D_{tr}^{c_i}$; *(ii)* the server cannot access training data and thus can only receive the clients' explanation for each prediction to be explained. In order to conduct our analysis given a test set D_{te} the following analytical methodology is applied:

- Each client c_i computes the SHAP explanation for each $x \in D_{te}$, i.e., it gets $\psi_{c_i}(x)$. Thus, each client produces a $k \times f$ matrix E^{c_i} where k is the number of records in D_{te} and f is the number of the features.

- A global explanation for each $x \in D_{te}$ is computed by averaging the clients' explanations as described above. Therefore, given the matrices $\{E^{c_1}, \ldots, E^{c_m}\}$ we can compute the matrix $\hat{E}$ where each element $e_{ij} = \frac{1}{|C|} \sum_{c \in C} e_{ij}^c$. We call this explanation *clients-based explanation*.
- A *server-based explanation* is computed by simulating the server's access to the client's training data. Accessing training data, the server can obtain the SHAP explainer ψ_S which applies to each $x \in D_{te}$ and the $k \times f$ matrix E_S.
- Finally, given the two matrices E_S and $\hat{E}$ we analyze the differences to understand the degree of approximation introduced by our approach which does not assume data access. We perform this analysis by computing: *(i)* a difference matrix $\Delta = E_S - \hat{E}$; *(ii)* the average importance for each feature j produced by the two methods in the dataset D_{te} and then, how the two methods differ, this means computing a vector having for each feature j a value $\delta_j = \frac{1}{|k|} \sum_{i \in [1 \ldots k]} \delta_{ij}$.

5 Experiments

This section presents the experimental results obtained by applying the analytical methodology described in the previous section. We use the `CoverType` and `Adult` tabular datasets available in the UCI Machine Learning Repository[3]. `CoverType` contains $581,012$ records, 54 attributes and 7 different class labels. The attributes represent cartographic variables, and the class labels represent forest cover types. The classification task involves recognizing forest cover types. On the other hand, `Adult` is composed of $48,842$ records and 13 variables (after discarding "fnlwgt" and "education-num"), both numerical and categorical. Information such as age, job, capital loss, capital gain, and marital status can be found in it. The labels have values $<= 50K$ or $> 50K$, indicating whether the person will earn more or less than $50K$ in a fiscal year.

We defined ML models using Keras. In particular, for `CoverType`, we developed a model with three dense layers consisting of 1024, 512, and 256 units and a final output layer, while for `Adult`, we used a model with three dense layers with ten units. In both models, we used Relu as an activation function in each layer except for the output layer, where we applied softmax. After each layer, we used Dropout to prevent overfitting. We employed Flower [3] to simulate FL training. The experiments were performed on a server with an Intel Core i9-10980XE processor with 36 cores and 1 GPU Quadro RTX 6000.

In our experiments, we tested architectures with a different number of clients $m \in \{8, 16, 32\}$ involved in the computation. Indeed, one of the objectives of our analysis is to understand how this parameter impacts the aggregated explanation. In this preliminary experimentation, we considered a scenario where the clients have IID data which we distribute by stratified sampling. Also, each client has the same amount of samples. We are perfectly aware that this scenario is unlikely in real applications, and indeed we plan to perform further experiments on non-IID data. Nevertheless, the experimented configuration allows us to analyze FL impact on SHAP explanations without excessive variability.

---

[3] https://archive.ics.uci.edu/ml/index.php.

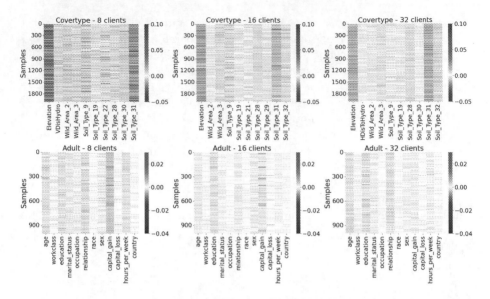

Fig. 2. Heatmaps showing the magnitude of the difference between server-based explanations and clients-based explanations for each sample. The first row shows the results for `CoverType` while the second one shows the results for `Adult`.

Results. In this section, we analyze the differences among the explanations with respect to two different aggregation criteria. Indeed, our goal is to investigate both the differences in the explanations from the point of view of the *features* and from the point of view of the *clients*.

In Fig. 2, we show through heatmaps, for each sample of the test set, the differences between the SHAP values of the server-based explanations and the ones of the clients-based explanations. These heatmaps are a graphical representation of the matrix Δ introduced in Sect. 4. To guarantee the readability of our results, in the plots of `CoverType`, we report only 10 features over 54, i.e., the features that, on average, have the highest discrepancy between the server-based explanations and clients-based explanations. As expected, the differences are negligible. For `CoverType` the features *"Soil_Type_31"* and *"Elevation"* have a greater divergence from 0. In particular, the clients-based explanation tends to overestimate the SHAP values of *"Elevation"* and underestimate the SHAP values of *"Soil_Type_31"*. We highlight that these two features present the highest divergence regardless of the number of clients involved in the training process. However, as we increase the number of clients, their divergence decreases. In `Adult`, we observe even smoother results in terms of divergence between server-based and clients-based explanations since the divergence varies in a smaller range with respect to `CoverType`. We can notice that, in any setting, we have only a couple of features having a magnitude of the difference more prominent with respect to the others. For example, in the setting with $m = 8$, clients *"capital_gain"* and *"realtionship"* present higher divergence.

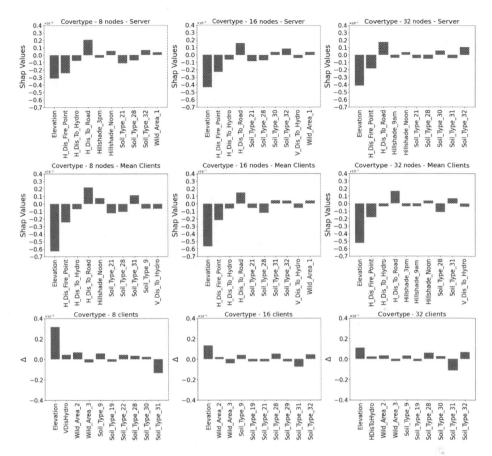

Fig. 3. SHAP values for `CoverType`. Top: calculated by the server. Middle: calculated by the clients. Bottom: Difference between SHAP values obtained by the server and those obtained by the clients.

We also conducted a more detailed analysis focused on the features. We report the results for `CoverType` in Fig. 3. The three plots in the first row depict the average SHAP values per feature of the server-based explanations, while the three in the middle row depict the average SHAP values per feature computed by clients-based explanations. As expected, these plots indicate that the two explanations almost always agree. The plots in the bottom row, instead, show the mean of the SHAP values for the top 10 features we selected for `CoverType`. They confirm our discussion based on the above heatmaps. Moreover, we observe that with an increasing number of clients m, some picks disappear, and the differences per feature vary in a smaller range of values.

Figure 4 shows the same analysis for `Adult`. As for `CoverType`, the two types of explanations almost always agree. Looking at the third row of the figure, we notice that, in general, the magnitude of the differences between the two

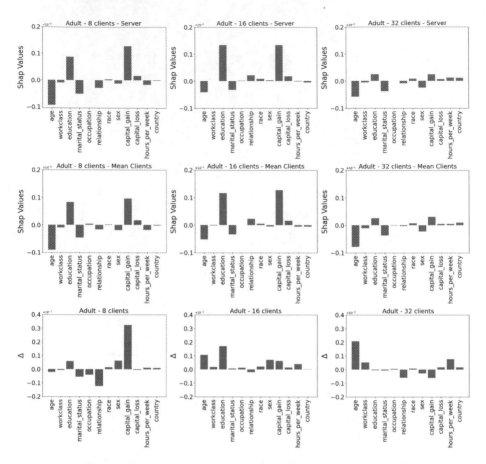

Fig. 4. SHAP values for `Adult`. Top: calculated by the server. Middle: calculated by the clients. Bottom: Difference between SHAP values obtained by the server and those obtained by the clients.

types of explanation decreases because, also in this case, some relevant picks disappear. As an example, the pick we have with the feature *"capital_gain"* in the experiment with $m = 8$ clients disappears as the number of clients increases.

Besides considering the differences in terms of SHAP values of *features*, we investigated the differences between the server-based explanation and the one performed on each client. This gives us the opportunity to understand if there are clients contributing more to the divergences between the two types of explanations. We report the results in Fig. 5. In `CoverType`, we observe that in the case of $m = 8$ clients, the difference with respect to the server is equal for all the clients. As the number of clients increases, we notice different behaviour among the various participants. Moreover, in the case with $m = 32$ clients, we observe an increase in the divergences with respect to the setting with $m = 16$ clients. This result is evident also in the last plot of the first row in Fig. 5.

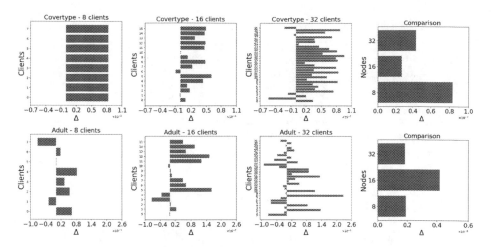

Fig. 5. Divergence of the server-based explanation w.r.t. clients-based. The first row reports results for `CoverType` and the second for `Adult`. For each setting, we plot the mean of the differences in the last plot of each row.

In `Adult`, we observe a different behaviour. The distance between the server and the various clients is different even when we use only 8 clients. As we increase the number of clients to 16, the distance increases, i.e., there are only a few clients with very low divergence and more clients with higher divergence. However, differently from the experiment with `CoverType`, when we increase the number of clients to 32, the overall difference decreases again (see the last plot of the second row in Fig. 5) because we have more clients with very low divergence.

In a nutshell, our results show that the clients-based explanation introduces a negligible approximation to SHAP values, proving that our method is promising.

6   Discussion of Findings

By aggregating local explanations, the proposed methodology investigates whether it is possible to derive an explanation for a model trained using Federated Learning. To achieve this goal, we exploited SHAP values' additive property. To be more specific, we aggregated the explanations computed by the individual clients to obtain a model explanation. We then compared this explanation with that of the server. The results obtained from the two datasets we considered support our initial guesses. Indeed, the differences between the aggregated explanation and the server explanation are minimal. Therefore, the explainer trained by the server and the one trained by the clients produce the same results. This means that they are both suitable for explaining a Federated Learning model. However, the explainer trained by the server requires some data to be transferred from the clients to the server to be trained. This is against the definition of Federated Learning [14]. By successfully showcasing the viability of aggregating local explanations, we proved that clients do not need to transmit their data to a central server. This ensures confidentiality and mitigates potential privacy risks due to data sharing.

By moving the explainers training from the server to the clients, we can also reduce the computation overhead on the server side. This is because it has only to perform the SHAP values aggregation. In addition, this approach could easily be extended and adapted to a peer-to-peer Federated Learning setting, where we would not have a server that could train an explainer. Instead, using our clients-based explanations, each client could first compute the explanations and then, after exchanging their SHAP values, aggregate them to derive the final explanation without sharing any data.

7   Conclusion

In this paper, we have presented a method for providing SHAP explanations in horizontal server-based Federated Learning systems. The basic idea is explaining an instance's prediction performed by the trained ML model by aggregating the explanation of the clients participating in the federation. Consequently, the proposed approach satisfies the strong requirements of a Federated Learning system by avoiding sharing clients' data with the server. We have presented empirical evidence that our proposal introduces an acceptable approximation to the SHAP explanations. In turn, it can be interpreted as a reasonable trade-off between privacy and utility. In future work, we intend to analyze the impact of adopting our method in a scenario with non-I.I.D. data distribution and in a peer-to-peer Federated learning setting where we do not have a central server. Moreover, we would also like to study the impact of a larger number of clients involved in the training. Lastly, we would also like to investigate the impact of privacy mitigation on explanation quality.

Acknowledgment. This work is partially supported by the EU NextGenerationEU programme under the funding schemes PNRR-PE-AI FAIR (Future Artificial Intelligence Research), "SoBigData.it - Strengthening the Italian RI for Social Mining and Big Data Analytics" - Prot. IR0000013, H2020-INFRAIA-2019-1: Res. Infr. G.A. 871042 *SoBigData++*, G.A. 761758 *Humane AI*, G.A. 952215 *TAILOR*, ERC-2018-ADG G.A. 834756 *XAI*, and CHIST-ERA-19-XAI-010 SAI, by MUR (N. not yet available), FWF (N. I 5205), EPSRC (N. EP/V055712/1), NCN (N. 2020/02/Y/ST6/00064), ETAg (N. SLTAT21096), BNSF (N. KP-06-AOO2/5).

References

1. Adadi, A., Berrada, M.: Peeking inside the black-box: a survey on explainable artificial intelligence (XAI). IEEE Access **6**, 52138–52160 (2018)
2. Bárcena, J.L.C., et al.: Fed-XAI: federated learning of explainable artificial intelligence models. In: XAI.it@AI*IA, CEUR Workshop Proceedings (2022)
3. Beutel, D.J., et al.: Flower: A friendly federated learning research framework (2020)
4. Bodria, F., Giannotti, F., Guidotti, R., Naretto, F., Pedreschi, D., Rinzivillo, S.: Benchmarking and survey of explanation methods for black box models. ArXiv: preprint, abs/2102.13076 (2021)

5. Doshi-Velez, F., Kim,B.: A roadmap for a rigorous science of interpretability. CoRR, abs/1702.08608 (2017)
6. Fiosina, J.: Explainable federated learning for taxi travel time prediction. In: VEHITS. SCITEPRESS (2021)
7. Freitas, A.A.: Comprehensible classification models: a position paper. SIGKDD Explor. **15**(1), 1–10 (2013)
8. Guidotti, R., Monreale, A., Ruggieri, S., Turini, F., Giannotti, F., Pedreschi, D.: A survey of methods for explaining black box models. ACM Comput. Surv. **51**(5), 1–42 (2019)
9. Haffar, R., Sánchez, D., Domingo-Ferrer, J.: Explaining predictions and attacks in federated learning via random forests. Appl. Intell. , 1–17 (2022). https://doi.org/10.1007/s10489-022-03435-1
10. Janzing, D., Minorics, L., Blöbaum, P.: Feature relevance quantification in explainable AI: a causal problem. In: Chiappa,S., Calandra, R., (eds.) The 23rd International Conference on Artificial Intelligence and Statistics, AISTATS 2020, 26–28 August 2020, [Palermo, Sicily, Italy], volume 108 of Proceedings of Machine Learning Research, pp. 2907–2916. PMLR (2020)
11. Li, Q., Wen, Z., Wu, Z., Hu, S., Wang, N., He, B.: A survey on federated learning systems: Vision, hype and reality for data privacy and protection. arXiv e-prints (2019)
12. Longo, L., Goebel, R., Lecue, F., Kieseberg, P., Holzinger, A.: Explainable artificial intelligence: concepts, applications, research challenges and visions. In: Holzinger, A., Kieseberg, P., Tjoa, A.M., Weippl, E. (eds.) CD-MAKE 2020. LNCS, vol. 12279, pp. 1–16. Springer, Cham (2020). https://doi.org/10.1007/978-3-030-57321-8_1
13. Lundberg, S.M., Lee, S.: A unified approach to interpreting model predictions. In: Guyon, I., et al., (eds.) Advances in Neural Information Processing Systems, vol. 30: Annual Conference on Neural Information Processing Systems 2017, 4–9 December 2017, Long Beach, CA, USA, pp. 4765–4774 (2017)
14. McMahan, B., Moore, E., Ramage, D., Hampson, S., Arcas, B.A.Y.: Communication-efficient learning of deep networks from decentralized data. In: Singh, A., Zhu, X.J., (eds.) Proceedings of the 20th International Conference on Artificial Intelligence and Statistics, AISTATS 2017, 20–22 April 2017, Fort Lauderdale, FL, USA, volume 54 of Proceedings of Machine Learning Research, pp. 1273–1282. PMLR (2017)
15. Molnar, C.: Interpretable machine learning. Lulu. com (2020)
16. Pedreschi, D., Giannotti, F., Guidotti, R., Monreale, A., Ruggieri, S., Turini, F.: Meaningful explanations of black box AI decision systems. In: The Thirty-Third AAAI Conference on Artificial Intelligence, AAAI 2019, The Thirty-First Innovative Applications of Artificial Intelligence Conference, IAAI 2019, The Ninth AAAI Symposium on Educational Advances in Artificial Intelligence, EAAI 2019, Honolulu, Hawaii, USA, 27 January–1 February 2019, pp. 9780–9784. AAAI Press (2019)
17. Tan, P., Steinbach, M.S., Kumar, V.: Introduction to Data Mining. Addison-Wesley, Boston (2005)
18. Wang, G.: Interpret federated learning with shapley values. ArXiv preprint, abs/1905.04519 (2019)
19. Wang, G., Dang, C.X., Zhou, Z.: Measure contribution of participants in federated learning. In: 2019 IEEE International Conference on Big Data (Big Data), Los Angeles, CA, USA, 9–12 December 2019, pp. 2597–2604. IEEE (2019)
20. Yang, Q., Liu, Y., Chen, T., Tong, Y.: Federated machine learning: concept and applications (2019)

PERFEX: Classifier Performance Explanations for Trustworthy AI Systems

Erwin Walraven[1](✉), Ajaya Adhikari[1], and Cor J. Veenman[1,2]

[1] Netherlands Organisation for Applied Scientific Research,
The Hague, The Netherlands
erwin.walraven@tno.nl
[2] Leiden University, Leiden, The Netherlands

Abstract. Explainability of a classification model is crucial when deployed in real-world decision support systems. Explanations make predictions actionable to the user and should inform about the capabilities and limitations of the system. Existing explanation methods, however, typically only provide explanations for individual predictions. Information about conditions under which the classifier is able to support the decision maker is not available, while for instance information about when the system is not able to differentiate classes can be very helpful. In the development phase it can support the search for new features or combining models, and in the operational phase it supports decision makers in deciding e.g. not to use the system. This paper presents a method to explain the qualities of a trained *base* classifier, called PERFormance EXplainer (PERFEX). Our method consists of a *meta* tree learning algorithm that is able to predict and explain under which conditions the base classifier has a high or low *error* or any other classification performance metric. We evaluate PERFEX using several classifiers and datasets, including a case study with urban mobility data. It turns out that PERFEX typically has high meta prediction performance even if the base classifier is hardly able to differentiate classes, while giving compact performance explanations.

Keywords: explainability · classification · decision support systems

1 Introduction

Decision support systems based on machine learning models are being developed for a growing number of domains. To deploy these systems for operational use, it is crucial that the system provides tangible explanations. It needs to be transparent about the underlying inference process of its predictions and about its own limitations. For example, in a medical setting it is important that a doctor knows under which circumstances the system is unable to provide reliable advice regarding a diagnosis [18]. Similarly, when a decision support system is used for investment decisions in policy making, then it is important that the users of

© The Author(s), under exclusive license to Springer Nature Switzerland AG 2023
L. Longo (Ed.): xAI 2023, CCIS 1902, pp. 164–180, 2023.
https://doi.org/10.1007/978-3-031-44067-0_9

the system get informed about the uncertainty associated with the advice it provides [2]. The importance of explanation capabilities is also emphasized by the guidelines on trustworthy AI from the European Commission [12], which includes explainability about capabilities and limitations of AI models as a key requirement.

Developing methods for explainability in machine learning has gained significant interest in recent years [6]. Global explanations give an overall view of the knowledge encoded in the model. This is very relevant for knowledge discovery like in biology or medical applications. Examples are model coefficients as in logistic regression [9] and indications of feature importance such as with random forests [4] and gradient boosting [8]. Local explanations on the other hand explain predictions for individual datapoints. For example, SHAP and LIME explain the class prediction of a datapoint by highlighting features which are locally most influencing the prediction [15,20].

In addition to explaining class predictions, methods are needed that explain the performance of a classifier. Such explanations can be used by a data scientist to understand under which circumstances a base classifier does or does not perform well. If the explanation defines that the model does not perform well for a specific subset of the data, then the data scientist may decide to look for additional data, additional features, or otherwise attempt to improve the model in a focused way. The explanations can also be used to inform e.g. a consultant or medical doctor about circumstances in which a model cannot be trusted, which is also relevant for engineers who bring models to production. In existing literature only a method for explaining the uncertainty of individual predictions has been proposed (e.g., by Antorán et al. [1]). For explaining the performance characteristics and limitations of classifiers globally, no methods have been published to the best of our knowledge.

This paper presents a model-agnostic PERFormance EXplainer (PERFEX) to derive explanations about characteristics of classification models. Given a *base* classifier, a dataset and a classification performance metric such as the prediction accuracy, we propose a *meta* learning algorithm that separates the feature space in regions with high and low prediction accuracy and enables to generate compact explanations for these regions. In the following sections we define the problem formally and overview related work. Then, we describe PERFEX in detail. We evaluate the method in experiments based on several classification methods and datasets including our own case study. The experiments show that PERFEX provides clear explanations in scenarios where explanations from SHAP and LIME are not sufficient to gain trust. We finalize the paper with our conclusions.

2   Problem Statement

We consider a classification task in which a base classifier $\mathcal{C}$ is trained to assign a datapoint x to a class. The set $\mathcal{K} = \{c_1, c_2, \ldots, c_k\}$ contains all k classes considered, and $\mathcal{C}(x) \in \mathcal{K}$ denotes the class to which datapoint x belongs according to $\mathcal{C}$. The classifier is trained using a tabular dataset $\mathcal{X}_t$ containing n datapoints,

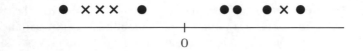

Fig. 1. One-dimensional dataset with correct predictions (dot) and incorrect predictions (cross)

and for each datapoint $x_i \in \mathcal{X}_t$ the true class label is denoted by $y_i \in \mathcal{K}$. Each datapoint in the dataset is defined by m feature values, and we use x^j to refer to feature value j of datapoint x.

The prediction performance of classifier $\mathcal{C}$ can be measured using standard metrics, such as accuracy, precision, recall, F1-score and expected calibration error [13]. We define the prediction performance metric $\mathcal{M}$ as a function that takes a classifier $\mathcal{C}$, test datapoints $x_1, \ldots, x_p$ and true labels $y_1, \ldots, y_p$ as input, and it computes a real-valued score as output. The problem we consider is: given a classifier $\mathcal{C}$, a metric $\mathcal{M}$, an independent dataset $\mathcal{X}$ and corresponding ground truth labels $\mathcal{Y}$, find a compact explanation for subgroups of the data having either low or high (sub) performance. The compactness refers to the amount of information that the explanation presents to the user.

As an example we consider prediction accuracy as performance metric $\mathcal{M}$, and we visually illustrate the problem based on a one-dimensional dataset with feature z, as shown in Fig. 1. The symbols indicate whether predictions from a given base classifier are correct (dot) or not (cross) when predicting for the ten datapoints that are shown. The overall prediction accuracy is 0.6. However, this number does not tell us under which circumstances the classifier performs well, and when it does not perform well. We would like to create explanations which tell that the classifier does not perform well for $z < 0$ (accuracy $2/5 = 0.4$), while it does perform well otherwise (accuracy $4/5 = 0.8$). Instead of accuracy other performance metrics $\mathcal{M}$ may be used, such as precision, recall, F1-score and expected calibration error.

3   Related Work

In this section we overview the work related to the stated problem ranging from model agnostic individual prediction to cluster based explanations and explaining uncertainties.

First, SHAP [15] and LIME [20] can be used to create explanations about individual predictions. SP-LIME [20] is a variant of LIME which aims to enable a user to assess whether a model can be trusted by providing an explanation for a group of samples as set of individual explanations. This is problematic in domains with many features, it requires that the user inspects many instances, and it is unclear whether a set of local explanations gives global understanding of a model. Anchors [21] is related to LIME and aims to explain how a model behaves on unseen instances, but only locally. K-LIME is another variant of

LIME, which is part of the H2O Driverless AI platform [14]. It performs a k-means clustering, and for each cluster it fits a linear model to explain features influencing the predictions in that cluster. In contrast to our problem, it uses a normal classification model fitting criterion instead of explaining a (base) learner using its performance metric.

Interpretable clustering [3] clusters data based on a tree structure. It derives an optimal clustering tree using mixed-integer optimization, and the branches in the tree structure make the clustering interpretable. Although this approach may deliver compact cluster explanations, like the LIME variants, it models the distribution of the data itself instead of the prediction structure of a base learner. A clustering based on the predictions of a model cannot be easily integrated in this exact optimization framework, especially if the computation of the performance metric is non-linear.

Explanations of prediction characteristics of a classifier is related to explanations of uncertainty. The CLUE method [1] can be used to explain which parts of the input of a deep neural network cause uncertainty by providing a counterfactual explanation in the input space. CLUE only provides an uncertainty explanation for an individual input, and it cannot be used to inform the user about the circumstances under which a model is uncertain. Our work also relates to Interpretable Confidence Measures (ICM), which uses the accuracy as a proxy for uncertainty [24]. A prediction for a datapoint is considered to be uncertain if the classifier makes mistakes for similar datapoints. Our problem is to provide e.g. uncertainty explanations for groups of datapoints, whereas ICM only focuses on individual datapoints.

For regression models regions with deviating performance can be identified by using subgroup mining, which creates Error Distribution Rules [19]. Instance spaces [16] also aim to identify groups of instances such that the strengths and weaknesses of a classifier can be studied. For both approaches it is important to emphasize that there is a strong focus on the accuracy of a classifier, whereas PERFEX can be used to create explanations for any metric.

Finally, there is a link with Emerging Pattern Mining (EPM), which can be used to capture contrasts between classes [10]. An important difference is that EPM aims at find patterns in data, while we aim at finding patterns in the modeled data (by potentially any classifier).

4   Classifier PERFormance EXplainer

This section describes our method to find compact explanations for subsets of datapoints based on local high or low performance of the base learner. As overviewed in the Related Work section applying clustering algorithms, such as k-means, is not suitable because k-means does not cluster based on $\mathcal{M}$. A clustering based on a decision tree can address this problem, because datapoints in leafs can be seen as clusters and the branch conditions in the tree can be used to extract explanations. If the classifier accuracy is used as metric $\mathcal{M}$, then a standard decision tree can be fitted which uses train targets which equal 1 if the

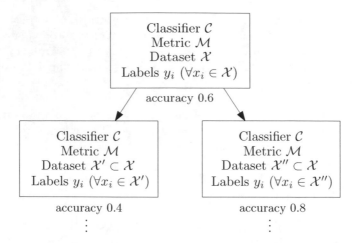

Fig. 2. Splitting dataset $\mathcal{X}$ into subsets $\mathcal{X}'$ and $\mathcal{X}''$

base classifier predicts correctly for a datapoint, and 0 otherwise. This would yield a tree which distinguishes subsets of data with low accuracy from subsets of data with high accuracy, and allows for explanations. However, for other performance metrics $\mathcal{M}$ such targets cannot be defined. We introduce PERFEX, model-agnostic method to explain the prediction performance of a base classifier for any performance metric $\mathcal{M}$.

4.1   Creating Subsets of Data Using Tree Structure

The basic idea of PERFEX is to divide $\mathcal{X}$ up in a hierarchical manner leading to a tree-structured meta learner. This enables us to naturally split the data based on a split condition that depends on $\mathcal{M}$, similar to the construction of classification trees. More importantly, through the hierarchical process the tree has typically a limited depth, such that when we use the branches as conditions in a decision rule, it leads to a compact explanation. The process is schematically illustrated in Fig. 2. For convenience we illustrate the tree construction based on the same accuracy values as in Fig. 1. In the root node we consider a classifier $\mathcal{C}$, metric $\mathcal{M}$, dataset $\mathcal{X}$ and the corresponding labels. The prediction metric score for $\mathcal{X}$ can be obtained by evaluating $\mathcal{M}$, which gives accuracy 0.6 in the figure. This value has been computed using the full dataset $\mathcal{X}$, but it does not enable the user to understand when this metric value is low or high. We provide this additional understanding to the user by decomposing $\mathcal{X}$ into two subsets $\mathcal{X}' \subset \mathcal{X}$ and $\mathcal{X}'' \subset \mathcal{X}$, such that $\mathcal{M}$ evaluates to a low value for $\mathcal{X}'$ and to a high value for $\mathcal{X}''$. This process is illustrated by the child nodes, which evaluate to an accuracy of 0.4 and 0.8, respectively. The branch conditions in the tree can be used to explain to a user when the performance metric evaluates to a low or high value.

The tree structure in Fig. 2 can be automatically created using an algorithm that closely resembles to procedure for generating decision trees for classifica-

---

Algorithm 1: PERFEX

> **input** : classifier $\mathcal{C}$, dataset $\mathcal{X}$, labels y_i ($\forall x_i \in \mathcal{X}$), prediction metric $\mathcal{M}$, minimum subset size α
>
> **output:** subsets $\mathcal{X}' \subset \mathcal{X}$ and $\mathcal{X}'' \subset \mathcal{X}$ with corresponding labels, split condition s

```
1  X' ← ∅,  X'' ← ∅,  s ← (0,0),   β ← 0
2  for j = 1,...,m do
3  │   foreach unique value v of feature j in X do
4  │   │   X̂' ← ∅,  X̂'' ← ∅
5  │   │   foreach x ∈ X do
6  │   │   │   if xʲ ≤ v then
7  │   │   │   │   X̂' ← X̂' ∪ {x}
8  │   │   │   else
9  │   │   │   │   X̂'' ← X̂'' ∪ {x}
10 │   │   │   end
11 │   │   end
12 │   │   e' ← evaluate M using C, X̂' and labels
13 │   │   e'' ← evaluate M using C, X̂'' and labels
14 │   │   β' ← |e' − e''|
15 │   │   if β' > β and |X̂'| ≥ α and |X̂''| ≥ α then
16 │   │   │   β ← β', X' ← X̂', X'' ← X̂'', s ← (j,β)
17 │   │   end
18 │   end
19 end
```

---

tion and regression [5]. A key difference is that we use a split condition based on $\mathcal{M}$ during the tree generation procedure, rather than using e.g. the Gini impurity. Algorithm 1 shows how to split a dataset $\mathcal{X}$ for all possible features into subsets $\mathcal{X}' \subset \mathcal{X}$ and $\mathcal{X}'' \subset \mathcal{X}$ using prediction metric $\mathcal{M}$ as split criterion. It enumerates all possible splits into subsets $\mathcal{X}'$ and $\mathcal{X}''$. For numerical and binary features a less-than-or-equal condition can be used on line 6, and for categorical features an equality condition should be used. For features with continuous values, it may be practical to consider only a fixed number of quantiles, rather than enumerating all unique values. After creating subsets on lines 4–11, it uses $\mathcal{M}$ to evaluate the metric value for both subsets, and it keeps track of the best split found so far. The quality of a split is determined by computing the difference between the performance metric values of both subsets. Since we want to distinguish subsets with low and high metric values, the algorithm returns the subsets with maximum difference. The split condition corresponding to the best split is stored in the tuple s, which contains both the index of the feature and the feature value used for splitting. Algorithm 1 shows how one node of the tree ($\mathcal{X}$) is divided into two child nodes ($\mathcal{X}'$, $\mathcal{X}''$). In order to create a full tree, the algorithm should be applied again to $\mathcal{X}'$ and $\mathcal{X}''$. This process repeats until a fixed depth is reached. Another stop criterion based on confidence intervals is discussed below.

4.2   Confidence Intervals on Values of $\mathcal{M}$

Splitting data using Algorithm 1 should terminate if the size of either $\mathcal{X}'$ or $\mathcal{X}''$ becomes too small to provide a good estimation of metric $\mathcal{M}$. This can be assessed based on a confidence interval on e' and e''. We only discuss the derivation for e' because for e'' the procedure is identical. The actual derivation is dependent on the chosen metric $\mathcal{M}$. Below we illustrate it for the metrics accuracy and precision.

For accuracy the estimator $e' = u \, / \, |\mathcal{X}'|$ can be used, in which u represents the total number of correct predictions. The estimator e' follows a binomial distribution, and therefore we can use a binomial proportion confidence interval:

$$\left(e' - z\sqrt{\frac{e'(1-e')}{|\mathcal{X}'|}}, e' + z\sqrt{\frac{e'(1-e')}{|\mathcal{X}'|}} \right), \tag{1}$$

in which z denotes the Z-score of the desired confidence level [17]. Given maximum interval width D, combined with the insight that the term $e'(1-e')$ takes a value that is at most 0.25, we obtain the minimum number of datapoints, which can be used as termination condition:

$$z\sqrt{\frac{0.25}{|\mathcal{X}'|}} = \frac{D}{2} \quad \Rightarrow \quad |\mathcal{X}'| = \frac{z^2}{D^2}. \tag{2}$$

For example, when using a 95 percent confidence level and maximum interval width 0.1, the minimum number of datapoints in $\mathcal{X}'$ equals $1.96^2 \, / \, 0.1^2 \approx 384$.

For other proportion metrics such as precision the derivation is slightly different, because precision does not depend on all datapoints in $\mathcal{X}'$. For example, the precision for class c_i equals $u \, / \, |\{x \in \mathcal{X}' \mid \mathcal{C}(x) = c_i\}|$, in which u denotes the number of datapoints in $\{x \in \mathcal{X}' \mid \mathcal{C}(x) = c_i\}$ which were predicted correctly. By applying the same derivation as above, it can be seen that the termination condition for tree generation should be based on the number of datapoints in $\{x \in \mathcal{X}' \mid \mathcal{C}(x) = c_i\}$ rather than $\mathcal{X}'$.

4.3   Tree Evaluation Using Test Set

The tree quality can also be evaluated using a separate test set $\bar{\mathcal{X}}$. First, the datapoints in $\bar{\mathcal{X}}$ are assigned to leafs. After that, the metric value in each leaf can be computed based on the assigned datapoints. Intuitively, it can be expected that the metric value for datapoints in a leaf of the tree is similar for $\mathcal{X}$ and $\bar{\mathcal{X}}$, regardless of the performance of the base classifier and regardless of the performance metric $\mathcal{M}$. For example, if the accuracy in all the leafs of the tree is low, then the estimated accuracy in the leafs will also be low when using another dataset from the same distribution. Algorithm 2 shows how the tree quality is determined by computing the mean absolute error based on the errors of the individual leafs. The output variable d can be used to assess to what extent PERFEX distinguishes subsets with low and high metric values.

Algorithm 2: Estimate quality of tree using test set

---

    input : tree $\mathcal{T}$ created by recursively applying Algorithm 1, metric $\mathcal{M}$,
                    classifier $\mathcal{C}$, dataset $\mathcal{X}$, test set $\bar{\mathcal{X}}$, and labels
    output: mean absolute error $\hat{e}$, metric difference d
1 $L \leftarrow$ set of leafs in $\mathcal{T}$, $\hat{e} \leftarrow 0$
2 **foreach** *leaf* $l \in L$ **do**
3 | $\mathcal{X}_l \leftarrow$ datapoints in leaf l after applying $\mathcal{T}$ to $\mathcal{X}$
4 | $\bar{\mathcal{X}}_l \leftarrow$ datapoints in leaf l after applying $\mathcal{T}$ to $\bar{\mathcal{X}}$
5 | $e_l \leftarrow$ evaluate $\mathcal{M}$ using $\mathcal{C}$, $\mathcal{X}_l$ and labels
6 | $\bar{e}_l \leftarrow$ evaluate $\mathcal{M}$ using $\mathcal{C}$, $\bar{\mathcal{X}}_l$ and labels
7 | $\hat{e} \leftarrow \hat{e} + |e_l - \bar{e}_l|$
8 **end**
9 $\hat{e} \leftarrow \hat{e} \ / \ |L|, \quad d \leftarrow (\max_{l \in L} e_l - \min_{l \in L} e_l)$

4.4   Generating Explanations

The tree structure created by Algorithm 1 can be used to extract explanations that can be presented to a user in a text-based format. Each leaf in the tree represents a subset of the data with a corresponding metric value. Therefore, we can print information about the leaf which explains to the user how the subset of data has been constructed, and what the metric value is, as illustrated below for one leaf:

```
There are 134 datapoints for which the
following conditions hold:
  length > 10.77, length <= 12.39
and for these datapoints accuracy is 0.68
```

For each leaf we print the number of datapoints, the prediction metric value computed on the same subset of data, and the conditions that were used to split the data. The conditions can be extracted from the tree by taking the conditions used in the nodes along the path from root to leaf.

    In order to create explanations that are understandable from a user point of view, it is important to limit the depth of the tree. It is expected that PERFEX works well if areas with low and high metric values can be distinguished by using a PERFEX tree with limited depth. If an extensive depth of the tree is required to distinguish these areas, then PERFEX is less suitable because this creates explanations with many conditions, which may be difficult to interpret for a user.

4.5   Example Using 2D Dataset

We provide an example using a dataset with two features, which shows visually how PERFEX creates an explanation. It will also show that explanations for the class prediction are not the same as the explanations based on $\mathcal{M}$. The dataset is shown in Fig. 3 and consists of the classes red and blue, generated

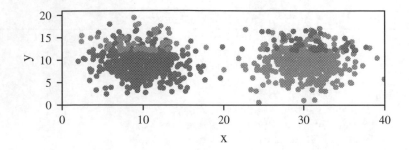

Fig. 3. Example dataset with two features and two classes

using Gaussian blobs with centers $(10, 10)$ and $(30, 10)$. For the purpose of the example we flip labels of some datapoints for which $y > 12$. The majority of the datapoints for which $x < 20$ belongs to red, and the majority belongs to blue if $x \geq 20$. Our base classifier is a decision tree with depth 1, predicting red if $x < 20$ and blue otherwise. We investigate when the base classifier has a low accuracy by applying Algorithm 1 with accuracy as metric $\mathcal{M}$:

```
There are 100 datapoints for which the
following conditions hold:
 y > 10.96
and for these datapoints accuracy is 0.72
```

```
There are 200 datapoints for which the
following conditions hold:
 y <= 10.96
and for these datapoints accuracy is 1.0
```

This explanation shows that the accuracy is lower if $y > 10.96$, which is also the area in which datapoints belong to two classes. More importantly, it shows that the explanation for accuracy depends on y, whereas the prediction made by the base classifier (and its explanation) only depend on x.

5   Experiments

We present the results of our experiments based on Gaussian data as well as several standard classifiers and datasets.

5.1   Evaluation of Tree Error with Gaussian Data

We start with two experiments to empirically study two hypotheses from the previous section. We use data from Gaussian distributions, allowing us to carefully control the difficulty of the prediction task. In our first experiment we show that PERFEX can be used to model a chosen prediction metric even if the

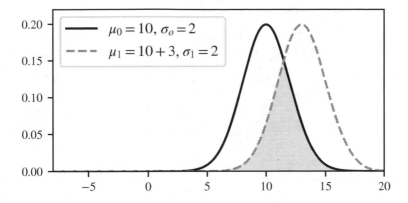

Fig. 4. Distribution with two classes defined by two Gaussians and one feature. The shaded area is the region of error.

original class prediction task is hard. We assume that the data comes from a one-dimensional dataset defined by two Gaussians, as shown in Fig. 4. The Gaussian with $\mu = 10$ and $\sigma = 2$ corresponds to the first class, and remains fixed. The datapoints of the second class follow a Gaussian distribution with $\mu = 10 + \delta$ and $\sigma = 2$. The parameter $\delta > 0$ is used to control the overlap of both Gaussians, which affects the difficulty of the prediction task. In the figure this is visualized for $\delta = 3$. Since the standard deviation of both distributions is the same, the difficulty of the prediction task can be expressed using the region of error, which is visualized using the shaded red area. We define a classifier which predicts the class for a datapoint x by taking the class for which the probability density is maximum: $\mathcal{C}(x) = \arg\max_{i \in \{0,1\}} f(\mu_i, \sigma_i, x)$, in which f denotes the probability density function. It can be expected that the prediction performance of the classifier drops if the region of error grows. This is confirmed in Fig. 5a, which shows the weighted F1 score of the classifier for an increasing region of error. We also created a PERFEX tree for accuracy, for which the mean absolute error (MAE, computed by Algorithm 2) is also shown. The error is close to zero, which confirms that PERFEX can model the accuracy of the classifier $\mathcal{C}$ even if the performance of this classifier is low.

Now we show that a generated tree can be used to model a prediction metric for a given classifier if the data used for creating the meta decision tree comes from the same distribution as the data used for creating the base classifier. We conduct an experiment in which we measure the error of the PERFEX tree, and we gradually shift the data distribution for creating the tree, which causes the error to increase. We use two Gaussians for creating the prediction model $\mathcal{C}$, with $\mu_0 = 10$, $\mu_1 = 13$ and $\sigma_0 = \sigma_1 = 2$. The data used for creating the PERFEX tree uses the same distributions, except that $\mu_1 = 13 + \delta$ with $\delta \geq 0$. If $\delta = 0$, then all datasets come from the same distribution, and in that case the error of the meta decision tree is low, as can be seen in Fig. 5b. If we shift the distribution of the data for creating our tree by setting $\delta > 0$, then we expect

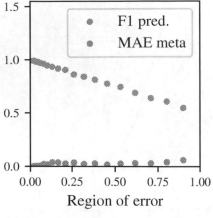

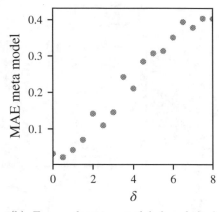

(a) Error for increasing region of error

(b) Error of meta model for shifted data distribution

Fig. 5. Results of experiments with Gaussian data

that the error increases due to this mismatch in the data. The figure confirms this, and it shows that a tree can be fitted only if its training data comes from the same distribution as the classifier training data.

5.2 Evaluation on Several Datasets and Models

We apply PERFEX to different datasets, classifiers and split conditions based on several metrics. Given that the meta tree needs sufficient data to create generalizable clusters, 4 classification datasets with at least 1000 datapoints from the UCI repository [11] were chosen: abalone, car evaluation, contraceptive method choice, and occupancy detection. While experimenting, we noticed that the classification of occupancy had almost perfect scores on the test-set. In that case, the meta model would not be able to create clusters. For that reason, we made the classification task more difficult by only including two features in the dataset: CO2 and temperature. Finally, we also included a fifth 2D dataset called *gaussian blobs*, which contains three clusters of datapoints that are partially overlapping. These clusters were sampled from a isotropic Gaussian distribution with cluster centers (10, 10), (20,12) and (15, 15), and a standard deviation of 3. We use this dataset to validate whether the tree is able to distinguish the non-overlapping regions with perfect scores and the overlapping regions with lower scores.

Each dataset was split into a train set (50%), test 1 set (25%) and test 2 set (25%), in a stratified manner according to the target. The train set was used to train 5 base classifiers: Logistic Regression (LR), Support Vector Machine with RBF kernel (SVM), Random Forest (RF), Decision Tree (DT), and KNN with K = 3. Test set 1 was used to evaluate the base classifier and to build the PERFEX tree with maximum depth 6. The tree is used to cluster the datapoints of test

Table 1. Evaluation of PERFEX using several datasets and base classifiers with accuracy as metric $\mathcal{M}$

Dataset	$\mathcal{C}$	Acc. of $\mathcal{C}$	L	D	Min acc.	Max acc.	MAE	STD AE
Abalone	SVC	53,6%	6	6	32,1%	84,3%	5,7%	4,6%
	LR	56,5%	6	6	37,2%	83,5%	4,9%	3,8%
	RF	54,5%	6	6	43,9%	82,7%	3,6%	2,7%
	DT	52,5%	6	6	37,0%	78,7%	5,1%	3,0%
	KNN	49,0%	6	6	32,2%	82,5%	4,2%	2,6%
Car evaluation	SVC	95,0%	2	2	87,6%	99,1%	1,1%	0,7%
	LR	90,5%	4	4	74,8%	100,0%	1,9%	2,9%
	RF	95,2%	2	2	89,2%	98,5%	1,4%	0,2%
	DT	94,8%	3	3	85,8%	100,0%	1,6%	0,9%
	KNN	87,5%	4	4	65,5%	99,4%	3,8%	3,9%
Contraceptive method choice	SVC	44,3%	3	3	33,0%	63,3%	7,2%	5,3%
	LR	53,4%	3	3	41,1%	63,8%	8,8%	2,0%
	RF	51,4%	4	4	38,3%	62,4%	4,3%	2,4%
	DT	52,3%	3	3	38,7%	62,6%	4,7%	1,3%
	KNN	48,2%	4	3	36,0%	62,4%	9,5%	6,2%
Occupancy detection	SVC	86,8%	12	6	20,6%	98,8%	3,6%	2,4%
	LR	81,9%	10	6	21,1%	98,5%	3,9%	3,6%
	RF	94,5%	7	6	80,3%	100,0%	2,0%	1,7%
	DT	93,5%	9	6	72,5%	98,3%	3,5%	2,0%
	KNN	88,6%	9	6	66,0%	98,6%	3,7%	2,0%
Gaussian blobs	SVC	80,3%	8	6	73,4%	100,0%	2,0%	2,8%
	LR	80,2%	8	6	73,1%	100,0%	1,2%	1,2%
	RF	78,6%	9	6	69,9%	100,0%	2,3%	1,5%
	DT	76,9%	7	6	70,1%	98,5%	2,8%	2,8%
	KNN	75,6%	8	6	67,7%	100,0%	3,5%	2,6%

set 1 and test set 2, separately. This tree is evaluated by comparing the accuracy scores of the corresponding clusters of the test sets using Mean Absolute Error (MAE), as described in Algorithm 2. This shows whether PERFEX is able to generalize the accuracy estimates to an unseen dataset.

Table 1 shows both the performance of the base classifiers and the corresponding PERFEX tree based on accuracy (abbreviated as 'acc' in the table columns). The classification models have a diverse accuracy, ranging from 51% to 95%. For PERFEX the table shows the amount of leaves (L), the depth of the tree (D), the minimum and maximum accuracies among the leaves, the MAE, and the STD of the Absolute Error (STD AE). PERFEX is able to separate datapoints with high and low accuracy, with the lowest difference of 9.3% (Car

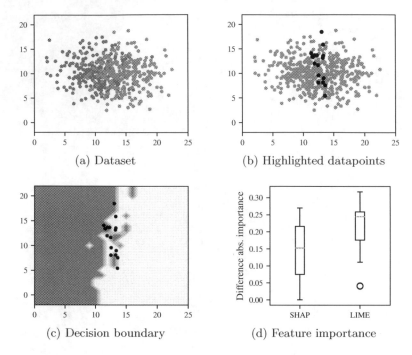

(a) Dataset

(b) Highlighted datapoints

(c) Decision boundary

(d) Feature importance

Fig. 6. Results of experiment with SHAP and LIME, with feature x^0 horizontal and feature x^1 vertical

RF) and the highest of 78.2% (Contraceptives SVC). For the gaussian blobs, we see clusters with perfect or almost perfect scores, as expected. The MAE is generally low, ranging from 1.1% to 9.5%. We also see a pattern in which classification models with high accuracy result in lower MAE. The supplement contains results for other metrics $\mathcal{M}$, and more details on the datasets and our code[1]

5.3   Limitations of SHAP and LIME

SHAP and LIME were introduced as methods to explain why a classifier makes a prediction, and to gain trust about the prediction. However, this can be dangerous in practice because SHAP and LIME provide explanations regardless of the classifier performance. We show that circumstances exist in which SHAP and LIME mark specific features as very important for a high-confidence prediction, while PERFEX clearly indicates that people should not rely on the classifier.

We consider a scenario in which a doctor uses a classifier to create predictions for patients that arrive, and SHAP and LIME are used to inform the doctor about the importance of features. The classifier is a random forest that was trained by

---

[1] The supplement and details on our code are available in a preliminary version of this article: https://arxiv.org/pdf/2212.06045.pdf.

a data scientist using the dataset shown in Fig. 6a. It can be seen that it may be difficult to predict in the area where both classes are overlapping. However, the doctor is not aware of this, and during model development the data scientist concluded based on accuracy (0.76) that the performance of the classifier is sufficient. Suppose that a patient arrives with features $x^0 = 10$ and $x^1 = 12$. It may happen that the classifier assigns a high score to one class, and SHAP and LIME highlight one feature as much more important than the other. This is not desirable, because the doctor gets the impression that the system can be trusted, while the classifier should not be used for such patients.

We now show that datapoints exist for which the described problem arises. According to PERFEX the cluster with the lowest accuracy (0.51) is defined by $11.2 \leq x^0 \leq 13.6$. In Fig. 6b we highlight datapoints that belong to this cluster, and for which two additional properties hold. First, the random forest assigns at least score 0.8 to the predicted class. Second, the prediction made by the random forest is not correct. For each highlighted datapoint we apply SHAP and LIME, which gives importance i_0 for feature x^0 and importance i_1 for feature x^1. Next, we compute $\max(|i_0|, |i_1|) - \min(|i_0|, |i_1|)$, which is high if the absolute importance of one feature is higher than the other. The results are summarized in Fig. 6d, in which we can see that both explanation methods give the impression that one feature is much more important than the other.

Suppose that the doctor would investigate one of the highlighted datapoints. It would get the impression that the model is very confident, because the output score is at least 0.8, while it is actually incorrect. Additionally, SHAP and LIME define that one feature is more important than the other. The prediction and explanation combined suggest that the model can be trusted. PERFEX is a crucial tool in this scenario because it would inform the doctor that classifier accuracy tends to be low for similar datapoints.

Finally, we investigate why SHAP and LIME indicate that one feature is more important than the other. The classifier decision boundary is shown in Fig. 6c. The highlighted datapoints are located close to the boundary. We can see that SHAP and LIME attempt to explain the behavior of the classifier locally, and due to the shape of the boundary both features have varying influence on the predictions. This also confirms our intuition that SHAP and LIME only explain local behaviour of the classifier.

6   Case Study: Modality Choices in Mobility

We present a case study in which we apply PERFEX in the context of mobility. Cities are facing a transition from conventional mobility concepts such as cars and bikes to so-called new mobility concepts such as ride sharing and e-scooters [22]. To support this transition, policy makers would like to predict and understand existing modality choices for trips in their city. They use a decision support system which uses a classifier to predict the modality that an individual chooses for a trip, based on trip properties as well as personal characteristics. The classes correspond to the modalities: car, car as a passenger, public transport, bike, walk. Each datapoint is a trip consisting of trip properties and characteristics of the traveler. The trip properties define the travel time for each modality, the cost for car and the cost for public transport. For the traveler a datapoint defines whether the traveler has a driving license, whether they own a car, and whether they are the main user of the car. Our dataset consists of 40266 trips from a travel survey conducted by Statistics Netherlands [7]. PERFEX is model-agnostic and applies to any base classifier, but for this specific case study we choose a random forest to illustrate the explanations. For prediction we train a random forest with 100 trees in the forest and at least 5 datapoints in each leaf. The accuracy of the final model is 0.91. We illustrate PERFEX based on two user questions.

User question 1. *When is the model not able to predict public transport trips as such?*

For a mobility researcher analyzing the use of public transport it is important to know whether the model is actually able to label public transport trips as such. This information can be provided to the researcher by applying our method with the recall of public transport as a performance metric.

```
There are 4163 trips for which the following
conditions hold:
  travel time public transport > 1800 seconds
  cost public transport > 0.74 euro
  travel time bike <= 1809 seconds
and for these trips the class recall is 0.07
```

User question 2. *When does the model assign high scores to both public transport and bike?*

Finally, we consider a mobility researcher that wants to investigate for which trips the model expects that both public transport and bike can be chosen. In order to answer this question we use a custom performance metric during tree construction. For each datapoint we take the minimum of the predicted scores for public transport and bike, and the metric $\mathcal{M}$ takes the mean of these values. The mean becomes high if the model assigns a high score to both classes. The explanation below intuitively makes sense: if walking takes a long time and if the traveler does not have a car, then both public transport and biking may be suitable choices.

```
There are 100 trips for which the following
conditions hold:
  cost public transport <= 21.78 euro
  traveler does not own a car
  travel time walk > 6069 seconds
and for these trips the model assigns on
average at least score 0.19 to both classes
```

7   Conclusions

We presented PERFEX, a model-agnostic method to create explanations about the performance of a given base classifier. Our method creates a clustering of a dataset based on a tree structure, such that subsets of data can be distinguished in which a given prediction metric is low or high. PERFEX can be used to e.g. explain under which circumstances predictions of a model are not accurate, which is highly relevant in the context of building trustworthy decision support systems. Our experiments have shown that PERFEX can be used to create explanations for various datasets and classification models, even if the base classifier hardly differentiates classes. It also shows that PERFEX is an important tool in scenarios in which SHAP and LIME are not sufficient to gain trust. PERFEX currently only uses subsets defined by AND-clauses, and therefore we aim to also investigate other types of subsets in future work [23].

Acknowledgement. We received funding from the TNO Appl.AI program, FATE flagship, the province of North Brabant in the Netherlands, the SmartwayZ.NL program, and the Human-Machine Teaming program at TNO (V2205 HMT). We also want to thank Taoufik Bakri and Bachtijar Ashari for preparing our mobility datasets.

References

1. Antorán, J., Bhatt, U., Adel, T., Weller, A., Hernández-Lobato, J.M.: Getting a CLUE: a method for explaining uncertainty estimates. In: Proceedings of the International Conference on Learning Representations (2021)
2. Arroyo, J., Corea, F., Jimenez-Diaz, G., Recio-Garcia, J.A.: Assessment of machine learning performance for decision support in venture capital investments. IEEE Access **7**, 124233–124243 (2019)
3. Bertsimas, D., Orfanoudaki, A., Wiberg, H.: Interpretable clustering: an optimization approach. Mach. Learn. **110**(1), 89–138 (2021)
4. Breiman, L.: Manual on setting up, using, and understanding random forests v3. 1. Statistics Department University of California Berkeley, CA, USA (2002)
5. Breiman, L., Friedman, J.H., Olshen, R.A., Stone, C.J.: Classification and Regression Trees. Routledge, Milton Park (1984)
6. Burkart, N., Huber, M.F.: A Survey on the explainability of supervised machine learning. J. Artif. Intell. Res. **70**, 245–317 (2021)
7. CBS: Onderweg in Nederland (ODiN) 2019 - Onderzoeksbeschrijving (2020)
8. Chen, T., Guestrin, C.: XGBoost: a scalable tree boosting system. In: Proceedings of the 22nd ACM SIGKDD International Conference on Knowledge Discovery and Data Mining, KDD 2016, pp. 785–794. ACM, New York (2016). https://doi.org/10.1145/2939672.2939785, http://doi.acm.org/10.1145/2939672.2939785
9. Cox, D.R.: The regression analysis of binary sequences. J. Roy. Stat. Soc.: Ser. B (Methodol.) **20**(2), 215–232 (1958)
10. Dong, G., Li, J.: Efficient mining of emerging patterns: discovering trends and differences. In: Proceedings of the ACM SIGKDD International Conference on Knowledge Discovery and Data Mining, pp. 43–52 (1999)
11. Dua, D., Graff, C.: UCI machine learning repository (2017). http://archive.ics.uci.edu/ml

12. EU High-Level Expert Group on AI: Ethics Guidelines for Trustworthy AI. European Commission (2019)
13. Guo, C., Pleiss, G., Sun, Y., Weinberger, K.Q.: On calibration of modern neural networks. In: Proceedings of the International Conference on Machine Learning, pp. 1321–1330. PMLR (2017)
14. Hall, P., Gill, N., Kurka, M., Phan, W.: Machine Learning Interpretability with H2O Driverless AI (2019)
15. Lundberg, S.M., Lee, S.I.: A unified approach to interpreting model predictions. In: Proceedings of the International Conference on Neural Information Processing Systems, pp. 4768–4777 (2017)
16. Muñoz, M.A., Villanova, L., Baatar, D., Smith-Miles, K.: Instance spaces for machine learning classification. Mach. Learn. **107**, 109–147 (2018)
17. Pan, W.: Approximate confidence intervals for one proportion and difference of two proportions. Comput. Stat. Data Anal. **40**(1), 143–157 (2002)
18. Papanastasopoulos, Z., et al.: Explainable AI for medical imaging: deep-learning CNN ensemble for classification of estrogen receptor status from breast MRI. In: Medical Imaging 2020: Computer-Aided Diagnosis, vol. 11314, pp. 228–235. International Society for Optics and Photonics, SPIE (2020)
19. Pimentel, J., Azevedo, P.J., Torgo, L.: Subgroup mining for performance analysis of regression models. Expert. Syst. **40**, e13118 (2023)
20. Ribeiro, M.T., Singh, S., Guestrin, C.: "Why should i trust you?" explaining the predictions of any classifier. In: Proceedings of the ACM SIGKDD International Conference on Knowledge Discovery and Data Mining, pp. 1135–1144 (2016)
21. Ribeiro, M.T., Singh, S., Guestrin, C.: Anchors: high-precision model-agnostic explanations. In: Proceedings of the AAAI Conference on Artificial Intelligence, pp. 1527–1535 (2018)
22. Schade, W., Krail, M., Kühn, A.: New mobility concepts: myth or emerging reality? In: Transport Research Arena (TRA) (2014)
23. Speakman, S., Somanchi, S., McFowland, E., III., Neill, D.B.: Penalized fast subset scanning. J. Comput. Graph. Stat. **25**(2), 382–404 (2016)
24. van der Waa, J., Schoonderwoerd, T., van Diggelen, J., Neerincx, M.: Interpretable confidence measures for decision support systems. Int. J. Hum Comput Stud. **144**, 102493 (2020)

The Duet of Representations and How Explanations Exacerbate It

Charles Wan[1]([✉]) [iD], Rodrigo Belo[2] [iD], Leid Zejnilović[2] [iD], and Susana Lavado[2] [iD]

[1] Rotterdam School of Management, Erasmus University,
Rotterdam, The Netherlands
wan@rsm.nl
[2] Nova School of Business and Economics, Universidade NOVA de Lisboa,
Lisbon, Portugal
{rodrigo.belo,leid.zejnilovic,susana.lavado}@novasbe.pt

Abstract. An algorithm effects a causal representation of relations between features and labels in the human's perception. Such a representation might conflict with the human's prior belief. Explanations can direct the human's attention to the conflicting feature and away from other relevant features. This leads to causal overattribution and may adversely affect the human's information processing. In a field experiment we implemented an XGBoost-trained model as a decision-making aid for counselors at a public employment service to predict candidates' risk of long-term unemployment. The treatment group of counselors was also provided with SHAP. The results show that the quality of the human's decision-making is worse when a feature on which the human holds a conflicting prior belief is displayed as part of the explanation.

Keywords: human-AI interaction · communication · causal representations · prior beliefs · biases · explanations · epistemic standpoint · salience · conflict · information processing

1 Introduction

Artificial intelligence is increasingly embedded in everyday business and consumer decision-making. For an array of reasons—technical, psychological, organizational, legal, and ethical—these decision-making systems are seldom fully automated. They require human input or, as components of larger socio-technical systems, interface to a significant degree with other components that are predominantly human-driven. Understanding how humans interact with algorithms *epistemically*, therefore, is of crucial importance whether the considerations are primarily economic and managerial or societal and ethical.

One principal way algorithms communicate with humans is via causal representations [35]. The algorithm effects a causal representation relating features and labels [4] in the human's perception. This is conveyed through the algorithm's observable output—typically predictions. For example, imagine a context where humans are using an algorithm as a decision-making aid to predict

L. Longo (Ed.): xAI 2023, CCIS 1902, pp. 181–197, 2023.
https://doi.org/10.1007/978-3-031-44067-0_10

the risk of loan default for different individuals. Upon observing the algorithm's output (predictions), the human might attribute to the algorithm a causal representation with the following semantics: longer job tenure leads to a lower risk of loan default.

Informed by history, humans form prior beliefs with respect to predictive tasks [22]. For example, in predicting loan default humans might associate lower income with a higher risk of loan default. This representation may conflict with the causal representation attributed to the algorithm. We call such a conflict the duet of representations. Because humans value simplicity, both their prior beliefs and the causal representations they attribute to algorithms are likely to be linear and sparse [21].

One way to facilitate communication between agents is through the provision of explanations. Explanatory methods can be viewed as tools that render the algorithm's causal representations human-interpretable. They extract simple representations via some model additive to the original algorithm. For example, LIME [26] use locally linear models to extract linear representations of relations between features and labels. SHAP [23] use cooperative games with features as players and extract representations in the form of sets of important features. Explanations direct human *attention* to sparse and cogent representations with clear semantics. They therefore increase the salience of any conflict with human priors. We present empirical evidences from a field experiment that explanations exacerbate the duet of representations and affect the quality of human decisions.

The results of our study suggest that fruitful and robust human-algorithm interaction requires a reconsideration of what constitutes "communication" between the algorithm and the human. Epistemically and communicatively, it is not sufficient to extract causal representations effected by algorithms. Effective communication depends on understanding the whys of a causal representation effected by the algorithm—the standpoint from which it is generated—as well as reciprocity, negotiability and the ability to refer to a shared objective reality. A set of desiderata for human-algorithm interaction is offered in Sect. 6.

2   Theory and Related Work

2.1   Human-Algorithm Collaboration

One literature stream on human-algorithm interaction adopts a managerial or engineering perspective and takes performance as the object of study. What matters is not the epistemic content of human-algorithm interaction but the effect it has on performance, evaluated against some metric. In this vein, [8] analyze how human-algorithm interaction can lead to the "cyborgization" of human thought. This results in the loss of unique human knowledge that can contribute to effective decision-making. [9] show that humans and AI working together can outperform AI alone when the latter delegates to the former. [30] study human deviations from algorithmic prescriptions in warehouse operations. They devise a machine learning algorithm to predict the deviations and show that incorporating them in logistics planning improves performance. Results from [18]'s field experiment show that the failure to adopt algorithmic recommendation can lead to a gap between the nominal and the actual performance of the algorithm. [11] develop a method that uses learning from bandit feedback to optimize human-AI collaboration.

The common thread behind this body of work is the conception of human-algorithm collaboration as a process that can and should be optimized in order to improve performance. To the extent that the process produces observable output in experiments, simulations, and real-world deployment, the data are used to understand decision quality and how it can be enhanced. This is an intellectual viewpoint that focuses on the "external"—measurements whose variances are related to observed variances in the structure of human-algorithm interaction. What is relatively less theorized is the epistemic content of this interaction. That is, beyond the fact that human knowledge and human actions can affect performance, how do humans process algorithmic predictions or recommendations *as information*?

2.2   Affective States

Another stream of literature focuses on internal psychological states induced by interaction with the algorithm. While the implicit goal might still be the improvement of a performance measure such as adoption, this body of work seeks to explain engagement psychologically or develop a normative framework for judging the conditions under which an internal psychological state is desirable. The literature has identified chiefly two affective states as important for human-algorithm interaction—trust and aversion. [5] introduces the concept of "algorithm aversion" and [6] shows that agency helps to attenuate it. [20] investigates how in medical diagnosis the opacity of AI diagnostics can lead to a loss of trust via an increase in epistemic uncertainty. [17] formalizes the notions of trust and trustworthiness in human-AI interaction and examine the criteria under which trust is normatively warranted. [14] reviews tangibility, transparency, reliability, and immediacy as factors that help to inculcate cognitive trust and anthropomorphism as a factor that helps to inculcate emotional trust in the AI. Lastly, [34] develops a multidimensional measure of trust in the context of robotics.

What underlies this body of work is an "internal" view that psychological states are determined by how humans interface with the algorithm and in turn drive aspects of human-algorithm interaction. Furthermore, there is a normative dimension in so far as certain psychological states such as trust are only warranted under specific conditions.

2.3   The Duet of Representations

While an affective state clearly disposes the human towards a particular set of actions vis-á-vis the algorithm, it lacks the adaptive rationality that allows agents to respond to changes. Feelings of trust and aversion, once developed, are relatively constant, at least on the timescale of human-algorithm interaction

[5,6,20]. They do not explain individual instances of interaction. Consider interpersonal dynamics. One might be inclined to accept suggestions from a trustworthy friend, with such inclination assumed to be relatively stable over time. There will nonetheless be variability in one's actions if one is not to surrender one's agency completely. If agency is the ability to perform a difference-making action (e.g. accept or reject a suggestion) as it pertains to one's goal, then affective states alone cannot account for the differences in actions. What enables difference-making actions and agency is representation. Humans build mental models of the world and also attribute mental models—via theory of mind—to other agents [19]. These models are often causal representations with interventionist[1] or counterfactual[2] semantics [25,36]. Human collaboration requires, in addition to a representation of the shared goal or task, representations of other agents—more precisely, representations of other agents' representations of the task [37]. When the human and the algorithm cooperate on a predictive task, it is the human's representation and the representation that she attributes to the algorithm that jointly enable the human to exercise her agency and perform difference-making actions.

Formally, the human constructs a representation R_h with respect to the predictive task from the space of human-interpretable representations $\mathcal{R}$. This representation could be a causal model with interventionist or counterfactual semantics [25,36]. It could also be a simpler heuristic [12,13]. For example, the representation for a binary classification task might be a sparse set of feature values that contributes to a negative prediction: $\{U = u_0\} \vee \{V = v_0\} \vee \{W = w_0\} \mapsto -1$. Since this representation defines the human's state of knowledge before using the algorithm, it can also be understood as the prior belief. The algorithm also effects a causal representation that relates features and labels. For example, a causal representation (that the human attributes to the algorithm) for a binary classification task might be that certain features values cause a positive prediction whereas others cause a negative prediction: $\{U = u_0\} \vee \{V = v_0\} \vee \{W = w_0\} \mapsto 1; \{X = x_1\} \vee \{Y = y_1\} \vee \{Z = z_1\} \mapsto -1$.

Given an instance from the input space $\mathcal{I}$, the representation the algorithm effects and the human prior belief interact to induce a human action from the action space $\mathcal{A}: \mathcal{I} \times \mathcal{R} \times \mathcal{R} \mapsto \mathcal{A}$. Using the binary classification example from above, consider the input instance $\{U = u_0\}$ for which the algorithm gives a positive prediction. The causal representation attributed to the algorithm $R_a : \{U = u_0\} \mapsto 1$ conflicts with the prior belief $R_h : \{U = u_0\} \mapsto -1$. This might prompt the human to reject or revise the algorithm's prediction. The set of possible actions as well as the exact process by which an action is selected will vary by the predictive task. Bayesian updating [1], for example, might be appropriate for continuous labels.

---

[1] Setting X to x_0, Y would be y_0.
[2] Had X been x_0, Y would have been y_0.

2.4 Explanations as Compressed Representations

[28] defines communication as "any process whereby decisional premises are transmitted from one member of an organization to another." Effective collaboration requires that the agents' states of knowledge be commensurate with the decision-making process. Sometimes routines and procedures encode past learning and constrain the agents to cooperate [3]. At other times explicit communication between the agents is needed to establish an adequate basis for action. With respect to predictive tasks where the human shares in decisional authority and responsibility, the latter means that the algorithm's representation would have to be communicated to the human. Explanations can render complex representations human-interpretable and help to close the gap in shared knowledge of decisional premises. Counterfactual and causal explanations [10,27] especially might be more aligned with human mental models.

In this capacity, explanations can be regarded as compressed representations: $R_a = \psi(h)$, where $|R_a| < |h|$. That is, an explanatory method $\psi(\cdot)$ extracts a compressed representation R_a of the original function h learned by the algorithm from the space of human-interpretable representations $\mathcal{R}$. The compressed representation R_a is more sparse than the underlying function h in some sense, e.g. the number of features. For example, LIME approximate the underlying model locally with sparse linear representations [26]. SHAP model features as players in a cooperative game and extract the most relevant ones as explanations [23]. Both have human-interpretable semantics—the former in the form of a sparse linear model, the latter in the form of a sparse set of relevant features.

A number of studies [15,16,24,29] have developed frameworks for evaluating the fidelity of explanatory methods with respect to the original models. Compressed representations generated by explanatory methods might also conflict with human priors. Explanations increase the *salience* of any conflict with human priors by commanding cognitive attention and directing it to sparse and cogent representations with clear semantics. The fact that an explanation is explicitly and concisely shown to the human—for SHAP it would be a set of relevant features—can make the disagreement more conspicuous. This exacerbates the conflict and can affect the quality of human decision-making.

[2] takes the view that explanations help human users to learn to meta-predict model predictions. While achieving an understanding of the model sufficient for meta-predicting its predictions is a normative good that can be useful for many tasks, this conceptualization underplays the fact that in many real-world settings learning per se is not the express goal—action is. It cannot be assumed that a human user would suspend her prior beliefs in making decisions as she might when the objective is explicitly learning. An explanation, therefore, is not simply a piece of information to be used for improving one's understanding. It represents a distinct epistemic standpoint which can conflict with that of the human user to an extent that is consequential for actions.

2.5 Psychological Salience and Information Processing

An explanation directs attention to a sparse representation with clear semantics. This increases the *salience* of features that form part of the explanation, especially if the human user has a strong prior belief on how they should be related to the label and this prior belief conflicts with what is implied by the explanation. For example, the human might hold the belief that $\{U = u_0\} \mapsto -1$ and an explanation that $\{U = u_0\}$ contributes to a positive prediction would put the conflict in the crosshairs.

Research in psychology has shown that salience can have a large impact on human judgment [31,33] and even affect causal attribution [7,32]. In the context of machine learning explanations, the focus of attention on a sparse set of features for which the human user holds strong prior beliefs can induce overconfidence [35]. By directing attention to features on which the human user has a conflicting prior belief, the explanation also directs attention *away* from other features which could have been part of the human user's information processing. This leads to causal overattribution. The conflict also exacts a cognitive cost. Both can affect the quality of human decision-making.

3 Field Experiment

3.1 Setting

The empirical context is a public employment service (PES) in the European Union. The PES provides services such as job referral and vocational training to unemployed individuals. When an individual becomes unemployed, she has to register at PES to receive financial support from the government. During the registration process, usually done in person, the registrant gives her data to a counselor who will review her case and support her in finding employment. According to an internal regulation, a counselor at the PES is obliged to assess the unemployed candidate's risk of LTU (long-term unemployment) upon registration, where LTU is defined as being involuntarily unemployed for a year or more.

We trained and implemented an XGBoost classification model that took as input candidate features and returned as output a raw probability score (risk score) and a risk assessment. Raw probability scores of LTU produced by XGBoost were converted into risk assessments of low, medium, and high, where high means a high probability of LTU. A risk assessment of high is equivalent to a positive prediction of LTU whereas a risk assessment of medium or low is equivalent to a negative prediction of LTU.

To explore the effect of explanations on human-algorithm interaction, we ran a field experiment from October 2019 to June 2020. The assignment of treatment was randomized at the level of job centers. Six centers were selected for the experiment, three for the treatment with 79 counselors and three for the control group with 77 counselors. Within a job center, candidates were assigned counselors available at the time of registration. After running the model, counselors were shown a risk assessment of low, medium or high and the raw probability score (risk score). The treatment group of counselors was additionally shown SHAP which comprised a set of six features. For a high (low) risk assessment, the top six features that increased (decreased) the probability of LTU were displayed; for a medium risk assessment, the top three features that, respectively, increased and decreased the probability of LTU were displayed. The counselors had the decisional authority and could either retain the algorithm's assessment or replace it with their own. They were also asked to rate their confidence in the final assessment on a Likert scale of 1 to 5. Data on the realized LTU outcomes of the candidates were collected in December 2021. Further information on the empirical setting can be found in Appendices A and B.

3.2 Research Ethics and Social Impact

Before launching the pilot, we obtained approval from the university's scientific council to run a study with human participants. All counselors taking part in the field experiment participated in a face-to-face information session. A presentation on the system they would be using was given and the counselors had the opportunity to ask the researchers questions. Counselors were also provided the researchers' e-mails and encouraged to get in touch with questions or concerns at any time. All the counselors agreed to participate in the study. After the end of the pilot, we conducted sessions presenting the results to representatives of all employment centers, which were recorded and made available to all PES (public employment service) counselors.

The researchers did not have access to any personal data that could potentially identify, directly or indirectly, the PES users. All the PES identification numbers were pseudonymized by the PES. All researchers with access to the data had training in personal data protection from the respective university's data protection office.

4 Methods

4.1 Identifying the Conflict

To extract a sparse causal representation effected by the algorithm in the human's perception, we regress the algorithm's LTU prediction r on candidate features using LASSO logistic regression with ten-fold cross-validation for the control group. The regression yields sparse linear models $p(r = i) = \mathbf{x}^\mathsf{T}\boldsymbol{\beta}_i$, where $p(r = i)$ is the probability of the prediction being i (positive or negative), $\boldsymbol{\beta}_i$ the set of coefficients associated with prediction i, and $\mathbf{x}$ the sparse set of features significant for driving variances in the algorithm's LTU predictions (Table 1).

Of the nine features, age, number of registrations, number of subsidy suspensions, and unemployment length are numeric variables. The rest are dummy variables derived from categorical variables. The representation attributed to the algorithm has the following possible semantics: if the unemployed candidate

Table 1. LASSO regression coefficients for the representation attributed to the algorithm

	LTU prediction	non-LTU	LTU
1	reason = contract ended	0.304	−0.304
2	reason = mutual agreement	−0.347	0.347
3	education = college	−0.127	0.127
4	social integration subsidy = true	−1.163	1.163
5	age	−0.133	0.133
6	number of registrations	0.037	−0.037
7	number of subsidy suspensions	0.012	−0.012
8	age group : > 56	−0.518	0.518
9	unemployment length	−0.023	0.023

left her previous employment by mutual agreement, is college-educated, receives social integration subsidy, is in the age group above 56, is older, has had a fewer number of registrations, has had a fewer number of subsidy suspensions, and/or has been unemployed for longer, then she is more likely to be (judged by the algorithm to be) in long-term unemployment. However, if the unemployed candidate left her previous employment because the contract ended, is younger, has had a greater number of registrations, has had a greater number of subsidy suspensions, and/or has been unemployed for shorter, then she is less likely to be (judged by the algorithm to be) in long-term unemployment.

R_a :

{reason = mutual agreement} ∨ {education = college}∨

{social integration subsidy = true} ∨ {age group :> 56} ∨ {age +}∨

{number of registrations -} ∨ {number of subsidy suspensions -}∨

{unemployment length +} ↦ LTU;

{reason = contract ended} ∨ {age -} ∨ {number of registrations +}∨

{number of subsidy suspensions +} ∨ {unemployment length -} ↦ non-LTU.

The counselor either retains or adjusts the algorithm's risk assessment. We construct a variable a, with actions $a = -1$ (adjusting the algorithm's risk assessment downward), $a = 0$ (retaining the algorithm's risk assessment as it is), and $a = 1$ (adjusting the algorithm's risk assessment upward). To identify features where the counselor have a strong prior belief, we regress a on candidate features using LASSO multinomial regression with ten-fold cross-validation for the control group. This yields sparse linear models $p(a = j) = \mathbf{w}^\mathsf{T}\boldsymbol{\alpha}_j$, where $p(a = j)$ is the probability of action j, $\boldsymbol{\alpha}_j$ the set of coefficients associated with action j, and $\mathbf{w}$ the sparse set of features likely, ceteris paribus, to induce the counselors to take a particular action. The regression is run over the counselors as an aggregate so the prior belief is assumed to be held collectively. Both the sparsity and the linearity dovetail with the inductive bias for human mental models, which tend to be sparse and linear [21] (Table 2)

Table 2. LASSO regression coefficients for the human prior belief

	action	down	same	up
1	reason = was student	0.099	−0.061	−0.037
2	nationality = non-EU/EEA	−0.007	−0.027	0.034
3	education = college	0.464	−0.075	−0.389
4	age	−0.001	0.004	−0.004
5	desired job = scientific research	0.012	−0.005	−0.008
6	personal employment plan = true	0.196	−0.131	−0.065
7	prior personal employment plan = true	−0.022	0.034	−0.012
8	number of interventions in job training	0.061	−0.034	−0.027
9	was LTU = true	0.052	0.064	−0.116

Except for age and number of interventions in job training, which are numeric variables, all are dummy variables derived from categorical variables. The human prior belief has the following semantics: if the unemployed candidate left her previous employment because she was a student, is college-educated, desires to find a job in scientific research, has a personal employment plan, and/or has had a greater number of interventions in job training, then she is less likely to be in long-term unemployment. However, if the candidate does not have EU/EEA nationality and/or has had a fewer number of interventions in job training, then she is more likely to be in long-term unemployment. The features age, prior personal employment plan = true, and was LTU = true have positive coefficients for $a = 0$ (retaining the algorithm's prediction). Thus there is not any strongly conflicting prior belief associated with them, although was LTU = true is slightly ambiguous as it also has a positive coefficient for downward adjustment.

R_h :
{reason = was student} ∨ {education = college}∨
{desired job = scientific research} ∨ {personal employment plan = true}∨
{number of interventions in job training + } ↦ non-LTU;
{nationality = non-EU/EEA}∨
{number of interventions in job training -} ↦ LTU.

Comparing R_a and R_h, we identify college education as the feature where the human prior belief conflicts with the causal representation effected by the algorithm as a statistical regularity. Whereas the algorithm effects a sparse causal representation college education to a higher risk of long-term unemployment, the human prior belief seems to be of the opposite view—that college education should lead to a lower risk of long-term unemployment.

4.2 Identifying the Effects of Explanations on Decision Quality and Confidence

We first partition the experimental data into instances for which the algorithm gives a positive prediction of LTU (a risk assessment of high) and instances for which the algorithm gives a negative prediction of LTU (a risk assessment of medium or low). This is done for two reasons. Firstly, a conflict is specified only for a given algorithmic prediction. Secondly, the covariates and dependent variables in our regressions have different distributions for the two subsets of observations.

We construct a dummy variable Conflict to indicate the presence or absence of features where R_a and R_h conflict with each other in the explanation (shown to the treatment but not the control group). We estimate the following equation as our first model using logistic regression:

$$\text{Decision Quality} = \gamma_0 + \gamma_1 \text{Exposed} + \gamma_2 \text{Conflict} + \gamma_3 \text{Exposed} \times \text{Conflict} + \gamma_4 \text{Risk Score} + \text{time fixed effects} + \varepsilon. \tag{1}$$

where Decision Quality is the accuracy of the final assessment and Exposed indicates treatment status. We use Risk Score, which is native to XGBoost, as a control variable that stratifies the data instances into bins of predictions of equal difficulty. The sign and statistical significance of γ_3 tell us whether showing features on which the counselors hold a conflicting prior belief as part of the explanation affects the decision quality.

A second model, similarly estimated using logistic regression, explores the heterogeneity of the mechanism by adding Adjustment as an interaction variable, where Adjustment is a dummy variable indicating whether the counselor has adjusted the algorithm's LTU prediction:

$$\text{Decision Quality} = \delta_0 + \delta_1 \text{Exposed} + \delta_2 \text{Conflict} + \delta_3 \text{Adjustment} + \delta_4 \text{Exposed} \times \text{Conflict} + \delta_5 \text{Exposed} \times \text{Adjustment} + \delta_6 \text{Conflict} \times \text{Adjustment} + \delta_7 \text{Exposed} \times \text{Conflict} \times \text{Adjustment} + \delta_8 \text{Risk Score} + \text{time fixed effects} + \eta. \tag{2}$$

The sign and statistical significance of δ_4 (δ_7) tell us whether showing features on which the counselors hold a conflicting prior belief as part of the explanation affects the decision quality, when the counselor retains (adjusts) the algorithm's prediction.

In a third model we examine the impact of explanations on counselors' confidence in the final assessment using linear regression:

$$\text{Confidence} = \zeta_0 + \zeta_1 \text{Exposed} + \zeta_2 \text{Conflict} + \zeta_3 \text{Adjustment}$$
$$+ \zeta_4 \text{Exposed} \times \text{Conflict} + \zeta_5 \text{Exposed} \times \text{Adjustment}$$
$$+ \zeta_6 \text{Conflict} \times \text{Adjustment} + \zeta_7 \text{Exposed} \times \text{Conflict} \times \text{Adjustment}$$
$$+ \zeta_8 \text{Risk Score} + \text{time fixed effects} + \xi. \tag{3}$$

The sign and statistical significance of ζ_4 (ζ_7) tell us whether showing features on which the counselors hold a conflicting prior belief as part of the explanation increases or decreases confidence, when the counselor retains (adjusts) the algorithm's prediction.

Models 1 and 2 are estimated as linear probability models and model 3 is estimated as a linear regression model.

5 Results

For model 1, Conflict is equal to 1 when college education is displayed as part of the explanation (or would have been displayed to the control group as part of the explanation had their treatment condition been different). Only the subset of instances for which the algorithm gives a positive prediction of LTU is included. The regression results show that a positive prediction with a higher Risk Score is more likely to be correct. The coefficient for Exposed × Conflict is negative and statistically significant. This means that displaying college education as part of the explanation degrades the quality of decision-making (Table 3).

Regression results for model 2 show that there is heterogeneity in the effects of explanations on decision quality with the larger part of the decrease coming from when counselors adjust the algorithm's positive prediction of LTU, as indicated by the negative and statistically significant coefficient for Exposed × Conflict × Adjustment.

Finally, regression results for model 3 show that displaying college education as part of the explanation has polarizing effects on confidence. It reduces confusion and increases confidence when counselors retain the algorithm's prediction, as indicated by the positive and statistically significant coefficient for Exposed × Conflict. On the other hand it draws attention to the conflict and decreases confidence when counselors adjust the algorithm's prediction, as indicated by the negative and statistically significant coefficient for Exposed × Conflict × Adjustment.

6 Discussion

Conflict between epistemic standpoints defines the kind of rationality that enables actions. If there is no *epistemic conflict*, agency—the ability to perform a difference-making action as it pertains to one's goal—would not be realized.

In our field experiment, the conflict between the human's prior belief that college education is negatively associated with long-term unemployment and the obverse representation attributed to the algorithm leads to actions that worsen

Table 3. Regression results

	Dependent variable:		
	Decision Quality	Decision Quality	Confidence
	LPM	LPM	Linear
	(1)	(2)	(3)
Exposed	−0.035*	−0.024	-0.006
	(0.015)	(0.016)	(0.018)
Exposed × Conflict	−0.104***	−0.049	0.171***
	(0.030)	(0.038)	(0.041)
Exposed × Conflict × Adjustment		−0.166**	−0.331***
		(0.058)	(0.063)
Conflict	0.031	−0.009	−0.100**
	(0.023)	(0.028)	(0.031)
Adjustment		−0.433***	−0.191***
		(0.024)	(0.027)
Exposed × Adjustment		0.047	0.108**
		(0.031)	(0.034)
Conflict × Adjustment		0.277***	0.349***
		(0.044)	(0.048)
Risk Score	0.834***	0.460***	0.164
	(0.085)	(0.081)	(0.089)
2020Q1	0.084***	0.082***	−0.030
	(0.016)	(0.015)	(0.016)
2020Q2	0.076***	0.084***	−0.199***
	(0.016)	(0.015)	(0.017)
Observations	5,728	5,728	5,728
R^2	0.029	0.1446	0.048
Adjusted R^2	0.028	0.1431	0.046

Note: *$p<0.05$; **$p<0.01$; ***$p<0.001$

the quality of decision-making for the time period during which the pilot was run. An alternative scenario, however, can be conceived where the human's prior beliefs encode useful information about the world that the algorithm is not privy to. In such a scenario, epistemic conflict can improve the quality of decision-making. Nevertheless it is not possible for an organization to determine ex-ante whether epistemic conflict would degrade or enhance the quality of decision-making.

Explanations perform an epistemic or communicative function by rendering complex representations human-interpretable. This however does not resolve the conflict of representations and may in fact—because explanations direct attention to cogent representations with explicit semantics—exacerbate it. As can be seen with positive predictions of LTU in our field experiment, showing college education as part of the explanation degrades the quality of decision-making.

Bare communication of representations, therefore, is not sufficient. Such communication is oddly solipsistic in that each representation is committed to its own epistemic standpoint. What should drive human-algorithm interaction is not the mere fact of epistemic conflict but its *whys*, just as human beings do not just insist on their differences but act to understand and bridge them. A more extensive communicative rationality is needed to enable actions that would improve the quality of decision-making.

We believe there are four desiderata for such communicative rationality. The first desideratum is *understanding*. The human should understand the algorithm's epistemic standpoint. In our empirical context, this means being imparted information about model training as well as possible reasons for certain representations (e.g. *why* college education is associated with higher risk of long-term unemployment). The second desideratum is *reciprocity*. Human-AI interaction tends to be unidirectional. Increasing the algorithm's understanding of the human's epistemic standpoint and prior beliefs can improve communication. The third desideratum is *negotiability*. Reciprocal understanding facilitates negotiation where arguments can be developed, evidences arrayed, biases identified, and confidences gauged. The last desideratum is a *shared reality*. In our empirical context, the counselors do not receive feedback on the accuracy of their judgment. Convergence to a shared reality is possible if the counselors are made aware of where each of the two parties has erred.

A   Empirical Setting

(See Table 4).

Table 4. Treatment assignment to job centers

job center	pre-pilot		pilot		treatment
	registrations	appointments/mo.	registrations	appointments/mo.	
1	11958	213	13139	169	0
2	9406	191	10263	160	1
3	3396	99	3743	72	0
4	5717	110	6022	88	1
5	3889	78	4379	69	0
6	7016	135	7336	100	1

B   User Interface

(See Figs. 1 and 2)

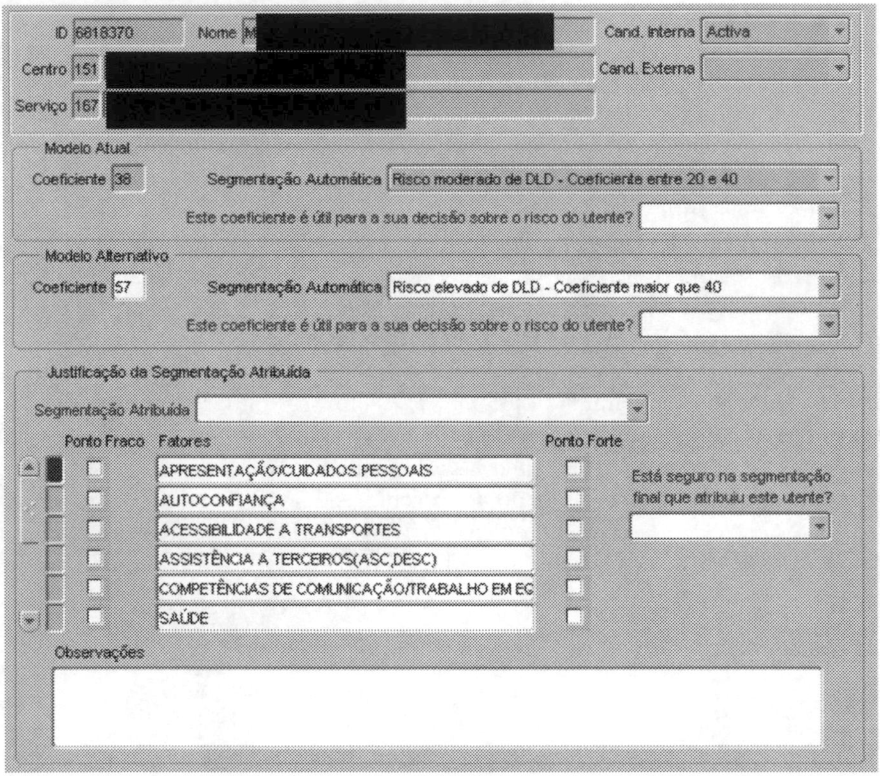

Fig. 1. User Interface for the Control Group. In the "Modelo Atual" panel the risk score and the risk assessment are shown. In the "Justificação da Segemntação Atribuída" panel the counselor has to select her own risk assessment on the top and her confidence level on the right.

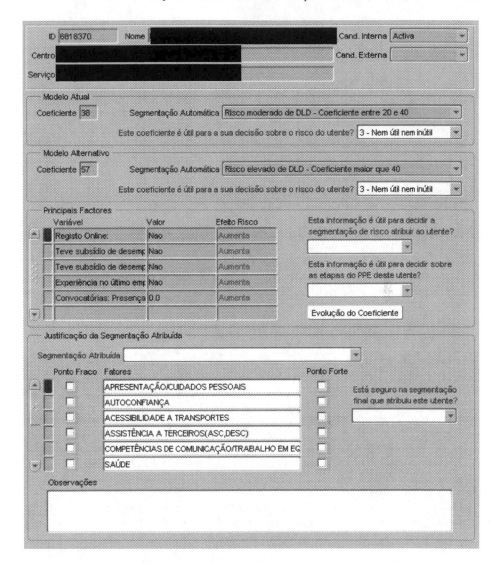

Fig. 2. User Interface for the Treatment Group. SHAP are shown in the "Principais Factores" panel with their respective effect on the risk of LTU.

References

1. Bundorf, K., Polyakova, M., Tai-Seale, M.: How do humans interact with algorithms? experimental evidence from health insurance. Technical report, National Bureau of Economic Research (2019)
2. Colin, J., Fel, T., Cadène, R., Serre, T.: What i cannot predict, i do not understand: a human-centered evaluation framework for explainability methods. Adv. Neural. Inf. Process. Syst. **35**, 2832–2845 (2022)

3. Cyert, R.M., March, J.G., et al.: A Behavioral Theory of the Firm, vol. 2. Englewood Cliffs, NJ (1963)
4. DeLanda, M.: Materialist Phenomenology: A Philosophy of Perception. Bloomsbury Publishing (2021)
5. Dietvorst, B.J., Simmons, J.P., Massey, C.: Algorithm aversion: people erroneously avoid algorithms after seeing them err. J. Exp. Psychol. Gen. **144**(1), 114 (2015)
6. Dietvorst, B.J., Simmons, J.P., Massey, C.: Overcoming algorithm aversion: people will use imperfect algorithms if they can (even slightly) modify them. Manage. Sci. **64**(3), 1155–1170 (2018)
7. Fiske, S.T., Kenny, D.A., Taylor, S.E.: Structural models for the mediation of salience effects on attribution. J. Exp. Soc. Psychol. **18**(2), 105–127 (1982)
8. Fügener, A., Grahl, J., Gupta, A., Ketter, W.: Will humans-in-the-loop become borgs? merits and pitfalls of working with AI. Manage. Inf. Syst. Q. (MISQ)-Vol **45** (2021)
9. Fügener, A., Grahl, J., Gupta, A., Ketter, W.: Cognitive challenges in human-artificial intelligence collaboration: investigating the path toward productive delegation. Inf. Syst. Res. **33**(2), 678–696 (2022)
10. Galhotra, S., Pradhan, R., Salimi, B.: Explaining black-box algorithms using probabilistic contrastive counterfactuals. In: Proceedings of the 2021 International Conference on Management of Data, pp. 577–590 (2021)
11. Gao, R., Saar-Tsechansky, M., De-Arteaga, M., Han, L., Lee, M.K., Lease, M.: Human-AI collaboration with bandit feedback. arXiv preprint arXiv:2105.10614 (2021)
12. Gigerenzer, G., Goldstein, D.G.: Reasoning the fast and frugal way: models of bounded rationality. Psychol. Rev. **103**(4), 650 (1996)
13. Gigerenzer, G., Todd, P., Group, A.: Simple heuristics that make us smart (1999)
14. Glikson, E., Woolley, A.W.: Human trust in artificial intelligence: review of empirical research. Acad. Manag. Ann. **14**(2), 627–660 (2020)
15. Guidotti, R.: Evaluating local explanation methods on ground truth. Artif. Intell. **291**, 103428 (2021)
16. Han, T., Srinivas, S., Lakkaraju, H.: Which explanation should i choose? a function approximation perspective to characterizing post hoc explanations. arXiv preprint arXiv:2206.01254 (2022)
17. Jacovi, A., Marasović, A., Miller, T., Goldberg, Y.: Formalizing trust in artificial intelligence: prerequisites, causes and goals of human trust in AI. In: Proceedings of the 2021 ACM Conference on Fairness, Accountability, and Transparency, pp. 624–635 (2021)
18. Kawaguchi, K.: When will workers follow an algorithm? a field experiment with a retail business. Manage. Sci. **67**(3), 1670–1695 (2021)
19. Lagnado, D.A.: Explaining the Evidence: How the Mind Investigates the World. Cambridge University Press, Cambridge (2021). https://doi.org/10.1017/9780511794520
20. Lebovitz, S., Lifshitz-Assaf, H., Levina, N.: To engage or not to engage with AI for critical judgments: how professionals deal with opacity when using AI for medical diagnosis. Organ. Sci. **33**(1), 126–148 (2022)
21. Lombrozo, T.: Simplicity and probability in causal explanation. Cogn. Psychol. **55**(3), 232–257 (2007)
22. Lu, H., Yuille, A.L., Liljeholm, M., Cheng, P.W., Holyoak, K.J.: Bayesian generic priors for causal learning. Psychol. Rev. **115**(4), 955 (2008)
23. Lundberg, S.M., Lee, S.I.: A unified approach to interpreting model predictions. In: Advances in Neural Information Processing Systems, pp. 4765–4774 (2017)

24. Nauta, M., et al.: From anecdotal evidence to quantitative evaluation methods: A systematic review on evaluating explainable ai. arXiv preprint arXiv:2201.08164 (2022)
25. Pearl, J., Mackenzie, D.: The Book of Why: The New Science of Cause and Effect. Basic books (2018)
26. Ribeiro, M.T., Singh, S., Guestrin, C.: " why should i trust you?" explaining the predictions of any classifier. In: Proceedings of the 22nd ACM SIGKDD international conference on knowledge discovery and data mining. pp. 1135–1144 (2016)
27. Ribeiro, M.T., Singh, S., Guestrin, C.: "Why should i trust you?" explaining the predictions of any classifier. In: Proceedings of the 22nd ACM SIGKDD International Conference on Knowledge Discovery and Data Mining, pp. 1135–1144 (2016)
28. Simon, H.A.: Administrative Behavior. Simon and Schuster, New York (2013)
29. Slack, D.Z., Hilgard, S., Singh, S., Lakkaraju, H.: Reliable post hoc explanations: modeling uncertainty in explainability. In: Beygelzimer, A., Dauphin, Y., Liang, P., Vaughan, J.W. (eds.) Advances in Neural Information Processing Systems (2021). https://openreview.net/forum?id=rqfq0CYIekd
30. Sun, J., Zhang, D.J., Hu, H., Van Mieghem, J.A.: Predicting human discretion to adjust algorithmic prescription: a large-scale field experiment in warehouse operations. Manage. Sci. **68**(2), 846–865 (2022)
31. Taylor, S.E., Crocker, J., Fiske, S.T., Sprinzen, M., Winkler, J.D.: The generalizability of salience effects. J. Pers. Soc. Psychol. **37**(3), 357 (1979)
32. Taylor, S.E., Fiske, S.T.: Point of view and perceptions of causality. J. Pers. Soc. Psychol. **32**(3), 439 (1975)
33. Taylor, S.E., Fiske, S.T.: Salience, attention, and attribution: top of the head phenomena. In: Advances in Experimental Social Psychology, vol. 11, pp. 249–288. Elsevier (1978)
34. Ullman, D., Malle, B.F.: What does it mean to trust a robot? steps toward a multi-dimensional measure of trust. In: Companion of the 2018 ACM/IEEE International Conference on Human-Robot Interaction, pp. 263–264 (2018)
35. Wan, C., Belo, R., Zejnilovic, L.: Explainability's gain is optimality's loss? how explanations bias decision-making. In: Proceedings of the 2022 AAAI/ACM Conference on AI, Ethics, and Society, pp. 778–787 (2022)
36. Woodward, J.: Causation with A Human Face: Normative Theory and Descriptive Psychology. Oxford University Press, Oxford (2021)
37. Xiang, Y., Vélez, N., Gershman, S.J.: Collaborative decision making is grounded in representations of other people's competence and effort (2022)

Closing the Loop: Testing ChatGPT to Generate Model Explanations to Improve Human Labelling of Sponsored Content on Social Media

Thales Bertaglia[1,3]([✉]) [iD], Stefan Huber[1,2,3], Catalina Goanta[2] [iD],
Gerasimos Spanakis[1] [iD], and Adriana Iamnitchi[1] [iD]

[1] Maastricht University, Maastricht, The Netherlands
t.costabertaglia@maastrichtuniversity.nl
[2] Utrecht University, Utrecht, The Netherlands
[3] Studio Europa, Maastricht, The Netherlands

Abstract. Regulatory bodies worldwide are intensifying their efforts to ensure transparency in influencer marketing on social media through instruments like the Unfair Commercial Practices Directive (UCPD) in the European Union, or Section 5 of the Federal Trade Commission Act. Yet enforcing these obligations has proven to be highly problematic due to the sheer scale of the influencer market. The task of automatically detecting sponsored content aims to enable the monitoring and enforcement of such regulations at scale. Current research in this field primarily frames this problem as a machine learning task, focusing on developing models that achieve high classification performance in detecting ads. These machine learning tasks rely on human data annotation to provide ground truth information. However, agreement between annotators is often low, leading to inconsistent labels that hinder the reliability of models. To improve annotation accuracy and, thus, the detection of sponsored content, we propose using chatGPT to augment the annotation process with phrases identified as relevant features and brief explanations. Our experiments show that this approach consistently improves inter-annotator agreement and annotation accuracy. Additionally, our survey of user experience in the annotation task indicates that the explanations improve the annotators' confidence and streamline the process. Our proposed methods can ultimately lead to more transparency and alignment with regulatory requirements in sponsored content detection.

Keywords: sponsored content detection · human-AI collaboration · legal compliance · social media

1 Introduction

The rise of influencers, content creators monetising online content through native advertising, has drastically changed the landscape of advertising on social

© The Author(s), under exclusive license to Springer Nature Switzerland AG 2023
L. Longo (Ed.): xAI 2023, CCIS 1902, pp. 198–213, 2023.
https://doi.org/10.1007/978-3-031-44067-0_11

media [8,13]. This shift has increased concern about hidden advertising practices that might harm social media users. For decades, advertising rules have been applied to legacy media in such a way as to separate commercial communication from other types of content. The primary rationale behind rules relating to mandated disclosures has been that hidden advertising leads to consumer deception. Despite the increasing legal certainty that native advertising, such as influencer marketing, must be clearly disclosed, monitoring and enforcing compliance remains a significant challenge [25].

The task of automatically detecting sponsored content aims to enable the monitoring and enforcement of such regulations at scale. For instance, in the United Kingdom, the Competition and Markets Authority is one of the enforcement agencies tasked with monitoring influencer disclosures on social media, which is done using some automated techniques developed by their internal data unit[1]. In published scholarship, most existing methods frame the problem as a machine learning task, focusing on developing models with high classification performance. The success of these models depends on the quality and consistency of human-annotated data, which often suffer from low inter-annotator agreement, compromising the reliability and performance of the models [9,27]. Moreover, fully-automated approaches are insufficient for regulatory compliance, where human decision-makers are ultimately responsible for imposing fines or pursuing further investigations.

To bridge this gap, we propose a novel annotation framework that augments the annotation process with AI-generated explanations, which, to our knowledge, is the first attempt in this domain. These explanations, presented as text and tokens or phrases identified as relevant features, aim to improve annotation accuracy and inter-annotator agreement. Our experiments show that our proposed framework consistently increases agreement metrics and annotation accuracy, thus leading to higher data quality and more reliable and accurate models for detecting sponsored content. Critically, our work tackles the need for explainability in AI tools used for regulatory compliance, ensuring that human decision-makers can better understand and trust the outputs of these models. This is particularly important for market surveillance activities, which have not yet caught up with the transparency and accountability issues at the core of discussions around individual surveillance [19].

2   Related Work

Sponsored content detection has primarily been studied as a text classification problem. Works in this field generally train models in a semi-supervised setting, using posts disclosed as ads with specific hashtags as weak labels. Generally, there is a lack of focus on evaluating model performance with labelled data. Most works collect their own datasets and do not describe whether (and how) data is annotated. Since social media platforms typically do not allow data sharing, there are no standardised datasets for evaluating the task; thus, comparing results is

---

[1] https://www.gov.uk/cma-cases/social-media-endorsements.

challenging. Furthermore, the absence of labelled data for evaluation affects the reliability of results, as models are often not tested on undisclosed ads.

From a technical perspective, previous studies have employed traditional machine learning models with basic text features [7,29], neural networks with text embeddings [32], and multimodal deep learning architectures combining text, image, and network features [16,17]. In this paper we experiment with some of these models in addition to chatGPT and GPT-4 for classification. Although peer-reviewed research is limited due to chatGPT's recent release, some technical reports have found chatGPT to achieve state-of-the-art performance in several text classification tasks [12,23,30].

Interdisciplinary research combining computational methods with fields such as communication and media studies and law has focused on identifying influencers, describing their characteristics, and mapping the prevalence of their disclosures [2,4,21]. In the context of using explanations to improve data labelling or decision-making, research has explored AI-human collaboration and investigated the optimal integration of explanations for human interaction [6,18,22,28]. To the best of our knowledge, our paper is the first to propose using AI-generated explanations to improve the detection of sponsored content, bridging the gap between explainable AI and regulatory compliance in the context of sponsored content on social media.

3   Experimental Setup

This section describes the dataset we use, how we selected the model for sponsored content detection, generated explanations to augment the annotation process, and designed the annotation task and the user-experience survey.

3.1   Data Collection

We collected and curated our own dataset of Instagram posts for this study. We manually selected 100 influencers based in the United States using the influencer discovery platform Heepsy[2]. We selected 50 micro-influencers (between $100k$ and $600k$ followers) and 50 mega-influencers (over $600k$ followers). Then, we collected all available data and metadata from all posts for each account using CrowdTangle[3], the Meta platform that provides access to social media data for (among others) academic purposes. Our dataset includes $294.6k$ posts, 66.1% from mega-influencers and 33.9% from micro-influencers. CrowdTangle's Terms of Service do not allow (re)sharing datasets that include user-generated content; thus, we cannot share the full dataset. However, the list of the *ids* of accounts and posts is publicly available on https://github.com/thalesbertaglia/chatgpt-explanations-sponsored-content/

---

[2] https://heepsy.com.
[3] https://www.crowdtangle.com/.

3.2   Detecting Sponsored Content

In the first step of our experimental setup, we aim to select the most suitable sponsored content classifier for generating explanations. We evaluate three previously proposed models: (1) a logistic regression classifier with term frequency inverse-document frequency (TF-IDF) features, analogous to the approach used by [7,29], (2) a pre-trained BERT model fine-tuned for our task, comparable to [17,32], and (3) OpenAI's chatGPT (GPT-3.5-turbo as of March 2022), which achieves state-of-the-art results in various text classification tasks [12,23]. We generate GPT predictions using OpenAI's API.

To evaluate the models' performance, we select a sample from our original dataset and split the data into training and test sets by year, using 2022 for testing and all prior posts for training. This division simulates a real-world scenario where a model is deployed and used to classify unseen data for regulatory compliance. By ensuring no temporal overlap between the sets, we prevent the model from learning features correlated with a specific period. Given the high imbalance in the data (only 1.72% of posts are disclosed as sponsored), we apply the random undersampling approach proposed by Zarei et al. (2020) [32] to balance the data. We include all disclosed posts (n) and randomly sample ($2 * n$) posts without disclosures as negative examples. We allocate 90% of the balanced data before 2022 to training and the remaining 10% to validation. We use all data in 2022 as the test set.

Additionally, we labelled a sample of the test set to evaluate the model's performance in detecting undisclosed ads. Four annotators labelled 1283 posts in total, with a sample of 50 posts labelled by all annotators for calculating agreement metrics. The inter-annotator agreement was 52% in absolute agreement and 53.37 in α, indicating moderate agreement. 654 posts were labelled as sponsored (50.97%) and 629 as non-sponsored (49.03%). 91.59% of the sponsored posts did not have disclosures – i.e., they were identified as undisclosed ads.

We employ a semi-supervised approach to train the models, treating disclosed sponsored posts as positive labels for the *sponsored* class. We consider *#ad*, *#advertisement*, *#spons*, and *#sponsored* as ad disclosures. We then remove disclosures from the posts to prevent models from learning a direct mapping between disclosure and sponsorship. We train the logistic regression model using TF-IDF features extracted from word-level n-grams from the captions (unigrams, bigrams, and trigrams). For the BERT-based model, we use the *bert-base-multilingual-uncased* pre-trained model weights from HuggingFace [31]. We fine-tuned the BERT-based model for three epochs using the default hyperparameters (specified in Devlin et al. (2019) [5]).

We apply various prompt-engineering techniques to enhance GPT's predictions. As we use the same methodology for generating explanations, we provide a detailed description in the following subsection. We evaluate all models using F1 for the positive and negative classes, Macro F1 (the simple average of both classes) and Accuracy in detecting undisclosed ads – a critical metric for determining the models' effectiveness in detecting sponsored posts without explicit disclosures, which is ultimately our goal. Table 1 presents the classification metrics for the three models, calculated based on the labelled test set.

Table 1. Performance of the different models on the labelled test set. Acc represents the models' accuracy in detecting undisclosed ads.

Model	Pos F1	Neg F1	Macro F1	Acc
Log Reg	45.33	66.50	55.92	28.71
BERT	29.30	68.84	49.07	10.85
GPT-3.5	76.09	63.93	70.01	88.98

GPT-3.5 outperforms the other models in Macro F1 and accuracy in detecting undisclosed ads. Logistic regression (Log Reg) and BERT achieve significantly low accuracy, suggesting their inability to identify undisclosed sponsored posts effectively. The difference in Macro F1 is smaller, highlighting that relying solely on this metric for evaluating models may not accurately reflect their actual performance. Therefore, having high-quality labelled data, including undisclosed ads, is crucial for proper evaluation.

BERT's inferior performance compared to Log Reg could be due to a few factors. Being pre-trained on longer texts, BERT might struggle to extract sufficient contextual information from short Instagram captions. In addition, Log Reg, when combined with TF-IDF features, effectively captures word-level n-grams that may be more effective at identifying sponsored content patterns. In contrast, BERT uses subword tokenisation, which could result in less efficient pattern recognition. Given GPT-3.5's superior performance, particularly in detecting undisclosed sponsored posts, we selected it as the model for generating explanations to augment the annotation task.

3.3   Generating Explanations with GPT

We investigated various prompts for all publicly accessible models from the GPT-3 series and GPT-4. We observed that even the smallest GPT-3 model, Ada (*text-ada-001*), performed well in sponsored content detection and identifying relevant words. Nevertheless, we noted significant performance improvements for larger models especially when employing chain-of-thought reasoning [30] and generating explanations – particularly for more ambiguous posts. Consequently, we focused on *GPT-3.5-turbo* (the default ChatGPT version as of March 2022) and GPT-4.

We found a conservative bias for both models, with a strong preference for predicting the *not sponsored* class or other negative labels over positive ones. This phenomenon appeared consistent across all *Davinci-* and *Curie*-based models, with the inverse being true for smaller *Babbage* and *Ada*-based models. We employed several prompt engineering techniques to mitigate this bias and calibrate the labels. First, we instructed the model to highlight relevant words and generate explanations before classifying a post. This chain-of-thought prompting approach, inspired by [30], significantly reduced bias and improved prediction interpretability. Second, we used few-shot learning to refine explanation calibration, address known failure modes, and further alleviate bias [3]. Third, we experimented with different label phrasings, such as "Likely (not) sponsored", to enhance the model's ability to make less confident predictions. Finally, we directly instructed the model to favour positive labels in cases of uncertainty, aiming to identify a higher proportion of undisclosed ads. The final prompt is available on the project's GitHub repository[4].

Upon qualitative evaluation, we found that GPT-4 outperformed GPT-3.5-turbo in explanation quality and classification accuracy, especially for ambiguous posts. However, for this study, we chose GPT-3.5-turbo (hereafter referred to as "GPT") due to its advantages in speed, cost, and public accessibility. Following this approach, we obtained the most important words in a post and generated explanations for why a post may or may not be sponsored to assist annotators. The following is an illustrative example of such an explanation; we omitted the actual brand name to ensure the post's anonymity:

```
Key indicators: '@BRAND', 'LTK'.
The post promotes a fashion brand and features a discount code,
indicating a partnership. Additionally, it features a @shop.LTK
link, a platform for paid partnerships.
```

3.4 Annotation Task

We conducted a user study to evaluate how explanations can help detect sponsored content. The study consisted of an annotation task in which participants labelled 200 Instagram posts from our dataset as *Sponsored* or *Non-Sponsored*. Our objective with the task was two-fold: i) Analyse explanations as a tool for improving annotation as a resource for ML tasks – i.e., to measure their impact on data quality, which, in turn, allows for the development of better models and evaluation methods. ii) Simulate regulatory compliance with sponsored content disclosure regulations – i.e., how a decision-maker would flag posts as sponsored.

We framed the annotation as a text classification task in which annotators had to determine whether an Instagram post was sponsored based on its caption. Generally, we followed the data annotation pipeline proposed by Hovy and Lavid (2010) [15]. We instructed annotators to consider a post as sponsored if the influencer who posted it was, directly or indirectly, promoting products or services for which they received any form of benefits in return. These benefits included direct financial compensation and non-monetary benefits, such as free products or services. Self-promotion was an exception: we considered posts promoting the influencer's content (e.g. YouTube channel or podcast) non-sponsored. However, posts advertising merchandise with their brand or directly selling other goods still fall under sponsored content. We explained these guidelines to each

---

[4] https://github.com/thalesbertaglia/chatgpt-explanations-sponsored-content/.

annotator and provided examples of sponsored and non-sponsored posts to help reinforce the definitions.

Eleven volunteer annotators with varying levels of expertise participated in the study. All were between 20 and 30 years old, active social media users, and familiar with influencer marketing practices on Instagram. Additionally, all annotators had or were working towards a high-education degree in a European university. Demographically, the participants came from various countries. We did not specifically collect country-level information, but at a continent level, participants were from Asia, Europe, and South America. While all participants were fluent in English, none were native speakers.

We split annotators into three groups according to their level of expertise in annotating sponsored content on social media. The first group, with three people, consisted of participants with no prior experience in data annotation. The second group included four participants who previously participated in annotation tasks but had no formal training. The third group, consisting of four legal experts, had specific legal expertise in social media advertisement regulations and had participated in annotations before. We further split the subgroups of annotators into two groups regarding annotation setup: one without explanations, in which annotators only had access to the captions, and one augmented with the generated explanations. One group of four annotators labelled the posts in both setups: with and without explanations. To summarise, our study includes three distinctive groups: novices with no prior annotation experience, intermediate annotators with previous experience but no formal training, and legal experts knowledgeable in social media regulations.

To select the 200 Instagram posts for our user study, we turned to a sample previously labelled by law students in another annotation task. Although the labels and definitions used in that task differed from ours, they provided a way to identify which posts were undisclosed ads, allowing us to include them in our study. We selected posts published between 2017 and 2020 by 66 different influencers based in the United States, with 62% being mega-influencers and 38% being micro-influencers. We also included 15% of posts with clear ad disclosures (such as the hashtag #ad) as an attention check to ensure annotators noticed the disclosures. Based on the labels from the previous annotations, we estimate that 65% (130) of the posts were likely sponsored, and 50% (100) were likely undisclosed ads.

We set up the study using the open-source annotation platform Doccano[5]. Each participant had a unique project, and although all annotators labelled the same 200 posts, the labels were not shared, and each participant only had access to their annotations. The annotation interface displayed the caption of the post and the two possible labels (Sponsored and Non-Sponsored) as buttons. After the post caption, we added the generated explanations with an explicit delimitation.

Accurately measuring inter-annotator agreement is crucial in data annotation tasks, as it allows us to estimate the annotated data's quality and the decision-making process's reliability. To assess inter-annotator agreement in our study,

---

[5] https://github.com/doccano/doccano.

we used three main metrics: Krippendorff's Alpha (α), absolute agreement, and accuracy in detecting disclosed posts. Krippendorff's Alpha measures the degree of agreement among annotators, considering the level of agreement expected by chance alone [14,20]. The absolute agreement indicates the proportion of annotations where all annotators agreed on the same label. We also used accuracy in detecting disclosed posts as an attention check mechanism, as it measures annotators' ability to correctly identify posts with clear disclosures as sponsored. This metric is crucial because disclosures may not always be easily visible in posts [21]. We also analysed additional metrics in some experiments, which we will introduce when describing the specific experiments.

3.5 User-Experience Survey

After the annotation, we conducted a user-experience survey to gather feedback from annotators on their experience using the explanations to assist with their decision-making process. The survey consisted of seven questions, with five closed-ended and two open-ended questions. We describe all questions and the rating scale used below:

- "On a scale of 1 (not helpful) to 5 (extremely helpful), how helpful were the explanations in identifying undisclosed advertisement partnerships?"
- "How accurate, from 1 (extremely inaccurate) to 5 (extremely accurate), did you think the explanations were?"
- "How often, from 1 (0% of the time) to 5 (100% of the time), did you agree with the AI explanations?"
- "Did the AI explanations help you feel more confident in your decision-making (Yes/No)?"
- "What aspects of the AI explanations were most helpful for your decision-making process?" This was a multiple-choice question with five options: *Reasoning, Identifying specific words or phrases, Clear examples, Other (specify),* and *None.*
- "In what ways did the AI explanations improve your understanding of what constitutes an undisclosed advertisement partnership?" Open-ended.
- "How could the AI explanations be further improved to better support your decision-making process? Did you find anything noticeable you want us to know?" Open-ended.

The participants who received annotations augmented with explanations all completed the questionnaires, and we ensured their anonymity by not collecting any identifiable information. Additionally, we made it clear to the annotators that their responses would be entirely anonymous.

4   Experimental Results

This section presents the main findings from the annotation task and user-experience survey. Table 2 shows the metrics comparing the agreement between

annotators who labelled the posts with and without explanations. Seven participants were in the **No Explanations** group (one with *no experience*, four with
some experience, and two *legal experts*). The **With Explanations** group had
eight people (three with *no experience*, three with *some experience*, and two *legal
experts*) – one participant from the *no experience* group and three from *some
experience* labelled in both settings. In addition to the metrics presented in Subsect. 3.4, we also evaluate the proportion of posts with at most one disagreement
(*1-Disag*) and show the percentage of posts labelled as sponsored (*Sponsored*).
The last two rows present the absolute and relative (normalised) differences in
metrics between the groups. The relative differences in metrics indicate the proportional change (in percentage). Positive differences represent an increase in
agreement.

Table 2. Agreement metrics comparing annotations with and without explanations.

	α	Abs	1-Disag	Acc	Sponsored
No Explanations	54.98	46.50	69.50	90.62	54.64
With Explanations	63.58	54.50	75.00	93.75	59.81
Absolute Diff	8.61	8.00	5.50	3.12	5.17
Relative Diff	15.65	17.20	7.91	3.45	9.46

Using explanations to enhance the annotations resulted in a consistent
improvement across all inter-annotator agreement metrics. Specifically, there was
a 15.65% increase in α and a 17.20% increase in absolute agreement. However, the
final values were still relatively low, typical of annotations in complex decision-
making tasks [9,10,27]. Accuracy in detecting disclosed posts also improved by
3.45%, but the final result was not perfect, suggesting that annotators still fail to
identify all disclosure hashtags, even with explanations highlighting them. Additionally, the proportion of posts labelled as sponsored increased by 9.46%, indicating that explanations led annotators to identify more as sponsored. We also
analyse the agreement between all pairs of annotators to measure the variation
in agreement and ensure the reliability of the annotations. Table 3 summarises
the pairwise agreement metrics. The *Min* and *Max* columns represent the lowest
and highest agreement metric values among the annotator pairs, respectively,
and the ± column denotes the standard deviation.

The pairwise metrics reveal considerable variation in the agreement between
annotator pairs. For the *No Explanation* group, there was a substantial difference of 46.23 in α between the pair with the lowest and highest agreement, with
a standard deviation of 10.83. This difference indicates that some annotators
are significantly less reliable than others. However, the group *With Explanations* showed a consistent improvement, with less variation between pairs. The
standard deviation decreased by 14.98% for absolute agreement and 7.62% for
α, indicating more reliable annotations. Even the lowest-agreement pair showed

Table 3. Pairwise agreement comparing annotations with and without explanations.

	Min Abs	Max Abs	±	Min α	Max α	±
No Explanations	66.00	88.50	5.28	30.81	77.04	10.83
With Explanations	73.00	90.00	4.49	43.13	79.53	10.00
Absolute Diff	7.00	1.50	−0.79	12.31	2.48	−0.82
Relative Diff	10.61	1.69	−14.98	39.96	3.22	−7.62

significant improvement, with an increase of 10.61% for absolute agreement and 39.96% for α. These results suggest that using explanations to augment annotations led to a higher inter-annotator agreement overall, improved consistency between pairs, and even increased agreement among the least reliable annotators. To better understand the impact of augmenting the annotation with explanations, we also investigated how it affects different subgroups of annotators. We divided the subgroups into three categories: legal experts, non-experts, and annotators who labelled in both settings (with and without explanations) – this category does not include legal experts. Table 4 presents the agreement metrics for each category in both subgroups of annotators, as well as the relative difference between them. # indicates the number of participants within the subgroup. For clarity, we did not report the proportion of annotations with at most one disagreement because some subgroups contain a single pair of annotators.

Table 4. Agreement metrics for different subgroups of annotators, aggregated according to their expertise level.

	α	Abs	Acc	Sponsored	#
Legal Experts No Explanations	52.11	76.50	96.88	57.25	2
Legal Experts With Explanations	61.94	83.00	100.00	66.50	2
Relative Diff	18.86	8.50	3.23	16.16	–
Non-Experts No Explanations	62.04	62.50	93.75	53.60	5
Non-Experts With Explanations	64.89	59.50	93.75	57.58	6
Relative Diff	4.59	−4.80	0.00	7.43	–
Labelled Both No Explanations	66.74	70.00	96.88	53.12	4
Labelled Both With Explanations	73.15	74.50	100.00	54.50	4
Relative Diff	9.60	6.43	3.23	2.59	–

The annotations augmented with explanations showed consistent improvements in all subgroups, except for absolute agreement within the non-expert group. Legal experts had the most significant improvement in α (18.86%). Additionally, the proportion of posts labelled as sponsored increased significantly (16.16%), with the subgroup *Legal Experts With Explanations* having the highest value (66.5%). This subgroup and *Labelled Both With Explanations* achieved

100% accuracy in detecting disclosed sponsored posts. *Labelled Both* also had the highest α in both settings. It is important to note that higher agreement does not necessarily imply higher accuracy in correctly identifying sponsored posts. The metrics measure how much a subgroup of annotators agree on the definitions they are applying to label; they could be wrongly applying a consistent judgement. Therefore, we cannot reliably conclude which group had the best performance. Moreover, the high agreement within the subgroup *Labelled Both* could be influenced by the annotators labelling the same posts twice in both settings. Although we randomly shuffled the posts to reduce the likelihood of memorisation, repetition could still affect agreement. Nevertheless, the high proportion of sponsored content and absolute agreement for the annotation within *Legal Experts With Explanations* indicate that experts agree that there are more sponsored posts than non-experts tend to identify.

While explanations can improve the quality of annotations, they may also introduce bias by influencing annotators to rely on specific cues presented in the explanation; annotator bias is a common challenge in text annotation tasks [1,11]. To investigate potential bias introduced by explanations in our study, we examine whether annotators tended to use the same label predicted by GPT. Although we did not explicitly provide GPT's prediction as part of the explanation, the model's reasoning and highlighted words and phrases might imply the predicted label, leading to over-reliance on the model and decreasing the accuracy of annotations. Thus, it is essential to analyse the impact of GPT's predictions on annotator behaviour to ensure the reliability and fairness of the annotations. Specifically, we calculate two metrics – the distribution of posts labelled as sponsored and the majority agreement with GPT predictions – to compare the agreement between annotators who received explanations and those who did not. We use majority agreement instead of absolute to reduce the impact of low-agreement pairs and fairly compare all groups. If the agreement with GPT predictions increased in the group with explanations, it could indicate that annotators followed the model's predictions. We hypothesise that, for the *Labelled Both* group, an increase in agreement with GPT predictions proportionally more than the percentage of sponsored posts would suggest that annotators changed their judgements based on the model's cues. Table 5 summarises the results of this analysis.

The majority agreement with GPT predictions is consistently high across all subgroups, ranging from 77.5% to 92%. All subgroups that received explanations had an increase in agreement with GPT predictions compared to the corresponding No Explanations subgroup. Specifically, except for *Labelled Both*, all subgroups showed proportional increases in both metrics, indicating no clear bias for GPT predictions. However, the *Labelled Both* subgroup demonstrated a significant increase in agreement with GPT predictions compared to the proportion of sponsored posts, suggesting that the annotators changed their decision-making process after having access to explanations. While this result indicates a bias towards the model's predictions, more experiments are needed to determine its impact on data quality. Given the generally high accuracy of GPT

Table 5. Proportion of posts labelled as sponsored and majority agreement with GPT predictions across subgroups of annotators.

	Sponsored	Agreement
No Explanations	54.64	85.50
With Explanations	59.81	90.50
Relative Diff	9.46	5.85
Legal Experts No Explanations	57.25	77.50
Legal Experts With Explanations	66.50	92.00
Relative Diff	16.16	18.71
Non-Experts No Explanations	53.60	81.00
Non-Experts With Explanations	57.58	88.50
Relative Diff	7.43	9.26
Labelled Both No Explanations	53.12	78.50
Labelled Both With Explanations	54.50	87.00
Relative Diff	2.59	10.83

demonstrated in our classification experiments, relying on them could improve annotation accuracy.

On the other hand, the difference in agreement with the predictions between the *Legal Experts* subgroups adds uncertainty about the model's accuracy. The subgroup of legal experts with no explanations had the lowest agreement with GPT predictions; in contrast, those with explanations had the highest. The groups include different annotators, and *Legal Experts No Explanations* had low inter-annotator agreement; therefore, we cannot effectively measure the model's accuracy. Although we found evidence of explanations biasing the annotators, further research is needed to investigate how this result impacts data quality.

Finally, we conducted a user-experience survey to gather feedback from annotators on their experience using the explanations to assist with their annotation process. All the responses are available online on https://tinyurl.com/sponsored-annotation-survey. We ensured that the document preserves the anonymity of all parties involved in the study.

The survey results showed that 87.5% of annotators felt more confident in their decision-making with the help of explanations. Additionally, 62.5% rated the explanations highly helpful and accurate (4 out of 5). Only one participant rated them as unhelpful (2 out of 5). The average estimate of agreement with the explanations was close to the agreement with GPT predictions, with 62.5% of annotators estimating that they agreed with the explanations between 80% and 100% of the time. Notably, all annotators selected the words and phrases highlighted by the model explanations as a helpful feature, while only 37.5% selected the reasoning behind the predictions. This result indicates a preference for precise explanations. Comparable explanations could be generated from any classifier using local-explainability methods such as LIME [24]. This shows that the methodology proposed and evaluated in our study does not rely on GPT's capability of generating longer text-based explanations and could be reproduced with simpler models.

The open-ended questions revealed two clear trends among participants. First, most participants found the highlighted words and phrases helpful in identifying brands and context-relevant hashtags in the posts. Second, participants suggested that adding the likelihood of a post being sponsored as a feature would be a useful improvement to the explanations. Overall, these results indicate that participants had a positive experience with the explanations, found them helpful and accurate, and felt they improved their decision-making.

5   Summary

Our experiments show that inter-annotator agreement metrics consistently improve when augmenting the annotation process with explanations. We observed a 15.65% increase in α and a 17.20% increase in absolute agreement among the general population of annotators. The accuracy in detecting disclosed sponsored posts improved by 3.45%, and the proportion of posts labelled as sponsored increased by 9.46%. These findings indicate that explanations not only help annotators identify more sponsored content but also enhance the reliability of annotations and reduce variation between annotator pairs. Our user-experience survey shows that most annotators found the explanations helpful and accurate, increasing their trust in decision-making. Therefore, our proposed annotation framework could lead to higher-quality data labelling and improve decision-makers' experience in regulatory compliance contexts. We made the *ids* of posts in our dataset, along with all the labels annotated by annotators and the GPT predictions, publicly available[6], offering a valuable resource that could benefit research in the field.

Nevertheless, our study has some limitations. One potential issue is the bias introduced by explanations, as annotators may rely on specific cues presented in the explanation. While we found no clear bias for most subgroups, we note that the group that labelled posts in both settings showed a significant increase in agreement with GPT predictions compared to the proportion of sponsored posts. Another area for improvement is the small sample size of legal experts and the variation in agreement metrics among different subgroups, which may impact the generalisability of our results.

Future research should investigate the impact of explanations on annotator bias and data quality and explore open-source models with greater transparency, such as LLaMA [26], instead of OpenAI's GPT – which is a privately-owned model with limited information regarding its training data. Moreover, conducting experiments with larger and more diverse samples of annotators, including more legal experts, could shed light on the role of expertise in the annotation process. Expanding the study to other annotation tasks and domains would also provide

---

[6] https://github.com/thalesbertaglia/chatgpt-explanations-sponsored-content/.

insights into the generalisability of our findings, potentially benefiting a broader range of applications.

Despite these limitations, it is important to consider that digital enforcement and market monitoring by authorities such as consumer agencies will exponentially grow in the coming years. Thus, monitoring techniques must consider transparency and explainability to avoid accuracy issues when applying legal sanctions.

References

1. Al Kuwatly, H., Wich, M., Groh, G.: Identifying and measuring annotator bias based on annotators' demographic characteristics. In: Proceedings of the Fourth Workshop on Online Abuse and Harms, pp. 184–190. Association for Computational Linguistics (2020). https://doi.org/10.18653/v1/2020.alw-1.21. https://aclanthology.org/2020.alw-1.21

2. Arriagada, A., Ibáñez, F.: "You need at least one picture daily, if not, you're dead": content creators and platform evolution in the social media ecology. Soc. Media + Soc. **6**(3), 2056305120944624 (2020). https://doi.org/10.1177/2056305120944624

3. Brown, T., Mann, B., Ryder, N., Subbiah, M., et al.: Language models are few-shot learners. In: Advances in Neural Information Processing Systems, vol. 33, pp. 1877–1901 (2020)

4. Christin, A., Lewis, R.: The drama of metrics: status, spectacle, and resistance among YouTube drama creators. Soc. Media + Soc. **7**(1), 2056305121999660 (2021). https://doi.org/10.1177/2056305121999660

5. Devlin, J., Chang, M.W., Lee, K., Toutanova, K.: BERT: pre-training of deep bidirectional transformers for language understanding. In: Proceedings of the 2019 Conference of the North American Chapter of the Association for Computational Linguistics, pp. 4171–4186. Association for Computational Linguistics (2019). https://doi.org/10.18653/v1/N19-1423. https://aclanthology.org/N19-1423

6. van Diggelen, J., et al.: Pluggable social artificial intelligence for enabling human-agent teaming. arXiv preprint arXiv:1909.04492 (2019)

7. Ershov, D., Mitchell, M.: The effects of influencer advertising disclosure regulations: evidence from instagram. In: Proceedings of the 21st ACM Conference on Economics and Computation, EC 2020, pp. 73–74. Association for Computing Machinery, New York (2020). https://doi.org/10.1145/3391403.3399477

8. Frithjof, M., et al.: The impact of influencers on advertising and consumer protection in the single market (2022). https://www.europarl.europa.eu/RegData/etudes/STUD/2022/703350/IPOL_STU(2022)703350_EN.pdf. Accessed 13 Oct 2022

9. Geiger, R.S., et al.: "Garbage in, garbage out" revisited: what do machine learning application papers report about human-labeled training data? CoRR abs/2107.02278 (2021). https://arxiv.org/abs/2107.02278

10. Geiger, R.S., et al.: Garbage in, garbage out? Do machine learning application papers in social computing report where human-labeled training data comes from? In: Proceedings of the 2020 Conference on Fairness, Accountability, and Transparency, pp. 325–336 (2020)

11. Geva, M., Goldberg, Y., Berant, J.: Are we modeling the task or the annotator? An investigation of annotator bias in natural language understanding datasets (2019)

12. Gilardi, F., Alizadeh, M., Kubli, M.: ChatGPT outperforms crowd-workers for text-annotation tasks (2023)
13. Goanta, C., Ranchordás, S.: The Regulation of Social Media Influencers. Edward Elgar Publishing (2020)
14. Hayes, A.F., Krippendorff, K.: Answering the call for a standard reliability measure for coding data. Commun. Methods Measures **1**(1), 77–89 (2007)
15. Hovy, E., Lavid, J.: Towards a 'science' of corpus annotation: a new methodological challenge for corpus linguistics. Int. J. Transl. **22**(1), 13–36 (2010)
16. Kim, S., Jiang, J.Y., Nakada, M., Han, J., Wang, W.: Multimodal post attentive profiling for influencer marketing. In: Proceedings of the Web Conference 2020, WWW 2020, pp. 2878–2884. Association for Computing Machinery, New York (2020). https://doi.org/10.1145/3366423.3380052
17. Kim, S., Jiang, J.Y., Wang, W.: Discovering undisclosed paid partnership on social media via aspect-attentive sponsored post learning. In: Proceedings of the 14th ACM International Conference on Web Search and Data Mining, WSDM 2021, pp. 319–327. Association for Computing Machinery, New York (2021). https://doi.org/10.1145/3437963.3441803
18. Kim, S.S.Y., Watkins, E.A., Russakovsky, O., Fong, R., Monroy-Hernández, A.: "Help me help the AI": understanding how explainability can support human-AI interaction. In: Proceedings of the 2023 CHI Conference on Human Factors in Computing Systems. ACM (2023). https://doi.org/10.1145/3544548.3581001
19. Kossow, N., Windwehr, S., Jenkins, M.: Algorithmic transparency and accountability. JSTOR (2021)
20. Krippendorff, K.: Computing Krippendorff's alpha-reliability. Annenberg School for Communication Departmental Papers, Philadelphia (2011)
21. Mathur, A., Narayanan, A., Chetty, M.: Endorsements on social media: an empirical study of affiliate marketing disclosures on youtube and pinterest. Proc. ACM Hum.-Comput. Interact. **2**(CSCW), 1–26 (2018). https://doi.org/10.1145/3274388
22. Neerincx, M.A., van der Waa, J., Kaptein, F., van Diggelen, J.: Using perceptual and cognitive explanations for enhanced human-agent team performance. In: Harris, D. (ed.) EPCE 2018. LNCS (LNAI), vol. 10906, pp. 204–214. Springer, Cham (2018). https://doi.org/10.1007/978-3-319-91122-9_18
23. Pikuliak, M.: ChatGPT survey: performance on NLP datasets (2023). https://www.opensamizdat.com/posts/chatgpt_survey
24. Ribeiro, M.T., Singh, S., Guestrin, C.: "Why should i trust you?": explaining the predictions of any classifier. In: Proceedings of the 22nd ACM SIGKDD International Conference on Knowledge Discovery and Data Mining, San Francisco, CA, USA, 13–17 August 2016, pp. 1135–1144 (2016)
25. Said, Z.K.: Mandated disclosure in literary hybrid speech. Wash. L. Rev. **88**, 419 (2013)
26. Touvron, H., et al.: LLaMA: open and efficient foundation language models (2023)
27. Vidgen, B., Derczynski, L.: Directions in abusive language training data, a systematic review: garbage in, garbage out. PLoS ONE **15**(12), e0243300 (2020)
28. van der Waa, J., van Diggelen, J., Cavalcante Siebert, L., Neerincx, M., Jonker, C.: Allocation of moral decision-making in human-agent teams: a pattern approach. In: Harris, D., Li, W.-C. (eds.) HCII 2020. LNCS (LNAI), vol. 12187, pp. 203–220. Springer, Cham (2020). https://doi.org/10.1007/978-3-030-49183-3_16
29. Waltenrath, A.: Empirical evidence on the impact of disclosed vs. undisclosed advertising in context of influencer marketing on Instagram. In: ECIS 2021 Research Papers, p. 17 (2021)

30. Wei, J., et al.: Chain-of-thought prompting elicits reasoning in large language models (2023)
31. Wolf, T., Debut, L., Sanh, V., et al.: Transformers: state-of-the-art natural language processing. In: Proceedings of the 2020 Conference on Empirical Methods in Natural Language Processing: System Demonstrations, pp. 38–45. Association for Computational Linguistics (2020). https://doi.org/10.18653/v1/2020.emnlp-demos.6. https://aclanthology.org/2020.emnlp-demos.6
32. Zarei, K., et al.: Characterising and detecting sponsored influencer posts on Instagram. arXiv:2011.05757 (2020)

Human-Computer Interaction and Explainability: Intersection and Terminology

Arthur Picard[1]([⊠]) , Yazan Mualla[1]([⊠]) , Franck Gechter[1,2] ,
and Stéphane Galland[1]

[1] UTBM, CIAD UMR 7533, 90010 Belfort Cedex, France
{arthur.picard,yazan.mualla,franck.gechter,stephane.galland}@utbm.fr
[2] SIMBIOT, LORIA UMR CNRS 7503, Université de Lorraine, 54506
Vandoeuvre-lès-Nancy, France

Abstract. Human-computer interaction (HCI) is generally considered the broader domain encompassing the study of the relationships between humans and types of technological artifacts or systems. Explainable AI (xAI) is involved in HCI to have humans better understand computers or AI systems which fosters, as a consequence, better interaction. The term "explainability" is sometimes used interchangeably with other closely related terms such as interpretability or understandability. The same can be said for the term "interaction". It is a very broad way to describe the relationship between humans and technologies, which is why it is often replaced or completed by more precise terms like cooperation, collaboration, teaming, symbiosis, and integration. In the same vein, the technologies are represented by several terms like computer, machine, AI, agent, and robot. However, each of these terms (technologies and relationships) has its specificity and properties which need to be clearly defined. Currently, the definitions of these various terms are not well established in the literature, and their usage in various contexts is ambiguous. The goals of this paper are threefold: First, clarify the terminology in the HCI domain representing the technologies and their relationships with humans. A few concepts specific to xAI are also clarified. Second, highlight the role that xAI plays or can play in the HCI domain. Third, study the evolution and tendency of the usage of explainability and interpretability with the HCI terminology throughout the years and highlight the observations in the last three years.

Keywords: Human-Computer Interaction · Explainability · Explainable AI · Terminology

1 Introduction

Human-computer interaction (HCI) is a discipline that was established early in the age of computers and has had to adapt and evolve, through many waves,

© The Author(s), under exclusive license to Springer Nature Switzerland AG 2023
L. Longo (Ed.): xAI 2023, CCIS 1902, pp. 214–236, 2023.
https://doi.org/10.1007/978-3-031-44067-0_12

together with the incredibly fast development of new technologies [6,23]. HCI includes the design, evaluation, and implementation of interactive systems for a wide range of tasks and applications. Since its inception, the discipline has drawn from multiple fields, mainly computer science, but also psychology, design, sociology, and more. It was never constrained to a specific area, and it is not surprising to see its field of study incorporating more and more topics following technological advancements in the computer industry [12].

Understanding the behavior of computers is crucial to guarantee smooth HCI since it is not straightforward for humans to understand the computer's state of mind. In the same vein, recent works in the literature highlighted explainability as one of the cornerstones for building understandable, trustworthy, responsible, and acceptable artificial intelligence (AI) systems [11,30,44,45]. Consequently, the field of explainable AI (xAI) gained momentum both in academia and industry [2,21]. xAI in HCI refers to the ability of a computer system to provide humans with clear and understandable explanations about their inner workings and why certain decisions were made.

HCI is generally considered to be the broader domain that encompasses the study of what type of relationship humans have with all types of technology, including computers, machines, agents, robots, and systems. One of the main issues that could be observed from the literature and technological works concerns the terminology representing both these types of technology and their relationships with humans. Indeed, the definitions of these terms are not well established in the literature, and their usage in various contexts is ambiguous and sometimes chaotic. Accordingly, before investigating the role that xAI plays or could play in the HCI domain, the relationships between humans and technologies needs to be fully analyzed. The relationships considered in this paper are between two parties: the first party is the human, and the second party is a term of the set {computer, machine, AI, agent, robot}. The relationship between these two parties could take several forms from the set {interaction, cooperation, collaboration, team, symbiosis, integration}. The previous two sets of terms are chosen based on our experience and knowledge.

The goals of this paper are threefold, organized into three main sections: *(i)* provide and clarify the terminology of both the technologies and their relationships with the human and how they are subdivided inside the HCI domain (Sect. 2). *(ii)* define common terms in xAI and investigate the role it plays or could play in the HCI domain (Sect. 3). *(iii)* analyze and study the results from research queries in Google Scholar to quantify the usages of terms (technologies and relationships) in the literature and better understand the evolution and tendency of the usage of explainability and interpretability with these terms throughout the years (Sect. 4). Finally, Sect. 5 discusses the limitations, and Sect. 6 concludes the paper.

2   Relationships Between Humans and Technologies

The relationships considered in this paper are between two parties: The first party is the human while the second is a term of the set {computer, machine,

AI, agent, robot}. Throughout the paper, variable "Y" is used to refer to the second party of the relationship. These relationships could take several forms from the set {interaction, cooperation, collaboration, team, symbiosis, integration}. Accordingly, the variable "X" is used to refer to these relationships.

2.1   Human-Y Interaction

This section focuses on the different terms representing the concepts used to describe "what" humans interact with. The concept of "interaction", representing the most general term for describing the mutual relationship between humans and technologies [17], is used throughout this section since it encompasses all the other and more detailed relationships. As such, the nature of the relationship is fixed to "interaction" to focus on the concept "Y", an element of the set computer, machine, AI, agent, robot.

Computer and Machine. A computer is defined as: "an electronic device for storing and processing data, typically in binary form, according to instructions given to it in a variable program." (Oxford Dictionary). While this definition is precise, it seems somewhat limited when looking at the literature. In the HCI domain, the term "computer" is not only used to refer to computational devices, but also includes devices or even systems that rely on computational devices to work [48]. Additionally, "computer" isn't only used to represent physical objects, but also the software that runs on them [10]. In other words, in HCI, "computer" can be defined as such: anything that relies on computation through processing units to function.

As highlighted in [12], computers have become part of almost every technological object, making the concepts of Human-computer interaction and Human-Technology Interaction strongly overlap [12]. However, the term "Technology" does not appear much, and the term "Computer" is generally used instead.

Another overlapping concept is Human-Machine Interaction. A machine is defined as "an apparatus using mechanical power and having several parts, each with a definite function and together performing a particular task" (Oxford Dictionary). As this definition is broad, it encompasses most of the devices focused on HCI. On top of that, the same idea of computers being part of almost all technological artifacts can be applied to machines. Fewer and fewer machines do not include a processing unit. According to the definition used here, software is not considered a machine as it does not have a physical body and does not rely on mechanical power. However, even software is sometimes included when using the term "machine" [18].

"Computer" and "machine" are the two broader used terms when it comes to Human-Y interaction, and as such, their meanings are somehow similar. The difference in usage mainly comes from the origins of the terms. "computer" is the most commonly used term as HCI was established as a discipline early on in the early 1980s, and has multiple renowned conferences directly including "HCI" or "Human-computer interaction" in their names. Overall, "machine" is more often found in domains closer to industry, robotics, and mechanical engineering and only rarely includes software. Even then, it makes sense to include "Human-machine interaction" as part of the overall "Human-computer interaction" research [25].

AI, Agent, and Robot. Terms other than "computer" and "machine" often used are "AI", "robot", and "agent". The formulation "Human-AI interaction" was not used for a long time (as shown in Sect. 4). However, it is starting to appear more and more in recent years.

AI is considered a "source of much confusion both within the field and among the public" [37]. Just like intelligence, the concept is both instinctively understood by many and hard to formally define [51]. This vagueness even extends to the legal and regulatory field, where it may be a source of problems [28]. In this work, the following definition of AI is considered: a software or virtual entity which can show behaviors that are usually believed to require intelligence.

A robot is defined as: "a machine capable of carrying out a complex series of actions automatically, especially one programmable by a computer" (Oxford Dictionary). The idea of "carrying out a complex series of actions automatically" can be described as seemingly intelligent, which fits with our definition of AI. As such, a robot is a machine that incorporates AI.

The term "agent" is often used to refer to a specific branch of AI and a way to represent AI and robots. In this context, an agent can be defined as: an autonomous entity with social skills to interact with other agents and can take reactive or proactive actions [52]. This definition is especially vague in the usage of the term "entity" which means that even humans can be modeled as human agents. Following this logic, papers about "Agent-agent interaction" can include "Human-agent interaction". However, as the focus here is on the formulation "Human-agent", which shows that humans are excluded from the agent model and focus on the relationship between humans and artificial agents, the definition of an agent is limited to artificial entities.

In a way, the relationship between the terms "agent" and "robot" is similar to the one between "computer" and "machine", respectively, with a large overlap, but the term "robot" focuses on a physical body while the term "agent" does include virtual agents. It is worth mentioning here the Human-Agent-Robot-Machine-Sensor (HARMS) mechanism [35,50] that connects parties over a network by a peer-to-peer manner and uses particular message types such that all parties are indistinguishable in terms of which type of party (e.g., robot, software agent, or even human) sends a message [36].

2.2 Human-Computer X

As aforementioned, a computer is the most common way to refer to "what" the human is interacting with and can be used to encompass the other concepts. As such, in this section, the term "computer" is fixed representing the second party of the relationship, to investigate the type of relationship "X" being part of the set interaction, teaming, cooperation, collaboration, symbiosis, integration.

Interaction. Since the 1960s, the idea of a human-computer interface, with its attributes of friendliness, usefulness, transparency, etc., has attracted the interest of researchers. Yet, a significant number of studies on human-automation relationship failures have been developed by cognitive ergonomics, which focus on what happens behind the interface [25,43]. Originally the term "interaction" referred to the interface between humans and computers, for example, chatbots. Nowadays, it refers to all types of human-computer relationships [17], and if further focus is needed, a more specific term is used. HCI also addresses a much broader range of research questions including, for example, the ergonomic issues raised by today's extremely sophisticated and dynamic human-computer systems [25]. From the point of view of humans, computers are not only tools, but also technological artifacts, and some coherence must be maintained between humans and these artifacts actions on the environment, whatever the interface is. This is why it is appealing to incorporate the paradigm of cooperation into the study of human-computer relationships.

Collaboration, Cooperation, and Teaming. The original focal point of HCI research was to improve workers' operational capabilities. While it is not limited to that anymore [12], it is still a predominant focus in the domain. This idea is reflected in the usage of terms like "collaboration", "cooperation", and "team"/"teaming" which all represent a relationship where humans work together with a computer. The terms "collaboration" and "cooperation" focus on the nature of interaction when working towards a specific goal, while the terms "team" or "teaming" focus on the efficient integration of computers into a formal organization that includes humans. In the following, the different relationships related to the aspect of humans and computers working together are discussed.

– *Human-Computer teaming:* In the context of work, teams are a small formal way to organize members together inside a larger organization. In traditional teams, there are at least two levels of authority, with normal members and a leader making global decisions and managing the rest of the members [7]. While each member can have their own level of autonomy and independence, concepts like communication, trust, cohesion, accountability, fairness, and even competition, are core to a team working properly. The topic of study of Human-Computer Teams is to create hybrid-intelligent teams composed of both humans and computers. It is an ambitious goal that presents numerous challenges, including the development of models adapted to mixed teams by either modifying existing human team models or creating new ones [15]. It also requires AI to be capable of filling properties such as accountability, fairness, and understandability [40].
– *Cooperation or Collaboration?:* "Cooperation" and "collaboration" types of relationships are very close. Usually, the difference between the two is not made in the HCI domain [54]. A very noticeable example of their use comes from the domain of multiagent systems, in which cooperation and collaboration are central concepts, [52]. In such context, there is also the field of collaborative working, in which humans are collaborating to solve a common

task. In both cases (cooperation and collaboration), humans and computers are working together towards the same goal, often sharing resources, including information. However, it can be interesting to look into the differences between the two in other disciplines to get a more precise definition [19]. Based on [27], cooperation can be as simple as having the work divided between all parties and realized independently. A collaboration, however, does not only mean that the different parties are working together towards a goal, but also that there is a close interdependence between the parties with reliance on each other, whether it is in decision-making or information sharing. As such, while the aim of HCI is mostly collaboration, it is often under the denomination "cooperation" which is a broader concept that regroups every way of working together towards a specific goal, including "collaboration", a specific way with a closer relationship between the parties [54].

Symbiosis. While it is not the most explored idea, the symbiosis relationship focuses on an interesting part of HCI. Instead of having humans and computers working together towards a specific goal, the explored relationship is based on mutual benefit [18]. The principle comes from biology, where it was first introduced by Anton de Bary in 1879 as "the living together of unlike named organisms" [41]. Although different forms of symbiosis are discussed in biology [34], the term is also used outside the field to describe a relationship of mutual benefit, which corresponds to "mutualism" symbiosis in biology [41]. In sociology, it is defined as "a mutually beneficial relationship between different people or groups" (Oxford Dictionary). By replacing "people or groups" with "human and computer", the human-computer symbiosis topic of the study appears. While it may be unusual to see computers as something that looks for benefits, they naturally inherit the goal of their creator and are made with purpose. Moreover, something like the common practice of allowing users to send feedback which is then used to improve the corresponding system is a direct benefit for the computer and can already be seen as a form of symbiosis. Thus, symbiosis is a step further in putting the link between humans and computers, moving from a simple task-sharing point of view to an integrative relationship in which humans and computers are parts of a whole system as described in the concept of a bio-physical system [14].

Integration. Integration takes a different approach as it starts by taking an outside perspective, considering humans and computers as a whole system before getting into the details of how to make it a seamless and effective system [17]. One approach to improving such a system is to take a long-term view of the relationship between the parties, specifically how humans adapt to the system and then how the computer adapts to humans, also called "co-adaptation" [33].

Adaptation and coadaptation are consequences of interaction over a long period. Co-adaptation is more clear when one looks at the relationship between human-centered design and goal-oriented design [16]. On the one hand, human-centered design (or user-centered design) focuses on grounding the design in understanding users, their needs, tasks, and the environment. Additionally, it tries to make user-friendly systems, allowing them to quickly integrate with the system [4]. However, such an approach can be limited by the fact that it only exposes a minimal amount of complexity to maximize usability. As such, it ends up limiting the performance a trained user would have in the system [16]. On the other hand, a goal-oriented design takes the opposite approach. It maximizes the performance a trained user would have with the system by allowing a maximum of available controls. It comes at the cost of usability. A user would need training to integrate properly into the system [16]. In other words, a human-centered design gives short-term advantages but has long-term drawbacks, while a goal-oriented design has the opposite. The purpose of studying co-adaptation is to reconcile the two ideas by understanding how humans adapt to the computer in the system and how to adapt the computers through their interaction with humans. As such, high usability early on can be achieved, and the system stays at an adequate complexity while the human users learn and maximize performance. At that time, human users can have in-depth control over the system [16].

After analyzing various types of relationships between humans and different kinds of technologies, the next section tackles the intersection between explainability and the HCI domain.

3   The Role of xAI in HCI

This section theoretically investigates the role that Explainable Artificial Intelligence (xAI) plays in the HCI domain. First, some definitions of explainability and some similar or related concepts like interpretability and understandability are analyzed. Then, the main contributions and opportunities that explainability could provide in the HCI domain are provided.

3.1   Definitions and Concepts

xAI is a study field that provides useful techniques and models for researchers to build AI-based systems that are explicable [21,24,39]. Primarily, the surge of interest in this field is explained by the often useful, but sometimes intriguing [49], results of black-box machine learning algorithms and the consequent need to understand how these data fed into the algorithm produced the given results [5, 22,46]. This field recognizes the need to incorporate explanations or explanations of explainability to improve transparency and trust [8,20,29].

In [2], a literature review of xAI is provided that focuses on goal-driven xAI, also called explainable agency. In [40], another review of the literature on xAI is presented, but in the field of healthcare. It focuses mainly on data-driven AI. The concepts of goal-driven and data-driven xAI emerged mainly to differentiate systems that rely on data analysis from those that are driven by actions. It highlights and defines the following goals of xAI: trustworthiness, causality, transferability, informativeness, confidence, fairness, accessibility, interactivity, and awareness of privacy.

In [3], the authors define some concepts related to xAI. While their work focuses on the xAI methods used in data-driven AI, some ideas are true in both goal-driven and data-driven AI. The differences between understandability, comprehensibility, interpretability, explainability, and transparency are also highlighted. The following goals of xAI are given: trustworthiness, causality, transferability, information, confidence, fairness, accessibility, interactivity, and privacy awareness.

From the literature, the three concepts of understandability, interpretability, and explainability could be differentiated as follows:

Understandability describes AI systems that are clear enough without explanations for the human user to understand how the model works. It does not mean that the user understands every detail of the model, but is mostly an instinctive but accurate understanding [3, 38].

Interpretability is similar to understandability in the fact that it is a "passive characteristic of models" [3] which allows humans to understand the AI's decision. However, with interpretability, it is achieved by giving insight into the inner working of the model [13, 47].

Explainability allows humans to understand the AI using methods like adding explanations or extracting relevant data that justify the AI's decision [26]. It can be seen as "post hoc interpretability" [13] where methods are used to compensate for the fact that the model used is not interpretable.

3.2 Key Contributions, Techniques, and Research Questions

As mentioned in the previous section, hybrid intelligent systems, where hybrid teams of humans and computers share decisions during complex operations, are gaining more interest in research. Hybrid Intelligence (HI) is the combination of human and computer intelligence, increasing human intellect and capabilities rather than replacing them and achieving goals that were unreachable to humans or computers [1]. For this purpose, xAI is an important part to make the interface from AI to human. The aim is to build adaptive, responsible, interactive, and human-centered intelligent systems that collaborate synergistically, proactively, and purposefully with humans. Hybrid teams highlight the need for effective interactions between computers and humans. This is to ensure that humans can understand the models and intelligent systems embodied in these computers. To have a good interaction with technology, humans need to trust it and, to trust it, humans need to understand it [40].

xAI Contributions in HCI. Understanding the behavior of computers is crucial to guarantee smooth HCI since it is not straightforward for humans to understand the computer's state of mind. xAI in HCI refers to the ability of a computer system to provide humans with clear and understandable explanations about their inner workings and why certain decisions were made. It is an important aspect of HCI because it helps humans trust and understand the behavior of intelligent systems, thus increasing the user satisfaction & acceptance and improving the decision making. Explainability is particularly indispensable for intelligent systems, such as decision-making systems, recommendation systems, and natural language processing systems, as these systems can be complex and difficult for users to understand. Explainability helps to coordinate and cooperate between humans and computers by providing a clear understanding of the goals, actions, and decisions of the system [1].

xAI played a more specific role in the HCI subdomains, i.e., Human-Y X. [53] is an example of applying xAI in HI in the field of predictive maintenance. Two main technical challenges are highlighted for the "optimizing human-machine collaboration in a predictive maintenance system". Furthermore, multiple social challenges are discussed regarding the acceptance of such systems by workers. Another example focuses on the benefit of xAI in teamwork [42]. As such, in a situation of collaboration between a human and a robot, it tests the impact of giving the human information on the actions of the robot, both with and without an explanation of the decision making. In the experiment, users are divided into two groups: expert and novice. The results show that adding xAI to the system helps to know the situation of the user. The novice group also shows better performance when working with xAI. The expert group, on the other hand, sees their performance degrade. These results highlight the objectivity feature of explanations and how situational the benefit from an explanation could be. As the metric of performance is the time taken to perform the task, the assumption is made that, since the expert is fast to realize the task anyway, the time lost by getting the information outweighs the time gained by knowing the robot status. We can also assume that if the task was complex enough to be difficult to complete even for an expert, the addition of xAI would lead to a gain in performance for both groups. This means that the explanation should be user- and context-sensitive, and this confirms other results in the literature [39].

Explainability Techniques in HCI. Explainability in HCI can be achieved through various techniques, such as:

- Providing human users with concise, understandable explanations of how a system operates, such as through visualizations or natural language explanations.
- Allowing users to view the components of an AI system's conclusion, such as the input data and the weights given to certain features.
- Allowing the users to investigate and interact with and explore the internal workings of a system, for example, through interactive visualizations or "what-if" simulations.
- Empowering the users with the ability to control and customize the behavior of a system, for example, by changing settings or offering feedback.

xAI Benefits to HCI. xAI not only targets data scientists and AI developer to facilitated models creation and optimization but also brings benefit to normal end users [3]. This is especially true for tasks with important decision making such as predictive visual analytic where both end-users and domain experts are strongly involved [9,32]. xAI can bring several of it's advantages to HCI: Increased trust & satisfaction, improved accountability & transparency, better user engagement, and improved decision-making. However, recent work in the literature has pointed out that the design of xAI systems should consider the user's background, cognitive skills, and prior knowledge [42]. Thus, various challenges must be considered: Balancing explainability & performance, user needs & preferences, addressing diversity, discrimination & bias, complexity & overhead, and ethical & social implications, evaluation & validation, and privacy & security.

HCI focuses on the interaction in terms of technology, while xAI focuses on ensuring that humans better understand and trust AI. AI is becoming more and more integrated into technology, so understanding the technology allows for better interactions with it. Therefore, we believe that further investigation of the role of explainability in HCI is a good direction of research that may facilitate better understandability, trust, and transparency of AI in the eyes of humans.

Research Questions. Several research questions could be considered in the context of applying explainability in HCI:

- How can users investigate and interact with and explore the internal workings of an intelligent system to control and customize its behavior?
- What are the different types of explanations that make the decision-making process in HI teams more transparent, understandable, and accountable?
- How can the explanations be communicated to human members of the HI team so that they improve human trust and lead to successful HCI? How can xAI be used to calibrated trust, foster interactions with users relying on the system while keeping a critical thinking i.e., trust without overtrust and excessive reliance ?
- How can explanations be personalized so that they align with human needs and capabilities? i.e., How to build a human-centered intelligent model?
- What potential could be achieved with the integration of learning and reasoning, i.e., symbolic and sub-symbolic AI as a hybrid solution to generate and communicate explanations?
- Unified explanations: Interpretability between humans and computers may not always align, and finding common ground can be challenging. How do we provide a unified explanation that is interpretable by both humans and computers?
- What objective and subjective metrics are needed to evaluate the reception and perception of computers' explanations by humans? How can the quality and strength of the explanations be evaluated? This question includes cognitive psychology, which can help us to understand how humans process and understand explanations.
- Accuracy and performance: Adding additional layers of explainability can slow down the decision-making process, which can be problematic in time-sensitive applications. How to maintain accuracy and performance when applying xAI techniques in HCI?

To quantify the theoretical analysis provided in this section, the next section provides a practical investigation of the tendency and evolution of the usage of xAI concepts (explainability and interpretability) associated with the terminology of the HCI subdomains that include the aforementioned various technologies (Sect. 2.1) and relationships (Sect. 2.2).

4   Tendency and Evolution in Usage of Terminology

This section evaluates the interest of the community over the years by taking a look at the number of Google Scholar search results of different queries. Since our purpose is to investigate a global interest in different topics, Google Scholar was chosen as it is the search engine that indexes the largest number of papers. Even if the results do include papers that are not peer reviewed, their inclusion still shows interest in the topics. Multiple formulations of the queries have been conducted, starting with less precise ones, which were refined to get results using precisely the keyword studied. The queries used for the data in this paper are:

  (i) "human-Y" AND "X"
 (ii) "human-Y" AND "X" AND "explainability"
(iii) "human-Y" AND "X" AND "interpretability"

With "Y" a term of the set {computer, machine, AI, agent, robot} and "X" a term of the set {interaction, cooperation, collaboration, team, symbiosis, integration, adaptation}. After running pilot queries, two concepts of xAI are chosen: explainability and interpretability. Consequently, in the queries, we have three choices: (i) without any keyword to represent xAI concepts; (ii) using the keyword "explainability"; (iii) using the keyword "interpretability". According to our definition (Sect. 3), the keyword "understandability" is mostly used to describe simpler models. As such, it is replaced by "interpretability" when insight into the model is purposefully given to make it more understandable and was not investigated further.

For all years between 2012 and 2022 (10 years), each type of query described above were run (3 types), with each X-Y combination (35 possible combination). Thus, resulting in a total of queries is 1050. The number of search results obtained from each query is recorded and used to make the graphs presented bellow. Two graphs are used to depict the data: (1) Heatmaps, where the number of results over a period of time are added to represent the relationship between each of the terms. The values are normalized over the total number of results in the graph and represented as a %. The scale is set between 0% and 23% on every map for comparison purposes. (2) Graphs that represent the number of search results as a function of years. As in Sect. 2, sometimes, "Y" is fixed as "computer" when considering the relationships only, and "X" as "interaction" when considering the technologies only. In all cases, curves for all options of the relationships or the technologies that are not fixed are displayed.

4.1   Query Formulation

In this section, the choices of the formulation of the queries are explained, especially when using quotation marks.

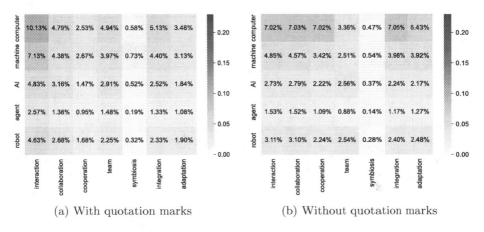

(a) With quotation marks   (b) Without quotation marks

Fig. 1. Normalized heatmap of the number of results using the queries: (a) "human-Y" AND "X" AND "explainability"; (b) human-Y X explainability, in the period [2020, 2022].

Figure 1 depicts the distribution of the search queries results of all values of variables "Y" and "X" with the keyword "explainability" in the period [2012, 2022]. This figure aims at showing the difference between using quotation marks (Fig. 1(a)) or not (Fig. 1(b)) around the keywords. An unexpected and large difference can be seen in the distribution of the results. Assuming the usage is the same as in the usual Google search engine, the purpose of the quotation marks is to get the exact keyword and not allow the algorithm to replace the quoted keyword with synonyms or similar keywords (such as "explainable" or "explanation" for "explainability" for example). This is supported by the fact that, in 2022, for the terms "computer" and "interaction", 3,880 results are found without quotation marks and only 1,750 with quotation marks. In Google Scholar, when manually searching for: [human-computer collaboration explainability], on the first page that the keywords "interaction" and "cooperation" are highlighted as corresponding to the search query, which means the algorithm handles them as synonyms of "collaboration". This explains the results in Fig. 1(b) which shows almost the same number of results for the keyword "computer" paired with "interaction", "collaboration", "cooperation" and "integration". In this context, all four terms are treated as synonyms. For this reason, we decided to keep the quotation marks in the rest of the experiments in the paper. "AND" are added for clarity. It's important to note that search queries using quotation marks may also introduce a certain bias, as this may not be the most commonly used way to refer to the topic. However, their usage is essential to avoid some keywords being treated as synonyms. Using the hyphen "-" between the two parties of the relationship, e.g., "Human" and "Y" excludes the results where the two keywords do not follow each other, which are likely to be papers that do not focus on the relationship between humans and "Y" but simply mention both concepts at some point.

Next, Sects. 4.2, 4.3, and 4.4 investigate, respectively, the usage of terms (relationships and technologies) of the HCI domain without the concepts of explainability and interpretability, with the keyword "explainability", and with the keyword "interpretability".

4.2 Without Explainability and Interpretability

The distribution of the usage of HCI terms is investigated when no keyword (neither "explainability" nor "interpretability") is used to represent the xAI concepts. This distribution is used as a baseline in comparison to the results when adding the xAI keywords.

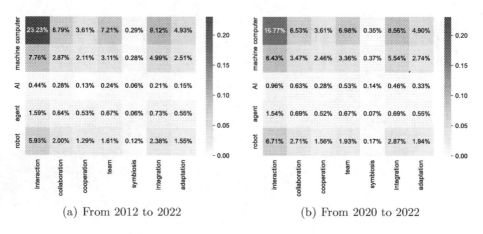

(a) From 2012 to 2022   (b) From 2020 to 2022

Fig. 2. Normalized heatmap of the number of results using the query: "human-Y" AND "X", in the periods [2012, 2022] (a), and [2020, 2022] (b).

Figure 2(a) shows the number of results of the search queries of all values of the variables "Y" and "X" in the last ten years (period [2012, 2022]). The main observation to highlight is that the overwhelming majority (23.23%) are found with the terms "Human-Computer interaction". As mentioned earlier, these results are to be expected since it has been established as a research domain early on. Additionally, it can be noted that the pairs (technology, relationship) of the terms {computer, integration}, {machine, interaction} and {computer, team} are also prominent focuses. Furthermore, it can be seen that the terms "AI", "agent", and "symbiosis" give the least amount of results.

Figure 2(b) shows the results when limiting the search queries to the last three years (period [2020, 2022]). The first observation, even though a bit trivial, is that the proportion of results of the terms pair {computer, integration} is remarkably reduced (16.77% in the last three years compared to 23.23% in the last ten years). This suggests that researchers tend to prefer, currently, to choose more specific terminology. The other pair of terms previously highlighted in Fig. 1(a), i.e., {computer, integration}, {machine, collaboration}, and {computer, team}, are still the main focuses, especially the two first pairs. The pair {computer, team} is currently at the same level as the pairs {computer, collaboration} and {robot, interaction}.

Overall, a movement of standardization can still be observed, with the majority gaining in proportion except for the results of the pair {computer, interaction} that diminish. The topic of HCI has always included an incredible diversity, both in the sciences used including psychology, ergonomics, and social sciences, on top of computer science [12], and in the topics focused on. The HCI community does not limit itself and includes every new technology in its research topics [31]. As such, it makes sense to use more precise keywords to describe the work, which can explain the relative decrease in the usage of the terms "Human-computer interaction".

4.3 Usage of the Keyword "explainability"

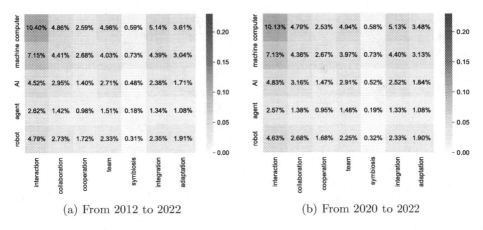

(a) From 2012 to 2022   (b) From 2020 to 2022

Fig. 3. Normalized heatmap of the number of results using the query: "human-Y" AND "X" **AND** "explainability", in the periods [2012, 2022] (a), and [2020, 2022] (b).

In this section, the focus is on the impact of adding the keyword "explainability" in the search queries. Figure 3 depicts the distribution of HCI terms usage together with the keyword "explainability" in the period [2012, 2022] (Fig. 3(a)) and in the period [2020, 2022] (Fig. 3(b)). The two heatmaps are almost identical. It can be explained by the fact that the usage of the keyword "explainability" is only recent. As such, the majority of results come from the last three years (period [2020, 2022]). This observation can also be asserted by Fig. 5(d) and Fig. 5(c) explained later in Sect. 4.5.

By comparing Fig. 2(b) and Fig. 3(b), the impact of the addition of the keyword "explainability" on the distribution and the proportions in the period [2020, 2022] can be observed. The first difference that draws attention is that adding the keyword "explainability" make the results tend towards a uniform distribution. That is to say that the results of the pair computer, interaction go from 16.77% to 10.13%. The number of results of the term "AI" which is almost non-existent in Fig. 2(b) is at the same level as the number of results of the term "robot" when adding the keyword. The term "Agent" is here the least used concept to describe the object of interaction, but is still relatively closer to the others. On the other axis, the number of the results of the term "symbioses" is still by far the least investigated term in both cases (with and without adding the keyword "explainability"). Explainability is a hot topic that continues to interest more and more people. Explainability is closely related to different subdomains of HCI and not only the pair computer, interaction. This means suggests that researchers tend to apply explainability in a specific subdomain of HCI.

4.4   Usage of the Keyword "interpretability"

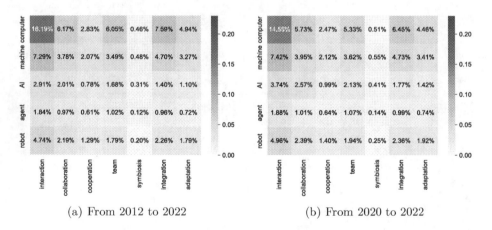

(a) From 2012 to 2022   (b) From 2020 to 2022

Fig. 4. Normalized heatmap of the number of results using the query: "human-Y" AND "X" **AND "interpretability"**, in the periods [2012, 2022] (a), and [2020, 2022] (b).

Figure 4 shows the distribution of HCI terms usage together with the keyword "interpretability". The comparison between 4(a) and 4(b) shows the difference in distribution between the period [2020, 2022], and the period [2020, 2022]. Just like with "explainability", the two heatmaps are pretty similar. The same reasoning can be made: the usage of the keyword "interpretability" became far more common in recent years. As such, the majority of results come from the last three years (period [2020, 2022]). This observation can be asserted in Fig. 5(f) and Fig. 5(e) that are explained later in Sect. 4.5. When compared to the results without the keywords "explainability" and "interpretability" shown in Fig. 2, the results are similar for the period [2020, 2022], with the proportion for the pair {computer, interaction} being close to 15% in both cases (16.77% and 14.55% respectively for: without "explainability" and "interpretability" and with "interpretability", in the last three years). However, like with the addition of the keyword "explainability", the proportion taken by both "AI" and "agent" is far greater when adding the keyword "interpretability". Overall, the differences in tendency when adding the keyword "interpretability" is similar to adding the keyword "explainability" but to a lesser extent.

4.5   Evolution in the Last Decade

This section will focus on the evolution in the last decade by displaying the number of results throughout the last decade. As displaying the results for all combinations would not be readable, "Y" is fixed to "computer" in half of the graphs and "X" to "interaction" in the other half. Both have one graph for each case: without "explainability" and "interpretability", with "explainability", with "interpretability".

In Fig. 5, the graphs are organized by lines and columns. The three graphs in the first columns show the search results with the keyword "computer" fixed, while the second columns show the results with the keyword "interaction" fixed. The graphs on the first line are the ones with neither "explainability" nor "interpretability", the second line is with "explainability" and the third line is with "interpretability".

One of the first observations is the difference in scale between the y-axis. With the addition of the keyword "explainability", the results go from 50 000 to 1750. It is a massive difference, however, it cannot be used to calculate the proportion of results incorporating "explainability". Explainability is often referred to as "explainable" or "xAI". Since the search is made using quotation marks, papers which are only referring to the concept with words other than "explainability" are excluded by the search algorithm. This is why the raw number cannot be compared between the different graphs, and the focus is on the relative proportion instead.

Figure 5(a) shows that when the query does not include the keywords "explainability" nor "interpretability", the term "interaction" gives far more results than any other term. However, this number of results stagnates since 2019 and even goes down in 2022. The number of results with either the keyword "explainability" or "interpretability" shows rapid growth in the last few years. This is especially visible for explainability, as it almost gave no results before 2016. With explainability, the results of the terms "integration", "team" and "collaboration" are the ones giving the most results after the term "interaction" and all three give almost the same value.

Figure 5(b) shows that without the keywords "explainability" and "interpretability", the term "computer" gives by far the highest number of results,

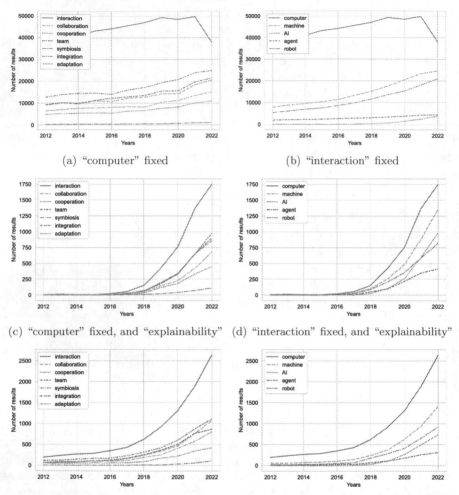

Fig. 5. Number of the search results using the queries (Y = computer): Number of the search results in the period [2012, 2022] using the query: "human-Y" AND "X" where (a, c, e) X in {interaction, cooperation, collaboration, team, symbiosis, integration} and Y = computer; (b, d, f) X = interaction and Y in {computer, machine, AI, agent, robot (c, d) AND "explainability" is added to the queries (e, f) AND "interpretability" is added to the queries

followed by the terms "machine" and "robot" which are close to each other, then by "agent" and "AI" which gives almost no results. The term "AI" is still notable due to its growth in the last few years. Figure 5(d) (with the keyword "explainability") shows the same growth mentioned before. The growth of the term "AI" is even more noticeable here, with its number of results, overtaking both those of the terms "agent" and "robot" in the last five years.

4.6   Results

The following summarizes the findings of this section:

- The proportion of the usage of the exact formulation "human-computer interaction" is less dominant in the last three years than before. It suggests that in recent years, researchers tend to prefer to choose more specific terminology (Fig. 2.)
- When adding the keyword "explainability", the distribution of usage of HCI terms becomes closer to being uniform (Figs. 2 and 3).
- The last observation is especially true for the usage of "human-AI" and "human-agent" which are almost non-existent in the distribution without "explainability" (Figs. 2 and 3).
- The last two observations are also true with "interpretability", but to a lesser degree (Figs. 2 and 4).
- The keyword "explainability" was virtually non-existent before 2016. It has experienced significant growth since then. This is especially true when paired with "AI" in which case the growth looks exponential (Figs. 5(c) and 5(d)).
- Although it was not common, the keyword "interpretability" was already used before 2016 but follow a similar growth (Figs. 5(e) and 5(f)).
- The keyword "symbiosis" is used the least out of our selection. It was expected as it is both uncommon and highly specific.

5   Limitations and Future Work

One aspect of this paper tries to tackle the knotty topic of terminology in HCI. One limitation of this paper is that the initial set of terms for the technologies and the relationships are chosen based on our experience and knowledge. A better solution is to rely on a systematic analysis of the literature. Other terms that were excluded from this paper are {automation, vehicle, system} to represent the technology and {partnership, interface, trust} to represent the relationship with the human. "Automation" and "vehicle" were judged to be too specific and only represent a small part of the query results. "System" can have multiple meanings and with a human interacting with a system, it is often seen as having the human incorporated as a part of the system. The latter is somehow discussed throughout the term "integration" in Sect. 2.2. The term "partnership" was not included because the terms "team" and "teaming" were used. The terms "Interface" and "trust" are out of the scope of this paper. While both are closely linked interactions, they do not define the purpose of the interaction or the nature of the relationship, but rather a result or a side effect.

xAI plays more specific roles in the subdomains of HCI, i.e., Human-Y X. Even though, the paper provided some examples about this point, not all combinations of "Y" and "X" were considered due to the space limit. Accordingly, future work could be to further investigate, systematically, the contributions of xAI in all subdomains of HCI.

When choosing the database in Sect. 4, we had the choice of using the Internet as the source, but we wanted to limit our scope to scientific works. Then, the choice was directed to databases like Association for Computing Machinery (ACM) and Web of Science (WoS). However, we did not want to limit the source to officially peer-reviewed works. Finally, we chose to use Google Scholar, which can be seen as a balanced trade-off between the massive works on the Internet and controlled scientific works as it includes various scholarly works (both peer-reviewed and not). It also has the advantage of accessibility but comes with the drawback of relying on an unknown algorithm for the analysis. Inconsistencies with the number of results were noticeable, like the number of results between 2012 and 2022 being different from the sum of the results obtained each year between 2012 and 2022. Other inconsistencies include having the number of results diminish when adding a term with the operator "OR". Because of that, the normalization was not done on the total number of unique papers.

It would be interesting to reproduce the experiments with other databases such as ACM and WoS as more accurate results can be expect, but with the drawback of limiting the results to only a small part of existing papers. We can also expect that such databases would come with a bias as the journals are selective. This bias is likely to be less present in Google Scholar as it indexes many more sources.

6   Conclusion

The paper aims to investigate the role of explainability in the HCI domain by analyzing its subdomains regarding the terminology representing various technologies that have relationships with humans and the nature of these relationships. Moreover, the paper studies the associations between these relationships and the xAI concepts (explainability and interpretability). The association of the two domains of xAI and HCI can provide several benefits: Trust, understandability, and acceptance; Human-centered AI that considers the human perspective and context; AI ethics that are transparent and accountable; and human-robot/agent teams. To further investigate this association, the paper quantifies the usage of the xAI concepts with the terms (technologies and relationships) that represent the subdomains of HCI.

The results mainly showed the recent growth in the usage of both the keywords "explainability" and "interpretability" together with HCI-related terms. The usage of the keyword "explainability" showed that the interest is spread out between most of the terms, with an important focus on AI in comparison to the results without this keyword. The same observation was made for the keyword "interpretability" but to a lesser degree.

The paper concludes that the terms "Computer" and "Machine" are mostly used as synonyms, with few exceptions in pure software and pure mechanical machines. Indeed, these terms are the two broader terms that encompass the terms "AI", "Agent", and "Robot" as well as more precise terms excluded from this paper like "automation" and "system". Moreover, an analogy can be made between the terms "Computer", "Machine" and the terms "Agent", "Robot" respectively, while the term "Robot" can be described as a "Machine" incorporating "AI". Furthermore, the term "collaboration" is a specific way of "cooperation" and should be the objective of most teamwork. The term "Symbiosis" differs in the purpose of the relationship, having both parties use each other for their own benefit. Finally, the term "integration" leads to a different approach and considers everything as a system composed of the two parties of the interaction.

The paper also concludes that when adding the keywords "explainability" and "interpretability" to the search queries, the distribution is found to be consistent between the period [2012, 2022] and [2020, 2022]. As shown by the curve representing the usage throughout the years, the distribution of both keywords is only recent and saw exponential growth in the last few years. As such, most of the results are found to come from the last three years, which makes its weight much more important than the previous years. This is one of the factors explaining the consistency between the distributions. The results show that when the query does not include the keywords "explainability" nor "interpretability", the term "interaction" gives far more results than any other term. However, this number of results stagnates since 2019. Additionally, the works that use explainability are shown to be more distributed to different subdomains of HCI and not closely related to the pair computer, interaction compared to the works that do not use explainability. The evolution of the usage of the terms throughout the years shows that the term "AI", or more precisely "human-AI" has faster growth than any other studied term, especially when paired with the keyword "explainability", but also visible otherwise. While the study of the interaction with AI is not something new, it shows that it is growing faster in recent years, and that the formulation "human-AI" may become more common with time.

References

1. Akata, Z., et al.: A research agenda for hybrid intelligence: augmenting human intellect with collaborative, adaptive, responsible, and explainable artificial intelligence. Computer **53**(08), 18–28 (2020)
2. Anjomshoae, S., Najjar, A., Calvaresi, D., Främling, K.: Explainable agents and robots: results from a systematic literature review. In: Proceedings of the 18th International Conference on Autonomous Agents and MultiAgent Systems, pp. 1078–1088. International Foundation for Autonomous Agents and Multiagent Systems (2019)
3. Barredo Arrieta, A., et al.: Explainable artificial intelligence (XAI): concepts, taxonomies, opportunities and challenges toward responsible AI. Inf. Fusion **58**, 82–115 (2020). https://doi.org/10.1016/j.inffus.2019.12.012
4. Bazzano, A.N., Martin, J., Hicks, E., Faughnan, M., Murphy, L.: Human-centred design in global health: a scoping review of applications and contexts. PLoS ONE **12**(11), e0186744 (2017). https://doi.org/10.1371/journal.pone.0186744
5. Biran, O., Cotton, C.: Explanation and justification in machine learning: A survey. In: IJCAI-17 workshop on explainable AI (XAI). pp. 8–13. No. 1 (2017)

6. Bødker, S.: When second wave HCI meets third wave challenges. In: Proceedings of the 4th Nordic Conference on Human-Computer Interaction: Changing Roles, pp. 1–8 (2006)
7. Bolman, L.G., Deal, T.E.: What makes a team work? Organ. Dyn. **21**(2), 34–44 (1992). https://doi.org/10.1016/0090-2616(92)90062-R
8. Bunt, A., Lount, M., Lauzon, C.: Are explanations always important? A study of deployed, low-cost intelligent interactive systems. In: Proceedings of the 2012 ACM International Conference on Intelligent User Interfaces, pp. 169–178 (2012)
9. Chatzimparmpas, A., Martins, R.M., Jusufi, I., Kerren, A.: A survey of surveys on the use of visualization for interpreting machine learning models. Inf. Vis. **19**(3), 207–233 (2020). https://doi.org/10.1177/1473871620904671
10. Cila, N.: Designing human-agent collaborations: commitment, responsiveness, and support. In: Proceedings of the 2022 CHI Conference on Human Factors in Computing Systems, pp. 1–18. CHI 2022, Association for Computing Machinery, New York, NY, USA (2022). https://doi.org/10.1145/3491102.3517500
11. Dhurandhar, A., Iyengar, V., Luss, R., Shanmugam, K.: TIP: typifying the interpretability of procedures. CoRR abs/1706.02952 (2017). http://arxiv.org/abs/1706.02952
12. Dix, A.: Human-computer interaction, foundations and new paradigms. J. Vis. Lang. Comput. **42**, 122–134 (2017). https://doi.org/10.1016/j.jvlc.2016.04.001
13. Ehsan, U., Riedl, M.O.: Human-centered explainable AI: towards a reflective sociotechnical approach (arXiv:2002.01092) (2020). http://arxiv.org/abs/2002.01092, arXiv:2002.01092 [cs]
14. Fass, D., Gechter, F.: Towards a theory for bio–cyber physical systems modelling. In: Duffy, V.G. (ed.) DHM 2015. LNCS, vol. 9184, pp. 245–255. Springer, Cham (2015). https://doi.org/10.1007/978-3-319-21073-5_25
15. Flathmann, C., Schelble, B.G., McNeese, N.J.: Fostering human-agent team leadership by leveraging human teaming principles. In: 2021 IEEE 2nd International Conference on Human-Machine Systems (ICHMS), pp. 1–6 (2021). https://doi.org/10.1109/ICHMS53169.2021.9582649
16. Gallina, P., Bellotto, N., Di Luca, M.: Progressive co-adaptation in human-machine interaction. In: 2015 12th International Conference on Informatics in Control, Automation and Robotics (ICINCO), vol. 02, pp. 362–368 (2015)
17. Gechter, F., Fass, D.: Bio-cyber-physical systems: from concepts to human-systems integration engineering. In: Human System Integration Conference INCOSE 2022 (2022)
18. Gerber, A., Derckx, P., Döppner, D.A., Schoder, D.: Conceptualization of the human-machine symbiosis - a literature review. In: Hawaii International Conference on System Sciences 2020 (HICSS-53) (2020). https://aisel.aisnet.org/hicss-53/cl/machines_as_teammates/5
19. Gervasi, R., Mastrogiacomo, L., Franceschini, F.: A conceptual framework to evaluate human-robot collaboration. Int. J. Adv. Manuf. Technol. **108**(3), 841–865 (2020). https://doi.org/10.1007/s00170-020-05363-1
20. Glass, A., McGuinness, D.L., Wolverton, M.: Toward establishing trust in adaptive agents. In: Proceedings of the 13th International Conference on Intelligent User Interfaces, pp. 227–236 (2008)
21. Guidotti, R., Monreale, A., Ruggieri, S., Turini, F., Giannotti, F., Pedreschi, D.: A survey of methods for explaining black box models. ACM Comput. Surv. (CSUR) **51**(5), 93 (2019)
22. Gunning, D.: Explainable artificial intelligence (XAI). In: Defense Advanced Research Projects Agency (DARPA), nd Web (2017)

23. Harrison, S., Tatar, D., Sengers, P.: The three paradigms of HCI. In: Alt. Chi. Session at the SIGCHI Conference on Human Factors in Computing Systems San Jose, California, USA, pp. 1–18 (2007)
24. Hemmer, P., Schemmer, M., Vössing, M., Kühl, N.: Human-AI complementarity in hybrid intelligence systems: a structured literature review. PACIS 78 (2021)
25. Hoc, J.M.: From human - machine interaction to human - machine cooperation. Ergonomics **43**(7), 833–843 (2000). https://doi.org/10.1080/001401300409044
26. Kirsch, A.: Explain to whom? putting the user in the center of explainable AI (2017)
27. Kozar, O.: Towards better group work: seeing the difference between cooperation and collaboration. Engl. Teach. Forum **48**(2), 16–23 (2010). eRIC Number: EJ914888
28. Krafft, P.M., Young, M., Katell, M., Huang, K., Bugingo, G.: Defining AI in policy versus practice. In: Proceedings of the AAAI/ACM Conference on AI, Ethics, and Society, pp. 72–78. AIES 2020, Association for Computing Machinery, New York, NY, USA (2020). https://doi.org/10.1145/3375627.3375835
29. Liao, Q.V., Gruen, D., Miller, S.: Questioning the AI: informing design practices for explainable AI user experiences. In: Proceedings of the 2020 CHI Conference on Human Factors in Computing Systems, pp. 1–15 (2020)
30. Lipton, Z.C.: The mythos of model interpretability. Commun. ACM **61**(10), 36–43 (2018). https://doi.org/10.1145/3233231
31. Liu, Y., Goncalves, J., Ferreira, D., Xiao, B., Hosio, S., Kostakos, V.: Chi 1994–2013: mapping two decades of intellectual progress through co-word analysis. In: Proceedings of the SIGCHI Conference on Human Factors in Computing Systems, pp. 3553–3562. CHI 2014, Association for Computing Machinery, New York, NY, USA (2014). https://doi.org/10.1145/2556288.2556969
32. Lu, Y., Garcia, R., Hansen, B., Gleicher, M., Maciejewski, R.: The state-of-the-art in predictive visual analytics. Comput. Graph. Forum **36**(3), 539–562 (2017). https://doi.org/10.1111/cgf.13210
33. Mackay, W.: Responding to cognitive overload: co-adaptation between users and technology. Intellectica **30**(1), 177–193 (2000)
34. Martin, B.D., Schwab, E.: Current usage of symbiosis and associated terminology. Int. J. Biol. **5**(1), 32–45 (2012). https://doi.org/10.5539/ijb.v5n1p32
35. Matson, E.T., Min, B.C.: M2M infrastructure to integrate humans, agents and robots into collectives. In: IEEE International Instrumentation and Measurement Technology Conference, pp. 1–6. IEEE (2011)
36. Matson, E.T., Taylor, J., Raskin, V., Min, B.C., Wilson, E.C.: A natural language exchange model for enabling human, agent, robot and machine interaction. In: The 5th International Conference on Automation, Robotics and Applications, pp. 340–345. IEEE (2011)
37. Monett, D., Lewis, C.W.P.: Getting clarity by defining artificial intelligence—a survey. In: Müller, V.C. (ed.) PT-AI 2017. SAPERE, vol. 44, pp. 212–214. Springer, Cham (2018). https://doi.org/10.1007/978-3-319-96448-5_21
38. Montavon, G., Samek, W., Müller, K.R.: Methods for interpreting and understanding deep neural networks. Digit. Signal Process. **73**, 1–15 (2018). https://doi.org/10.1016/j.dsp.2017.10.011
39. Mualla, Y., et al.: The quest of parsimonious XAI: A human-agent architecture for explanation formulation. Artif. Intell. **302**, 103573 (2022). https://doi.org/10.1016/j.artint.2021.103573

40. Nazar, M., Alam, M.M., Yafi, E., Su'ud, M.M.: A systematic review of human-computer interaction and explainable artificial intelligence in healthcare with artificial intelligence techniques. IEEE Access **9**, 153316–153348 (2021). https://doi.org/10.1109/ACCESS.2021.3127881
41. Oulhen, N., Schulz, B., Carrier, T.: English translation of Heinrich Anton de Bary's 1878 speech, "die erscheinung der symbiose" ('de la symbiose'). Symbiosis **69**, 131–139 (2016). https://doi.org/10.1007/s13199-016-0409-8
42. Paleja, R., Ghuy, M., Ranawaka Arachchige, N., Jensen, R., Gombolay, M.: The utility of explainable AI in ad hoc human-machine teaming. In: Advances in Neural Information Processing Systems, vol. 34, pp. 610–623. Curran Associates, Inc. (2021). https://proceedings.neurips.cc/paper/2021/hash/05d74c48b5b30514d8e9bd60320fc8f6-Abstract.html
43. Parasuraman, R., Mouloua, M., Molloy, R.: Effects of adaptive task allocation on monitoring of automated systems. Hum. Factors **38**(4), 665–679 (1996)
44. Preece, A.: Asking 'Why'in AI: explainability of intelligent systems-perspectives and challenges. Intell. Syst. Account. Financ. Manage. **25**(2), 63–72 (2018)
45. Rosenfeld, A., Richardson, A.: Explainability in human-agent systems. Auton. Agent. Multi-Agent Syst. **33**, 673–705 (2019)
46. Samek, W., Wiegand, T., Müller, K.R.: Explainable artificial intelligence: understanding, visualizing and interpreting deep learning models. arXiv preprint arXiv:1708.08296 (2017)
47. Silva, A., Schrum, M., Hedlund-Botti, E., Gopalan, N., Gombolay, M.: Explainable artificial intelligence: Evaluating the objective and subjective impacts of XAI on human-agent interaction. Int. J. Hum. Comput. Interact. **39**(7), 1390–1404 (2023). https://doi.org/10.1080/10447318.2022.2101698
48. Stephanidis, et al.: Seven HCI grand challenges. Int. J. Hum. Comput. Interact. **35**(14), 1229–1269 (2019). https://doi.org/10.1080/10447318.2019.1619259
49. Szegedy, C., et al.: Intriguing properties of neural networks. arXiv preprint arXiv:1312.6199 (2013)
50. Wagoner, A.R., Matson, E.T.: A robust human-robot communication system using natural language for harms. In: FNC/MobiSPC, pp. 119–126 (2015)
51. Wang, P.: On defining artificial intelligence. J. Artif. Gen. Intell. **10**(2), 1–37 (2019). https://doi.org/10.2478/jagi-2019-0002
52. Weiss, G., Wooldridge, M.: Multiagent Systems: A Modern Approach to Distributed Artificial Intelligence. MIT Press, Cambridge (1999). google-Books-ID: JYcznFCN3xcC
53. Wellsandt, S., et al.: 45 - hybrid-augmented intelligence in predictive maintenance with digital intelligent assistants. Annu. Rev. Control. **53**, 382–390 (2022). https://doi.org/10.1016/j.arcontrol.2022.04.001
54. Yang, C., Zhu, Y., Chen, Y.: A review of human-machine cooperation in the robotics domain. IEEE Trans. Hum. Mach. Syst. **52**(1), 12–25 (2022). https://doi.org/10.1109/THMS.2021.3131684

Explaining Deep Reinforcement Learning-Based Methods for Control of Building HVAC Systems

Javier Jiménez-Raboso(✉) ⓘ, Antonio Manjavacas ⓘ,
Alejandro Campoy-Nieves ⓘ, Miguel Molina-Solana ⓘ,
and Juan Gómez-Romero ⓘ

Department of Computer Science and Artificial Intelligence,
Universidad de Granada, 18014 Granada, Spain
jajimer@correo.ugr.es

Abstract. Deep reinforcement learning (DRL) has emerged as a powerful tool for controlling complex systems, by combining deep neural networks with reinforcement learning techniques. However, due to the black-box nature of these algorithms, the resulting control policies can be difficult to understand from a human perspective. This limitation is particularly relevant in real-world scenarios, where an understanding of the controller is required for reliability and safety reasons. In this paper we investigate the application of DRL methods for controlling the heating, ventilation and air-conditioning (HVAC) system of a building, and we propose an Explainable Artificial Intelligence (XAI) approach to provide interpretability to these models. This is accomplished by combining different XAI methods including surrogate models, Shapley values, and counterfactual examples. We show the results of the DRL-based controller in terms of energy consumption and thermal comfort and provide insights and explainability to the underlying control strategy using this XAI layer.

Keywords: XAI · Deep Reinforcement Learning · Building Control

1 Introduction

Deep Reinforcement Learning (DRL) has emerged as a powerful technique for training agents that can learn to solve complex tasks through trial and error. However, the black-box nature of the neural networks used by DRL algorithms makes it challenging to understand why an agent behaves in a particular way. This lack of transparency can be problematic, especially in high-stakes applications such as healthcare or autonomous driving, where incorrect decisions can have severe consequences.

By incorporating Explainable Artificial Intelligence (XAI) [3] techniques into DRL models, we can develop algorithms that not only perform well but also provide interpretable explanations for their decisions. This can help increasing trust

© The Author(s), under exclusive license to Springer Nature Switzerland AG 2023
L. Longo (Ed.): xAI 2023, CCIS 1902, pp. 237–255, 2023.
https://doi.org/10.1007/978-3-031-44067-0_13

and transparency, allowing stakeholders to better understand and potentially correct the agent's behavior if needed. Additionally, XAI can provide insights into the underlying mechanisms of DRL-based solutions, allowing us to improve the overall performance and generalizability of these systems. Nevertheless, XAI methods for DRL have not been extensively studied, particularly in industrial problems [18].

One of the most promising industrial applications of DRL is the mitigation of climate change and, more specifically, energy efficiency of buildings, which according to the International Energy Agency (IEA), are responsible for 17% and 10% of global direct and indirect CO_2 emissions [19], respectively. On this basis, DRL has been proposed as a viable alternative for building energy optimization frameworks, mostly focused on improving energy consumption and sustainability of the Heating, Ventilation, and Air-Conditioning (HVAC) systems, which represent more than 50% of buildings' energy demand [38]. DRL can learn sophisticated control strategies from building simulations [2,4,6,12,37,51], avoiding the short-term horizon of proportional-integral-derivative controllers (PID) [14] and being more computationally efficient than Model Predictive Control (MPC) methods [15,52].

This research paper proposes applying XAI techniques to Deep Reinforcement Learning (DRL) algorithms for building energy control. This study applies three post-hoc explanation methods [3]: (1) training a decision tree as an explainable surrogate model of the agent's policy, (2) computation of Shapley values [44] to evaluate the features importance, and (3) generating counterfactual examples that involve hypothetical scenarios in which the agent's decision is modified. The tree-based model offers interpretable rules describing the underlying control logic, enabling building operators to interpret and potentially correct it. Shapley values assess the contribution of each input variable in the DRL policy, thus providing insights into the factors that influence the control decisions the most. In addition, the counterfactual examples help to evaluate the reliability of the controller and establish decision boundaries.

Overall, our experiments show that these XAI methods are useful for interpreting DRL-based controllers, as they allow to discover the underlying rules and main factors driving the policy. Additionally, they have the potential of improving the performance through the selection of the state variables.

The remainder of this paper is organized as follows. Section 2 presents the fundamental concepts of DRL and reviews the related work on DRL and XAI, analysing existing proposals and gaps in the literature. We present our proposed methodology in Sect. 3, describing the problem formulation, the experimental setup and the explainability methods to be used. Section 4 presents the results of the experimentation, which are discussed in Sect. 5. Finally, we summarize the main conclusions of our work and identify future lines of research in Sect. 6.

2   Background

2.1   Fundamentals of DRL

Reinforcement learning (RL) is a widely used machine learning framework for solving continuous control problems, based on the interaction of an agent with its environment. Such interaction can be represented as a Markov Decision Process (MDP) in which learning takes place over a sequence of discrete timesteps $\mathcal{T} = \{0, 1, 2, ...\}$. At each time step t, the agent starts from the current state of the environment $s_t \in \mathcal{S}$ and selects an action $a_t \in \mathcal{A}$ based on a policy function π, such that $a_t \sim \pi(\cdot|s_t)$. As a result of performing this action, the environment transitions into a new state $s_{t+1} \in \mathcal{S}$, emitting a reward signal $r_t \in \mathbb{R}$ which represents how good or bad the performed action has been.

The objective of the RL agent is learning an optimal policy function that maximizes the sum of discounted rewards over time, i.e. the *return*, defined as: $G_t = \sum_{k=0}^{\infty} \gamma^k R_{t+k+1}$, with $\gamma \in [0, 1]$ being a *discount rate* used to weight rewards based on their temporal proximity. Learning an optimal policy can be carried out in contexts with limited state and action spaces by using dynamic programming methods, such as value or policy iteration, or classical reinforcement learning algorithms, such as Monte Carlo, SARSA or Q-learning [46,50]. However, these classical methods have proven to be incapable of scaling to environments where $\mathcal{S}$ or $\mathcal{A}$ are too large, or even infinite for continuous problems.

In recent years, this limitation has motivated the development of Deep Reinforcement Learning (DRL) algorithms, which leverage the abstraction capability of neural networks to approximate value functions or policies in complex environments. DRL algorithms assume a parameterized policy π_θ, i.e., a neural network with weights θ, whose expected return is iteratively approximated to that of an optimal policy by adjusting the parameters θ. The way this policy is approximated depends on the type of algorithm we are dealing with. Some of the most used DRL algorithms constituting the state of the art are the following: Deep Q-Networks (DQN) [31], Deep Deterministic Policy Gradient (DDPG) [24], Advantage Actor-Critic (A2C) and Asynchronous Advantage Actor-Critic (A3C) [30], Proximal Policy Optimization (PPO) [43], Trust Region Policy Optimization (TRPO) [42], Twin Delayed DDPG (TD3) [13] or Soft Actor-Critic (SAC) [17], with all their variants.

2.2   Related Work

Explainability in Deep Reinforcement Learning (XAI-DRL) has been a topic of interest in recent years. In [10], one of the nine most relevant challenges of real-world reinforcement learning is providing system operators with explainable policies. As highlighted in the paper, the ability to comprehend the ultimate intentions of a policy is crucial for securing stakeholder support, particularly when the policy may present an unforeseen and alternative strategy for regulating a system. Additionally, in cases where policy errors occur, gaining a posteriori comprehension of the origins of the error is imperative. However, this is the less researched challenge of the suite. For example in [9], the authors provide an open-source benchmark of control environments, but explicitly leave XAI out since an objective evaluation of the explainability of a policy is not trivial.

Since DRL is driven by deep neural networks, most of the existing methods for explaining deep learning models can also be applied for explaining reinforcement learning policies. [3] offers a taxonomy of existing post-hoc explainability methods, which can be divided in model-agnostic and model-specific methods. While neural networks-specific methods can take advantage of the differentiable nature of these algorithms [32,35], model-agnostic methods can be applied to any machine learning model. Among them, the authors of [3] also identified several trends regarding how explainability is achieved; namely by simplification [5], feature relevance [25], locally [22] or visually [11].

Most of the existing methods of XAI-DRL are adaptations of those for explaining supervised learning algorithms. Several reviews have been proposed for categorizing existing methods [18,29,39,49]. [18] distinguishes between transparent algorithms, which explicitly learn a representation for the explanations, or post-hoc explainability methods. Both [29] and [39] create a taxonomy based on the RL component where explanations are aimed: policies, states, rewards, transition dynamics or tasks. Similarly, [49] exposes the different paradigms for XAI-DRL depending on whether local actions, policies or global properties of the agent are to be explained. Additionally, we highlight several works proposing specific methods for XAI-DRL. In [21] rewards are decomposed into meaningful types, allowing to explain action selection process in terms of them. Other works focus on expressing policies in an interpretable form, using decision trees [41] or symbolic expressions [23]. In [27], an approach for learning a structural causal model is proposed for encoding causal relationships between input states and actions. Lastly, authors of [16] propose a self-explainable model which captures time step importance in order to predict cumulative reward over episodes.

A limited number of works have investigated the usage of XAI methods in HVAC-related scenarios, predominantly focusing on supervised learning problems [26,28]. Despite the growing interest in the applications of DRL for solving energy management problems [53], there is a lack of experiments and proposals focusing on XAI-DRL in real-world scenarios. To the best of our knowledge, only two papers have considered this matter: in [54] the authors use Shapley values for quantifying the feature importance of a DRL-based controller for a power system, and in [8] the authors use a decision tree to simplify the policy of a DQN algorithm for controlling a building cooling system.

Given the relevance of having explainable and reliable controllers and the potential of DRL algorithms for improving energy efficiency of building HVAC systems, this research aims to address the existing gap in the literature by proposing a methodology for XAI-DRL for controlling the HVAC system of a building, introducing an XAI layer with several methods of explainability.

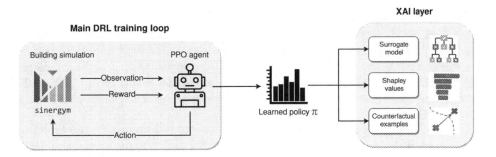

Fig. 1. Schematic representation of the proposed methodology.

3   Methodology

3.1   Problem Formulation

In this paper we address a continuous and multi-objective HVAC control problem, where an agent must learn to minimise the power consumption of the HVAC system while simultaneously ensuring occupants' thermal comfort. The control is performed by selecting the heating and cooling temperature setpoints of the system.

In this formulation, the *state* $s_t \in \mathcal{S}$ encodes information about the current status of the building at time t; including weather conditions, indoor temperature and humidity, comfort metrics, power consumption, number of occupants, etc. An *action* $a_t \in \mathcal{A}$ consists on the selection of the HVAC heating and cooling setpoints. By selecting this action the building transitions into a new state s_{t+1}, given by $s_{t+1} = f(s_t, a_t)$ where $f : \mathcal{S} \times \mathcal{A} \rightarrow \mathcal{S}$ is some unknown *transition function* driving the dynamics of the building.

Based on building state variables, we can obtain information about its current *power consumption*, $P(s_t)$ (measured in W). In turn, we can also compute different *comfort* metrics, such as the distance from the current indoor temperature to a target comfort range, $C(s_t, s_{target})$. We can combine both terms in a weighted sum, yielding the following *reward* signal:

$$r(s_t, a_t) = -(1 - \omega)\lambda_P P(s_t) - \omega \lambda_C C(s_t, s_{target}) \tag{1}$$

where ω weights the importance of comfort and consumption, and λ_P, λ_C are constants used to balance both magnitudes. Note that reward is expressed in negative terms, and thus we aim at maximizing it.

3.2   Building Simulation

Learning an optimal DRL-based control policy usually requires a large amount of data which, in a real environment, would take several years to gather. Therefore, most approaches in the literature use building simulators —such as EnergyPlus or Modelica— to design controllers and evaluate their performance, thus allowing us to simulate, in a affordable computing time, the equivalent to several long time real-world periods [48,55]. Building simulation also allows for a greater quantity and variety of data, enabling the consideration of extreme situations or under designer's criteria. Moreover, it is possible to pre-train agents in simulated environments and then continue their training online once deployed. This avoids cold starts, reducing the time it takes to obtain an acceptable control policy from which to start acting [47,48].

Usually, training DRL agents for HVAC control involves connecting building simulators with DRL libraries, such as StableBaselines3. Since the communication between controllers and simulators is not trivial, different frameworks have been proposed in the literature. In this work we used Sinergym [20], which offers a Python interface for EnergyPlus, fully compliant with the Gymnasium API, the de facto standard for DRL.

3.3   Experimental Settings

The experimentation of this work is based on the `5ZoneAutoDXVAV` building available in Sinergym. It is a single-story building divided into 1 indoor and 4 outdoor zones, comprising an area of $463.6\,\text{m}^2$, and it is equipped with a packaged variable air volume HVAC system with dual setpoints. The building is simulated on different weather conditions, randomly sampled on each training episode (see [20] for details on weather data).

The agent interacts with the building environment on a hourly basis, receiving information from the current state of the building. The complete list of variables conforming the observation space is described in Table 3 of Appendix A. We define a 5-dimensional discrete action space, where each action corresponds to a particular combination of values for the heating and cooling setpoints of the HVAC system. These values are shown in Table 1.

Table 1. Action space for the HVAC setpoints control.

Action index	Heating and cooling setpoints ($^\circ$C)
0	[10, 40]
1	[18, 30]
2	[22, 40]
3	[15, 27]
4	[15, 23]

The reward function is expressed by (1). In this case, the comfort term $C(s_t, s_{target})$ is defined as the absolute value between current indoor temperature and the comfort range, and therefore it will be 0 if thermal comfort is satisfied. We considered a comfort range of [20, 23.5] for winter (October-May) and [23, 26] for summer (June-September), based on ASHRAE recommendations

[1]. The parameter ω takes different values depending on the hour of the day to give importance to thermal comfort only during working hours, being $\omega = 0.5$ from 7AM to 6PM, and $\omega = 0$ the for the rest of the day. The constants shown in (1) were set to $\lambda_P = 0.0001$W and $\lambda_C = 1°$ C.

Finally, the DRL algorithm employed was the PPO [43] implementation of StableBaselines3. We trained the model for 30 episodes using the hyperparameters shown in Appendix B. After training, the model was executed for 10 evaluation episodes for collecting samples of states and actions produced by the agent. This dataset, composed of 87,600 samples, was used for training the XAI methods.

3.4   Explainability Methods

Once the policy was trained and we collected data from evaluation episodes, we included an extra XAI layer to interpret the controller behavior. We applied several explainability methods in order to draw different conclusions from the underlying control logic. In particular, we aim to answer the following three questions regarding explainability of the DRL-based controller:

– **Q1**: How could we approximate the policy learned by the agent by some simple *if-else* rules, in order to better understand its behavior?
– **Q2**: What are the main input features for the control, i.e., what are the most relevant variables for the controller?
– **Q3**: How would the outputs of the agent change if the inputs changed (*what-if* scenarios)?

It is worth noting that these questions complement each other, as each one allows to understand the model from different angles. For example, answering Q1 would improve interpretation from a human perspective, while Q2 and Q3 would be more appropriate to ensure reliability or compliance requirements.

In the following, we discuss the XAI methods applied in this work for answering such questions.

Q1: Training a Surrogate Model. Surrogate models are simple models intended to explain a more complex model, typically a black-box one. They are trained on the black-box model's outputs in order to approximate and interpret its predictions. The most used surrogates are linear and decision tree models, since they are easy to understand by a human reader.

We used a decision tree [7] as surrogate model for approximating the policy of the DRL algorithm. This question can be addressed as a multi-class classification problem, where each class corresponds to one of the 5 possible actions available to the agent. We trained the model using data collected from the 10 evaluation episodes, with a 5-fold cross-validation strategy for selecting the maximum depth of the tree, using a grid search between 2 and 6. After training, the model was pruned by aggregating terminal nodes with the same predicted action. Scikit-learn [36] was employed for implementing and training the decision tree.

Q2: Shapley Values for Feature Importance. Another relevant aspect for explainability is quantifying the importance of each input variable in the trained policy, both for understanding the action selection process and for gaining insights on the main aspects that drive the HVAC control.

We used Shapley values [44] for estimating the contribution of each input variable in the model's output. These values provide a theoretically robust manner to distribute the importance among the features, by considering all possible permutations of the inputs and averaging their marginal contributions. Additionally, Shapley values are additive, meaning that the sum of Shapley values for a particular data sample is equal to the difference between model's output for that sample and the model average response.

The implementation from [25] was used to calculate Shapley values of the DRL policy, treating its output as the probability distribution for selecting each action. Then, we used these values for measuring feature contribution in two flavors: (1) locally, by explaining individual data samples and (2) globally, by aggregating Shapley values over the full dataset to extract the global feature importance.

Q3: Counterfactual Examples. This approach involves the generation of synthetic data samples that modify the output of the controller, i.e., counterfactual examples. These examples allow us to analyse the boundaries of the decision function by slightly changing input variables, thus creating *what-if* scenarios to better understand the model. An interesting property of counterfactual examples from an XAI point of view is that they can be translated into natural language, in the form of *"If input variable X were to change its value from x to x', then the controller would select action a' instead of a"*.

We used the implementation from [33] to generate these counterfactual samples. The generation process is as follows. First, given a query sample x_i with action $a_i = \pi(x_i)$, we generate up to 1,000 candidates $C(x_i)$ by incrementally changing input values (first one feature at a time, then two at a time, etc.) until we obtain a different action $a_i' = \pi(C(x_i))$ from the policy. Then, the best candidate is selected as the counterfactual example considering diversity and proximity to the query sample, as also discussed in [33].

We let only a subset of the input features from the observation to be varied; namely weather conditions (temperature, relative humidity, wind speed and direction and direct and diffuse solar radiation), temperature and relative humidity inside the building and number of occupants. The rationale behind this decision is to only generate intuitive and meaningful counterfactual examples that allow us to better understand the HVAC control.

4   Results

The results of our experimentation are discussed in the following subsections. First, we present the results of the DRL algorithm for controlling the HVAC system, and we compare its performance with a baseline controller in terms of cumulative reward, energy consumption and thermal comfort. Next, we present the results of the XAI layer using the aforementioned methods for interpreting the control policy.

4.1 DRL Results

We trained the PPO algorithm for 30 episodes and evaluated on 10 episodes. We compared its performance using the default control of the building as a baseline, which modifies the temperature setpoints of the HVAC system based only on the hour and season. Then, we compared both methods using the cumulative reward of Equation (1) over the entire episode, i.e., the aggregation of the total power consumption and the thermal comfort violation. The results are shown in Table 2.

Table 2. Evaluation of baseline and PPO controllers. Metrics are calculated on a full episode, which represents one year of simulation. Results show the mean and standard deviation over 10 evaluation episodes

Evaluation metric	Baseline	PPO
Cumulative reward	-3532 ± 619	$\mathbf{-2838 \pm 554}$
Total power consumption (GW)	$\mathbf{32.5 \pm 8.0}$	34.4 ± 7.0
Mean comfort violation (°C)	1.26 ± 0.12	$\mathbf{0.97 \pm 0.11}$

The DRL-based method outperformed the default controller in terms of cumulative reward, with an improvement of 24%. Regarding thermal comfort, PPO was capable of reducing the mean deviation from the comfort range from 1.26° C to 0.97° C, which represents a 30% improvement. However, PPO had a trade-off in terms of energy efficiency, increasing the mean power consumption by a 6%. Note that, by modifying the parameters of the reward function (1), different results may be obtained.

4.2 Explainability Results

After training the policy, we incorporated an extra layer of XAI techniques to interpret the black-box controller and address the questions on explainability raised above.

Decision Tree. We trained the decision tree using data collected from the evaluation episodes, using the same input features as the policy. This surrogate model achieved a mean accuracy of 74.9% in predicting actions made by the DRL agent.

The visualization of the trained decision tree is shown in Fig. 2. The final model has a depth of 5 and 10 terminal nodes, representing the predicted action.

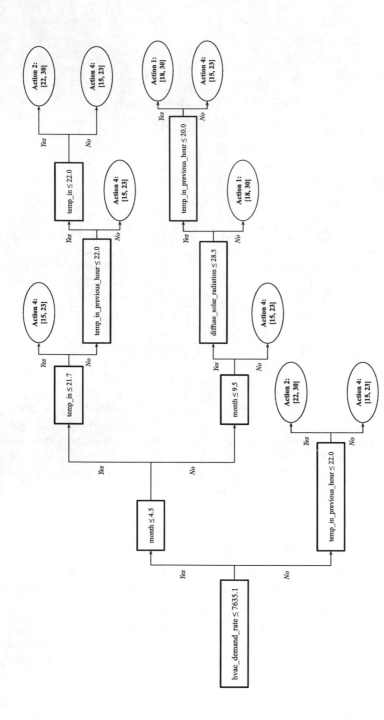

Fig. 2. Visualization of the trained decision tree. This surrogate model achieves a mean accuracy of 74.9% in predicting actions made by the DRL policy

We can see that only 5 features are considered in the decision path; namely the month, indoor temperatures in current and previous hour, the diffuse solar radiation and the HVAC electricity demand rate. It is also worth mentioning that the surrogate model selects only 3 of the 5 actions (1, 2 and 4), which is in line with the original policy where these actions are performed 15%, 14% and 59% of the timesteps respectively.

Feature Importance. The results of the calculation of the Shapley values are summarized in Figs. 3 and 4. Local explanations are shown in Fig. 3 for four individual samples. In the first case (3a), action 4 is selected with a probability of 0.885, which is 0.291 greater than the baseline. We observe that the direct solar radiation is the feature contributing the most towards selecting this action (+0.17), while the number of occupants is subtracting 0.11, resulting in a negative contribution. By interpreting these local Shapley values we can conclude that this sample corresponds to a warm day, and the controller is selecting a cooling setpoint of 23° C to maintain indoor temperature in the comfort range. In the second example (3a), action 1 is selected with a probability of 0.326, being 0.183 greater than its baseline. The hour of the day and the number of occupants are the most influential features in this case. The example 3c illustrates a sample where action 4 is selected with a similar probability (0.592) than the baseline, since there are both positive and negative contributing variables. Lastly, in example 3d action 1 is selected with a probability of 0.446 and having a positive contribution from the number of occupants and month and hour of the sample; while all other features are essentially ignored.

Global feature importance is shown in Fig. 4. We can see that the most influential variables for the controller are the month, hour of the day, number of occupants and the direct solar radiation. Additionally, these values also allow us to compare how each action is dependent on different features. For example, direct solar radiation has great impact on selecting a cooling setpoint of 23° C (action 4), while action 1 is mostly driven by the month and the number of occupants.

Counterfactual Examples. Three examples of these counterfactual explanations are shown in Listing 1. In example A, a modification of both the indoor temperature and the number of occupants leads to changing from action [15, 23] to action [18, 30]. The second case (example B) shows that the presence of direct solar radiation also modifies the selected setpoints, moving from [10, 40] to [18, 30]. Lastly, example C shows that a change in weather conditions such as the direct solar radiation and the wind direction switches the setpoints from [18, 30] to [10, 40].

5 Discussion

The above results show how different XAI methods can be adapted to interpret and understand the policy of DRL-based controllers. By combining different

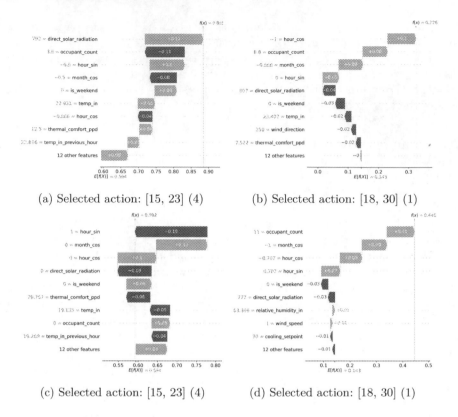

(a) Selected action: [15, 23] (4)   (b) Selected action: [18, 30] (1)

(c) Selected action: [15, 23] (4)   (d) Selected action: [18, 30] (1)

Fig. 3. Shapley values for four individual data samples. $f(x)$ represents the probability given by the policy to the selected action, while $E[f(x)]$ is the average probability of that action over the full dataset.

Listing 1. Counterfactual examples. For each query sample, a set of counterfactual candidates are generated. We select and report the one with highest diversity and proximity to the original, as discussed in [33].

- Example A: *If variable* `temp_in` *changed its value from 20 to 16 and variable* `occupant_count` *changed its value from 0 to 10, then action [18, 30] would have been selected instead of [15, 23].*
- Example B: *If variable* `direct_solar_radiation` *changed its value from 0 to 887, then action [18, 30] would have been selected instead of [10, 40].*
- Example C: *If variable* `direct_solar_radiation` *changed its value from 792 to 311 and variable* `wind_direction` *changed its value from 230 to 27, then action [10, 40] would have been selected instead of [18, 30].*

post-hoc techniques we can reach a better comprehension of the underlying control logic, as each method may provide different answers regarding explainability.

It is worth mentioning that each XAI method has its own advantages and limitations. Using a decision tree as surrogate model provided an accurate and

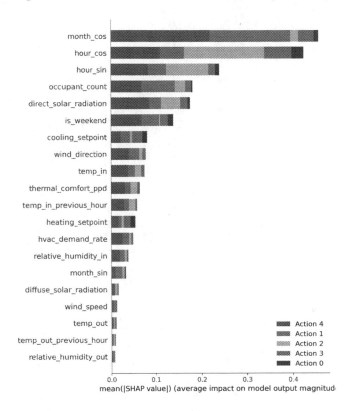

Fig. 4. Shapley values for global feature importance.

simple approximation of the policy (Fig. 2), however, since decision trees partition the input space one feature at a time, they may be not well-suited for more complex policies or control settings. In this sense Shapley values are a convenient method for explaining feature importance in HVAC control, providing robust theoretical guarantees for both local and global explanations. In our case study, the main features affecting the control policy are the hour and month of the day, building occupation and the direct solar radiation (Fig. 4). These two methods are complemented with the generation of counterfactual examples (Listing 1), which show how the variation of one or two variables may modify the setpoint selection. This kind of examples are useful for assessing the performance of the controller under different conditions or for ensuring safety requirements.

The results obtained by the DRL-based controller (Table 2) show an improvement of 30% with respect to the baseline controller in terms of thermal comfort, but at the cost of 6% higher energy consumption. In HVAC control problems there is a trade-off between these two objectives [34], so properly designing and tuning the reward function has a major impact on final performance. Additionally, in this case study keeping the temperature setpoints fixed provides good results, which is not the case in more complex scenarios [2,47,48,56]. Our proposed methodology (Fig. 1) is intended to explain any DRL-based controller and therefore it could be easily adapted to other building control problems, since it is agnostic to the reward function, algorithm or observation space to be used. However, the results and insights obtained in this work are specific to the problem setting we considered, and they may change for other use cases.

As final remarks, we would like to highlight the ethical concerns of having DRL-based controllers in real buildings without properly assessing or explaining their behavior. Despite their high performance in a wide variety of tasks, the black-box nature of these algorithms may be problematic in scenarios where their operation can affect people, as it is the case of HVAC control problems. Therefore, incorporating XAI methods in the development of DRL algorithms is crucial to find reliable and transparent control solutions for stakeholders. We believe an XAI layer for interpreting DRL-based controllers, like the one presented in this work, could be included in both the development, training and evaluation pipelines of these methods.

6   Conclusions

In this paper we presented a methodology for explaining DRL-based methods for controlling HVAC systems using several XAI techniques. We trained a surrogate model for approximating the original policy with a simple decision tree, we calculated Shapley values of input feature for measuring their importance both locally and globally, and we generated counterfactual examples for evaluating *what-if* scenarios where the action selection varies. Our results show that combining different XAI methods improves interpretability and allows for assessing the reliability of the controller.

Future work should be oriented towards further exploring explainability in DRL-based methods for building control, including other scenarios like demand response [48] or microgrid coordination [45]. We will also intend to include other XAI methods, such as LIME [40], in order to address explainability from different perspectives. Finally, we plan to explore intrinsically explainable DRL-based methods in order to provide interpretable control policies by design.

Acknowledgements. This work has been partially funded by the European Union – NextGenerationEU (IA4TES project, MIA.2021.M04.0008), Junta de Andalucía (D3S project, 30.BG.29.03.01 – P21.00247) and the Spanish Ministry of Science (SPEEDY, TED2021.130454B.I00). A. Manjavacas is also funded by FEDER/Junta de Andalucía (IFMIF-DONES project, SE21_UGR_IFMIF-DONES).

Appendix

A. Observation space description

Table 3. Observation space used for training the DRL agent. It is composed of 20 variables normalized into range $[0, 1]$ using min-max strategy.

Variable name	Description
month_cos	Cosine of the current month
month_sin	Sine of the current month
is_weekend	Flag indicating weekday or weekend
hour_cos	Cosine of the current hour
hour_sin	Sin of the current hour
temp_out	Outdoor temperature
temp_out_previous_hour	Outdoor temperature in the previous hour
relative_humidity_out	Outdoor relative humidity
wind_speed	Wind speed
wind_direction	Wind direction
diffuse_solar_radiation	Diffuse solar radiation
direct_solar_radiation	Direct solar radiation
heating_setpoint	Current value of the heating setpoint
cooling_setpoint	Current value of the cooling setpoint
temp_in	Current indoor temperature of the building
temp_in_previous_hour	Indoor temperature of the building in the previous hour
relative_humidity_in	Indoor relative humidity inside the building
thermal_comfort_ppd	PPD thermal comfort index
occupant_count	Current number of occupants of the building
hvac_demand_rate	Electricity demand rate of the HVAC system

B. PPO hyperparameters

The trained PPO model has the default architecture of the `ActorCriticPolicy` class of StableBaselines3. This architecture is similar for policy and value nets, and consists of a feature extractor followed by 2 fully-connected hidden layers with 64 units per layer. The activation function is `tanh`.

The remaining hyperparameters are listed in Table 4.

Table 4. Hyperparameters for training PPO model

Hyperparameter	Value
learning_rate	0.0003
n_steps	2048
batch_size	64
n_epochs	10
gamma	0.99
gae_lambda	0.95
clip_range	0.2
ent_coef	0
vf_coef	0.5
max_grad_norm	0.5

References

1. ASHRAE: Guideline 36–2021: High Performance Sequences of Operation for HVAC Systems. ASHRAE (2021)
2. Azuatalam, D., Lee, W.L., de Nijs, F., Liebman, A.: Reinforcement learning for whole-building HVAC control and demand response. Energy AI **2**, 100020 (2020). https://doi.org/10.1016/j.egyai.2020.100020
3. Barredo Arrieta, A., et al.: Explainable artificial intelligence (XAI): concepts, taxonomies, opportunities and challenges toward responsible AI. Inf. Fusion **58**, 82–115 (2020). https://doi.org/10.1016/j.inffus.2019.12.012. https://www.sciencedirect.com/science/article/pii/S1566253519308103
4. Barrett, E., Linder, S.: Autonomous HVAC control, a reinforcement learning approach. In: Bifet, A., et al. (eds.) ECML PKDD 2015. LNCS (LNAI), vol. 9286, pp. 3–19. Springer, Cham (2015). https://doi.org/10.1007/978-3-319-23461-8_1
5. Bastani, O., Kim, C., Bastani, H.: Interpretability via model extraction (2018). https://doi.org/10.48550/arXiv.1706.09773
6. Biemann, M., Scheller, F., Liu, X., Huang, L.: Experimental evaluation of model-free reinforcement learning algorithms for continuous HVAC control. Appl. Energy **298**, 117164 (2021). https://doi.org/10.1016/j.apenergy.2021.117164
7. Breiman, L., Friedman, J., Stone, C.J., Olshen, R.: Classification and Regression Trees. Chapman and Hall/CRC, Wadsworth, Belmont, CA (1984). https://doi.org/10.1201/9781315139470
8. Cho, S., Park, C.S.: Rule reduction for control of a building cooling system using explainable AI. J. Build. Perform. Simul. **15**(6), 832–847 (2022). https://doi.org/10.1080/19401493.2022.2103586
9. Dulac-Arnold, G., et al.: Challenges of real-world reinforcement learning: definitions, benchmarks and analysis. Mach. Learn. **110**(9), 2419–2468 (2021). https://doi.org/10.1007/s10994-021-05961-4
10. Dulac-Arnold, G., Mankowitz, D., Hester, T.: Challenges of real-world reinforcement learning. arXiv preprint arXiv:1904.12901 (2019)
11. Fong, R.C., Vedaldi, A.: Interpretable explanations of black boxes by meaningful perturbation. In: Proceedings of the IEEE International Conference on Computer Vision (ICCV) (2017)

12. Fu, Q., Han, Z., Chen, J., Lu, Y., Wu, H., Wang, Y.: Applications of reinforcement learning for building energy efficiency control: a review. J. Build. Eng. (2022). https://doi.org/10.1016/j.jobe.2022.104165
13. Fujimoto, S., Hoof, H., Meger, D.: Addressing function approximation error in actor-critic methods. In: International Conference on Machine Learning, pp. 1582–1591 (2018). https://doi.org/10.48550/arXiv.1802.09477
14. Geng, G., Geary, G.: On performance and tuning of PID controllers in HVAC systems. In: Proceedings of IEEE International Conference on Control and Applications, pp. 819–824. IEEE (1993). https://doi.org/10.1109/CCA.1993.348229
15. Gomez-Romero, J., et al.: A probabilistic algorithm for predictive control with full-complexity models in non-residential buildings. IEEE Access **7**, 38748–38765 (2019)
16. Guo, W., Wu, X., Khan, U., Xing, X.: Edge: explaining deep reinforcement learning policies. In: Ranzato, M., Beygelzimer, A., Dauphin, Y., Liang, P., Vaughan, J.W. (eds.) Advances in Neural Information Processing Systems, vol. 34, pp. 12222–12236. Curran Associates, Inc. (2021). https://proceedings.neurips.cc/paper_files/paper/2021/file/65c89f5a9501a04c073b354f03791b1f-Paper.pdf
17. Haarnoja, T., Zhou, A., Abbeel, P., Levine, S.: Soft actor-critic: Off-policy maximum entropy deep reinforcement learning with a stochastic actor. In: International Conference on Machine Learning, pp. 1861–1870. PMLR (2018). https://doi.org/10.48550/arXiv.1801.01290
18. Heuillet, A., Couthouis, F., Díaz-Rodríguez, N.: Explainability in deep reinforcement learning. Knowl.-Based Syst. **214**, 106685 (2021). https://doi.org/10.1016/j.knosys.2020.106685
19. International Energy Agency: Tracking buildings (2021). https://www.iea.org/reports/tracking-buildings-2021
20. Jiménez-Raboso, J., Campoy-Nieves, A., Manjavacas-Lucas, A., Gómez-Romero, J., Molina-Solana, M.: Sinergym: a building simulation and control framework for training reinforcement learning agents. In: Proceedings of the 8th ACM International Conference on Systems for Energy-Efficient Buildings, Cities, and Transportation, pp. 319–323. Association for Computing Machinery, New York, USA (2021). https://doi.org/10.1145/3486611.3488729
21. Juozapaitis, Z., Koul, A., Fern, A., Erwig, M., Doshi-Velez, F.: Explainable reinforcement learning via reward decomposition. In: Proceedings at the International Joint Conference on Artificial Intelligence. A Workshop on Explainable Artificial Intelligence (2019)
22. Krause, J., Perer, A., Ng, K.: Interacting with predictions: visual inspection of black-box machine learning models. In: Proceedings of the 2016 CHI Conference on Human Factors in Computing Systems, pp. 5686–5697. CHI 2016, Association for Computing Machinery, New York, NY, USA (2016). https://doi.org/10.1145/2858036.2858529
23. Landajuela, M., et al.: Discovering symbolic policies with deep reinforcement learning. In: Meila, M., Zhang, T. (eds.) Proceedings of the 38th International Conference on Machine Learning. Proceedings of Machine Learning Research, vol. 139, pp. 5979–5989. PMLR (2021). https://proceedings.mlr.press/v139/landajuela21a.html
24. Lillicrap, T.P., et al.: Continuous control with deep reinforcement learning. arXiv preprint arXiv:1509.02971 (2015). https://doi.org/10.48550/arXiv.1509.02971
25. Lundberg, S.M., Lee, S.I.: A unified approach to interpreting model predictions. In: Guyon, I., et al. (eds.) Advances in Neural Information Processing Systems, vol.

30, pp. 4765–4774. Curran Associates, Inc. (2017). http://papers.nips.cc/paper/7062-a-unified-approach-to-interpreting-model-predictions.pdf

26. Madhikermi, M., Malhi, A.K., Främling, K.: Explainable artificial intelligence based heat recycler fault detection in air handling unit. In: Calvaresi, D., Najjar, A., Schumacher, M., Främling, K. (eds.) EXTRAAMAS 2019. LNCS (LNAI), vol. 11763, pp. 110–125. Springer, Cham (2019). https://doi.org/10.1007/978-3-030-30391-4_7

27. Madumal, P., Miller, T., Sonenberg, L., Vetere, F.: Explainable reinforcement learning through a causal lens (2019). https://doi.org/10.48550/arXiv.1905.10958

28. Meas, M., et al.: Explainability and transparency of classifiers for air-handling unit faults using explainable artificial intelligence (XAI). Sensors 22(17), 6338 (2022). https://doi.org/10.3390/s22176338

29. Milani, S., Topin, N., Veloso, M., Fang, F.: A survey of explainable reinforcement learning (2022). https://doi.org/10.48550/arXiv.2202.08434

30. Mnih, V., et al.: Asynchronous methods for deep reinforcement learning. In: International Conference on Machine Learning, pp. 1928–1937. PMLR (2016). https://doi.org/10.48550/arXiv.1602.01783

31. Mnih, V., et al.: Playing Atari with deep reinforcement learning. arXiv preprint arXiv:1312.5602 (2013). https://doi.org/10.48550/arXiv.1312.5602

32. Montavon, G., Lapuschkin, S., Binder, A., Samek, W., Müller, K.R.: Explaining nonlinear classification decisions with deep Taylor decomposition. Pattern Recogn. 65, 211–222 (2017). https://doi.org/10.1016/j.patcog.2016.11.008. https://www.sciencedirect.com/science/article/pii/S0031320316303582

33. Mothilal, R.K., Sharma, A., Tan, C.: Explaining machine learning classifiers through diverse counterfactual explanations. In: Proceedings of the 2020 Conference on Fairness, Accountability, and Transparency, pp. 607–617. FAT 2020, Association for Computing Machinery, New York, NY, USA (2020). https://doi.org/10.1145/3351095.3372850

34. Papadopoulos, S., Kontokosta, C.E., Vlachokostas, A., Azar, E.: Rethinking HVAC temperature setpoints in commercial buildings: the potential for zero-cost energy savings and comfort improvement in different climates. Build. Environ. 155, 350–359 (2019). https://doi.org/10.1016/j.buildenv.2019.03.062

35. Papernot, N., McDaniel, P.: Deep k-nearest neighbors: towards confident, interpretable and robust deep learning (2018). https://doi.org/10.48550/arXiv.1803.04765

36. Pedregosa, F., et al.: Scikit-learn: machine learning in Python. J. Mach. Learn. Res. 12, 2825–2830 (2011)

37. Perera, A., Kamalaruban, P.: Applications of reinforcement learning in energy systems. Renew. Sustain. Energy Rev. 137, 110618 (2021). https://doi.org/10.1016/j.rser.2020.110618

38. Pérez-Lombard, L., Ortiz, J., Pout, C.: A review on buildings energy consumption information. Energy Build. 40(3), 394–398 (2008). https://doi.org/10.1016/j.enbuild.2007.03.007

39. Qing, Y., Liu, S., Song, J., Wang, H., Song, M.: A survey on explainable reinforcement learning: concepts, algorithms, challenges (2022). https://doi.org/10.48550/arXiv.2211.06665

40. Ribeiro, M., Singh, S., Guestrin, C.: "why should I trust you?": explaining the predictions of any classifier. In: Proceedings of the 2016 Conference of the North American Chapter of the Association for Computational Linguistics: Demonstrations, pp. 97–101. Association for Computational Linguistics, San Diego, Califor-

nia (2016). https://doi.org/10.18653/v1/N16-3020. https://aclanthology.org/N16-3020

41. Roth, A.M., Topin, N., Jamshidi, P., Veloso, M.: Conservative q-improvement: reinforcement learning for an interpretable decision-tree policy (2019). https://doi.org/10.48550/arXiv.1907.01180

42. Schulman, J., Levine, S., Moritz, P., Jordan, M.I., Abbeel, P.: Trust region policy optimization (2017). https://doi.org/10.48550/arXiv.1502.05477

43. Schulman, J., Wolski, F., Dhariwal, P., Radford, A., Klimov, O.: Proximal policy optimization algorithms. arXiv preprint arXiv:1707.06347 (2017). https://doi.org/10.48550/arXiv.1707.06347

44. Shapley, L.S.: A Value for n-Person Games, pp. 307–318. Princeton University Press, Princeton (1953). https://doi.org/10.1515/9781400881970-018

45. Shuai, H., He, H.: Online scheduling of a residential microgrid via Monte-Carlo tree search and a learned model. IEEE Trans. Smart Grid **12**(2), 1073–1087 (2021). https://doi.org/10.1109/TSG.2020.3035127

46. Sutton, R.S., Barto, A.G.: Reinforcement Learning: An Introduction. MIT Press, Cambridge (2018). https://doi.org/10.1109/tnn.1998.712192

47. Valladares, W., et al.: Energy optimization associated with thermal comfort and indoor air control via a deep reinforcement learning algorithm. Build. Environ. **155**, 105–117 (2019)

48. Vázquez-Canteli, J.R., Ulyanin, S., Kämpf, J., Nagy, Z.: Fusing TensorFlow with building energy simulation for intelligent energy management in smart cities. Sustain. Urban Areas **45**, 243–257 (2019). https://doi.org/10.1016/j.scs.2018.11.021

49. Vouros, G.A.: Explainable deep reinforcement learning: state of the art and challenges. ACM Comput. Surv. **55**(5), 92:1–92:39 (2022). https://doi.org/10.1145/3527448

50. Watkins, C.J., Dayan, P.: Q-learning. Mach. Learn. **8**(3–4), 279–292 (1992)

51. Yang, Y., Srinivasan, S., Hu, G., Spanos, C.J.: Distributed control of multizone HVAC systems considering indoor air quality. IEEE Trans. Control Syst. Technol. **29**(6), 2586–2597 (2021). https://doi.org/10.1109/TCST.2020.3047407

52. Yao, Y., Shekhar, D.K.: State of the art review on model predictive control (MPC) in heating ventilation and air-conditioning (HVAC) field. Build. Environ. **200**, 107952 (2021). https://doi.org/10.1016/j.buildenv.2021.107952

53. Yu, L., Qin, S., Zhang, M., Shen, C., Jiang, T., Guan, X.: A review of deep reinforcement learning for smart building energy management. IEEE Internet Things J. (2021). https://doi.org/10.1109/JIOT.2021.3078462

54. Zhang, K., Zhang, J., Xu, P.D., Gao, T., Gao, D.W.: Explainable AI in deep reinforcement learning models for power system emergency control. IEEE Trans. Comput. Soc. Syst. **9**(2), 419–427 (2022). https://doi.org/10.1109/TCSS.2021.3096824

55. Zhang, Z., Chong, A., Pan, Y., Zhang, C., Lam, K.P.: Whole building energy model for HVAC optimal control: a practical framework based on deep reinforcement learning. Energy Build. **199**, 472–490 (2019)

56. Zhong, X., Zhang, Z., Zhang, R., Zhang, C.: End-to-end deep reinforcement learning control for HVAC systems in office buildings. Designs **6**(3), 52 (2022). https://doi.org/10.3390/designs6030052

Handling Missing Values in Local Post-hoc Explainability

Martina Cinquini[1,2](✉)[iD], Fosca Giannotti[2,3][iD], Riccardo Guidotti[1,2][iD],
and Andrea Mattei[1]

[1] University of Pisa, Pisa, Italy
{martina.cinquini,andrea.mattei}@unipi.it
[2] ISTI-CNR, Pisa, Italy
riccardo.guidotti@isti.cnr.it
[3] Scuola Normale Superiore, Pisa, Italy
fosca.giannotti@sns.it

Abstract. Missing data are quite common in real scenarios when using Artificial Intelligence (AI) systems for decision-making with tabular data and effectively handling them poses a significant challenge for such systems. While some machine learning models used by AI systems can tackle this problem, the existing literature lacks post-hoc explainability approaches able to deal with predictors that encounter missing data. In this paper, we extend a widely used local model-agnostic post-hoc explanation approach that enables explainability in the presence of missing values by incorporating state-of-the-art imputation methods within the explanation process. Since our proposal returns explanations in the form of feature importance, the user will be aware also of the importance of a missing value in a given record for a particular prediction. Extensive experiments show the effectiveness of the proposed method with respect to some baseline solutions relying on traditional data imputation.

Keywords: Explainable AI · Local Post-hoc Explanation · Decision-Making · Missing Values · Missing Data · Data Imputation

1 Introduction

Missing data is a pervasive problem across various domains that arises when some values in a dataset, typically tabular datasets, are unavailable due to factors such as measurement errors, incomplete data collection, or the intrinsic nature of the data [7,14]. The presence of missing values, and therefore the absence of some information, can significantly affect the performance of Machine Learning (ML) models used by Artificial Intelligence (AI) systems for decision-making in these contexts, often resulting in biased outcomes and inferior accuracy [13]. In particular, issues related to missing values are particularly relevant in applications where accurate data is critical for decision-making, such as medical diagnosis, risk assessment, and credit scoring [17,38,46]. Hence, addressing missing values

© The Author(s), under exclusive license to Springer Nature Switzerland AG 2023
L. Longo (Ed.): xAI 2023, CCIS 1902, pp. 256–278, 2023.
https://doi.org/10.1007/978-3-031-44067-0_14

is crucial to improve the reliability and usefulness of ML models used by AI systems in real-world scenarios. In the last years, researchers realized various data preprocessing methods to impute missing values [12,29], and designed predictive ML models which can deal by design with datasets affected by missing values such as XGBoost [8], LightGBM [26], and CatBoost [41].

Besides missing values, another issue against which researchers are fighting nowadays is the eXplainability of AI systems (XAI), particularly when ML techniques are employed to model the logic of the AI system in high-stakes decision fields [20,28]. Indeed, some of the most effective ML predictors are considered "black-box" models [20,37] due to their complexity, which causes the non-interpretability of the decision process [28,34]. However, explainability is a fundamental requirement in sensitive domains where the AI system is meant to offer support to experts instead of making decisions for them [15,33].

Even though the current research in XAI is flourishing [1,5,30,50], there is an apparent research vacuum at the intersection between these two issues in AI and ML, i.e., XAI approaches able to deal with missing values. To understand a real practical scenario in which it may be important to have an explanation method also working in the presence of missing values, we can think of a predictive model in the healthcare context that tries to assess the severity of a disease or to recommend a treatment plan. Indeed, models in such contexts are typically trained and applied on incomplete patient data due to missing values [17,38, 46]. For instance, the record describing a patient can be incomplete because they cannot undergo particular medical examinations. In such cases, the AI recommendation should be questioned and inspected thoroughly to check the correctness of the decision process. In addition, even if the model's performance may appear promising, the model might be biased towards a particular group of patients due to missing data and thus make incorrect predictions and recommend wrong treatments. Consequently, an explainer working in this context is needed to verify the decision logic learned and applied by the AI system.

Since the literature shows a lack of efforts toward the design of XAI methods able to handle missing values, we extend one of the most widely used and applied post-hoc explanation approaches. In this paper, we propose LIMEMV for Local Interpretable Model-Agnostic Explanations with Missing Values. LIMEMV extends LIME [42] by removing the need for imputing missing data before explaining the record under analysis. Indeed, LIMEMV handle missing values within the explanation process by employing state-of-the-art imputation methods. Specifically, (i) we replace the synthetic data generation performed by LIME with a neighborhood generation strategy creating synthetic records with missing data, and (ii) we substitute the linear model adopted by LIME with a surrogate model able to handle missing values. As a result, LIMEMV is able to return an explanation in the form of feature importance for a record with missing values, for a predictive model working on missing values, and for considering a dataset with missing values. We highlight that our proposal for a missing-value-compliant explanation method can be easily adapted to extend and improve other model-agnostic explainers like LORE [19], or SHAP [31]. However, we restrict our investigation and the enabling of the native treatment of missing values into the explanation extraction process of LIME due to the easiness of the integration. Our experiments on various datasets show that LIMEMV explanations are relatively similar to those of LIME and that it approximates well the decisions taken by the black-box classifier without impacting the fidelity in mimicking the black-box.

The rest of this paper is organized as follows. Section 2 describes the state-of-the-art related to missing values and XAI. Section 3 formalizes the problem treated and recalls basic notions for understanding our proposal that is defined in Sect. 4. Section 5 presents experimental results. Conclusions, limitations and future works are discussed in Sect. 6.

2   Related Works

In this section, we provide the reader with a brief review of XAI approaches, taking into account missing values and LIME, that is at the basis of our proposal.

In [2] are presented the challenges of imputation in XAI methods showing different settings where AI models with imputation can be problematic, as optimizing for explainability with post-hoc models while simultaneously optimizing for performance via imputation may lead to unsafe results. Our proposal can be adapted to answer many issues raised in this paper. In [25] is confirmed that the presence of missing values is among the common issues faced by data scientists working with explainability. However, despite the presence of many researchers both in the fields of missing values [7,14] and XAI [15,20,28,33,34] there is a clear lack of effort at the intersection of these two fields. To the best of our knowledge, we can refer to decision trees [49] as interpretable-by-design approaches dealing with missing data. Indeed, during training, if an attribute a has missing values in some of the training instances associated with a node, a way to measure the gain in purity for a is to exclude instances with missing values of the records of a in the counting of instances associated with every child node generated for every possible outcome. Further, suppose a is chosen as the attribute test condition at a node. In that case, training instances with missing values of a can be propagated to the child nodes by distributing the records to every child according to the probability that the missing attribute has a particular value. The same can be done at query time. Obviously, such approaches, despite being interpretable, are only sometimes effective for solving complex decision problems. Another possibility for decision trees is the CHAID approach [24] that treats missing values as separate categorical values. Also, the BEST approach [4] selects a certain feature to split the dataset only when in the current partition there are no missing values. Furthermore, CART trees [47] employ recursive partitioning based on feature thresholds to split data into homogeneous subsets. Recently, in [22] has been presented a procedure for data imputation based on different data type values and their association constraints that not only imputes the missing values but also generates human-readable explanations describing the significance of attributes used for every imputation.

Again to the best of our knowledge, there are no post-hoc local explanation approaches able to handle natively missing values. Consequently, we decided to extend LIME [42], the most well-known model-agnostic explainer that returns local explanations as feature importance vectors. Further details about LIME are presented in Sect. 3. Although LIME is effective and straightforward, it has several weak points. A possible downside is the required transformation of any data into a binary format claimed to be human-interpretable. Another aspect worth highlighting is that the random perturbation method results in shifts in data and instability in explanations. Indeed, for the same record and prediction, LIME can generate different explanations over several iterations [51]. This lack of stability is among the main weaknesses of an interpretable model, especially in critical domains [51]. Lastly, in [16] is shown that *additive* explanations like those returned by LIME cannot be trusted in the presence of noisy interactions introduced in the reference set used to extract the explanations.

Over recent years, numerous researchers have analyzed LIME limitations and proposed several subsequent works extending or improving it. Most of the modifications have been in selecting relevant data for training the local interpretable model. For instance, KLIME [21] runs the K-Means clustering algorithm to partition the training data and then fit local models within each cluster instead of perturbation-based data generation around an instance being explained. A weakness of KLIME is that it is non-deterministic, as the default implementation of K-Means picks initial centroids randomly. In [23] is proposed LIME-SUP that approximates the original LIME better than KLIME by using supervised partitioning. Furthermore, KL-LIME [40] adopts the Kullback-Leibler divergence to explain Bayesian predictive models. Within this constraint, both the original task and the explanation model can be arbitrarily changed without losing the theoretical information interpretation of the projection for finding the explanation model. ALIME [45] presents modifications by employing an autoencoder as a better weighting function for the local surrogate models. In QLIME [6], the authors consider nonlinear relationships using a quadratic approximation. Another approach proposed in [44] utilizes a Conditional Tabular Generative Adversarial Network (CTGAN) to generate more realistic synthetic data for querying the model to be explained. Theoretically, GAN-like methods can learn possible dependencies. However, as empirically demonstrated in [9], these relationships are not directly represented, and there is no guarantee that they are followed in the data generation process. In [51] is proposed DLIME, a Deterministic Local Interpretable Model-Agnostic Explanations. In DLIME, random perturbations are replaced with hierarchical clustering to group the data. After that, a kNN is used to select the cluster where the instance to be explained belongs. The authors showed that DLIME is superior to LIME with respect to three medical datasets. We highlight that, besides this deterministic enhancement, clusters may have a few points affecting the fidelity of explanations. In [52] is presented a Bayesian local surrogate model called BAY-LIME, which exploits prior knowledge and Bayesian reasoning to improve both the consistency in repeated explanations of a single prediction and the robustness to kernel settings. Finally, in [10] is presented CALIME, a causal-aware version of LIME that discover causal relationships and exploits them for the synthetic neighborhood generation.

Although a considerable number of solutions proposed to overcome the limitations of LIME, no state-of-the-art variants allow to handle missing values. This research vacuum motivates our interest in developing such a methodology.

3   Setting the Stage

In this paper, we address the problem of designing a XAI method able to solve the *black-box outcome explanation problem* [20] in the presence of incomplete data. A black-box classifier is defined as a function $b : \mathcal{X}^{(m)} \to \mathcal{Y}$ that maps data instances $x = \{(a_1, v_1), \ldots, (a_m, v_m)\}$ from a feature space $\mathcal{X}^{(m)}$ with m input features (where a_i is the attribute name and v_i is the corresponding value) to a decision y in a target space $\mathcal{Y}$ of size $l = |\mathcal{Y}|$, i.e., y can assume one of the l different labels ($l = 2$ is binary classification, $l > 2$ is multi-class classification). We write $b(x) = y$ to denote the decision y taken by b, and $b(X) = Y$ as a shorthand for $\{b(x) \mid x \in X\} = Y$. A classifier b is *black-box* when its internals are unknown to the observer or they are known but uninterpretable by humans. If b is a probabilistic classifier, we denote with $b_p(x)$ the vector of probabilities for the different labels. Hence, $b(x) = y$ is the label with the highest probability among the l values in $b_p(x)$. In this paper, we assume that *(i)* some values v_i of the records used to train the classifier b can be missing, i.e., $v_i = *$, *(ii)* b can return a decision $y = b(x)$ even when values $v_i = *$ in x are missing. Let $A = \{a_1, \ldots, a_m\}$ be the set of all the features. We name $M(x) = \{a_j | \forall j = 1, \ldots m \wedge v_j = *\}$ the set of features with a missing value for a record x, and $\neg M(x) = A - M(x)$ the set of features for which values are not missing. We write $M(X)$, respectively $\neg M(X)$, as a shorthand to indicate the set of features for which at least a record has a missing value in X. Thus, we can model the input domain of a predictive model b as $\mathcal{X}^{(m)} = (A_1 \cup \{*\}) \times \cdots \times (A_m \cup \{*\})$ where A_i identifies the set of known values for attribute a_i. We complete our formalism using $|X|$ to indicate the size of a dataset X, and X_j to indicate the jth feature, i.e., column, of X.

Given a black-box b and an instance x classified by b, i.e., $b(x) = y$, the *black-box outcome explanation problem* aims at providing an explanation e belonging to a human-interpretable domain. According to the domain, in our work, we focus on feature importance modeling the explanation as a vector $e = \{e_1, e_2, \ldots, e_m\}$, in which the value $e_i \in e$ is the importance of the ith feature for the decision made by $b(x)$. To understand each feature's contribution, the sign and the magnitude of e_i are considered. If $e_i < 0$, the feature a_i contributes negatively to the outcome y; otherwise, the feature a_i contributes positively. The magnitude represents how significant the feature's contribution is to the prediction.

In this context, our aim is to design an explanation method that can return a valid and meaningful explanation e even in the presence of missing values in x and/or X without requiring any a priori imputation.

We keep this paper self-contained by summarizing in the following the key concepts necessary to comprehend our proposal.

3.1   Missing Values Imputation

In statistics [43], the mechanisms of missing values are categorized into three types depending on the relationship between $M(X)$ and $\neg M(X)$.

First, Missing Completely At Random (MCAR) if $M(X)$ is independent of A, i.e., when the probability of a record having a missing value for an attribute does not depend on either the known values or the missing data itself.

Second, Missing At Random (MAR) if $M(X)$ depends only on $\neg M(X)$, i.e., when the probability of a record having a missing value for an attribute may depend on the value of other attributes without missing values. In other words, MAR occurs when the distribution of a record having missing values for an attribute depends on the observed data. Considering missing data as MAR instead of MCAR is a safer assumption since any analysis valid for MAR data, e.g., multiple imputations, is correct also if the data is MCAR [39].

Finally, Missing Not At Random (MNAR) if $M(X)$ depends on $M(X)$, i.e., MNAR occurs when the probability of a record having a missing value for an attribute may depend on the value of that attribute. MNAR data is also called "non-ignorable" since treating it with techniques designed to work on MCAR or MAR, like imputation, will produce misleading results. A peculiar case of MNAR is when data is structurally missing, i.e., data that is missing for a logical reason. A typical example can be a survey where some questions are only asked participants who answered in a certain way to previous questions. In this case, the mechanism is easy to analyze, while MNAR data can pose more of a challenge since the logic behind the missing data might be difficult to understand. We conduct experiments with the MCAR mechanism only, as most researchers are reported doing in the survey in [29]. The extensive adoption of the MCAR approach underlines its credibility and efficacy in addressing missing data, making it a compelling and well-founded choice for our investigations. In future works, we intend to explore also other settings such as MAR or MNAR.

In the following, we summarize two missing values imputation approaches that we adopted as competitors and as a component of our proposal.

K-Nearest Neighbours. k-Nearest Neighbours (kNN) is a supervised ML method widely employed with good results for imputing missing values [29]. KNN identifies the nearest neighbors of an instance based on a distance function, e.g., the Euclidean distance. The distance computation is performed w.r.t. the features in $\neg M(x)$. A majority vote is then conducted among the top k neighbors to determine the most appropriate value for replacing the missing one.

MICE. Multivariate Imputation by Chained Equations (MICE) [3] is a multiple imputation method [36] that can be used whenever missing data is assumed to be MAR or MCAR. MICE works by imputing values in multiple copies of the dataset and then pooling together the results. On each copy of the available data, MICE performs an iterative process in which, at each iteration, a feature in the dataset is imputed using the knowledge of the other attributes. In particular, at each iteration, the first step replaces the missing values in $M(X)$ with placeholder

---

Algorithm 1: LIME(x, b, X, k, N)

Input : x - instance to explain, b - classifier, X - reference dataset,
k - nbr of features N - nbr of samples
Output: e - features importance

1   $Z \leftarrow \emptyset, Z' \leftarrow \emptyset, W \leftarrow \emptyset, S \leftarrow \emptyset$;   // init. empty synth data, weights, ad stats

2   **for** $j \in [1, m]$ **do**

3    $S \leftarrow S \cup \{(\mu(X_j), \sigma(X_j))\}$;   // compute statistics

4   **for** $i \in [1, \ldots, N]$ **do**

5    $z \leftarrow sampling(x, S)$;   // random permutation

6    $z' \leftarrow \{(a_j, \mathbb{1}(x_{v_j} = z_{v_j})) | j = 1, \ldots, m\}$;   // features changed

7    $Z \leftarrow Z \cup \{z\}$; $Z' \leftarrow Z' \cup \{z'\}$;   // add synthetic instance

8    $W \leftarrow W \cup \{exp(\frac{-\pi(x,z)^2}{\sigma^2})\}$;   // add weights

9   $e \leftarrow solve\_Lasso(Z', b_p(Z), W, k)$;   // get coefficients

10 **return** e;

---

values that do not consider the other features, e.g., the mean of the available data for that attribute or random values. Then, let $X' \subset X$, for each attribute $a \in M(X')$, MICE imputes it with a linear regression model trained on another slice of the dataset $X'' \subset X$ such that $a \in \neg M(X'')$. An iteration is completed when all the features are processed. This process is repeated up to a user-specified number of times or until convergence is reached.

3.2 LIME

A widely adopted, local, model-agnostic, post-hoc explanation method is LIME (Local Interpretable Model-Agnostic Explanations) [42], which acts as a foundation for our proposal. The main idea of LIME is that the explanation can be derived locally from records generated randomly in the synthetic neighborhood Z of the instance x that has to be explained.

Algorithm 1 illustrates the pseudo-code of LIME. In line 1, two empty sets Z and Z' are initialized. Z will be populated with the synthetic data sampled around the instance x represented in the real domain, while Z' will contain a representation of the synthetic records in Z in a binary version signaling the features that have been changed, i.e., given $z' \in Z'$ and $z \in Z$, the value of the jth features in z' is equal to one ($z'_{v_j} = 1$) if $z_{v_j} = x_{v_j}$, $z'_{v_j} = 0$ otherwise. The vector W will contain the weights associated with the records Z generated, expressed in terms of their distance from x. S will contain the statistics of every feature j with $j = \{1, \ldots, m\}$ where m is the number of features. Indeed, the loop in lines 2–3 populates S with the mean μ and standard deviation σ of every feature X_j. Subsequently, LIME runs N times a loop (lines 4–8), populating Z, Z' and W at each iteration with a new synthetic instance. LIME randomly samples N instances similar to x by drawing values according to the statistics S (line 5). The function $\mathbb{1}(condition)$ in line 6 returns one when the *condition* is verified, zero otherwise. It highlights how LIME creates the binary version Z' of the synthetic records Z. Then, LIME weights proximity of the records z' with

x w.r.t. a certain distance function π and store the result in W (line 8). Finally, LIME adopts the perturbed sample of instances Z to fed to the black-box b and obtain the classification probabilities $b_p(Z)$ with respect to the class $b(x) = y$. The binary synthetic instances Z' with the weights W are used to train a linear regressor with Lasso regularization using the classification probabilities $b_p(Z)$ as the target variable and considering only the top k most essential features (line 9). The k coefficients of the linear regressor are returned as explanation e.

4   Local Explainability with Missing Values

We present LIMEMV (Local Interpretable Model-Agnostic Explanations with Missing Values). LIMEMV extends LIME [42] with the ability to handle incomplete data during the explanation process. This eliminates the need of imputing missing values both on the training dataset and on the records for which the explanation is required. The presence of the missing values in X impacts the calculus of the statistics S used to generate the synthetic neighborhood (line 3, Algorithm 1), while missing values in the record x to be explained impacts the sampling function generating the synthetic records z (line 5, Algorithm 1). LIMEMV is able to deal with both of these issues.

Before outlining the details of LIMEMV, we aim at clarifying when this approach is crucial. Given a dataset X with missing values, a user can decide *(i)* to adopt a model b which is not able to handle missing values, such as a SVM or a Neural Network, *(ii)* to use a model b able to handle missing values, such as XGBoost and LightGBM. In the first case, in order to train b, the user needs to preprocess X by applying a data imputation approach. As a consequence, given a test record x possibly having missing values, the same imputation approach should be applied on x before querying b to obtain the decision $y = b(x)$. Thus, if an explanation e is desired for the decision $y = b(x)$, the classic LIME approach can be used. Instead, in the second case, the dataset X can be directly used to train b, and any test record x can be passed to b without requiring any data imputation. However, if an explanation e is desired, for the decision $y = b(x)$, the classic LIME approach cannot be used, as it cannot work in the presence of missing data. A naive solution consists in applying an imputation approach on X and x before passing them to LIME (see Algorithm 1). However, in this case, the explainer is applied to a dataset and on a record that differ from those adopted by the decision model b. On the other hand, with LIMEMV, the user does not need to apply any imputation approach, and it can be used directly to obtain the explanation e for the decision $y = b(x)$ in the presence of missing data.

The pseudo-code of LIMEMV is reported on Algorithm 2, with the main differences from LIME highlighted in blue. In the following, we detail such differences. Also, Fig. 1 visualizes with an example the various steps of LIMEMV.

4.1   Input Parameters

First, we can notice that *(i)* LIMEMV does not require the user to specify the number of important features k as these are identified by design by the surrogate

---

Algorithm 2: LIMEMV(x, b, X, k, N)

Input : x - instance to explain, b - classifier, X - reference dataset,
N - nbr of samples, ψ - imputation function

Output: e - features importance

1 $Z \leftarrow \emptyset, W \leftarrow \emptyset, S \leftarrow \emptyset$;   // init. empty synth data, weights, ad stats
2 **for** $j \in [1, m]$ **do**
3      $X'_j \leftarrow \{(a_i, v_i)|\forall i = 1, \ldots, |X| \wedge v_i \neq *\}$;   // consider only non missing values
4      $S \leftarrow S \cup \{(\mu(X'_j), \sigma(X'_j), 1 - |X'_j|/|X|)\}$;   // compute statistics
5 **for** $i \in [1, \ldots, N]$ **do**
6      $z \leftarrow sampling\_imputation(x, \psi_X, S)$;   // random permutation with imputation
7      $Z \leftarrow Z \cup \{z\}$;   // add synthetic instance
8      $W \leftarrow W \cup \{exp(\frac{-\pi'(x,z)^2}{\sigma^2})\}$;   // add weights
9 $T \leftarrow train\_tree(Z, b_p(Z), W))$;   // train regressor tree
10 $e \leftarrow tree\_feature\_imp(x, T)$;   // get coefficients
11 **return** e;

---

model adopted; *(ii)* it requires as input an imputation function ψ, i.e., a function that given a dataset X fills the missing values using a certain strategy. Examples of ψ functions are kNN [29] and MICE [3]. Other naive approaches may consist in using the mean (or the mode) of each feature to fill in missing values.

4.2 Dataset Statistics

The next difference is in the loop computing the statistics (lines 3–4). Indeed, rather than of calculating the mean and standard deviations for the complete set of features X_j, it calculates them on a subset $X'_j \subseteq X_j$ such that X_j only contains not missing values (as formalized in line 3). This setting solves the possible presence of the missing values in X. Another difference w.r.t. LIME is an addition to the set of computed statistics, i.e., the information about the distribution of missing values in each attribute. Since a priori we need to assume MCAR data, this boils down to the relative number of missing values for each feature, i.e., $1 - |X'_j|/|X|$. However, when dealing with MAR data, information about the relationships with other features can be exploited if available. Figure 1 shows an example of S content resulting from a dataset.

4.3 Synthetic Neighborhood Generation

The knowledge stored in S is then applied when generating the synthetic neighborhood in the subsequent loop (lines 5–8) that is responsible for the synthetic neighborhood generation, where the sampling function has been changed w.r.t. LIME (line 6, Algorithm 2) to fix the possible presence of missing values in the record x. The problem we face is relative to how to sample values around a coordinate that is absent from x. A naive strategy consists in generating the N

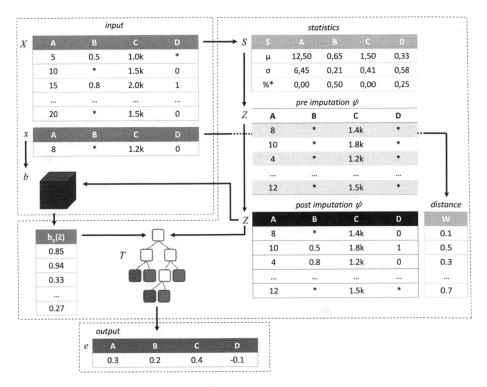

Fig. 1. LIMEMV takes as input the reference dataset X, the instance to explain x and the black-box b, and returns as output a feature importance explanation e. The workflows highlights the statistics S calculated considering missing values and shows the synthetic neighborhood Z before and after the imputation with ψ. Finally, e is returned as feature importance extracted from a local regressor tree using as target variable the probability $b_p(x)$ for the decision $y = b(x)$.

synthetic neighbors Z only considering the features in $\neg M(x)$. This would practically remove those attributes from the explanation, thus preventing the user from understanding the impact of features with missing values. On the other hand, the *sampling_imputation* adopted by LIMEMV works as follows. The values for the features in $\neg M(x)$ are drawn as in the classic approach exploiting the means and standard deviations in S, while for the features in $M(x)$ the values are set as missing $*$. After that, an imputation function ψ is used to fill a number of missing values in z proportionate with the ratio stored in S, i.e., $1 - |X_j|/|X|$ for feature j. We implemented ψ as kNN [29] and MICE [3]. In other words, with LIMEMV we obtain a set Z of synthetic records where the features without missing values in $\neg M(x)$ are randomly sampled around the observed values or left the same, while some of the records of some of the features with missing values in $M(x)$ are filled w.r.t. the records in X, i.e., with plausible values for non missing features. Hence, in this way, the imputation is performed exclusively at explanation time and to generate a plausible synthetic dataset in the proximity of x and respect the missing values in X. Figure 1 shows an example of a synthetic neighborhood Z before and after the application of the imputation function ψ. We notice that the number of missing values per feature remains coherent with those in the observed dataset X and captured by S.

Like in LIME, the importance of the synthetic records in Z is stored in W and it is evaluated w.r.t. their proximity with x. Differently from LIME, since the synthetic records z have missing values, we employ a function (π') calculating the Euclidean distances in the presence of missing values by ignoring features with a missing value in both x and z and scaling the result as m divided by the features without missing values [11], i.e., $|(\neg M(x)) \cap (\neg M(z))|$.

4.4   Local Interpretable Surrogate Model

At this stage, differently from LIME, the synthetic neighborhood Z contains missing values. As a consequence, the linear Lasso regression model cannot be used as it is not capable of handling training sets containing missing values. Thus, inspired by [19], we decided to employ a decision tree T that is able to deal with missing data by design [49] (line 9). As a side effect, in LIMEMV there is no need for the user to specify the number of important features k for which the explanation is required as the explanation e is going to be formed only by the features appearing in the branch of T responsible for the decision on x. However, differently from LIME instead of training the surrogate tree regressor T on Z', i.e., the binary version of Z modeling the changes w.r.t. x, like in [19], we train the surrogate T directly on Z, permitting in this way to understand in terms of values, and not in terms of presence/absence, the dependencies between the features Z and the prediction probability of the target label $b_p(Z)$.

4.5   Explanation with Missing Values

Finally, LIMEMV extracts the explanation e of x in terms of feature importance with the function *tree_feature_imp* as follows. First, as the magnitude of the feature importance e_j, it is used the normalized total reduction of the impurity criterion brought by the jth feature, i.e., the Gini importance[1] [49]. Second, as the sign of the feature importance e_j, LIMEMV adopts the sign of the difference between the average value on the qth node in the tree (with $q = 0$ indicating the root) and the subsequent one w.r.t. the path from the root to the leaf followed on T for the prediction of the record x, i.e., $sign(T_q(x) - T_{q+1}(x))$, where $T_q(x)$ indicates the average value on the qth node T for the prediction of x. Thus, each feature j receives a score that depends on the decision path followed on x. We should note that, while considering e_j could be reasonable, it requires more investigation and might also be of interest outside the missing data domain.

For example, suppose that a certain local surrogate tree T for the record x in the root separates the data using the attribute $a_j =age$. If the normalized

---

[1] The Gini importance could be biased regarding cardinality as pointed out in [48] but its effect is mitigated from the normalization.

Gini importance of a_j is 0.4, and, for x, $T_0(x) - T_1(x) < 0$, than, we will have $e_j = -0.4$, meaning that *age* has a negative contribution of 0.4 in the decision taken by b on x. We underline that, according to our definition, the value of *age* for x might also be unspecified in this setting. However, we still have access to its local importance for the decision $y = b(x)$.

5   Experiments

We report here the experiments carried out to validate LIMEMV[2]. We present the evaluation measures adopted, the datasets used, the experimental setup, and the explainers selected as baselines. Then, we demonstrate that LIMEMV outperforms LIME used in pipeline with standard imputation approaches. Since it is not generally possible to access the ground truth for explanations [18], we decided to adopt a controlled experiment to check the validity of the explanations returned by LIMEMV and by the baseline competitors to judge their effectiveness.

In particular, we adopt datasets without missing data in which we insert missing values in a controlled way. Formally, let X be the original dataset, and $\tilde{X}$ the same dataset where some records are modified by inserting missing values for certain features according to a procedure detailed in the following sections. Let b be the black-box able to deal with missing trained on X and $\tilde{b}$ the same black-box trained on $\tilde{X}$. Also, let x be a record to predict and explain and $\tilde{x}$ the same record but with some missing values. Given an explanation method *expl* that is implemented in the experiments by LIMEMV or by one of the baselines, we name e and $\tilde{e}$ the feature importance explanations returned by $expl(x, b, X)$ and $expl(\tilde{x}, \tilde{b}, \tilde{X})$, respectively. Then, by comparing sets of e and $\tilde{e}$, i.e., the explanations obtained for records with and without missing values, we can establish the impact of the treatment of the missing values in the explanation process: the lower the discrepancy between the explanations, the less impactful is the treatment of the missing values made by the explainer.

5.1   Evaluation Measures and Explanations Normalization

In order to compare explanations expressed as feature importance, we normalize the magnitude e_i of the values present in each explanation e. Given an explanation e, we aim at guaranteeing that the following property holds $\sum_{j=1}^{m} |e_j| = 1$. Thus, we normalize the value e_j obtaining the normalized value e_i' as

$$e_i' = e_i / \sum_{j=1}^{m} |e_j|.$$

We underline that this normalization is useful not only to compare explanations, but also to make the explanations more intuitive for human users. In the following, we assume that all the explanations returned by the different explainers tested are normalized as described in this section.

---

[2] The implementation is available here: https://github.com/marti5ini/LIMEMV..

Table 1. Datasets statistics and classifiers accuracy. Specifically, we present the number of samples of each dataset (n), the number of features (m), the number of labels that can assume the class (l), the number of training records for the black-box (X_b) and the number of records for which we seek predictions (X_t). Additionally, we report the accuracy of the black-box without missing values (b) and with missing values $(\tilde{b})$ across various levels of missingness (p).

	n	m	l	$|X_b|$	$|X_t|$	b	$\tilde{b}$				
							$p=10$	$p=20$	$p=30$	$p=40$	$p=50$
adult	32561	13	2	2600	50	.88	.87 ± .01	.87 ± .01	.70 ± .01	.87 ± .01	.87 ± .01
compas	6907	11	2	1381	50	.81	.79 ± .01	.79 ± .02	.80 ± .01	.79 ± .01	.79 ± .02
diabetes	768	8	2	154	50	.73	.73 ± .02	.70 ± .03	.71 ± .04	.69 ± .02	.70 ± .04
fico	10459	22	2	1822	50	.67	.70 ± .01	.70 ± .00	.70 ± .00	.70 ± .01	.69 ± .01
german	1000	20	2	200	50	.83	.79 ± .02	.77 ± .03	.77 ± .02	.77 ± .04	.76 ± .02
iris	150	4	3	30	30	1.0	.96 ± .03	.99 ± .02	.95 ± .08	.98 ± .03	.96 ± .04
titanic	715	4	2	143	50	.78	.77 ± .02	.78 ± .02	.76 ± .02	.76 ± .02	.76 ± .02

Given a couple of normalized explanations with and without missing values e and $\tilde{e}$, we adopted the *Cosine Similarity* (CS) [49] and the Kendall Tau (KT) [27] to measure their similarity. The CS ranges in $[-1, 1]$, the closer to one the better it is. In addition, inspired by [16,32], we measure the discrepancy between two explanations by calculating the *Absolute Deviation* (AD) as feature-wise and record-wise means of the vector of differences $\delta = \{|e_1 - \tilde{e_1}|, \ldots, |e_m - \tilde{e_m}|\}$. The AD ranges in $[0, +\infty]$, the closer to zero the better it is. In particular, we group the features to analyze the differences between the features contained in $M(\tilde{X})$ versus those contained in $\neg M(\tilde{X})$. We use ADW to indicate the AD for features With missing values, and ADO for the AD of features with Out missing values.

Furthermore, in line with the literature in XAI [5,20], we measure the *Fidelity* (FI) of the local surrogate models in approximating the behavior of the black-box as the difference between the predicted probability of the black-box for the decision, i.e., $b_p(x)$, and the prediction of the surrogate, i.e., T. We measure the FI as $1 - |b_p(x) - T(x)|$ such that it is in $[0, 1]$, the closer to one the better it is.

Finally, we also report the *Explanation Time* (ET) expressed in seconds.

5.2   Datasets and Experimental Setting

We experimented on seven benchmarking datasets from UCI Machine Learning Repository and Kaggle[3], namely iris, titanic, adult, german, diabetes, compas, and fico, which belong to diverse yet critical real-world applications. These datasets have very different properties in terms of number of records and features and type of features, i.e., their attributes are numeric, categorical, or mixed. Table 1 (left) presents a summary of each dataset. The datasets are preprocessed by removing all the records with missing values, and normalized using

---

[3] https://archive.ics.uci.edu/ml/index.php, https://www.kaggle.com/.

the Z-Score normalization [49]. Categorical features are label encoded. We split each dataset into two partitions: X_b, is the set of records to train the black-box models b and $\tilde{b}$ when trained on the training with and without missing values, respectively, while is X_t the partition that contains the records for which we want a prediction b and $\tilde{b}$ and an explanation from the explainers detailed in the following section. We highlight that both X_b and X_t are used at training and explanation time in the two versions with and without missing values. We underline that X_b is used to train the black-box but also by LIMEMV and by the baselines tested to gather information to generate the synthetic neighborhood.

Our objective is to re-create a scenario in which missing values are present both in the observable data and in the records for which the explanation is required[4]. In this work, we experiment with the MCAR setting, which is typically assumed in the presence of missing values when additional knowledge is unavailable. We leave the study on MAR and MNAR for future work.

Since often the most important features for individual predictions are in overlap with features globally important for the classifier, we aim at stressing the experimental scenario by inserting missing values among the features most important globally. Thus, for each dataset, we train a Random Forest (RF) classifier on X_b with default hyper-parameters. We exploit the RF to obtain a ranking of the m features $\{j_1, \ldots, j_m\}$, where j_r says that the jth features is ranked r^{th} w.r.t. its importance, *which is determined using Gini importance*. Thus, we randomly select $p\%$ features among the most important ones with respect to the ranking obtained with $p \in \{10, 20, 30, 40, 50\}$, i.e., $|M(X)| = |X| * p/100$. Then, for each feature in $M(X)$ we select the percentage q of missing values with $q \in \{4, 8, 16, 32\}$. Hence, we are able to observe the impact of different configurations of missing values in the explanation process.

As black-box we trained an XGBoost [8] implemented as the `xgboost` library[5] using default parameters both in the training set with and without missing values to avoid possible biases. The partitioning sizes and the classification accuracy in presence of missing values and without them are in Table 1 (right). When in presence of missing values for a certain percentage of features p, it is reported the average accuracy w.r.t. the various percentages of missing values in the features q. We notice that, even in presence of missing values with various p, the accuracy of the various black-boxes $\tilde{b}$ remains close to the accuracy of b.

5.3   Baseline Explainers

We compare LIMEMV against some naive approaches that can be adopted to solve the problem faced in this paper without requiring a novel implementation. These solutions consist in using *a data imputation approach* on the dataset X_b and on

---

[4] In preliminary experimentation considering missing values present only in the observable data X_b or only in the explained records X_t we noticed that the overall performance are similar to those reported in this paper. Thus we preferred to illustrate and discuss results only for the most realistic and complex scenario.

[5] https://xgboost.readthedocs.io/en/stable/.

the test record x, and then relying on the explanation returned by the classic LIME version since there are no missing values disturbing the explanation process. As data imputation approaches we experiment with the mean value of the feature with missing values, kNN, and MICE. We adopt the names LB-M, LB-K, and LB-C, to refer to these baseline explainers relying on mean, kNN, and MICE imputations and LIME, respectively. On the other hand, we use LMV-K and LMV-C to refer to the two versions of LIMEMV implementing the imputation function ψ with kNN and MICE, respectively. For future work, it could be also interesting to investigate LIME with a tree-based local model and pre-hoc imputation as a competitor. To make the LIME and LIMEMV methods comparable, since LIMEMV automatically selects the most important features that will appear with non-zero features importance, for LIME we set $k = m$ such that all the features are considered by the surrogate Lasso regressor. For all the explainers we keep the size of the synthetic neighborhood as in the original LIME implementation, i.e., $N = 5000$. We remark on the fact that with p and q we refer to the percentages of features among the most important ones and those with missing values and they do not impact with k.

5.4   Case Study Explanation

Before presenting the experimental results, we show in Fig. 2 a case study explanation for a record of the `adult` dataset where missing values are inserted among $p = 50\%$ of the most important features according to a RF and such that there are at least $q = 20\%$ missing values for each feature with missing. The features' importance of the explanations is reported as bars for the features having a value e_j different from zero. Thus, the taller the bar, the higher the magnitude of the feature importance e_j. For completeness, we also report the values. The plot on the left shows the feature importance returned by LIME using kNN as data imputation method at the preprocessing time, while the one on the right shows the feature importance returned by LIMEMV using kNN as an imputation function ψ.

In this particular example, the record has two missing values for the attributes *age* and *relationship*. By comparing the two plots, we immediately realize two aspects. First, due to the usage of the Lasso regressor as a local surrogate, LIME returns much more features than LIMEMV with non-zero feature importance e_j[6]. On the other hand, the local surrogate tree regressor adopted by LIMEMV is able to identify by-design the most important features, and indeed, due to the experimental setting adopted, among them, we find also *age* and *relationship*. Second, we visually see a clear discrepancy between the feature importance of the explanations with and without missing values when LIME or LIMEMV are adopted. Indeed, LIMEMV is considerably more adherent than LIME to the explanation without missing values as to *capital-gain* is assigned almost

---

[6] Such an outcome is due to the choice of $k = m$. However, regardless of how we set k, the same result occurs when k is smaller than m and greater than the minimum number of features required to obtain a high-performing linear regressor surrogate.

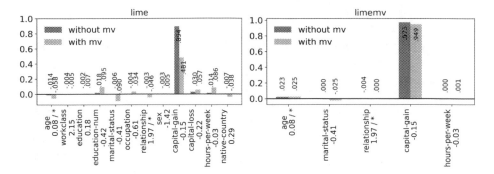

Fig. 2. Explanations of a record of the `adult` dataset with and without missing values for LIME using kNN as imputer at preprocessing time, and LIMEMV using kNN as imputation function ψ. Normalized/missing values (*) of the record are on the x-axis.

the same value. Furthermore, also for the features with missing values, we notice a minor discrepancy for the explanation of LIMEMV: *age* passes from 0.023 to 0.025 for LIMEMV while it changes from -0.14 to -0.58 for LIME, *relationship* passes from -0.004 to 0.00 for LIMEMV while it changes from -0.003 to -0.046 for LIME.

In the next section, we observe numerically these phenomena on various datasets and with various settings for inserting missing values.

5.5   Results

According to our experimental setting, we are able to evaluate the explanations with the measures previously presented for each record in X_t of each dataset, for each explanation method, and for each couple of parameters p and q tested. Table 2 reports the mean and standard deviations for the various settings where the measures obtained for the local explanations of the records in X_t of each setting are aggregated using the interquartile range mean, i.e., the mean of the values in the range defined by the 25th and 75th percentile. The score of the best performer for each dataset and measure is highlighted in bold.

We immediately realize that LMV-K exhibits superior performance in all qualitative measures for `adult`, `compas`, and `titanic`. Furthermore, LMV-K is always the best performer in terms of ADO, i.e., it is the explainer treating missing values with a smaller impact on features without missing values. This characteristic is particularly significant since missing values are usually a minority among the records in a dataset, and therefore, their importance should remain unchanged regardless of their presence or absence. On the contrary, LIMEMV adopting MICE, i.e., LMV-C, is often among the worst in terms of ADO. This underlines how the choice of a certain imputation function ψ can affect the explanation process that is not necessarily the best with more advanced imputation functions.

Concerning the similarity measures CS and KT we notice that there is not a clear winner. Indeed, regarding CS for three datasets, the best approach is LMV-

Table 2. Mean and standard deviation of the evaluation measures observed for each dataset, explainer, and setting of missing values w.r.t. the number of features with missing and percentage of missing values. The best performer is highlighted in bold.

		CS ↑	KT ↑	ADW ↓	ADO ↓	FI ↑	ET ↓
adult	LB-M	.024 ± .38	.271 ± .05	.299 ± .20	.029 ± .02	.691 ± .11	.047 ± .00
	LB-K	.465 ± .14	.396 ± .04	.211 ± .09	.026 ± .01	.796 ± .02	.048 ± .00
	LB-C	.132 ± .28	.304 ± .03	.276 ± .16	.027 ± .01	.697 ± .07	.577 ± .00
	LMV-K	**.770 ± .06**	**.437 ± .08**	**.112 ± .05**	**.012 ± .01**	**.834 ± .02**	8.75 ± 1.08
	LMV-C	.071 ± .28	.026 ± .06	.317 ± .18	.031 ± .01	.697 ± .07	**.040 ± .00**
compas	LB-M	.314 ± .11	.243 ± .09	.176 ± .04	.072 ± .02	.870 ± .02	.059 ± .01
	LB-K	.360 ± .07	.248 ± .07	.194 ± .05	.041 ± .01	.871 ± .04	.059 ± .01
	LB-C	.258 ± .06	.206 ± .05	.210 ± .05	.057 ± .01	.869 ± .02	.210 ± .01
	LMV-K	**.380 ± .07**	**.387 ± .07**	**.071 ± .10**	**.028 ± .02**	.858 ± 0.03	1.82 ± .26
	LMV-C	.311 ± 0.07	.119 ± .06	.301 ± .10	.058 ± .01	**.871 ± .02**	**.039 ± .00**
diabetes	LB-M	.235 ± .15	.143 ± .14	.284 ± .05	.087 ± .02	.772 ± .03	.037 ± .00
	LB-K	.315 ± .12	.228 ± .12	.266 ± .04	.060 ± .01	.771 ± .03	.041 ± .00
	LB-C	**.316 ± .12**	.215 ± .13	**.261 ± .04**	.069 ± .01	.774 ± .02	.099 ± .00
	LMV-K	.248 ± .17	**.303 ± .10**	.364 ± .17	**.030 ± .03**	**.809 ± .05**	.227 ± .03
	LMV-C	.210 ± .07	.165 ± .08	.400 ± .14	.076 ± .02	.774 ± .02	**.035 ± .00**
fico	LB-M	.340 ± .14	.334 ± .08	.094 ± .03	.023 ± .00	.816 ± .03	.086 ± .00
	LB-K	.681 ± .11	.466 ± .06	.066 ± .02	.018 ± .00	.842 ± .02	.093 ± .00
	LB-C	**.731 ± .07**	**.500 ± .05**	**.062 ± .01**	.018 ± .00	**.844 ± .02**	1.56 ± .00
	LMV-K	.491 ± .52	.129 ± .17	.223 ± .11	**.010 ± .01**	.781 ± .03	3.19 ± .40
	LMV-C	.273 ± .20	.047 ± .05	.141 ± .04	.038 ± .01	**.844 ± .02**	**.081 ± .00**
german	LB-M	.483 ± .10	.405 ± .07	**.079 ± .01**	.027 ± .00	.832 ± .03	.063 ± .00
	LB-K	.521 ± .11	.433 ± .09	**.079 ± .01**	.025 ± .00	.838 ± .02	.074 ± .00
	LB-C	**.526 ± .11**	**.436 ± .08**	.079 ± .02	.024 ± .00	.851 ± .03	.547 ± .00
	LMV-K	.445 ± .13	.396 ± .11	.126 ± .03	**.012 ± .01**	.849 ± .03	.345 ± .04
	LMV-C	.398 ± .07	.210 ± .04	.127 ± .02	.034 ± .01	**.851 ± .01**	**.059 ± .00**
iris	LB-M	.565 ± .24	.317 ± .22	.285 ± .11	.162 ± .06	.758 ± .07	.063 ± .00
	LB-K	**.619 ± .18**	**.503 ± .11**	**.232 ± .09**	.087 ± .03	.791 ± .04	.064 ± .00
	LB-C	.599 ± .22	.450 ± .16	.252 ± .11	.097 ± .02	.698 ± .06	.114 ± .00
	LMV-K	.525 ± .36	.446 ± .28	.337 ± .20	**.050 ± .04**	**.834 ± .10**	.110 ± .00
	LMV-C	.456 ± .17	.377 ± .12	.269 ± .13	.134 ± .05	.698 ± .06	**.061 ± .00**
titanic	LB-M	.156 ± .17	.151 ± .19	.558 ± .09	.168 ± .06	.618 ± .07	.053 ± .00
	LB-K	.172 ± .14	.157 ± .14	.542 ± .07	.113 ± .05	.658 ± .05	.054 ± .00
	LB-C	.151 ± .12	.133 ± .16	.541 ± .07	.110 ± .04	.630 ± .07	.080 ± .00
	LMV-K	**.182 ± .11**	**.168 ± .16**	**.521 ± .09**	**.100 ± .11**	**.678 ± .05**	.232 ± .02
	LMV-C	.086 ± .18	.075 ± .13	.663 ± .14	.116 ± .05	.630 ± .07	**.051 ± .00**

K, for the other three is LB-C, and for one is LB-K. On the other hand, for KT, LMV-K is the winner on four datasets, LB-C on two, and for one dataset LB-K. The insights from this analysis are the following. First, relying only on the mean at a preprocessing time does not guarantee at all coherence for explanations, and using LMV-C can be even worse. Some approaches are favoring similarity among the scores (measured in terms of CS), while others are favoring that the ordering of the scores, i.e., the order of the importance, is respected. Overall, adopting kNN as an imputation function is a reliable solution at a preprocessing time with LIME but is even better at explanation time with LIMEMV.

Regarding the absolute deviation with missings (ADW), the situation is even more unclear as it is considerably difficult to leave untouched the level of importance of a feature when the value is missing. A possible future research direction might re-frame this measure into a loss function and learn an explanation model from simulated situations of missing values (like the proposed experiment) such that these errors can be avoided by relying on the other features with values to estimate the importance of the features with missing values.

For the fidelity (FI) of the local surrogate, we observe that the proposed approaches in the LIMEMV family have always the best results. This is probably due to the usage *(i)* of the regressor tree that is better in approximating the behavior of the black-box, *(ii)* of a synthetic neighborhood that includes missing values and resembles the real data where the black-box is trained and applied.

Finally, for the explanation time (ET), we observe that LMV-K is the slowest approach compared to the others that always have an ET smaller than a second for explaining a single instance. This is caused by the kNN imputation approach that is applied for each instance in the synthetic neighborhood Z having at least a missing value and every time it needs to calculate the distance with all the other synthetic records in Z. Since the size of Z is $N = 5000$, this causes a not negligible increment in the ET w.r.t. the other explainers for large datasets.

In Fig. 3 and Fig. 4, we observe the impact of the different percentages of features with missing values (p) and different percentages of missing values in features (q) on the evaluation measures CS, KT, ADW, and ADO, for the datasets `adult` and `german`, respectively. Similar behaviors can be observed for the other datasets. In particular, for `compas`, `diabetes`, `titanic` and `iris` results are similar to `adult`, while for `fico` results are similar to `german`. We do not report the same plots for FI and ET as the variation of p and q do not impact these measures significantly enough.

As we know from the previous discussion and from Table 2, LMV-K is, on average, the best performer for the `adult` dataset. However, Fig. 3 unveils that this is not true for all combinations of p and q. Besides highlighting the best performers, through these plots, we can understand that the situation is even more variegated than expected, independently from the explainer we are interested in. Indeed, from Fig. 3, we can realize that for the explainers the increment of the percentage of features with missing values p has an impact w.r.t. certain measures. The measures more impacted by p are CS and ADW, as we observe an increasing performance trend when p grows. Indeed, the explainers are more coherent in explaining the corresponding record without missing values when the number of missing values is smaller. This may seem surprising. However, it makes sense that when there are fewer features with missing values, it is eas-

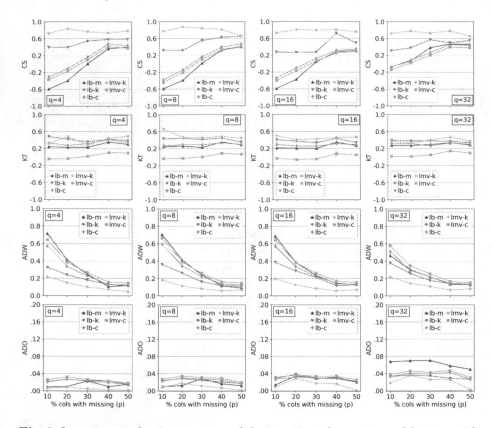

Fig. 3. Impact on evaluation measures of the variation of percentage of features with missing values (p) and percentage of missing values in features (q) for `adult`.

ier to create a discrepancy with the real importance value as by experimental setting, these are the globally most important. In comparison, when there are more features with missing values, their overall relative importance might be balanced among them, and the measures suffer less from their incorrect evaluation. A future research direction might consist in designing unbiased evaluation measures. All the explainers gain an improvement of ADW with LMV-K being constantly the best while concerning CS LMV-K and LB-K seem to be more robust, and their performance remains constant when varying p. On the other hand, KT and ADO are less impacted by the variation of p. Concerning q, we notice that nearly all the plots have slight changes from left to right, except for $q = 32$ for ADO. Indeed, in this case, especially for LB-M, we observe a degradation of the performance in terms of discrepancy for the features without missing values, i.e., having 32% of missing values in the features negatively affects the estimation of the importance of features without missing values.

In Fig. 4 are shown the same results reported in Fig. 3 but for `german`. In this case, we can notice that the percentage of features with missing values p has a

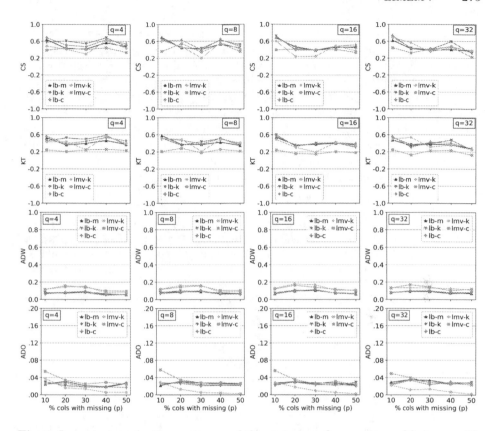

Fig. 4. Impact on evaluation measures of the variation of percentage of features with missing values (p) and percentage of missing values in features (q) for `german`.

negligible impact w.r.t. almost measures. For ADO, we observe an improvement in the performance when p grows, but this is not evident as it was in Fig. 3 for CS and ADW. In addition, the scores of all the explainers are quite similar to each other and do not follow a clear increasing or decreasing trend. Therefore, these approaches are not very sensitive to the characteristics of the missing values for `german`, for the configurations studied.

6   Conclusion

We have presented LIMEMV, the first proposal in the research area of post-hoc local model-agnostic explanation methods that is able to handle the presence of missing values directly in the explanation process. An experimental evaluation empirically proves that using LIMEMV leads to more reliable explanations than using any imputation approach in the pipeline with the classic LIME regarding coherence for features without missing values and fidelity of the local surrogate model. However, we cannot state that LIMEMV is always the best solution as it seems that various issues are tied to the type of dataset processed by the black-box, with the type of missing values and how disruptive their presence is.

As future research direction, we would like to implement the missing value-compliant version of other post-hoc explanation approaches such as SHAP [31], LORE [19] or DICE [35] by following the same strategies used for LIMEMV. Also, we intend to study these techniques not only in the MCAR setting but also in MAR and MNAR. Furthermore, we aim to adapt the neighborhood generation process by extending its capability to handle categorical, continuous, and discrete data simultaneously. Finally, to completely cover LIME applicability, we would like to study to which extent it is possible to handle missing data on data types different from tabular data, such as images, textual data, and time series.

Acknowledgment. This work is partially supported by the EU NextGenerationEU programme under the funding schemes PNRR-PE-AI FAIR (Future Artificial Intelligence Research), "SoBigData.it - Strengthening the Italian RI for Social Mining and Big Data Analytics" - Prot. IR0000013, H2020-INFRAIA-2019-1: Res. Infr. G.A. 871042 *SoBigData++*, G.A. 761758 *Humane AI*, G.A. 952215 *TAILOR*, ERC-2018-ADG G.A. 834756 *XAI*, and CHIST-ERA-19-XAI-010 SAI, by MUR (N. not yet available), FWF (N. I 5205), EPSRC (N. EP/V055712/1), NCN (N. 2020/02/Y/ST6/00064), ETAg (N. SLTAT21096), BNSF (N. KP-06-AOO2/5).

References

1. Adadi, A., Berrada, M.: Peeking inside the black-box: a survey on explainable artificial intelligence (XAI). IEEE Access **6**, 52138–52160 (2018)
2. Ahmad, M.A., Eckert, C., Teredesai, A.: The challenge of imputation in explainable artificial intelligence models. In: AISafety@IJCAI, vol. 2419 of CEUR Workshop Proceedings. CEUR-WS.org (2019)
3. Azur, M.J., Stuart, E.A., Frangakis, C., Leaf, P.J.: Multiple imputation by chained equations: what is it and how does it work? Int. J. Meth. Psychiatr. Res. **20**(1), 40–49 (2011)
4. Beaulac, C., Rosenthal, J.S.: BEST: a decision tree algorithm that handles missing values. Comput. Stat. **35**(3), 1001–1026 (2020). https://doi.org/10.1007/s00180-020-00987-z
5. Bodria, F., Giannotti, F., Guidotti, R., Naretto, F., Pedreschi, D., Rinzivillo, S.: Benchmarking and survey of explanation methods for black box models. CoRR, abs/2102.13076 (2021)
6. Bramhall, S., Horn, H., Tieu, M., Lohia, N.: Qlime-a quadratic local interpretable model-agnostic explanation approach. SMU Data Sci. Rev. **3**(1), 4 (2020)
7. Brick, J.M., Kalton, G.: Handling missing data in survey research. Stat. Meth. Med. Res. **5**(3), 215–238 (1996)
8. Chen, T., Guestrin, C.: XGBoost: a scalable tree boosting system. In: KDD, pp. 785–794. ACM (2016)
9. Cinquini, M., Giannotti, F., Guidotti, R.: Boosting synthetic data generation with effective nonlinear causal discovery. In: CogMI, pp. 54–63. IEEE (2021)
10. Cinquini, M., Guidotti, R.: CALIME: causality-aware local interpretable model-agnostic explanations. CoRR, abs/2212.05256 (2022)

11. Dixon, J.K.: Pattern recognition with partly missing data. IEEE Trans. Syst. Man Cybern. **9**(10), 617–621 (1979)
12. Donders, A.R.T., Van Der Heijden, G.J., Stijnen, T., Moons, K.G.: A gentle introduction to imputation of missing values. J. Clin. Epidemiol. **59**(10), 1087–1091 (2006)
13. Emmanuel, T., Maupong, T., Mpoeleng, D., Semong, T., Mphago, B., Tabona, O.: A survey on missing data in machine learning. J. Big Data **8**(1), 1–37 (2021). https://doi.org/10.1186/s40537-021-00516-9
14. Fletcher Mercaldo, S., Blume, J.D.. Missing data and prediction: the pattern submodel. Biostatistics **21**(2), 236–252 (2020)
15. Freitas, A.A.: Comprehensible classification models: a position paper. SIGKDD Explor. **15**(1), 1–10 (2013)
16. Gosiewska, A., Biecek, P.: Do not trust additive explanations. CoRR, abs/1903.11420 (2019)
17. Groenwold, R.H., White, I.R., Donders, A.R.T., Carpenter, J.R., Altman, D.G., Moons, K.G.: Missing covariate data in clinical research: when and when not to use the missing-indicator method for analysis. CMAJ **184**(11), 1265–1269 (2012)
18. Guidotti, R.: Evaluating local explanation methods on ground truth. Artif. Intel. **291**, 103428 (2021)
19. Guidotti, R., Monreale, A., Giannotti, F., Pedreschi, D., Ruggieri, S., Turini, F.: Factual and counterfactual explanations for black box decision making. IEEE Intell. Syst. **34**(6), 14–23 (2019)
20. Guidotti, R., Monreale, A., Ruggieri, S., Turini, F., Giannotti, F., Pedreschi, D.: A survey of methods for explaining black box models. ACM Comput. Surv. **51**(5):93:1–93:42 (2019)
21. Hall, P., Gill, N., Kurka, M., Phan, W.: Machine learning interpretability with H2O driverless AI. H2O. AI (2017)
22. Hans, S., Saha, D., Aggarwal, A.: Explainable data imputation using constraints. In: COMAD/CODS, pp. 128–132. ACM (2023)
23. Hu, L., Chen, J., Nair, V.N., Sudjianto, A.: Locally interpretable models and effects based on supervised partitioning (LIME-SUP). CoRR, abs/1806.00663 (2018)
24. Kass, G.V.: An exploratory technique for investigating large quantities of categorical data. J. Roy. Stat. Soc.: Ser. C (Appl. Stat.) **29**(2), 119–127 (1980)
25. Kaur, H., Nori, H., Jenkins, S., Caruana, R., Wallach, H., Wortman Vaughan, J.: Interpreting interpretability: understanding data scientists' use of interpretability tools for machine learning. In: CHI, pp. 1–14. ACM (2020)
26. Ke, G., et al.: LightGBM: a highly efficient gradient boosting decision tree. In: NeurIPS, pp. 3146–3154 (2017)
27. Kendall, M.G.: A new measure of rank correlation. Biometrika **30**(1/2), 81–93 (1938)
28. Li, X., et al.: A survey of data-driven and knowledge-aware explainable AI. IEEE Trans. Knowl. Data Eng. **34**(1), 29–49 (2022)
29. Lin, W., Tsai, C.: Missing value imputation: a review and analysis of the literature (2006–2017). Artif. Intel. Rev. **53**(2), 1487–1509 (2020)
30. Longo, L., Goebel, R., Lecue, F., Kieseberg, P., Holzinger, A.: Explainable artificial intelligence: concepts, applications, research challenges and visions. In: Holzinger, A., Kieseberg, P., Tjoa, A.M., Weippl, E. (eds.) CD-MAKE 2020. LNCS, vol. 12279, pp. 1–16. Springer, Cham (2020). https://doi.org/10.1007/978-3-030-57321-8_1
31. Lundberg, S.M., Lee, S.: A unified approach to interpreting model predictions. In: NIPS, pp. 4765–4774 (2017)

32. Manerba, M.M., Guidotti, R.: Investigating debiasing effects on classification and explainability. In: AIES, pp. 468–478. ACM (2022)
33. Mehrabi, N., Morstatter, F., Saxena, N., Lerman, K., Galstyan, A.: A survey on bias and fairness in machine learning. ACM Comput. Surv. **54**(6), 115:1–115:35 (2022)
34. Miller, T.: Explanation in artificial intelligence: insights from the social sciences. Artif. Intel. **267**, 1–38 (2019)
35. Mothilal, R.K., Sharma, A., Tan, C.: Explaining machine learning classifiers through diverse counterfactual explanations. In: FAT*, pp. 607–617. ACM (2020)
36. Murray, J.S.: Multiple imputation: a review of practical and theoretical findings (2018)
37. Pasquale, F.: The black box society: The secret algorithms that control money and information. Harvard University Press (2015)
38. Payrovnaziri, S.N., et al.: The impact of missing value imputation on the interpretations of predictive models: a case study on one-year mortality prediction in ICU patients with acute myocardial infarction. MedRxiv **10**(2020.06), 06–20124347 (2020)
39. Pedersen, A.B. et al.: Missing data and multiple imputation in clinical epidemiological research. Clin. Epidemiol. **9**, 157–166 (2017)
40. Peltola, T.: Local interpretable model-agnostic explanations of Bayesian predictive models via Kullback-Leibler projections. CoRR, abs/1810.02678 (2018)
41. Prokhorenkova, L., Gusev, G., Vorobev, A., Dorogush, A.V., Gulin, A.: CatBoost: unbiased boosting with categorical features. In: NeurIPS, pp. 6639–6649 (2018)
42. Ribeiro, M.T., Singh, S., Guestrin, C.: "Why should I trust you?": explaining the predictions of any classifier. In: HLT-NAACL Demos, pp. 97–101. The Association for Computational Linguistics (2016)
43. Rubin, D.B.: Inference and missing data. Biometrika **63**(3), 581–592 (1976)
44. Saito, S., Chua, E., Capel, N., Hu, R.: Improving LIME robustness with smarter locality sampling. CoRR, abs/2006.12302 (2020)
45. Shankaranarayana, S.M., Runje, D.: ALIME: autoencoder based approach for local interpretability. In: Yin, H., Camacho, D., Tino, P., Tallón-Ballesteros, A.J., Menezes, R., Allmendinger, R. (eds.) IDEAL 2019. LNCS, vol. 11871, pp. 454–463. Springer, Cham (2019). https://doi.org/10.1007/978-3-030-33607-3_49
46. Sharafoddini, A., Dubin, J.A., Maslove, D.M., Lee, J., et al.: A new insight into missing data in intensive care unit patient profiles: observational study. JMIR Med. Inform. **7**(1), e11605 (2019)
47. Steinberg, D.: Cart: classification and regression trees. In: The Top Ten Algorithms in Data Mining, pp. 193–216. Chapman and Hall/CRC (2009)
48. Strobl, C., Boulesteix, A.L., Zeileis, A., Hothorn, T.: Bias in random forest variable importance measures: illustrations, sources and a solution. BMC Bioinform. **8**, 1–21 (2007)
49. Tan, P.N., Steinbach, M., Kumar, V.: Introduction to Data Mining. Addison-Wesley, Boston (2005)
50. Vilone, G., Longo, L.: Explainable artificial intelligence: a systematic review. CoRR, abs/2006.00093 (2020)
51. Zafar, M.R., Khan, N.: Deterministic local interpretable model-agnostic explanations for stable explainability. Mach. Learn. Knowl. Extr. **3**(3), 525–541 (2021)
52. Zhao, X., Huang, W., Huang, X., Robu, V., Flynn, D.: BayLIME: Bayesian local interpretable model-agnostic explanations. In: Uncertainty in Artificial Intelligence, pp. 887–896. PMLR (2021)

Necessary and Sufficient Explanations of Multi-Criteria Decision Aiding Models, with and Without Interacting Criteria

Christophe Labreuche[1,2](✉) and Roman Bresson[1,2]

[1] Thales Research & Technology, Palaiseau, France
{christophe.labreuche,roman.bresson}@thalesgroup.com
[2] SINCLAIR AI Lab, Palaiseau, France

Abstract. We are interested in explaining models from Multi-Criteria Decision Aiding. These can be used to perform pairwise comparisons between two options, or classify an instance in an ordered list of categories, on the basis of multiple and conflicting criteria. Several models can be used to achieve such goals ranging from the simplest one assuming independence among criteria - namely the weighted sum model - to complex models able to represent complex interaction among criteria, such as the Hierarchical Choquet Integral (HCI). We consider two complementary explanations of these two models under these two goals: sufficient explanation (a.k.a. Prime Implicants) and necessary explanations (a.k.a. Counterfactual explanations). The idea of prime implicants is to identify the parts of the instance that need to be kept unchanged so that the decision remains the same, while the other parts are replaced by any value. We generalize the notion of information that needs to be kept not only on the values of the criteria (values of the instance of the criteria) but also on the weights of criteria (parameters of the model). For the HCI model, we propose a Mixed-Integer Linear Program (MILP) formulation to compute the prime implicants. We also propose a weak version of prime implicants to account for the case where the requirements of changing the other criteria in any possible way is too strong. Finally, we also propose a MILP formulation for computing counterfactual explanations of the HCI model.

Keywords: Prime Implicants · Counterfactual Explanation · Multi-Criteria Decision Aiding · Choquet integral

1 Introduction

We are interested in explaining Multi-Criteria Decision Aiding (MCDA). The aim of MCDA is to capture the preferences of a decision maker regarding alternatives described over multiple criteria. Such criteria are conflicting in the sense that one can usually not maximize all of them at the same time [13]. One thus needs to perform tradeoffs among criteria, as one criterion may compensate another one. MCDA aims at solving several types of problems. This first one, *ranking* aims at constructing a preference relation among a set of alternatives. This relation can be used for instance to determine the preferred option. Another goal is *sorting* and aims at assigning options

© The Author(s), under exclusive license to Springer Nature Switzerland AG 2023
L. Longo (Ed.): xAI 2023, CCIS 1902, pp. 279–302, 2023.
https://doi.org/10.1007/978-3-031-44067-0_15

to an ordered list of categories. An essential component of decision support, once the preference model is constructed, is to explain the recommendation to the user.

The ranking and sorting problems in MCDA can be solved by a utility model which maps each alternative onto a utility scale. The essential component of this utility function is the so-called *aggregation function*, which aggregates the outcomes of the criteria and returns an overall utility score. The simplest aggregation function is the weighted sum. It is sufficient to represent tradeoffs among criteria. However, this model is limited by the fact that it requires the criteria to be independant, which is not the case in many real-life situations. In this case, a more versatile model is the Choquet integral (CI) [10, 15]. CIs have the ability to capture complex interaction among criteria, such as sinergy or redundancy. It is common to organize such models in a hierarchical way, thereby decomposing the aggregation process into a tree of smaller aggregations. The corresponding model is the Hierarchical Choquet Integral (HCI), which is a nest composition of Choquet integrals [8]. One reason chosen for using HCI is its by-design explainability, which we will detail now.

Explainability can take very different forms [2]. An explanation can be constructed independently from the model (model-agnostic explanation) or be dedicated to a particular class of models (model specific). One can then try to explain the model as a whole (global explanation) or focus on explaining a particular instance (local explanation) [21]. One may think of applying a model agnostic explanation to an MCDA model. Feature-attributions techniques represent good candidates, as they are widely used in Machine Learning. We may mention the LIME or SHAP frameworks [35, 40]. Note that the Shapley value has been extended to models decomposed in trees, through the concept of Winter value [34, 51]. While being fully adapted to the hierarchical MCDA models, this approach does not provide any concrete and actionable explanation.

We thus consider other types of explanations. The first type is called *sufficient explanation*. It corresponds to the concept of *Prime Implicants*. The idea is that if changing the value of a feature by any other value does not modify the outcome of the model, then this feature has no influence on the result. This approach provides a safe and compelling way to remove non-influential features from the explanation, unlike the feature attribution methods, which require to introduce a -subjective- threshold to decide whether the features should be displayed to the user. While Prime Implicants simplify only on the feature values of the instance, we propose in this work to simplify on both the values of the instance on the features and the weights of criteria. We propose efficient approaches to compute the sufficient explanations for the weighted sum model. For the non-linear HCI model, prime implicants can be obtained thanks to a Mixed-Integer Linear Program (MILP) formulation. Prime implicants imply that we can replace the value on a feature that is not in the prime implicant by any other value without changing the outcome of the decision model. This condition might be too restrictive in some applications. Moreover, operating a reasonable modification of the value on a feature might be sufficient to remove this feature from the explanation. This yields a weaker version of prime implicants, which we develop later.

The second type of explanation is called *necessary explanation* – also called counterfactual explanation. We look for the smallest modification of the values on the features that yield a different outcome. We also show that this problem can be turned into a MIP formulation in the case of a HCI model.

The paper is organized as follows: Section 3 recalls the background in MCDA. The following sections present our contribution: the construction of necessary and sufficient explanations, for the decision and classification problems, applied to the weighted sum and the Choquet integral models. First, Sect. 4 considers sufficient explanations for the decision problem. Then we tackle sufficient explanations for the classification problem (Sect. 5). Necessary explanations are treated separately (Sect. 6). Finally Sect. 7 discusses the impact of our approaches on the xAI field. Note that, in order to make the formal sessions easier to read, the proofs of lemmas are given in Sect. 9.

2   Related Works

2.1   Related Works in MCDA

Various models have been explored in MCDA to capture different types of preferences [13]. The basic ingredient in MCDA is a binary relation called *preference* relation, which compares any pair of alternatives. The two main classes of MCDA models for representing such a relation differ on the order in which the operations of aggregation of the attributes and comparison of the two alternatives are made. In the *outranking* methods, one first compares the two alternatives attribute by attribute, then these comparisons are aggregated [43]. The ELECTRE method is a popular MCDA method in this category [42]. The other approach consists in aggregating the values over all attributes for each alternative, into an overall utility. Only then do we decide between both alternatives by comparing their utilities [27]. Often, a marginal utility function is applied to the value on each attribute. One then simply sum-up these partial utility to obtain the overall utility. The corresponding model is the *additive-utility* [27]. When the value of utilities are commensurate and can be compared, then the marginal utilities are combined with criteria weights to construct the overall utility. This yields to the *weighted sum*. Many elicitation methods have been designed to construct the additive utility with the UTA approach [25], or the weighted sum with AHP [46] or MACBETH [3]. Apart from these two branches, *rough sets* methodology brings a way to explicitly capture preferences through (at-least or at-most) rules [19].

We will follow the second, that is the utility-based approach. The assumption of independence of criteria, which characterizes the weighted sum, is often violated in applications. To overcome this limitation, the *Choquet integral* [10] is used in MCDA to represent interacting criteria and complex decision strategies [15, 16].

2.2   Related Works in xAI

Many xAI techniques have been defined. The first category of methods provides formal definition of explanation. Prime implicants define sufficient interpretation in first-order logic [36]. They can be used to explain a particular instance, which yields the concepts of *sufficient reason* [11], *PI-explanation* [47] and *abductive explanation* [24]. An explanation is a subset of the literals of the instance that entails the same conclusion.

A sufficient cause is a subset of literals such that if they were modified, the conclusion would have been different [22]. An actual cause is a minimal sufficient cause [22].

It has been shown that humans often reason in a contrastive way. This means that the explanation of "*Why x?*" is cast into "*why x and not y?*", where x is the *fact* and y is called the *foil* [37]. A counterfactual explanation aims at finding the minimal change in the values of the instance on the features so that its classification is changed [48,50]. The main difficulty of these approaches is to generate modification recommendations that are realistic for the user [26,28].

Anchors generates an if-then rule to explain an instance with high precision, in the sense that the accuracy of the local rule is quite good [41]. This is also a sufficient explanation in the sense that when some features are missing from the premises of the rule, then changing the value on those features do not influence the outcome (with high accuracy). *LORE* is a local interpretator that generates for a given instance, a rule explaining the instance together with several counterfactual rules proposing different ways to change the instance outcome [20].

Other methods are less formal and in particular simply aim at allocating an importance to each feature for a given instance (feature attribution methods) [40]. These techniques highlight the most important features. Their main added-value is that they are model-agnostic, meaning that they can be applied to any (even black-box) model. The *LIME* approach constructs a linear model to approach the separation border close to the instance to explain (where this model is trained from data selected according to their proximity to the instance) [40]. The weights of this linear model provide the importance of features for the given instance. The Shapley value has recently become popular in Machine Learning (ML) for feature attribution [12,35,49]. What distinguishes these methods is the game on which the Shapley value is computed. A major difficulty in assessing the game is to take into account the interdependencies among the features in a consistent way [1].

3   Setting

A Multi-Criteria Decision Aiding (MCDA) problem consists of a set $N = \{1, \dots, n\}$ of features or attributes. Each feature is associated to its domain of definition X_i. The instances are elements of $X = X_1 \times \cdots \times X_n$. We assume we are given for each feature $i \in N$ a *binary preference relation* $\succsim_i$ over X_i such that $x_i \succsim_i x_i'$ (for $x_i, x_i' \in X_i$) means that x_i is at least as good as x_i' on this feature.

MCDA aims at representing the preferences of a user regarding options in X. These preferences can be mapped into different problems.

Definition 1. *In a* sorting *problem, the aim is to assign any element in X into ordered classes – typically $C = \{0, 1\}$, where 0 is the lower class and 1 is the higher class – thanks to a function $f : X \to C$, where f is a* classification function.

Definition 2. *In a* ranking *problem, the aim is to construct a preference relation $\succsim$ over $X \times X$ such that $x \succsim y$ (with $x, y \in X$) means that x is at least as good as y.*

If $\succsim$ is a weak order, one may for instance deduce the best elements in X. These two problems can be represented with the help of a so-called utility function $u : X \to \mathbb{R}$. The sorting problem is obtained by discretizing function u:

$$f(x) = 1 \quad \Leftrightarrow \quad u(x) > \alpha, \tag{1}$$

where α is a threshold, and the ranking of alternatives also follows from the utility:

$$x \succsim y \quad \Longleftrightarrow \quad u(x) \geq u(y). \tag{2}$$

An important property of MCDA is monotonicity with respect to $\succsim_i$: for all $x, y \in X$, $[\forall i \in N \ x_i \succsim_i y_i]$ implies that $u(x) \geq u(y)$.

Utility model u is taken in the *decomposable form* [27]:

$$u(x) = F(u_1(x_1), \ldots, u_n(x_n)), \tag{3}$$

where $u_i : X_i \to [0,1]$ (for every $i \in N$) is a so-called utility function transforming feature i into a utility in satisfaction scale $[0,1]$ (where 0 is total non-satisfaction, and 1 is the total satisfaction), and $F : [0,1]^N \to [0,1]$ is an aggregation function.

We assume here that the model is already constructed. We can assume without loss of generality that the X_i's are already normalized, so that the marginal utility functions are the identity functions and that $X_i = [0,1]$.

The simplest aggregation function is the weighted sum (w_i is criterion i's weight):

$$u(x) = F(x) = \sum_{i \in N} w_i\, x_i. \tag{4}$$

In order to ease its interpretability, function F is taken as a hierarchical model, described by a tree T characterized by the set N of leaves, a set of other nodes M and a root $r \in M$. The children of a node $i \in M$ are denoted $C(i) \subseteq M \cup N$. We define thus a local aggregation function $F_i : [0,1]^{C(i)} \to [0,1]$ for each $i \in M$. For $x \in X = [0,1]^N$, we recursively set $x_i = F_i(t_{C(i)})$ for any $i \in M$, and $u(x) = F(x) = x_r$.

A weighted sum can be equivalently described on any hierarchy, without consequence on the mathematical expression, provided that the weights are correctly assigned to each node. A more versatile aggregation function than the weighted sum is the Choquet integral [10]. The two-additive Choquet integral takes the following form:

$$F_i(x_{C(i)}, m) = \sum_{j \in C(i)} m_j\, x_j + \sum_{\{j,k\} \in E(i)} m_{j,k}\, x_j \wedge x_k, \tag{5}$$

where $E(i) \subseteq \{\{j,k\} \subseteq C(i)\}$ is the set of pairs having non-zero interaction. We note that $m_{j,k}$ and m_j correspond to the Möbius coefficients for the two-additive Choquet integral. A hierarchy of Choquet integrals is called a HCI model.

4 Sufficient Explanation of the Preference Relation $\succsim$

We wish to explain preference $x \succsim y$, with $x, y \in X = [0,1]^N$.

Prime Implicants (PI) represent a standard explanation approach. It consists in simplifying the known values on the features while the decision remains the same. The idea is that *a set T of criteria explains the decision if the decision remains unchanged regardless of what values are assigned on the other criteria.* In this approach, the simplification is done on the feature space.

Following [32], the arguments explaining a weighted sum shall mention the values on the features and/or the parameters of the model (e.h. the importance of criteria). We take this idea by extending the concept of explanation in which the process of simplification or modification shall not be done only on the value of the features but also on the parameters of the model.

4.1   General Approach for the Weighted Sum Model

We consider the weighted sum model:

$$x \succsim y \quad \Longleftrightarrow \quad H(\Delta, w) := \sum_{i \in N} w_i \, \Delta_i \geq 0$$

where $\Delta_i = x_i - y_i$. Let $D = [-1, 1]^N$ be the set of possible values of Δ, and W be the set of normalized weights:

$$W = \left\{ w \in \mathbb{R}^N \; : \; \sum_{i \in N} w_i = 1 \text{ and } \forall i \in N, \; w_i \geq 0 \right\}.$$

An explanation is a subset of the utilities of x and y (it is sufficient to know the difference Δ), but also a subset of the criteria weights w, such that the preference remains the same, whatever the remaining values of the utilities and of the weights. One wishes to display to the user the simplest explanation, i.e. to show the least number of elements of Δ and w. If one keeps only the utility discrepancy Δ on criteria $S \subseteq N$ and the weights w on a subset $T \subseteq N$ of criteria, and if Δ_S can be completed by anything on $N \backslash S$ and w_T can be completed by anything on $N \backslash T$ while x remains preferred to y, then the explanation can focus on the pair $\langle S, T \rangle$. More generally, one may enforce some constraints on the completion of Δ_S and w_T. We denote by $D(S) \subseteq D$ the set of admissible preferences given that Δ is known only in S, and by $W(T) \subseteq W$ the set of admissible weights given that w is known only for criteria in T.

Definition 3. *We define the set of* sufficient explanations *(or* implicants*) as:*

$$Ex_{\mathrm{Suf}} := \{ \langle S, T \rangle \text{ with } S, T \subseteq N \; : \forall \Delta' \in D(S), \; \forall v \in W(T), \; H(\Delta', v) \geq 0 \}.$$

Several definitions of $D(S)$ and $W(T)$ will be proposed. We assume that

$$D(S) \subseteq \{ \Delta' \in D \; : \; \Delta'_i = \Delta_i \; \forall i \in S \},$$
$$W(T) \subseteq \{ v \in W \; : \; v_i = w_i \; \forall i \in T \}.$$

We have that $\langle N, N \rangle \in Ex_{\mathrm{Suf}}$ (since x is preferred to y from Δ and w) and that $\langle \emptyset, \emptyset \rangle \notin Ex_{\mathrm{Suf}}$ (since one can of course obtain that y is preferred to x if we consider other preference information on the options or importance of criteria).

We assume that $D(\cdot)$ and $W(\cdot)$ are antimonotone:

$$\forall S \subseteq S' \subseteq N \qquad D(S) \supseteq D(S'), \tag{6}$$
$$\forall T \subseteq T' \subseteq N \qquad W(T) \supseteq W(T'). \tag{7}$$

If $S \subseteq S'$, then $D(S)$ is composed of weights whose value is fixed on S' to Δ, and thus is also fixed on $S \subseteq S'$. Hence $D(S') \subseteq D(S)$. The same argument applies for $W(\cdot)$.

Lemma 1. *Under (6) and (7), we have*

$$\langle S, T \rangle \in Ex_{\mathrm{Suf}} \implies \forall S' \supseteq S \, \forall T' \supseteq T \quad , \quad \langle S', T' \rangle \in Ex_{\mathrm{Suf}}.$$

The proof of this lemma and the other results is given in Sect. 9.

Starting from a sufficient explanation $\langle S, T \rangle \in Ex_{\mathrm{Suf}}$, adding extra information Δ_i (for $i \in N \backslash S$) regarding the utilities or w_j (for $j \in N \backslash T$) on the criteria weights also yields a sufficient explanation. We are thus looking for the simplest explanation, that is the minimal ones.

Definition 4. *We define the set $Ex_{\mathrm{Suf}}^{\min}$ of minimal sufficient explanations (or prime implicants) as the minimal elements of Ex_{Suf} w.r.t. set inclusion.*

Remark 1. If the decision is clear-cut, then it is possible to change a lot of weights without inverting the decision. In this case, the elements of $Ex_{\mathrm{Suf}}^{\min}$ contain only a small number of criteria. Hence the explanation is simple when the decision is clear-cut. On the opposite side, if the decision is tight, then a little change in the utilities or criteria weights is enough to switch the decision. Hence, the elements of $Ex_{\mathrm{Suf}}^{\min}$ contain a relatively large number of criteria. Hence the explanation is relatively complex when the decision is tight.

We propose several definitions of $D(\cdot)$ and $W(\cdot)$ depending on whether we simplify only on the utilities of x and y, only on the criteria weights w, or on both. These these three possibilities are explored in the next sections.

4.2   Case of the Weighted Sum: Simplification w.r.t. the Utilities

The first approach is the standard way to conceive Prime Implicants, that is, by simplifying only on the values of the features. No simplification is done on the weights of the model. Simplifying only on the utilities means that the weights of criteria are known to the recipient of the explanation. They only wants to know which values of x and y are essential to understand the preference of x over y. We set

$$D(S) = \{\Delta' \in D \; : \; \Delta_i' = \Delta_i \, \forall i \in S\},$$
$$W(T) = \{w\}.$$

For $D(S)$, we keep the values of utilities in S and consider any possible value on the other criteria. We keep all criteria weights, so that $W(T)$ is only composed of the full vector of weights. The second argument in $\langle S, T \rangle \in Ex_{\mathrm{Suf}}$ is not relevant and is removed. Hence we keep only the first argument S of the elements of Ex_{Suf}.

Lemma 2. *We have*

$$Ex_{\mathrm{Suf}} = \Big\{ S \subseteq N \ : \ L(S) \geq 0 \Big\},$$

where $L(S) := \sum_{k \in S} w_k \, \Delta_k - \sum_{k \in N \setminus S} w_k = \sum_{k \in S} w_k \, (\Delta_k + 1) - 1.$

Proof. When the value of Δ is unknown, the most pessimistic value is -1.

■

Let

$$c_k := w_k \, (\Delta_k + 1). \tag{8}$$

We have

$$L(S) - L(S \setminus \{k\}) = c_k \geq 0 \tag{9}$$

Define a permutation π such that

$$c_{\pi(1)} \geq c_{\pi(2)} \geq \cdots \geq c_{\pi(n)}. \tag{10}$$

The k that are selected are the ones with the small values of c_k. Relation $c_k \approx 0$ means:

– criterion k is not important ($w_k \approx 0$);
– or criterion k is very negative ($\Delta_k \approx -1$).

Lemma 3. *Let p the smallest integer such that $\{\pi(1), \pi(2), \ldots, \pi(p)\} \in Ex_{\mathrm{Suf}}$. Then $\{\pi(1), \pi(2), \ldots, \pi(p)\} \in Ex_{\mathrm{Suf}}^{\min}$ and there is no element of $Ex_{\mathrm{Suf}}^{\min}$ with a smaller cardinality.*

The minimal explanation generated by this lemma focuses on the strongest and most positive arguments, which makes sense.

Let us start with an example in which very few simplifications are obtained.

Example 1. Consider the following examples with 5 criteria.

Criteria	1	2	3	4	5
x	0.5	0.4	0.1	0.7	0.9
y	0.2	0.6	0.5	0.4	0.2
Δ	0.3	-0.2	-0.4	0.3	0.7
w	0.2	0.2	0.1	0.4	0.1
c	0.26	0.16	0.06	0.52	0.17

We have $u(x) = 0.56$ and $u(y) = 0.39$ so that $x \succ y$. Even though, there is some margin on the utility of x compared to that of y, the set of minimal explanations is:

$$Ex_{\mathrm{Suf}}^{\min} = \big\{\{1,2,3,4\}, \{1,3,4,5\}, \{1,2,4,5\}\big\}.$$

Explanation $\{1, 2, 3, 4\}$ yields an exact indifference between x and y, as $L(\{1, 2, 3, 4\}) = 0$. We see that we can remove criteria 2, 3 or 5 in the explanation.

Criteria 2 and 3 are the two negative arguments. Criterion 5 correspond to a weak positive argument as its weight is small.

We also note that $c_4 > c_5 > c_2 > c_1 > c_3$, i.e. $\pi(1) = 4, \pi(2) = 5, \pi(3) = 2, \pi(4) = 1, \pi(5) = 3$. Hence the minimal explanation (according to Lemma 3) is $\{\pi(1), \pi(2), \pi(3), \pi(4)\} = \{1, 2, 4, 5\}$, as $L(\{\pi(1), \pi(2), \pi(3), \pi(4)\}) \geq 0$ but $L(\{\pi(1), \pi(2), \pi(3)\}) < 0$. We only remove criterion 3 from this explanation.   ∎

The next example illustrates a much more efficient simplification.

Example 2. Consider the following examples with 5 criteria. We have $u(x) = 0.75$,

Criteria	1	2	3	4	5
x	0.7	0.9	0.4	0.8	0.9
y	0.2	0.6	0.5	0.4	0.2
Δ	0.5	0.3	−0.1	0.4	0.7
w	0.3	0.1	0.1	0.5	0.1
c	0.45	0.13	0.09	0.56	0.17

$u(y) = 0.35$ and thus $x \succ y$. One can now simplify on much more criteria. We note that $c_4 > c_1 > c_5 > c_2 > c_3$. Hence the minimal explanation (according to Lemma 3) is $\{\pi(1), \pi(2)\} = \{1, 4\}$.   ∎

4.3 Case of a Weighted Sum: Simplification w.r.t. the Weights

The second approach supposes that we keep all information on the values of criteria, thereby the simplification only operates on the criteria weights. We set

$$D(S) = \{\Delta\}$$
$$W(T) = \{v \in W : v_i = w_i \ \forall i \in T\}.$$

We keep all utilities so that $D(S)$ is reduced to Δ. For $W(T)$, we keep the criteria weights in T and we complete this vector in any possible way. The first argument in $\langle S, T \rangle \in Ex_{\text{Suf}}$ is not considered. We only keep the second argument T of the elements of Ex_{Suf}. The following lemma provides a means to compute the sufficient explanations.

Lemma 4. *We have*

$$Ex_{\text{Suf}} = \left\{ T \subseteq N : \forall i \in N \backslash T \quad \Delta_i \geq -\frac{\sum_{k \in T} w_k \, \Delta_k}{1 - \sum_{k \in T} w_k} \right\}, \tag{11}$$

and equivalently

$$Ex_{\text{Suf}} = \left\{ T \subseteq N : H(T) \geq 0 \right\}, \tag{12}$$

where $H(T) := \left(\sum_{k \in N \backslash T} w_k \right) \min_{i \in N \backslash T} \Delta_i + \sum_{k \in T} w_k \, \Delta_k.$

The idea is that the criteria $N\backslash T$ are not selected since, once w is known on T, the remaining amount of weight $1 - \sum_{k \in T} w_k$ for criteria $N\backslash T$ can be assigned in any way without switching the preference between x and y.

By Lemma 1, if $T \in Ex_{\mathrm{Suf}}$ and $i \in N\backslash T$ then $T \cup i \in Ex_{\mathrm{Suf}}$. We have

$$H(N) - H(T) = \sum_{k \in N\backslash T} w_k \left(\Delta_k - \min_{i \in N\backslash T} \Delta_i \right) \geq 0.$$

Hence for $T \in Ex_{\mathrm{Suf}}$, we have $0 \leq H(T) \leq H(N)$. In order to find the smallest possible explanation T, we wish to find the smallest T such that $H(N) - H(T) \leq H(N)$. In order to have $H(N) - H(T)$ small, we have two options:

– the Δ_k have more or less the same value for all $k \in N\backslash T$;
– or $w_k \approx 0$ for all $k \in N\backslash T$.

Example 3 (Example 1 cont.). With the same values as in Example 1, we now obtain

$$Ex_{\mathrm{Suf}}^{\min} = \Big\{ \{1, 2, 4\}, \{2, 3, 5\}, \{2, 4, 5\}, \{3, 4\} \Big\}.$$

The explanation with minimal cardinality is $\{3, 4\}$ and contains the two negative arguments. ∎

Comparing Examples 1 and 3, the approach of simplification w.r.t. utilities exhibits the most important and positive arguments, whereas the approach of simplification w.r.t. weights seem to highlight the negative arguments. The reason for this is that if a negative argument is not selected, it will receive all weights of the unselected criteria, which is very penalizing to keep the same decision – see Lemma 4. The so-obtained explanation $\{3, 4\}$ looks counter-intuitive. Moreover, $N\backslash\{i\} \in Ex_{\mathrm{Suf}}$ for any $i \in N$, as if we just remove one criterion, its weight can of course be deduced from all other ones (they sum-up to one). For these reasons, we will not consider this part of simplifying only on criteria weights in the remaining of the paper.

4.4 Case of the Weighted Sum: Simplification w.r.t. both the Weights and the Utilities

In the last approach, we assume that we can simplify on both the values of the features and the weights. We set

$$D(S) = \{\Delta' \in D \ : \ \Delta'_i = \Delta_i \ \forall i \in S\}$$
$$W(T) = \{v \in W \ : \ v_i = w_i \ \forall i \in T\}.$$

Lemma 5. *We have*

$$Ex_{\mathrm{Suf}} = \Big\{ \langle S, T \rangle \in 2^N \times 2^N \ : \ M(S, T) \geq 0 \Big\},$$

where

$$M(S, T) := \begin{cases} \sum_{k \in S \cap T} w_k \Delta_k - \sum_{k \in T \backslash S} w_k - (1 - \sum_{k \in T} w_k) \ \textit{if } T \cup S \neq N \\ \sum_{k \in S \cap T} w_k \Delta_k - \sum_{k \in T \backslash S} w_k + \left(\min_{k \in S \backslash T} \Delta_k \right) \sum_{k \in S \backslash T} w_k \ \textit{else} \end{cases}$$

Lemma 6. *Assume that $T \cup S \neq N$. If $\langle S, T \rangle \in Ex_{\mathrm{Suf}}$, then $\langle S \cap T, S \cap T \rangle \in Ex_{\mathrm{Suf}}$.*

The previous lemma shows that the minimal elements of Ex_{Suf} for which $T \cup S \neq N$ select the same criteria for Δ and w. For $\langle S, S \rangle$ with $S \neq N$, we have

$$M(S, S) = \sum_{k \in S} w_k \, \Delta_k - \sum_{k \in N \setminus S} w_k = L(S), \tag{13}$$

with the same function L as in Lemma 2. We can thus apply the results of Sect. 4.3.

Let us consider $\langle S, T \rangle$ with $S \cup T = N$. It does not seem very interesting to keep values of criteria and weights that cover all inputs but that are not identical. Starting from pair $\langle S, T \rangle$ we remove $i \in S \cap T$ on both terms:

$$L(S, T) - L(S \setminus \{i\}, T \setminus \{i\}) = \left[w_i \, \Delta_i + \sum_{k \in (S \cap T) \setminus \{i\}} w_k \, \Delta_k + \left(\min_{k \in S \setminus T} \Delta_k \right) \sum_{k \in S \setminus T} w_k \right]$$

$$- \left[\sum_{k \in (S \cap T) \setminus \{i\}} w_k \, \Delta_k - \underbrace{\sum_{k \in N \setminus (T \setminus \{i\})} w_k}_{= w_i + \sum_{k \in S \setminus T} w_k} \right]$$

$$= w_i \, (\Delta_i + 1) + \sum_{k \in S \setminus T} w_k \left(\min_{k \in S \setminus T} \Delta_k + 1 \right)$$

Applying this to $\langle N, N \rangle$, we obtain

$$L(N, N) - L(N \setminus \{i\}, N \setminus \{i\}) = w_i \, (\Delta_i + 1) = c_i.$$

by (8). We also recover the same case as in Sect. 4.3.

In sum, we can use exactly the same algorithm than in Sect. 4.3 to compute a minimal explanation. In particular, let p be the smallest integer such that $\langle S, S \rangle \in Ex_{\mathrm{Suf}}$ with $S = \{\pi(1), \pi(2), \dots, \pi(p)\}$. As in Lemma 3, this is a minimal explanation, thanks to Lemma 6.

Example 4 (Example 1 cont.). Applying the previous heuristics, we obtain the minimal explanation $\langle \{1, 2, 4, 5\}, \{1, 2, 4, 5\} \rangle$. ∎

Comparing Sects. 4.2 and 4.4, we see that the explanations obtained by simplifying only the utilities, or both the utilities and the criteria weights are similar. This completely makes sense, as when S and T are similar (we align the knowledge on the utilities and the criteria weights), we can allocate the weights on the criteria which utility is not known in any way.

4.5   Case of the HCI Model

Following the discussion at the end of the previous section, we are interested in explanation based only on the simplification w.r.t. utilities. We wish here to compute a minimal explanation for the HCI model given by (5). In Sect. 4.2, we have described a linear algorithm to find the minimal explanation with the smallest cardinality. As the HCI model is composed of nested Choquet integrals, and each Choquet is non-linear, we cannot compute a minimal explanation in linear time. We propose a MILP (Mixed-Integer Linear Program) formulation of the problem of finding a minimum explanation on the utilities.

We introduce the following MILP:

$$\min \sum_{i \in N} \lambda_i \tag{14}$$

$$\text{under } \forall i \in N \quad \lambda_i \in \{0,1\} \, , \, t_i^x, t_i^y \in [0,1] \tag{15}$$

$$\forall i \in N \; t_i^x = x_i \, \lambda_i \tag{16}$$

$$\forall i \in N \; t_i^y = y_i \, \lambda_i + (1 - \lambda_i) \tag{17}$$

$$\forall i \in M \; \forall \{j,k\} \in E(i) \quad t_{j,k}^x \in [0,1] \, , \, \varepsilon_{j,k}^x \in \{0,1\} \tag{18}$$

$$t_{j,k}^x \leq t_j^x \quad , \quad t_{j,k}^x \leq t_k^x \tag{19}$$

$$t_{j,k}^x \geq t_j^x + \varepsilon_{j,k}^x \tag{20}$$

$$t_{j,k}^x \geq t_k^x + 1 - \varepsilon_{j,k}^x \tag{21}$$

$$\forall i \in M \qquad t_i^x = \sum_{\{j,k\} \in E(i)} m_{j,k} \, t_{j,k}^x + \sum_{j \in C(i)} m_j \, t_j^x \tag{22}$$

$$\forall i \in M \; \forall \{j,k\} \in E(i) \quad t_{j,k}^y \in [0,1] \, , \, \varepsilon_{j,k}^y \in \{0,1\} \tag{23}$$

$$t_{j,k}^y \leq t_j^y \quad , \quad t_{j,k}^y \leq t_k^y \tag{24}$$

$$t_{j,k}^y \geq t_j^y + \varepsilon_{j,k}^y \tag{25}$$

$$t_{j,k}^y \geq t_k^y + 1 - \varepsilon_{j,k}^y \tag{26}$$

$$\forall i \in M \qquad t_i^y = \sum_{\{j,k\} \in E(i)} m_{j,k} \, t_{j,k}^y + \sum_{j \in C(i)} m_j \, t_j^y \tag{27}$$

$$t_r^x \geq t_r^y \tag{28}$$

We simplify here with respect to the values of the features. The implicant S is the set of indices $i \in N$ such that $\lambda_i = 1$. As we look for prime implicants, we wish to minimise the number of indices $i \in N$ taking value 1 for λ_i. Constraints (18)–(21) implies that $t_{j,k}^x = \min(t_j^x, t_k^x)$ (classic reformulation trick from LP). Hence (22) is exactly the expression of the 2-additive Choquet integral for $(x_S, 0_{N \setminus S})$. Likewise (27) is the 2-additive Choquet integral for $(x_S, 1_{N \setminus S})$. Finally, x shall be preferred to y – see (28).

The interest of this formulation is to directly handle a HCI model.

Example 5. Consider the following examples with 5 criteria.

Criteria	1	2	3	4	5
x		0.5	0.6	0.4	0.7	0.9
y		0.4	0.8	0.1	0.4	0.2

$$x_6 = 0.4\,x_1 + 0.6\,\min(x_2, x_3)$$
$$x_7 = 0.3\,\min(x_3, x_4) + 0.7\,\min(x_3, x_5)$$
$$u(x) = x_8 = 0.5\,\min(x_6, x_7) + 0.1\,x_6 + 0.4\,x_7$$

$x_6 = 0.5$, $x_7 = 0.4$, $u(x) = x_8 = 0.41$, $y_6 = 0.4$, $y_7 = 0.1$ and $u(y) = y_8 = 0.13$. Hence $x \succ y$.

$$Ex_{\text{Suf}}^{\min} = \Big\{\{1, 2, 3, 4\}, \{1, 3, 5\}\Big\}.$$

The MILP returns explanation $\{1, 3, 5\}$.   ∎

5   Sufficient Explanation of a Classification Function

We consider a binary classification problem and $x \in X$ with $f(x) = 1$. We wish to find a sufficient explanation the class of x.

5.1   Case of the Weighted Sum

We consider first a weighted sum. The PI of the class 1 assigned to x are:

$$Ex_{\text{Suf}} := \{\langle S, T \rangle \text{ with } S, T \subseteq N \;:\; \forall x' \in U(S)\;\forall w' \in W(T)\quad \sum_{i \in N} w_i'\, x_i' > \alpha\}.$$

where α is a decision threshold – see (1).

   We usually assume that

$$U(S) \subseteq \{x' \in [0, 1]^N \;:\; x_i' = x_i\ \forall i \in S\},$$
$$W(T) \subseteq \{w' \in W \;:\; w_i' = w_i\ \forall i \in T\}.$$

As in Sect. 4, we can either simplify the explanation only on the first argument (i.e. the utilities), only on the second argument (i.e. the criteria weights), or on both. We focus on the first case, in which the explanation reduces to $S \subseteq N$.

Lemma 7. *We have*

$$Ex_{\text{Suf}} = \Big\{S \subseteq N \;:\; F_S(x, w) > \alpha\Big\}.$$

where $F_S(x, w) = \sum_{i \in S} w_i\, x_i$.

Proof. When the value of t' is unknown, the most pessimistic value is 0.

                                                                              ∎

   Let

$$d_k := w_k\, t_k^x$$

Define a permutation π such that

$$d_{\pi(1)} \geq d_{\pi(2)} \geq \cdots \geq d_{\pi(n)}.$$

Lemma 8. *Let p the smallest integer such that $\{\pi(1), \pi(2), \ldots, \pi(p)\} \in Ex_{\text{Suf}}$. Then the set $\{\pi(1), \pi(2), \ldots, \pi(p)\}$ is minimal in PI and there is no element of Ex_{Suf} with a smaller cardinality.*

5.2   Case of a HCI Model

We can adapt the MILP of Sect. 4.5 to binary classification. A sufficient explanation of a classification problem for a HCI model can thus be obtained by the following MILP:

$$\min \& \sum_{i \in N} \lambda_i \tag{29}$$

$$\text{under } \forall i \in N \quad \lambda_i \in \{0,1\} \,,\; t_i^x \in [0,1] \tag{30}$$

$$\forall i \in N \; t_i^x = x_i \, \lambda_i + r_i \, (1 - \lambda_i) \tag{31}$$

$$\text{constraints (18)--(22)}$$

$$t_r^x > \alpha \tag{32}$$

where $r = (0, \ldots, 0)$ is the worst case for x being in class 1, when its value is not known on some feature. Condition (32) indicates that the class is still 1. Unknown vector λ takes value 1 for the criteria on which the value of x is kept – the other values of x being removed. Finally, the explanation is the vector of literals

$$\Big\{ (i, x_i) \; : \; i \in N \text{ and } \lambda_i = 1 \Big\}.$$

The interest of this formulation is to directly handle a HCI model.

5.3   Weak Prime Implicants

A sufficient explanation is a strong condition as we only remove the literals whose value can be replaced by any other value. The following example illustrates the fact that the prime implicants may not simplify the values of x.

Example 6. Consider the following example with $n = 5$: with $\alpha = 0.5$. One can easily

	1	2	3	4	5
score x	0.9	0.7	0.5	0.4	0.6
weights w	0.1	0.1	0.2	0.3	0.3

check that $F_N(x, w) = 0.55 > \alpha$ so that $f(x) = 1$. However, removing any value of x yields an overall score that is lower than α:

$$F_{\{2,3,4,5\}}(t, w) = 0.48 \,,\; F_{\{1,3,4,5\}}(t, w) = 0.45 \,,\; F_{\{1,2,4,5\}}(t, w) = 0.43 \,,$$
$$F_{\{1,2,3,5\}}(t, w) = 0.47 \,,\; F_{\{1,2,3,4\}}(t, w) = 0.37.$$

Therefore, we cannot simplify vector of x while keeping the same class.   ∎

A weaker version consists in stating that the prediction $f(x) = 1$ would not change if value x_i on attribute i is changed with some intensity, which can belong to for instance *infinitely*, *a lot*, *significantly*, or *a little bit*. Of course, the larger the intensity, the better for the stability of the explanation. For the end-user, not mentioning an attribute that does not influence the decision if we change it a lot is fine, even if changing it extremely would finally change the decision. The idea is that this extreme change would put the option in a completely different situation, and the end-user does not care about this situation. We define thus a set of $\bar{q}$ categories of intensity of change on the attributes: $Q = \{0, 1, \ldots, \bar{q}\}$, where 0 means that no change is allowed and $\bar{q}$ means that any change is allowed. We define nested sets of allowed values on the attributes, for $q \in Q$

$$X_i^q(x_i) = \{y_i \in X_i \, , \, |y_i - x_i| \le s_i^q(x_i)\},$$

satisfying

$$\{x_i\} = X_i^0(x_i) \subset X_i^1(x_i) \subset \cdots \subset X_i^{\bar{q}-1}(x_i) \subset X_i^{\bar{q}}(x_i) = X_i.$$

This implies the following conditions

$$0 = s_i^0(x_i) < s_i^1(x_i) < \cdots < s_i^{\bar{q}-1}(x_i) < s_i^{\bar{q}}(x_i) = \infty.$$

Then

$$Ex^q(x, c) = \{x_S \, , \, S \subseteq N \text{ s.t. } \forall y_{N\setminus S} \in X_{N\setminus S}^q(x_{N\setminus S}) \ f(x_S, y_{N\setminus S}) = c\}.$$

Example 7 (Example 6 cont.). We weaken sufficient explanations, by allowing a modification of the utilities up to intensity $s_i^q(x_i) = 0.3$ in the $[0, 1]$ scale. We obtain

$$Ex^q(x, c) = \Big\{ \{1, 2\}, \{3\} \Big\}.$$

We can in particular avoid mentioning criteria 1 and 2, under the assumption that they can vary in a given range.   ∎

We choose the largest value of q such that $PI^q(x, c)$ is significantly smaller than the full set of values of x. We can apply MILP (29)–(32) with $r_i = x_i - s_i^q(x_i)$ for some $q \in Q$.

6   Necessary Explanation

In the so-called *necessary approach*, we wish to know the smallest modification in the preference information that changes the decision. This approach corresponds to a robustness analysis.

6.1   Explanation of $\succsim$ for a Weighted Sum

Following Sect. 4.1, a counterfactual example can be a pair $\langle S, T \rangle$ composed of a subset of criteria values and a subset of criteria weights. We define the set of *necessary explanations* as

$$Ex_{\text{Nec}} := \{\langle S, T \rangle \text{ with } S \subseteq N \text{ and } T \subseteq N :$$
$$\exists \Delta' \in D(N\setminus S), \ \exists v \in W(N\setminus T), \ H(\Delta', v) \le 0\}$$

We have that $\langle N, N \rangle \in Ex_{\text{Nec}}$ and that $\langle \emptyset, \emptyset \rangle \notin Ex_{\text{Nec}}$.

Necessary and sufficient explanations are dual of one another, as shown in the following result.

Lemma 9. $\langle S, T \rangle \in Ex_{\text{Nec}} \iff \langle N \backslash S, N \backslash T \rangle \notin Ex_{\text{Suf}}$.

However, recommending changing criteria weights is not realistic in the case of an actionable explanation. The end-user takes the model as granted, and cannot act on it. The only action at the hand of the user is to improve (after producing some effort) his evaluation on some criteria. So we restrict an explanation to $S \subseteq N$.

$$\widehat{Ex}_{\text{Nec}} := \{S \subseteq N \, : \, \exists \Delta' \in D(N \backslash S), H(\Delta', N) \le 0\}$$

We have then to turn vector Δ' into new values x' and y' of x and y such that $x' - y' = \Delta$.

If the decision is clear-cut, then one needs a lot of changes in the weights to invert the decision. Hence, the minimal elements of Ex_{Nec} contain a relatively large number of criteria. This is rather counter-intuitive since one would expect that a clear-cut decision is explained only with a few arguments. On the opposite side, if the decision is tight, then a little change in the weights is enough to switch the decision. Hence, the minimal elements of Ex_{Nec} contain only a small number of criteria. Once again, this is counter-intuitive since the explanation is relatively simple when the decision is tight.

6.2 Explanation of the Preference Relation $\succsim$ for the HCI Model

A counterfactual explanation of $x \succsim y$ for the HCI model consists of finding t^x close to x and t^y close to y such that $t^x \prec t^y$. We can adapt the MILP of Sect. 4.5 to this case:

$$\min \sum_{i \in N} (|t_i^x - x_i| + |t_i^y - y_i|)$$
$$\text{under } \forall i \in N \quad t_i^x, t_i^y \in [0, 1]$$
$$\text{constraints (18)–(27)}$$
$$t_r^x < t_r^y - \varepsilon$$

for a small constant $\varepsilon > 0$. The last constraint indicates that t^x shall be strictly less preferred than t^y.

6.3 Explanation of a Classification Function for the HCI Model

Given $x \in X$ with $f(x) = 0$, we look at $y \in X$ s.t. $f(y) = 1$ that is close to x.

$$\min \sum_{i \in N} |t_i^x - x_i|$$
$$\text{under\&} \forall i \in N \; t_i \in [0, 1]$$
$$\text{constraints (18)–(22)}$$
$$\text{constraint (32)}$$

This is also a MILP. The counterfactual explanation is t^x.

7   Contribution to the XAI Field

One of the main focus of MCDA has been to build models that are interpretable and constrained by design [44]. They are justified by axiomatic characterizations which provide necessary and sufficient conditions under which a given model is the unique admissible one (each condition is an interpretable property of the model) [30], and by behavioral studies in cognitive science showing the cognitive biases that are captured by each model. The idea behind such models is to be trustable for advising a human end user in making a specific decision. The CI model is rooted in this philosophy [16], with a natural intelligibility and formal guarantees over their behavior, making them suitable for use in safety-critical settings [18], in particular as it offers guarantees that are not provided by post-hoc analysis of black-box models [45]. Its main source of explainability is the ability to extract indicators, such as the Shapley value, in a straight-forward manner from a closed-form formula. Interaction indices can be computed in a similar manner [17]. Together, these indices allow to quickly summarize, analyze and ultimately validate a given model on a global, holistic scale. Local (or instance-wise) Shapley values are also extractable, allowing for a fine-grained, instance-specific analysis, which an end user can exploit for understanding a given model's decision, granting interpretation at runtime. Finally, the formal constraints of the model restrict its behavior to follow expert-validated properties, ensuring no unpredictable phenomenon to occur at runtime.

The hierarchical generalization of the CI, called HCI in this paper, has the same strengths in terms of interpretability and behavioral properties. First of all, all nodes in the hierarchy are constructed with a decision maker, and thus make sense to the user. This is the contrary of Deep learning in which the intermediate nodes and layers are latent variables which are not interpretable. When discussing on the outcome of a MCDA model on a particular alternative with the user, we can communicate on the elementary criteria (i.e. the leaves of the tree) but also on the higher level nodes which represent a more comprehensive viewpoint than elementary criteria. These hierarchical models can be globally interpreted with approaches being developed for generalizing Shapley values to tree structures [34,51]. The hierarchical model offers even higher interpretability, allowing through its structure to decompose nicely the reasoning of the model. In particular, explanations can now be obtained at different levels, with different granularity, depending on what information the end user requires. Moreover, using a hierarchy is a way to ensure model sparsity, in turn easing the cognitive effort on the end user. Finally, the robustness and trustability of HCIs was further reinforced by these models' identifiability [7], ensuring the unicity of the interpretation of a given model.

While CIs were traditionally built using constrained optimization based on information provided by a domain expert, several approaches have been recently proposed to learn the parameter of a fuzzy integral such as a CI [6,23]. A noticeable example is the learning a HCI from data through the use of neural networks [8]. These works further reinforce the bond between xAI and MCDA, allowing to use methods from machine learning to learn models which offer all the strength of MCDA models, preserving their interpretability and constrainedness.

Even though MCDA offers naturally interpretable models, some work has been pursued to generate local explanations. The first level of explainability refers to the interpretation of the model parameters. The weighted sum proposes such a framework by distinguishing between the concepts of marginal utility (level of satisfaction of criterion by criterion) and criteria importance in the model (their weight). One may say for instance that an alternative is preferred to another one as the first one has a high satisfaction on important criteria [32]. This has lead to several approaches generating argumentation schemas [32,39]. Alternatively, one can also produce an argumentation graph [52]. The drawback of these approaches is that the identification of the arguments (criteria that are displayed to the user) is based on heuristics, which introduces biases and subjectivity, making these models questionable for safety-critical settings.

Another approach for explaining MCDA is to assign a level of contribution to each criterion. The concept of *compellingness* has been defined in MCDA long time before feature attribution techniques have been developed in machine learning [9,29]. This concept has been extended to the Choquet integral [38], but this yields instability [34]. To overcome this drawback, the Shapley value has been extended to hierarchical structures such as HCI [34]. An axiomatic characterization of these indices has been proposed in the framework of Game Theory [34]. Lastly, Främling introduced two indices per criteria instead of one, where the first one (Contextual Importance) represents the importance of a criterion relatively to a given instance, and the second one (Contextual Utility) is interpreted as the utility of the instance on a criterion [14]. The drawback of all these methods computing degrees is that, at some point, one needs to introduce a threshold above which the values of this value are displayed to the user. The choice of this threshold is again questionable.

Another approach has been proposed – based on *robust entailment*. The decision is done not from fixed values of the parameters, but for the set of all parameters that are compatible with a set of preferential data. It has been shown that the entailment is necessarily a linear combination (with integer coefficients) of some preferential data [4,5,33]. The drawback is on the use of the robust entailment, which might be (nearly) empty. It fails to recommend a decision in most of the cases, which is not acceptable.

We propose in this paper two alternative approaches – namely sufficient and necessary explanations. Their main asset is that they do not rely on any threshold or other parameter. They provide a grounded method for recommending sufficient criteria (the other criteria can be removed without any consequence on the outcome) or minimal modification to perform on criteria values to change the model outcome.

Sufficient Explanations: Sufficient explanations aims at identifying the criteria and/or model parameters that can be discarded (i.e. replaced by any possible value) without any consequence on the model outcome (a decision or a class). The main asset of this approach is that it provides a justification to safely discard those elements from the explanation. This is not the case with approaches based on indices, as their interpretation is not clear and their are not designed for feature selection. We have seen that simplifying only on the model parameters may yield explanations which are difficult to understand. We have also seen that for the weighted sum, it is equivalent to simplify only on the utilities or on both the utilities and criteria weights (see Sect. 4.4).

The use of prime implicants provides a baseline for restricting the set of criteria, which avoids mentioning non-relevant criteria in the explanation. Assume that subset S is a minimal sufficient explanation: it is completely useless to mention criteria in $N \setminus S$ at all. This approach can be seen as a baseline for safely selecting relevant criteria, and can be complemented to another xAI approach. One can think for instance of explanations based on argumentation schemas [32,39]. The difficulty here is to make sure that such approach mentions no criterion in $N \setminus S$. We have of course no guarantee on that. In order to ensure this constraint, we can construct from the decision model u defined on N, a restricted decision model $u_{[S]}$ defined only on S, as in [31]. As criteria $N \setminus S$ do not influence u when criteria S take value x, there are several ways to construct $u_{[S]}$. For instance $u_{[S]}(x_S)$ is an average of quantity $u(x_S, y_{N \setminus S})$ over several values of $y_{N \setminus S}$ [31]. Then the other explanation approach is used on this restricted model $u_{[S]}$. As its arguments are criteria S, we are sure that the explanation of $u_{[S]}$ is only restricted to S.

Necessary Explanations: Necessary explanations aim at finding the smallest modification that yields the opposite decision or class. The interest of these explanations is that they are actionable, that is that they can be applied by the user. As it is complex to generate realistic modification recommendations, one can imagine extending the MILP to include user feedback. It can take the form of a constraint on some criteria – e.g. the value of this criterion cannot exceed some value, or one cannot improvetwo criteria at the same time.

8   Conclusion and Future Works

In this paper, we have explicited the notion of prime implicants with regards to the hierarchical Choquet integral model. We have proposed to formulate this problem as an MILP to extract the PIs in several settings. We also exploit the same method to extract counterfactual explanations.

A practical challenge is to generate an instance that is *realistic*. This means that some points in X are not realistic, even though they are close, in terms of distance, to a real point x. In practice, given an unsupervised set of instances, one can construct a normality score with a one-class SVM for example. Another idea would be to be able to quantify the relationships between the variables, which can be done either explicitly if there is a theoretical background (for instance in physical systems) or through learning the manifold of data, then sampling from it.

A realistic counterfactual example is then an instance y that is close to x, has the opposite class than x and has a large normality score. This is loosely analogous to generating adversarial examples.

We denote by $\overline{X}$ the set of realistic instances. We can also use $\overline{X}$ in Prime Implicants, by avoiding modifications of the instances that are not realistic. It is to be noted, though, that this can lead to values that are so constrained that the possibilities are restricted to a small, or even empty, set.

9   Proofs

Proof of Lemma 1: Assume that $\langle S, T \rangle \in Ex_{\text{Suf}}$. Let S' and T' such that $S' \supseteq S$ and $T' \supseteq T$.

Let $\Delta' \in D(S')$ and $v \in W(T')$. By the assumptions (6) and (7), $\Delta' \in D(S)$ and $v \in W(T)$. Hence since $\langle S, T \rangle \in Ex_{\text{Suf}}$, we obtain that $H(\Delta', v) > 0$. We conclude that $\langle S', T' \rangle \in Ex_{\text{Suf}}$. ∎

Proof of Lemma 9: We have

$$\langle S, T \rangle \in Ex_{\text{Nec}} \iff \exists \Delta' \in D(N \setminus S) \ \exists v \in W(N \setminus T) \quad H(\Delta', v) \leq 0$$

$$\iff \text{NOT}\Big[\forall \Delta' \in D(N \setminus S) \ \forall v \in W(N \setminus T) \quad H(\Delta', v) > 0\Big]$$

$$\iff \text{NOT}\Big[\langle N \setminus S, N \setminus T \rangle \in Ex_{\text{Suf}}\Big]$$

$$\iff \langle N \setminus S, N \setminus T \rangle \notin Ex_{\text{Suf}}$$

∎

Proof of Lemma 4: The set $\mathcal{T} := \{v_{N \setminus T} \in [0,1]^{N \setminus T} \ : \ (w_T, v_{N \setminus T}) \in \mathcal{W}\}$ forms a polytope. Since the constraint $x \succ_{(w_T, v_{N \setminus T})} y$ is linear, it is sufficient to check this condition at the vertices of $\mathcal{T}$. Clearly the vertices of $\mathcal{T}$ are of the form for all $i \in N \setminus T$

$$v_k = w_k, \ \forall k \in T \,, \ v_i = 1 - \sum_{k \in T} w_k \text{ and } v_k = 0 \ \forall k \in N \setminus (T \cup i).$$

Then the constraint gives $(1 - \sum_{k \in T} w_k) \Delta_i + \sum_{k \in T} w_k \Delta_k > 0$ for all $i \in N \setminus T$. Hence (11) holds.

The condition in (11) is equivalent to

$$\min_{i \in N \setminus T} \Delta_i > -\frac{\sum_{k \in T} w_k \Delta_k}{1 - \sum_{k \in T} w_k} = -\frac{\sum_{k \in T} w_k \Delta_k}{\sum_{k \in N \setminus T} w_k}$$

which is equivalent to the condition in (12). ∎

Proof of Lemma 3: Let p given in the lemma and $P = \{\pi(1), \pi(2), \ldots, \pi(p)\}$. Then $P \setminus \{\pi(p)\} \notin Ex_{\text{Suf}}$. This means that $L(P \setminus \{\pi(p)\}) \leq 0$. Let $l \in \{1, 2, \ldots, p\}$. Then

$$L(P \setminus \{\pi(l)\}) - L(P \setminus \{\pi(p)\}) = c_{\pi(p)} - c_{\pi(l)} \leq 0.$$

Hence $L(P \setminus \{\pi(l)\}) \leq 0$ and thus $P \setminus \{\pi(l)\} \notin Ex_{\text{Suf}}$. This proves that P is minimal in Ex_{Suf}.

The fact that P has the smallest cardinality follows from the relation $L(S) = \sum_{k \in S} c_k - 1$. ∎

Proof of Lemma 5: We have

$$\langle S, T \rangle \in Ex_{\text{Suf}} \iff \forall \Delta' \in D(S) \ \forall v \in W(T) \quad H(\Delta', v) > 0$$

$$\iff H(\Delta', v) > 0 \text{ for } \Delta'_i = \begin{cases} \Delta_i & \text{if } i \in S \\ -1 & \text{otherwise} \end{cases} \text{ and } v_i = \begin{cases} w_i & \text{if } i \in T \\ 1 - \sum_{j \in T} w_j & \text{if } i = k \\ 0 & \text{otherwise} \end{cases}$$

where $k \in N\backslash(T \cup S)$ if $T \cup S \neq N$ and $k \in S\backslash T$ that has the smallest value of Δ_k otherwise. This later condition is equivalent to

$$\sum_{i \in S \cap T} w_i\, \Delta_i - \sum_{i \in T\backslash S} w_i - \left(1 - \sum_{j \in T} w_j\right) \geq 0$$

if $T \cup S \neq N$ (when $T \cup S \neq N$, the worst choice of $k \notin T$ is obtained with for $k \notin S$, in which case $\Delta'_k = -1$), and is equivalent to

$$\sum_{i \in S \cap T} w_i\, \Delta_i - \sum_{i \in T\backslash S} w_i + \left(\min_{k \in S\backslash T} \Delta_k\right) \sum_{j \in S\backslash T} w_j \geq 0$$

otherwise (when $T \cup S = N$, the worst choice of $k \notin T$ is obtained for $k \in S\backslash T$). ∎

Proof of Lemma 6: Let $\langle S, T \rangle \in Ex_{\mathrm{Suf}}$ and $i \in T\backslash S$. We have, as $S \cap T = S \cap (T\backslash\{i\})$

$$M(S,T) - M(S,T\backslash\{i\}) = \left[-\left(w_i + \sum_{k \in (T\backslash S)\backslash\{i\}} w_k\right) - \left(1 - w_i - \sum_{k \in T\backslash\{i\}} w_k\right)\right]$$

$$- \left[-\sum_{k \in (T\backslash S)\backslash\{i\}} w_k - \left(1 - \sum_{k \in T\backslash\{i\}} w_k\right)\right]$$

$$= 0$$

so that $\langle S, T\backslash\{i\}\rangle \in Ex_{\mathrm{Suf}}$. Iterating over all $i \in T\backslash S$, we obtain that $\langle S, S \cap T\rangle \in Ex_{\mathrm{Suf}}$.

From the expression of M, $M(S,T)$ is independant of $S\backslash T$. Hence $M(S, S \cap T)$ is also independant of $S\backslash T$. This implies that $\langle S \cap T, S \cap T\rangle \in Ex_{\mathrm{Suf}}$. ∎

Proof of Lemma 8: Let p given in the lemma and $P = \{\pi(1), \pi(2), \ldots, \pi(p)\}$. Then $\sum_{\ell=1}^{p} c_{\pi(\ell)} > \alpha$ and $\sum_{\ell=1}^{p-1} c_{\pi(\ell)} \leq \alpha$. By definition of π, for every $S \subseteq N$ with $|S| < p$

$$\sum_{i \in S} c_i \leq \sum_{\ell=1}^{p-1} c_{\pi(\ell)} \leq \alpha.$$

Hence P is minimal and there is subset of cardinality strictly lower than p that is a prime implicant. ∎

References

1. Aas, K., Jullum, M., Løland, A.: Explaining individual predictions when features are dependent: more accurate approximations to shapley values. Artif. Intell. **298**, 103502 (2021)
2. Arrieta, A.B., et al.: Explainable artificial intelligence (XAI): concepts, taxonomies, opportunities and challenges toward responsible AI. Inf. Fusion **58**, 82–115 (2020)
3. Bana e Costa, C.A., De Corte, J., Vansnick, J.C.: MACBETH. Int. J. Inf. Technol. Decis. Making **11**, 359–387 (2012)

4. Belahcène, K., Chevaleyre, Y., Labreuche, C., Maudet, N., Mousseau, V., Ouerdane, W.: Accountable approval sorting. In: Proceedings of the Twenty-Seventh International Joint Conference on Artificial Intelligence (IJCAI 2018), pp. 70–76. Stockholm, Sweden (2018)
5. Belahcène, K., Labreuche, C., Maudet, N., Mousseau, V., Ouerdane, W.: Comparing options with argument schemes powered by cancellation. In: Proceedings of the Twenty-Eight International Joint Conference on Artificial Intelligence (IJCAI 2019), pp. 1537–1543. Macao, China (2019)
6. Benabbou, N., Perny, P., Viappiani, P.: Incremental elicitation of Choquet capacities for multicriteria choice, ranking and sorting problems. Artif. Intell. **246**, 152–180 (2017)
7. Bresson, R., Cohen, J., Hüllermeier, E., Labreuche, C., Sebag, M.: On the identifiability of hierarchical decision models. In: Proceedings of the 18th International Conference on Principles of Knowledge Representation and Reasoning (KR 2021), pp. 151–162. Hanoi, Vietnam (2021)
8. Bresson, R., Cohen, J., Hüllermeier, E., Labreuche, C., Sebag, M.: Neural representation and learning of hierarchical 2-additive Choquet integrals. In: Proceedings of the Twenty-Eight International Joint Conference on Artificial Intelligence (IJCAI 2020), pp. 1984–1991. Yokohoma, Japan (2020)
9. Carenini, G., Moore, J.: Generating and evaluating evaluative arguments. Artif. Intell. **170**, 925–952 (2006)
10. Choquet, G.: Theory of capacities. Annales de l'Institut Fourier **5**, 131–295 (1953)
11. Darwiche, A., Hirth, A.: On the reasons behind decisions. In: Proceedings of the European Conference on Artificial Intelligence (ECAI 2020), pp. 712–720. Santiago, Spain (2020)
12. Datta, A., Sen, S., Zick, Y.: Algorithmic transparency via quantitative input influence: theory and experiments with learning systems. In: IEEE Symposium on Security and Privacy. San Jose, CA, USA (2016)
13. Figueira, J., Greco, S., Ehrgott, M. (eds.): Multiple Criteria Decision Analysis: State of the Art Surveys, 2nd edn. Kluwer Acad Publisher, New York (2016)
14. Främling, K.: Decision theory meets explainable AI. In: Calvaresi, D., Najjar, A., Winikoff, M., Främling, K. (eds.) EXTRAAMAS 2020. LNCS (LNAI), vol. 12175, pp. 57–74. Springer, Cham (2020). https://doi.org/10.1007/978-3-030-51924-7_4
15. Grabisch, M.: The application of fuzzy integrals in multicriteria decision making. Eur. J. Oper. Res. **89**, 445–456 (1996)
16. Grabisch, M., Labreuche, C.: A decade of application of the Choquet and Sugeno integrals in multi-criteria decision aid. Ann. Oper. Res. **175**, 247–286 (2010)
17. Grabisch, M., Murofushi, T., Sugeno, M., Kacprzyk, J.: Fuzzy Measures and Integrals. Theory and Applications. Physica Verlag, Berlin (2000)
18. Grabisch, M., Labreuche, C.: Interpretation of multicriteria decision making models with interacting criteria. In: Doumpos, M., Figueira, J.R., Greco, S., Zopounidis, C. (eds.) New Perspectives in Multiple Criteria Decision Making. MCDM, pp. 151–176. Springer, Cham (2019). https://doi.org/10.1007/978-3-030-11482-4_6
19. Greco, S., Matarazzo, B., Słowinski, R.: Rough sets methodology for sorting problems in presence of multiple attributes and criteria. Eur. J. Oper. Res. **138**, 247–259 (2002)
20. Guidotti, R., Monreale, A., Ruggieri, S., Pedreschi, D., Turini, F., Giannotti, F.: Local rule-based explanations of black box decision systems. In: CoRR abs/1805.10820 (2018)
21. Guidotti, R., Monreale, A., Ruggieri, S., Turini, F., Giannotti, F., Pedreschi, D.: A survey of methods for explaining black box models. ACM Comput. Surv. **51**(5), 1–42 (2018). Article 93
22. Halpern, J.Y., Pearl, J.: Causes and explanations: a structural-model approach - part II: explanations. Br. J. Philos. Sci. **56**(4), 889–911 (2005)
23. Havens, T.C., Anderson, D.T.: Machine Learning of Choquet integral regression with respect to a bounded capacity (or non-monotonic fuzzy measure). In: FUZZ-IEEE-18 (2018)

24. Ignatiev, A., Narodytska, N., Marques-Silva, J.: Abduction-based explanations for machine learning models. In: AAAI, pp. 1511–1519. Honolulu, Hawai (2019)
25. Jacquet-Lagrèze, E., Siskos, Y.: Assessing a set of additive utility functions for multicriteria decision making: the UTA method. Eur. J. Oper. Res. **10**, 151–164 (1982)
26. Keane, M., Kenny, E., Delaney, E., Smyth, B.: If only we had better counterfactual explanations: five key deficits to rectify in the evaluation of counterfactual XAI techniques. In: Proceedings of the Thirtieth International Joint Conference on Artificial Intelligence (IJCAI-21), pp. 4466–4474 (2021)
27. Keeney, R.L., Raiffa, H.: Decision with Multiple Objectives. Wiley, New York (1976)
28. Kenny, E., Keane, M.: On generating plausible counterfactual and semi-factual explanations for deep learning. In: Thirty-Fifth AAAI Conference on Artificial Intelligence (AAAI-21), pp. 11575–11585 (2021)
29. Klein, D.: Decision Analytic Intelligent Systems: Automated Explanation and Knowledge Acquisition. Lawrence Erlbaum Associates (1994)
30. Krantz, D., Luce, R., Suppes, P., Tversky, A.: Foundations of measurement: Additive and Polynomial Representations, vol. 1. Academic Press, New York (1971)
31. Labreuche, C., Destercke, S.: How to handle missing values in multi-criteria decision aiding? In: Proceedings of the Twenty-Eight International Joint Conference on Artificial Intelligence (IJCAI 2019), pp. 1756–1763. Macao, China (2019)
32. Labreuche, C.: A general framework for explaining the results of a multi-attribute preference model. Artif. Intell. **175**, 1410–1448 (2011)
33. Labreuche, C., Maudet, N., Ouerdane, W.: Justifying dominating options when preferential information is incomplete. In: European Conference on Artificial Intelligence (ECAI), pp. 486–491. Montepellier, France (2012)
34. Labreuche, C., Fossier, S.: Explaining multi-criteria decision aiding models with an extended shapley value. In: Proceedings of the Twenty-Seventh International Joint Conference on Artificial Intelligence, IJCAI-18, pp. 331–339. International Joint Conferences on Artificial Intelligence Organization (2018)
35. Lundberg, S., Lee, S.: A unified approach to interpreting model predictions. In: Guyon, I., Luxburg, U.V., Bengio, S., Wallach, H., Fergus, R., Vishwanathan, S., Garnett, R. (eds.) 31st Conference on Neural Information Processing Systems (NIPS 2017), pp. 4768–4777. Long Beach, CA, USA (2017)
36. Marquis, P.: Consequence Finding Algorithms. In: Handbook of Defeasible Reasoning and Uncertainty Management Systems, pp. 41–145 (2000)
37. Miller, T.: Explainable AI: Insights from the social sciences. Artif. Intell. **267**, 1–38 (2019)
38. Montmain, J., Mauris, G., Akharraz, A.: Elucidation and decisional risk in a multi criteria decision based on a Choquet integral aggregation: a cybernetic framework. Int. J. Multi-Criteria Decision Anal. **13**, 239–258 (2005)
39. Nunes, I., Miles, S., Luck, M., Barbosa, S., Lucena, C.: Pattern-based explanation for automated decisions. In: European Conference on Artificial Intelligence (ECAI), pp. 669–674. Prague, Czech Republic (2014)
40. Ribeiro, M., Singh, S., Guestrin, C.: "Why should i trust you?": explaining the predictions of any classifier. In: KDD 2016 Proceedings of the 22nd ACM SIGKDD International Conference on Knowledge Discovery and Data Mining, pp. 1135–1144. San Francisco, California, USA (2016)
41. Ribeiro, M., Singh, S., Guestrin, C.: Anchors: high-precision model-agnostic explanations. In: Thirty-Second AAAI Conference on Artificial Intelligence, pp. 1527–1535 (2018)
42. Roy, B.: Classement et choix en présence de points de vue multiples (la méthode ELECTRE). R.I.R.O. 2, 57–75 (1968)

43. Roy, B.: How outranking relations helps multiple criteria decision making. In: Cochrane, J.L., Zeleny, M. (eds.) Multiple Criteria Decision Making, pp. 179–201. University of South California Press, Columbia (1973)

44. Roy, B.: Decision aiding today: what should we expect? In: Gal, T., Stewart, T., Hanne, T. (eds.) Multicriteria decision making: advances in MCDM models, algorithms, theory and applications, pp. 1.1-1.35. Kluwer Academic Publishers, Boston (1999)

45. Rudin, C.: Stop explaining black box machine learning models for high stakes decisions and use interpretable models instead (2019)

46. Saaty, T.L.: A scaling method for priorities in hierarchical structures. J. Math. Psychol. **15**, 234–281 (1977)

47. Shih, A., Choi, A., Darwiche, A.: A symbolic approach to explaining Bayesian network classifiers. In: Proceedings of the Twenty-Seventh International Joint Conference on Artificial Intelligence (IJCAI 2018), pp. 5103–5111. Stockholm, Sweden (2018)

48. Stepin, I., Alonso, J., Catala, A., Pereira-Farina, M.: A survey of contrastive and counterfactual explanation generation methods for explainable artificial intelligence. IEEE Access **9**, 11974–12001 (2021)

49. Strumbelj, E., Kononenko, I.: An efficient explanation of individual classifications using game theory. J. Mach. Learn. Res. **11**, 1–18 (2010)

50. Verma, S., Dickerson, J., Hines, K.: Counterfactual explanations for machine learning: a review. In: arXiv preprint arxiv:2010.10596 (2020)

51. Winter, E.: A value for cooperative games with levels structure of cooperation. Int. J. Game Theory **18**(2), 227–40 (1989)

52. Zhong, Q., Fan, X., Toni, F., Luo, X.: Explaining best decisions via argumentation. In: Proceedings of the European Conference on Social Intelligence (ECSI-2014), pp. 224–237. Barcelona, Spain (2014)

XInsight: Revealing Model Insights for GNNs with Flow-Based Explanations

Eli Laird[✉][ID], Ayesh Madushanka[ID], Elfi Kraka[ID], and Corey Clark[ID]

Southern Methodist University, Dallas, TX, USA
{ejlaird,amahamadakalapuwage,ekraka,coreyc}@smu.edu

Abstract. Progress in graph neural networks has grown rapidly in recent years, with many new developments in drug discovery, medical diagnosis, and recommender systems. While this progress is significant, many networks are 'black boxes' with little understanding of the 'what' exactly the network is learning. Many high-stakes applications, such as drug discovery, require human-intelligible explanations from the models so that users can recognize errors and discover new knowledge. Therefore, the development of explainable AI algorithms is essential for us to reap the benefits of AI.

We propose an explainability algorithm for GNNs called eXplainable Insight (XInsight) that generates a distribution of model explanations using GFlowNets. Since GFlowNets generate objects with probabilities proportional to a reward, XInsight can generate a diverse set of explanations, compared to previous methods that only learn the maximum reward sample. We demonstrate XInsight by generating explanations for GNNs trained on two graph classification tasks: classifying mutagenic compounds with the MUTAG dataset and classifying acyclic graphs with a synthetic dataset that we have open-sourced. We show the utility of XInsight's explanations by analyzing the generated compounds using QSAR modeling, and we find that XInsight generates compounds that cluster by lipophilicity, a known correlate of mutagenicity. Our results show that XInsight generates a distribution of explanations that uncovers the underlying relationships demonstrated by the model. They also highlight the importance of generating a diverse set of explanations, as it enables us to discover hidden relationships in the model and provides valuable guidance for further analysis.

Keywords: Explainable AI · Graph Neural Networks · GFlowNets

1 Introduction

Graph neural networks (GNNs) have emerged as a popular and effective machine learning algorithm for modeling structured data, particularly graph data. As GNNs continue to gain popularity, there is an increasing need for explainable GNN algorithms. Explainable AI refers to machine learning algorithms that can provide understandable and interpretable results. Explainable AI algorithms

L. Longo (Ed.): xAI 2023, CCIS 1902, pp. 303–320, 2023.
https://doi.org/10.1007/978-3-031-44067-0_16

have the ability to uncover hidden relationships or patterns that deep learning models use in making their decisions. This means that researchers can use these methods to understand why a model arrived at a certain decision. In the case of GNNs, the need for explainability arises from the fact that they are often used in applications where the decision-making process needs to be transparent and easily understood by humans. For example, in the field of drug discovery, GNNs are used to predict the efficacy of a drug by analyzing its molecular structure [49]. In this case, it is crucial to understand how the GNN arrived at its prediction, as it can have significant implications for patient health and safety.

Explainable AI algorithms also uncover erroneous correlations in deep learning models. For instance, in a study by Narla et al. [25], the researchers found that their model had incorrectly learned that images with rulers were more likely to be cancerous. The use of explainable AI methods helped them uncover this error and highlighted the need for methods that can explain the underlying relationships that deep learning models rely on to make predictions.

In response to this need, we propose a novel GNN explainability algorithm, *eXplainable Insight (XInsight)*, that generates diverse model-level explanations using Generative Flow Networks (GFlowNets) [3]. XInsight represents the first application of GFlowNets to explain graph neural networks. Unlike previous model-level algorithms, that only learn the maximum reward sample, XInsight generates objects with probabilities proportional to a reward. We demonstrate the effectiveness of XInsight by applying it to GNNs trained on two graph classification tasks: classifying mutagenic compounds with the MUTAG dataset and classifying acyclic graphs with a synthetic dataset. In our experiments, we demonstrate that XInsight's explanations for the MUTAG dataset [24] can be analyzed using data mining techniques and QSAR [14] modeling to uncover hidden relationships in the model. For instance, when analyzing the compounds generated by XInsight, we found that they clustered by lipophilicity, which is a known correlate of mutagenicity. Our results demonstrate that XInsight generates a distribution of explanations that enables the discovery of hidden relationships in the model.

The key contributions of this paper are summarized below:

(i) We proposed eXplainable Insight (XInsight), an explainability algorithm for Graph Neural Networks (GNNs) that uses GFlowNets to generate a distribution of model explanations.

(ii) We applied XInsight to explain two classification tasks, one of which was a newly open-sourced synthetic dataset, and the other was a real-world molecular compound dataset.

(iii) We analyzed XInsight's generated explanations using a clustering method and chemical analysis tool, which helped us to discover important underlying patterns and relationships of the examined model.

2   Related Work

2.1   Graph Neural Networks

Graph neural networks (GNNs) have emerged as a popular deep learning technique to model structured data that can be represented as graphs. Unlike traditional neural networks that operate on structured data like images and sequences, GNNs operate on non-Euclidean data, such as social networks [9,34], chemical molecules [5,11,12,49], and 3D point clouds [10,31]. GNNs typically use a message-passing approach [12], where the feature representations of nodes, edges, and the overall graph are iteratively updated by aggregating the features of their neighbors and combining them with the learned features from the previous step. This message-passing process is repeated for a fixed number of iterations or until convergence. Expanding upon traditional message-passing GNNs, many other GNN architectures have been proposed, such as Graph Convolutional Networks (GCNs) [48] that use convolutional operations similar to Euclidean Convolutional Neural Networks, Graph Isomorphism Networks (GINs) [41] that employ multilayer perceptrons to aggregate neighboring features, and Graph Attention Networks (GATs) [36] that apply an attention mechanism to weigh contributions of neighboring nodes/edges based on their importance. With the development of GNNs, we can now model and make predictions based on structured data in a way that was not possible before.

2.2   Explaining Graph Neural Networks

Graph neural networks (GNNs) are widely used in various domains such as drug discovery [5,11,12,49], recommendation systems [39,40,43], and medical diagnosis [1,18,19]. However, as with other machine learning models, GNNs are often considered to be 'black boxes', providing little insight into how they make predictions. Therefore, explainable AI algorithms for GNNs have gained increasing attention in recent years.

There are several approaches to developing explainable GNN algorithms that can conveniently be categorized as *instance-level* and *model-level* approaches. Instance-level algorithms provide explanations for individual predictions of the GNN and include methods that utilize the gradients of the features to determine input importance, such as sensitivity analysis, Guided BP, and Grad-CAM [2,30,33], perturb inputs to observe changes in output as in GNNExplainer and PGExplainer [20,42], and learn relationships between the input and its neighbors using surrogate models [15,38]. While there are several instance-level explainability methods for GNNs, there is still a lack of effective model-level explainability methods [46].

Model-level explanations help identify how the GNN approaches the task at hand, and can reveal patterns and structures that may not be immediately evident from the graph data alone. They also help identify when a model is not performing well on the given task, or when it is exhibiting unwanted behavior. Outside of the graph-learning world, input optimization is a popular model-level approach for image classification models, where the goal is to generate an image that maximizes the predicted class label [8, 21, 26–28, 32]. In contrast, model-level explanations for GNNs have received relatively less attention. One of the most prominent model-level explainability methods for GNNs is XGNN (eXplainable Graph Neural Networks) [45]. XGNN leverages reinforcement learning techniques to generate graphs that provide insights into how the GNN is making predictions. XGNN generates a graph explanation that maximizes a target prediction, thereby revealing the optimized class pattern learned by the model.

To gain more insight into the model, it is often necessary to analyze a diverse distribution of examples that cover different scenarios and edge cases. Furthermore, generating a distribution of explanations opens the door to applying statistical analysis and data mining techniques, such as dimensionality reduction or t-tests, to uncover hidden relationships in the data. For instance, in this paper we use dimensionality techniques to uncover clusters within XInsight explanations. When then used these clusters to verify that the model correctly learned a known correlation within the data.

2.3 XGNN

XGNN, which stands for eXplainable Graph Neural Networks, is a novel model-level explainability framework introduced by Yuan et al. in 2020 [45]. The goal of XGNN is to generate a graph that maximizes a specific target class of a graph classification model. XGNN employs a reinforcement learning approach to iteratively build a graph using actions that add nodes or edges to the graph at each time step. During each time step, the model calculates the reward based on the probability of the target class, which encourages the algorithm to select actions that generate graphs of a particular class. This process is repeated until the model converges or until a maximum number of time steps is reached.

Like Graph Convolutional Policy Networks [44], XGNN learns a generator model using a policy gradient. The generator produces a graph that contains patterns that maximize the target class in question. In contrast to instance-level explainability methods that identify subgraphs that contribute to the model's output, XGNN focuses on the entire graph and the relationships between its nodes and edges. XGNN is currently the only model-level explanation method that has been proposed for GNNs, according to a recent survey [46].

While XGNN is a powerful model-level explainability method for GNNs, it generates a single maximum reward explanation, which limits its ability to explain the full extent of the model's behavior. XGNN is also limited in its utility to discover hidden insights related to the classification task due to the inability to perform a more detailed analysis of the explanations, such as clustering. Due to these limitations, there is no way of directly comparing XGNN to techniques that generate a distribution of explanations, such as XInsight.

2.4 GFlowNets

Generative Flow Networks (GFlowNets) are a type of generative model that generate a diverse set of objects by iteratively sampling actions proportional to a reward function [3,4]. The objective of GFlowNets is to learn to sample from a distribution of diverse and high-reward samples instead of generating a single sample to maximize a reward function. GFlowNets can be viewed as Markov Decision Processes (MDP) represented by a directed acyclic graph (DAG), where the edges represent the actions that can be taken in the states. The flows coming into a state represent the actions that can be taken to reach that state, while the flows leaving a state represent the actions that can be taken in that state to reach the next state. The DAG is traversed iteratively by sampling flows, which generates a flow trajectory that ends when a terminal state is reached. The flow entering a terminal state is the total flow of the trajectory and is equal to the reward function assigned to that state.

Trajectory Balance Objective. In [22], Malkin et al. introduced the *Trajectory Balance Constraint*, shown in Eq. 1, which ensures that the flow of the trajectory leading to a state is equal to the flow of the trajectory leaving that state and terminating at a terminal state. Satisfying this constraint allows the GFlowNet to sample objects with probability proportional to its reward.

$$Z \prod_t P_F(s_{t+1}|s_t) = R(\tau) \prod_t P_B(s_t|s_{t+1}) \tag{1}$$

where Z is the 'total flow'. The right side of Eq. 1 represents the fraction of the total reward going through the trajectory, while the left represents the fraction of the total flow going through the trajectory. This constraint can be turned into the *Trajectory Balance Objective* [22] for training a GFlowNet, shown below:

$$L_{TB}(\tau) = \left(\log \frac{Z \prod_t P_F(s_{t+1}|s_t)}{R(\tau) \prod_t P_B(s_t|s_{t+1})} \right)^2 \tag{2}$$

Applications of GFlowNets. GFlowNets have been applied to many generative applications, including molecular sequence generation [3,16,22] and MNIST image generation [47]. And due to their ability to generate diverse samples, GFlowNets trained to generate model explanations, as in XInsight, provide the machine learning user a greater breadth of human-readable explanations of what their models are learning from the data.

3   eXplainable Insight (XInsight)

3.1   Explaining Graph Neural Networks

Graph classification networks can be difficult for humans to interpret since graph structures can be less intuitive to humans compared to visual features which humans are naturally equipped to interpret. Therefore when seeking to understand a graph classification model, a quality explainability algorithm should take advantage of the natural pattern matching capabilities of its human users by producing concise explanations that highlight patterns that are easily interpreted by humans. To make it even easier for its users, a quality explainability algorithm should produce a distribution of explanations in order to provide the user with multiple perspectives into the model; however, most algorithms to date lack one or both of these qualities.

XInsight not only produces concise explanations that highlight important patterns but also produces a distribution of explanations that allows the user to develop a more robust understanding of what the examined model is learning from the data. XInsight trains a GFlowNet to generate a diverse set of model-explanations for a graph classification model. The explanations that XInsight generates highlight general patterns that the classification model attributes to specified target class in question.

In the context of model explanations as a whole, the explanations that XInsight produces are particularly useful for discovering relationships within the trained model. For example, they can help determine if a model incorrectly associates an artifact in the data with the target class, like rulers with skin cancer as discussed in [25]. XInsight empowers users to do this by generating a distribution of explanations, which can then be passed through traditional data mining techniques, such as clustering, to uncover what the model is learning from the data.

3.2   Generating Graphs with XInsight

XInsight employs a GFlowNet that it is trained to generate graphs with probabilities proportional to their likelihood of belonging to a target class. Specifically, the GFlowNet generates a graph by iteratively sampling actions that determine whether to add a new node or edge to the existing structure. It is important to note that the likelihood of a sample belonging to a particular class is defined by the trained model that is being explained. Therefore, the distribution of generated samples is dependent upon the trained model and not the true class distribution, which in the context of explaining a trained model is desirable since the goal is to understand the model itself.

Action Space. The action space, $\mathcal{A}$, is split into two flows: the first selecting a starting node and the second selecting the ending node. The starting node is selected from the set of nodes N in the current incomplete graph G_t. The ending node is selected from the union of the same $\mathcal{N}$, excluding the starting node and a set of building blocks $\mathcal{B}$. Together, the starting and ending nodes form the combined action $\mathcal{A}(n_s, n_e)$ sampled from the forward flow P_F. Taking this action generates a new graph G_{t+1} as shown below:

$$G_{t+1} \sim P_F(\mathcal{A}(n_s, n_e)|G_t) \tag{3}$$

$$p_{start}(n_s \in N|G_t) \tag{4}$$

$$p_{end}(n_e \in N \cup \mathcal{B}; n_e \neq n_s | G_t) \tag{5}$$

3.3 Proxy

The proxy f in classical GFlowNets is used to generate the reward for a generated object. For example, in [3] Bengio et al. used a pretrained model as their proxy to predict the binding energy of a generated molecule to a protein target. In XInsight, we use the model to be explained as the proxy since the generated objects are treated as explanations of the model.

Reward. The reward in XInsight guides the underlying GFlowNet to generate graphs that explain the proxy. In XInsight, we define the reward as the proxy's predicted probability that the generated graph belongs to the target class c, as shown in Eq. 6. To encourage the generation of objects explaining the target class, we define the reward to be zero if the generated object is classified as the opposite class. In addition, we add a scalar multiplier α to magnify the reward for the target class, where $\alpha > 0$.

$$R(G_t) = \begin{cases} \alpha * softmax(f(G_t)) & \text{if } argmax\{f(G_t)\} = Target\ Class \\ 0 & \text{if } argmax\{f(G_t)\} \neq Target\ Class \end{cases} \tag{6}$$

3.4 Training XInsight

We train XInsight using the trajectory balance objective, following [22]. We define the trajectory balance objective for a complete graph G generated over a trajectory τ actions in Eq. 7.

$$L_{TB}(G) = \left(\log \frac{Z \prod_t^\tau P_F(G_{t+1}|G_t)}{R(G_t) \prod_t^\tau P_B(G_t|G_{t+1})} \right)^2 \tag{7}$$

The training loop consists of sampling trajectories (i.e. generating graphs), calculating forward and backward flows and the reward, and updating the underlying GFlowNet parameters until convergence. We highlight the in-depth steps of XInsight's training loop in Algorithm 1.

For every epoch in the training loop, we start by initializing the GFlowNet and creating an initial graph G_0. Then we generate a graph by iteratively sampling actions from the forward policy P_F that add nodes or edges to the graph at each step G_t. Once a trajectory is complete, either by the reaching the $MAX\_ACTIONS$ limit or by sampling a *stop* action, the reward is computed for G_t using the *Proxy*. Finally, we calculate the trajectory balance loss, update the GFlowNet's parameters and repeat.

Algorithm 1. XInsight Training Loop

Input: $EPOCHS$, $Proxy(\cdot)$, $TARGET\_CLASS$, $MAX\_ACTIONS$

  $XI(\cdot; \theta) \leftarrow$ GFlowNet
  for epoch in $EPOCHS$ **do**
    $actions \leftarrow 0$
    $G_t \leftarrow G_0$ ▷ Initialize new graph
    $\tau \leftarrow \emptyset + \{G_t\}$
    repeat
      $P_F, P_B \leftarrow XI(G_t; \theta)$ ▷ Generate flows
      $n_s, n_e \sim P_F$ ▷ Sample start & end node
      if $n_s = stop$ **then**
        $STOP \leftarrow True$ ▷ Stop if stop action sampled
      end if
      $G_{new} \leftarrow \mathcal{T}(n_s, n_e)$ ▷ Add node/edge
      $P_F, P_B \leftarrow XI(G_{new}; \theta)$ ▷ Recompute flows
      $G_t = G_{new}$
      $\tau \leftarrow \tau + \{G_t\}$ ▷ Append G_t to trajectory
      $actions + +$
    until $actions > MAX\_ACTIONS$ or $STOP$
    $Reward = softmax(Proxy(G_t))_{TARGET\_CLASS}$ ▷ Calculate reward
    $\theta \leftarrow \theta - \eta \nabla Loss_{TB}(Reward, log_Z, \tau)$ ▷ Update parameters
  end for

---

4 Experiment Design

4.1 Datasets

The Acyclic Graph dataset includes 2405 synthetically generated graphs labeled as either acyclic or cyclic. We generated graphs using graph generation functions from the NetworkX software package [13]. To improve the diversity of the dataset, we trained a GFlowNet with a brute-force cycle checker as a reward function to generate acyclic and cyclic graphs to add to the dataset. The code used to generate this dataset can be found in [17].

The MUTAG dataset [24], included in Pytorch Geometric, contains 188 graphs representing chemical compounds used in an Ames test on the S. Typhimurium TA98 bacteria with the goal of measuring the mutagenic effects of the compound. This dataset was used in a study to measure the correlation between the chemical structure of the compounds and their mutagenic activity [7]. The nodes and edges in the graphs in MUTAG represent 7 different atoms (Carbon, Nitrogen, Oxygen, Fluorine, Iodine, Chlorine, and Bromine) and their chemical bonds. In the graph learning community, the dataset is used as a benchmark dataset for graph classification models labeling each graph as 'Mutagenic' or 'Non-Mutagenic'.

4.2 Verifying XInsight's Generative Abilities Setup

To validate that XInsight can generate graphs belonging to a target class, we trained XInsight to generate acyclic graphs because of their simple and human-interpretable form. For the proxy, we trained a graph convolutional neural network (GCN) to classify acyclic graphs using the Acyclic Graph dataset and node degree as the node features, achieving 99.58% accuracy. This GCN is composed of three graph convolutional layers (GCNConv) with 32, 48, 64 filters, respectively, a global mean pooling layer, and two fully connected layers with 64 and 32 hidden units. We also used dropout and the ReLU activation function. The GFlowNet was also a GCN made up of three GCNConv layers with 32, 64, and 128 filters, two fully connected layers with 128 and 512 hidden units, and a scalar parameter representing $log(Z)$ from the reward function, see Sect. 3.3. The building blocks used for action selection consisted of a single node of degree 1.

4.3   Revealing MUTAG Relationships Setup

Due to their highly qualitative nature, there is no established method for evaluating model-level explanation methods for graphs, particularly for methods that generate a distribution of explanations. Despite this barrier, we demonstrate XInsight's explanatory abilities by applying it to the task of knowledge discovery within the mutagenic compound domain. Particularly, we evaluated XInsight for its ability to uncover meaningful relationships learned by a graph neural network trained to classify mutagenic compounds and verify that these relationships exist in the ground truth data.

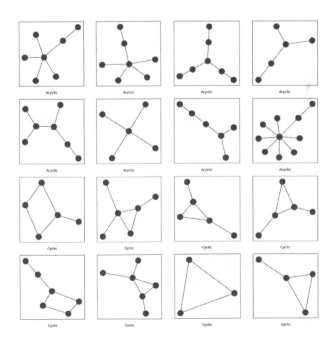

Fig. 1. Generated graphs (8 with cycles and 8 without cycles) to verify XInsight's ability to generate graphs of a specified target class.

For the proxy, we trained a graph convolutional neural network (GCN) to classify mutagenic compounds using the MUTAG dataset. Following [45], we used node features which were seven-dimensional one-hot encoded vectors encoding the seven different atoms in the dataset. The architecture of this GCN mirrored that used for the Acyclic classification task, with the addition of another GCNConv layer with 64 filters and LeakyReLU as the activation function. With this architecture, we achieved 89% accuracy on the MUTAG classification task. The GFlowNet architecture was also the same as the one used for the Acyclic classification task, except we used seven nodes representing the different atoms as the building blocks. The initial graph G_0, used in training the GFlowNet, was set to a single node graph with the feature value set to carbon, as in [45].

5   Results

5.1   Verifying XInsight's Generative Abilities Using the Acyclic Dataset

To verify that XInsight is capable of generating graphs of a particular class defined by a classification model, we conducted an experiment in which we trained XInsight to generate graphs from a graph convolutional network, previously trained on the Acyclic Graphs dataset. This synthetic dataset contains two classes, acyclic and cyclic, and is described in detail in Sect. 4.1.

Following XInsight training, we generated a distribution of 16 graphs (8 acyclic and 8 cyclic), shown in Fig. 1. The results of the experiment indicate that XInsight is indeed capable of generating acyclic graphs, which is consistent with the nature of the dataset. This provides evidence that XInsight is capable of generating graphs guided by the predictions of a simple classification model.

5.2   Revealing Distinct Relationships Learned by the MUTAG Classifier

Generating Explanations. In our second experiment, we trained XInsight to explain a GCN trained on the MUTAG dataset. Our objective was to uncover hidden patterns and relationships that the trained GCN classifier associates with the mutagenic class. To achieve this, we used XInsight to generate a distribution of 16 compounds, illustrated in Fig. 2, and then fed the generated graphs through the trained GCN to produce graph embeddings. In order to visualize the 32-dimensional graph embeddings we used the UMAP dimensionality reduction algorithm, which preserves global and local structure of the data [23], to project the embeddings onto a 2-dimensional plane. From this visualization, we identified five distinct groupings of compounds that we hypothesize group by an unknown factor related to mutagenicity. To uncover the factor behind these groupings, we continued our analysis by analyzing the chemical properties of the generated compounds using QSAR modeling [14] (Fig. 3).

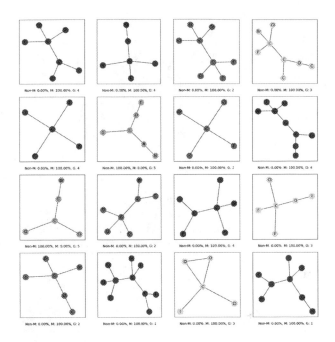

Fig. 2. Distribution of explanations for the *Mutagenic* classifier generated by the trained XInsight model, with MUTAG class probabilities according to the trained proxy. Colors represent UMAP clusters of graph embeddings for the generated compounds. Blue: Group 1, Red: Group 2, Yellow: Group 3, Purple: Group 4, Orange: Group 5. (Color figure online)

Knowledge Discovery. Quantitative Structure-Activity Relationship (QSAR) modeling is a well-established methodology that is used to differentiate between mutagenic and non-mutagenic compounds, which have been identified by the Ames test [14]. Various features of typical drugs, such as lipophilicity, polarizability, hydrophilicity, electron density, and topological analysis, have been utilized in the literature to establish QSAR models for mutagenicity [35]. Among these features, lipophilicity has been identified as a major contributing factor for mutagenicity, as it facilitates the penetration of lipophilic compounds through cellular membranes.

To establish a relationship between the clusters of compounds generated by XInsight and their mutagenicity, we calculated the lipophilicity of all the generated structures using the XLOGP3 method [6], samples shown in Fig. 4. This method has been shown to provide reliable results that are comparable to those obtained using the calculation of the octanol water partition coefficient for $logP$ [37]. It is essential to note that we added hydrogens to O (-OH) and N (-NH2) groups to represent the aqueous environment within the human body, since hydrogen atoms were not included in the building blocks for the MUTAG dataset.

In Fig. 5 we see that in general the lipophilicity value is higher for the generated mutagenic compounds compared to the non-mutagenic compounds. We

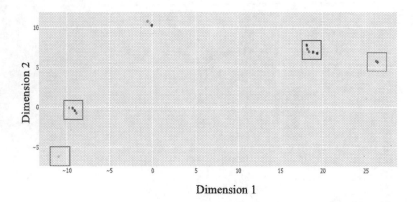

Fig. 3. Generated graph embeddings projected onto 2-dimensional plane using UMAP. UMAP was fit using the cosine similarity metric, 2 neighbors, and a minimum distance of 0.1.

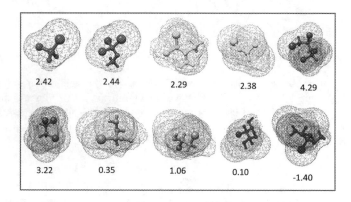

Fig. 4. Lipophilicity calculations for 10 of the clustered compounds generated by XInsight using the XLOGP3 method. Surface mesh and 3 dimensional structures were generated by Chimera visualization software [29].

observed that the highest lipophilicity was associated with compounds of Group 4 (purple), followed by those of Group 2 (red) and Group 3 (yellow). The purple cluster exhibited significant differences in lipophilicity when compared to the red and yellow clusters, which explains why purple is a distinct cluster. However, groups 1 (blue) and 5 (orange) showed lower levels of lipophilicity values but still exhibited significant differences. Thus, lipophilicity appears to be a factor related to the mutagenicity of these compounds.

Knowledge Verification. To verify that the discovered relationship between lipophilicity and mutagenicity is valid, we randomly sampled 32 compounds from the MUTAG dataset, with 16 compounds for each class, and calculated lipophilicity for each. We then performed a t-test to determine whether there is a statistically significant difference in lipophilicity for mutagenic and non-mutagenic compounds. In Table 1 we show a statistically significant difference between the mean lipophilicity values for the mutagenic and non-mutagenic classes, thus verifying that the relationship uncovered using XInsight's generated distribution is a true relationship exhibited in the training data. Additionally, this shows how XInsight can be used to discover knowledge about the model.

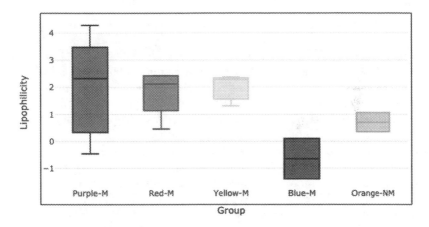

Fig. 5. XLOGP3 Lipophilicity values for UMAP clustered compounds colored by group with classified labels, Mutagenic: *M*, Non-Mutagenic: *NM*. (Color figure online)

Further Insights. The distribution of explanations provided us with another significant insight, which is that the compounds in Group 1 (blue) and Group 5 (orange) have low lipophilicity, even though Group 1 is classified as mutagenic and Group 5 as non-mutagenic. This raises two possible assumptions: first, the classifier might be incorrectly classifying compounds that are similar to those in Groups 1 as mutagenic, or second, there might be another underlying factor that is responsible for the hydrophilic nature of these compounds. Furthermore, as mentioned earlier, lipophilicity is not the only factor determining the mutagenicity of the compounds. To explain the clustering of the Group 1, additional quantum-mechanical calculations are necessary.

This analysis underscores the considerable advantages of generating a distribution of explanations, as opposed to a single explanation that maximizes the reward. By having a distribution of explanations, we can uncover hidden insights into what the classification model associates with the target class. Without a distribution of explanations, we are restricted in the types of analysis we can perform to more effectively explain the model being examined.

Table 1. *t-test* results showing a statistically significant difference between Mutagenic and Non-Mutagenic lipophilicity values for 32 randomly sampled compounds from the MUTAG dataset, $\alpha = 0.05$.

	Mutagenic	Non-Mutagenic
Mean	4.1444	2.1750
Variance	0.6812	1.3963
t-statistic	\-5.2917	
p-value	0.00001022	

6   Conclusion

In this paper, we proposed XInsight, a novel explainability algorithm for graph neural networks, that generates a diverse set of model explanations using Generative Flow Networks. Our approach is designed to provide human-understandable explanations for GNNs that uncover the hidden relationships of the model. We demonstrated the effectiveness of XInsight by generating explanations for GNNs trained for two graph classification tasks, including the classification of acyclic graphs and the classification of mutagenic compounds. Our results indicate that XInsight uncovers underlying relationships and patterns demonstrated by the model, and provides valuable guidance for further analysis.

Our findings emphasize the importance of generating a diverse set of explanations, as it enables us to discover hidden relationships in the model and identify important features in the data. Furthermore, we show that the generated explanations from XInsight can be used in combination with data mining and chemical analysis methods to uncover relationships within the model. For instance, we analyzed the generated compounds from XInsight using QSAR modeling, and we observe that XInsight generates compounds that cluster by Lipophilicity, a known correlate of mutagenicity.

Overall, XInsight provides a promising direction for developing explainable AI algorithms for graph-based applications, with implications for many real-world domains. We believe that XInsight has the potential to make a significant impact in various real-world domains, particularly in high-stakes applications, such as drug discovery, where interpretability and transparency are essential.

References

1. Ahmedt-Aristizabal, D., Armin, M.A., Denman, S., Fookes, C., Petersson, L.: Graph-based deep learning for medical diagnosis and analysis: past, present and future. Sensors **21**(14), 4758 (2021). https://doi.org/10.3390/s21144758. https://www.mdpi.com/1424-8220/21/14/4758
2. Baehrens, D., Schroeter, T., Harmeling, S., Kawanabe, M., Hansen, K., Mueller, K.R.: How to explain individual classification decisions (2009). https://doi.org/10.48550/arXiv.0912.1128. http://arxiv.org/abs/0912.1128. arXiv:0912.1128

3. Bengio, E., Jain, M., Korablyov, M., Precup, D., Bengio, Y.: Flow network based generative models for non-iterative diverse candidate generation (2021). https://doi.org/10.48550/arXiv.2106.04399. http://arxiv.org/abs/2106.04399. arXiv:2106.04399

4. Bengio, Y., Lahlou, S., Deleu, T., Hu, E.J., Tiwari, M., Bengio, E.: GFlowNet Foundations (2022). https://doi.org/10.48550/arXiv.2111.09266. arXiv:2111.09266

5. Bongini, P., Bianchini, M., Scarselli, F.: Molecular graph generation with Graph Neural Networks. Neurocomputing **450**, 242–252 (2021). https://doi.org/10.1016/j.neucom.2021.04.039. http://arxiv.org/abs/2012.07397, arXiv:2012.07397

6. Cheng, T., et al.: Computation of octanol-water partition coefficients by guiding an additive model with knowledge. J. Chem. Inf. Model. **47**(6), 2140–2148 (2007). https://doi.org/10.1021/ci700257y. https://pubs.acs.org/doi/10.1021/ci700257y

7. Debnath, A.K., Lopez De Compadre, R.L., Debnath, G., Shusterman, A.J., Hansch, C.: Structure-activity relationship of mutagenic aromatic and heteroaromatic nitro compounds. Correlation with molecular orbital energies and hydrophobicity. J. Med. Chem. **34**(2), 786–797 (1991). https://doi.org/10.1021/jm00106a046

8. Dosovitskiy, A., Brox, T.: Inverting visual representations with convolutional networks. In: 2016 IEEE Conference on Computer Vision and Pattern Recognition (CVPR), pp. 4829–4837. IEEE, Las Vegas, NV, USA (2016). https://doi.org/10.1109/CVPR.2016.522

9. Fan, W., et al.: Graph Neural Networks for Social Recommendation (2019). https://doi.org/10.48550/arXiv.1902.07243. http://arxiv.org/abs/1902.07243. arXiv:1902.07243

10. Gao, J., et al.: VectorNet: encoding HD maps and agent dynamics from vectorized representation (2020). https://doi.org/10.48550/arXiv.2005.04259. arXiv:2005.04259

11. Gasteiger, J., Groß, J., Günnemann, S.: Directional message passing for molecular graphs (2022). https://doi.org/10.48550/arXiv.2003.03123. http://arxiv.org/abs/2003.03123. arXiv:2003.03123

12. Gilmer, J., Schoenholz, S.S., Riley, P.F., Vinyals, O., Dahl, G.E.: Neural message passing for quantum chemistry (2017). https://doi.org/10.48550/arXiv.1704.01212. arXiv:1704.01212

13. Hagberg, A., Swart, P., S Chult, D.: Exploring network structure, dynamics, and function using networkx (2008). https://www.osti.gov/biblio/960616

14. Honma, M., et al.: Improvement of quantitative structure-activity relationship (QSAR) tools for predicting Ames mutagenicity: outcomes of the Ames/QSAR International Challenge Project. Mutagenesis **34**(1), 3–16 (2019). https://doi.org/10.1093/mutage/gey031. https://academic.oup.com/mutage/article/34/1/3/5142926

15. Huang, Q., Yamada, M., Tian, Y., Singh, D., Yin, D., Chang, Y.: GraphLIME: local interpretable model explanations for graph neural networks (2020). https://doi.org/10.48550/arXiv.2001.06216. http://arxiv.org/abs/2001.06216. arXiv:2001.06216

16. Jain, M., et al.: Biological sequence design with GFlowNets (2022). https://arxiv.org/abs/2203.04115v2

17. Laird, E.: Acyclic graph dataset. https://github.com/elilaird/acyclic-graph-dataset

18. Li, Y., Qian, B., Zhang, X., Liu, H.: Graph neural network-based diagnosis prediction. Big Data **8**(5), 379–390 (2020). https://doi.org/10.1089/big.2020.0070. https://www.liebertpub.com/doi/10.1089/big.2020.0070

19. Lu, H., Uddin, S.: A weighted patient network-based framework for predicting chronic diseases using graph neural networks. Sci. Rep. **11**(1), 22607 (2021). https://doi.org/10.1038/s41598-021-01964-2. https://www.nature.com/articles/s41598-021-01964-2

20. Luo, D., et al.: Parameterized explainer for graph neural network. In: Proceedings of the 34th International Conference on Neural Information Processing Systems. NIPS 2020, Curran Associates Inc., Red Hook, NY, USA (2020)

21. Mahendran, A., Vedaldi, A.: Understanding deep image representations by inverting them. In: 2015 IEEE Conference on Computer Vision and Pattern Recognition (CVPR), pp. 5188–5196. IEEE, Boston, MA, USA (2015). https://doi.org/10.1109/CVPR.2015.7299155

22. Malkin, N., Jain, M., Bengio, E., Sun, C., Bengio, Y.: Trajectory balance: improved credit assignment in GFlowNets (2022). https://doi.org/10.48550/arXiv.2201.13259. http://arxiv.org/abs/2201.13259. arXiv:2201.13259

23. McInnes, L., Healy, J., Melville, J.: UMAP: uniform manifold approximation and projection for dimension reduction (2020). https://doi.org/10.48550/arXiv.1802.03426. arXiv:1802.03426

24. Morris, C., Kriege, N.M., Bause, F., Kersting, K., Mutzel, P., Neumann, M.: TUDataset: a collection of benchmark datasets for learning with graphs (2020). https://doi.org/10.48550/arXiv.2007.08663. arXiv:2007.08663

25. Narla, A., Kuprel, B., Sarin, K., Novoa, R., Ko, J.: Automated classification of skin lesions: from pixels to practice. J. Invest. Dermatol. **138**(10), 2108–2110 (2018). https://doi.org/10.1016/j.jid.2018.06.175. https://linkinghub.elsevier.com/retrieve/pii/S0022202X18322930

26. Nguyen, A., Clune, J., Bengio, Y., Dosovitskiy, A., Yosinski, J.: Plug & play generative networks: conditional iterative generation of images in latent space. In: 2017 IEEE Conference on Computer Vision and Pattern Recognition (CVPR), pp. 3510–3520. IEEE, Honolulu, HI (2017). https://doi.org/10.1109/CVPR.2017.374

27. Nguyen, A., Yosinski, J., Clune, J.: Deep neural networks are easily fooled: High confidence predictions for unrecognizable images. In: 2015 IEEE Conference on Computer Vision and Pattern Recognition (CVPR), pp. 427–436. IEEE, Boston, MA, USA (2015). https://doi.org/10.1109/CVPR.2015.7298640

28. Olah, C., Mordvintsev, A., Schubert, L.: Feature visualization. Distill **2**(11), e7 (2017). https://doi.org/10.23915/distill.00007

29. Pettersen, E.F., et al.: UCSF chimera?A visualization system for exploratory research and analysis. J. Comput. Chem. **25**(13), 1605–1612 (2004). https://doi.org/10.1002/jcc.20084. https://onlinelibrary.wiley.com/doi/10.1002/jcc.20084

30. Selvaraju, R.R., Cogswell, M., Das, A., Vedantam, R., Parikh, D., Batra, D.: Grad-CAM: visual explanations from deep networks via gradient-based localization. Int. J. Comput. Vis. **128**(2), 336–359 (2020). https://doi.org/10.1007/s11263-019-01228-7. http://arxiv.org/abs/1610.02391. arXiv:1610.02391

31. Sheng, Z., Xu, Y., Xue, S., Li, D.: Graph-based spatial-temporal convolutional network for vehicle trajectory prediction in autonomous driving. IEEE Trans. Intell. Transp. Syst. **23**(10), 17654–17665 (2022). https://doi.org/10.1109/TITS.2022.3155749. http://arxiv.org/abs/2109.12764. arXiv:2109.12764

32. Simonyan, K., Vedaldi, A., Zisserman, A.: Deep inside convolutional networks: visualising image classification models and saliency maps (2014). https://doi.org/10.48550/arXiv.1312.6034. arXiv:1312.6034

33. Springenberg, J.T., Dosovitskiy, A., Brox, T., Riedmiller, M.: Striving for simplicity: the all convolutional net (2015). https://doi.org/10.48550/arXiv.1412.6806. http://arxiv.org/abs/1412.6806. arXiv:1412.6806

34. Tan, Q., Liu, N., Hu, X.: Deep representation learning for social network analysis. Front. Big Data **2**, 2 (2019). https://doi.org/10.3389/fdata.2019.00002.https://www.frontiersin.org/article/10.3389/fdata.2019.00002/full

35. Tuppurainen, K.: Frontier orbital energies, hydrophobicity and steric factors as physical QSAR descriptors of molecular mutagenicity. A review with a case study: MX compounds. Chemosphere **38**(13), 3015–3030 (1999). https://doi.org/10.1016/S0045-6535(98)00503-7.https://linkinghub.elsevier.com/retrieve/pii/S0045653598005037

36. Veličković, P., Cucurull, G., Casanova, A., Romero, A., Lió, P., Bengio, Y.: Graph attention networks (2018). https://doi.org/10.48550/arXiv.1710.10903. arXiv:1710.10903

37. Viana, R.D.S., Aquino, F.L.T.D., Barreto, E.: Effect of trans -cinnamic acid and p -coumaric acid on fibroblast motility: a pilot comparative study of in silico lipophilicity measure. Nat. Prod. Res. **35**(24), 5872–5878 (2021). https://doi.org/10.1080/14786419.2020.1798664. https://www.tandfonline.com/doi/full/10.1080/14786419.2020.1798664

38. Vu, M.N., Thai, M.T.: PGM-explainer: probabilistic graphical model explanations for graph neural networks (2020). https://doi.org/10.48550/arXiv.2010.05788.arXiv:2010.05788

39. Wang, X., He, X., Wang, M., Feng, F., Chua, T.S.: Neural graph collaborative filtering. In: Proceedings of the 42nd International ACM SIGIR Conference on Research and Development in Information Retrieval, pp. 165–174 (2019). https://doi.org/10.1145/3331184.3331267. http://arxiv.org/abs/1905.08108. arXiv:1905.08108

40. Wu, J., et al.: Self-supervised graph learning for recommendation. In: Proceedings of the 44th International ACM SIGIR Conference on Research and Development in Information Retrieval. pp. 726–735 (2021). https://doi.org/10.1145/3404835.3462862. http://arxiv.org/abs/2010.10783. arXiv:2010.10783

41. Xu, K., Hu, W., Leskovec, J., Jegelka, S.: How Powerful are Graph Neural Networks? (2019). https://doi.org/10.48550/arXiv.1810.00826. arXiv:1810.00826

42. Ying, R., Bourgeois, D., You, J., Zitnik, M., Leskovec, J.: GNNExplainer: generating explanations for graph neural networks. In: Proceedings of the 33rd International Conference on Neural Information Processing Systems. Curran Associates Inc., Red Hook, NY, USA (2019)

43. Ying, R., He, R., Chen, K., Eksombatchai, P., Hamilton, W.L., Leskovec, J.: Graph convolutional neural networks for web-scale recommender systems. In: Proceedings of the 24th ACM SIGKDD International Conference on Knowledge Discovery & Data Mining, pp. 974–983 (2018). https://doi.org/10.1145/3219819.3219890. http://arxiv.org/abs/1806.01973. arXiv:1806.01973

44. You, J., Liu, B., Ying, R., Pande, V., Leskovec, J.: Graph convolutional policy network for goal-directed molecular graph generation. In: Proceedings of the 32nd International Conference on Neural Information Processing Systems, pp. 6412–6422. NIPS 2018, Curran Associates Inc., Red Hook, NY, USA (2018)

45. Yuan, H., Tang, J., Hu, X., Ji, S.: XGNN: towards model-level explanations of graph neural networks. In: Proceedings of the 26th ACM SIGKDD International Conference on Knowledge Discovery & Data Mining, pp. 430–438. ACM, Virtual Event CA USA (2020). https://doi.org/10.1145/3394486.3403085

46. Yuan, H., Yu, H., Gui, S., Ji, S.: Explainability in graph neural networks: a taxonomic survey. IEEE Trans. Pattern Anal. Mach. Intell. 45, 1–19 (2022). https://doi.org/10.1109/TPAMI.2022.3204236. https://ieeexplore.ieee.org/document/9875989/

47. Zhang, D., Malkin, N., Liu, Z., Volokhova, A., Courville, A., Bengio, Y.: Generative flow networks for discrete probabilistic modeling (2022). https://arxiv.org/abs/2202.01361v2
48. Zhang, H., Lu, G., Zhan, M., Zhang, B.: Semi-supervised classification of graph convolutional networks with Laplacian rank constraints. Neural Process. Lett. **54**(4), 2645–2656 (2022). https://doi.org/10.1007/s11063-020-10404-7
49. Zhang, Z., et al.: Graph neural network approaches for drug-target interactions. Curr. Opin. Struct. Biol. **73**, 102327 (2022). https://doi.org/10.1016/j.sbi.2021.102327. https://linkinghub.elsevier.com/retrieve/pii/S0959440X2100169X

What Will Make Misinformation Spread: An XAI Perspective

Hongbo Bo[1]([⊠]), Yiwen Wu[2], Zinuo You[1], Ryan McConville[2], Jun Hong[3], and Weiru Liu[2]

[1] Department of Computer Science, University of Bristol, Bristol, UK
hongbo.bo@bristol.ac.uk
[2] Department of Engineering Mathematics, University of Bristol, Bristol, UK
[3] School of Computing and Creative Technologies,
University of the West of England, Bristol, UK

Abstract. Explainable Artificial Intelligence (XAI) techniques can provide explanations of how AI systems or models make decisions, or what factors AI considers when making the decisions. Online social networks have a problem with misinformation which is known to have negative effects. In this paper, we propose to utilize XAI techniques to study what factors lead to misinformation spreading by explaining a trained graph neural network that predicts misinformation spread. However, it is difficult to achieve this with the existing XAI methods for homogeneous social networks, since the spread of misinformation is often associated with heterogeneous social networks which contain different types of nodes and relationships. This paper presents, MisInfoExplainer, an XAI pipeline for explaining the factors contributing to misinformation spread in heterogeneous social networks. Firstly, a prediction module is proposed for predicting misinformation spread by leveraging GraphSAGE with heterogeneous graph convolution. Secondly, we propose an explanation module that uses gradient-based and perturbation-based methods, to identify what makes misinformation spread by explaining the trained prediction module. Experimentally we demonstrate the superiority of MisinfoExplainer in predicting misinformation spread, and also reveal the key factors that make misinformation spread by generating a global explanation for the prediction module. Finally, we conclude that the perturbation-based approach is superior to the gradient-based approach, both in terms of qualitative analysis and quantitative measurements.

Keywords: Misinformation Spread · Graph Neural Networks · Explainable Artificial Intelligence

1 Introduction

Explainable Artificial Intelligence (XAI) [2] is a set of techniques used to make AI more explainable and understandable to humans. By using XAI techniques, developers and users of AI can understand how AI makes decisions or produces outputs, including the factors considered when making the decisions. XAI

L. Longo (Ed.): xAI 2023, CCIS 1902, pp. 321–337, 2023.
https://doi.org/10.1007/978-3-031-44067-0_17

has become popular because AI techniques are now prevalent in people's daily lives [30,36], and it is important to know how AI makes decisions that can increase trust and confidence in AI systems by making AI more understandable to humans which can lead to better acceptance of and improvements in AI methods [12]. XAI methods can be divided into local explanation methods and global explanation methods. The local explanation methods [20,29] provide the explanation for a specific decision or output of the system, while the global XAI methods [2] explain the behavior of the system as a whole.

Misinformation, which can cause negative effects, is pervasive on social media. A research question of interest to us is to understand the factors, for example, the content of the misinformation or the relationships between users, that enable the spread of misinformation on online social networks. Previous studies [24,33] on this topic have largely cooperated with social scientists, relying on specialized knowledge for subjective analysis, which is not efficient when social media data is huge. However, a global explanation may be able to identify which factors enable misinformation spread, but this relies on an accurate underlying machine learning model. Graph Neural Networks (GNNs) have seen increasing use in many applications, including social network analysis [6,7,27], and have been demonstrated success at classifying misinformation on social networks [4,21]. Several explainable approaches for GNNs have been explored, such as GNNExplainer [37], GraphLIME [16], and GraphSHAP [25].

However, these existing methods are insufficient to explain the misinformation spread. Social networks are often studied as homogenous networks between users [5,39], but it can be argued that they are better modeled as heterogeneous networks of different types of nodes [23]. Some of these methods, such as GraphLIME [16], can only generate explanations for a homogeneous graph that contains the same types of nodes and edges. Some other explanation methods are limited to classification tasks and may not be suitable for explaining the spread of misinformation, such as PGM-Explainer [34] which is designed for node and graph classification tasks. To address the limitations of the existing XAI methods, this paper explores two research challenges. Firstly, how to train an effective graph neural network that can accurately predict the spread of misinformation on large complex heterogeneous social networks. Secondly, given this model, how to explain the factors contributing to misinformation spread.

To address these two challenges, this paper presents MisInfoExplainer, an XAI pipeline designed to explore the factors contributing to the spread of misinformation. The key contributions of this paper are as follows: First, we provide a new formulation of the spread of misinformation problem where the objective is to predict the spread value of each source of misinformation quantitatively. Second, we introduce a misinformation spread prediction approach that leverages the GraphSAGE model with the heterogeneous graph convolution (HeteroGraphConv) to accurately predict the spread of misinformation on heterogeneous social networks. Third, we propose a GNN-based explanation approach that uses both gradient-based and perturbation-based methods to identify what node feature types and edge types contribute to the spread of misinformation.

Furthermore, we apply MisInfoExplainer to a large social network dataset to demonstrate how it can be used to identify the node feature types and edge types that contribute to the spread of misinformation. Finally, we conclude that the explanations generated by the perturbation-based approach are superior to those produced by the gradient-based approach by conducting both qualitative analysis and quantitative measurements.

2   Related Work

Our study closely relates to two distinct topics of interest. The first topic centers around the analysis of misinformation spread, aiming to gain insights into its dynamics and effects. The second topic explores the domain of GNN-based Explainable AI (XAI), with a focus on interpreting and providing transparent insights into the decision-making process of Graph Neural Networks.

2.1   Misinformation Spread

Misinformation is false or inaccurate information by concealing the correct facts, also called 'fake news' or 'rumor'. Misinformation has the potential to spread rapidly through social media due to users' behaviors, leading to various negative effects. Consequently, the detection of misinformation has emerged as an important research topic. One category of studies involves using Natural Language Processing (NLP) technology to determine whether a post contains misinformation [9,17] and the explanations are also involved during detection, such as dEFEND [31] which is to capture the features from the comments on a message to explain why a message is considered as fake. Other studies have used information propagation models for graph structures or GNNs to detect the spread of false information [4,21].

Our study, however, focuses on the spread of known misinformation rather than whether a message is misinformation. Some research studies the spread of misinformation by using propagation models [22,33], while few have used GNN models. However, the spread of known misinformation can be framed as an information propagation problem and GNNs are currently the most commonly used approach for modeling the relationships between users in information spread prediction models for social networks. Examples of such models include CasCN [11], MUCas [10], and coupledGNN [8], which all focus on homogeneous graphs rather than heterogeneous graphs.

There are also studies that aim at explaining the misinformation spread. For instance, [33] examined why fake information spreads faster than true information, and [24] provided a psychological framework for understanding the spread of misinformation. However, none of them used the XAI method to explain a prediction model. To the best of our knowledge, we are the first to explore the prediction and explanation of misinformation spread with the model-based XAI method.

2.2 GNN-Based XAI

Graph Neural Networks (GNNs) have demonstrated their effectiveness in numerous graph machine learning tasks, as many real-world problems can be naturally represented as graphs [14]. The XAI approaches to explaining GNNs are broadly categorized into the following groups. Gradient-based methods leverage the input gradient, representing the rate of change of input features in a deep learning model, to quantify the importance values of the input features. Initially proposed for image explanation, these methods have been successfully extended to graphs, exemplified by techniques like Grad-CAM and Guided BP [26]. Perturbation-based methods assess the significance of input features by introducing perturbations to the inputs and observing the subsequent changes in model predictions. Several examples of perturbation-based Graph Neural Networks (GNNs) for Explainable AI (XAI) are GNNExplainer [37], GraphSHAP [25], and Graph-Mask [28]. Surrogate-based methods involve employing a simple surrogate model to approximate the outputs of a complex GNN model, and the feature importance in the surrogate model is utilized to explain the original model. Examples of surrogate-based Graph Neural Networks (GNNs) for Explainable AI (XAI) include GraphLIME [16] and PGM-Explainer [34]. These GNN-based XAI methods are designed for GNNs with homogeneous graphs, if the explanations are required for heterogeneous GNNs, extensions to these methods would be needed.

3 Problem Formulation

The social network with misinformation is represented as a heterogeneous graph that consists of multiple types of nodes, such as *users*, *misinformation*, *claims*, etc. and different types of relationships between nodes. For example, a user *following* another user, a user *posting* a misinformation tweet, a reply tweet *replying* to a misinformation tweet, a misinformation tweet *belonging* to a particular claim, etc. where *following*, *posting*, *replying* are edge types.

Definition 1 *Heterogeneous Social Network.* *A heterogeneous social network is defined as a heterogeneous graph* $G = (V, E)$, *consisting of a node set* V *and an edge set* E. *A heterogeneous graph is also associated with a node type mapping function* $\xi : V \to R_V$ *and an edge type mapping function* $\psi : E \to R_E$. R_V *and* R_E *denote the predefined sets of node types and edge types, respectively, with* $|R_V| + |R_E| > 2$.

A heterogeneous graph can also be represented as $G = (X, A)$, where $A = \{A_1, A_2, .., A_{|R_E|}\}$ is the set of adjacency matrices corresponding to the edge types R_E and $X = \{x_1, ..., x_v, ...,\}$ denotes the node feature vectors of nodes $v \in V$. A heterogeneous graph is also associated with a node feature type mapping function $\zeta : X \to R_X$, where R_X denotes the predefined set of node feature types and $|\zeta(x_v)| >= 1$. In a heterogeneous graph representing a social network, the misinformation (i.e., misinformation tweets) can be represented as a type of nodes $M \subset V$.

The first challenge this paper solves is to quantitatively predict the spread value, y_i, of each misinformation tweet, $m_i \in M$, on a social network G, which functionally depends on the number of reply tweets rp_i, the number of retweets rt_i, and the number of quote tweets qt_i for m_i:

$$y_i = log(rp_i + rt_i + qt_i + 1), \tag{1}$$

where y_i is the spread value of a source of misinformation $m_i \in M$.

Research Challenge 1 *Misinformation Spread Prediction. The objective of misinformation spread prediction is to use a learned misinformation spread prediction model ϕ to predict the spread value of a misinformation node $m_i \in M$ on a social network G. The model predicts the spread value of m_i on G which is represented as $\overline{y}_i = \phi(m_i, G)$ approximating the true spread value y_i.*

The second research challenge this paper solves is to analyze what causes a misinformation tweet to spread by explaining ϕ. The explanation focuses on the node feature types R_X and edge types R_E, specifically which node feature types in R_X and which edge types in R_E contribute to the misinformation spread.

Research Challenge 2 *Misinformation Spread Explanation. Given the social network G and the trained misinformation spread prediction model ϕ, the objective of the misinformation spread explanation is to calculate a set of important values $Im_i \in [0, 1]$ for $i = 1, ..., |R_X| + |R_E|$ with each Im_i representing the contribution of an $Input_i \in \{R_X \cup R_E\}$, which is an input node feature or edge type to ϕ.*

4   Methodolodgy

In this section, we describe MinInfoExplainer, our proposed GNN-based explanation pipeline for predicting and explaining the spread of misinformation on social networks. The pipeline begins with training a misinformation spread prediction model ϕ to solve the problem of misinformation spread prediction (Research Challenge 1) using a heterogenous convolutional graph neural network (see Sect. 4.1). Then two XAI methods, a gradient-based method and a perturbation-based method, are used to explain the misinformation spread (Research Challenge 2), which is predicted by the model ϕ (see Sect. 4.2).

4.1   Misinformation Spread Prediction Module

We have implemented an extended version of GraphSAGE [13] to solve the misinformation spread prediction in Research Challenge 1, which is to predict the spread values $\overline{y}_i$ of the misinformation node m_i, which approximates the corresponding ground truth y_i. GraphSAGE is a GNN for node representation learning by aggregating information from each node's neighborhood. For a homogeneous graph, a GraphSAGE layer updates the hidden representation for each node v based on the features of its neighbors $\mathcal{N}(v)$:

$$h_{\mathcal{N}(v)}^{(l+1)} = aggregate(\{h_u^l, \forall u \in \mathcal{N}(v)\}), \tag{2}$$

$$h_v^{(l+1)} = \sigma(W \cdot concat(h_v^l, h_{\mathcal{N}(v)}^{(l+1)})), \tag{3}$$

where l represents the l-th layer and W is the weight matrix. When $l = 0$, we have the $h_v^0 = x_v$, where $x_v \in X$ representing the features of v. The *aggregate* process in Eq. 2 determines how to combine the representations of v's neighbors and we use the LSTM (Long Short-Term Memory) [15] function as the *aggregate* function. Then the aggregated representation of $\mathcal{N}(v)$ and the representation of v are concatenated to generate a new representation for v (as shown in Eq. 3).

However, when the social network G used to predict the misinformation spread is heterogeneous, hence the different types of nodes and edges need to be taken into consideration. Each node is connected to its neighbor nodes by different types of edges and a heterogeneous graph convolution (HeteroGraphConv) provided by the Deep Graph Library [35] is used to initiate the GraphSAGE layer for each edge type $r \in R_E$. The different GraphSAGE layers in the same HeteroGraphConv module do not share the parameters and the HeteroGraphConv module passes the message from a source node to a target node based on the GraphSAGE layer given for the corresponding edge type. HeteroGraphConv updates the hidden representations for the nodes that are connected by the same type of edges and then a function *conv_agg* aggregates the representations for each node v that is connected by the different types of edges:

$$h_{\mathcal{N}_r(v)}^{(l+1)} = aggregate(\{h_u^l, \forall u \in \mathcal{N}_r(v)\}), \tag{4}$$

$$h_{v,r}^{(l+1)} = \sigma(W_r \cdot concat(h_v^l, h_{\mathcal{N}_r(v)}^{(l+1)})), \tag{5}$$

$$h_v^{(l+1)} = conv\_agg(\sum_{r \in R_E} h_{v,r}^{(l+1)}), \tag{6}$$

where Eq. 4 and 5 are the GraphSAGE layer for the the edge type $r \in R_E$ and $\mathcal{N}_r(v)$ represents the set of neighbors of node v with edge type r. We use a sum function as the *conv_agg* function in this work.

The entire prediction module is called HeteroGraphSAGE which outputs the prediction on the spread value, $\overline{y}_i = \phi(m_i, G), \overline{y}_i \in \overline{Y}$, for each misinformation node $m_i \in M$, with the MSE loss between $\overline{y}_i$ and y_i calculated as the feedback for the optimisation process. The prediction module is formally described in Algorithm 1.

Algorithm 1. HeteroGraphSAGE

Input: Social network G; Misinformation Nodes M; Spread Values Y
Output: The trained ϕ for predicting the spread values of M.
1: Initial ϕ;
2: **while** Training **do**
3:     **for** Each HeteroGraphConv layer in ϕ **do**
4:         **for** Each relation type in R_E **do**
5:             Initiate a GraphSAGE layer;
6:             Calculate the hidden representation for each node based on Eq. 4 and 5;
7:         **end for**
8:         Aggregate multiple relations to nodes by $conv\_agg$ (Eq. 6);
9:     **end for**
10:     Update weights in ϕ based on the loss between $\overline{Y}$ and Y.
11: **end while**

4.2 GNN-Based Explanation Module

With the prediction model ϕ trained, we propose a GNN-based explanation module that incorporates treating both node feature types R_X and edge types R_E together as the input to the model to identify the factors that contribute to the prediction on the spread of misinformation by the model. Gradient-based and perturbation-based methods are the two most common methods for explaining deep learning models. We extend these two methods to heterogeneous GNNs to explain the prediction model ϕ. Gradient-based methods use the gradients of the inputs in the deep learning model to measure the importance of the inputs, while perturbation-based methods perturb the inputs to measure the importance of the inputs. Both gradient-based and perturbation-based methods can output the importance values $Im_i \in [0, 1]$ that represents the contribution of the input feature or edge type $Input_i \in \{R_X \cup R_E\}$ to the model ϕ.

Gradient-Based Method. We use a widely used gradient-based attribution method, called Integrated Gradient (IG) [32], to help us understand which features are more important in making predictions. As we need to explain a heterogeneous graph model with different types of node features and edges, the IG method needs to be extended to compute the importance value of each node feature type and edge type. Given a trained model ϕ and the node feature set X, IG takes as input k different versions of the modified $\{\hat{X}_1, .., \hat{X}_k\}$ which only modified the node features values of the type that needs to be calculated. For each type of node feature, IG calculates the change in the output of the model as each feature $x^i \in X$ in the input is gradually changed. Then IG output the attribution score for each x^i by integrating the gradients of the model output with respect to x^i:

$$IG_i = (x^i - \hat{x}^i) \sum_{j=1}^{k} \left(\frac{\partial \phi(M, (A, \hat{X}_j + j/k(X - \hat{X}_j)))}{\partial x^i} \right) \tag{7}$$

where $\hat{X}_j + j/k(X - \hat{X}_j)$ is the combined modified node feature input and $\partial\phi(M, (A, \hat{X}_j + j/k(X - \hat{X}_j)))/\partial x^i$ is the gradient of output with respect to feature x^i, where M is the misinformation nodes set and A is the adjcency matrices set.

The explanation of edge types is based on a general principle of GraphSAGE, that training a model without edge weights is equivalent to training the model with all edge weights $w_e = 1, w_e \in W_e$ equal to 1, which is $\phi(M, (A, X, W_e))$. For each edge type, we first need to generate an edge weight vector w_e with values set to 1 for each type of edge and then use a similar equation to calculate the IG value for each edge type:

$$IG_e = (w_e - \hat{w}_e) \sum_{j=1}^{k} (\frac{\partial\phi(M, (A, X, \hat{w}_{ej} + j/k(w_e - \hat{w}_{ej}))}{\partial w_e})) \qquad (8)$$

Since the explanation of misinformation spread in our proposed pipeline needs to be meaningful, we integrate the IG_i and IG_e absolute values into Im_i which corresponds to $Input_i$. This is done by mapping the node features corresponding to IG_i to the node feature types R_X and the edges corresponding to IG_e to edge types R_E, using the mapping functions ζ and ψ respectively. After this integration, Im_i is normalized so that $\sum_{i=1}^{N}(Im_i) = 1$.

Perturbation-Based Method. We use a similar idea in GNNExplainer [37], to iteratively mask the node features and edges to identify the impact on the output of a GNN model. Given the trained ϕ, we use the node feature mask $Xm \in [0, 1]$ and edge mask $Am \in [0, 1]$ to perturb the node feature X and the set of adjacency matrix A, by $\hat{X} = X \odot Xm$ and $\hat{A} = A \odot Am$, where $\odot$ denotes element-wise multiplication. The intuition is that if a node feature or edge is not important to the model ϕ (with a low Im_i), even with a large perturbation (with small values in the masks), the model output $\hat{Y} = \phi(M, (\hat{A}, \hat{X})$ will not change much from the original output $\overline{Y} = \phi(M, (A, X))$. We want to obtain Xm and Am that can perturb the unimportant node feature or edge as much as possible that makes little change to the model output, then the elements in Xm and Am can indicate the importance of the node feature or edge types $Input_i$, based on the mapping functions ζ or ψ.

To generate an explanation module, the Xm and Am are trained by optimizing the following objective function:

$$\mathcal{L}_{all} = \mathcal{L}(\hat{Y}, \overline{Y}) + \alpha_1||Xm||_1 + \beta_1||Am||_1 + \alpha_2 H(Xm) + \beta_2 H(Am), \qquad (9)$$

where $\mathcal{L}(\hat{Y}, \overline{Y})$ is to calculate the MSE loss of output changing after perturbation, $||Xm||_1$ and $||Am||_1$ is to make as many elements in two masks change as possible, $H(\cdot)$ is the entropy function which can make the masks as stable as possible, and $\alpha_1, \alpha_2, \beta_1, \beta_2$ are hyper-parameters.

For each node feature type or edge type, the Im_i is integrated using Xm and Am, which is the same operation used in the gradient-based method for integrating IG_i and IG_e.

5   Experimental Results

This section shows the experimental results of predicting misinformation spread and exploring factors contributing to the spread using our proposed MisinfoExplainer on a misinformation-labeled social network dataset. We also perform the evaluation of the two proposed XAI methods described in the previous section on this dataset.

5.1   Dataset

We perform our experiments on a large-scale misinformation social network dataset, MuMiN [23], to quantitatively evaluate the proposed MisinfoExplainer. The MuMiN dataset is a public misinformation graph dataset with three different versions that contain multimodal information from Twitter. Specifically, MuMiN associates multitopic and multilingual tweets with fact-checked claims, and it also includes textual and visual content from tweets. We only keep the data that are fact-checked tweets discussing misinformation and filter out the tweets discussing factual claims. The statistics of the different node types R_V in the MuMiN dataset after filtering are shown in Table 1. The data we use contains 9 types of node features, denoted as 'n1' to 'n9' in Table 2, which consist of the node feature type set R_X and 12 different types of edges, denoted 'e1' to 'e12' shown in Fig. 1, which are the edge type set R_E. In our experiment, we predict the misinformation spread which is to predict the spread value $\overline{Y}$ of the *misinformation* type of nodes, and reveal the key factors that make misinformation spread which is to measure the importance values Im_i for each $Input_i \in \{R_X \cup R_E\}$.

Table 1. Three versions of the dataset. The 6 node types in R_V and the numbers of nodes in these node types are shown in the table. Misinformation is a type of nodes representing tweets that have been labelled as discussing a non-factual claim, a claim is a short description of the misinformation provided by a fact-checker and a reply is a tweet that replies to a tweet.

Dataset	Misinformation	Claim	User	Hashtag	Image	Reply
MuMiN-Small	3,589	2,049	140,113	25,472	986	163,113
MuMiN-Medium	9,326	5,318	290,199	49,575	2,397	356947
MuMiN-Large	22,835	12,509	564,789	85,501	6,309	754,097

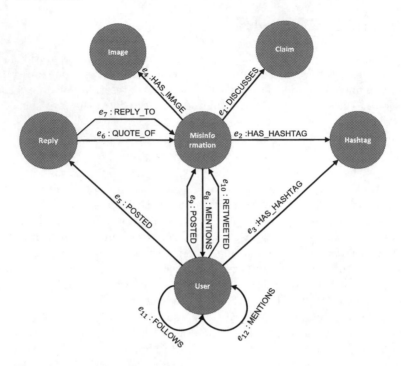

Fig. 1. The edge types R_E present in the data we use, denoted as e_1 to e_{12}. The figure shows a metagraph that consists of the nodes representing all 6 different node types in the dataset and all the edge types between them.

5.2 Prediction Module Evaluation

To comprehensively evaluate the performance of our prediction module, Hetero-GraphSAGE, we conducted a series of comparative experiments on the MuMiN dataset. These experiments allow us to assess the effectiveness and efficiency of HeteroGraphSAGE in comparison to other state-of-the-art methods, providing valuable insights into its capabilities for handling heterogeneous graph data.

Experiment Setup. This experimental evaluation aims to measure the effectiveness of HeteroGraphSAGE. We selected two GNNs that are commonly used in the field of social network analysis, Graph Convolutional Networks (GCN) and Graph Attention Networks (GAT), as the baseline methods. Since both GCN and GAT are designed for homogeneous graphs, we extended them to HeteroGCN and HeteroGAT, respectively, by applying HeteroGraphConv. The performance is evaluated in terms of Mean Absolute Percentage Error (MAPE), Mean Squared Error (MSE), and R-squared (R2).

The baseline methods and our proposed method are all based on 2-layer HeteroGraphConv and the dimension of each layer is set to 512. All parameters are trained using the AdmaW [19] optimizer with a learning rate $3e^{-4}$ and a dropout rate 0.2. For HeteroGAT, each layer contains 3 attention heads. We

Table 2. The node feature types R_X and node types. (The claim_reviewer is the URL for the fact-checking website that reviewed the claim and the 'lang' is an abbreviation of 'language').

Input	Features Types	Associated Node Types
n1	misinformation_text	Misinformation
n2	misinformation_lang	Misinformation
n3	claim_embedding	Claim
n4	claim_reviewer	Claim
n5	image_embedding	Image
n6	hashtag_embedding	Hashtag
n7	user_profile	User
n8	reply_text	Reply
n9	reply_lang	Reply

used the pre-set train/valid/test splits provided by the MuMiN dataset, which claims that these pre-set splits can better cover distinct events [23] and thus better measure the ability of the model to generalise to unseen misinformation topics. The number of training epochs is set to 100.

Comparison Results. The results of the experiments are shown in Table 3. HeteroGraphSAGE has significant advantages for misinformation spread prediction tasks on all three versions MuMiN dataset. The quality of our proposed regression model was assessed using three metrics, with the best performance on MAPE and MSE indicating the accurate prediction of the misinformation spread values y_i, and the best performance on R2 showing the good fit of the data.

Table 3. Performance of the prediction module based on different GNN models. For the MSE and MAPE evaluation metrics, a smaller value indicates better performance, whereas, for R2, a larger value indicates better performance.

Data	Model	MAPE	MSE	R2
MuMiN-Small	HeteroGCN	0.1752	0.5412	0.7684
	HeteroGAT	0.1660	0.5558	0.7622
	HeteroGraphSAGE	**0.1511**	**0.4214**	**0.8197**
MuMiN-Medium	HeteroGCN	0.1351	0.3213	0.8241
	HeteroGAT	0.1436	0.4000	0.7810
	HeteroGraphSAGE	**0.1239**	**0.3091**	**0.8308**
MuMiN-Large	HeteroGCN	0.1321	0.2692	0.8372
	HeteroGAT	0.1308	0.2792	0.8312
	HeteroGraphSAGE	**0.1134**	**0.2091**	**0.8735**

5.3   What Factors Make Misinformation Spread?

We then trained the HeteroGraphSAGE on the MuMiN-small dataset to obtain the trained model ϕ and then explained ϕ by using our gradient-based and perturbation-based XAI methods respectively. We considered the 9 types of node features and 12 types of edges as shown in Table 2 and Fig. 1 as the *Inputs* which are the factors we aim to measure the *Im*.

Experiment Setup. The HeteroGraphSAGE was trained with the same settings as in the previous experiments in Subsect. 5.2. For the gradient-based method, the number of modified inputs k is set to 50. For the perturbation-based method, the number of training epochs is set to 100, the learning rate is set to 0.1. The purpose of hyper-parameters in Eq. 9 is to make the terms of the loss function balance during optimizing, and we set α_1, α_2, β_1 and β_2 to 0.05, 1.0, 1.0 and 0.1.

Experiment Results and Qualitative Analysis. The explanation results using perturbation-based and gradient-based methods are shown in Fig. 2. Both methods consider the text of the misinformation ($n1$: *misinformation_text*) to be the most important factor in the spread of misinformation, which is also corroborated by marketing research, for example [3], which claims the message content itself can contribute to the virality.

The perturbation-based explanation considers that the four important factors after the text of the tweet are the text of reply ($n8$: *reply_text*), the embedding of the claim ($n3$: *claim_embedding*), the embedding of image ($n5$: *image_embedding*) and the users description ($n7$: *user_profile*). The reply text can include other users' opinions, stimulating engagement, which can amplify the original tweet and then contribute to spreading further, engaging more users. The claim is a short description of the misinformation, which can be seen as a summary of the misinformation. The explanation considers that images can help the spread of related misinformation, where a similar conclusion is also found in marketing research [18] that high-quality images can lead to engagement with related Tweets.

The gradient-based explanation considers four different types of edges as important factors for spreading misinformation: a user follows another user ($e11$: User *follows* User), a user retweeted misinformation ($e10$: User *retweeted* Misinformation), a user has a hashtag ($e3$: User *has_hashtag* Hashtag), and a misinformation tweet has a hashtag ($e2$: Misinformation *has_hashtag* Hashtag). In contrast to the perturbation-based approach, the gradient-based approach gives a less plausible explanation. The following relationship and retweeting interactions are utilized in many studies [1,27] about information diffusion, but it is difficult to explain intuitively how the hashtag relationship contributes to the spread of misinformation.

In summary, the perturbation-based method considers node features to be more important, while the gradient-based method considers edges to be more

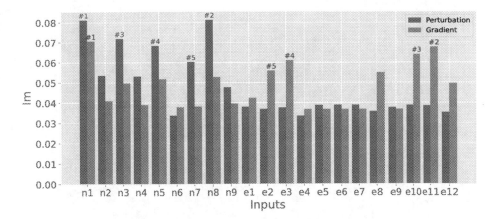

Fig. 2. *Im* values calculated by two different explanation methods. The top five *Inputs* which are considered as important in each method are marked.

important. In the following subsection, we compare the two explanation methods quantitatively to see which one is more plausible.

5.4 Which Explanation Shall We Believe?

While visualizations can provide insights regarding whether the explanations are reasonable to humans, such evaluations are not entirely trustworthy due to the lack of ground truth. In this subsection, we calculate the fidelity which can quantitatively measure the explanation methods.

The *Fidelity*$^+$ metric was originally proposed in [26,38] based on the intuition that if the important factors identified by explanation methods are discriminative to the model, the predictions should change significantly when these features are removed. In this study, we extend *Fidelity*$^+$ to be defined as the difference between the original predictions $\phi(M, G)$ and the new predictions $\phi(M, G^{1-\sum_{i=1}^{N} Input_i})$ after masking out N important *Inputs*, as follows:

$$Fidelity^+ = \frac{1}{N}(\phi(M, G) - \phi(M, G^{1-\sum_{i=1}^{N} Input_i})), \tag{10}$$

where i is the ith most important *Input* indicated by the explainer, N is the number of *Inputs* to be removed and $G^{1-\sum_{i=1}^{N} Input_i}$ indicates the graph removed N most important *Inputs*. For *Fidelity*$^+$, higher values indicate better explanations, and more discriminative *Inputs* are identified.

In contrast, the *Fidelity*$^-$ [26,38] was proposed to study prediction change by keeping important input features and removing unimportant features. The *Fidelity*$^-$ is defined as the difference between the original predictions $\phi(M, G)$ and the new predictions $\phi(M, G^{\sum_{i=1}^{N} Input_i})$ where G only contains the important *Inputs*:

$$Fidelity^- = \frac{1}{N}(\phi(M, G) - \phi(M, G^{\sum_{i=1}^{N} Input_i})) \tag{11}$$

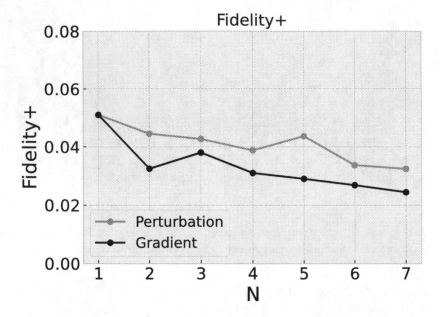

Fig. 3. *Fidelity*$^{+}$. The higher values indicate better explanations.

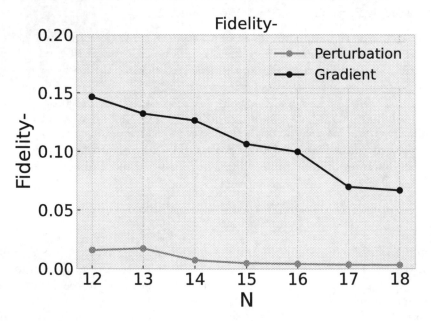

Fig. 4. *Fidelity*$^{-}$. The lower values mean the explanations are better.

For *Fidelity*$^{-}$, lower values indicate less important *Inputs* are removed so that the explanations results are better.

For the measurement of $Fidelity^+$, we conducted experiments by removing the top 1 to top 7 most important *Inputs*, with N ranging from 1 to 7. However, for the $Fidelity^-$ measurement, it was challenging to keep only a few *Inputs* and still construct a graph. Therefore, we set N from 12 to 18 for this measurement. The results are shown in Fig. 3 and Fig. 4. We can observe that the perturbation-based approach works better, which supports the previous intuitive observation in Subsect. 5.3.

6 Conclusion and Future Works

In this paper, we proposed a novel XAI pipeline, called MisinfoExplainer, to explore the factors contributing to misinformation spread on social networks. The proposed MisinfoExplainer made use of the heterogenous convolutional GraphSAGE (HeteroGraphSAGE) to predict the misinformation spread with the trained model explained by XAI methods. We provided two XAI methods for explaining the trained model: a gradient-based method that exploits the gradients of the input in the model, and a perturbation-based method that perturbs the input of the model to obtain explanations. The experimental results showed that our proposed pipeline can obtain an accurate model for misinformation spread prediction, and that HeteroGraphSAGE is superior to other methods on a large-scale misinformation-labelled social network dataset. We obtained the factors that contribute to misinformation spread by explaining the prediction model using the two proposed XAI methods. Through qualitative analysis and quantitative measurement, we concluded that the perturbation-based method provides better explanations than the gradient-based method.

Limitations and Future Work. All experiments in this study are conducted under the assumption that the dataset has classified certain tweets as misinformation. Our XAI method is constrained by the model of misinformation spread, which incorporates the use of spread indicators, such as the number of retweets. In future work, we aim to develop more precise models of misinformation spread and explore advanced XAI techniques to provide comprehensive explanations for the spread process. Nonetheless, we firmly believe that the current research approach in this study, which involves modeling the spread and utilizing XAI to investigate the factors contributing to its occurrence, is a valid and valuable research direction.

References

1. Amati, G., Angelini, S., Capri, F., Gambosi, G., Rossi, G., Vocca, P.: Twitter temporal evolution analysis: comparing event and topic driven retweet graphs. IADIS Int. J. Comput. Sci. Inf. Syst. **11**(2), 155–162 (2016)
2. Arrieta, A.B., et al.: Explainable artificial intelligence (XAI): concepts, taxonomies, opportunities and challenges toward responsible AI. Inf. Fusion **58**, 82–115 (2020)
3. Berger, J., Milkman, K.L.: What makes online content viral? J. Mark. Res. **49**(2), 192–205 (2012)

4. Bian, T., et al.: Rumor detection on social media with bi-directional graph convolutional networks. In: Proceedings of the AAAI Conference on Artificial Intelligence. vol. 34, pp. 549–556 (2020)
5. Bo, H., McConville, R., Hong, J., Liu, W.: Social network influence ranking via embedding network interactions for user recommendation. In: Companion Proceedings of the Web Conference 2020, pp. 379–384 (2020)
6. Bo, H., McConville, R., Hong, J., Liu, W.: Social influence prediction with train and test time augmentation for graph neural networks. In: 2021 International Joint Conference on Neural Networks (IJCNN), pp. 1–8. IEEE (2021)
7. Bo, H., McConville, R., Hong, J., Liu, W.: Ego-graph replay based continual learning for misinformation engagement prediction. In: 2022 International Joint Conference on Neural Networks (IJCNN), pp. 01–08. IEEE (2022)
8. Cao, Q., Shen, H., Gao, J., Wei, B., Cheng, X.: Popularity prediction on social platforms with coupled graph neural networks. In: Proceedings of the 13th International Conference on Web Search and Data Mining, pp. 70–78 (2020)
9. Chen, T., Li, X., Yin, H., Zhang, J.: Call attention to rumors: deep attention based recurrent neural networks for early rumor detection. In: Ganji, M., Rashidi, L., Fung, B.C.M., Wang, C. (eds.) PAKDD 2018. LNCS (LNAI), vol. 11154, pp. 40–52. Springer, Cham (2018). https://doi.org/10.1007/978-3-030-04503-6_4
10. Chen, X., Zhang, F., Zhou, F., Bonsangue, M.: Multi-scale graph capsule with influence attention for information cascades prediction. Int. J. Intell. Syst. **37**(3), 2584–2611 (2022)
11. Chen, X., Zhou, F., Zhang, K., Trajcevski, G., Zhong, T., Zhang, F.: Information diffusion prediction via recurrent cascades convolution. In: 2019 IEEE 35th International Conference on Data Engineering (ICDE), pp. 770–781 (2019). https://doi.org/10.1109/ICDE.2019.00074
12. Došilović, F.K., Brčić, M., Hlupić, N.: Explainable artificial intelligence: a survey. In: 2018 41st International Convention on Information and Communication Technology, Electronics and Microelectronics (MIPRO), pp. 0210–0215. IEEE (2018)
13. Hamilton, W., Ying, Z., Leskovec, J.: Inductive representation learning on large graphs. In: Advances in Neural Information Processing Systems, vol. 30 (2017)
14. Hamilton, W.L.: Graph representation learning. Synth. Lect. Artif. Intell. Mach. Learn. **14**(3), 1–159 (2020)
15. Hochreiter, S., Schmidhuber, J.: Long short-term memory. Neural Comput. **9**(8), 1735–1780 (1997)
16. Huang, Q., Yamada, M., Tian, Y., Singh, D., Chang, Y.: Graphlime: local interpretable model explanations for graph neural networks. IEEE Trans. Knowl. Data Eng. **35**, 6968–6972 (2022)
17. Kumar, S., Asthana, R., Upadhyay, S., Upreti, N., Akbar, M.: Fake news detection using deep learning models: a novel approach. Trans. Emerg. Telecommun. Technol. **31**(2), e3767 (2020)
18. Li, Y., Xie, Y.: Is a picture worth a thousand words? an empirical study of image content and social media engagement. J. Mark. Res. **57**(1), 1–19 (2020)
19. Loshchilov, I., Hutter, F.: Decoupled weight decay regularization. arXiv preprint arXiv:1711.05101 (2017)
20. Ma, H., McAreavey, K., McConville, R., Liu, W.: Explainable AI for non-experts: energy tariff forecasting. In: 2022 27th International Conference on Automation and Computing (ICAC), pp. 1–6. IEEE (2022)
21. Monti, F., Frasca, F., Eynard, D., Mannion, D., Bronstein, M.M.: Fake news detection on social media using geometric deep learning. arXiv preprint arXiv:1902.06673 (2019)

22. Nekovee, M., Moreno, Y., Bianconi, G., Marsili, M.: Theory of rumour spreading in complex social networks. Phys. A **374**(1), 457–470 (2007)
23. Nielsen, D.S., McConville, R.: Mumin: a large-scale multilingual multimodal fact-checked misinformation social network dataset. In: Proceedings of the 45th International ACM SIGIR Conference on Research and Development in Information Retrieval, pp. 3141–3153 (2022)
24. Pennycook, G., Rand, D.G.: The psychology of fake news. Trends Cogn. Sci. **25**(5), 388–402 (2021)
25. Perotti, A., Bajardi, P., Bonchi, F., Panisson, A.: Graphshap: motif-based explanations for black-box graph classifiers. arXiv preprint arXiv:2202.08815 (2022)
26. Pope, P.E., Kolouri, S., Rostami, M., Martin, C.E., Hoffmann, H.: Explainability methods for graph convolutional neural networks. In: Proceedings of the IEEE/CVF Conference on Computer Vision and Pattern Recognition, pp. 10772–10781 (2019)
27. Qiu, J., Tang, J., Ma, H., Dong, Y., Wang, K., Tang, J.: Deepinf: social influence prediction with deep learning. In: Proceedings of the 24th ACM SIGKDD International Conference on Knowledge Discovery & Data Mining, pp. 2110–2119 (2018)
28. Schlichtkrull, M.S., De Cao, N., Titov, I.: Interpreting graph neural networks for NLP with differentiable edge masking. arXiv preprint arXiv:2010.00577 (2020)
29. Shi, Y., McAreavey, K., Liu, W.: Evaluating contrastive explanations for AI planning with non-experts: a smart home battery scenario. In: 2022 27th International Conference on Automation and Computing (ICAC), pp. 1–6. IEEE (2022)
30. Shi, Z., Cartlidge, J.: State dependent parallel neural Hawkes process for limit order book event stream prediction and simulation. In: Proceedings of the 28th ACM SIGKDD Conference on Knowledge Discovery and Data Mining, pp. 1607–1615 (2022)
31. Shu, K., Cui, L., Wang, S., Lee, D., Liu, H.: defend: explainable fake news detection. In: Proceedings of the 25th ACM SIGKDD International Conference on Knowledge Discovery & Data Mining, pp. 395–405 (2019)
32. Sundararajan, M., Taly, A., Yan, Q.: Axiomatic attribution for deep networks. In: International Conference on Machine Learning, pp. 3319–3328. PMLR (2017)
33. Vosoughi, S., Roy, D., Aral, S.: The spread of true and false news online. Science **359**(6380), 1146–1151 (2018)
34. Vu, M., Thai, M.T.: PGM-explainer: probabilistic graphical model explanations for graph neural networks. Adv. Neural. Inf. Process. Syst. **33**, 12225–12235 (2020)
35. Wang, M., et al.: Deep graph library: a graph-centric, highly-performant package for graph neural networks. arXiv preprint arXiv:1909.01315 (2019)
36. Yang, X., Burghardt, T., Mirmehdi, M.: Dynamic curriculum learning for great ape detection in the wild. Int. J. Comput. Vis. **131**, 1–19 (2023)
37. Ying, Z., Bourgeois, D., You, J., Zitnik, M., Leskovec, J.: GNNExplainer: generating explanations for graph neural networks. In: Advances in Neural Information Processing Systems, vol. 32 (2019)
38. Yuan, H., Yu, H., Gui, S., Ji, S.: Explainability in graph neural networks: a taxonomic survey. IEEE Trans. Pattern Anal. Mach. Intell. **45**(5), 5782–5799 (2022)
39. Zuo, W., Raman, A., Mondragón, R.J., Tyson, G.: Set in stone: analysis of an immutable web3 social media platform. In: Proceedings of the ACM Web Conference 2023, pp. 1865–1874 (2023)

MEGAN: Multi-explanation Graph Attention Network

Jonas Teufel[ID], Luca Torresi[ID], Patrick Reiser[ID], and Pascal Friederich[(✉)][ID]

Institute of Theoretical Informatics (ITI), Karlsruhe Institute of Technology (KIT),
Karlsruhe, Germany
jonas.teufel@student.kit.edu,
{luca.torresi,patrick.reiser,pascal.friederich}@kit.edu

Abstract. We propose a multi-explanation graph attention network (MEGAN). Unlike existing graph explainability methods, our network can produce node and edge attributional explanations along multiple channels, the number of which is independent of task specifications. This proves crucial to improve the interpretability of graph regression predictions, as explanations can be split into positive and negative evidence w.r.t a reference value. Additionally, our attention-based network is fully differentiable and explanations can actively be trained in an explanation-supervised manner. We first validate our model on a synthetic graph regression dataset with known ground-truth explanations. Our network outperforms existing baseline explainability methods for the single- as well as the multi-explanation case, achieving near-perfect explanation accuracy during explanation supervision. Finally, we demonstrate our model's capabilities on multiple real-world datasets. We find that our model produces sparse high-fidelity explanations consistent with human intuition about those tasks.

Keywords: Graph Neural Network · Self-Explaining Model · Explanation Supervision

1 Introduction

Explainable AI (XAI) methods aim to provide explanations complementing a model's predictions to make it's complex inner workings more transparent to humans with the intention to improve trust and reliability, provide tools for model analysis, and comply with anti-discrimination laws [8]. The majority of existing work on graph explainability focuses on post-hoc methods, which can be used to generate explanations for already trained models, which have been proven to perform well. While post-hoc methods are an important area of development to add explainability to time-tested models, we want to emphasize the potential of *self-explaining* methods. In their literature review, Jiminez-Luna *et al.* [17] describe these methods as being explainable by design. One example of this class are the simpler, traditional machine learning approaches that are

ⓒ The Author(s), under exclusive license to Springer Nature Switzerland AG 2023
L. Longo (Ed.): xAI 2023, CCIS 1902, pp. 338–360, 2023.
https://doi.org/10.1007/978-3-031-44067-0_18

naturally interpretable, such as decision tree methods [11]. However, we want to focus on self-explaining graph neural networks, which produce the attributional explanations for the nodes and edges of the input graph directly alongside each prediction. We emphasize this class of methods specifically due to their capability for explanation-supervised training. During explanation-supervised training, a model is additionally trained to produce explanations that are similar to a given set of reference explanations. Recently, there has been promising progress on the topic of explanation supervision in the domains of image processing [2,19,29] and natural language processing [10,28,37]. Previous work is able to improve model interpretability by training models to generate more human-like explanations and even improve main prediction performance by training models on human-generated image saliency maps. In the graph domain, however, there has been little work on explanation supervision [13,21] yet. Inspired by the successes recently demonstrated in other domains, we propose the self-explaining *multi-explanation graph attention network* (MEGAN) architecture. In this work, we demonstrate that our model shows significantly improved capability to learn explanations during explanation-supervised training, outperforming the baseline method [13] from the literature.

In addition to its properties w.r.t. explanation supervision, we design our network to output explanations along *multiple channels*, the number of which is independent of the main prediction task. Like the majority of existing GNN explainability methods, we focus on attributional explanations, which attribute a value of importance to each element of the input graph. For existing methods, the number of these attribution values is dictated by the details of the main prediction task. For single-value graph regression tasks for example a single value would be assigned to each node and edge. For our multi-explanation method, however, this number of attributions is a property of the network rather than restricted by task specifications.

We want to emphasize the importance of this property especially in regard to graph regression problems. For the prediction of a single regression value, existing methods only produce a single attribution for each node and edge. We argue that such explanations are insufficient for the interpretation of regression predictions. In reality, one often encounters structure-property explanations of opposing *polarity*. One practical example of this is the prediction of water solubility, where large non-polar carbon structures generally cause low solubility values and polar functional groups cause higher values. A single attributional explanation may highlight all the important motifs, but is not able to capture this crucial detail about their polarity. For this reason, we decouple the number of explanations from the task specification to be able to produce two explanations (negative and positive influence) for graph regression problems. We introduce an explanation co-training method which uses only the generated explanation masks to solve an approximation of the prediction problem to promote each explanation channel to behave according to their intended interpretation. In our experiments, we find that this explanation co-training is an effective method to guide the generation of the explanation channels to contribute faithfully to the prediction outcome according to pre-determined interpretations. We validate this finding on several real-world datasets, where our model produces explanations consistent with human intuition about those tasks. Beyond that, we apply our model to one real-world task of molecular property prediction without common human intuition and are able to support previously published hypotheses about structure-property relationships and propose several new potential explanatory motifs.

2 Related Work

GNN Explanation Methods. Yuan et al. [41] provide a taxonomic overview of XAI methods for graph neural networks. Some methods have been adapted from similar approaches in other domains, such as GradCAM [26], GraphLIME [16] and LRP [33]. Other methods were developed specifically for graph neural networks. Notable ones include GNNExplainer [40], PGExplainer [20], and Zorro [12]. Jiminez-Luna et al. [17] present another literature review about the applications of XAI in drug discovery. Henderson et al. [15] for example introduce regularization terms to improve GradCAM-generated explanations for chemical property prediction. Sanchez-Lenglin et al. [32] introduce new benchmark datasets for attributional graph explanations based on molecular graphs and compare several existing explanation methods.

Generally, most explanation methods aim to produce attributional explanations, which explain a prediction by assigning importance values to the nodes and edges of the input graph. However, there exists some criticism about this class of explanations [1,18], which is partially why recently different modalities of explanations have been explored for the graph domain as well. Magister et al. [22] for example propose GCExplainer, which can be used to generate *concept-based* explanations for graph neural networks in a post-hoc fashion. Shin et al. [34] for example propose PAGE, a method to generate *prototype-based* explanations. *Counterfactuals* are yet another popular explanation modality, for which Tan et al. [38] and Prado-Romero and Stilo [27] have recently proposed methods for graph neural networks.

Self-explaining Graph Neural Networks. In their literature review, Jiminez-Luna et al. [17] define *self-explaining* methods as those that are explainable by design. One large fraction of this category is represented by simpler traditional machine learning methods. Friederich et al. [11] for example use an interpretable decision tree approach to structure-property relationships for several real-world graph datasets. However, there is also recent progress for more complex self-explaining models such as graph neural networks. Dang and Wang [4] and Zhang et al. [43] independently introduce self-explaining graph neural networks for prototype-based explanations. Magister et al. [21] introduce a self-explaining network for concept-based explanations. Furthermore, Müller et al. [24] propose DT+GNN, an interesting method that combines the capabilities of GNNs with the inherent interpretability of decision trees.

Explanation Supervision. During explanation supervision, models are not only trained to perform a main prediction task through ground truth target labels but also to produce explanations that are similar to a given set of reference explanations. Most interestingly explanation supervision provides the possibility to train models to produce more human-like explanations. Beyond that, several works are able to show that the inclusion of human saliency maps has the potential to increase the task performance of the models [2,19]. In that context, Linseley *et al.* [19] for example show that human saliency maps improve the performance of an image classifier. Boyd et al. [2] demonstrate that human saliency annotations improve the performance of a deep fake detection model. In the domain of natural language processing, Pruthi *et al.* [28] use explanation-supervised models to substitute human participants in artificial simulatability studies to assess the quality of explanations. Fernandes *et al.* [10] even take this concept one step further and train an explainer to optimize this property of simulatability.

3   Multi-explanation Graph Attention Network

3.1   Task Description

We assume a directed graph $\mathcal{G} = (\mathcal{V}, \mathcal{E})$ is represented by a set of node indices $\mathcal{V} \subset \mathbb{N}^V$ and a set of edges $\mathcal{E} \subseteq \mathcal{V} \times \mathcal{V} \subset \mathbb{R}^E$, where a tuple $(i,j) \in \mathcal{E}$ denotes an edge from node i to node j. Every node i is associated with a vector of initial node features $\mathbf{h}_i^{(0)} \in \mathbb{R}^{N_0}$, combining into the initial node feature tensor $\mathbf{H}^{(0)} \in \mathbb{R}^{V \times N_0}$. Each edge is associated with a feature vector $\mathbf{u}_i \in \mathbb{R}^M$, combining into the edge feature tensor $\mathbf{U} \in \mathbb{R}^{E \times M}$.

We consider graph classification and regression problems, which means graphs are associated with a target vector $\mathbf{y} \in \mathbb{R}^C$ which is either a one-hot class encoding or continuous regression values. In addition, node and edge attributional explanations for graphs are considered. We define explanations as masks that assign $[0,1]$ values to each node and each edge, representing the importance of the corresponding graph element toward the outcome of the prediction. We generally assume that any prediction may be explained by K individual importance channels, where K is an independent hyperparameter. The node explanations are given as the *node importance* tensor $\mathbf{V}^{\text{im}} \in [0,1]^{V \times K}$ and the edge explanations are given as the *edge importance* tensor $\mathbf{E}^{\text{im}} \in [0,1]^{E \times K}$.

3.2   Architecture Overview

To solve the previously defined task we propose the following *multi-explanation graph attention network* (MEGAN) architecture, for which Fig. 1 provides a visual overview. The network consists of L attention layers, where the number of layers L and the hidden units of each layer are hyperparameters. Each of these layers consists of K individual, yet structurally identical GATv2 [3] attention heads, one for each of the K expected explanation channels. Assuming the

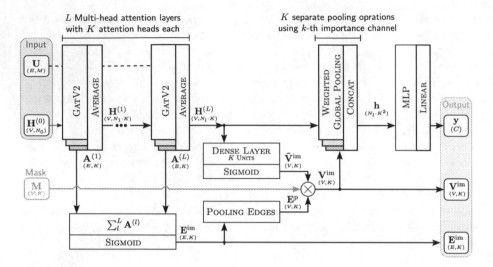

Fig. 1. Multi-explanation graph attention network (MEGAN) architecture overview. Rectangle boxes represent layers; arrows indicate layer interconnections. Rounded boxes represent tensors. Intermediate tensors are also named annotated arrows. Tuples beneath variable names indicate the tensor shape, with batch dimension omitted, but implicitly assumed as the first dimension for all.

attention heads in the l-th layer have N_l hidden units, then each attention head produces its own node embeddings $\mathbf{H}^{(l,k)}$, where $k \in \{1, \dots, K\}$ is the head index. The final node embeddings $\mathbf{H}^{(l)} \in \mathbb{R}^{V \times N_l \cdot K}$ of layer l are then produced by averaging all these individual matrices along the feature dimension:

$$\mathbf{H}^{(l)} = \frac{1}{K} \sum_{k}^{K} \mathbf{H}^{(l,k)} \tag{1}$$

This node embedding tensor is then used as the input to *each* of the K attention heads of layer $l + 1$. Aside from the node embeddings, each attention head also produces a vector $\mathbf{A}^{(l,k)} \in \mathbb{R}^E$ of attention logits which are used to calculate the attention weights

$$\boldsymbol{\alpha}^{(l,k)} = \mathrm{softmax}(\mathbf{A}^{(l,k)}) \tag{2}$$

of the k-the attention head in the l-th layer. The edge importance tensor $\mathbf{E}^{\mathrm{im}} \in [0,1]^{E \times K}$ is calculated from the concatenation of these attention logit tensors in the feature dimension and summed up over the number of layers:

$$\mathbf{E}^{\mathrm{im}} = \sigma \left(\sum_{l=1}^{L} \left(\mathbf{A}^{(l,1)} \,\|\, \mathbf{A}^{(l,2)} \,\|\, \dots \,\|\, \mathbf{A}^{(l,K)} \right) \right) \tag{3}$$

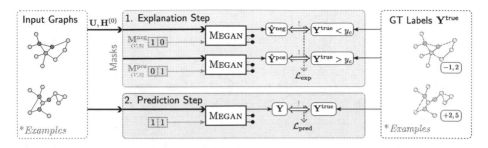

Fig. 2. Illustration of the split training procedure for the regression case. The explanation-only train step attempts to find an approximate solution to the main prediction task, by using only a globally pooled node importance tensor. After the weight update for the explanation step was applied to the model, the prediction step performs another weight update based on the actual output of the model and the ground truth labels.

Based on this, a local pooling operation is used to derive the pooled edge importance tensor $\mathbf{E}^\mathrm{P} \in [0,1]^{V \times K}$ for the *nodes* of the graph. This local pooling operation can be seen as the aggregation step in a message-passing framework, where the edge importance values are treated as the corresponding messages.

The final node embeddings $\mathbf{H}^{(L)}$ are then used as the input to a dense network, whose final layer is set to have K hidden units, producing the node importance embeddings $\tilde{\mathbf{V}}^\mathrm{im} \in [0,1]^{V \times K}$. The node importance tensor is then calculated as the product of those node importance embeddings $\tilde{\mathbf{V}}^\mathrm{im} \in [0,1]^{V \times K}$ and the pooled edge importance tensor $\mathbf{E}^\mathrm{P} \in [0,1]^{V \times K}$:

$$\mathbf{V}^\mathrm{im} = \tilde{\mathbf{V}}^\mathrm{im} \cdot \mathbf{E}^\mathrm{P} \cdot \mathbf{M}. \tag{4}$$

The mask $\mathbf{M}$ introduced in Fig. 1 is only optionally used to compute the fidelity metric, which is introduced in Sect. 3.4. At this point, the edge and node importance matrices, which represent the explanations generated by the network, are already accounted for, which leaves only the primary prediction to be explained. The first remaining step is a global sum pooling operation which turns the node embedding tensor $\mathbf{H}^{(L)}$ into a vector of global graph embeddings. For this, K separate weighted global sum pooling operations are performed, one for each explanation channel. Each of these pooling operations uses the same node embeddings $\mathbf{H}^{(L)}$ as input, but a different slice $V^\mathrm{im}_{:,k}$ of the node importance tensor as weights. In that way, K separate graph embedding vectors

$$\mathbf{h}^{(k)} = \sum_{i=0}^{V} \left(\mathbf{H}^{(L)} \cdot \mathbf{V}^\mathrm{im}_{:,k} \right)_{i,:} \tag{5}$$

are created, which are then concatenated into a single graph embedding vector

$$\mathbf{h} = \mathbf{h}^{(1)} \| \mathbf{h}^{(2)} \| \cdots \| \mathbf{h}^{(K)} \tag{6}$$

where $\mathbf{h} \in \mathbb{R}^{N_L \cdot K}$. This graph embedding vector is then passed through a generic MLP whose final layer either has linear activation for graph regression or softmax activation for graph classification to create an appropriate output

$$\mathbf{y} = \mathrm{MLP}(\mathbf{h}) \tag{7}$$

3.3   Explanation Co-training

With the architecture as explained up to this point, there is no mechanism yet to ensure that individual explanation channels learn the appropriate explanations according to their intended interpretation (for example positive vs negative evidence). We use a special explanation co-training procedure to guide the individual explanation channels to develop according to pre-determined interpretations. This is illustrated in Fig. 2. For this purpose, the loss function consists of two parts: The prediction loss and the explanation loss. The explanation loss is based only on the node importance tensor produced by the network. A global sum pooling operation is used to turn the importance values of each separate channel into a single *alternate output tensor* $\hat{\mathbf{Y}} \in \mathbb{R}^{B \times K}$, where B is the training batch size. This alternate output tensor is then used to solve an approximation of the original prediction problem: This can be seen as a reduction of the problem into a set of K separate and independent subgraph counting problems, where each of those only uses the subset of training batch samples that aligns with the respective channel's intended interpretation.

Regression. For regression, we assume $K = 2$, where the first channel represents the negative and the second channel the positive influences relative to the reference value y_c, which is a hyperparameter of the model and usually set as the arithmetic mean of the target value distribution in the train set. We select all samples of the current training batch lesser and greater than the reference value and use these to calculate a mean squared error (MSE) loss:

$$\mathcal{L}_{\exp} = \frac{1}{2 \cdot B} \sum_{b=1}^{B} \begin{cases} (\hat{\mathbf{Y}}_{b,0} - y_c - \mathbf{Y}_b^{\mathrm{true}})^2 & \text{if } \mathbf{Y}_b^{\mathrm{true}} < y_c \\ (\hat{\mathbf{Y}}_{b,1} - y_c - \mathbf{Y}_b^{\mathrm{true}})^2 & \text{if } \mathbf{Y}_b^{\mathrm{true}} > y_c \end{cases} \tag{8}$$

Classification. We assume the number of channels $K = C$ is equal to the number of possible output classes C. We use the alternate output channel to compute an individual binary cross entropy (BCE) loss for each channel:

$$\mathcal{L}_{\exp} = \frac{1}{C \cdot B} \sum_{b=1}^{B} \sum_{c=1}^{C} \mathcal{L}_{\mathrm{BCE}}(\mathbf{Y}_{b,c}^{\mathrm{true}}, \hat{\mathbf{Y}}_{b,c}) \tag{9}$$

For regression as well as classification, the total loss during model training consists of these task-specific terms and an additional term for explanation sparsity:

$$\mathcal{L}_{\mathrm{total}} = \mathcal{L}_{\mathrm{pred}} + \gamma \mathcal{L}_{\exp} + \beta \mathcal{L}_{\mathrm{sparsity}} \tag{10}$$

where γ and β are hyperparameters of the training process. Explanation sparsity $\mathcal{L}_{\text{sparsity}}$ is calculated as L1 regularization over the node importance tensor. Based on this loss the gradients are calculated and the model weights are updated.

We will henceforth use the notation MEGAN_γ^K to refer to specific model configurations with K explanation channels, γ explanation co-training weight and use the superscript $\text{MEGAN}^{(S)}$ to indicate when models where trained in an explanation-supervised fashion.

3.4   Multi-channel Fidelity

A particular challenge in the field of explainable AI is the question of how to properly assess the quality of explanations [8]. One commonly used metric is the *fidelity* of explanations w.r.t. the model predictions. It quantifies the extent to which the explanation is responsible for the corresponding prediction. Yuan *et al.* [41] define the Fidelity$^+$ metric as the deviation of the predicted model output if all the nodes and edges that are part of the explanation are removed from the input. The reasoning is that the higher this resulting output deviation, the more important the explanation must have been for the original prediction. This metric is usually computed by setting all the features of the corresponding nodes and edges of the input graph to zero. However, one issue with this approach is that zero might be an in-distribution value for the input features. Therefore, the masked input elements may have an effect on the model that is different than their intended removal.

To address this issue we introduce the multi-channel Fidelity* metric to assess the faithfulness of MEGAN's predictions. Since our network directly incorporates the explanations into the prediction process as weights of the final global pooling operation, we can directly manipulate these explanations to quantify their impact on the prediction. This can be done by providing an additional importance mask $\mathbf{M} \in [0,1]^{V \times K}$ during the prediction of the network (see Fig. 1). For each explanation channel k, we construct a mask $\mathbf{M}^k$ which only suppresses that channel from the final pooling operation. The model is then queried with that mask to produce the modified output $\hat{\mathbf{y}}^k$, which we use to calculate the deviation $\Delta^k = |\mathbf{y} - \hat{\mathbf{y}}_k|$ w.r.t. the original output. The fidelity is then calculated as:

$$\text{Fidelity}^* = \frac{1}{K} \sum_k^K \begin{cases} +\Delta^k & \text{if deviation as expected for channel } k \\ -\Delta^k & \text{if deviation } not \text{ as expected for channel } k \end{cases} \quad (11)$$

What kind of deviation counts as *expected* for a given channel k is defined by the interpretation that is assigned to that channel. In the case of regression, for example, we assign the interpretation of the first explanation channel to be the negatively influencing evidence and the second channel to be the positively influencing evidence. In that case, if all the negative evidence is omitted from the result, it would be expected that the output becomes more positive than the original prediction and vice versa. For classification on the other hand, if

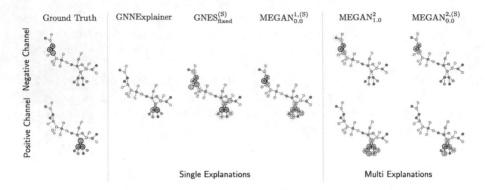

Fig. 3. Examples for explanations generated for one element of the RbMotifs dataset using selected methods. Explanations are represented as bold highlights of the corresponding graph elements. Left: The ground truth explanations split by the polarity of their influence on the graph target value. Middle: Explanations generated by some selected single-explanation methods. Right: Explanations generated by the multi-explanation MEGAN models.

all evidence for one specific class is suppressed it would be expected that the confidence of that respective class decreases.

Consequently, a positive Fidelity* indicates that the channels of the model generally have an effect on the prediction outcome that matches with their predefined interpretation.

4   Computational Experiments

We conduct computational experiments to demonstrate the capabilities of our network. Primarily, we emphasize two key strengths of our proposed model: (1) The inherent advantage of multi channel-explanations especially in regard to the interpretability of regression problems. On a specifically designed synthetic dataset we show that, unlike other post-hoc methods, by using explanation co-training our model is able to correctly capture the *polarity* of existing sub-graph evidence. (2) Our model's significantly increased capability for explanation-supervised training, where our model correctly learns to replicate the ground truth explanations that it was trained on. Additionally, we conduct experiments with real-world graph classification and regression datasets that provide anecdotal evidence for the correctness of the model's explanations for more complex tasks as well.

4.1   Synthetic Graph Regression

We create a synthetic graph regression dataset called *RbMotifs* consisting of 5000 randomly generated graphs, where each node is associated with 3 node features representing an RGB color code. Graphs are additionally randomly seeded with specific simple sub-graph motifs, which either consist dominantly of red nodes or blue nodes. If a red-based motif exists within a graph, it contributes a constant positive value to the overall target value of a graph. Likewise, a blue-based motif contributes a negative value. Thus, the overall target value associated with each graph is the sum of all the sub-graph contributions and a small random value. The dataset represents a simple motif-based graph regression problem, where the individual sub-graph motifs are considered the perfect ground truth explanations. Most importantly, the explanations have a clear *opposing polarity* which is crucial to the understanding of the dataset's underlying structure-property relationship.

Single Explanations. Although many regression tasks may exhibit such explanations of different polarity, existing post-hoc attributional XAI methods are only able to provide a single explanation. These single explanations are only able to point out which parts of the graph are generally important for the prediction but do not capture in what manner they contribute to the outcome. Therefore, to compare our proposed MEGAN model to some established existing post-hoc explanation methods, we conduct a first experiment that only considers such single explanations. For this case, we concatenate all of the relevant sub-graphs into a single channel which will be considered the ground truth explanation for each element of the dataset.

We conduct the experiment for explanations obtained from Gradients [26], GNNExplainer [40], GNES [13] and MEGAN. For all the post-hoc methods we train a 3-layer GATv2 network as the basis for the explanations. The results of this experiment can be found in Table 1. We report on the overall prediction performance of the network, the explanation accuracy, the sparsity, and the fidelity of the explanations. The explanation accuracy is given as the node and edge AUROC score resulting from a comparison with the ground truth explanations, as it is proposed by McCloskey *et al.* [23]. The fidelity is given as the relative value $\text{Fidelity}_{\text{rel}}^{+}$, which is the difference between the predicted explanation's fidelity and the fidelity of random explanations of the same sparsity (see Appendix A). In addition, we perform experiments with explanation supervision. To our knowledge, MEGAN and GNES are currently the only methods capable of explanation supervision for node and edge attributional explanations. For both of these cases, the models are trained with ground truth explanations in addition to the target values.

The results show that the explanations generated by all the methods achieve reasonable results for predictive performance, the node accuracy w.r.t. the explanation ground truth, as well as sparsity and fidelity. The explanation supervised methods show the best results for explanation accuracy. The supervised $\text{MEGAN}_{0.0}^{1,(S)}$ model achieves a near-perfect accuracy, with the explanation-supervised GNES method being second-best.

The differences in prediction performance between the baseline methods and MEGAN models can be explained by the slightly different model architectures. However, one particularly interesting result is the small but significant perfor-

Table 1. Results for 25 independent repetitions of the computational experiments on the RbMotifs dataset. We report the mean in black and the standard deviation in gray. The upper section contains results for the single-explanation experiments and the lower section for multi-explanation experiments. We highlight the best results in each section in bold and underline the second-best.

Explanations	r^2 ↑	Node AUC ↑	Edge AUC ↑	Sparsity ↓	Fidelity$_{\mathrm{ref}}^{+}$ ↑
Gradients	0.89±0.05	0.73±0.05	0.60±0.03	0.12±0.01	0.57±0.14
GnnExplainer	0.89±0.05	0.70±0.04	0.52±0.03	0.22±0.06	<u>0.78±0.20</u>
$\mathrm{GNES}_{\mathrm{original}}^{(S)}$	0.88±0.02	0.63±0.04	0.58±0.03	0.10±0.01	0.50±0.22
$\mathrm{GNES}_{\mathrm{fixed}}^{(S)}$	0.88±0.02	<u>0.85±0.04</u>	0.66±0.02	0.12±0.01	0.74±0.13
$\mathrm{MEGAN}_{0.0}^{1}$	<u>0.92±0.05</u>	0.82±0.12	<u>0.79±0.08</u>	0.14±0.08	**1.10±0.03**
$\mathrm{MEGAN}_{0.0}^{1,(S)}$	**0.95±0.02**	**0.98±0.00**	**0.99±0.00**	0.18±0.00	0.53±0.17
$\mathrm{MEGAN}_{1.0}^{2}$	<u>0.95±0.01</u>	<u>0.94±0.02</u>	<u>0.85±0.06</u>	0.10±0.06	<u>2.06$^{(*)}$±0.65</u>
$\mathrm{MEGAN}_{0.0}^{2,(S)}$	**0.95±0.03**	**0.99±0.00**	**0.99±0.00**	0.09±0.06	**2.11$^{(*)}$±0.36**

(S) Explanation-supervised models. These models were trained on the ground truth explanation annotations in addition to the main target values.

(*) Values of the multi-channel Fidelity* metric. Note that these are *not* comparable to the other fidelity values obtained in a single channel setting.

mance difference between $\mathrm{MEGAN}_{0.0}^{1}$ and the supervised $\mathrm{MEGAN}_{0.0}^{1,(S)}$ version. In both cases, the same model architecture and hyperparameters are used, the only difference being that the latter additionally receives the explanatory information during training. This indicates that the explanations provide the model with some additional level of information about the task, which is useful for the main prediction task as well.

Aside from the numerical results, Fig. 3 illustrates one example for these explanations. It shows that the single-explanation methods are able to capture the ground truth explanations to various degrees of success. However, in the presence of motifs with opposing influence, we often observe the issue that single-explanation methods focus on only one of these motifs and fail to highlight the other. An example of this can be seen with the explanation generated by GNNExplainer in Fig. 3, where it only highlights the positive explanation as being important. Although this is not always the case, we believe this effect contributes to the lower explanation accuracy results of these methods. Explanation-supervised training can be used to effectively counter this property, as is evident from the examples and the numerical results. However, even if all the explanatory motifs are correctly highlighted, we argue that single-explanations still don't provide the crucial information about *how* each motif contributes to the prediction outcome, as the polarity information cannot be retrieved from a single channel.

Multi-explanations. To demonstrate the advantages of multi-channel explanations, we conduct an experiment with the RbMotifs dataset, where the ground truth explanatory motifs of each graph are separated into two channels according to their influence on the target values. All blue-based motifs with a negative influence are sorted into one channel and all red-based motifs with positive influence are sorted into another.

We train two models to solve the prediction task: A two-channel $MEGAN^2_{1.0}$ model, which uses explanation co-training to promote the generation of explanations according to the previously introduced explanations and a $MEGAN^{2,(S)}_{0.0}$ which is explanation-supervised with the ground truth explanations instead. The results can be found in the lower section of Table 1.

Both models achieve nearly equal predictive performance, explanation sparsity, and Fidelity*. The explanation-supervised model achieves near-perfect explanation accuracy for nodes and edges. However, the explanation co-training model also achieves a very good explanation accuracy. The right-hand side of Fig. 3 shows an example of these results. As can be seen, both versions of the model are able to correctly capture the ground truth explanatory motifs according to their respective influence on the target value. The highly positive Fidelity* results in both cases prove that both of the model's channels actually contribute to the prediction outcome according to their assigned interpretations of negative and positive influence. The results of this experiment present solid evidence that our proposed explanation co-training is an effective method to accurately capture the polarity of ground truth explanations even in the absence of ground truth explanations during training.

4.2   Real World Datasets

MovieReviews - Sentiment Classification. The *MovieReviews* dataset is originally a natural language processing dataset from the ERASER benchmark [7] consisting of 2000 movie reviews from the IMDB database. The general sentiment of each review is labeled as either "positive" or "negative", where both classes are represented equally. Since this is a text classification dataset in its original form, we first process it in a manner similar to Rathee *et al.* [30]. First, the raw strings are converted into token lists, where tokens are either words or other sentence elements such as punctuation. Each token is converted into a 50-dimensional feature vector through a pre-trained GLOVE model [25]. We finally convert the token list into a graph by applying a sliding window method, where each token is considered to be a node and connected to its four closest neighbors through an undirected edge.

We train a three-layer $MEGAN^2_{1.0}$ model to solve the binary sentiment classification task for each graph using the classification version of the explanation co-training procedure. The explanation co-training procedure promotes the first explanation channel of the network to contain evidence for the "negative" class label and the second channel for the "positive" class label.

In terms of classification performance our model achieves similar results (F1 ≈ 0.85) as previously reported by Rathee *et al.* [30], who also use GNN and GLOVE embeddings. However, these results are significantly worse than results obtained with state-of-the-art NLP models, as they are for example reported by DeYoung *et al.* [7] (F1 ≈ 0.92). We believe the main reason for this difference

Table 2. Example explanations generated for both sentiment classes for a review about the movie "Avengers Endgame". Larger importance values are represented by stronger color highlights.

Negative	Positive
overall avengers endgame was a remarkable movie and a worthy culmination of the mcu up to this point there were some genuinely heartbreaking moments and breathtaking action sequences but to be honest some of the movies i had to sit through to get here were not worth it some of the early mcu movies and series leading up to this finale i found rather bland unfunny and sometimes just downright bad but this movie was one of the best movies i have seen in a while	overall avengers endgame was a remarkable movie and a worthy culmination of the mcu up to this point there were some genuinely heartbreaking moments and breathtaking action sequences but to be honest some of the movies i had to sit through to get here were not worth it some of the early mcu movies and series leading up to this finale i found rather bland unfunny and sometimes just downright bad but this movie was one of the best movies i have seen in a while

to be the use of the token embeddings derived from the 2014 GLOVE model. In the future, it would be interesting to see if GNNs could achieve competitive performance by using a state-of-the-art encoder such as BERT [6].

In regard to the generated explanations, Table 2 shows one example of a movie review. As can be seen, the model correctly learns negative adjectives such as "bad" as evidence for the "negative" class and positive adjectives such as "breathtaking" and "best" as evidence for the "positive" class. Despite this encouraging result, we still find there to be some errors in regard to the model's explanations about sentiment classification. On the one hand, the model also highlights unrelated words as explanations as well, such as "criminal" showing up as an explanation for negative reviews and "director" as positive evidence. On the other hand, the model is also not capable of accurately identifying negations and sarcasm to cause an inversion of sentiment.

AqSolDB - Molecular Regression. The *AqSolDB* [35] dataset consists of roughly 10000 molecular graphs which are annotated with experimentally determined values of their water solubility. In chemistry, there exists some general intuition about what kinds of molecular structures are responsible for higher solubility values and which are responsible for lower ones. In a simplified manner, one can say that non-polar substructures such as carbon rings and long carbon chains generally result in lower solubility values, while polar structures such as certain nitrogen and oxygen functional groups are associated with higher values.

In this experiment, we train a dual-channel three-layer $\text{MEGAN}^2_{1.0}$ model to predict the continuous solubility values for the molecular graphs. We make use of the previously described regression version of the co-training procedure, which promotes the first channel to highlight negatively influencing motifs and the

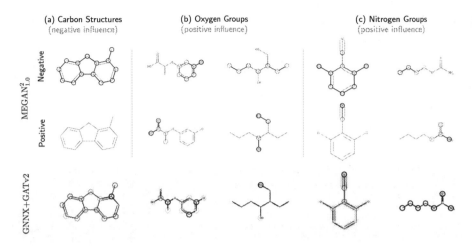

Fig. 4. Example explanations generated by MEGAN and GNNExplainer for the prediction of water solubility. Explanations are represented as bold highlights of the corresponding graph elements. Explanations are represented as bold highlights of the corresponding graph elements. (a) Examples of molecules dominated by large carbon structures which are known as negative influences on water solubility. (b) Examples of molecules containing oxygen functional groups which are known to be a positive influence on water solubility. (c) Examples of molecules containing nitrogen groups which are also known as positive influences.

second channel to highlight positively influencing motifs. Additionally, we train a comparable GATv2 model on the solubility dataset as well and use GNNExplainer to produce single explanations as a comparison.

Both the MEGAN model and the GATv2 model are able to match the predictive performance which was previously reported in the literature by Sorkunen *et al.* [36]. Both approaches also generate explanations with low sparsity and high fidelity values, as it can be seen in Table 3. Figure 4 illustrates some example explanations generated by MEGAN and GNNExplainer. The examples show that the explanations generated by MEGAN match the general human intuition about the structure-property relationships of water solubility. Large carbon structures are consistently highlighted in the negative explanation channel. The positive explanation channel on the other hand mostly contains polar nitrogen and oxygen functional groups. The explanations generated by GNNExplainer on the basis of the GATv2 model, however, do not show any such discernible pattern.

Despite an equally high predictive performance and high explanation fidelity, we argue that the single-explanation case contributes significantly less useful information for a human understanding of the predictions. We think this example reinforces the importance of the multi-explanation approach, especially for graph regression problems. By considering the polarity of structure-property explanations in graph regression problems, the MEGAN model is able to provide explanations that are more consistent with human intuition and are thus more interpretable.

Table 3. Results for 5 independent repetitions of the experiments with the AqSolDB dataset for water solubility. We report the mean in black and the standard deviation in gray.

Model	R^2 ↑	Sparsity ↓	Fidelity[(*)] ↑
GNNX+GATv2	0.93±0.01	0.34±0.27	1.26±0.90
MEGAN$^2_{1.0}$	0.93±0.01	0.22±0.14	2.50[(*)]±2.29
Consensus Model[†]	0.93	-	-

[†] Previously published results by Sorkun *et al.* [35].

[(*)] Multi-explanation case measures Fidelity* metric

TADF - Molecular Regression.

TADF - Molecular Regression. Previous experiments were able to provide exemplary evidence for the correctness of MEGAN's explanations through real-world datasets for which human intuition exists. In this final experiment, we choose a dataset where almost no human intuition exists to investigate potential applications to reveal novel insights about structure-property relationships. The *TADF* dataset consists of roughly half a million molecular graphs. Target value annotations were during a high-throughput virtual screening experiment conducted by Gómez-Bombarelli *et al.* [14] with the objective to discover novel materials for an application in OLED technology. Specifically, the authors aimed to discover materials that show a specific characteristic of thermally delayed fluorescence (TADF). This class of materials is a promising approach to avoid the high cost of typically used phosphorescent OLED materials [9,42]. Along the delayed fluorescent rate constant k_{TADF}, the elements of the dataset are annotated with the singlet-triplet energy gap ΔE_{st} and the oscillator strength f.

In this experiment, we train a three-layer MEGAN$^2_{1.0}$ model to estimate the singlet-triplet gap ΔE_{st} for each element. As before, the explanation co-training promotes the first channel to contain the negative influences and the second channel to contain the positive influences.

Our model achieves overall good predictivity ($R^2 \approx 0.90$) for the main prediction task and a positive Fidelity* value validating that the individual channels indeed affect the model prediction according to their pre-determined interpretations. Figure 5 illustrates some example explanations obtained from the model. Most importantly, we show that our model is able to replicate one of the few known structure-property relationships about the singlet-triplet energy. Triphenylamine bridges are known to be associated with low energy gaps, as they cause the necessary twist angles between the fragments, decoupling electron-donating and electron-accepting parts of a molecule to reduce the exchange interaction between the frontier orbitals which would otherwise lower the triplet state compared to the singlet state, thus preventing undesired singlet-triplet splittings. This fact is reflected in Fig. 5(a), where a triphenylamine bridge is highlighted as a negative influence on the prediction outcome. Furthermore, our model is able to support hypotheses published in previous work by Friederich *et al.* [11],

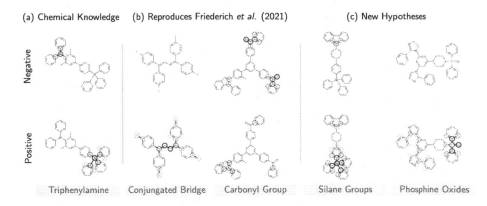

Fig. 5. Example explanations obtained from the MEGAN model for the prediction of the singlet-triplet energy gap of the TADF dataset. (a) Explanations that reproduce known chemical intuition about the task. (b) Explanations that reproduce hypotheses previously published by Friederich *et al.* [11]. (c) New explanatory sub-graph motifs proposed through an observation of the explanations generated by MEGAN.

who use an interpretable decision tree method to generate explanation hypotheses for the same task. As shown in Fig. 5(b) our model replicates their findings of conjugated bridges as a positive influence on the energy gap and carbonyl groups as a negative influence. Beyond that, our model finds several novel hypotheses about structure-property relationships, two of which are shown in Fig. 5(c): We can propose silane groups and phosphine oxides as positive influences to the singlet-triplet energy gap.

5   Limitations

Despite the encouraging experimental results, there are limitations to the proposed MEGAN architecture: Firstly, there is no hard guarantee that each channel's explanations align correctly according to their pre-determined interpretations. This alignment is mainly promoted through the explanation co-training, whose influence on the network is dependent on a hyperparameter. We occasionally observed "explanation leakage" and "explanation flipping" during training. In those rare cases, explanations factually belonging to one channel may either faintly appear in the opposite channel or a particularly disadvantageous initialization of the network causes explanations to develop in the exact opposite channel relative to their assigned interpretation. Ultimately, the alignment of a particular channel with its intended interpretation has to be tested through a Fidelity* analysis after the model training.

The second limitation is in the design of the explanation co-training itself, which essentially reduces the problem to a subgraph counting task. While there are many important real-world applications that can be approximated as such, it still presents an important limit to the expressiveness of the models produced by our model.

6   Conclusion

In this work, we introduce the self-explaining multi-explanation graph attention network (MEGAN) architecture, which produces node and edge attributional explanations for graph regression and classification tasks. Our model implements the number K of generated explanations as a hyperparameter of the network itself, instead of being dependent on the task specification. Based on several exemplary synthetic and real-world datasets, we show that this property is especially crucial for graph regression problems. By being able to generate attributional explanations for a single regression target along multiple explanation channels, our model is able to account for the *polarity* of explanations. In many graph regression applications certain sub-graph motifs influence the predicted outcome in opposing directions: Some motifs present a negative influence on the overall prediction, while others are a positive influence. We achieve the alignment of the model's multiple explanation channels according to these predetermined interpretations by introducing an explanation co-training procedure. Beside the main prediction loss, an additional explanation loss is generated from an approximate solution of the prediction problem based only on each channels explanation masks. We can validate the channel's alignment to their respective intended interpretations through the Fidelity* metric, which extends the concept of explanation fidelity to our multi-channel case.

Additionally, we demonstrate the capabilities of our model for explanation-supervised training, where a model is trained to produce explanations based on a set of given ground truth explanations. For a synthetic graph regression dataset, we show that our model is able to learn the given ground truth explanations almost perfectly, significantly outperforming an existing baseline method from literature.

One particularly interesting result is the improvement of the prediction performance for the explanation-supervised training during the first synthetic experiment but not during the second one. Similar effects have already been shown in the domain of image processing, where various authors are able to demonstrate a performance increase when models are additionally trained to emulate human saliency maps [2,19]. One promising direction for future work will be to investigate the conditions under which (human) explanations have the potential to improve predictive performance for graph-related tasks as well.

7   Reproducibility Statement

We make our experimental code publically available at https://github.com/ aimat-lab/graph_attention_student. The code is implemented in the Python 3.9 programming language. Our neural networks are built with the KGCNN library by Reiser *et al.* [31], which provides a framework for graph neural network implementations with TensorFlow and Keras. We make all data used in our experiments publically available on a file share provider https://bwsyncandshare.kit. edu/s/E3MynrfQsLAHzJC. The datasets can be loaded, processed, and visualized with the visual graph datasets package https://github.com/aimat-lab/ visual_graph_datasets. All experiments were performed on a system with the following specifications: Ubuntu 22.04 operating system, Ryzen 9 5900 processor, RTX 2060 graphics card and 80 GB of memory. We have aimed to package the various experiments as independent modules and our code repository contains a brief explanation of how these can be executed.

A   Evaluation Metrics

Fidelity. Fidelity metrics are used to quantify the degree to which explanations are actually responsible for a model's prediction. In our experiments, we use the definition of the Fidelity$^+$ metric as defined by Yuan *et al.* [41]. It is calculated as the difference between the original predicted value and the predicted value if the elements of the explanation are removed from the input graph. It is generally assumed the higher this value, the more important those elements are for the prediction. This metric generally works well by itself for classification problems, where confidence values are limited to the range between 0 and 1. In such a case, a fidelity value of 0.8 would be considered quite high because there exists a frame of reference that defines 1 as the maximum possible value. However, for this reason, we find that the metric is not immediately applicable to the regression problems since there exists no frame of reference as to what would be considered a particularly high or low value.

Instead, for our regression experiments, we use a relative fidelity value which is defined relative to a point of reference.

$$\text{Fidelity}^+_{\text{rel}} = \text{Fidelity}^+ - \text{Fidelity}^+_{\text{random}} \tag{12}$$

As the frame of reference, we use the fidelity value which results from a purely random input graph mask, which has the *same sparsity* as the given explanation. The random fidelity value is calculated as the arithmetic mean resulting from 10 such randomly sampled input masks per explanation.

B   GNES Implementation

In our experiments, we use the GNES method by Gao *et al.* [13] as a baseline approach from the literature that supports explanation supervision. In their framework, the authors propose using existing differentiable post-hoc explanation methods for explanation supervision. For that, they introduce a generic framework to describe node and edge attributional explanations. For example, they define node the attributional explanation for node n at layer l as

$$M_n^{(l)} = \| \text{ReLU}(g(\frac{\partial y_c}{\partial F_n^{(l)}}) \cdot h(F_n^{(l)})) \| \tag{13}$$

where $F_n^{(l)}$ is the activation of node n at layer l. $g(\cdot)$ and $h(\cdot)$ are generic functions that can be defined for specific implementations of explanation methods. Edge explanations are defined in a similarly generic way. Explanation supervision is then achieved through additional loss MAE loss terms between these generated explanations and the given reference explanations.

For our experiments, we were not able to use the original code at https://github.com/YuyangGao/GNES as that implementation only supports binary classification problems and is limited to a batch size of 1. We re-implement their method in the KGCNN framework. We follow the original paper as closely as possible for the version we call GNES$_{original}$. However, we find that the used ReLU($\cdot$) operation does not work well with regression operations as it cuts off negative values and thus actively discards explanatory motifs with *opposing influence*. Consequently, we modify the method to use an absolute value operation $|| \cdot ||$ instead of the ReLU($\cdot$) for the version we call GNES$_{fixed}$. We find that this version works much better with regression tasks as it is able to properly account for positive and negative influences.

C   GNN Benchmarks

Aside from its capability for explanation supervision, we also find that our model generally shows a good prediction performance as well, when compared to other state-of-the-art GNNs. Figure 6 shows the benchmarking results of the MEGAN model compared to several other GNNs from the literature for two datasets of molecular property prediction. The benchmarking results were obtained from the KGCNN library https://github.com/aimat-lab/gcnn_keras/tree/master/training/results. To produce the results, all models were subjected to a cursory hyperparameter optimization on the respective datasets. The MEGAN models trained for this comparison use neither explanation supervision nor the co-training method.

The results show that MEGAN achieves the second-best results for both tasks.

(a) Results for the ESOL dataset [5] which consists of 1128 molecular graphs and their respective values for water solubility.

(b) Results for the LIPOP dataset [39] which consists of 4200 molecular graphs and their respective octanol/water distribution coefficient.

Model	MAE ↓	RMSE ↓	Model	MAE ↓	RMSE ↓
GAT	$0.49_{\pm0.02}$	$0.70_{\pm0.04}$	GAT	$0.50_{\pm0.02}$	$0.70_{\pm0.04}$
GIN	$0.50_{\pm0.02}$	$0.70_{\pm0.03}$	INorp	$0.46_{\pm0.01}$	$0.65_{\pm0.01}$
CMPNN	$0.48_{\pm0.03}$	$0.68_{\pm0.02}$	Schnet	$0.48_{\pm0.00}$	$0.65_{\pm0.00}$
INorp	$0.49_{\pm0.01}$	$0.68_{\pm0.03}$	GIN	$0.45_{\pm0.01}$	$0.64_{\pm0.03}$
GATv2	$0.47_{\pm0.03}$	$0.67_{\pm0.03}$	AttentiveFP	$0.45_{\pm0.01}$	$0.62_{\pm0.01}$
Schnet	$0.46_{\pm0.03}$	$0.65_{\pm0.04}$	GATv2	$0.41_{\pm0.01}$	$0.59_{\pm0.01}$
DMPNN	$0.45_{\pm0.02}$	$0.63_{\pm0.02}$	PAiNN	$0.40_{\pm0.01}$	$0.58_{\pm0.03}$
AttentiveFP	$0.46_{\pm0.01}$	$0.63_{\pm0.03}$	CMPNN	$0.41_{\pm0.01}$	$0.58_{\pm0.01}$
MEGAN	$\underline{0.44}_{\pm0.03}$	$\underline{0.60}_{\pm0.05}$	MEGAN	$\underline{0.40}_{\pm0.01}$	$\underline{0.56}_{\pm0.01}$
PAiNN	$\mathbf{0.43}_{\pm0.02}$	$\mathbf{0.60}_{\pm0.02}$	DMPNN	$\mathbf{0.38}_{\pm0.01}$	$\mathbf{0.55}_{\pm0.03}$

Fig. 6. Benchmarking results obtained from the KGCNN library from a random 5-fold cross-validation for the ESOL dataset [5] and the LIPOP dataset [39].

References

1. Adebayo, J., Gilmer, J., Muelly, M., Goodfellow, I., Hardt, M., Kim, B.: Sanity checks for saliency maps. In: Advances in Neural Information Processing Systems, vol. 31. Curran Associates, Inc. (2018). https://proceedings.neurips.cc/paper_files/paper/2018/hash/294a8ed24b1ad22ec2e7efea049b8737-Abstract.html

2. Boyd, A., Tinsley, P., Bowyer, K., Czajka, A.: CYBORG: blending human saliency into the loss improves deep learning (2022). https://doi.org/10.48550/arXiv.2112.00686. http://arxiv.org/abs/2112.00686. arXiv:2112.00686

3. Brody, S., Alon, U., Yahav, E.: How attentive are graph attention networks? (2022). https://openreview.net/forum?id=F72ximsx7C1

4. Dai, E., Wang, S.: Towards self-explainable graph neural network. In: Proceedings of the 30th ACM International Conference on Information & Knowledge Management, CIKM 2021, pp. 302–311. Association for Computing Machinery, New York (2021). https://doi.org/10.1145/3459637.3482306

5. Delaney, J.S.: ESOL: estimating aqueous solubility directly from molecular structure. J. Chem. Inf. Comput. Sci. **44**(3), 1000–1005 (2004). https://doi.org/10.1021/ci034243x

6. Devlin, J., Chang, M.W., Lee, K., Toutanova, K.: BERT: pre-training of deep bidirectional transformers for language understanding. In: Proceedings of the 2019 Conference of the North American Chapter of the Association for Computational Linguistics: Human Language Technologies, Volume 1 (Long and Short Papers), Minneapolis, Minnesota, pp. 4171–4186. Association for Computational Linguistics (2019). https://doi.org/10.18653/v1/N19-1423. https://aclanthology.org/N19-1423

7. DeYoung, J., et al.: ERASER: a benchmark to evaluate rationalized NLP models. In: Proceedings of the 58th Annual Meeting of the Association for Computational Linguistics, pp. 4443–4458. Association for Computational Linguistics (2020). https://doi.org/10.18653/v1/2020.acl-main.408. https://aclanthology.org/2020.acl-main.408

8. Doshi-Velez, F., Kim, B.: Towards a rigorous science of interpretable machine learning. arXiv:1702.08608 (2017). http://arxiv.org/abs/1702.08608

9. Endo, A., et al.: Efficient up-conversion of triplet excitons into a singlet state and its application for organic light emitting diodes. Appl. Phys. Lett. **98**(8), 083302 (2011). https://doi.org/10.1063/1.3558906. https://aip.scitation.org/doi/full/10.1063/1.3558906

10. Fernandes, P., Treviso, M., Pruthi, D., Martins, A.F.T., Neubig, G.: Learning to scaffold: optimizing model explanations for teaching (2022). https://doi.org/10.48550/arXiv.2204.10810. http://arxiv.org/abs/2204.10810. arXiv:2204.10810

11. Friederich, P., Krenn, M., Tamblyn, I., Aspuru-Guzik, A.: Scientific intuition inspired by machine learning-generated hypotheses. Mach. Learn. Sci. Technol. **2**(2), 025027 (2021). https://doi.org/10.1088/2632-2153/abda08

12. Funke, T., Khosla, M., Rathee, M., Anand, A.: ZORRO: valid, sparse, and stable explanations in graph neural networks. IEEE Trans. Knowl. Data Eng. **35**(8), 8687–8698 (2023). https://doi.org/10.1109/TKDE.2022.3201170. https://ieeexplore.ieee.org/document/9866587/

13. Gao, Y., Sun, T., Bhatt, R., Yu, D., Hong, S., Zhao, L.: GNES: learning to explain graph neural networks. In: 2021 IEEE International Conference on Data Mining (ICDM), pp. 131–140 (2021). https://doi.org/10.1109/ICDM51629.2021.00023. ISSN: 2374-8486

14. Gómez-Bombarelli, R., et al.: Design of efficient molecular organic light-emitting diodes by a high-throughput virtual screening and experimental approach. Nat. Mater. **15**(10), 1120–1127 (2016). https://doi.org/10.1038/nmat4717. https://www.nature.com/articles/nmat4717

15. Henderson, R., Clevert, D.A., Montanari, F.: Improving molecular graph neural network explainability with orthonormalization and induced sparsity. In: Proceedings of the 38th International Conference on Machine Learning, pp. 4203–4213. PMLR (2021). https://proceedings.mlr.press/v139/henderson21a.html. ISSN: 2640-3498

16. Huang, Q., Yamada, M., Tian, Y., Singh, D., Chang, Y.: GraphLIME: local interpretable model explanations for graph neural networks. IEEE Trans. Knowl. Data Eng. **35**(7), 6968–6972 (2022). https://doi.org/10.1109/TKDE.2022.3187455

17. Jiménez-Luna, J., Grisoni, F., Schneider, G.: Drug discovery with explainable artificial intelligence. Nat. Mach. Intell. **2**(10), 573–584 (2020). https://doi.org/10.1038/s42256-020-00236-4. https://www.nature.com/articles/s42256-020-00236-4

18. Kindermans, P.-J., et al.: The (un)reliability of saliency methods. In: Samek, W., Montavon, G., Vedaldi, A., Hansen, L.K., Müller, K.-R. (eds.) Explainable AI: Interpreting, Explaining and Visualizing Deep Learning. LNCS (LNAI), vol. 11700, pp. 267–280. Springer, Cham (2019). https://doi.org/10.1007/978-3-030-28954-6_14

19. Linsley, D., Shiebler, D., Eberhardt, S., Serre, T.: Learning what and where to attend (2019). https://openreview.net/forum?id=BJgLg3R9KQ

20. Luo, D., et al.: Parameterized explainer for graph neural network. ArXiv (2020). https://www.semanticscholar.org/paper/Parameterized-Explainer-for-Graph-Neural-Network-Luo-Cheng/d9f5ec342df97e060b527a8bc18ae4e97401f246

21. Magister, L.C., et al.: Encoding concepts in graph neural networks (2022). https://doi.org/10.48550/arXiv.2207.13586. http://arxiv.org/abs/2207.13586. arXiv:2207.13586

22. Magister, L.C., Kazhdan, D., Singh, V., Liò, P.: GCExplainer: human-in-the-loop concept-based explanations for graph neural networks (2021). https://doi.org/10.48550/arXiv.2107.11889. http://arxiv.org/abs/2107.11889. arXiv:2107.11889

23. McCloskey, K., Taly, A., Monti, F., Brenner, M.P., Colwell, L.J.: Using attribution to decode binding mechanism in neural network models for chemistry. Proc. Natl. Acad. Sci. **116**(24), 11624–11629 (2019). https://doi.org/10.1073/pnas.1820657116. https://www.pnas.org/doi/10.1073/pnas.1820657116

24. Müller, P., Faber, L., Martinkus, K., Wattenhofer, R.: DT+GNN: a fully explainable graph neural network using decision trees (2022). https://doi.org/10.48550/arXiv.2205.13234. http://arxiv.org/abs/2205.13234. arXiv:2205.13234

25. Pennington, J., Socher, R., Manning, C.: GloVe: global vectors for word representation. In: Proceedings of the 2014 Conference on Empirical Methods in Natural Language Processing (EMNLP), Doha, Qatar, pp. 1532–1543. Association for Computational Linguistics (2014). https://doi.org/10.3115/v1/D14-1162. https://aclanthology.org/D14-1162

26. Pope, P.E., Kolouri, S., Rostami, M., Martin, C.E., Hoffmann, H.: Explainability methods for graph convolutional neural networks, pp. 10772–10781 (2019). https://openaccess.thecvf.com/content_CVPR_2019/html/Pope_Explainability_Methods_for_Graph_Convolutional_Neural_Networks_CVPR_2019_paper.html

27. Prado-Romero, M.A., Stilo, G.: GRETEL: graph counterfactual explanation evaluation framework. In: Proceedings of the 31st ACM International Conference on Information & Knowledge Management, CIKM 2022, pp. 4389–4393. Association

for Computing Machinery, New York (2022). https://doi.org/10.1145/3511808.
3557608. https://dl.acm.org/doi/10.1145/3511808.3557608

28. Pruthi, D., Gupta, M., Dhingra, B., Neubig, G., Lipton, Z.C.: Learning to deceive
with attention-based explanations. In: Proceedings of the 58th Annual Meeting of the Association for Computational Linguistics, pp. 4782–4793. Association
for Computational Linguistics (2020). https://doi.org/10.18653/v1/2020.acl-main.
432. https://aclanthology.org/2020.acl-main.432

29. Qiao, T., Dong, J., Xu, D.: Exploring human-like attention supervision in visual
question answering. In: Thirty-Second AAAI Conference on Artificial Intelligence
(2018). https://www.aaai.org/ocs/index.php/AAAI/AAAI18/paper/view/16485

30. Rathee, M., Funke, T., Anand, A., Khosla, M.: BAGEL: a benchmark for assessing
graph neural network explanations (2022). https://doi.org/10.48550/arXiv.2206.
13983. http://arxiv.org/abs/2206.13983. arXiv:2206.13983

31. Reiser, P., Eberhard, A., Friederich, P.: Graph neural networks in TensorFlow-
Keras with RaggedTensor representation (KGCNN). Softw. Impacts **9**, 100095
(2021). https://doi.org/10.1016/j.simpa.2021.100095. https://www.sciencedirect.
com/science/article/pii/S266596382100035X

32. Sanchez-Lengeling, B., et al.: Evaluating attribution for graph neural networks.
In: Advances in Neural Information Processing Systems, vol. 33, pp. 5898–5910.
Curran Associates, Inc. (2020). https://proceedings.neurips.cc/paper/2020/hash/
417fbbf2e9d5a28a855a11894b2e795a-Abstract.html

33. Schwarzenberg, R., Hübner, M., Harbecke, D., Alt, C., Hennig, L.: Layerwise rel-
evance visualization in convolutional text graph classifiers. In: Proceedings of the
Thirteenth Workshop on Graph-Based Methods for Natural Language Processing
(TextGraphs-2013), Hong Kong, pp. 58–62. Association for Computational Lin-
guistics (2019). https://doi.org/10.18653/v1/D19-5308. https://aclanthology.org/
D19-5308

34. Shin, Y.M., Kim, S.W., Shin, W.Y.: PAGE: prototype-based model-level explanations for graph neural networks (2022). https://doi.org/10.48550/arXiv.2210.
17159. http://arxiv.org/abs/2210.17159. arXiv:2210.17159

35. Sorkun, M.C., Khetan, A., Er, S.: AqSolDB, a curated reference set of
aqueous solubility and 2D descriptors for a diverse set of compounds. Sci.
Data **6**(1), 143 (2019). https://doi.org/10.1038/s41597-019-0151-1. https://www.
nature.com/articles/s41597-019-0151-1

36. Sorkun, M.C., Koelman, J.M.V.A., Er, S.: Pushing the limits of solubility prediction via quality-oriented data selection. iScience **24**(1), 101961 (2021). https://doi.
org/10.1016/j.isci.2020.101961. https://www.sciencedirect.com/science/article/
pii/S2589004220311585

37. Stacey, J., Belinkov, Y., Rei, M.: Supervising model attention with human explanations for robust natural language inference (2022). https://doi.org/10.48550/
arXiv.2104.08142. http://arxiv.org/abs/2104.08142. arXiv:2104.08142

38. Tan, J., et al.: Learning and evaluating graph neural network explanations based on
counterfactual and factual reasoning. In: Proceedings of the ACM Web Conference
2022, WWW 2022, pp. 1018–1027. Association for Computing Machinery, New
York (2022). https://doi.org/10.1145/3485447.3511948

39. Wu, Z., et al.: MoleculeNet: a benchmark for molecular machine learning. Chem.
Sci. **9**(2), 513–530 (2018). https://doi.org/10.1039/C7SC02664A. https://pubs.rsc.
org/en/content/articlelanding/2018/sc/c7sc02664a

40. Ying, Z., Bourgeois, D., You, J., Zitnik, M., Leskovec, J.: GNNExplainer: generating explanations for graph neural networks. In: Advances in Neural Information

Processing Systems, vol. 32. Curran Associates, Inc. (2019). https://papers.nips.cc/paper/2019/hash/d80b7040b773199015de6d3b4293c8ff-Abstract.html

41. Yuan, H., Yu, H., Gui, S., Ji, S.: Explainability in graph neural networks: a taxonomic survey. IEEE Trans. Pattern Anal. Mach. Intell. **45**(5), 5782–5799 (2022). https://doi.org/10.1109/TPAMI.2022.3204236

42. Zhang, Q., et al.: Design of efficient thermally activated delayed fluorescence materials for pure blue organic light emitting diodes. J. Am. Chem. Soc. **134**(36), 14706–14709 (2012). https://doi.org/10.1021/ja306538w

43. Zhang, Z., Liu, Q., Wang, H., Lu, C., Lee, C.: ProtGNN: towards self-explaining graph neural networks. In: Proceedings of the AAAI Conference on Artificial Intelligence, vol. 36, no. 8, pp. 9127–9135 (2022). https://doi.org/10.1609/aaai.v36i8.20898. https://ojs.aaai.org/index.php/AAAI/article/view/20898

Quantifying the Intrinsic Usefulness of Attributional Explanations for Graph Neural Networks with Artificial Simulatability Studies

Jonas Teufel, Luca Torresi, and Pascal Friederich[✉]

Institute of Theoretical Informatics (ITI), Karlsruhe Institute of Technology (KIT),
Karlsruhe, Germany
jonas.teufel@student.kit.edu, {luca.torresi,pascal.friederich}@kit.edu

Abstract. Despite the increasing relevance of explainable AI, assessing the quality of explanations remains a challenging issue. Due to the high costs associated with human-subject experiments, various proxy metrics are often used to approximately quantify explanation quality. Generally, one possible interpretation of the quality of an explanation is its inherent value for teaching a related concept to a student. In this work, we extend artificial simulatability studies to the domain of graph neural networks. Instead of costly human trials, we use explanation-supervisable graph neural networks to perform simulatability studies to quantify the inherent *usefulness* of attributional graph explanations. We perform an extensive ablation study to investigate the conditions under which the proposed analyses are most meaningful. We additionally validate our method's applicability on real-world graph classification and regression datasets. We find that relevant explanations can significantly boost the sample efficiency of graph neural networks and analyze the robustness towards noise and bias in the explanations. We believe that the notion of usefulness obtained from our proposed simulatability analysis provides a dimension of explanation quality that is largely orthogonal to the common practice of faithfulness and has great potential to expand the toolbox of explanation quality assessments, specifically for graph explanations.

Keywords: Graph Neural Networks · Explainable AI · Explanation Quality · Simulatability Study

1 Introduction

Explainable AI (XAI) methods are meant to provide explanations alongside a complex model's predictions to make its inner workings more transparent to human operators to improve trust and reliability, provide tools for retrospective model analysis, as well as to comply with anti-discrimination laws [6]. Despite

© The Author(s), under exclusive license to Springer Nature Switzerland AG 2023
L. Longo (Ed.): xAI 2023, CCIS 1902, pp. 361–381, 2023.
https://doi.org/10.1007/978-3-031-44067-0_19

recent developments and a growing corpus of XAI methods, a recurring challenge remains the question of how to assess the quality of the generated explanations.

Since explainability methods aim to improve human understanding of complex models, Doshi-Velez and Kim [6] argue that ultimately the quality of explanations has to be assessed in a human context. To accomplish this, the authors propose the idea of simulatability studies. In that context, human subjects are tasked to simulate the behavior of a machine-learning model given different amounts of information. While a control group of participants receives only the model input-output information, the test group additionally receives the explanations in question. If, in that case, the test group performs significantly better at simulating the behavior, the explanations can be assumed to contain information useful to human understanding of the task. However, human trials such as this are costly and time-consuming, especially considering the number of participants required to obtain a statistically significant result. Therefore, the majority of XAI research is centered around more easily available proxy metrics such as explanation sparsity and faithfulness.

While proxy metrics are an integral part of the XAI evaluation pipeline, we argue that the quantification of usefulness obtained through simulatability studies is an important next step toward comparing XAI methods and thus increasing the impact of explainable AI. Recently, Pruthi *et al.* [21] introduce the concept of *artificial simulatability studies* as a trade-off between cost and meaningfulness. Instead of using human subjects, the authors use explanation-supervisable neural networks as participants to conduct simulatability studies for natural language processing tasks.

In this work, we extend the concept of artificial simulatability studies to the domain of graph neural networks and specifically node and edge attributional explanations thereof. This application has only been enabled through the recent development of sufficiently explanation-supervisable graph neural network approaches [26]. We will henceforth refer to this artificial simulatability approach as the student-teacher analysis of explanation quality: The explanations in question are considered to be the "teachers" that are evaluated on their effectiveness of communicating additional task-related information to explanation-supervisable "student" models. We show that, under the right circumstances, explanation supervision leads to significantly improved main task prediction performance w.r.t. to a reference. We first conduct an extensive ablation study on a specifically designed synthetic dataset to highlight the conditions under which this effect can be optimally observed. Most importantly, we find that the underlying student model architecture has to be sufficiently capable to learn explanations during explanation-supervised training. Our experiments show, that this is especially the case for the self-explaining MEGAN architecture, which was recently introduced by Teufel *et al.* [26].

Additionally, we find that the target prediction problem needs to be sufficiently challenging to the student models to see a significant effect. We can furthermore show that while ground truth explanations cause an increase in performance, deterministically incorrect/adversarial explanations cause a significant decrease in performance. In the same context, random explanation noise merely diminishes the benefit of explanations, but neither causes a significant advantage nor a disadvantage.

Finally, we validate the applicability of our method on explanations for one real-world molecular classification and one molecular regression dataset.

2 Related Work

Simulatability Studies. Doshi-Velez and Kim [6] introduce the concept of simulatability studies, in which human participants are asked to simulate the forward predictive behavior of a given model. Explanations about the model behavior should be considered useful if a group of participants with access to these explanations performs significantly better than a control group without them. Such studies are only rarely found in the growing corpus of XAI literature due to the high effort and cost associated with them. Nonetheless, some examples of such studies can be found. Chandrasekaran *et al.* [4] for example conduct a simulatability study for a visual question answering (VQA) task. The authors investigate the effect of several different XAI methods such as GradCAM and attention among other aspects. They find no significant performance difference for participants when providing explanations. Hase and Bansal [10] conduct a simulatability study for a sentiment classification task. They can only report significant improvements for a small subset of explanation methods. Lai *et al.* [13,14] conduct a simulatability study for a deception detection task. Unlike previously mentioned studies, the authors ask participants to predict ground truth labels instead of simulating a model's predictions. Among different explanation methods, they also investigate the effects of other assistive methods on human performance, such as procedurally generated pre-task tutorials and real-time feedback. The study shows that real-time feedback is crucial to improve human performance. In regard to explanations, the authors find that especially simplistic explanations methods seem to be more useful than more complicated deep-learning-based ones and that providing the polarity of attributional explanations is essential.

Beyond the cost and effort associated with human trials, previous studies report various additional challenges when working with human subjects. One issue seems to be the limited working memory of humans, where participants report forgetting previously seen relevant examples along the way. Another issue is the heterogeneity of participants' abilities, which causes a higher variance in performance results, necessitating larger sample sizes to obtain statistically significant results. Overall, various factors contribute to such studies either not observing any effect at all or reporting only on marginal explanation benefits.

One possible way to address this is proposed by Arora *et al.* [2], who argue to rethink the concept of simulatability studies itself. In their work, instead of merely using human subjects as passive predictors, the participants are encouraged to interactively engage with the system. In addition to guessing the model prediction, participants are asked to make subsequent single edits to the input text with the goal of maximizing the difference in model confidence. The metric of the average confidence deviation per edit can then also be seen as a measure of human understanding of the model's inner workings. The authors argue that such an explorative and interactive study design is generally more suited to the strengths of human subjects and avoids their respective weaknesses.

Another approach is represented by the emergent idea of *artificial simulatability studies*, which generally aim to substitute human participants in these kinds of studies with machine learning models that are able to learn from explanations in a similar manner. There exist early variations of this basic idea [11,27], for which conceptional problems have been pointed out [21]. Most notably, some methods expose explanations during test time, which may cause label leakage. Recently, Pruthi *et al.* [21] devise a method that does not expose explanations during test time by leveraging explanation-supervised model training. They are able to show a statistically significant test performance benefit for various explanation methods, as well as for explanations derived from human experts in natural language processing tasks. In our work, we build on the basic methodology proposed by Pruthi *et al.* and use explanation-supervisable student models to avoid the label-leakage problem. Furthermore, we extend their basic approach toward a more rigorous method. The authors consider the *absolute* performance of the explanation supervised student by itself as an indicator of simulatability. We argue that, due to the stochastic nature of neural network training, potential simulatability benefits should only be considered on a statistical level obtained through multiple independent repetitions, only *relative* to a direct reference, and verified by tests of statistical significance.

Explanation Supervision for GNNs. Artificial simulatability studies, as previously discussed, require student models which are capable of *explanation supervision*. This means that it should be possible to directly train the generated explanations to match some given ground truth explanations during the model training phase. Explanation supervision has already been successfully applied in the domains of image processing [16] and natural language processing [3]. However, only recently was the practice successfully adapted to the domain of graph neural networks as well. First, Gao *et al.* [8] propose the GNES framework, which aims to use the differentiable nature of various existing post-hoc explanation methods such as GradCAM and LRP to perform explanation supervised training. Teufel *et al.* [26] on the other hand introduce the MEGAN architecture which is a specialized attention-based architecture showing especially high potential for explanation-supervision. To the best of our knowledge, these two methods remain the only existing methods for explanation-supervision of graph *attributional* explanations until now.

In addition to attributional explanations, several other types of explanations have been introduced. Noteworthy examples are prototype-based explanations [23] and concept-based explanations [19]. In the realm of prototype explanations, Zhang *et al.* [28] and Dai and Wang [5] introduce self-explaining prototype-based graph neural networks, although it has not yet been demonstrated if and how explanation-supervision could be applied to them. For concept-based explanations, on the other hand, Magister *et al.* [18] demonstrate explanation supervision, opening up the possibility to extend artificial simulatability studies to explanation modalities beyond simple attributional explanations as well.

3   Student-Teacher Analysis of Explanation Quality

Simulatability studies aim to assess how useful a set of explanations is in improving human understanding of a related task. To offset the high cost and uncertainty associated with human-subject experiments, Pruthi *et al.* [21] introduce artificial simulatability studies, which substitute human participants with explanation-aware neural networks, for natural language processing tasks. In this section, we describe our extension of this principle idea to the application domain of graph neural networks and introduce the novel STS metric which we use to quantify the explanation-induced performance benefit.

We assume a directed graph $\mathcal{G} = (\mathcal{V}, \mathcal{V})$ is represented by a set of node indices $\mathcal{V} = \mathbb{N}^V$ and a set of edges $\mathcal{E} \subseteq \mathcal{V} \times \mathcal{V}$, where a tuple $(i, j) \in \mathcal{E}$ denotes a directed edge from node i to node j. Every node i is associated with a vector of initial node features $\mathbf{h}_i^{(0)} \in \mathbb{R}^{N_0}$, combining into the initial node feature tensor $\mathbf{H}^{(0)} \in \mathbb{R}^{V \times N_0}$. Each edge is associated with an edge feature vector $\mathbf{u}_{ij}^{(0)} \in \mathbb{R}^M$, combining into the edge feature tensor $\mathbf{U} \in \mathbb{R}^{E \times M}$. Each graph is also annotated with a target value vector $\mathbf{y}^{\text{true}} \in \mathbb{R}^C$, which is either a one-hot encoded vector for classification problems or a vector of continuous values for regression problems. For each graph exists node and edge attributional explanations in the form of a node importance tensor $\mathbf{V} \in [0, 1]^{V \times K}$ and an edge importance tensor

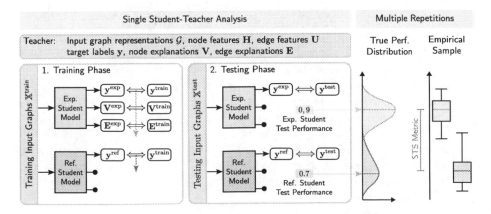

Fig. 1. Illustration of the student teacher training workflow as well as the setting of our artificial simulatability study.

$\mathbf{E} \in [0,1]^{E \times K}$ respectively. K is the number of explanation channels and is usually equal to the size C of the target vector, meaning that for every target value each element of the input graph is annotated with a 0 to 1 value indicating that element's importance.

In the framework of artificial simulatability studies, human participants are replaced by explanation-aware machine learning models which will be referred to as *students*. In this analogy, the *teacher* is represented by the dataset of input graphs and target value annotations, as well as the explanations whose quality is to be determined. Figure 1 illustrates the concept of such a *student-teacher analysis* of explanation quality. The set $\mathbb{X}$ of input data consists of tuples $(G, \mathbf{H}^{(0)}, \mathbf{U}^{(0)})$ of graphs and their features. The set $\mathbb{Y}$ consists of tuples $(\mathbf{y}, \mathbf{V}, \mathbf{E})$ of target value annotations, as well as node and edge attributional explanations. A student is defined as a parametric model $\mathcal{S}_\theta : (G, \mathbf{H}^{(0)}, \mathbf{U}^{(0)}) \rightarrow (\mathbf{y}, \mathbf{V}, \mathbf{E})$ with the trainable model parameters $\boldsymbol{\theta}$. This firstly implies that every student model has to directly output explanations alongside each prediction. Moreover, these generated explanations have to be actively *supervisable* to qualify as an explanation-aware student model.

During a single iteration of the student-teacher analysis, the sets of input and corresponding output data are split into a training set $\mathbb{X}^{\text{train}}, \mathbb{Y}^{\text{train}}$ and an unseen test set $\mathbb{X}^{\text{test}}, \mathbb{Y}^{\text{test}}$ respectively. Furthermore, two architecturally identical student models are initialized with the same initial model parameters $\boldsymbol{\theta}$: The reference student model $\mathcal{S}_\theta^{\text{ref}}$ and the explanation-aware student model $\mathcal{S}_\theta^{\text{exp}}$. During the subsequent training phase, the reference student only gets to train on the main target value annotations $\mathbf{y}$, while the explanation student is additionally trained on the given explanations. After the two students were trained on the same training elements and the same hyperparameters, their final prediction performance is evaluated on the unseen test data. If the explanation student outperforms the reference student on the final evaluation, we can assume that the given explanations contain additional task-related information and can thus be considered useful in this context.

However, the training of complex models, such as neural networks, is a stochastic process that generally only converges to a local optimum. For this reason, a single execution of the previously described process is not sufficient to assess a possible performance difference. Rather, a repeated execution is required to confirm the statistical significance of any result. Therefore, we define the student-teacher analysis as the R repetitions of the previously described process, resulting in the two vectors of test set evaluation performances $\mathbf{p}^{\text{ref}}, \mathbf{p}^{\text{exp}} \in \mathbb{R}^R$ for the two student models respectively. The concrete type of metric used to determine the final performance may differ, as is the case with classification and regression problems for example. Based on this definition we define the *student-teacher simulatability* metric

$$\text{STS}_R = \text{median}(\mathbf{p}^{\text{exp}} - \mathbf{p}^{\text{ref}})$$

as the median of the pairwise performance differences between all the individual explanation students' and reference students' evaluation results. We choose the median here instead of the arithmetic mean, due to its robustness towards outliers, which may occur when models sporadically fail to properly converge in certain iterations of the procedure.

In addition to the calculation of the STS metric, a paired t-test is performed to assure the statistical significance of the results. Only if the p-value of this test is below a 5% significance level should the analysis results be considered meaningful.

4   Computational Experiments

4.1   Ablation Study for a Synthetic Graph Classification Dataset

We first conduct an ablation study on a specifically designed synthetic graph dataset to show the special conditions under which a performance benefit for the explanation student can be observed.

We call the synthetic dataset created for this purpose *red and blue adversarial motifs* and a visualization of it can be seen in Fig. 2. The dataset consists of 5000 randomly generated graphs where each node is associated with 3 node features representing an RGB color code. Each graph is seeded with one primarily red motif: Half of the elements are seeded with the red and yellow star motif and are consequently labeled as the "active" class. The other half of the elements are seeded with a red and green ring motif and labeled as "inactive". The dataset represents a binary classification problem where each graph will have to be classified as either active or inactive. As each class assignment is entirely based on the existence of the corresponding sub-graph motifs, these motifs are considered the perfect ground truth explanations for that dataset. In addition to the primarily red motifs, each graph is also seeded with one primarily blue motif: Either a blue-yellow ring motif or a blue-green star motif. These blue motifs are seeded such that their distribution is completely uncorrelated with the true class label of the elements. Thus, these motifs are considered deterministically incorrect/adversarial explanations w.r.t. the main classification task.

Student Model Implementations. We conduct an experiment to assess the suitability of different student model implementations. As previously explained, a student model has to possess two main properties: Node and edge explanations have to be generated alongside each prediction and more importantly it has to be possible to train the models based on these explanations in a supervised manner. To the best of our knowledge, there exist two methods from literature, which do this for *attributional* explanations: The GNES framework of Gao et al. [8] and the MEGAN architecture of Teufel et al. [26]. We conduct an experiment with $R = 25$ repetitions of the student-teacher analysis for three different models: A lightweight MEGAN model, GNES explanations based on a simple GCN network, and GNES explanations based on a simple GATv2 network. In each iteration, 100 elements of the dataset are used to train the student model while the rest is used during testing. Table 1 shows the results of this experiment. We report the final STS value, as well as the node and edge AUC metrics, which indicate how well the explanations of the corresponding models match the ground truth explanations of the test set.

Table 1. Results for 25 repetitions of the student-teacher analysis for different reference models (Ref) and explanation supervised student model (Exp) implementations.

Student Model	STS_{25} ↑	Node AUC ↑		Edge AUC ↑	
		Ref	Exp	Ref	Exp
$GNES_{GCN}$	0.02	$0.55_{\pm 0.04}$	$0.59_{\pm 0.03}$	$0.64_{\pm 0.04}$	$0.66_{\pm 0.04}$
$GNES_{GATv2}$	0.01	$0.59_{\pm 0.05}$	$0.61_{\pm 0.05}$	$0.51_{\pm 0.05}$	$0.55_{\pm 0.04}$
$MEGAN_{0.0}^{2}$	$\mathbf{0.12}^{(*)}$	$0.64_{\pm 0.15}$	$\mathbf{0.94}_{\pm 0.01}$	$0.66_{\pm 0.14}$	$\mathbf{0.96}_{\pm 0.02}$

$^{(*)}$ Statistically significant according to a paired T-test with $p < 5\%$

Since the perfect ground truth explanations are used for this experiment, we expect the explanation student to have the maximum possible advantage w.r.t to the explanations. The results show that only the MEGAN student indicates a statistically significant STS value of a median 12% accuracy improvement for the explanation-aware student. The GNES experiments on the other hand do not show statistically significant performance benefits. We believe that this is due to the limited effect of the explanation supervision that can be observed in these cases: While the node and edge accuracy of the GNES explanation student only improves by a few percent, the MEGAN explanation student almost perfectly learns the ground truth explanations. This is consistent with the results

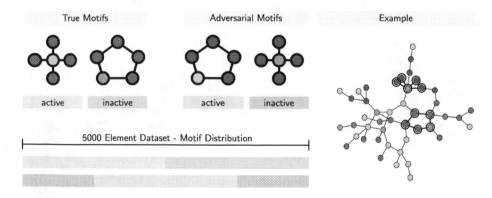

Fig. 2. Synthetic dataset used to quantify the usefulness of attributional graph explanations, incl. testing the robustness toward adversarial explanations. (Color figure online)

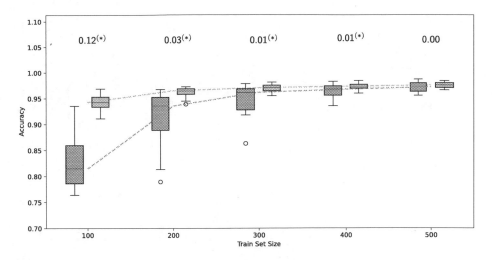

Fig. 3. Results of student-teacher analyses ($R = 25$) for different training dataset sizes. Each column shows the performance distribution for the reference student (blue) and the explanation student (green) of the student-teacher procedure. The number above each column is the resulting STS value. (*) indicates statistical significance according to a paired T-test with $p < 5\%$ (Color figure online)

reported by Teufel *et al.* [26], who report that MEGAN outperforms the GNES approach in capability for explanation supervision. A possible explanation for why that is the case might be that the explanation-supervised training of the already gradient-based explanations of GNES relies on a second derivative of the network, which might provide a generally weaker influence on the network's weights.

Based on this result, we only investigate the MEGAN student in subsequent experiments.

Training Dataset Size Sweep. In this experiment, we investigate the influence of the training dataset size on the explanation performance benefit. For this purpose, we conduct several student-teacher analyses with $R = 25$ repetitions using the MEGAN student architecture. We vary the number of elements used for training between 100, 200, 300, 400, and 500 elements out of a total of 5000. In each iteration, the training dataset with that number of elements is randomly sampled from the entire dataset and the rest is used during testing. Figure 3 shows the results of this experiment. We visualize the performance distributions of explanation and reference students for each dataset size and provide the STS metric in each case.

The results show the greatest performance benefit for the smallest training set size of just 100 elements. Afterward, the STS value converges to 0 for 500 elements, losing statistical significance as well. We believe that this is caused by the convergence of *both* students to the near-perfect performance of approx. 98%

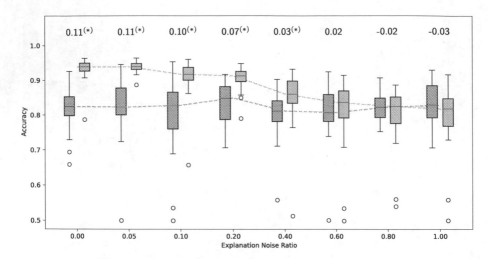

Fig. 4. Results of student-teacher analyses ($R = 25$) for explanations with different ratios of additional explanation noise. Each column shows the performance distribution for the reference student (blue) and the explanation student (green) of the student-teacher procedure. The number above each column is the resulting STS value. (*) indicates statistical significance according to a paired T-test with $p < 5\%$ (Color figure online)

accuracy. In other words: A larger train set size represents a smaller difficulty for the student models. With decreasing difficulty, the students can solve the task almost perfectly by themselves, diminishing any possible benefit of the explanations. We can therefore formulate the rule of thumb that explanations have the potential to provide the greatest benefit when tasks are *more difficult*, and cannot be so easily solved without explanations. As shown in this experiment, a reduction of the train set size sufficiently provides such an increase in difficulty.

Based on this result, we conduct subsequent experiments with a training set size of 100 to observe the most pronounced effect.

Explanation Noise Sweep. For the majority of real-world tasks, perfect ground truth explanations are generally not available. Instead, explanations can be generated through a multitude of XAI methods that have been proposed in recent years. Since complex machine learning models and XAI methods generally only find local optima, it is reasonable to assume that generated explanations are not perfect but rather contain some amount of noise as well. The question is how such explanation noise affects the results of our proposed student-teacher analysis. In this experiment, we perform different student-teacher analyses, where in each case the explanations are overlaid with a certain ratio $P\%$ of random noise, where $P \in \{0, 5, 10, 20, 40, 60, 80, 100\}$. A ratio $P\%$ means that the explanation importance value for every element (nodes and edges) in every graph has a $P\%$ chance of being randomly sampled instead of the ground truth value being used.

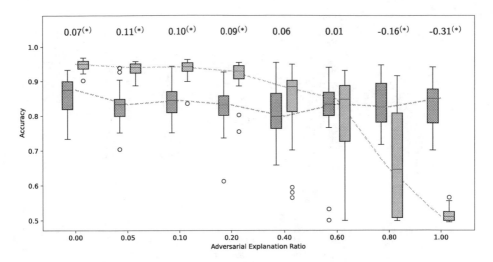

Fig. 5. Results of student-teacher analyses ($R = 25$) for datasets containing different amounts of adversarial incorrect explanations. Each column shows the performance distribution for the reference student (blue) and the explanation student (green) of the student-teacher procedure. The number above each column is the resulting STS value. (*) indicates statistical significance according to a paired T-test with $p < 5\%$ (Color figure online)

Each student-teacher analysis is conducted with a MEGAN student architecture and 100 training data points. Figure 4 shows the results of this experiment.

The results show that there is a statistically significant performance benefit for the explanation student until 40% explanation noise is reached. Afterward, the STS value converges towards zero and loses statistical significance as well. One important aspect to note is that even for high ratios of explanation noise the performance difference converges toward zero. This indicates that explanations consisting almost entirely of *random noise* do not benefit the performance of a student model, but they do *not negatively influence* it either. We believe this is the case because random explanations do not cause any learning effect for the model. In our setup of explanation-supervised training, actual explanation labels are not accessible to either student during the testing phase, instead, the models have to learn to replicate the given explanations during training through their own internal explanation-generating mechanisms. Only through these learned replications can any potential advantage or disadvantage be experienced by the models during performance evaluation. Completely random explanations cannot be learned by the models and consequently have no effect during performance evaluation.

Adversarial Explanation Sweep. The previous experiment indicates that purely random explanations do not negatively affect the model performance. By contrast, it could be expected that deterministic incorrect explanations on

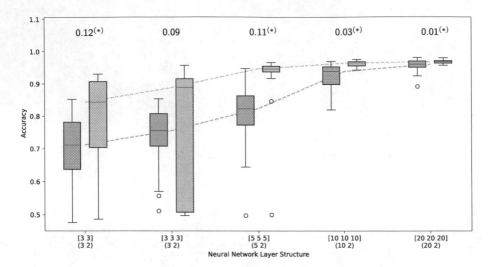

Fig. 6. Results of student-teacher analyses ($R = 25$) for different layer structures of the MEGAN student model. The square brackets indicate the number of hidden units in each layer of the main convolutional part of the network. The normal brackets beneath indicate the number of hidden units in the fully connected layers in the tail-end of the network. Each column shows the performance distribution for the reference student (blue) and the explanation student (green) of the student-teacher procedure. The number above each column is the resulting STS value. (*) indicates statistical significance according to a paired T-test with $p < 5\%$ (Color figure online)

the other hand should have a negative influence on the performance. The used dataset is seeded with two families of sub-graph motifs (see Fig. 2): The red-based motifs are completely correlated with the two target classes and can thus be considered the perfect explanations for the classification task. The blue-based motifs on the other hand are completely uncorrelated to the task and can thus be considered *incorrect/adversarial* explanations w.r.t. to the target labels. In this experiment, increasing amounts of these adversarial explanations are used to substitute the true explanations during the student-teacher analysis to investigate the effect of incorrect explanations on the performance difference. In each iteration, $Q\%$ of the true explanations are replaced by adversarial explanations, where $Q \in \{0, 5, 10, 20, 40, 60, 80, 100\}$. Each student-teacher analysis is conducted with a MEGAN student architecture and 100 training elements.

The results in Fig. 5 show that a statistically significant explanation performance benefit remains for ratios of adversarial explanations for up to 20%. For increasingly large ratios, the STS value still remains positive although the statistical significance is lost. For ratios of 80% and above, statistically significant *negative* STS values can be observed. This implies that incorrect explanations negatively influence the performance of the explanation-aware student model.

Student Network Layer Structure. In this experiment, we investigate the influence of the concrete student network layout on the explanation performance benefit. For this purpose, we conduct several student-teacher analyses with $R = 25$ repetitions using the MEGAN student architecture. We vary the number of convolutional and fully-connected layers, as well as the number of hidden units in these layers. Starting with a simple two-layer 3-unit network layout, the number of model parameters, and thus its complexity is gradually increased until the most complex case of a three-layer 20-unit network is reached. Figure 6 shows the results of this experiment. We visualize the performance distributions of explanation and reference students for each dataset size and provide the STS metric in each case.

The results show that the students' prediction performance generally improves for more complex models. However, this is true for the explanation as well as the reference student. While there still is a statistically significant effect for the most complex network layout, it is very marginal because the reference student achieves almost perfect accuracy in these cases as well. On the other hand, the most simple student network layout shows the largest performance benefit. However, for the simple network layouts, the standard variation of the performance over the various repetitions is greatly increased for reference and explanation students, but seemingly more so for the explanation student. We generally conclude that both extreme cases of simplistic and complex student network architectures have disadvantages w.r.t. to revealing a possible explanation performance benefit. In the end, the best choice is a trade-off between variance in performance and overall capability.

Node Versus Edge Explanations. We conduct an experiment to determine the relative impact of the node and edge explanations individually. We conduct a student-teacher analysis with $R = 25$ repetitions. We use a simple three-layer MEGAN student, where each iteration uses 100 randomly chosen training samples. We investigate three cases: As a baseline case, the explanation student uses ground truth node and edge explanations during explanation-supervised training. In another case, the explanation student is only supplied with the node attributional explanations. In the last case, only the edge attributional explanations are used. This is achieved by setting the corresponding weighting factors to 0 during training. Table 2 shows the results of this experiment. We report the final STS value, as well as the node and edge AUC metrics, which indicate how well the explanations of the corresponding models match the ground truth explanations of the test set.

The results show that all three cases achieve statistically significant STS values indicating a performance benefit of the given explanations. Furthermore, in all three cases, the explanations learned by the explanation student show high similarity (AUC > 0.9) to the ground truth explanations for node *as well as* edge attributions. This implies that the student model is able to infer the corresponding explanation edges for the ground truth explanatory motifs, even if it is only trained on the nodes, and vice versa. We believe the extent of this property is

Table 2. Results for 25 repetitions of the student-teacher Analysis conducted with either only node explanations, only edge explanations, or both.

Explanations	STS_{25} ↑	Node AUC ↑		Edge AUC ↑	
		Ref	Exp	Ref	Exp
Both	$0.12^{(*)}$	$0.62_{\pm 0.14}$	$0.95_{\pm 0.03}$	$0.62_{\pm 0.16}$	$0.94_{\pm 0.03}$
Nodes	$0.12^{(*)}$	$0.65_{\pm 0.13}$	$0.93_{\pm 0.03}$	$0.65_{\pm 0.13}$	$0.92_{\pm 0.04}$
Edges	$0.10^{(*)}$	$0.67_{\pm 0.15}$	$0.93_{\pm 0.03}$	$0.67_{\pm 0.12}$	$0.94_{\pm 0.03}$

$^{(*)}$ Statistically significant according to a paired T-test with $p < 5\%$

a consequence of the used MEGAN student architecture. The MEGAN network architecture implements an explicit architectural co-dependency of node and edge explanations to promote the creation of connected explanatory sub-graphs. These results imply that it may be possible to also apply the student-teacher analysis in situations where only node or edge explanations are available.

4.2   Real-World Datasets

In addition to the experiments on the synthetic dataset, we aim to provide a validation of the student-teacher analysis' effectiveness on real-world datasets as well. For this purpose, we choose one graph classification and one graph regression dataset from the application domain of chemistry. We show how the student-teacher analysis can be used to quantify *usefulness* of the various kinds of explanations for these datasets.

Mutagenicity - Graph Classification. To demonstrate the student-teacher analysis of GNN-generated explanations on a real-world graph classification task, we choose the Mutagenicity dataset [9] as the starting point. By its nature of being real-world data, this dataset does not have ground truth explanations as it is, making it hard to compare GNN-generated explanations to the ground truth. However, the dataset can be transformed into a dataset with ground truth explanatory subgraph motifs. It is hypothesized that the nitro group (NO_2) is one of the main reasons for the property of mutagenicity [15,17]. Following the procedure previously proposed by Tan *et al.* [25], we extract a subset of elements containing all molecules which are labeled as mutagenic and contain the benzene-NO_2 group as well as all the elements that are labeled as non-mutagenic and do not contain that group. Consequently, for the resulting mutagenicity subset, the benzene-NO_2 group can be considered as the definitive ground truth explanation for the mutagenic class label. We call the resulting dataset *MutagenicityExp*. It consists of roughly 3500 molecular graphs, where about 700 are labeled as mutagenic. Furthermore, we designate 500 random elements as the test set, which are sampled to achieve a balanced label distribution.

Based on this dataset, we train GNN models to solve the classification problem. Additionally, we use multiple different XAI methods to generate attributional explanations for the predictions of those GNNs on the previously mentioned test set of 500 elements. These explanations, generated by the various XAI methods, are then subjected to student-teacher analysis, along with some baseline explanations. The results of an analysis with 25 repetitions can be found in Table 3. The hyperparameters of the student-teacher analysis have been chosen through a brief manual search. We use the same basic three-layer MEGAN student architecture as with the synthetic experiments. In each repetition, 10 random elements are used to train the students, and the remainder is used to assess the final test performance. Each training process employs a batch size of 10, 150 epochs, and a 0.01 learning rate. The student-teacher analysis is performed solely on the previously mentioned 500-element test set, which remained unseen to any of the trained GNN models.

Table 3. Results for 25 repetitions of the student-teacher analysis for different explanations on the MutagenicityExp dataset. We mark the best result in bold and underline the second best.

Explanations by	STS_{25} ↑	Node AUC ↑		Edge AUC ↑	
		Ref	Exp	Ref	Exp
Ground Truth	$\mathbf{0.13}^{(*)}$	$0.42_{\pm 0.05}$	$\mathbf{0.97}_{\pm 0.05}$	$0.41_{\pm 0.05}$	$\mathbf{0.96}_{\pm 0.04}$
GNNExplainer	$0.09^{(*)}$	$0.50_{\pm 0.09}$	$0.69_{\pm 0.05}$	$0.50_{\pm 0.11}$	$0.71_{\pm 0.04}$
Gradient	$0.07^{(*)}$	$0.54_{\pm 0.18}$	$0.84_{\pm 0.06}$	$0.46_{\pm 0.17}$	$0.67_{\pm 0.10}$
$MEGAN^2_{1.0}$	$\underline{0.12}^{(*)}$	$0.55_{\pm 0.15}$	$\underline{0.91}_{\pm 0.01}$	$0.55_{\pm 0.14}$	$\underline{0.92}_{\pm 0.02}$
Random	0.01	$0.50_{\pm 0.04}$	$0.50_{\pm 0.03}$	$0.50_{\pm 0.04}$	$0.50_{\pm 0.04}$

$^{(*)}$ Statistically significant according to a paired T-test with $p < 5\%$

As expected, the results show that the reference random explanations do not produce a statistically significant STS result. These explanations are included as a baseline sanity check because previous experiments on the synthetic dataset imply that purely random explanation noise should not have any statistically significant effect on the performance in either direction. The benzene-NO_2 ground truth explanations on the other hand show the largest statistically significant STS value of a median 13% accuracy improvement, as well as the largest explanation accuracy of the explanation student models. GNNexplainer and Gradient explanations also show statistically significant STS values of 9% and 7% median accuracy improvement respectively. The MEGAN-generated explanations show the overall second-best results with an STS value just slightly below the ground truth.

We hypothesize that high values of explanation accuracy are a necessary but not sufficient condition for high STS results. A higher learned explanation accuracy indicates that the explanations are generally based on a more consistent set of underlying rules and can consequently be replicated more easily by the student network, which is the basic prerequisite to show any kind of effect during the student evaluation phase. This is a necessary but not sufficient condition because as shown in the previous adversarial explanation experiment, explanations can be highly deterministic yet conceptionally incorrect and thus harmful to model performance.

AqSolDB - Graph Regression. The AqSolDB [24] dataset consists of roughly 10000 molecular graphs annotated with experimentally determined logS values for their corresponding solubility in water. Of these, we designate 1000 random elements as the test set.

For the concept of water solubility, there exist no definitive attributional explanations. However, there exists some approximate intuition as to what molecular structures should result in higher/lower solubility values: In a simplified manner, one can say that non-polar substructures such as carbon rings and long carbon chains generally result in lower solubility values, while polar structures such as certain nitrogen and oxygen groups are associated with higher solubility values.

Based on this dataset, we train a large MEGAN model on the training split of the elements to regress the water solubility and then generate the dual-channel attributional explanations for the previously mentioned 1000-element test split. For this experiment, we only use a MEGAN model as it is the only XAI method able to create dual-channel explanations for single value graph regression tasks [26]. These dual-channel explanations take the previously mentioned *polarity of evidence* into account, where some substructures have an opposing influence on the solubility value. The first explanation channel contains all negatively influencing sub-graph motifs, while the second channel contains the positively influencing motifs. In addition to the MEGAN-generated explanations, we provide two baseline explanation types. Random explanations consist of randomly generated binary node and edge masks with the same shape. Trivial explanations represent the most simple implementation of the previously introduced human intuition about water solubility: The first channel contains all carbon atoms as explanations and the second channel contains all oxygen and nitrogen atoms as explanations.

The hyperparameters of the student-teacher analysis have been chosen through a brief manual search. We use the same basic three-layer MEGAN student architecture as with the synthetic experiments. In each repetition, 300 random elements are used to train the students, and the remainder is used to assess the final test performance. Each training process employs a batch size of 32, 150 epochs, and a 0.01 learning rate. The student-teacher analysis is performed solely on the previously mentioned 1000-element test set, which remained unseen to the predictive model during training (Table 4).

Table 4. Results for 25 repetitions of the student-teacher analysis for different explanations on the AqSolDB dataset. We highlight the best result in bold and underline the second best.

Model	STS_{25} ↑	Node AUC ↑		Edge AUC ↑	
		Ref	Exp	Ref	Exp
Random	0.00	$0.50_{\pm 0.04}$	$0.50_{\pm 0.03}$	$0.50_{\pm 0.04}$	$0.50_{\pm 0.04}$
Trivial	<u>0.03</u>	$0.40_{\pm 0.05}$	$\mathbf{0.99}_{\pm 0.05}$	$0.42_{\pm 0.05}$	$\mathbf{0.99}_{\pm 0.04}$
$MEGAN_{1.0}^2$	$\mathbf{0.23}^{(*)}$	$0.55_{\pm 0.15}$	$\underline{0.90}_{\pm 0.01}$	$0.55_{\pm 0.14}$	$\underline{0.89}_{\pm 0.02}$

$^{(*)}$ Statistically significant according to a paired T-test with $p < 5\%$

The results show that neither the random nor the trivial explanations result in any significant performance improvement. The MEGAN-generated explanations on the other hand result in a significant improvement of a median 0.23 for the final prediction MSE. This implies that the MEGAN-generated explanations do in fact encode additional task-related information, which goes beyond the most trivial intuition about the task. However, a possible pitfall w.r.t. to this conclusion needs to be pointed out: The MEGAN-generated explanations are evaluated by a MEGAN-based student architecture. It could be that the effect is so strong because these explanations are especially well suited to that kind of architecture, as they were generated through the same architecture. We believe that previous experiments involving architecture-independent ground truth explanations have weakened this argument to an extent. Still, it will be prudent to compare these results with explanations of a different origin in the future, such as the explanations of human experts.

5   Limitations

We propose the student-teacher analysis as a means to measure the content of *useful* task-related information contained within a set of attributional graph explanations. This methodology is inspired by human simulatability studies but with the decisive advantages of being vastly more time- and cost-efficient as well as being more reproducible. However, there are currently also some limitations to the applicability of this approach. Firstly, the approach is currently limited to attributional explanations, which assign a 0 to 1 importance value to each element. These kinds of explanations have been found to have issues [1,12] and recently many different kinds of explanations have been proposed. Some examples are *counterfactuals* [20], *concept-based* explanations [19], and *prototype-based* explanations [23].

Another limitation is that the student-teacher analysis process itself depends on a lot of parameters. As we show in previous sections, the size of the training dataset and the specific student architectures have an impact on how pronounced the effect can be observed. For these reasons, the proposed STS metric cannot be used as an absolute measure of quality such as accuracy for example. Rather, it can be used to relatively *compare* different sets of explanations under the condition that all experiments are conducted with the same parameters. We propose certain rules of thumb for the selection of these parameters, however, it may still be necessary to conduct a cursory parameter search for each specific application. Despite these limitations, we believe that artificial simulatability studies, as proposed in this work, are still an important step toward better practices for the evaluation of explainable AI methods. The currently most widespread metric of explanation quality is the concept of explanation *faithfulness*, which only measures how decisive an explanation is for a model's prediction. We argue, that the concept of artificial simulatability is a first step towards a measure of how intrinsically *useful* explanation can be for the *communication* of additional task-related information.

6   Conclusion

In this work, we extend the concept of artificial simulatability studies to the application domain of graph classification and regression tasks. We propose the student-teacher analysis and the *student-teacher simulatability* (STS) metric to quantify the content of intrinsically *useful* task-related information for a given set of node and edge attributional explanations. We conduct an ablation study on a synthetic dataset to investigate the conditions under which an explanation benefit can be observed most clearly and propose several rules of thumb for an initial choice of experimental parameters: Analysis requires a sufficient number of repetitions for statistical significance, a small number of training elements and a light-weight layer structure for the student model. Furthermore, we show evidence that the analysis method is robust towards small amounts of explanation noise and adversarial explanations. Interestingly, random explanation noise merely suppresses any explanation benefit while deterministically incorrect explanations cause significant performance degradation. This indicates that the method cannot only be used to identify good explanations but also to detect actively harmful ones. Furthermore, we can validate the applicability of our proposed analysis for several real-world datasets of molecular classification and regression.

We believe that artificial simulatability studies can provide a valuable additional tool for the evaluation of graph explanations. The student-teacher analysis measures the *usefulness* of explanations in communicating task-related knowledge, which can be seen as a complementary dimension to the current widespread practice of measuring explanation faithfulness.

For future work, it will be interesting to extend this process to other kinds of graph explanations that have recently emerged such as concept-based explanations or prototype-based explanations. Since this is a method of measuring the content of task-related information within explanations, another application may be in educational science. The method could be used to assess explanation annotations created by human students to provide quantitative feedback on their understanding of a given graph-related problem. Another line of future work is demonstrated by Fernandes *et al.* [7] which uses the differentiable nature of Pruthi *et al.*'s [21] original artificial simulatability procedure itself in a meta-optimization process that attempts to optimize an explanation generator for this property of explanation usefulness.

7   Reproducibility Statement

We make our experimental code publically available at https://github.com/aimat-lab/gnn_student_teacher. The code is implemented in the Python 3.9 programming language. Our neural networks are built with the KGCNN library by Reiser *et al.* [22], which provides a framework for graph neural network implementations with TensorFlow and Keras. We make all data used in our experiments publically available on a file share provider https://bwsyncandshare.kit.edu/s/E3MynrfQsLAHzJC. The datasets can be loaded, processed, and visualized with the visual graph datasets package https://github.com/aimat-lab/visual_graph_datasets. All experiments were performed on a system with the following specifications: Ubuntu 22.04 operating system, Ryzen 9 5900 processor, RTX 2060 graphics card and 80GB of memory. We have aimed to package the various experiments as independent modules and our code repository contains a brief explanation of how these can be executed.

References

1. Adebayo, J., Gilmer, J., Muelly, M., Goodfellow, I., Hardt, M., Kim, B.: Sanity checks for saliency maps. In: Advances in Neural Information Processing Systems, vol. 31. Curran Associates, Inc. (2018). https://proceedings.neurips.cc/paper_files/paper/2018/hash/294a8ed24b1ad22ec2e7efea049b8737-Abstract.html
2. Arora, S., Pruthi, D., Sadeh, N., Cohen, W.W., Lipton, Z.C., Neubig, G.: Explain, edit, and understand: rethinking user study design for evaluating model explanations. In: Proceedings of the AAAI Conference on Artificial Intelligence, vol. 36, no. 5, pp. 5277–5285 (2022). https://doi.org/10.1609/aaai.v36i5.20464. https://ojs.aaai.org/index.php/AAAI/article/view/20464
3. Boyd, A., Tinsley, P., Bowyer, K., Czajka, A.: CYBORG: blending human saliency into the loss improves deep learning (2022). https://doi.org/10.48550/arXiv.2112.00686. http://arxiv.org/abs/2112.00686. arXiv:2112.00686
4. Chandrasekaran, A., Prabhu, V., Yadav, D., Chattopadhyay, P., Parikh, D.: Do explanations make VQA models more predictable to a human? (2018). https://doi.org/10.48550/arXiv.1810.12366. http://arxiv.org/abs/1810.12366. arXiv:1810.12366
5. Dai, E., Wang, S.: Towards self-explainable graph neural network. In: Proceedings of the 30th ACM International Conference on Information & Knowledge Management, CIKM 2021, pp. 302–311. Association for Computing Machinery, New York (2021). https://doi.org/10.1145/3459637.3482306
6. Doshi-Velez, F., Kim, B.: Towards a rigorous science of interpretable machine learning. arXiv:1702.08608 (2017). http://arxiv.org/abs/1702.08608

7. Fernandes, P., Treviso, M., Pruthi, D., Martins, A.F.T., Neubig, G.: Learning to scaffold: optimizing model explanations for teaching (2022). https://doi.org/10.48550/arXiv.2204.10810. http://arxiv.org/abs/2204.10810. arXiv:2204.10810

8. Gao, Y., Sun, T., Bhatt, R., Yu, D., Hong, S., Zhao, L.: GNES: learning to explain graph neural networks. In: 2021 IEEE International Conference on Data Mining (ICDM), pp. 131–140 (2021). https://doi.org/10.1109/ICDM51629.2021.00023. ISSN: 2374-8486

9. Hansen, K., et al.: Benchmark data set for in silico prediction of Ames mutagenicity. J. Chem. Inf. Model. **49**(9), 2077–2081 (2009). https://doi.org/10.1021/ci900161g

10. Hase, P., Bansal, M.: Evaluating explainable AI: which algorithmic explanations help users predict model behavior? (2020). https://doi.org/10.48550/arXiv.2005.01831. http://arxiv.org/abs/2005.01831. arXiv:2005.01831

11. Hase, P., Zhang, S., Xie, H., Bansal, M.: Leakage-adjusted simulatability: can models generate non-trivial explanations of their behavior in natural language? (2020). https://doi.org/10.48550/arXiv.2010.04119. http://arxiv.org/abs/2010.04119. arXiv:2010.04119

12. Kindermans, P.-J., et al.: The (un)reliability of saliency methods. In: Samek, W., Montavon, G., Vedaldi, A., Hansen, L.K., Müller, K.-R. (eds.) Explainable AI: Interpreting, Explaining and Visualizing Deep Learning. LNCS (LNAI), vol. 11700, pp. 267–280. Springer, Cham (2019). https://doi.org/10.1007/978-3-030-28954-6_14

13. Lai, V., Liu, H., Tan, C.: "Why is 'Chicago' deceptive?" Towards building model-driven tutorials for humans. In: Proceedings of the 2020 CHI Conference on Human Factors in Computing Systems, CHI 2020, pp. 1–13. Association for Computing Machinery, New York (2020). https://doi.org/10.1145/3313831.3376873

14. Lai, V., Tan, C.: On human predictions with explanations and predictions of machine learning models: a case study on deception detection. In: Proceedings of the Conference on Fairness, Accountability, and Transparency, FAT* 2019, pp. 29–38. Association for Computing Machinery, New York (2019). https://doi.org/10.1145/3287560.3287590. https://dl.acm.org/doi/10.1145/3287560.3287590

15. Lin, W., Lan, H., Li, B.: Generative causal explanations for graph neural networks. In: Proceedings of the 38th International Conference on Machine Learning, pp. 6666–6679. PMLR (2021). https://proceedings.mlr.press/v139/lin21d.html. ISSN: 2640-3498

16. Linsley, D., Shiebler, D., Eberhardt, S., Serre, T.: Learning what and where to attend (2019). https://openreview.net/forum?id=BJgLg3R9KQ

17. Luo, D., et al.: Parameterized explainer for graph neural network. In: Advances in Neural Information Processing Systems, vol. 33, pp. 19620–19631. Curran Associates, Inc. (2020). https://proceedings.neurips.cc/paper/2020/hash/e37b08dd3015330dcbb5d6663667b8b8-Abstract.html

18. Magister, L.C., et al.: Encoding concepts in graph neural networks (2022). https://doi.org/10.48550/arXiv.2207.13586. http://arxiv.org/abs/2207.13586. arXiv:2207.13586

19. Magister, L.C., Kazhdan, D., Singh, V., Liò, P.: GCExplainer: human-in-the-loop concept-based explanations for graph neural networks (2021). https://doi.org/10.48550/arXiv.2107.11889. http://arxiv.org/abs/2107.11889. arXiv:2107.11889

20. Prado-Romero, M.A., Stilo, G.: GRETEL: graph counterfactual explanation evaluation framework. In: Proceedings of the 31st ACM International Conference on Information & Knowledge Management, CIKM 2022, pp. 4389–4393. Association for Computing Machinery, New York (2022). https://doi.org/10.1145/3511808.3557608. https://dl.acm.org/doi/10.1145/3511808.3557608

21. Pruthi, D., et al.: Evaluating explanations: how much do explanations from the teacher aid students? arXiv:2012.00893 (2021). http://arxiv.org/abs/2012.00893

22. Reiser, P., Eberhard, A., Friederich, P.: Graph neural networks in TensorFlow-Keras with RaggedTensor representation (KGCNN). Softw. Impacts **9**, 100095 (2021). https://doi.org/10.1016/j.simpa.2021.100095. https://www.sciencedirect.com/science/article/pii/S266596382100035X

23. Shin, Y.M., Kim, S.W., Shin, W.Y.: PAGE: prototype-based model-level explanations for graph neural networks (2022). https://doi.org/10.48550/arXiv.2210.17159. http://arxiv.org/abs/2210.17159. arXiv:2210.17159

24. Sorkun, M.C., Khetan, A., Er, S.: AqSolDB, a curated reference set of aqueous solubility and 2D descriptors for a diverse set of compounds. Sci. Data **6**(1), 143 (2019). https://doi.org/10.1038/s41597-019-0151-1. https://www.nature.com/articles/s41597-019-0151-1

25. Tan, J., et al.: Learning and evaluating graph neural network explanations based on counterfactual and factual reasoning. In: Proceedings of the ACM Web Conference 2022, WWW 2022, pp. 1018–1027. Association for Computing Machinery, New York (2022). https://doi.org/10.1145/3485447.3511948

26. Teufel, J., Torresi, L., Reiser, P., Friederich, P.: MEGAN: multi-explanation graph attention network (2022). https://doi.org/10.48550/arXiv.2211.13236. http://arxiv.org/abs/2211.13236. arXiv:2211.13236

27. Treviso, M.V., Martins, A.F.T.: The explanation game: towards prediction explainability through sparse communication (2020). https://doi.org/10.48550/arXiv.2004.13876. http://arxiv.org/abs/2004.13876. arXiv:2004.13876

28. Zhang, Z., Liu, Q., Wang, H., Lu, C., Lee, C.: ProtGNN: towards self-explaining graph neural networks. In: Proceedings of the AAAI Conference on Artificial Intelligence, vol. 36, no. 8, pp. 9127–9135 (2022). https://doi.org/10.1609/aaai.v36i8.20898. https://ojs.aaai.org/index.php/AAAI/article/view/20898

Evaluating Link Prediction Explanations
for Graph Neural Networks

Claudio Borile[✉], Alan Perotti, and André Panisson

CENTAI Institute, Corso Inghilterra, 3, 10138 Turin, Italy
{claudio.borile,alan.perotti,andre.panisson}@centai.eu

Abstract. Graph Machine Learning (GML) has numerous applications, such as node/graph classification and link prediction, in real-world domains. Providing human-understandable explanations for GML models is a challenging yet fundamental task to foster their adoption, but validating explanations for link prediction models has received little attention.

In this paper, we provide quantitative metrics to assess the quality of link prediction explanations, with or without ground-truth. State-of-the-art explainability methods for Graph Neural Networks are evaluated using these metrics. We discuss how underlying assumptions and technical details specific to the link prediction task, such as the choice of distance between node embeddings, can influence the quality of the explanations.

Keywords: Graph Machine Learning · Explainable Artificial Intelligence · Link Prediction · Explanation Evaluation

1 Introduction

Intelligent systems in the real world often use machine learning (ML) algorithms to process various types of data. However, graph data present a unique challenge due to their complexity. Graphs are powerful data representations that can naturally describe many real-world scenarios where the focus is on the connections among numerous entities, such as social networks, knowledge graphs, drug-protein interactions, traffic and communication networks, and more [9]. Unlike text, audio, and images, graphs are embedded in an irregular domain, which makes some essential operations of existing ML algorithms inapplicable [17]. GML applications seek to make predictions, or discover new patterns, using graph-structured data as feature information: for example, one might wish to classify the role of a protein in a biological interaction graph, predict the role of a person in a collaboration network, or recommend new friends in a social network.

Unfortunately the majority of GML models are black boxes, thanks to their fully subsymbolic internal knowledge representation - which makes it hard for humans to understand the reasoning behind the model's decision process. This

L. Longo (Ed.): xAI 2023, CCIS 1902, pp. 382–401, 2023.
https://doi.org/10.1007/978-3-031-44067-0_20

widely recognized fundamental flaw has multiple negative implications: (i) difficulty of adoption from domain experts [19], (ii) non-compliance to regulation, (e.g. GDPR) [14], (iii) inability to detect learned spurious correlations [34], and (iv) risk of deploying biased models [25]. The eXplainable Artificial Intelligence (XAI) research field tackles the problem of making modern ML models more human-understandable. The goal of XAI techniques is to extract from the trained ML model comprehensible information about their decision process. Explainability is typically performed *a posteriori* - it is a process that takes place after the ML model has been trained, and possibly even deployed. Despite a growing number of techniques for explaining GML models, most of them target node and graph classification tasks [47]. Link Prediction (LP) is a paradigmatic problem, but it has been relatively overlooked from the explainability perspective - especially since it has been often ascribed to knowledge graphs. There are many ML techniques to tackle the LP problem, but the most popular approaches are based on an encoder/decoder architecture that learns node embeddings. In this case, LP explanations are based on the interaction of pairs of node representations. It is still not clear how different graph ML architectures affect the explainer's behavior, and in the particular case of link prediction we have observed how explanations can be susceptible to technical choices for the implementation of both the encoding and the decoding stages.

Regarding the validation of explanation and explainers, few works have considered the study and evaluation of GML explainers for LP [20]. Furthermore, despite growing interest regarding the validation of explanations, there is currently no consensus on the adoption of any standard protocol or set of metrics. Given a formal definition for the problem of explaining link predictions, our Research Questions are therefore the following:

- **RQ1.** How can we validate LP explainers and measure the quality of their explanations?
- **RQ2.** What hidden characteristics of LP models can be revealed by the explainers? What can we learn about the different LP architectures, given the explanations to their decisions?

In this paper, we propose a theoretical framing and a set of experiments for the attribution of GML models on the LP task, considering two types of Graph Neural Networks: Variational Graph Auto-Encoders (VGAE) [21] and Graph Isomorphism Networks (GIN) [42]. We first perform a validation of the explanation methods on synthetic datasets such as Stochastic Block Models and Watts-Strogatz graphs, where we can define the ground truth for the explanations and thus compute the confusion matrices and report sensitivity (TPR) and specificity (TNR) for the attribution results. For real-world datasets with no ground-truth (CORA, PubMed and DDI) [31, 39], we exploit an adaptation of the insertion/deletion curves, a technique originally designed to validate computer vision models [26] that allows to quantitatively compare the produced explanations against a random baseline by inserting/removing features and/or edges based on their importance with respect to the considered attribution method.

2   Related Work

2.1   State-of-the-Art Explainers for GML Models

Considering the blooming research in the field of XAI for GNNs, and the increasing quantity of new methods that are proposed, we refer to the taxonomy identified in Yuan et al. [47] to pinpoint the basic foundational principles underlying the different methods and choose few well-known models as representatives for broader classes of methods and use them in the remainder of the paper. Namely, we consider attribution methods based on perturbation methods, gradient-based approaches, decomposition - plus a hybrid one. A more detailed description of these classes and the selected explainers will be given in Sect. 3. We note that all these methods were originally discussed only in the context of node/graph classification.

Perturbation-based explainers study the output variations of a ML model with respect to different input perturbations. Intuitively, when important input information is retained, the predictions should be similar to the original predictions. Existing methods for computer vision learn to generate a mask to select important input pixels to explain deep image models. Brought to GML, perturbation-based explainers learn masks that assign an importance to edges and/or features of the graph [24,29,48]. Arguably, the most widely-known perturbation-based explainer for GNNs is *GNNExplainer* [45]. Gradients/features-based methods decompose and approximate the input importance considering the gradients or hidden feature map values [30,32,33,35,52]. While other techniques just need to query the ML black-box at will (*model-agnostic* methods), explainers of this class require access to the internal weights of the ML model, and are therefore labelled as *model-aware* or *model-dependent*. Another popular way to explain ML models is decomposition methods, which measure the importance of input features by decomposing the final output of the model layer-by-layer according to layer-specific rules, up to the input layer. The results are regarded as the importance scores of the corresponding input features.

2.2   Link Prediction

Link prediction is a key problem for network-structured data, with the goal of inferring missing relationships between entities or predict their future appearance. Like node and graph classification, LP models can exploit both node features and the structure of the network; typically, the model output is an estimated probability, for a non-existing link. Due to the wide range of real-world domain that can be modelled with graph-based data, LP can be applied to solve a high number of tasks. In social networks, LP can be used to infer social interactions or to suggest possible friends to the users [11]. In the field of network biology and network medicine, LP can be leverage in predicting results from drug-drug, drug-disease, and protein-protein interactions to advance the speed of drug discovery [1]. As a ML task, LP has been widely studied [22], and there exists a wide range of link prediction techniques. These approaches span from information-theoretic to clustering-based and learning-based; deep learning models represent the most recent techniques [50]. The idea of enriching link prediction models with semantically meaningful auxiliary information has been seldom explored for simpler models, such as recommender systems [7], or with hand-crafted feature extraction [12]. These approaches do not pair with the complex nature of deep GML models, where the feature extraction phase is part of the learning process, and models learn non-interpretable embeddings for each node. Finally, even though there are many LP approaches more advanced than VGAE and GIN, these two architectures are the base of many popular LP approaches [4] and should be sufficient for the evaluation of the selected explanation techniques.

Regarding methods explicitly proposed to explain/interpret GNN-based LP models, Wang et al. [37] follow the intuition of focusing on the embeddings of pairs of nodes. Their explanations correspond to the attention scores of the aggregation step for the contexts interactions, and therefore they only give a first useful indication of important edges (and not features) for the prediction, but this preliminary information should be paired with a downstream explainer, as the authors point out. For Xie et al. [40], an explanation is a subgraph of the original graph that focuses on important edges, but ignores node features in the explanation, which are an important aspect in the decision process of a GNN. While the overall settings have differences, our work and their approach share the idea of considering embedding representations to produce graph explanations.

The task of explaining LP black-box models has been considered in the context of Knowledge Graphs [16,27], but KGs consider labeled relations that must be taken into account and contribute actively to the explanation. When considering unlabeled edges, a different approach for explaining the LP task is required. Regarding the LP frameworks that incorporate features such as distance encoding and hyperbolic encoding [10,43,51,54], we believe that there should be a community-wide discussion about how such features can be incorporated in the proposed explanations. In our view, while these frameworks are very powerful for capturing features that are important for the LP task, none of the current attribution methods is able to assign an explanation to such features.

Closely related to our work, recent attention has been posed onto the topic of systematically evaluating the produced explanations [2,3,13,28], but exclusively for node/graph classification tasks. Here we fill the gap for the LP task.

3   Explaining Link Predictions

Given a graph $G = (V, E)$ with set of nodes V and set of edges $E \subseteq 2^{V \times V}$, and a node-feature matrix $X \in \mathbb{R}^{|V| \times F}$, link prediction estimates the probability that an unseen edge between two nodes $i, j \in V$, $(i, j) \notin E$ is missing (e.g. when reconstructing a graph or predicting a future edge). Formally, a link prediction model is a function $\phi_{G,X} : V \times V \mapsto [0, 1]$ that given G and X maps every pair of nodes in V to a probability $p \in [0, 1]$. A common approach for LP tasks is to learn a node representation in a vector space (*encoder* $\mathrm{Enc}_{G,X} : V \mapsto \mathbb{R}^d$), and then estimate edge probability from pairwise distances in this latent space (*decoder* $\mathrm{Dec} : \mathbb{R}^d \times \mathbb{R}^d \mapsto [0,1]$). Most encoders are currently based on a message-passing mechanism that learns a latent representation of the nodes via a aggregate-update iterative mechanism. At each iteration, of each node in the graph receives messages coming from neighboring nodes (their current embeddings). The messages are then aggregated through a permutation-invariant function and the node embedding is subsequently updated using a non-linear learnable function of the current node embedding and the aggregated messages, such as a multi-layer perceptron [8,53]. Decoders for link prediction usually compute a similarity function between node embeddings, such as the inner product between two node embeddings, followed by a normalization function, such as a sigmoid function, to obtain the probability of a link between the two nodes.

3.1   Attribution Methods for Link Prediction

A LP explainer implements a function that, given an edge (i,j) and a model to explain, maps the edges in E and the node features in X to their respective explanation scores. The higher the explanation score, the more important the edge (or the feature) is for the model to estimate the probability of (i,j). For this work, we have selected representative LP explainers basing our choice on *(i)* their belonging to different classes of the taxonomy described by Yuan et al. [47] to have a representative set of explainers, and *(ii)* their adoption and availability of code. Namely, we consider attribution methods based on perturbation (*GNNExplainer* [23]), gradient-based approaches (*Integrated Gradients* (IG) [36]), decomposition (*Deconvolution* [49]) - plus a hybrid one (*Layer-wise relevance propagation* (LRP) [5]).

GNNExplainer [23] searches for a subgraph G_S, and a subset of features X_S of the original dataset G, X that maximises the mutual information between the outputs of G, X and G_S, X_S. Since LP outputs a probability, the goal is reduced to finding a G_S that maximizes the probability of the model output while enforcing sparseness in G_S. Therefore, explanation scores are defined as a mask on edges and node features. GNNExplainer provides explanations for LP with no change to its optimization goal, but the model's encoder and decoder must be plugged in so that the edge and feature masks can be properly estimated. In our setting, when a model predicts a link (i,j), GNNExplainer learns a single mask over all links and features that are in the computation graphs of i and j.

Integrated Gradients (IG) [36] is an axiomatic attribution method that aims to explain the relationship between a model's predictions in terms of its features. It oughts to satisfy two axioms: sensitivity and implementation invariance, by analysing the gradients of the model with respect to its input features. In the case of link prediction, IG assigns positive and negative explanation scores to each link and each node feature, depending on how sensible the model's prediction is as these inputs change.

Deconvolution [49], first introduced for the explanation of convolutional neural networks in image classification, is a saliency method that uses a deconvolution operation to perform a backward propagation of the original model. It allows to highlight which feature or edge is activated the most and the attribution output consists in positive and negative scores for edges and node features.

Layer-wise relevance propagation (LRP) [5] is based on a backward propagation mechanism applied sequentially to all layers of the model. For a target neuron, its score is represented as a linear approximation of neuron scores from the previous layer. Here, the model output score represents the initial relevance which is decomposed into values for each neuron of the underlying layers, based on predefined rules. In this paper we use the $\varepsilon - stabilized$ rule as in [6].

To illustrate how the above attribution methods work in practice for LP, we start with a white-box message-passing model for link prediction on a toy example given by the graph shown in Fig. 1(left) with 5 nodes and 3 edges, $V = (a, b, x, y, z)$, $E = \{(a, x), (a, y), (a, z)\}$ and a feature matrix X with two node features defined as

$$X = \begin{bmatrix} 0.5 & 0.5 \\ 1 & 0 \\ 1 & 0 \\ 0 & 1 \\ 0.5 & 0.5 \end{bmatrix}. \tag{1}$$

We define the embeddings $e_i \in \mathbb{R}^d, i \in V$ of the graph nodes as

$$e_{ia} = \frac{1}{|\partial i|} \sum_{j \in \partial i} X_{ja} + X_{ia}, \quad a = 1, \ldots, d, \tag{2}$$

where $\partial i \equiv \{j \in V : i \neq j, (i, j) \in E\}$ indicates the set of first neighbors to node i. The probability of an edge between two nodes (the decoder) is the cosine similarity between the node embeddings.

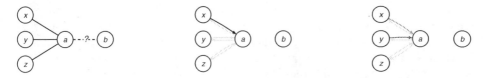

Fig. 1. Toy graph (left) and explanations (mask and attribution) for the link (a, b) in the toy graph for GNNExplainer (center) and Integrated Gradients (right) attribution methods. The edge color in the right panel indicates positive (orange) and negative (blue) importance. The explanations produced by Deconvolution and LRP are similar to Integrated Gradients. (Color figure online)

We ask to explain the prediction for link (a, b). Here the edge (a, x) has positive score because it "pulls" the embedding of a closer to b, while the edge (a, y) has negative score because it "pushes" the embedding of a away from b. The edge (a, z) is neutral. Figure 1 shows the edge explanations provided by GNNExplainer (center) and IG (right). IG is able to reflect the ground truth as it provides both positive and negative scores, while GNNExplainer considers positive masks only, thus returning a partial result. The explanations from Deconvolution and LRP are similar to the one produced with IG.

3.2   Validating Explanations

The validation of explanations is a generally overlooked topic in XAI, and LP tasks are no exceptions. Here, we suggest two different approaches, respectively to deal with ground-truth cases, and with no-ground-truth cases.

When ground truth is available, we use metrics from information retrieval. The ground truth is defined as a binary mask over E and X where (i, j) is true if the edge is important to the model prediction (and false otherwise), and a binary mask over features that follows the same logic. The explanation scores are binarized, fixing a standard threshold for the explanation scores, e.g. 0.5 for the positive defined masks of GNNExplainer and 0 for the other explainers considered here, or selecting the optimal threshold based on the ROC curve of true positive rate and false positive rate obtained varying the threshold, so that we can calculate a confusion matrix. True positives are considered when a high explanation score is assigned to an edge (or a feature) that is important according to the ground truth. False positives are considered when high explanation scores are assigned to non-important edges (or features). True negatives (and accordingly, false negatives) are considered when low explanation scores are assigned to unimportant (or important) edges or features. Finally, metrics such as precision, recall, specificity and sensitivity are calculated for each explainability technique. Here we focus on specificity and sensitivity, i.e., the true positive and true negative rates.

When ground truth explanations are not available, we resort to a validation method borrowed from explainability for computer vision, proposed first by Petsiuk et al. [26], that we adapt for graph explanations. To the best of our knowledge this is the first time this validation method is used in this context. This method consists in progressively removing/inserting features and/or edges based on their importance with respect to the attribution method considered. The feature and edge attributions are sorted by decreasing score and in the *deletion* case they are gradually removed. In the *insertion* case, they are gradually inserted in decreasing order of score starting with no features/edges. Intuitively, if the explainer's output is correct, removing or adding the most important features will cause the greatest change in the model output. The area under the curve of the fraction of features inserted/removed versus the output of the model provides a quantitative evaluation of the explanation.

To quantitatively compare different attribution methods, we define the following *area score*: referring to Fig. 2, for the insertion case, consider the area A_+ comprised between the explainer curve γ_e and the random curve γ_r when $\gamma_e > \gamma_r$, and the area above γ_r, U. The ratio $\frac{A_+}{U} \in [0, 1]$ describes the portion of the graph where the explainer performs better than the random baseline. Consider then the area A_- comprised between the explainer curve γ_e and the random curve γ_r when $\gamma_e < \gamma_r$, and the area below γ_r, L. The ratio $\frac{A_-}{L} \in [0, 1]$

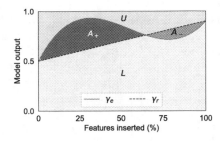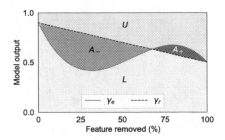

Fig. 2. Illustration of the area score for the feature insertion (left) and feature deletion (right) procedures. γ_e is the insertion (deletion) curve when features are sorted according to their explanation scores, while γ_r is the random insertion (deletion) curve. The area score for the insertion procedure is given by $\frac{A_+}{U} - \frac{A_-}{L}$. The area score for the deletion procedure is $\frac{A_-}{L} - \frac{A_+}{U}$.

corresponds to the portion of the graph where the explainer performs worse than the random baseline. We define the final score as

$$s_{ins} \equiv \frac{A_+}{U} - \frac{A_-}{L} \in [-1, 1]. \tag{3}$$

Similarly, for the deletion case the score is given by

$$s_{del} \equiv \frac{A_-}{L} - \frac{A_+}{U} \in [-1, 1]. \tag{4}$$

The area score is a summary metric for the insertion and deletion procedures, and reflects the ability of the explainer to assign higher scores to the most influential features/edges for the considered prediction. Ideally, a perfect explainer should give high scores to very few edges and/or features that carry almost all the information necessary for the prediction. In this case, inserting these features would be sufficient to recover the output of the model when all the features/edges are present, and deleting it would cause a great drop in the output of the model. In this case the area score would be equal or close to 1. In the case of random explanation scores, removing/inserting the features/edges with the highest score would not have, on average, a strong impact on the output of the model. In this case the area score would be 0. A negative value of the area score indicates a performance worse than the random baseline.

Note that the absolute values of the area score for the insertion and deletion procedure are not directly comparable since the normalization is different. This score is particularly useful for comparing the performance of different explainers with respect to the random baseline under the same procedure. The deletion curve is closely related to the fidelity and sparsity metrics [47], but the area score has the advantage of providing a single metric that coherently summarizes the two for easier readability. The insertion curve complement the deletion curve, in the sense that instead of considering the distance between the original model output and the output obtained by iteratively removing the most important feature by explanation score, it considers the distance between the original model and the output obtained by starting with all null features and iteratively adding the most important features by explanation score.

4   Experiments

In this section we report the results of evaluating LP explanations in two distinct scenarios – one with ground-truth explanations, and another without. In the first scenario, we use synthetic data, where graph datasets are generated along with their respective ground truth explanations for the created edges. This approach allows us to assess the explanations in a controlled setting, where we know the true explanations.

In the second scenario, we turn to empirical data from three different datasets. Here, without the availability of ground-truth explanations, we assess the quality of explanations produced by the explanation methods through the area score defined in Sect. 3.2. This provides a means to measure the performance of explanation methods in real-world, less controlled conditions.

Our experiments consist of four steps: (i) dataset preparation, (ii) model training, (iii) attribution, and (iv) attribution evaluation. Edges are split into training and test sets, with the same proportion of positive and negative edges, and attributions are performed on the test set. To ensure reproducibility and fair comparison, we test all explainers with the same trained model and train-test sets for each dataset. Multiple realizations of the attribution process with different random seeds account for the stochastic nature of ML training. For each dataset, we consider 2 encoders (VGAE, GIN), 2 decoders (Inner product, Cosine distance), and 4 explainers (GNNExplainer, Integrated Gradients, Deconvolution, and LRP). In Fig. 3 we show an example of the explanations given by each of the explainers considered for a GIN network predicting a missing edge on the Watts-Strogatz dataset (see Sect. 4.1).

4.1   Synthetic Data

We consider two generative models, namely the Stochastic Block Model (SBM) [18] and the Watts-Strogatz model (WS) [38], as examples of graphs where we can reconstruct the ground truth attributions for the link prediction task. In these experiments, whether an edge is present or not is clearly defined by the generative model. The small proportion of random edges introduced by the two stochastic generative models are not used to evaluate the explainers. We assume that a model trained on a sufficient number of data points is able to reflect the logic of the generative model, therefore an explainer should reflect this aspect in its attributions. For the SBM, a link should be present if two nodes belong to the same block, while for WS a link should be predicted if two nodes belong to a triangle completion. The node features in both cases are simply the one-hot encodings of the node ids, i.e. X corresponds to the identity matrix.

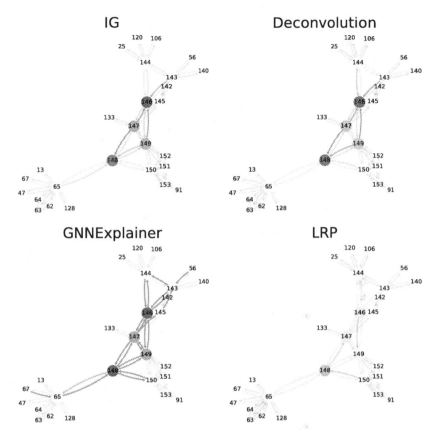

Fig. 3. Explanations for GIN trained on Watts-Strogatz graph data for the presence of an edge between the two nodes in red. The two nodes should be connected based on the triangle closure (green nodes). IG and Deconvolution give good explanations, while GNNExplainer considers important most of the computational graph, and LRP fails to identify the important edges. (Color figure online)

This is a common choice to use as node features in the absence of meaningful ones [46].

For both models, the experiments are designed as follows: we generate a graph $G = (V, E)$ of given size $|V|$, and we train a GML model for the LP task on a training fold of G. Then, the explainer is asked to explain each edge in the test set (except for the random edges). We compare the attributions to the ground truth, computing a confusion matrix of the results. We get a score for each predicted edge, obtaining the error distribution for the explainer.

For the sake of readability, we summarize the results with two metrics, namely specificity and sensitivity. Specificity measures the proportion of true negatives, that is, the number of edges that receive small importance from the explainer and that are in fact not important for the considered edge, over the number of true negatives; similarly, sensitivity is the ratio between predicted and true positives. Sensitivity and specificity together completely describe the quality of the attribution, but should not be considered separately. Figure 4 shows the sensitivity and specificity distributions for the four explainers tested on a GIN model trained on SBM (left) and WS (right) graphs.

In the SBM case (left), GNNExplainer demonstrates better specificity than other explainers but suffers from poor sensitivity due to numerous true positives in an SBM block. This is because it tends to produce sparse masks, often missing many true positives. This issue is particularly evident in SBM, where explanations involve numerous nodes, while in the WS graph, GNNExplainer's performance is in line with other explainers due to the sparse explanation.

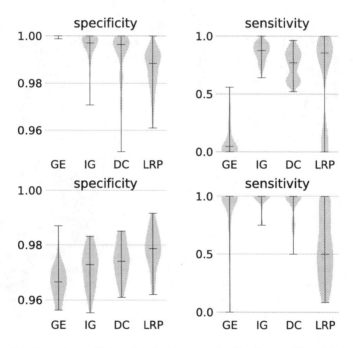

Fig. 4. Sensitivity and specificity distributions on the Stochastic Block Model (top) and Watt-Strogatz (bottom) graphs for the four considered attribution methods: GNNExplainer (GE), Integrated Gradients (IG), Deconvolution (DC) and Layer-wise Relevance Propagation (LRP).

The similarity measure used in the decoder significantly impacts the explanation quality. Common measures like cosine similarity pose challenges for current explainability techniques. Issues arise when nodes become more similar as information is masked, leading to degenerate solutions like empty subgraphs and the masking of all features. Consequently, for explainers that search for a subgraph that maximizes the model output such as GNNExplainer, no edges or features are deemed important when using cosine similarity between node embeddings. To highlight the impact of the decoder in producing explanations, we show in

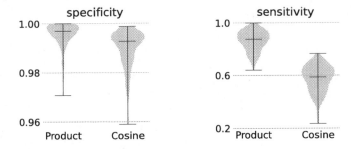

Fig. 5. Difference in the performance (specificity and sensitivity) of the IG attribution method for two GCN models with same encoder but different decoders, one based on scalar product and other based on cosine similarity, respectively.

Fig. 5 the sensitivity and specificity distributions for the IG explainer (but the results are similar for all explainers) when applied to two different GNN models that differ only in the decoder: the first uses a inner product of the node embeddings followed by a sigmoid, and the second uses a cosine similarity decoder. The explanation quality drops drastically if the model uses the cosine distance. This metric, due to normalization, is prone to produce explanation scores that are close to zero.

4.2   Empirical Data

In this section we focus on the validation of explainability methods when ground truth explanations are not available. In order to do so, we consider three empirical datasets: Cora and PubMed [31], plus a drug-drug interaction (DDI) network obtained from DrugBank [39]. The graph G and the node features X are constructed according to Yang et al. [44]: the bag-of-words representation is converted to node feature vectors and the graph is based on the citation links. The Cora dataset has 2,708 scientific publications classified into seven classes, connected through 5,429 links. The PubMed dataset has 19,717 publications classified into three classes, connected through 44,338 links. Although originally introduced for the node classification task, these two datasets are common benchmarks for the evaluation of current state-of-the-art GML models for the LP task, allowing a precise comparison of the performance of the models that we are explaining. The DDI dataset has 1,514 nodes representing drugs approved by the U.S. Food and Drug Administration, and 48,514 edges representing interaction between drugs. The dataset does not provide node features, that are provided as node embedding vectors of fixed dimension 128 computed using Node2Vec [15]. For this dataset, link prediction is a critical task, aiming to anticipate potential drug-drug interactions that have yet to be observed. Predicting these interactions can mitigate their adverse effects and health risks, thereby promoting patient safety through preventive healthcare measures.

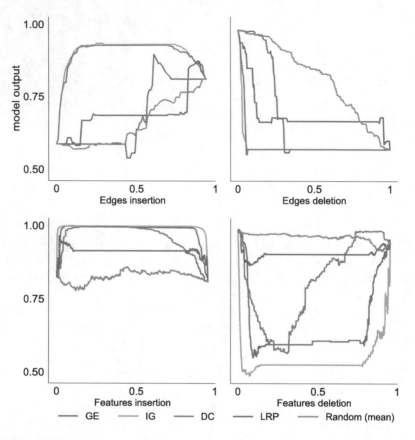

Fig. 6. Examples of insertion and deletion curves for edges (top) and features (bottom) for a GIN model with Inner product decoder.

We train two state-of-the art types of GNN encoders that are suitable for the link prediction task, namely the VGAE [21] and GIN [41]. For both encoder architectures, we use the inner product of node embeddings followed by a sigmoid as the decoder. Training the GNNs on CORA we reach an AUC test score of 0.952 ($accuracy$ = 0.744) for VGAE and an AUC test score of 0.904 ($accuracy$ = 0.781) for GIN. Training on PubMed we reach AUC test score of 0.923 ($accuracy$ = 0.724) for VGAE and AUC test score of 0.893 ($accuracy$ = 0.742) for GIN. Lastly, on DDI we reach AUC test score of 0.881 ($accuracy$ = 0.667) for VGAE and AUC test score of 0.920 ($accuracy$ = 0.751) for GIN. Once the model is trained we consider the edges in the test set and look at the explanation scores for node features and edges resulting from the attribution methods. These scores define insertion and deletion curves as described in Sect. 3.2. In Fig. 6 we show an example of insertion and deletion curves for node features and edges attributions obtained for a single edge predicted by a GIN model trained on CORA. The x axis refers to the ratio of edges/features that

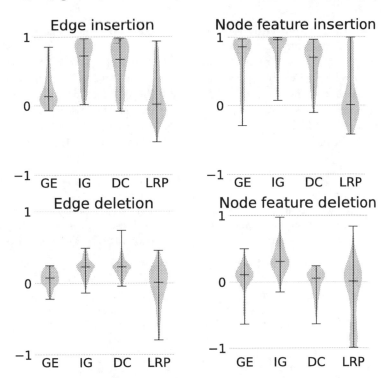

Fig. 7. Score distribution for feature and edge insertion and deletion. For each edge in the test set, we produce their respective insertion and deletion curves for features and edges, and calculate the area score according to the procedure illustrated in Fig. 2. The violin plots show the distribution of scores for each explainability method: GNNExplainer (GE), Integrated Gradients (IG), Deconvolution (DC) and Layer-wise Relevance Propagation (LRP).

have been inserted/removed by attribution importance, and the y axis shows the variation in the model output, for the selected class, in presence/absence of these features or edges. Each curve represents a single explainer, plus a curve (in purple) that represents the random insertion/deletion baseline. The random baseline is computed by adding/removing features or edges at random without taking in consideration any attribution score. Many realization of the random curve are then averaged in order to obtain a robust baseline. We then compute the area score defined in Sect. 3.2 for all the considered attribution methods and all the edges in the test set. In Fig. 7 we show the distribution of scores obtained from the CORA dataset with a GIN model. In Table 1 we report the results for all tested explainability methods for the three datasets using the GIN architecture as the encoder.

The case of edge deletion/insertion is particularly interesting when comparing the two different GNN architectures. Even if they perform comparably on the task of link prediction, the area score for the attribution on the VGAE model drops drastically for all attribution methods, suggesting that most of the signal of the data is taken from the node features alone, while the GIN model shows a very different scenario, where also the edges, and thus the network structure, are important for the model. In Fig. 8 we show the distribution of gain in the area score when inserting/deleting edges ordered by the IG mask versus random deletion, both for the VGAE and GIN models. We can see that while the VGAE has almost no gain, the GIN model is consistently better than the random baseline. We obtained similar results for the other explainers (not shown).

Table 1. Area scores (median ± std) for insertion (top) and deletion (bottom) for the selected explainers: GNNExplainer (GE), Integrated Gradients (IG), Deconvolution (DC) and Layer-wise Relevance Propagation (LRP). Area scores are calculated by taking into consideration the explanation scores produced by the explainers for LP models with GIN architecture as the encoder, trained with the three datasets: Cora, PubMed and DDI.

		Cora		PubMed		DDI	
		edge	feature	edge	feature	edge	feature
Insertion scores	GE	0.13 ± 0.22	0.86 ± 32	0.28 ± 0.30	0.68 ± 0.32	0.93 ± 0.38	0.71 ± 0.31
	IG	$\mathbf{0.72 \pm 0.27}$	$\mathbf{0.96 \pm 22}$	$\mathbf{0.89 \pm 0.25}$	$\mathbf{0.92 \pm 0.24}$	$\mathbf{0.96 \pm 0.29}$	$\mathbf{0.88 \pm 0.24}$
	DC	0.67 ± 0.31	0.70 ± 0.27	0.77 ± 0.29	0.65 ± 0.30	0.92 ± 0.27	-0.12 ± 0.10
	LRP	0.02 ± 0.32	0.01 ± 0.40	0.03 ± 0.40	0.13 ± 0.41	-0.1 ± 0.35	-0.04 ± 0.28
Deletion scores	GE	0.08 ± 0.11	0.11 ± 0.20	0.03 ± 0.10	0.05 ± 0.20	0.22 ± 0.12	0.10 ± 0.14
	IG	$\mathbf{0.23 \pm 0.11}$	$\mathbf{0.31 \pm 0.18}$	$\mathbf{0.26 \pm 0.15}$	$\mathbf{0.26 \pm 0.22}$	$\mathbf{0.43 \pm 0.15}$	$\mathbf{0.19 \pm 0.21}$
	DC	0.23 ± 0.11	0.05 ± 0.18	0.24 ± 0.15	0.12 ± 0.11	0.38 ± 0.13	0.01 ± 0.15
	LRP	0.01 ± 0.25	0.01 ± 0.44	-0.11 ± 0.38	-0.36 ± 0.39	0.23 ± 0.31	0.03 ± 0.33

5   Discussion of Findings

In the previous section we devised different approaches for a quantitative comparison of explanation methods applied to the link prediction task.[1] Synthetic data offers the advantage of having a ground truth available and complete control over its construction, but methods for a quantitative evaluation of real-world data, where no information is available *a priori*, are also necessary. For the latter we introduced the *area score*, a single-valued metric based on the insertion and deletion curves introduced in [26] that quantifies the gain in performance with respect to the random baseline when node features and/or edges are inserted/removed according to the attribution scores.

IG performs better in all cases, and this is coherent with previous results on GCNs for node and graph classification tasks [13, 28]. Deconvolution is a good alternative. We note that GNNExplainer, despite the acceptable performance, needs to be trained, and its output is strongly dependent on the choice of its hyperparameters. This makes it difficult to use GNNExplainer as a plug-and-play method for the attribution of GNN models. It has the advantage of being model-agnostic, contrary to the other methods.

---

[1] The complete source code is available at https://github.com/cborile/eval_lp_xai.

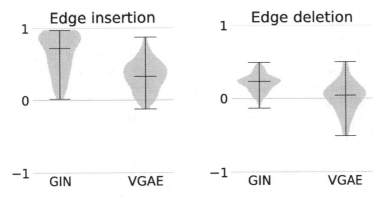

Fig. 8. Area score difference between VGAE and GIN models for edge insertion (left) and deletion (right) on the CORA dataset. The VGAE model has almost no gain with respect to the random baseline, while the GIN model is consistently better. This is suggestive of a different exploitation of topological features, that is, edges, in the graph by different encoder architectures when learning the link prediction task.

Applied to the DDI dataset, the utility of the area score and the insertion and deletion curves is particularly clear, since the drug-drug interaction graph is much more dense than the other examples. When looking for the reason of a link prediction output obtained through a Black-Box GML model, there are normally too many neighboring edges contributing to the model output even for 1- or 2- layers Graph Neural Networks, i.e., GNNs that consider only 1- or 2-hop neighborhoods in their computation graphs. A good area score on the edges means that most of the neighboring edges can be discarded for explaining the model output, thus increasing the interpretability for experts of what drugs can explain the interaction between a new candidate drug and existing ones.

Finally, we showed that technical details of the GNN black-box models can result in very different attributions for the same learned task, and even make some explanation methods completely inapplicable. Some of these details, like the choice of the distance function in the decoder stage, are inherent for the link prediction task and must be taken carefully into account when explainability is important. Also, different graph neural network architectures can result in drastic changes in the explanations, as some architectures can weigh more the network structure, while others can extract more signal from the node features.

6   Conclusions and Future Work

We introduced quantitative metrics for evaluating GML model explanations in LP tasks using a synthetic dataset testbed with known ground truth and adapted insertion/deletion curves for empirical datasets. This provided metrics for validating attribution methods when ground truth is unavailable. We tested representative XAI methods on GML models with different architectures and datasets, and our metrics enabled comparison of LP explanations with each other and with random baselines.

The thorough comparison of explanations we performed revealed hidden pitfalls and unexpected behaviors. For example, we identified cases where two models with similar performance produce drastically different explanations, and how seemingly minor choices, like embedding similarity in decoders, significantly impact explanations. The integration of feature and edge explanation scores, often overlooked in GML XAI, is a promising area for future research. We strongly advocate for comparative validation of XAI techniques, enabling informed selection of explainers, and we believe that the development of validation metrics and benchmarks is the first step towards establishing quantitative, comparative validation protocols for XAI techniques. This, in turn, would enable awareness in the choice of both GML models and explainers, and critical acceptance of the produced explanations.

Besides its technical challenges, explainable LP is a task that might positively impact several real-world scenarios, spanning from social networks, to biological networks and financial transaction networks. Each of these application domains displays unique characteristics and behaviors, both on the pragmatical and semantic level, and might therefore require the careful selection of an explainer in order to trust the final explanation. A pipeline that seamlessly integrates a GML model with an explainer, combining results of both model performance and explanation accuracy with the area score, might help mitigate the well-known black-box problems: difficulty of adoption from domain experts and debugging from developers, legal risk of non-compliance to regulation, and moral risk of inadvertently deploying biased models.

References

1. Abbas, K., et al.: Application of network link prediction in drug discovery. BMC Bioinform. **22**(1), 187 (2021). https://doi.org/10.1186/s12859-021-04082-y
2. Agarwal, C., Queen, O., Lakkaraju, H., Zitnik, M.: Evaluating explainability for graph neural networks. Sci. Data **10**(1), 144 (2023)
3. Agarwal, C., Zitnik, M., Lakkaraju, H.: Probing GNN explainers: a rigorous theoretical and empirical analysis of GNN explanation methods. In: Proceedings of the 25th International Conference on Artificial Intelligence and Statistics, pp. 8969–8996 (2022)
4. Ahn, S.J., Kim, M.: Variational graph normalized autoencoders. In: Proceedings of the 30th ACM International Conference on Information & Knowledge Management, pp. 2827–2831 (2021)
5. Bach, S., Binder, A., Montavon, G., Klauschen, F., Müller, K.R., Samek, W.: On pixel-wise explanations for non-linear classifier decisions by layer-wise relevance propagation. PLoS ONE **10**(7), e0130140 (2015)
6. Baldassarre, F., Azizpour, H.: Explainability techniques for graph convolutional networks. arXiv preprint arXiv:1905.13686 (2019)
7. Barbieri, N., Bonchi, F., Manco, G.: Who to follow and why: link prediction with explanations. In: Proceedings of the 20th ACM SIGKDD International Conference on Knowledge Discovery and Data Mining, pp. 1266–1275 (2014)

8. Bronstein, M.M., Bruna, J., Cohen, T., Veličković, P.: Geometric deep learning: grids, groups, graphs, geodesics, and gauges. arXiv preprint arXiv:2104.13478 (2021)
9. Chami, I., Abu-El-Haija, S., Perozzi, B., Ré, C., Murphy, K.: Machine learning on graphs: a model and comprehensive taxonomy. J. Mach. Learn. Res. **23**(89), 1–64 (2022)
10. Chami, I., Ying, Z., Ré, C., Leskovec, J.: Hyperbolic graph convolutional neural networks. In: Advances in Neural Information Processing Systems, vol. 32 (2019)
11. Daud, N.N., Ab Hamid, S.H., Saadoon, M., Sahran, F., Anuar, N.B.: Applications of link prediction in social networks: a review. J. Netw. Comput. Appl. **166**, 102716 (2020)
12. van Engelen, J.E., Boekhout, H.D., Takes, F.W.: Explainable and efficient link prediction in real-world network data. In: Boström, H., Knobbe, A., Soares, C., Papapetrou, P. (eds.) IDA 2016. LNCS, vol. 9897, pp. 295–307. Springer, Cham (2016). https://doi.org/10.1007/978-3-319-46349-0_26
13. Faber, L., Moghaddam, A.K., Wattenhofer, R.: When comparing to ground truth is wrong: on evaluating GNN explanation methods. In: Proceedings of the 27th ACM SIGKDD Conference on Knowledge Discovery & Data Mining, pp. 332–341 (2021)
14. Goodman, B., Flaxman, S.: EU regulations on algorithmic decision-making and a "right to explanation". AI Mag. **38** (2016)
15. Grover, A., Leskovec, J.: node2vec: scalable feature learning for networks. In: Proceedings of the 22nd ACM SIGKDD International Conference on Knowledge Discovery and Data Mining, pp. 855–864 (2016)
16. Halliwell, N., Gandon, F., Lecue, F.: A simplified benchmark for ambiguous explanations of knowledge graph link prediction using relational graph convolutional networks. In: 36th AAAI Conference on Artificial Intelligence (2022)
17. Hamilton, W.L.: Graph Representation Learning. Synthesis Lectures on Artificial Intelligence and Machine Learning, vol. 14, no. 3, pp. 1–159 (2020)
18. Holland, P.W., Laskey, K.B., Leinhardt, S.: Stochastic blockmodels: first steps. Soc. Netw. **5**(2), 109–137 (1983)
19. Jiang, H., Kim, B., Guan, M., Gupta, M.: To trust or not to trust a classifier. In: Advances in Neural Information Processing Systems, pp. 5541–5552 (2018)
20. Kang, B., Lijffijt, J., De Bie, T.: Explanations for network embedding-based link predictions. In: Kamp, M., et al. (eds.) ECML PKDD 2021. CCIS, vol. 1524, pp. 473–488. Springer, Cham (2021). https://doi.org/10.1007/978-3-030-93736-2_36
21. Kipf, T.N., Welling, M.: Variational graph auto-encoders. arXiv preprint arXiv:1611.07308 (2016)
22. Kumar, A., Singh, S.S., Singh, K., Biswas, B.: Link prediction techniques, applications, and performance: a survey. Phys. A **553**, 124289 (2020)
23. Lucic, A., ter Hoeve, M., Tolomei, G., de Rijke, M., Silvestri, F.: CF-GNNExplainer: counterfactual explanations for graph neural networks (2022). arXiv: 2102.03322
24. Luo, D., et al.: Parameterized explainer for graph neural network. In: Advances in Neural Information Processing Systems, vol. 33, pp. 19620–19631. Curran Associates, Inc. (2020)
25. Obermeyer, Z., Powers, B., Vogeli, C., Mullainathan, S.: Dissecting racial bias in an algorithm used to manage the health of populations. Science **366**(6464), 447–453 (2019)
26. Petsiuk, V., Das, A., Saenko, K.: RISE: randomized input sampling for explanation of black-box models. In: British Machine Vision Conference (BMVC) (2018)

27. Rossi, A., Firmani, D., Merialdo, P., Teofili, T.: Explaining link prediction systems based on knowledge graph embeddings. In: Proceedings of the 2022 International Conference on Management of Data, pp. 2062–2075 (2022)
28. Sanchez-Lengeling, B., et al.: Evaluating attribution for graph neural networks. In: Advances in Neural Information Processing Systems, vol. 33, pp. 5898–5910 (2020)
29. Schlichtkrull, M.S., De Cao, N., Titov, I.: Interpreting graph neural networks for NLP with differentiable edge masking. In: International Conference on Learning Representations (2020)
30. Selvaraju, R.R., Cogswell, M., Das, A., Vedantam, R., Parikh, D., Batra, D.: Grad-CAM: visual explanations from deep networks via gradient-based localization. In: Proceedings of the IEEE International Conference on Computer Vision, pp. 618–626 (2017)
31. Sen, P., Namata, G., Bilgic, M., Getoor, L., Galligher, B., Eliassi-Rad, T.: Collective classification in network data. AI Mag. **29**(3), 93–93 (2008)
32. Simonyan, K., Vedaldi, A., Zisserman, A.: Deep inside convolutional networks: visualising image classification models and saliency maps. arXiv preprint arXiv:1312.6034 (2013)
33. Smilkov, D., Thorat, N., Kim, B., Viégas, F., Wattenberg, M.: SmoothGrad: removing noise by adding noise. arXiv preprint arXiv:1706.03825 (2017)
34. Steging, C., Schomaker, L., Verheij, B.: The XAI paradox: systems that perform well for the wrong reasons. In: BNAIC/BENELEARN (2019)
35. Sundararajan, M., Taly, A., Yan, Q.: Axiomatic attribution for deep networks. In: Proceedings of the 34th International Conference on Machine Learning, ICML 2017, vol. 70, pp. 3319–3328. JMLR.org (2017)
36. Sundararajan, M., Taly, A., Yan, Q.: Axiomatic attribution for deep networks. In: International Conference on Machine Learning, pp. 3319–3328. PMLR (2017)
37. Wang, Z., Zong, B., Sun, H.: Modeling context pair interaction for pairwise tasks on graphs. In: Proceedings of the 14th ACM International Conference on Web Search and Data Mining, pp. 851–859 (2021)
38. Watts, D.J., Strogatz, S.H.: Collective dynamics of 'small-world' networks. Nature **393**(6684), 440–442 (1998)
39. Wishart, D.S., et al.: DrugBank 5.0: a major update to the DrugBank database for 2018. Nucl. Acids Res. **46**(D1), D1074–D1082 (2017)
40. Xie, Y., et al.: Task-agnostic graph explanations. arXiv preprint arXiv:2202.08335 (2022)
41. Xu, K., Hu, W., Leskovec, J., Jegelka, S.: How powerful are graph neural networks? arXiv preprint arXiv:1810.00826 (2018)
42. Xu, K., Hu, W., Leskovec, J., Jegelka, S.: How powerful are graph neural networks? In: International Conference on Learning Representations (2019)
43. Yan, Z., Ma, T., Gao, L., Tang, Z., Chen, C.: Link prediction with persistent homology: an interactive view. In: International Conference on Machine Learning, pp. 11659–11669. PMLR (2021)
44. Yang, Z., Cohen, W., Salakhudinov, R.: Revisiting semi-supervised learning with graph embeddings. In: International Conference on Machine Learning, pp. 40–48. PMLR (2016)
45. Ying, Z., Bourgeois, D., You, J., Zitnik, M., Leskovec, J.: GNNExplainer: generating explanations for graph neural networks. In: Advances in Neural Information Processing Systems, vol. 32 (2019)
46. You, J., Gomes-Selman, J.M., Ying, R., Leskovec, J.: Identity-aware graph neural networks. In: Proceedings of the AAAI Conference on Artificial Intelligence, vol. 35, pp. 10737–10745 (2021)

47. Yuan, H., Yu, H., Gui, S., Ji, S.: Explainability in graph neural networks: a taxonomic survey. IEEE Trans. Pattern Anal. Mach. Intell. **45**(5), 5782–5799 (2022)
48. Yuan, H., Yu, H., Wang, J., Li, K., Ji, S.: On explainability of graph neural networks via subgraph explorations. arXiv preprint arXiv:2102.05152 (2021)
49. Zeiler, M.D., Fergus, R.: Visualizing and understanding convolutional networks. In: Fleet, D., Pajdla, T., Schiele, B., Tuytelaars, T. (eds.) ECCV 2014. LNCS, vol. 8689, pp. 818–833. Springer, Cham (2014). https://doi.org/10.1007/978-3-319-10590-1_53
50. Zhang, M., Chen, Y.: Link prediction based on graph neural networks. In: Proceedings of the 32nd International Conference on Neural Information Processing Systems, NIPS 2018, Red Hook, NY, USA, pp. 5171–5181. Curran Associates Inc. (2018)
51. Zhang, M., Chen, Y.: Link prediction based on graph neural networks. In: Advances in Neural Information Processing Systems, vol. 31 (2018)
52. Zhou, B., Khosla, A., Lapedriza, A., Oliva, A., Torralba, A.: Learning deep features for discriminative localization. In: Proceedings of the IEEE Conference on Computer Vision and Pattern Recognition, pp. 2921–2929 (2016)
53. Zhou, J., et al.: Graph neural networks: a review of methods and applications. AI Open **1**, 57–81 (2020)
54. Zhu, Z., Zhang, Z., Xhonneux, L.P., Tang, J.: Neural bellman-ford networks: a general graph neural network framework for link prediction. In: Advances in Neural Information Processing Systems, vol. 34, pp. 29476–29490 (2021)

Actionable eXplainable AI, Semantics and Explainability, and Explanations for Advice-Giving Systems

Propaganda Detection Robustness Through Adversarial Attacks Driven by eXplainable AI

Danilo Cavaliere[1], Mariacristina Gallo[1(✉)], and Claudio Stanzione[2]

[1] Department of Management and Innovation Systems, University of Salerno,
84084 Fisciano, SA, Italy
{dcavaliere,mgallo}@unisa.it

[2] Defence Analysis and Research Institute, Center for Higher Defence Studies,
00165 Rome, RM, Italy
stanzione.dottorando@casd.difesa.it

Abstract. Pre-trained language models like BERT have shown remarkable success in many areas, including the detection of propaganda in text messages. However, recent studies have uncovered the vulnerability of these language models to adversarial text attacks. Attacks are perpetrated by perturbing or paraphrasing original text instances to hack the detection model. A crucial task for performing the attack is identifying critical message words on which the detection model leverages. In this sense, this work focuses on the role of the malicious use of eXplainable Artificial Intelligence (xAI) in increasing the effectiveness of adversarial text attacks or, dually, the aid its correct use may provide in measuring the robustness of propaganda detection models. The approach proposed here leverages xAI and Adversarial Text Generation techniques to simulate malicious attacks and measure the robustness of a propaganda detection model based on BERT. The attacks involve generating a new dataset by perturbing critical words in the original one identified with the aid of xAI (SHAP and LIME). The effectiveness of terms determined using xAI methods is compared with a statistical keyword extractor (YAKE!). These methods are adopted to detect the most important words as perturbation targets. The goal is to quantify the impact of disrupted instances on learning model performance. Experiments on the SemEval 2020 task 11 dataset reveal that modifying words detected by xAI methods significantly affects classification performance by reducing accuracy by 30%. These results demonstrate the effectiveness of xAI methods in system fooling attempts, highlighting the need to enhance learning system robustness.

Keywords: Propaganda detection · xAI · Adversarial Text Generation · Model Fooling · Cybersecurity

© The Author(s), under exclusive license to Springer Nature Switzerland AG 2023
L. Longo (Ed.): xAI 2023, CCIS 1902, pp. 405–419, 2023.
https://doi.org/10.1007/978-3-031-44067-0_21

1   Introduction

The spread of fast and low-budget access to the Internet encouraged people to share their own thoughts about different topics (politics, social events, etc.) through posts published on social networks (e.g., Facebook, Reddit, Twitter, etc.) or personal blog/site reaching a vast audience worldwide. On the one hand, this increasing trend indeed promotes the freedom of speech, but on the other hand, it makes the society vulnerable and undefended in the presence of eventual news manipulation coming from multiple sources. This is evident in the recent large-scale misinformation and disinformation events concerning US presidential campaign and Brexit in 2016, as well as the global infodemic related to the Covid-19 pandemic and vax-no-vax debate. Social networks can boost the effectiveness and spread of disinformation so that tailor-made content may strongly affect users' beliefs by using persuasive language. Contrary to classical disinformation (e.g., hoaxes, fake news), propaganda is not based on false statements but appeals to the user's sentiment to drive his/her opinions to meet the writer's needs and intents that may be of different kinds (e.g., economic, political, social, etc.).

The propaganda detection problem has been approached mainly through Machine and Deep Learning-based solutions [4,6] that had a relevant explosion in the last years in many areas. Moreover, parallel with the spread of such techniques, eXplainable Artificial Intelligence (xAI) reached great attention for building result explanations and helping experts in making decisions. However, if, on the one hand, xAI substantially improves the transparency of results of "black-box" models, on the other hand, it leaves the system vulnerable to adversary attacks [3]. Employing a specific jargon (e.g., argot, cryptolect) or word manipulations can easily fool detection systems. An example of a similar trick regards supporters of QAnon (an American political conspiracy theory and political movement) who may use different nicknames (e.g., "17Anon") to identify themselves and avoid the banning from social media sites [18].

Fooling learning models, especially in disinformation counterfeiting, can be seen as a form of cyber-attack aiming at leading detection systems to fail. This paper presents a framework that utilizes xAI technologies, namely SHAP and LIME, and a statistical keyword extractor (i.e., YAKE!) to test the robustness of a pre-trained Transformer-based propaganda detection classifier and its capacity to withstand cyber-attacks. By simulating a text manipulation attack through Adversarial Text Generation, the framework identifies and changes the most critical words for propaganda detection and reclassifies the text for analyzing system performances. The study reveals the superiority of xAI-based methods in detecting significant words for propaganda detection and their potential to combat cyber-attacks on propaganda detection systems. That outcome suggests that devoting efforts to cybersecurity solutions by leveraging xAI methods could give good results.

The paper is organized as follows: Sect. 2 introduces the topic background; Sect. 3 discusses related work; Sect. 4 presents the method and its features; Sect. 5 reports experiments and results achieved. Conclusions close the paper.

2 Preliminaries

This section presents a complete background about xAI domain and frameworks for feature selection.

2.1 xAI Technologies

In 2017, USA Defense Advanced Research Projects Agency (DARPA) started the Explainable AI (xAI) Program [13]. The main rationale behind the xAI program is to allow design and building of new models easier to understand without affecting model performances and high accuracy rate (accuracy of predictions) achieved with AI methods. Furthermore, another xAI aim is to allow humans understand, completely trust, and deal with the next generation of AI partners.

xAI techniques can work on generating explanations on local aspects (i.e., specific inputs) or at global level (i.e., explanations of the entire model). The main xAI principles are summarized below:

- **Model Specific or Model Agnostic:** This refers to evaluate if the interpretation method is restricted or not to a specific model. In details, Model-Specific methods and tools have been clearly designed for a specific model. On the contrary, Model Agnostic methods are not constrained to work with a specific ML model. In this latter case, accessing to Internal model data, including weights and structural details, is not allowed.
- **Intrinsic or Extrinsic (post-hoc):** This feature is meant to distinguish among models that are interpretable on their own and models requiring external methods examining models after training for achieving explainability. For instance, easy-to-understand models (e.g., decision trees) are intrinsic. The employment of an interpretation strategy after training to get interpretations lies within extrinsic techniques.
- **Local or Global:** This is intended to classify interpretation methods among those meant to depict one single data record and those describing a global behavior of the model considered. Therefore, Global methods are in charge of interpreting the whole model, whereas Local methods are targeted to explain a single prediction.

2.2 Frameworks for Feature Selection

The extraction of meaningful document keywords is a well-established problem and solutions to deal with it have been proven to be successful for solving many tasks, including text summarization, clustering, opinion mining, thesaurus building, recommendation, query expansion, information visualization, retrieval and more [2,9]. Generally, solutions may be designed for two broad tasks: keyword assignment and keyword extraction. The former concerns multi-label text classification associating a set of keywords taken from a controlled vocabulary (dictionary or thesaurus) with an instance of data (documents). The latter, instead, refers to the mere process of extracting keywords from the documents by using unsupervised [2] or supervised [9] methods. These methods focus on local text features and statistical information, such as term co-occurrence and frequencies, to extract keywords [2,9]. Other approaches employ xAI technologies to allow feature extraction explainability [16,22].

In this paper, three frameworks have been considered: two xAI-based (LIME and SHAP) and a statistical one (YAKE!). Their features are summarized below.

LIME. Local Interpretable Model-agnostic Explanations (LIME) is a framework that aims to provide an individual-level explanation of single predictions (*Local*) in an extrinsic (*Post-hoc*) way and can explain a model without having to 'peak' into it (*Model-Agnostic*) [22]. After perturbing input in its neighborhood, it evaluates the model predictions to establish which portions of the interpretable input contribute to the prediction itself. Then it creates an entirely novel dataset of modified samples and the corresponding black box model predictions. Based on how similar the sampled examples are to the instance of interest, LIME weights the interpretable model it trains on this new dataset.

SHAP. SHapley Additive exPlanations (SHAP) framework [16] evaluates the contribution of each feature to the final prediction of an instance x in order to explain the prediction of that instance. It is a *Local*-based, *Post-hoc*, and *Model-Agnostic* paradigm, similar to LIME. Coalitional game theory is used by the SHAP explanation approach to calculate Shapley values. Shapley values are feature values of a data instance acting as coalition members. Shapley values indicate how evenly dispersed the forecast is across the characteristics. A player could consist of several feature values or just one. In contrast to LIME, SHAP does not need the establishment of a local model; instead, the Shapley values for each dimension are computed using the same function.

YAKE!. Yet Another Keyword Extractor (YAKE!) [2] library allows the detection of the most important keywords exploiting methods to extract text statistical features from the article. YAKE! consists in five principal steps: (1) text pre-processing and identification of candidate terms; (2) feature extraction; (3) term score computation; (4) n-gram generation and candidate keyword score calculation; and (5) data deduplication and ranking. The first step is in charge of turning the document into a machine-readable format for detection of potential candidate terms. The second phase receives a list of individual terms in input that are represented as a set of statistical features. The third step employs a heuristic to asses a unique score from the combination of the acquired features to represent term importance. The fourth step employs an n-gram construction method to produce the candidate keywords so that each one of them is associated with a score based on candidate importance. Last step exploits the deduplication distance similarity measure to spot similar keywords.

3   Related Work

This section explores related work in two reference domains: online propaganda detection and monitoring, and text manipulation cyberattacks.

3.1   Propaganda

Concerning online propaganda, the most explored topic in literature is propaganda detection from texts [7,10,14,19]. In [14], authors introduce a technique for dataset labeling on persuasive text, run topic modeling, and then perform a corpora imbalance assessment to detect propaganda. In [7], a method is designed exploiting different methodologies and technologies, including GloVe, BERT and LSTM, to build word representation, pre-train the model and detect propagandistic text, respectively. Another approach [10] designs a method to analyze text at the fragment level, bridging TF/IDF, word and character n-grams, which are then used to build a propagandistic text classifier. In [19], authors propose a Machine Learning model for propaganda detection, including a preliminary data process, feature extraction algorithms and a binary classification to detect propaganda at the article and sentence level. Other trends are directed at analyzing propaganda on social networks to help countermeasure definitions, such as [11] proposing a framework to analyze social dynamics of social influence within ISIS supporters by using activity-connectivity maps based on patterns related to network and temporal activities. Another study focuses on sentiment employment [21] by introducing a hybrid deep learning approach bridging Word2Vec for word semantics extraction and an emotional dictionary built with VADER sentiment analysis to detect propaganda from texts better. A reference work for the classification of propaganda is [6], where the authors present 14 different classes that characterize the world of propaganda. Another work [4] presents ensemble models employing RoBERTa-based neural architectures, additional CRF layers, and transfer learning to handle span identification and technique learning.

Concerning methods that employed xAI techniques to explain results accomplished by pre-trained models, in [23], the authors propose an approach that processes BERT model results with two xAI techniques, namely Local Interpretable Model-Agnostic Explanations (LIME) and Anchors, to check fake news data including short pieces of text such as tweets or headlines. However, no xAI approach working on BERT models has been found dealing with propaganda detection. To the best of our knowledge, this paper introduces, for the first time, an xAI-based approach to extracting the most significant words for detecting propaganda from texts.

3.2   Adversarial Attacks

The main objective of adversarial attacks is to lead Machine Learning and Deep Learning systems to fail on purpose by giving them adversarial examples as input data which forces the system to get incorrect outputs. To prevent real cyberattacks, techniques of Adversarial Attacks may be used to improve existing models and achieve more robust learning systems to withstand cyberattacks better. In this regard, the approach proposed in [8] helps discover vulnerabilities for Deep Learning models by introducing an attack algorithm generating adversarial malware binaries to make DL models more robust.

Adversarial attacks have also been explored to improve the performances of DL methods for tasks in specific domains. An example of such a use is the study proposed in [5] that demonstrates the efficacy of adversarial attacks to improve fake news detection and social bot detection models.

Other researchers investigated the combination of xAI technologies and adversarial attacks to enhance the trustworthiness of AI methods. To this purpose, the authors in [12] demonstrated that Adversarial Perturbations could strongly affect the xAI outcomes, even in the case of failed attacks.

Some other trends focus on the employment of adversarial techniques to outwit hackers by making AI systems robust against attacks. In this regard, some researchers propose new solutions to improve existing models; for example, the authors in [24] improved the adversarial robustness of DNN classifiers without using adversarial training. Some other approaches are targeted at re-defining adversarial attacks to be used for adversarial robustness evaluation of specific models. To this purpose, the authors in [25] design new attacks to generate adversarial examples over affine transformations.

From the xAI point of view, the term robustness usually refers to the effects of small changes to the input on explanations provided by xAI techniques [17]. However, in this work, robustness is associated with the learning model and its capacity to react to adversarial attacks (i.e., examples constructed to fool the model). In this sense, xAI techniques, studied to give an explanation to the model's responses, can become a double-edged sword leveraged to intercept features to modify that most affecting final results [20]. So, Adversarial Text Generation is employed jointly with xAI frameworks to detect the most significant words for propaganda detection and change them in the dataset to fool the model and test its robustness.

4   Methodology

This section introduces the proposed methodology to analyze the robustness of a propaganda detection model toward adversarial attacks aimed at deceiving the system in the classification process. A complete workflow is shown in Fig. 1. The first step concerns the detection of propaganda from texts by using a pre-trained Transformer-based model; the achieved results are then processed to extract features ranked by their impact; the third step allows changing the extracted features in the dataset by using Adversarial Text Generation (ATG) techniques. Finally, the last step runs the pre-trained Transformer-based model on the updated dataset to get newer propaganda classification results, that are compared to the early ones for assessing the robustness of the evaluated model against adversarial attacks.

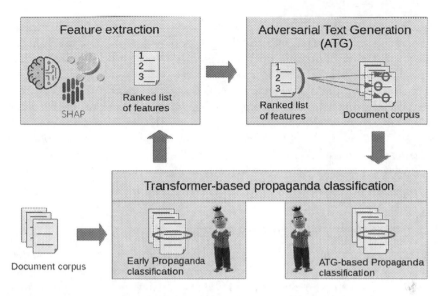

Fig. 1. Methodology Workflow: 1) Propaganda in texts is detected using a pre-trained Transformer model; 2) xAI methods extract impactful features; 3) the dataset is updated using Adversarial Text Generation (ATG) on features previously selected; 4) the updated dataset is used to run the pre-trained Transformer-based model again, generating newer propaganda classification results.

4.1   Transformer-Based Propaganda Classification

A Transformer network based on a DistilBERT pre-trained model is employed to classify text propaganda. The pre-trained model is fine-tuned on the SemEval 2023 Task 3 training dataset (which, at the time of writing, is yet to be public but only available for competition participants) for the propaganda detection task [1]. The dataset provided by the SemEval-2023 Task 3 organizers for Subtask 3 specific for the English language contains 446 training news and web articles and 9498 paragraphs, where 5738 are labeled as "No Propaganda" and 3760 fall under at least one of the 23 propaganda techniques. Data is subjected to a preprocessing step to clean the text and remove punctuation. To fine-tune the Transformer Distilbert-Base-Uncased, the following hyperparameters are used: the batch size of 16; learning rate of $2e^{-5}$; AdamW optimizer; 4 epochs.

The constructed model is tested on the corresponding dev set consisting of 90 articles and 3127 paragraphs whose 2007 are "No Propaganda" and 1120 "Propaganda". Tests provide an accuracy of around 90%.

4.2   Feature Extraction

To extract the features (i.e., words) with the highest impact on propaganda detection results, frameworks described in Sect. 2.2 are adopted. In detail, two different xAI technologies (i.e., SHAP and LIME) and a statistical keyword extractor (i.e., YAKE!) are used for the task. The three methods return as much as ranked lists of words that mostly affected propaganda predictions. Such words are selected at this stage to change the original dataset and then test the robustness of the propaganda detection model.

Let us show a running example for which the classification changes after the adversarial attempts. Starting from the following instance, *"Are You Kidding Me, Ted Cruz? Don't "Blame The Police Office" Who Admitted Killing Botham Jean? FOX 26 asked Cruz to respond to his Democratic midterm rival, Beto O'Rourke, who called for officer Guyger to be fired"* the system extracts the first five most important words by each method. In particular, LIME detects the subsequent ones: *midterm, Killing, rival, officer, Democratic*.

4.3   Adversarial Text Generation (ATG)

At this stage, each word detected as crucial at the previous step is looked for in the dataset and replaced with alternative words calculated using Adversarial Text Generation (ATG) techniques. ATG refers to the practice of generating new instances by slightly perturbing inputs to fool the learning models. Algorithms for ATG can select words among nearest neighbors in the embedding space, out-of-vocabulary, or through generative models. In this work, five different methods are used for generating words that are semantically and syntactically similar to the original ones; they are (1) space insert, (2) character delete, (3) character swap, (4) Substitute-C (Sub-C), (5) Substitute-W (Sub-W) [15]. Method (1) consists in inserting a space into the word, method (2) deletes a middle character, method (3) swaps two adjacent characters in a word, method (4) replaces a character in a word with a visually similar one (i.e., '1' with 'l') and method (5) replaces a word with its top k nearest neighbors in a context-aware word vector space. The word replacement algorithm applies the five methods in sequence to the extracted N-ranked words, from the highest-ranked word to the lowest-ranked one. Finally, the updated dataset is processed with the Transformer-based propaganda classification model to get the propaganda detection results after the ATG-based changes.

Recalling the example in the previous section, by applying the character delete technique to all five words, the starting instance becomes as follows: *"Are You Kidding Me, Ted Cruz? Don't "Blame The Police Office" Who Admitted* **Kiling** *Botham Jean? FOX 26 asked Cruz to respond to his* **Demoratic** **miderm rial***, Beto O'Rourke, who called for* **officer** *Guyger to be fired"*. Then, the propaganda detection model classifies the new instance and the changed others, and performance is registered.

Comparing the accuracy of the updated dataset and the original one allows for determining how much the extracted words contributed to determining propaganda sentences. In detail, the higher the accuracy gap, the higher the impact of words in detecting propaganda and, consequently, the risk of corrupting the model by modifying them.

5   System Evaluation

The experimentation was aimed at evaluating the proposed methodology. It is carried out by comparing the performance of the propaganda detection model before and after adversarial attacks conducted systematically on words identified as significant by the three chosen methods: XAI-based (SHAP and LIME) and statistical keyword extraction (YAKE!). More in detail, the experimentation follows subsequent steps:

- Creation of the dataset;
- Feature extraction and ATG attempts generation;
- Results collection.

The steps are detailed in the following subsections.

5.1   Creation of the Dataset

The dataset used for the experimentation is SemEval 2020 task 11, subtask Technique Classification. The task aims to associate labels representing the propaganda technique employed by choosing from an inventory of 14, given a specific text fragment in the context of a whole document [6]. The dataset is provided with the start and end coordinates of the span within a paragraph and the propaganda technique or techniques, if more than one, that characterize such paragraph. The label "Propaganda" is associated with paragraphs containing these spans. Paragraphs without any propaganda spans are labeled as "No Propaganda". An operation of down-sampling assures the balancing of the dataset with 1000 final instances.

Applying the constructed propaganda detection model on the described dataset returns an accuracy of 88%.

5.2   Feature Extraction and ATG Attempts Generation

Given the propaganda detection model and the dataset, LIME, SHAP and YAKE! are asked to extract features (in this case, words) crucial for the final classification. First, each framework produces a ranked list of words. Then, adversarial attacks on these words are generated. Attacks, as previously described, are inspired by the TextBugger framework consisting of five text editing techniques. Thus, five correlated words are generated for each word extracted, corresponding to five new instances, which the propaganda detection model must classify. The performance of new classifications is described in the following subsection.

5.3   Results Collection

Table 1 presents the prediction results after modifying the most important word for each method. On average, modifying words detected by two xAI-based methods significantly decreases the model performance, leading it to lose 10% accuracy. In particular, with the SUB-C technique on the words identified by LIME, there is a quite significant decrease of 13%. Regarding the YAKE! statistical method, its performance decrease is at maximum around 3%, which is way less significant than that observed for the two xAI methods.

Table 1. Performance of Propaganda Detection Model with and without adversarial attacks on the most important word extracted by each method. The table shows how the accuracy of the model changes after the first word deemed most relevant by the different methods is perturbed with the different ATG techniques.

METHODS	NO ATG	INSERT	DELETE	SWAP	SUB-C	SUB-W
SHAP	0,88	0,78	0,79	0,79	0,80	0,80
LIME	0,88	0,79	0,79	0,81	0,75	0,83
YAKE!	0,88	0,85	0,85	0,86	0,85	0,88

Table 2. Performance of Propaganda Detection Model after attacks on the five most important words extracted by the SHAP method. The table shows the accuracy for each ATG technique as the perturbations progressed. For example, in column '2', the model was tested by making perturbations on the first and second most important words extracted from SHAP. In column '5', the model is tested on a text where the first five most relevant words have been perturbed.

SHAP	0	1	2	3	4	5
INSERT	0,88	0,78	0,74	0,71	0,68	0,67
DELETE	0,88	0,79	0,74	0,70	0,68	0,65
SWAP	0,88	0,79	0,74	0,71	0,68	0,66
SUB-C	0,88	0,80	0,73	0,69	0,66	0,64
SUB-W	0,88	0,80	0,74	0,69	0,67	0,64

After an initial experiment attacking only the first-ranked word in terms of importance, the investigation is extended to the first five words extracted by each technique. Results shown in Tables 2, 3 and 4 confirm what was already experienced for the first-ranked word: words detected by SHAP and LIME are more relevant for the final accuracy, leading the model to fail more often, even with small perturbations. After perturbing five words, SHAP and LIME cause a decrease in model accuracy, which is greater than 20%, except for the SUB-W technique on LIME. Regarding LIME, it is impressive to analyze the impact of the SUB-C technique, in which case the model accuracy decreases by 31%. The other techniques also perform very well, with the most significant decrease, with the SHAP method being 24%. The same thing does not happen when using YAKE!: with this method, the most significant decrease always occurs with the SUB-C technique, scoring 14%, much lower than the 31% of LIME. Moreover, YAKE! causes a 10% accuracy decrease, on average, by perturbating the first five words, while the other methods cause an equivalent decrease after perturbating just the first word.

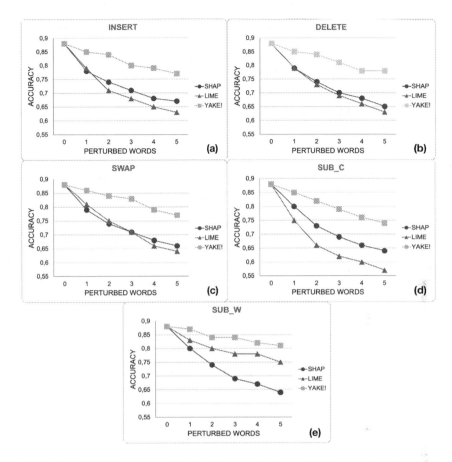

Fig. 2. Technical ATGs compare the first five words for each feature extraction method. The figure shows on each graph how the accuracy decreases as the number of perturbed words increases. In particular, (a) shows the comparison using the INSERT technique, (b) the DELETE technique, (c) the SWAP technique, (d) the SUB-C technique and finally, (e) the SUB-W technique.

Another consideration should be made about the techniques: SUB-C is the most effective. Figure 2(d) shows how performance drops steadily by adopting this technique focused on a visual perturbation. The least effective technique is SUB-W which replaces the word with the top k nearest neighbors in a context-aware word vector space. Figure 3, which shows a numerical comparison between the accuracy of the initial model and the model after perturbing the first five words for each method, confirms what has been analyzed so far: the SUB-C technique is the most effective in deceiving the model. Finally, let us notice that the words identified by LIME also cause a higher accuracy decrease than those detected by the other methods, except for the SUB-W technique (see Fig. 2). Therefore, the last analysis consists in measuring the accuracy decrease after

Table 3. Performance of Propaganda Detection Model after attacks on the five most important words extracted by the LIME method. The table shows the accuracy for each ATG technique as the perturbations progressed, meaning that in column '5', the model is tested on a text where all the first five most relevant words have been perturbed.

LIME	0	1	2	3	4	5
INSERT	0,88	0,79	0,71	0,68	0,65	0,63
DELETE	0,88	0,79	0,73	0,69	0,66	0,63
SWAP	0,88	0,81	0,75	0,71	0,66	0,64
SUB-C	0,88	0,75	0,66	0,62	0,60	0,57
SUB-W	0,88	0,83	0,80	0,78	0,78	0,75

Table 4. Performance of Propaganda Detection Model after attacks on the five most important words extracted by the YAKE! method. The table shows the accuracy for each ATG technique as the perturbations progressed, meaning that in column '5', the model is tested on a text where the all first five most relevant words have been perturbed.

YAKE!	0	1	2	3	4	5
INSERT	0,88	0,85	0,84	0,80	0,79	0,77
DELETE	0,88	0,85	0,84	0,81	0,78	0,78
SWAP	0,88	0,86	0,84	0,83	0,79	0,77
SUB-C	0,88	0,85	0,82	0,79	0,76	0,74
SUB-W	0,88	0,87	0,84	0,84	0,82	0,81

each perturbation. In particular, Fig. 4 shows the average decrease after each perturbation for each technique and each word extraction method. Let us notice that the reported statistics display the relevance of the SUB-C technique, with an average decrease of 6% after each attack. The figure also shows how YAKE! is less effective than the other two methods.

The results emerging from the experimentation can be summarized as follows:

1. xAI-based framework performs better than a statistical one in selecting the most important feature (i.e., words) of a Transformer-based classifier for propaganda detection;
2. Perturbing words can significantly decrease the performance of a propaganda detection model;
3. Among perturbation techniques proposed by the TextBugger framework (i.e., space insert, character delete, character swap, Sub-C, Sub-W), the most effective in terms of model tricking is Sub-C, namely replacing a character with a visually similar one (i.e., '1' with 'l').

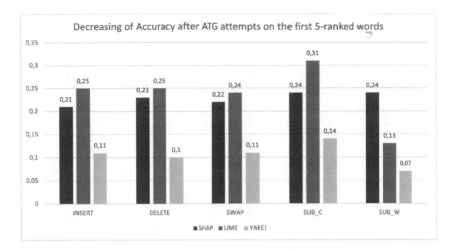

Fig. 3. Decreasing of Accuracy after ATG attempts on the first five-ranked words. The figure describes with a bar graph how much the model's accuracy decreases with the perturbation of each technique's first five words identified by each method.

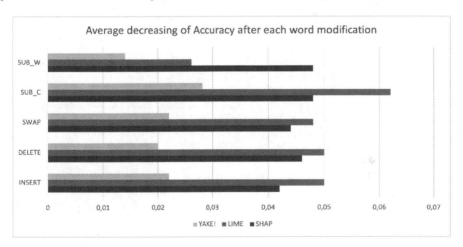

Fig. 4. The average decreases in accuracy after each word modification. The figure describes how much, on average, the model declines in accuracy after each perturbation. It does so for each technique for each method.

6   Conclusion

This paper proposed a novel framework that employs xAI and statistical methods (SHAP, LIME, and YAKE!) with Adversarial Text Generation techniques to simulate malicious attacks and measure the robustness of a pre-trained Transformer-based propaganda classifier. Experimental results on the SemEval 2020 task 11 dataset showed that perturbing critical words detected by xAI methods significantly affect classification performance, pointing out the effectiveness of xAI methods in the system fooling attempts. The findings highlight the need for xAI-based solutions to enhance the robustness of learning models and prevent potential cyberattacks on propaganda detection systems.

Overall, the proposed framework can be extended in terms of the application domain and adopted models. Moreover, solutions against Adversarial Text Generation attacks can be studied by, for example, enhancing the training model leveraging just adversarial attacks suggested by xAI methods.

Acknowledgement. This work was partially supported by project SERICS (PE00000014) under the MUR National Recovery and Resilience Plan funded by the European Union - NextGenerationEU.

References

1. Bangerter, M., et al.: Unisa at SemEval-2023 task 3: a shap-based method for propaganda detection. In: Proceedings of the 17th International Workshop on Semantic Evaluation, SemEval 2023, Toronto, Canada (2023)
2. Campos, R., Mangaravite, V., Pasquali, A., Jorge, A., Nunes, C., Jatowt, A.: YAKE! Keyword extraction from single documents using multiple local features. Inf. Sci. **509**, 257–289 (2020)
3. Capuano, N., Fenza, G., Loia, V., Stanzione, C.: Explainable artificial intelligence in cybersecurity: a survey. IEEE Access **10**, 93575–93600 (2022)
4. Chernyavskiy, A., Ilvovsky, D., Nakov, P.: Aschern at SemEval-2020 task 11: it takes three to tango: RoBERTa, CRF, and transfer learning. In: Proceedings of the Fourteenth Workshop on Semantic Evaluation, pp. 1462–1468 (2020)
5. Cresci, S., Petrocchi, M., Spognardi, A., Tognazzi, S.: Adversarial machine learning for protecting against online manipulation. IEEE Internet Comput. **26**(2), 47–52 (2021)
6. Da San Martino, G., Barrón-Cedeño, A., Wachsmuth, H., Petrov, R., Nakov, P.: SemEval-2020 task 11: detection of propaganda techniques in news articles. In: Proceedings of the Fourteenth Workshop on Semantic Evaluation, pp. 1377–1414 (2020)
7. Dao, J., Wang, J., Zhang, X.: YNU-HPCC at SemEval-2020 task 11: LSTM network for detection of propaganda techniques in news articles. In: Proceedings of the Fourteenth Workshop on Semantic Evaluation, pp. 1509–1515 (2020)
8. Demetrio, L., Biggio, B., Giovanni, L., Roli, F., Alessandro, A., et al.: Explaining vulnerabilities of deep learning to adversarial malware binaries. In: CEUR Workshop Proceedings, vol. 2315 (2019)
9. Duari, S., Bhatnagar, V.: Complex network based supervised keyword extractor. Expert Syst. Appl. **140**, 112876 (2020)
10. Ermurachi, V., Gifu, D.: UAIC1860 at SemEval-2020 task 11: detection of propaganda techniques in news articles. In: Proceedings of the Fourteenth Workshop on Semantic Evaluation, pp. 1835–1840 (2020)
11. Ferrara, E.: Contagion dynamics of extremist propaganda in social networks. Inf. Sci. **418**, 1–12 (2017)
12. Galli, A., Marrone, S., Moscato, V., Sansone, C.: Reliability of eXplainable artificial intelligence in adversarial perturbation scenarios. In: Del Bimbo, A., et al. (eds.)

ICPR 2021. LNCS, vol. 12663, pp. 243–256. Springer, Cham (2021). https://doi. org/10.1007/978-3-030-68796-0_18

13. Gunning, D., Aha, D.: DARPA's explainable artificial intelligence (XAI) program. AI Mag. **40**(2), 44–58 (2019)

14. Kirill, Y., Mihail, I.G., Sanzhar, M., Rustam, M., Olga, F., Ravil, M.: Propaganda identification using topic modelling. Procedia Comput. Sci. **178**, 205–212 (2020)

15. Li, J., Ji, S., Du, T., Li, B., Wang, T.: TextBugger: generating adversarial text against real-world applications. In: 26th Annual Network and Distributed System Security Symposium (2019)

16. Lundberg, S.M., Lee, S.I.: A unified approach to interpreting model predictions. In: Advances in Neural Information Processing Systems, vol. 30 (2017)

17. Mishra, S., Dutta, S., Long, J., Magazzeni, D.: A survey on the robustness of feature importance and counterfactual explanations. arXiv preprint arXiv:2111.00358 (2021)

18. Morrish, L.: How QAnon content endures on social media through visuals and code words (2020). http://firstdraftnews.org/articles/how-qanon-content-endures-on-social-media-through-visuals-and-code-words/. Accessed 20 Apr 2023

19. Oliinyk, V.A., Vysotska, V., Burov, Y., Mykich, K., Fernandes, V.B.: Propaganda detection in text data based on NLP and machine learning. In: MoMLeT+ DS, pp. 132–144 (2020)

20. Pawelczyk, M., Agarwal, C., Joshi, S., Upadhyay, S., Lakkaraju, H.: Exploring counterfactual explanations through the lens of adversarial examples: a theoretical and empirical analysis. In: International Conference on Artificial Intelligence and Statistics, pp. 4574–4594. PMLR (2022)

21. Polonijo, B., Šuman, S., Šimac, I.: Propaganda detection using sentiment aware ensemble deep learning. In: 2021 44th International Convention on Information, Communication and Electronic Technology (MIPRO), pp. 199–204. IEEE (2021)

22. Ribeiro, M.T., Singh, S., Guestrin, C.: "Why should i trust you?" Explaining the predictions of any classifier. In: Proceedings of the 22nd ACM SIGKDD International Conference on Knowledge Discovery and Data Mining, pp. 1135–1144 (2016)

23. Szczepański, M., Pawlicki, M., Kozik, R., Choraś, M.: New explainability method for BERT-based model in fake news detection. Sci. Rep. **11**(1), 23705 (2021)

24. Wei, J., Yao, L., Meng, Q.: Self-adaptive logit balancing for deep neural network robustness: defence and detection of adversarial attacks. Neurocomputing **531**, 180–194 (2023)

25. Xiang, W., Su, H., Liu, C., Guo, Y., Zheng, S.: Improving the robustness of adversarial attacks using an affine-invariant gradient estimator. Comput. Vis. Image Underst. **229**, 103647 (2023)

Explainable Automated Anomaly Recognition in Failure Analysis: is Deep Learning Doing it Correctly?

Leonardo Arrighi[1]([✉])(iD), Sylvio Barbon Junior[2](iD), Felice Andrea Pellegrino[2](iD), Michele Simonato[3](iD), and Marco Zullich[4](iD)

[1] Department of Mathematics and Geosciences, University of Trieste, Trieste, Italy
leonardo.arrighi@phd.units.it
[2] Department of Engineering and Architecture, University of Trieste, Trieste, Italy
{sylvio.barbonjunior,fapellegrino}@units.it
[3] ASAC srl, Cessalto, (TV), Italy
michele.simonato@asac.it
[4] Department of Artificial Intelligence, University of Groningen, Groningen, The Netherlands
m.zullich@rug.nl

Abstract. EXplainable AI (XAI) techniques can be employed to help identify points of concern in the objects analyzed when using image-based Deep Neural Networks (DNNs). There has been an increasing number of works proposing the usage of DNNs to perform Failure Analysis (FA) in various industrial applications. These DNNs support practitioners by providing an initial screening to speed up the manual FA process. In this work, we offer a proof-of-concept for using a DNN to recognize failures in pictures of Printed Circuit Boards (PCBs), using the boolean information of (non) faultiness as ground truth. To understand if the model correctly identifies faulty connectors within the PCBs, we make use of XAI tools based on Class Activation Mapping (CAM), observing that the output of these techniques seems not to align well with these connectors. We further analyze the *faithfulness* of these techniques with respect to the DNN, observing that often they do not seem to capture relevant features according to the model's decision process. Finally, we *mask out* faulty connectors from the original images, noticing that the DNN predictions do not change significantly, thus showing that the model possibly did not learn to base its predictions on features associated with actual failures. We conclude with a warning that FA using DNNs should be conducted using more complex techniques, such as object detection, and that XAI tools should not be taken as *oracles*, but their correctness should be further analyzed.

Keywords: Convolutional Neural Network · Explainable Artificial Intelligence · Class Activation Mapping · Faithfulness · Printed Circuit Board

L. Longo (Ed.): xAI 2023, CCIS 1902, pp. 420–432, 2023.
https://doi.org/10.1007/978-3-031-44067-0_22

1   Introduction

In the last decade, Deep Neural Networks (DNNs) and, more specifically, Convolutional Neural Networks (CNNs) have been widely adopted to solve several classification and regression problems involving images, consistently achieving state-of-art results on several vision benchmark tasks [1,2] and often surpassing human accuracy. One field where DNNs have been extensively used in recent times is Failure Analysis (FA). FA can be seen as the activity to identify and trace back the root of failures. A failure is defined as «the termination of the ability of an item to perform a required function» [3]. Human-led FA is often applied *in-situ* by human experts, who carefully examine potentially faulty objects in search of possible anomalies and defects [4]. The examination can be carried out visually or with the aid of other tools or methodologies. While these tests are usually accurate, they can be time-consuming and expensive since they have to be executed by expert figures. Thus, there have been many attempts to design semi-autonomous tools to aid human experts in speeding up their evaluations. In many cases, these systems work on raw images of the objects to be inspected: thus, CNN-based techniques are a natural direction for their development.

In the present work, we start by training a CNN to perform FA on Printed Circuit Motherboards (PCBs) of a model specifically created for the project by the company ASAC srl. We will provide additional information on these boards in Sect. 3.1. Our initial aim is to furnish a professional figure with an automatic diagnosis specifying whether a given PCB is faulty, possibly highlighting areas the CNN considers defective. The training is performed on several images of these PCBs on the premise that the ground truth fed to the CNN is a boolean value indicating whether the motherboard is defective or not. We are able to obtain a validation-set accuracy of 91.61%.

We follow this initial training by conducting an extensive qualitative and quantitative critical analysis of the results produced by the CNN. Specifically, we aim to provide a proof-of-concept using eXplainable Artificial Intelligence (XAI) tools, namely Class Activation Mapping (CAM) [5] and Gradient-weighted CAM (GradCAM) [6] based techniques, to answer the following research questions:

i. Is the CNN able to identify components of the defective PCBs? We investigate this aspect by comparing the output of the XAI tools with the underlying ground truth (i.e., the defective components). We show that these outputs do not align well with the actual faulty areas of the PCBs, sometimes highlighting parts of the motherboards containing no circuits or even parts of the background.

ii. Are these XAI tools *faithful* or *correct*? I.e., are they highlighting areas of the images that are effectively relevant to CNN for producing its output? We show that in 94.5% of our test images, *masking out* the portions of the images which seem most relevant according to those XAI tools do not lead to a change in classification, thus revealing low faithfulness. We continue the analysis by showing that even masking out *all* of the faulty components of the PCBs does not lead to a change in classification, highlighting the ineffectiveness of the CNN to capture areas that are connected to faultiness.

Thus, we conclude that, despite showcasing good results accuracy-wise on a validation set, performing FA using a CNN trained with the sole information that a given PCB is faulty/healthy does not yield semantically good results, as the CNN seems unable to correctly identify defective components of the PCB.

In addition, we provide a warning for the community not always to trust the heatmaps produced by CAM and its variants, as they *could* display a low level of *faithfulness* or *correctness* with respect to the model they are applied to, and can, thus, result in inaccurate representations of the inner functioning of a CNN.

Our code and dataset are available on https://github.com/LeonardoArrighi/PCB_Analysis.

2   Related Works

2.1   Failure Analysis on PCBs

Failure analysis on PCBs is a critical procedure for determining the underlying cause of PCB malfunctions. PCBs are widely utilized in electronic devices and may fail due to a variety of reasons, such as design flaws, manufacturing defects, environmental stress, and aging. Typically, these steps encompass visual inspection of the faulty PCB to detect any apparent damage or defects, along with non-destructive testing techniques. FA on PCBs is a crucial process that ensures the reliability and performance of electronic devices.

Lewis [7] exhaustively described the principles of FA applicable to polymers. These principles are therefore suited to the identification of failures in PCBs. In particular, identifying corrosion-related defects, such as rust formation, color changes, and other possible evidence, is primarily performed by visual inspection. Kanimozhi and Krishnan [8] proposed an excellent survey summarizing the state-of-art of automatic FA techniques on PCBs. In particular, as in, e.g., [9], the usefulness of studying techniques based on a visual inspection of the PCB was highlighted. For a thorough review of the PCB failure detection approaches proposed in the last three decades, we refer the reader to Ling and Isa [4].

2.2   Explainable Artificial Intelligence

Many XAI techniques have been proposed in order to make ANNs more transparent, explainable, and interpretable [10–12]. Concentrating on CNNs, of particular interest, are methods focused on *visualizing* internal representations or dynamics learned by the networks. Bach et al. [13] underlined the importance of understanding and interpreting classification decisions of automated image classification systems; they proposed using a layer-wise relevance propagation technique to visualize, by means of a heatmap, the *relevant* part of an input in the decision process of a neural network. Their technique makes use of a linear approximation of the class scoring function in the neighborhood of a data point.

Building on the same ideas of visualization-based XAI tools, Zhou et al. [5] proposed a technique called Class Activation Mapping (CAM); the method aims to visualize predicted class scores on any image fed to CNNs for classification using a *heatmap* that can highlight which parts of the image are most significant for the network itself to perform the task. Inspired by CAM, numerous other techniques have been proposed to generalize the technique to different DNNs or to improve its precision [6, 14–20].

CAM-based techniques have been used to perform localization in CNNs trained on image classification (i.e., without explicit information on the position of an object within an image): Zhou et al. [5] applied CAM to a classification-trained CNN to perform object detection without using bounding boxes for training. Cheng et al. [21,22] developed a similar idea, expanding the so-called *weakly supervised* object detection concept by exploiting CAM-based techniques.

Despite seeing extended usage, XAI tools are difficult to assess quantitatively. Studies that apply these techniques to DNNs are often limited to qualitative considerations on a subset of their datasets, offering mere visual evaluations, e.g., the overlap between semantic features and the outputs of these tools [23,24]. An extensive line of research exists to develop quantitative or objective ways of evaluating XAI techniques. Nauta et al. [25] summarized many of these works by proposing a unified framework to review these tools. Popular metrics for CAM include the aforementioned correctness or faithfulness or localization, i.e., the ability to localize instances of objects within the images correctly.

An additional point of concern is that these tools are frequently applied as *oracles* without investigating their correctness. Some works have raised concerns with CAM-based techniques, such as low faithfulness [20,26], or inability to capture multiple instances of objects in an image [27], or still difficulty in precise instance localization [28]. These considerations serve as a base for a critical usage of CAM-based techniques.

3   Materials and Methods

3.1   The Dataset

To begin the present work, we constructed a dataset of images of PCBs specifically designed to run lifetime testing. All standard updated technical features are presented and suitable for investigation/testing. For the present research, three features have been investigated. We considered circular welding bases (used to assemble discrete components such as power line capacitors), rectangular welding bases (used to assemble Surface-Mount Device components such as microcontrollers), and parallel electrical tracks (used to transfer signals). Specifically, such electrical tracks are designed with different interspace distances, distributed on single and multi-layers, to cover all configurations used in actual PCBs.

The dataset was constructed starting from a batch of 7 PCBs of the described model. Six of these boards were rendered faulty by subjecting them to an aging process: they were immersed in a saline solution (5% salt) for 96 hours, observing the procedure described in [29]. The remaining one was left untouched. This procedure aimed at reproducing faults to the PCBs, which can be attributed to age/corrosion in a realistic usage setting.

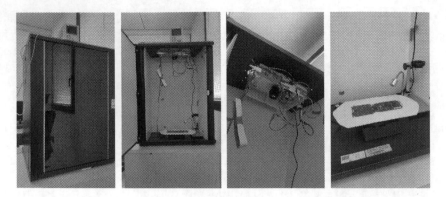

Fig. 1. The structure assembled to take pictures for creating the dataset. It is composed of a rack server as a dark room, a Raspberry Pi 4 with which the whole mechanism is controlled, a Raspberry camera with a 1:1 (magnification of the lens) lens, an RGBW LED lamp mounted on the top of the rack server, a LED lamp mounted on the side of the rack server, and a 3D printed rotating platform.

In order to artificially increase the number of samples, each PCB image was acquired using a rotating platform where we placed one PCB, a fixed camera, and a set of lights. We could control the orientation and rotation of the board with respect to the camera and toggle light conditions. Some pictures of the structure assembled to take pictures can be seen in the Fig. 1. Each board was divided into 4 regions of equal size. Each picture included only one specific region of the PCB. After each shot, the board was rotated by 10° (without contextually rotating the camera), and the next shot of the same region was taken. The whole method was repeated three times: we introduced two sets of different light colors in distinct positions, which were combined in different ways:(i) one white lamp above the board, on the axis of rotation of the platform, and (ii) a natural soft yellow placed on the cabinet wall to form an angle of 30° with the center of the platform, of which we modulated the intensity. This process was aimed at reproducing different light conditions and shot angles. We took the pictures at a resolution of 1024×768 pixels. An example of the images obtained using this protocol can be appreciated in Fig. 2. Our goal was to have models, which we trained on this dataset, robust with respect to various factors (such as light conditions and object pose). This would enable the final user to employ it without using a standardized protocol for shooting pictures, even concentrating solely on specific regions of the PCB. We remain available to provide additional information concerning the creation of the dataset for reproducibility purposes.

Once the images were obtained, they were classified as "Defective" (3207 images) or "Non-defective" (2653 images) according to a visual inspection of the components carried out by an expert. We further divided the dataset into a train, validation, and test split: 70% of the images were randomly allocated to the training set (for a total of 4102 pictures), leaving 20% of them in the validation split, and 10% of them in the test set.

(a)   (b)

Fig. 2. Examples of two images composing our dataset: both pictures depict the same PCB with the same pose with respect to the camera but with different light conditions, which significantly alter its appearance.

3.2   CNN for PCB Classification

For performing the PCB classification task, we used a ResNet50d CNN [2,30], characterized by a sequential stack of residual blocks. Residual blocks are structures containing multiple convolutional layers. The input to a block is *cloned* along two paths, the first being processed sequentially by the convolutional layers and the second being left untouched (*skip connection*), or, in some instances, downsampled by means of other convolutional layers. The data in the skip connection is then summed to the output of the last convolutional layer of the first path. The residual block is designed as in Fig. 3. This architecture stacks 12 of these blocks for a total of 50 convolutional layers. Finally, a fully-connected layer for performing the final classification is applied.

3.3   Implementation Details

We conducted the experiments on a computing node with an Nvidia Tesla V100 GPU, employing Python version 3.8.12 and the Pytorch[1] library. We fine-tuned the ResNet50d pre-trained model on ImageNet [31]. We recovered the pre-trained parameters released alongside the timm library[2]. We made use of the RAdam optimizer [32]. We trained the model for 300 epochs. We set the batch size to 64. We employed dropout [33] with the dropout rate set to 0.1. We used the categorical cross-entropy loss function. Considering that the dataset was built by encompassing a certain variability in rotation and light conditions, we used a small set of additional data augmentation techniques: horizontal and vertical flip and planar homography.

---

[1] https://pytorch.org/.

[2] https://github.com/huggingface/pytorch-image-models.

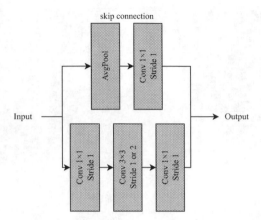

Fig. 3. The schematization of the residual block used in the ResNet50d. The input is duplicated along the two paths. The bottom path passes through a sequence of 3 convolutional layers (orange) with different kernel sizes and stride values. The upper path (the skip connection) is left untouched unless a downsampling of the input is needed: in this case, a sequence of two layers, depicted in green,—an average pooling ("AvgPool") and a convolutional layer of kernel size 1 and stride 1—are applied.

3.4 XAI Techniques Used

We used several XAI tools to assess whether the trained CNN correctly identifies features relevant to the FA task on our PCBs. The various techniques adopted are based on CAM [5], an XAI technique specific for CNNs used to display, through an approximate activation map, the parts of an image the CNN has used to classify that specific image in a specific category. According to the definitions provided by Dwivedi et al. [34], CAM, and CAM techniques are *local post hoc* XAI tools. *Post hoc* means they are applied to a model *after* it has been trained without modifying its parameters, while *local* indicates that they produce explanations for single data points which are input to the CNN, rather than giving explanations which are valid globally for the whole model, regardless of its input.

The first relevant technique employed is GradCAM, proposed by Selvaraju et al. [6]. It produces an activation map G_C given by the linear combination of the feature map activations of the last convolutional layer of the network (A_k), weighted by the gradients of the loss function with respect to the neurons of this layer (w_k^C):

$$G_C = \mathrm{ReLU} \left(\sum_k w_k^C \cdot A_k \right). \tag{1}$$

GradCAM++ [14] is a more advanced version of GradCAM: it calculates the weights w_k using a more elaborate procedure, which includes both the aforementioned activations and gradients of the loss function.

Axiom-based GradCAM (XGradCAM) [18] integrates into the generation of the map a series of axioms such as sensitivity (i.e., that each component of the explanation should be proportional to the impact of removing the corresponding feature from the input on the model's output) or conservation (i.e., the property that the sum of the components of the explanation should match the magnitude of the model's output).

LayerCAM [19] generates attention maps for all layers of the CNN, employing GradCAM, and then combines them into a single attention map for the whole image. Thus, LayerCAM provides an interpretation of the model's decision-making process that considers the contribution of each layer of the CNN.

High-Resolution CAM (HiResCAM) [20] aims at improving GradCAM. The latter calculates weights by averaging gradients (Eq. (1)); this leads to an approximation of the heatmap, corresponding to a deficiency in its representation. The attention map in HiResCAM is generated by element-wise multiplying the gradient and the activations (as in Eq. (1)) but without computing the average of the gradients.

FullGrad [15], is fundamentally different. It generates heatmaps by computing the gradients of the output of the CNN with respect to both the input image and the bias term in the network. It does not depend on the class used to compute the gradient being propagated; it can produce similar outputs across different classes.

AblationCAM [16] proposes a substantial change to the way the map is generated: the weights of the Eq. (1) are calculated using the *slope*, i.e., a function defined as the measure of the effect of ablation of unit k (i.e., an individual activation cell in the feature map A_k of the final convolutional layer of the CNN) on the class activation score y.

Finally, EigenCAM [17] is based on a hypothesis: important spatial features in the input image that the CNN model learns are preserved during the optimization process. Non-relevant or unnecessary features are either smoothed out or regulated, ensuring only relevant spatial features are used to generate the localization map. The activation map of EigenCAM is generated by projecting the output of the last convolutional layer of the CNN onto the first eigenvector of its singular value decomposition.

3.5 Evaluation Metrics

We evaluated our model on accuracy (i.e., the fraction of images correctly classified by the model) and the area under the receiver operating characteristics curve (AUC-ROC), a popular metric for binary classification problems. In addition, we provide the confusion matrix to quickly quantify the number of false positives and negatives. All these quantities were calculated on the validation split of the dataset.

Table 1. Metrics (Table 1a) and confusion matrix (Table 1b) for the model ResNet50d evaluated on the validation datset.

(a) Metrics evaluation

Metric	Value (%)
Accuracy	91.61
AUC-ROC	97.78

(b) Confusion matrix

	Prediction	
Ground truth	Defective	Non-defective
Defective	318	27
Non-defective	25	250

4   Results

The performances of the proposed ResNet model are summarized in the Table 1a. The model achieved an accuracy of 91.61%: as seen from the Confusion Matrix (Table 1b), 568 out of 620 test set images are correctly classified. Furthermore, an AUC-ROC of 97.78% reinforces the conclusion that the model behaved effectively.

Among the 318 images of the test set correctly classified by the network as "Defective", we randomly selected 10 of them to perform the following investigation. We analyzed those pictures with the CAM techniques described in Sect. 3.4 using the implementations by Gildenblat and contributors [35]. We evaluated the output of the CAM models choosing as target the last convolutional layer of the ResNet50d.

As we can notice in Fig. 4, the first aspect is that the CNN is apparently unable to identify specific patterns that refer to the failures: semantically meaningless areas are highlighted by the various techniques. In many cases, these areas are not even located within the boundaries of the PCBs. At this point, we were interested in determining whether these areas represent relevant features for the classification by the CNN. As mentioned in Sect. 2.2, we removed the topical areas identified by CAM-based techniques. Following a visual inspection, we set a threshold at 0.4 and binarized the outputs of CAM-based methods according to this value, thus creating a binary mask that identifies the topical regions. We then applied these masks to the original images by replacing the pixels of these areas with specific colors/patterns, as shown in Fig. 5. After the masking, the new dataset comprised 400 pictures. We re-evaluated these images on the CNN. The result is that 22 of the 400 photos (5.5%) were reclassified as "Non-Defective", while the remaining ones (94.5%) were still classified as "Defective". As a last test, to check whether the CNN was learning relevant features for the classification, we operated directly on the original 10 images by masking out the faulty components with the same 5 modalities mentioned above. Of the 50 images thus obtained, 45 were evaluated as "Defective" by the model. Therefore, in 90% of the images, the classification did not change. This shows how the CNN, originally thought to perform well on our dataset, is, on a deeper level, unable to learn features connected to true failures.

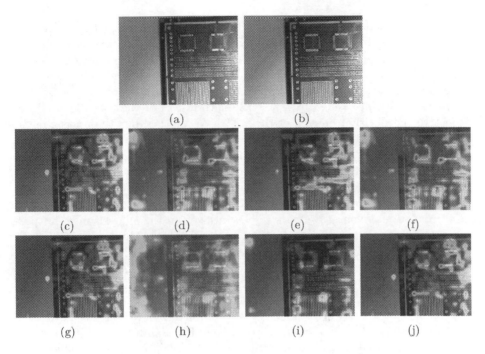

Fig. 4. Examples of a single image analyzed through CAM-based techniques: the picture of a region of a PCB (a), classified as "Defective" due to the defective components highlighted in (b), is overlapped with the heatmaps generated by GradCAM (c), GradCAM++ (d), AblationCAM (e), LayerCAM (f), XGradCAM (g), FullGrad (h), EigenCAM (i), and HiResCAM (j).

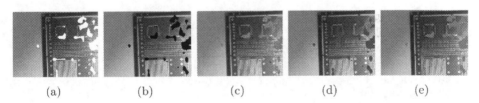

Fig. 5. Examples of masks applied to original images by transforming GradCAM output. The patterns adopted are: all white (a), all black (b), random pixels (c), the color of the green surface of the board (d), and the color of the background of the area outside the board (e). (Color figure online)

5   Conclusions

In this paper, we proposed using a Deep Neural Network (DNN) to identify failures on Printed Circuit Motherboards (PCBs) by classifying images of portions of the boards as flawless when there were no evident defects and as defective when there was a visible defect. We showed how we obtained a seemingly accurate and robust binary classifier with a Convolutional Neural Network (CNN), specifically a ResNet50d. We also provided a proof-of-concept using Class Activation Mapping (CAM)-based eXplainable Artificial Intelligence (XAI) techniques to investigate whether the model could identify defective PCB components within pictures of portions of motherboards. We showed that, by and large, the techniques we employed did not correctly highlight the defective areas of the boards. Furthermore, we proceeded to assess the faithfulness of these techniques with respect to the decision process of the CNN. We masked out the areas emphasized by the CAM-based techniques in the test images. We found that these areas did not correspond to significant features used by the CNN for the classification. We also proceeded to mask out the defective PCB components in a selection of test images, showing that this did not significantly change the classification operated by the CNN. Based on the evidence, it can be inferred that the Convolutional Neural Network (CNN) utilized in the analysis may not possess an accurate understanding of the concept of failure. This suggests that the classification of the images may have been influenced by various visual cues and features identified by the model.

Our findings prompt us to posit that Failure Analysis using DNNs should be conducted using more suitable and complex methods like object detection or segmentation to capture the defective components better and that the sole PCB-level information of defect is insufficient for training a well-functioning model. Furthermore, we conclude with a call towards a more responsible usage of local post hoc XAI tools, specifically CAM-based techniques: they should not be regarded as *oracles* since, as we showed in the present work, their outputs might be misleading. We advocate in favor of a critical usage of such tools—appropriate in-depth analyses should always be carried out to confirm their reliability.

References

1. Krizhevsky, A., Sutskever, I., Hinton, G.E.: ImageNet classification with deep convolutional neural networks. Commun. ACM **60**(6), 84–90 (2017). https://doi.org/10.1145/3065386
2. He, K., Zhang, X., Ren, S., Sun, J.: Deep residual learning for image recognition. In: Proceedings of the IEEE Conference on Computer Vision and Pattern Recognition, pp. 770–778 (2016)
3. Rausand, M., Øien, K.: The basic concepts of failure analysis. Reliab. Eng. Syst. Saf. **53**(1), 73–83 (1996)
4. Ling, Q., Isa, N.A.M.: Printed circuit board defect detection methods based on image processing, machine learning and deep learning: a survey. IEEE Access **11**, 15921–15944 (2023). https://doi.org/10.1109/ACCESS.2023.3245093
5. Zhou, B., Khosla, A., Lapedriza, A., Oliva, A., Torralba, A.: Learning deep features for discriminative localization. In: Proceedings of the IEEE Conference on Computer Vision and Pattern Recognition, pp. 2921–2929 (2016)
6. Selvaraju, R.R., Cogswell, M., Das, A., Vedantam, R., Parikh, D., Batra, D.: Grad-CAM: visual explanations from deep networks via gradient-based localization. In: Proceedings of the IEEE International Conference on Computer Vision, pp. 618–626 (2017)

7. Lewis, P.R.: Sample examination and analysis. In: Lewis, P.R. (ed.), Forensic Polymer Engineering (Second Edition), pp. 33–69. Woodhead Publishing (2016). ISBN 978-0-08-101055-6, https://doi.org/10.1016/B978-0-08-101055-6.00002-1

8. Kanimozhi, S., Krishnan, K.G.: A review on automatic bare PCB board testing. Int. J. Sci. Technol. ISSN (2013)

9. Salahinejad, E., Eslami-Farsani, R., Tayebi, L.: Corrosion failure analysis of printed circuit boards exposed to H2S-containing humid environments. Eng. Fail. Anal. **79**, 538–546 (2017). ISSN 1350–6307, https://doi.org/10.1016/j.engfailanal.2017.05.038

10. Angelov, P.P., Soares, E.A., Jiang, R., Arnold, N.I., Atkinson, P.M.: Explainable artificial intelligence: an analytical review. WIREs Data Min. Knowl. Discovery **11**(5), e1424 (2021). ISSN 1942–4795, https://doi.org/10.1002/widm.1424

11. Arrieta, A.B., et al.: Explainable artificial intelligence (XAI): concepts, taxonomies, opportunities and challenges toward responsible AI. Inf. Fusion **58**, 82–115 (2020). https://doi.org/10.1016/j.inffus.2019.12.012

12. Schwalbe, G., Finzel, B.: A comprehensive taxonomy for explainable artificial intelligence: a systematic survey of surveys on methods and concepts (2023). ISSN 1573–756X. https://doi.org/10.1007/s10618-022-00867-8

13. Bach, S., Binder, A., Montavon, G., Klauschen, F., Müller, K.R., Samek, W.: On pixel-wise explanations for non-linear classifier decisions by layer-wise relevance propagation. Plos One **10**(7), e0130140 (2015). https://doi.org/10.1371/journal.pone.0130140

14. Chattopadhay, A., Sarkar, A., Howlader, P., Balasubramanian, V.N.: Grad-CAM++: improved visual explanations for deep convolutional networks. In: 2018 IEEE Winter Conference on Applications of Computer Vision, pp. 839–847 (2018). https://doi.org/10.1109/WACV.2018.00097

15. Srinivas, S., Fleuret, F.: Full-gradient representation for neural network visualization. In: Advances in Neural Information Processing Systems, vol. 32 (2019). https://doi.org/10.5555/3454287.3454658

16. Ramaswamy, H.G., et al.: Ablation-CAM: visual explanations for deep convolutional network via gradient-free localization. In: Proceedings of the IEEE/CVF Winter Conference on Applications of Computer Vision, pp. 983–991 (2020). https://doi.org/10.1109/WACV45572.2020.9093360

17. Muhammad, M.B., Yeasin, M.: Eigen-CAM: class activation map using principal components. In: 2020 International Joint Conference on Neural Networks (IJCNN), pp. 1–7 (2020)

18. Fu, R., Hu, Q., Dong, X., Guo, Y., Gao, Y., Li, B.: Axiom-based Grad-CAM: towards accurate visualization and explanation of CNNs. arXiv preprint arXiv:2008.02312 (2020)

19. Jiang, P.-T., Zhang, C.-B., Hou, Q., Cheng, M.-M., Wei, Y.: LayerCAM: exploring hierarchical class activation maps for localization. IEEE Trans. Image Process. **30**, 5875–5888 (2021). https://doi.org/10.1109/TIP.2021.3089943

20. Draelos, R.L., Carin, L.: Use HiResCAM instead of Grad-CAM for faithful explanations of convolutional neural networks. arXiv e-prints (2020)

21. Cheng, G., Yang, J., Gao, D., Guo, L., Han, J.: High-quality proposals for weakly supervised object detection. IEEE Trans. Image Process. **29**, 5794–5804 (2020). ISSN 1941–0042, https://doi.org/10.1109/TIP.2020.2987161

22. Inbaraj, X.A., Jeng, J.H.: Mask-GradCAM: object identification and localization of visual presentation for deep convolutional network. In: 6th International Conference on Inventive Computation Technologies, pp. 1171–1178 (2021). https://doi.org/10.1109/ICICT50816.2021.9358569

23. Lopes, J.F., da Costa, V.G.T., Barbin, D.F., Cruz-Tirado, L.J.P., Baeten, V., Barbon Junior, S.: Deep computer vision system for cocoa classification. Multimed. Tools Appl. **81**(28), 41059–41077 (2022). https://doi.org/10.1007/s11042-022-13097-3

24. Joo, H.T., Kim, K.J.: Visualization of deep reinforcement learning using grad-CAM: how AI plays Atari games? In: 2019 IEEE Conference on Games (CoG), pp. 1–2. IEEE (2019). https://doi.org/10.1109/CIG.2019.8847950

25. Nauta, M., et al.: From anecdotal evidence to quantitative evaluation methods: a systematic review on evaluating explainable AI. ACM Comput. Surv. **55**, 1–42 (2023). ISSN 0360–0300, https://doi.org/10.1145/3583558

26. Li, J., Lin, D., Wang, Y., Xu, G., Ding, C.: Towards a reliable evaluation of local interpretation methods. Appl. Sci. **11**(6), 2732 (2021). ISSN 2076–3417. https://doi.org/10.3390/app11062732

27. Singh, P., Sharma, A.: Interpretation and classification of arrhythmia using deep convolutional network. IEEE Trans. Instrum. Meas. **71**, 1–12 (2022). https://doi.org/10.1109/TIM.2022.3204316

28. Xiao, M., Zhang, L., Shi, W., Liu, J., He, W., Jiang, Z.: A visualization method based on the grad-cam for medical image segmentation model. In: 2021 International Conference on Electronic Information Engineering and Computer Science (EIECS), pp. 242–247 (2021). https://doi.org/10.1109/EIECS53707.2021.9587953

29. Mostofizadeh, M., Pippola, J., Marttila, T., Frisk, L.K.: Effect of thermal aging and salt spray testing on reliability and mechanical strength of SN-58BI lead-free solder. IEEE Trans. Compon. Packag. Manuf. Technol. **3**, 1778–1785 (2013). https://doi.org/10.1109/TCPMT.2013.2267333

30. He, T., Zhang, Z., Zhang, H., Zhang, Z., Xie, J., Li, M.: Bag of tricks for image classification with convolutional neural networks. In: 2019 IEEE/CVF Conference on Computer Vision and Pattern Recognition (CVPR), pp. 558–567. IEEE, ISBN 978-1-72813-293-8, https://doi.org/10.1109/CVPR.2019.00065

31. Deng, J., Dong, W., Socher, R., Li, L.J., Li, K., Fei-Fei, L.: ImageNet: a large-scale hierarchical image database. In: 2009 IEEE Conference on Computer Vision and Pattern Recognition, pp. 248–255 (2009). https://doi.org/10.1109/CVPR.2009.5206848

32. Liu, L., et al.: On the variance of the adaptive learning rate and beyond. arXiv preprint arXiv:1908.03265 (2019)

33. Srivastava, N., Hinton, G., Krizhevsky, A., Sutskever, I., Salakhutdinov, R.: Dropout: a simple way to prevent neural networks from overfitting. J. Mach. Learn. Res. **15**(1), 1929–1958 (2014). https://doi.org/10.5555/2627435.2670313 https://dl.acm.org/doi/10.5555/2627435.2670313

34. Dwivedi, R., et al.: Explainable AI (XAI): core ideas, techniques, and solutions. ACM Comput. Surv. **55**(9), 1–33 (2023). https://doi.org/10.1145/3561048

35. Gildenblat, J., et al.: Pytorch library for CAM methods (2021). https://github.com/jacobgil/pytorch-grad-cam

DExT: Detector Explanation Toolkit

Deepan Chakravarthi Padmanabhan[1] , Paul G. Plöger[1] ,
Octavio Arriaga[2] , and Matias Valdenegro-Toro[3]([✉])

[1] Bonn-Rhein-Sieg University of Applied Sciences, Sankt Augustin, Germany
[2] University of Bremen, Bremen, Germany
arriagac@uni-bremen.de
[3] University of Groningen, Groningen, The Netherlands
m.a.valdenegro.toro@rug.nl

Abstract. State-of-the-art object detectors are treated as black boxes
due to their highly non-linear internal computations. Even with unprece-
dented advancements in detector performance, the inability to explain
how their outputs are generated limits their use in safety-critical applications. Previous work fails to produce explanations for both bounding
box and classification decisions, and generally make individual explanations for various detectors. In this paper, we propose an open-source
Detector Explanation Toolkit (DExT) which implements the proposed
approach to generate a holistic explanation for all detector decisions
using certain gradient-based explanation methods. We suggests various
multi-object visualization methods to merge the explanations of multiple objects detected in an image as well as the corresponding detections in a single image. The quantitative evaluation show that the Single
Shot MultiBox Detector (SSD) is more faithfully explained compared to
other detectors regardless of the explanation methods. Both quantitative
and human-centric evaluations identify that SmoothGrad with Guided
Backpropagation (GBP) provides more trustworthy explanations among
selected methods across all detectors. We expect that DExT will motivate practitioners to evaluate object detectors from the interpretability
perspective by explaining both bounding box and classification decisions.

Keywords: Object detectors · Explainability · Quantitative
evaluation · Human-centric evaluation · Saliency methods

1 Introduction

Object detection is imperative in applications such as autonomous driving [15],
medical imaging [5], and text detection [18]. An object detector outputs bounding
boxes to localize objects and categories for objects of interest in an input image.
State-of-the-art detectors are deep convolutional neural networks [54] with high
accuracy and fast processing compared to traditional detectors. However, convolutional detectors are considered black boxes [37] due to over-parameterization

---

Supplementary Information The online version contains supplementary material
available at https://doi.org/10.1007/978-3-031-44067-0_23.

and hierarchically non-linear internal computations. This non-intuitive decision-making process restricts the capability to debug and improve detection systems. The user trust in model predictions has decreased and consequently using detectors in safety-critical applications is limited. In addition, the process of verifying the model and developing secure systems is challenging [12,52]. Numerous previous studies state interpreting detectors by explaining the model decision is crucial to earning the user's trust [32,40,48], estimating model accountability [20], and developing secure object detector systems [12,52].

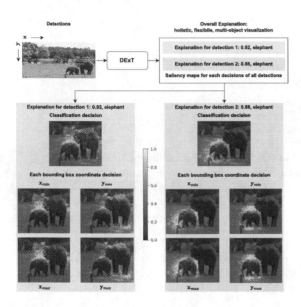

Fig. 1. A depiction of the proposed approach to interpret all object detector decisions. The corresponding explanations are provided in the same colored boxes. This breakdown of explanations offers more flexibility to analyze decisions and serves as a holistic explanation for all the detections.

With a range of users utilizing detectors for safety critical applications, providing humanly understandable explanations for the category and each bounding box coordinate predictions together is essential. In addition, as object detectors are prone to failures due to non-local effects [30], the visualization techniques for detector explanations should integrate explanations for multiple objects in a single image at the same time. Previous saliency map-based methods explaining detectors [17,26,46] focus on classification or localization decisions individually, not both at the same time.

In this paper, we consider three deficits in the literature: methods to explain each category and bounding box coordinate decision made by an object detector, visualizing explanations of multiple bounding boxes into the same output explanation image, and a software toolkit integrating the previously mentioned aspects.

This work concentrates on providing individual humanly understandable explanations for the bounding box and classification decisions made by an object detector for any particular detection, using gradient-based saliency maps. Figure 1 provides an illustration of the proposed solution by considering the complete output information to generate explanations for the detector decision.

Explanations for all the decisions can be summarized by merging the saliency maps to achieve a high-level analysis and increasing flexibility to analyze detector decisions, improving improving model transparency and trustworthiness. We suggest methods to combine and visualize explanations of different bounding boxes in a single output explanation image as well as an approach to analyze the detector errors using explanations.

This work contributes DExT, software toolkit, to explain each decisions (bounding box regression and object classification jointly), evaluate explanations, and identify errors made by an object detector. A simple approach to extend gradient-based explanation methods to explain bounding box and classification decisions of an object detector. An approach to identify reasons for the detector failure using explanation methods. Multi-object visualization methods to summarize explanations for all output detections in a single output explanation. And an evaluation of gradient-based saliency maps for object detector explanations, including quantitative results and a human user study.

We believe our work reveals some major conclusions about object detector explainability. Overall quantitative metrics do not indicate that a particular object detector is more interpretable, but visual inspection of explanations indicates that recent detectors like EfficientDet seem to be better explained using gradient-based methods than older detectors (like SSD or Faster R-CNN, shown in Fig. 2), based on lack of artifacts on their heatmaps. Detector backbone has a large impact on explanation quality (Fig. 6).

The user study (Sect. 4.4) reveals that humans clearly prefer the convex polygon representation, and Smooth Guided Backpropagation provides the best detector explanations, which is consistent with quantitative metrics. We believe these results are important for practitioners and researchers of object detection interpretability. The overall message is to explain both object classification and bounding box decisions and it is possible to combine all explanations into a single image using the convex polygon representation of the heatmap pixels. The appendix of this paper is available at https://arxiv.org/abs/2212.11409.

2 Related Work

Interpretability is relatively underexplored in detectors compared to classifiers. There are post hoc [17,26,46] and intrinsic [21,51] detector interpretability approaches. Detector Randomized Input Sampling for Explanation (D-RISE) [26] in a model-agnostic manner generates explanations for the complete detector output. However, saliency map quality depends on the computation budget, the method is time consuming, and individual explanations for bounding boxes are not evaluated. Contrastive Relevance Propagation (CRP) [46] extends Layer-wise Relevance Propagation (LRP) [7] to explain individually the bounding box and classification decisions of Single Shot MultiBox Detector (SSD). This procedure includes propagation rules specific to SSD. Explain to fix (E2X) [17] contributes a framework to explain the SSD detections by approximating SHAP [24] feature importance values using Integrated Gradients (IG), Local Interpretable Model-agnostic Explanations (LIME), and Probability Difference Analysis (PDA) explanation methods. E2X identifies the detection failure such as false negative errors using the explanations generated. The individual explanations for bounding box decisions and classification decisions are unavailable.

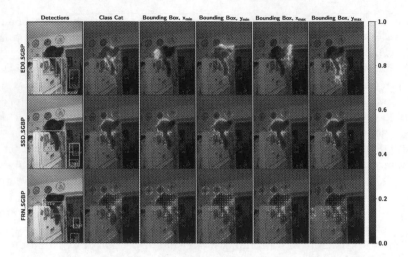

Fig. 2. Comparison of the classification and all bounding box coordinate explanations corresponding to the cat detection (red-colored box) across different detectors using SGBP is provided. The bounding box explanations from EfficientDet-D0 illustrate the visual correspondence to the respective bounding box coordinates. The explanations from Faster R-CNN illustrate a sharp checkerboard pattern. (Color figure online)

The intrinsic approaches majorly focus on developing detectors that are inherently interpretable. Even though the explanations are provided for free, currently, most of the methods are model-specific, do not provide any evaluations on the explanations generated, and includes complex additional designs.

Certain attention-based models such as DEtector TRansformer (DETR) [10] and detectors using non-local neural networks [49] offer attention maps improving model transparency. A few previous works with attention reveal contradicting notions of using attention for interpreting model decisions. [19,35] illustrate attention maps are not a reliable indicator of important input region as well as attention maps are not explanations, respectively. [8] have revealed saliency methods provide better explanations over attention modules.

We select the post hoc gradient-based explanation methods because they provide better model translucency, computational efficiency, do not affect model performance, and utilize the gradients in DNNs. Finally, saliency methods are widely studied in explaining DNN-based models [3]. A detailed evaluation of various detectors reporting robustness, accuracy, speed, inference time as well as energy consumption across multiple domains has been carried out by [4]. In this work, the authors compare detectors from the perspective of explainability.

3 Proposed Approach

3.1 Explaining Object Detectors

This work explains various detectors using gradient-based explanation methods as well as evaluate different explanations for bounding box and classification decisions. The selected detectors are: SSD512 (SSD) [23], Faster R-CNN (FRN) [28], and EfficientDet-D0 (ED0) [43]. The short-form tags are provided in the bracket. SSD512 and Faster R-CNN are widely used single-stage and two-stage approaches, respectively. Explaining the traditional detectors will aid in extending the explanation procedure to numerous similar types of recent detectors. EfficientDet is a relatively recent state-of-the-art single-stage detector with higher accuracy and efficiency. It incorporates a multi-scale feature fusion layer called a Bi-directional Feature Pyramid Network (BiFPN). EfficientDet-D0 is selected to match the input size of SSD512. The variety of detectors selected aids in evaluating the explanation methods across different feature extractors such as VGG16 (SSD512), ResNet101 (Faster R-CNN), and EfficientNet (EfficientDet-D0). The gradient-based explanation methods selected in this work to explain detectors are: Guided Backpropagation (GBP) [41], Integrated Gradients (IG) [42], SmoothGrad [39] + GBP (SGBP), and SmoothGrad + IG (SIG). GBP produces relatively less noisy saliency maps by obstructing the backward negative gradient flow through a ReLU. For instance, an uncertainty estimate of the most important pixels influencing the model decisions is carried out using GBP and certain uncertainty estimation methods [50]. This combines uncertainty estimation and interpretability to better understand DNN model decisions. IG satisfies the implementation and sensitivity invariance axioms that are failed by various other state-of-the-art interpretation methods. SmoothGrad aids in sharpening the saliency map generated by any interpretation method and improves the explanation quality. These four explanation methods explain a particular detector decision by computing the gradient of the predicted value at the output target neuron with respect to the input image.

The object detector decisions for a particular detection are bounding box coordinates $(x_{\min}, y_{\min}, x_{\max}, y_{\max})$, and class probabilities $(c_1, c_2, ..., c_k)$, where k is the total number of classes predicted by the detector. Usually these are output by heads at the last layer of the object detector. The classification head is denoted as $\text{model}_{\text{cls}}(x)$, while the bounding box regression head is $\text{model}_{\text{bbox}}(x)$. Considering that an explanation method computes a function $\text{expl}(x, \hat{y})$ of the input x and scalar output prediction $\hat{y}$ (which is one output layer neuron), then a classification explanation e_{cls} is:

$$\hat{c} = \text{model}_{\text{cls}}(x) \quad k = \arg\max_i \hat{c}_i \quad e_{\text{cls}} = \text{expl}\left(x, \hat{l}_k\right) \tag{1}$$

A bounding box explanation consists of four different explanations, one for each bounding box component $e_{x_{\min}}, e_{y_{\min}}, e_{x_{\max}}, e_{y_{\max}}$:

$$\hat{x}_{\min}, \hat{y}_{\min}, \hat{x}_{\max}, \hat{y}_{\max} = \text{model}_{\text{bbox}}(x) \tag{2}$$

$$e_{x_{\min}} = \text{expl}\left(x, \hat{x}_{\min}\right) \quad e_{y_{\min}} = \text{expl}\left(x, \hat{y}_{\min}\right) \tag{3}$$

$$e_{x_{\max}} = \text{expl}\left(x, \hat{x}_{\max}\right) \quad e_{y_{\max}} = \text{expl}\left(x, \hat{y}_{\max}\right) \tag{4}$$

In case of explaining the bounding box coordinates, the box offsets predicted by an object detectors are converted to normalized image coordinates before computing the gradient. In case of classification decisions, the logits ($\hat{l}_k$, before

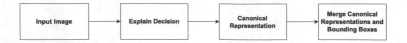

Fig. 3. Overview of the Multi-object visualizations pipeline to jointly visualize all detections.

softmax probability, $\hat{c} = \text{softmax}(\hat{l})$) are used to compute the gradient. Figure 2 illustrates the explanations generated for each decisions of the cat detection by across detectors. Saliency explanations can be computed for each bounding box of interest in the image.

3.2 Multi-object Visualization

In order to summarize the saliency maps of all detections, the individual saliency maps corresponding to each detection are represented using a canonical form. This representation illustrates the most important pixels for the decision explanation. This paper proposes four different methods for combining detection explanations into a single format: principal components, contours, density clustering, and convex polygons. Each method uses a different representation, allowing for detected bounding box, and category to be marked using same colors on the input image. The general process is described in Fig. 3. An example the four multi-object visualizations are illustrated in Fig. 4. Appendix F provides additional details on the multi-object visualization approaches and how different combination methods work. including explanation heatmap samples.

(a) Principal compo-   (b) Contour   (c) Density cluster   (d) Convex polygon
nent

Fig. 4. Multi-object visualizations generated to jointly visualize all detections from EfficientDet-D0 and the corresponding classification explanations generated using SIG in the same color. The combination approach is specified in sub-captions. Explanation pixels are colored same as the corresponding bounding box that is being explained.

4   Experiments

Section 4.1 visually analyzes the explanations generated for different detector and explanation method combinations. Section 4.3 provides the quantitatively evaluates different detector and explanation method combinations. Finally, Sect. 4.4

estimates an overall ranking for the explanation methods based on user preferences of the explanations produced for each decision. In addition, the multi-object visualization methods are ranked based on user understandability of the detections. In Section G (Appendix), the procedure to analyze the failures of detector using the proposed approach is discussed.

Most of the experiments use ED0, SSD, and FRN detectors detecting common objects from COCO [22]. The additional details about these detectors are provided in Table 2 (Appendix). In cases requiring training a detector, different versions of SSD with various pre-trained backbones detecting marine debris provided in Table 3 are used. The marine debris detectors are trained using a train split of the Marine Debris dataset [47] and explanations are generated for the test images. These detectors are used only to study how are the explanations change across different backbones and different performance levels (epochs) in Sect. 4.1.

4.1   Visual Analysis

Across Target Decision and Across Detectors. The saliency maps for the classification and bounding box decisions generated using a particular explanation method for a specific object change across different detectors as shown in Fig. 2. All the bounding box explanations of EfficientDet-D0 in certain scenarios provide visual correspondence to the bounding box coordinates.

Across Different Target Objects. Figure 5 illustrate that the explanations highlight different regions corresponding to the objects explained. This behavior is consistent in most of the test set examples across the classification and bounding box explanations for all detectors.

Figure 6 illustrates the classification explanations for the wall detection across the 6 different backbones. Apart from the attribution intensity changes, the pixels highlight different input image pixels, and the saliency map texture changes. MobileNet and VGG16 illustrate thin horizontal lines and highlight other object pixels, respectively. ResNet20 highlights the wall as a thick continuous segment. Figure 18 illustrate the y_{min} and y_{max} bounding box coordinate explanations for the chain detection across different backbones. The thin horizontal lines of MobileNet are consistent with the previous example. In addition, VGG16 illustrates a visual correspondence with the y_{min} and y_{max} bounding box coordinate by highlighting the upper half and lower half of the bounding box respectively. However, this is not witnessed in other detectors. This behavior is consistent over a set of 10 randomly sampled test set images from the Marine Debris dataset.

The explanations generated using SSD model instances with ResNet20 backbone at different epochs are provided in Fig. 7. The model does not provide any final detections at lower epochs. Therefore, the explanations are generated using the target neurons of the output box corresponding to the interest decision in the final detections from the trained model. Figure 7 illustrate variations in the saliency maps starting from a randomly initialized model to a completely

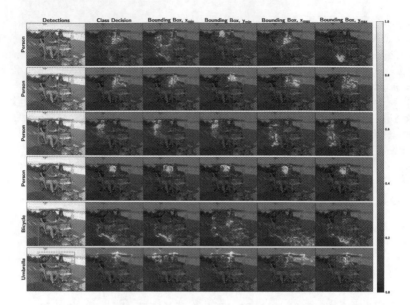

Fig. 5. Comparison of classification and bounding box explanations for all detections from EfficientDet-D0 using SIG is provided. Each row provides the detection (red-colored box) followed by the corresponding classification and all bounding box explanation heatmaps. (Color figure online)

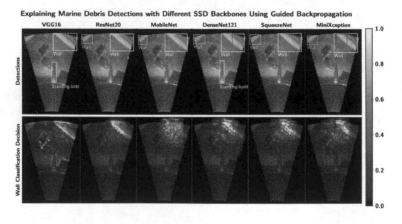

Fig. 6. Comparison of class "wall" classification explanations across different SSD backbones. The detections from each SSD backbone are provided in the first row. The explanations of the wall detection (white-colored box) vary across each backbone.

trained model for the classification decision of the chain detection. The explanations extracted using the random model are dispersed around the features. The explanations slowly concentrate along the chain object detected and capture the object feature to a considerable amount. This behavior is qualitatively analyzed by visualizing the explanation of 10 randomly sampled test set images from the Marine Debris dataset. In the case of the small hook explained in Appendix Fig. 19, the variations between the random model and the trained model are not as considerable as the previous chain example. This illustrates the variations change with respect to each class.

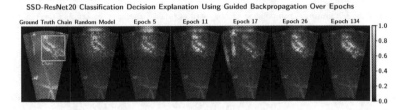

SSD-ResNet20 Classification Decision Explanation Using Guided Backpropagation Over Epochs

Fig. 7. Classification explanation for class "chain" across different epochs (along columns) of SSD-ResNet20 using GBP is illustrated. The first column is the chain ground truth annotation (white-colored box).

4.2 Error Analysis

The section analyzes detector errors by generating explanations using the proposed detector explanation approach. The saliency map highlighting the important regions can be used as evidence to understand the reason for the detector failure rather than assuming the possible reasons for detector failure. The failure modes of a detector are wrongly classifying an object, poorly localizing an object, or missing a detection in the image [26]. As the error analysis study requires ground truth annotations, the PASCAL VOC 2012 images are used. The PASCAL VOC images with labels mapping semantically to COCO labels are only considered as the detectors are trained using the COCO dataset. For instance, the official VOC labels such as sofa and tvmonitor are semantically mapped to couch and tv, respectively, by the model output trained on COCO.

The procedure to analyze a incorrectly classified detection is straightforward. The output bounding box information corresponding to the wrongly classified detection can be analyzed in two ways. The target neuron can be the correct class or the wrongly classified class to generate the saliency maps (Fig. 8). More examples of error analysis are available in Section G in the appendix.

4.3 Quantitative Evaluation

Evaluating detector explanations quantitatively provides immense understanding on selecting the explanation method suitable for a specific detector. This section performs the quantitative evaluation of saliency explanations.

Fig. 8. Example error analysis using gradient-based explanations. EfficientDet-D0 wrongly classifies the dog (red-colored box) in ground truth as cat (red-colored box). We display two saliency explanations (GBP and SIG). In this figure, it is clear the model is imagining a long tail for the dog (GBP) and wrongly classifies the dog as a cat. The saliency map highlights certain features of the dog and the background stripes pattern along the edges of the dog body (GBP and SIG). In order to illustrate the tail clearly which is predominant in cats available in COCO dataset, the saliency map is only shown without overlaying on the input image. (Color figure online)

Evaluation Metrics. The quantitative evaluation of the explanations of a detector incorporates causal metrics to evaluate the bounding box and classification explanations. This works by causing a change to the input pixels and measuring the effect of change in model decisions. The evaluation aids in estimating the faithfulness or truthfulness of the explanation to represent the cause of the model decision. The causal metrics discussed in this work are adapted from the previous work [25,26,33]. The two variants of causal evaluation metrics based on the cause induced to alter the prediction are deletion and insertion metric. The deletion metric evaluates the saliency map explanation by removing the pixels from the input image and tracking the change in model output. The pixels are removed sequentially in the order of the most important pixels starting with a larger attribution value and the output probability of the predicted class is measured. The insertion metric works complementary to the deletion metric by sequentially adding the most important pixel to the image and causing the model decision to change. Using deletion metric, the explanation methods can be compared by plotting the fraction of pixels removed along x-axis and the predicted class probability along y-axis. The method with lower Area Under the Curve (AUC) illustrates a sharp drop in probability for lesser pixel removal. This signifies the explanation method can find the most important pixels that can cause a significant change in model behavior. The explanation method with less AUC is better. In the case of insertion metric, the predicted class probability increases as the most relevant pixels are inserted. Therefore, an explanation method with a higher AUC is relatively better. [26] utilize constant gray replacing pixel values and blurred image as the start image for deletion and insertion metric calculation respectively.

Effects Tracked. The previous work evaluating the detector explanations utilize insertion and deletion metric to track the change in the bounding box Intersection over Union (IoU) and classification probability together. [26] formulate a vector representation involving the box coordinates, class, and probability. The similarity score between the non-manipulated and manipulated vectors are tracked. However, this work performs an extensive comparison of explanation methods for each decision of a detector by tracking the change in maximum probability of the predicted class, IoU, distance moved by the bounding box (in pixels), change in box height (in pixels), change in box width (in pixels), change in top-left x coordinate of the box (in pixels), and change in top-left y coordinate of the box (in pixels). The box movement is the total movement in left-top and right-bottom coordinates represented as euclidean distance in pixels. The coordinates distances are computed using the interest box corresponding to the current manipulated image and the interest box corresponding to the non-manipulated image. This extensive evaluation illustrates a few explanation methods are more suitable to explain a particular decision. As declared in the previous sections, the image origin is at the top-left corner. Therefore, a total of 7 effects are tracked for each causal evaluation metric.

Evaluation Settings. The previous section establishes the causal deletion and insertion metric along with the 7 different effects. In this section, two different settings used to evaluate the detectors using the causal metrics are discussed.

Single-box Evaluation Setting. The detector output changes drastically when manipulating the input image based on saliency values. We denote principal box to the bounding box detecting the object in the original image. In this setting, seven principal box effects are tracked across insertion and deletion of input pixels. This aids in capturing how well the explanation captures true causes of the principal box prediction. The effects measured for the single-box setting are bounded because the principal box value is always measurable. This is called a single-box setting because only the changes in the principal box are tracked.

Realistic Evaluation Setting. In this evaluation setting, all 7 effects are tracked for the complete object detector output involving all bounding boxes after the post-processing steps of a detector. In this setting, the current detection for a particular manipulated input image is matched to the interest detection by checking the same class and an IoU threshold greater than 0.9. For various manipulated input images, there is no current detection matching the interest detection. Therefore, depending on the effect tracked and to calculate AUC, a suitable value is assigned to measure the effect. For instance, if the effect tracked is the class probability for deletion metric and none of the current detection matches with the interest detection, a zero class probability is assigned. Similarly, if the effect tracked is box movement in pixels for deletion metric, the error in pixels increases to a large value.

Interpretation Through Curves. Given the causes induced to change model output, effects tracked, and evaluation setting for the detector, this work uses 28 causal evaluation metrics. These correspond to causes ↓ Deletion (**D**) and ↑ Insertion (**I**), Effects tracked Class Maximum Probability (**C**), Box IoU (**B**), Box Movement Distance (**M**), Box X-top (**X**), Box Y-top (**Y**), Box Width (**W**), Box Height(**H**), and evaluation settings Single-box (**S**) and Realistic (**R**).

To interpret a causal evaluation metric, a graph is drawn tracking the change of the effect tracked along the y-axis and the fraction of pixels manipulated along the x-axis. For instance, consider the scenario of deleting image pixels sequentially to track the maximum probability of the predicted class at single-box evaluation setting. The x-axis is the fraction of pixels deleted. The y-axis is the maximum probability of the predicted class at the output of the box tracked. In this work, the curve drawn is named after the combination of the causal evaluation metrics, effects tracked, end evaluation settings. The curves are the DCS curve, DBS curve, ICS curve. For instance, the DCS curve is the change in the maximum probability for the predicted class (C) at the single output box (S) due to removing pixels (D). The curves are the evaluation metrics used in this work and also called as DCS evaluation metric (deletion + class maximum probability + single-box setting), DBS (deletion + box IoU + single-box setting) evaluation metric, and so on.

In order to compare the performance of explanation methods to explain a single detection, as stated before, the AUC of a particular evaluation metric curve is estimated. The corresponding AUC is represented as $\text{AUC}_{<evaluation\_metric>}$. In order to estimate a global metric to compare the explanation methods explaining a particular decision of a detector, the average AUC, represented as $\text{AAUC}_{<evaluation\_metric>}$, is computed. As the explanations are provided for each detection, the evaluation set is given by the total number of detections. The total detections in the evaluation set are the sum of detections in each image of the evaluation set. The average evaluation metric curve is computed by averaging the evaluation metric curve at each fraction of pixels manipulated across all detections. AAUC of a particular evaluation metric curve is the AUC of the average evaluation metric curve.

Results. Figure 9 illustrates the AAUC computed by evaluating the explanations of each bounding box coordinate is similar across different evaluation metrics curves. This similarity is consistent for all the detectors and explanation methods combinations evaluated. Therefore, the explanation methods quantitatively explain each bounding box coordinate decisions with similar performance. In this work, the AAUC for the bounding box decision is computed by averaging the AUC of all the evaluation metric curves corresponding to all the box coordinate explanations. This offers the means to evaluate the explanation methods across all the bounding box coordinate decisions.

Figure 10 and Fig. 11 illustrate quantitatively complementary trends in the evaluation metric curves plotted by tracking box movement distance in pixels and box IoU. The IoU decreases and box movement distance increases as the pixels

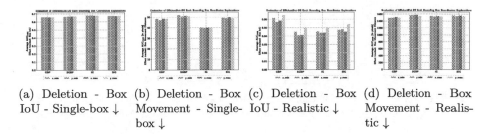

(a) Deletion - Box IoU - Single-box ↓

(b) Deletion - Box Movement - Single-box ↓

(c) Deletion - Box IoU - Realistic ↓

(d) Deletion - Box Movement - Realistic ↓

Fig. 9. The figure illustrates the average AUC, AAUC, for the evaluation metric curves obtained by tracking box IoU (a, c) and box movement distance (b, d) as the pixels are deleted sequentially. Each bar corresponds to the AAUC estimated by evaluating explanations generated for each bounding box coordinate decisions using the explanation methods specified in the x-axis of all detection made by EfficientDet-D0 in the evaluation set images. AAUC is computed by averaging the AUC of all the evaluation metric curves generated using the combination specified in the sub-captions. Lower AAUC is better in all the plots.

are deleted sequentially as shown in Fig. 10. Similarly, Fig. 11 illustrates the increase in box IoU and decrease in box movement distance as pixels are inserted to a blurred version of the image. There is a large difference in the AAUC between the single-stage and two-stage detectors. This is primarily due to the RPN in the two-stage detectors. The proposals from RPN are relatively more sensitive to the box coordinate change than the predefined anchors of the single-stage detectors. In addition, Fig. 10d and Fig. 11d indicates the steady change of box coordinates in the final detections of the EfficientDet-D0. However, SSD and Faster R-CNN saturate relatively sooner. In the remainder of this work, the ability of the box IoU effect is used for quantitative evaluation. This is only because the box IoU effect offers the same scale between 0 to 1 as the class maximum probability effect. In addition, both box IoU and class maximum probability effect follow the trend lower AUC is better for the deletion case. However, it is recommended to consider all the box IoU and box movement distance effects at the level of each box coordinate for a more accurate evaluation.

Figure 12 and Appendix Fig. 17 aids in understanding the explanation method interpreting both the classification and bounding box decision of a particular detector more faithful than other explanation methods. Figure 12a illustrate SSD512 classification decisions are better explained by SGBP at single-box setting for deletion metrics. However, the bounding box decisions are not explained as well as the classification decisions. Figure 12b illustrate a similar scenario for SGBP with EfficientDet-D0 and Faster R-CNN at the realistic setting for deletion metrics. However, all selected explanation methods explain the bounding box and classification decisions of SSD512 relatively better at the single-box setting for insertion metrics. In general, none of the selected explanation methods explain both the classification and bounding box regression decisions substantially well compared to other methods for all detectors. This answers EQ13. Similarly, none of the detectors is explained more faithfully for

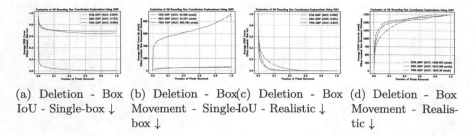

(a) Deletion - Box IoU - Single-box ↓

(b) Deletion - Box Movement - Single-box ↓

(c) Deletion - Box IoU - Realistic ↓

(d) Deletion - Box Movement - Realistic ↓

Fig. 10. Comparison of average curves obtained by tracking box IoU (a, c) and box movement distance (b, d) as the pixels are deleted sequentially. Each average curve is the average of the evaluation curves plotted by evaluating the explanations of all bounding box coordinate decisions across all the detections by the respective detector. The explanations are generated using GBP. The evaluation metric curve is generated using the combination specified in the sub-captions.

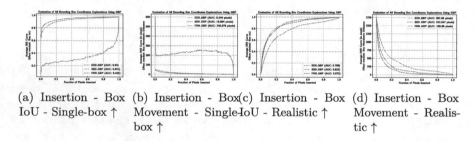

(a) Insertion - Box IoU - Single-box ↑

(b) Insertion - Box Movement - Single-box ↑

(c) Insertion - Box IoU - Realistic ↑

(d) Insertion - Box Movement - Realistic ↑

Fig. 11. Comparison of average curves obtained by tracking box IoU (a, c) and box movement distance (b, d) as the pixels are inserted sequentially. Each average curve is the average of the evaluation curves plotted by evaluating the explanations of all bounding box coordinate decisions across all the detections by the respective detector. The explanations are generated using GBP. The evaluation metric curve is generated using the combination specified in the sub-captions.

both classification and bounding box decisions among the selected detectors by a single method across all evaluation metrics discussed. This is illustrated by no explanation methods (by different colors) or no detectors (by different characters) being represent in the lower left rectangle or upper right rectangle in Fig. 12 and Appendix Fig. 17 respectively.

Figure 14a and Fig. 14c illustrate AAUC of the classification saliency maps and the saliency maps combined using different merging methods are different in certain scenarios while tracking the maximum probability. The AAUC of all the box coordinate saliency maps is provided for a baseline comparison. This denotes the effect on maximum probability by removing pixels in the order of most important depending on the all box coordinates saliency maps. Similarly, Fig. 14b and Fig. 14d illustrate the similarity in the AAUC of all box coordinate explanations and the merged saliency maps while tracking the box IoU. In Fig. 14a, the evaluation of the GBP classification saliency map is less faith-

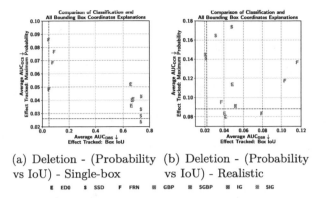

(a) Deletion - (Probability vs IoU) - Single-box

(b) Deletion - (Probability vs IoU) - Realistic

E ED0   S SSD   F FRN   ⊠ GBP   ⊠ SGBP   ⊠ IG   ⊠ SIG

Fig. 12. Comparison between the Deletion AAUC of the evaluation metric curves for the classification and all bounding box coordinate explanations generated across the chosen explanation methods and detectors. Explanation methods (highlighted with different colors) placed at a lower value in the x-axis and y-axis perform relatively better at explaining the box coordinates and classification decisions respectively. Detectors (marked with different characters) placed at a lower value in x-axis and y-axis are relatively better explained for the box coordinates and classification decisions respectively.

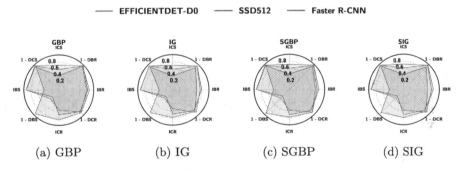

(a) GBP   (b) IG   (c) SGBP   (d) SIG

Fig. 13. Multi-metric comparison of quantitative results. According to these metrics, all methods perform similarly when considering all object detectors. The user study and visual inspection of explanation heatmaps reveal more information.

ful than the merged saliency map. Therefore, the merged saliency map represents the classification decision more faithfully than the standalone classification explanation in the case of EfficientDet-D0. However, Fig. 14a and Fig. 14c illustrate in the case of SGBP explaining EfficientDet-D0 and certain cases of Faster R-CNN respectively separately classification saliency maps are more faithful in depicting the classification decision. The larger AAUC for all the box coordinate saliency maps generated using each method for Faster R-CNN indicate the box saliency maps are not faithful to the bounding box decisions of Faster R-CNN. This is coherent with the visual analysis. Therefore, in certain scenarios merg-

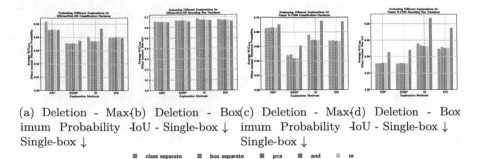

(a) Deletion - Max(b) Deletion - Box(c) Deletion - Max(d) Deletion - Box imum Probability -IoU - Single-box ↓ imum Probability -IoU - Single-box ↓ Single-box ↓   Single-box ↓

Fig. 14. Comparison of average AUC, AAUC, for the evaluation metric curves obtained by tracking maximum probability (a, c) and box IoU (b, d) as the most important pixels based on the explanation generated using the explanation methods specified in the x-axis are deleted sequentially. All the explanations are generated for detection made by EfficientDet-D0 (left) and Faster R-CNN (right) in the evaluation set images. Lower AAUC is better in both plots.

ing is helpful to represent the reason for a particular decision. However, each individual saliency map provides peculiar information about the detection. For instance, the visual correspondence shown in Fig. 2 to each bounding coordinate information is seen only at the level of individual box coordinate explanations.

An overall comparison of all quantitative metrics is shown in Fig. 13. For the purpose of understanding, the ranking of explanation methods explaining a particular detector is provided in Table 1. SGBP performs relatively better across all selected detectors. In addition, IG is ranked least across all the selected detectors. SSD detector is better explained by all the explanation methods. One of the reasons can be SSD is a simpler architecture compared to EfficientDet-D0 and Faster R-CNN. EfficientDet-D0 and Faster R-CNN include a Bi-directional Feature Pyramid Network (BiFPN) and Region Proposal Network (RPN) respectively. However, further experiments should be conducted for validation.

4.4   Human-Centric Evaluation

The human-centric evaluation ranks the explanation methods for each detector and ranks the multi-object visualization methods with a user study. All important details of the user study are presented in Appendix H.

Ranking Explanation Methods. Previous work assess the user trust in the model explanations generated by a particular explanation method [26,29,34]. As user trust is difficult to evaluate precisely, this work in contrast to previous works estimate the user preferability of the explanation methods. The user preferability for the methods GBP, SGBP, IG, and SIG are evaluated by comparing two explanations corresponding to a particular predictions. In this study, the explanation methods are compared directly for a particular interest detection and

Table 1. Ranking of all the explanation methods for a particular detector based on the quantitative evaluation metrics. A lower value is a better rank. The explanation method better explaining a particular detector is awarded a better rank. Each detector is ranked with respect to each evaluation metric considering a particular explanation method. The column names other than the last column and the first two columns represent the average AUC for the respective evaluation metric. The overall rank is computed by calculating the sum along the row and awarding the best rank to the lowest sum. OD - Object detectors, IM - Interpretation method.

OD	IM	DCS	ICS	DBS	IBS	DCR	ICR	DBR	IBR	Overall Rank
ED0	GBP	4	3	1	2	4	3	3	1	3
	SGBP	1	2	2	4	1	2	2	2	2
	IG	3	4	4	3	3	4	4	4	4
	SIG	2	1	3	1	2	1	1	3	1
SSD	GBP	2	3	2	3	1	3	2	3	3
	SGBP	1	2	1	2	2	2	1	1	1
	IG	4	4	4	4	4	4	7	4	4
	SIG	3	1	3	1	3	1	3	2	2
FRN	GBP	4	3	1	2	2	1	1	1	1
	SGBP	1	1	2	1	1	3	2	2	2
	IG	3	4	4	4	4	4	4	4	4
	SIG	2	2	3	3	3	2	3	3	3

interest decision across SSD, EDO, and FRN detector separately. The evaluation identifies the relatively more trusted explanation method by the users for a particular detector. The explanation methods are ranked by relatively rating the explanations generated using different explanation methods for a particular detection made by a detector. The rating serves as a measure of user preference.

A pair of explanations generated by different explanation methods using the same interest decision and same interest detection for the same detector is shown to a number of human users as shown in Fig. 38. The detector, interest decision, interest detection, and explanation method used to generate explanations are randomly sampled for each question and each user. In addition, the image chosen for a particular question is randomly sampled from an evaluation set. The evaluation set is a randomly sampled set containing 50 images from the COCO test 2017. This avoids incorporating any bias into the question generation procedure. Each question is generated on the fly for each user performing the task. The explanations are named Robot A explanation and Robot B explanation to conceal the names of the explanation methods to the user. The robots are not detectors. In this study, the robots are treated as explanation methods. Robot A explanation and Robot B explanation for each question is randomly assigned with a pair of explanation method output. This is done to reduce the bias due

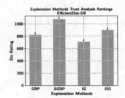 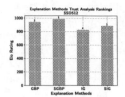 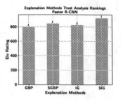

Fig. 15. Ranking obtained for the explanation methods from the user trust study for each detector selected in this work. An initial Elo rating of 1000 is used for all explanation methods. The explanation method with a higher Elo rating has gained relatively more user preferability in the random pair-wise comparisons of explanations for each detector. The rank of a particular method is provided on the top of the bar corresponding to the method.

to positioning and ordering bias of the explanations as shown to users. The task provided for the user is to rate the quality of the Robot A explanation based on the Robot B explanation. The scoring gives scores in the range $[-2, 2]$ depending if Robot A or B is better. The available options are provided in Table 5.

A single question in the evaluation is treated as a game between two randomly matched players. The explanation methods are the players. The game result depends on the explanation quality produced by the competing explanation methods for a particular detection decision. In case of a draw, both explanation methods receive the same score. During non-draw situations, the points won by a particular explanation method are the points lost by the other explanation method. By treating all the questions answered by numerous users as individual games, the global ranking is obtained using the Elo rating system [13]. Each explanation method is awarded an initial Elo rating of 1000.

Ranking Multi-object Visualization Methods. The rank for multi-object visualization methods is obtained by voting for the method producing the most understandable explanation among the four methods. Each user is asked a set of questions showing the multi-object visualization generated by all four methods. The user is provided with a *None of the methods* option to chose during scenarios where all the multi-object visualizations generated are confusing and incomprehensible to the user. The methods are ranked by counting the total number of votes each method has obtained. The experiment is performed using COCO 2017 test split and the VOC 2012.

Results. Each user is requested to answer 10 questions, split as 7 and 3 between Task 1 and Task 2, respectively. 52 participants have answered the user study for both task 1 and task 2. The participants range across researchers, students, deep learning engineers, office secretaries, and software engineers.

Figure 15 indicates SGBP provide relatively more reasonable explanations with higher user preferability for both single-stage detectors. Similarly, SIG is preferred for the two-stage detector. Figure 16a illustrates the top two ranks are obtained by SmoothGrad versions of the SGBP and IG for all detectors. GBP relatively performs in the middle rank in the majority of cases. SGBP achieves the first rank in both the human-centric evaluation and functional evaluation. Figure 16a illustrates the overall ranking taking into account all the bounding box and classification explanations together. The ranking is similar in analyzing the bounding box and classification explanations separately.

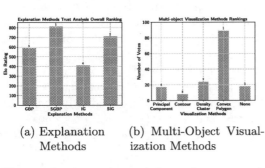

(a) Explanation Methods

(b) Multi-Object Visualization Methods

Fig. 16. Ranking obtained from the user study considering all user answers. The rank of a particular method is provided on the top of the bar corresponding to the method.

The ranking of multi-object visualization methods clearly illustrate that majority of the users are able to understand convex polygon-based explanations. 18 answers among the total 156 are *None of the methods* because none of the four other methods provided a legible summary of all the explanation methods and detections. The users have selected principal component-based visualization in cases involving less than 3 detections in an image. In addition, *None of the methods* is chosen in most of the cases involving more than 9 detections or more than 3 overlapping detections in an image. Among the total participants, only 89 users (57%) agree with the convex polygon-based visualization. Therefore, by considering the remaining 43% users, there is a lot of need to improve the multi-object visualization methods discussed in this work and achieve a better summary.

5   Conclusions and Future Work

Explaining convolutional object detectors is crucial given the ubiquity of detectors in autonomous driving, healthcare, and robotics. We extend post-hoc gradient-based explanation methods to explain both classification and bounding box decisions of EfficientDet-D0, SSD512, and Faster R-CNN. In order to integrate explanations and summarize saliency maps into a single output images, we propose four multi-object visualization methods: PCA, Contours, Density clustering, and Convex polygons, to merge explanations of a particular decision.

We evaluate these detectors and their explanations using a set of quantitative metrics (insertion and deletion of pixels according to saliency map importance) and with a user study to understand how useful these explanations are to humans. Insertion and deletion metrics indicate that SGBP provides more faithful explanations in the overall ranking. In general there is no detector that clearly provides better explanations, as a best depends on the criteria being used, but visual inspection indicates a weak relationship that newer detectors (like EfficientDet) have better explanations without artifacts (Fig. 2), and that different backbones do have an influence on the saliency map quality (Fig. 6).

The user study reveals a human preference for SGBP explanations for SSD and EfficientDet (and SIG for Faster R-CNN), which is consistent with the quantitative evaluation, and for multi-object explanation visualizations, convex polygons are clearly preferred by humans.

We analyze certain failure modes of a detector using the formulated explanation approach and provide several examples. The overall message of our work is to always explain both object classification and bounding box decisions, and that it is possible to combine explanations into a single output image through convex polygon representation of the saliency map.

Finally, we developed an open-source toolkit, DExT, to explain decisions made by a detector using saliency maps, to generate multi-object visualizations, and to analyze failure modes. We expect that DExT and our evaluation will contribute to the development of holistic explanation methods for object detectors, considering all their output bounding boxes, and both object classification and bounding box decisions.

Limitations. Firstly, the pixel insertion/deletion metrics might be difficult to interpret [16] and more advanced metrics could be used [45]. However, the metric selected should consider the specifics of object detection and evaluate both classification and bounding box regression. Moreover, as detectors are prone to non-local effects, removing pixels from the image [30] can cause bounding boxes to appear or disappear. Therefore, special tracking of a particular box is needed. We extend the classic pixel insertion/deletion metrics [3] for object detection considering these two aspects.

The second limitation is about the user study. Given the challenges in formulating a bias-free question, we ask users to select which explanation method is better. This is a subjective human judgment and does not necessarily have to correspond with the true input feature attribution made by the explanation method. Another part of the user study is comparing multi-object visualization methods, where we believe there is a much clearer conclusion. The novelty of our work is to combine quantitative, qualitative, and a user study, to empirically evaluate saliency explanations for detectors considering object classification and bounding box regression decisions.

In general, saliency methods are prone to heavy criticisms questioning the reliability of the methods. This study extends a few gradient-based saliency methods for detectors and conducts extensive evaluation. However, we acknowledge that there are other prominent saliency methods to study.

Our work evaluates and explains real-world object detectors without any toy example. The literature has previously performed basic sanity checks on toy usecases that does not include multiple localization and classification outputs. In addition, object detectors are categorized on the basis of number of stages (single-stage [23,43] and two-stage [28]), availability of anchors (anchor-based [23,43] and anchor-free [27,44]), and vision transformer based detectors [9,10]. We explain detectors specific to certain groups (SSD512, Faster R-CNN, and EfficientDet) and leave anchor-free and transformer-based detectors for future.

Even though fully white-box interpretable models would be the best solution [31], this is not yet available at the model scale required for high object detection performance.

References

1. Abdulla, W.: Mask R-CNN for object detection and instance segmentation on Keras and TensorFlow. GitHub (2017). Accessed 20 Sept 2021
2. Ancona, M., Ceolini, E., Öztireli, C., Gross, M.: Towards better understanding of gradient-based attribution methods for deep neural networks. In: 6th International Conference on Learning Representations (ICLR) Conference Track Proceedings (2018)
3. Ancona, M., Ceolini, E., Öztireli, C., Gross, M.: Gradient-based attribution methods. In: Samek, W., Montavon, G., Vedaldi, A., Hansen, L.K., Müller, K.-R. (eds.) Explainable AI: Interpreting, Explaining and Visualizing Deep Learning. LNCS (LNAI), vol. 11700, pp. 169–191. Springer, Cham (2019). https://doi.org/10.1007/978-3-030-28954-6_9
4. Arani, E., Gowda, S., Mukherjee, R., Magdy, O., Kathiresan, S.S., Zonooz, B.: A comprehensive study of real-time object detection networks across multiple domains: a survey. Trans. Mach. Learn. Res. (2022). Survey Certification
5. Araújo, T., Aresta, G., Galdran, A., Costa, P., Mendonça, A.M., Campilho, A.: UOLO - automatic object detection and segmentation in biomedical images. In: Stoyanov, D., et al. (eds.) DLMIA/ML-CDS -2018. LNCS, vol. 11045, pp. 165–173. Springer, Cham (2018). https://doi.org/10.1007/978-3-030-00889-5_19
6. Arriaga, O., Valdenegro-Toro, M., Muthuraja, M., Devaramani, S., Kirchner, F.: Perception for Autonomous Systems (PAZ). Computing Research Repository (CoRR) abs/2010.14541 (2020)
7. Bach, S., Binder, A., Montavon, G., Klauschen, F., Müller, K., Samek, W.: On pixel-wise explanations for non-linear classifier decisions by layer-wise relevance propagation. PLoS ONE **10**(7), 1–46 (2015)
8. Bastings, J., Filippova, K.: The elephant in the interpretability room: why use attention as explanation when we have saliency methods? In: Alishahi, A., Belinkov, Y., Chrupala, G., Hupkes, D., Pinter, Y., Sajjad, H. (eds.) Proceedings of the Third BlackboxNLP Workshop on Analyzing and Interpreting Neural Networks for NLP, BlackboxNLP@EMNLP, pp. 149–155. Association for Computational Linguistics ACL (2020)
9. Beal, J., Kim, E., Tzeng, E., Park, D.H., Zhai, A., Kislyuk, D.: Toward transformer-based object detection. CoRR abs/2012.09958 (2020)
10. Carion, N., Massa, F., Synnaeve, G., Usunier, N., Kirillov, A., Zagoruyko, S.: End-to-end object detection with transformers. In: Vedaldi, A., Bischof, H., Brox, T., Frahm, J.-M. (eds.) ECCV 2020. LNCS, vol. 12346, pp. 213–229. Springer, Cham (2020). https://doi.org/10.1007/978-3-030-58452-8_13
11. Padmanabhan, D.C., Plöger, P. G., Arriaga, O., Valdenegro-Toro, M.: Sanity checks for saliency methods explaining object detectors. In: Proceedings of the 1st World Conference on Explainable Artificial Intelligence (2023)
12. Doshi-Velez, F., Kim, B.: Towards a rigorous science of interpretable machine learning. arXiv preprint arXiv:1702.08608 (2017)
13. Elo, A.E.: The Rating of Chess Players. Past and Present, BT Batsford Limited (1978)

14. Ester, M., Kriegel, H., Sander, J., Xu, X.: A density-based algorithm for discovering clusters in large spatial databases with noise. In: Simoudis, E., Han, J., Fayyad, U.M. (eds.) Proceedings of the Second International Conference on Knowledge Discovery and Data Mining (KDD), pp. 226–231. AAAI Press (1996)
15. Feng, D., et al.: Deep multi-modal object detection and semantic segmentation for autonomous driving: datasets, methods, and challenges. IEEE Trans. Intell. Transp. Syst. (TITS) **22**(3), 1341–1360 (2021)
16. Grabska-Barwinska, A., Rannen-Triki, A., Rivasplata, O., György, A.: Towards better visual explanations for deep image classifiers. In: eXplainable AI Approaches for Debugging and Diagnosis (2021)
17. Gudovskiy, D.A., Hodgkinson, A., Yamaguchi, T., Ishii, Y., Tsukizawa, S.: Explain to fix: a framework to interpret and correct DNN object detector predictions. Computing Research Repository (CoRR) abs/1811.08011 (2018)
18. He, P., Huang, W., He, T., Zhu, Q., Qiao, Y., Li, X.: Single shot text detector with regional attention. In: 2017 IEEE International Conference on Computer Vision (ICCV), pp. 3066–3074. IEEE (2017)
19. Jain, S., Wallace, B.C.: Attention is not explanation. In: Burstein, J., Doran, C., Solorio, T. (eds.) Proceedings of the 2019 Conference of the North American Chapter of the Association for Computational Linguistics: Human Language Technologies (NAACL-HLT) Volume 1 (Long and Short Papers), pp. 3543–3556. Association for Computational Linguistics (ACL) (2019)
20. Kim, B., Doshi-Velez, F.: Machine learning techniques for accountability. AI Mag. **42**(1), 47–52 (2021)
21. Kim, J.U., Park, S., Ro, Y.M.: Towards human-like interpretable object detection via spatial relation encoding. In: 2020 IEEE International Conference on Image Processing (ICIP), pp. 3284–3288. IEEE (2020)
22. Lin, T.-Y., et al.: Microsoft COCO: common objects in context. In: Fleet, D., Pajdla, T., Schiele, B., Tuytelaars, T. (eds.) ECCV 2014. LNCS, vol. 8693, pp. 740–755. Springer, Cham (2014). https://doi.org/10.1007/978-3-319-10602-1_48
23. Liu, W., et al.: SSD: single shot MultiBox detector. In: Leibe, B., Matas, J., Sebe, N., Welling, M. (eds.) ECCV 2016. LNCS, vol. 9905, pp. 21–37. Springer, Cham (2016). https://doi.org/10.1007/978-3-319-46448-0_2
24. Lundberg, S.M., Lee, S.: A unified approach to interpreting model predictions. In: Guyon, I., et al. (eds.) Proceedings of the 31st International Conference on Neural Information Processing Systems (NIPS), pp. 4768–4777. NIPS 2017, Curran Associates, Inc. (2017)
25. Petsiuk, V., Das, A., Saenko, K.: RISE: randomized input sampling for explanation of black-box models. In: British Machine Vision Conference (BMVC), p. 151. BMVA Press (2018)
26. Petsiuk, V., et al.: Black-box explanation of object detectors via saliency maps. In: Proceedings of the IEEE/CVF Conference on Computer Vision and Pattern Recognition (CVPR), pp. 11443–11452 (2021)
27. Redmon, J., Divvala, S.K., Girshick, R.B., Farhadi, A.: You only look once: unified, real-time object detection. In: 2016 IEEE Conference on Computer Vision and Pattern Recognition (CVPR), pp. 779–788. IEEE (2016)
28. Ren, S., He, K., Girshick, R.B., Sun, J.: Faster R-CNN: towards real-time object detection with region proposal networks. IEEE Trans. Pattern Anal. Mach. Intell. (PAMI) **39**(6), 1137–1149 (2017)
29. Ribeiro, M.T., Singh, S., Guestrin, C.: "Why Should I Trust You?": explaining the predictions of any classifier. In: Krishnapuram, B., Shah, M., Smola, A.J., Aggarwal, C.C., Shen, D., Rastogi, R. (eds.) Proceedings of the 22nd ACM SIGKDD

International Conference on Knowledge Discovery and Data Mining, pp. 1135–1144. Association for Computing Machinery (ACM) (2016)

30. Rosenfeld, A., Zemel, R.S., Tsotsos, J.K.: The elephant in the room. Computing Research Repository (CoRR) abs/1808.03305 (2018)

31. Rudin, C.: Stop explaining black box machine learning models for high stakes decisions and use interpretable models instead. Nature Mach. Intell. 1(5), 206–215 (2019)

32. Rudin, C., Wagstaff, K.L.: Machine learning for science and society. Mach. Learn. 95(1), 1–9 (2014)

33. Samek, W., Montavon, G., Lapuschkin, S., Anders, C.J., Müller, K.: Explaining deep neural networks and beyond: a review of methods and applications. Proc. IEEE 109(3), 247–278 (2021)

34. Selvaraju, R.R., Cogswell, M., Das, A., Vedantam, R., Parikh, D., Batra, D.: Grad-CAM: visual explanations from deep networks via gradient-based localization. Int. J. Comput. Vision 128(2), 336–359 (2020)

35. Serrano, S., Smith, N.A.: Is attention interpretable? In: Korhonen, A., Traum, D.R., Màrquez, L. (eds.) Proceedings of the 57th Conference of the Association for Computational Linguistics (ACL), pp. 2931–2951. Association for Computational Linguistics (ACL) (2019)

36. Shrikumar, A., Greenside, P., Kundaje, A.: Learning important features through propagating activation differences. In: Precup, D., Teh, Y.W. (eds.) Proceedings of the 34th International Conference on Machine Learning (ICML) 2017. Proceedings of Machine Learning Research, vol. 70, pp. 3145–3153. Proceedings of Machine Learning Research (PMLR) (2017)

37. Shwartz-Ziv, R., Tishby, N.: Opening the black box of deep neural networks via information. Computing Research Repository (CoRR) abs/1703.00810 (2017)

38. Simonyan, K., Vedaldi, A., Zisserman, A.: Deep inside convolutional networks: visualising image classification models and saliency maps. In: Bengio, Y., LeCun, Y. (eds.) 2nd International Conference on Learning Representations (ICLR) Workshop Track Proceedings (2014)

39. Smilkov, D., Thorat, N., Kim, B., Viégas, F.B., Wattenberg, M.: SmoothGrad: removing noise by adding noise. Computing Research Repository (CoRR) abs/1706.03825 (2017)

40. Spiegelhalter, D.: Should we trust algorithms? Harvard Data Sci. Rev. 2(1), 1 (2020)

41. Springenberg, J.T., Dosovitskiy, A., Brox, T., Riedmiller, M.A.: Striving for simplicity: the all convolutional net. In: Bengio, Y., LeCun, Y. (eds.) 3rd International Conference on Learning Representations (ICLR) Workshop Track Proceedings (2015)

42. Sundararajan, M., Taly, A., Yan, Q.: Axiomatic attribution for deep networks. In: Precup, D., Teh, Y.W. (eds.) Proceedings of the 34th International Conference on Machine Learning (ICML) 2017. Proceedings of Machine Learning Research, vol. 70, pp. 3319–3328. Proceedings of Machine Learning Research (PMLR) (2017)

43. Tan, M., Pang, R., Le, Q.V.: EfficientDet: scalable and efficient object detection. In: 2020 IEEE/CVF Conference on Computer Vision and Pattern Recognition (CVPR), pp. 10778–10787. IEEE (2020)

44. Tian, Z., Shen, C., Chen, H., He, T.: FCOS: fully convolutional one-stage object detection. In: 2019 IEEE/CVF International Conference on Computer Vision, ICCV 2019, Seoul, Korea (South), 27 October– 2 November 2019, pp. 9626–9635. IEEE (2019)

45. Tomsett, R., Harborne, D., Chakraborty, S., Gurram, P., Preece, A.: Sanity checks for saliency metrics. In: Proceedings of the AAAI Conference on Artificial Intelligence, vol. 34, pp. 6021–6029 (2020)

46. Tsunakawa, H., Kameya, Y., Lee, H., Shinya, Y., Mitsumoto, N.: Contrastive relevance propagation for interpreting predictions by a single-shot object detector. In: 2019 International Joint Conference on Neural Networks (IJCNN), pp. 1–9. IEEE (2019)

47. Valdenegro-Toro, M.: Forward-looking sonar marine debris datasets. GitHub (2019). Accessed 01 Dec 2021

48. Wagstaff, K.L.: Machine learning that matters. In: 2012 Proceedings of the 29th International Conference on Machine Learning (ICML) (2012). https://icml.cc/, Omnipress

49. Wang, X., Girshick, R.B., Gupta, A., He, K.: Non-local neural networks. In: 2018 IEEE/CVF Conference on Computer Vision and Pattern Recognition (CVPR), pp. 7794–7803. IEEE (2018)

50. Wickstrøm, K., Kampffmeyer, M., Jenssen, R.: Uncertainty and interpretability in convolutional neural networks for semantic segmentation of colorectal polyps. Med. Image Anal. **60**, 101619 (2020)

51. Wu, T., Song, X.: Towards interpretable object detection by unfolding latent structures. In: 2019 IEEE/CVF International Conference on Computer Vision (ICCV), pp. 6032–6042. IEEE (2019)

52. Zablocki, É., Ben-Younes, H., Pérez, P., Cord, M.: Explainability of vision-based autonomous driving systems: review and challenges. Computing Research Repository (CoRR) abs/2101.05307 (2021)

53. Zeiler, M.D., Fergus, R.: Visualizing and understanding convolutional networks. In: Fleet, D., Pajdla, T., Schiele, B., Tuytelaars, T. (eds.) ECCV 2014. LNCS, vol. 8689, pp. 818–833. Springer, Cham (2014). https://doi.org/10.1007/978-3-319-10590-1_53

54. Zou, Z., Shi, Z., Guo, Y., Ye, J.: Object detection in 20 years: a survey. Computing Research Repository (CoRR) abs/1905.05055 (2019)

Unveiling Black-Boxes: Explainable Deep Learning Models for Patent Classification

Md Shajalal[1,2]($\boxtimes$), Sebastian Denef[3], Md. Rezaul Karim[4], Alexander Boden[1,5], and Gunnar Stevens[2]

[1] Fraunhofer-Institute for Applied Information Technology FIT, Sankt Augustin, Germany
md.shajalal@fit.fraunhofer.de
[2] University of Siegen, Siegen, Germany
[3] AGENTS.inc., Berlin, Germany
[4] RWTH Aachen University, Aachen, Germany
[5] Bonn-Rhein-Sieg University of Applied Sciences, Sankt Augustin, Germany

Abstract. Recent technological advancements have led to a large number of patents in a diverse range of domains, making it challenging for human experts to analyze and manage. State-of-the-art methods for multi-label patent classification rely on deep neural networks (DNNs), which are complex and often considered black-boxes due to their opaque decision-making processes. In this paper, we propose a novel deep explainable patent classification framework by introducing layer-wise relevance propagation (LRP) to provide human-understandable explanations for predictions. We train several DNN models, including Bi-LSTM, CNN, and CNN-BiLSTM, and propagate the predictions backward from the output layer up to the input layer of the model to identify the relevance of words for individual predictions. Considering the relevance score, we then generate explanations by visualizing relevant words for the predicted patent class. Experimental results on two datasets comprising two-million patent texts demonstrate high performance in terms of various evaluation measures. The explanations generated for each prediction highlight important relevant words that align with the predicted class, making the prediction more understandable. Explainable systems have the potential to facilitate the adoption of complex AI-enabled methods for patent classification in real-world applications.

Keywords: Patent Classification · Explainability · Layer-wise relevance propagation · Deep Learning · Interpretability

1 Introduction

Patent classification is an important task in the field of intellectual property management, involving the categorization of patents into different categories based on their technical contents [1]. Traditional approaches to patent classification have relied on manual categorization by experts, which can be time-consuming

© The Author(s), under exclusive license to Springer Nature Switzerland AG 2023
L. Longo (Ed.): xAI 2023, CCIS 1902, pp. 457–474, 2023.
https://doi.org/10.1007/978-3-031-44067-0_24

and subjective [2]. However, due to the exponential growth of patent applications in recent times, it has become increasingly challenging for human experts to classify patents. The international patent classification (IPC) system, which consists of 645 labels for the general classes and over 67,000 labels for the subgroups, reflects the magnitude of challenges in multi-level patent classification tasks [1]. Furthermore, patent texts are generally lengthy and contain irregular scientific terms, making them a challenging field of application for text classification approaches, as patents often include highly technical and scientific terms that are not commonly used in everyday language, and authors often use jargon to make their patents unique and innovative [3]. These factors contribute to the significant challenges associated with patent classification.

However, recent advancements in machine learning (ML) and deep neural network (DNN) have made significant progress in automating the patent classification process. In the past, classical ML models, such as support vector machine (SVM), K-nearest neighbour, and naive bayes, have been widely used to automatically classify patent texts [4]. However, more recently, several DNN models have been proposed to address the challenges associated with patent classification. Generally, these models represent patent text using word embedding and transformer-based pre-trained models [1,2,5–7]. The DNN models, including recurrent neural networks (RNN) and their variants such as convolutional neural networks (CNN), long short-term memory networks (LSTM), bidirectional LSTM (Bi-LSTM), and gated recurrent unit (GRU), can learn to classify patents based on their textual content [2,5,7–9]. Hence, these enable faster and more reliable categorization of patents and scientific articles.

Mathematically, DNN-based classification approaches are often complex in their architecture, and the decision-making procedures can be opaque [10,11]. While these approaches may exhibit efficient performance in classifying patents, the decisions they make are often not understandable to patent experts, or even to practitioners of artificial intelligence (AI). As a result, it is crucial to ensure that the methods and decision-making procedures used in patent classification are transparent and trustworthy, with clear explanations provided for the reasons behind each prediction. This is particularly important because patents are legal documents, and it is essential to comprehend the reasoning behind the classification decisions made by the model. Therefore, patent classification models should be designed to be explainable, allowing the reasons and priorities behind each prediction to be presented to users. This will help build trust in the predictive models and promote transparency among users and stakeholders.

For text-based uni-modal patent classification tasks, explanations can be provided by highlighting relevant words and their relevance to the prediction, thus increasing trust of users in the accuracy of predictions. In recent years, there has been a growing interest in developing explainable artificial intelligence (XAI) to unveil the black-box decision-making process of DNN models in diverse fields, including image processing [12], text processing, finance [13,14], and health applications [15,16]. These XAI models can provide insights into the decision-making process, explaining the reasoning behind specific predictions, the overall model's priorities in decision making, and thereby enhancing the transparency and trust-worthiness of the application [10–12,17,18].

In this paper, our goal is to develop a patent classification framework that not only predicts the classes of patents but also provides explanations for the predicted classes. To achieve this, we propose a new explainable method for patent classification based on layer-wise relevance propagation (LRP). This method can break down the contribution of patent terms that are crucial in classifying a given patent into a certain class. We start by representing the patent terms using a high-dimensional distributed semantic feature vector obtained from pre-trained word-embedding models. Next, we proceed to train several DNN-based models, including Bi-LSTM, CNN, and CNN-BiLSTM, which are capable of predicting the patent class. Finally, the LRP-enabled explanations interface highlights relevant words that contributed to the final prediction, providing an explanation for the model's decision.

We conducted experiments using two benchmark patent classification datasets, and the experimental results demonstrated the effectiveness of our approach in both classifying patent documents and providing explanations for the predictions. Our contributions in this paper are twofold:

1. We propose an LRP-based explainability method that generates explanations for predictions by highlighting relevant patent terms that support the predicted class.
2. Our developed DNN models show effective performance in terms of multiple evaluation metrics on two different benchmark datasets, and performance comparison with existing works confirms their consistency and effectiveness.

Overall, explainable DNN models offer promising solutions for patent classification, enabling faster and more accurate categorization while providing insights into the decision-making process. With the increasing volume of patent applications, the development of such explainable models could be beneficial in automatically categorizing patents with efficiency and transparency.

The rest of the paper is structured as follows: Sect. 2 presents the summary of existing research on patent classification. Our proposed explainable deep patent classification framework is presented in Sect. 3. We demonstrate the effectiveness of our methods in classifying patents and explaining the predictions in detail in Sect. 4. Finally, Sect. 5 concluded our findings with some future directions in explainable patent classification research.

2   Related Work

In recent years, the patent classification task has gained significant attention in the field of natural language processing (NLP) research, as evidenced by several notable studies [2,3,19]. Various methods have been employed for classifying and analyzing patent data, and the methods can be categorized based on different factors such as the techniques utilized, the tasks' objectives (e.g., multi-class or multi-level classification), and the type of resources used to represent the patent data (i.e., uni-modal vs multi- modal) [7,9,20]. However, traditional approaches have relied on classical ML and bag-of-words (BoW)-based text representation, which have limitations in capturing semantic and contextual information of the text, as they can only capture lexical information. With the advent of different word-embedding techniques such as *word2vec* by Mikolov et al. [21,22], *Glove* by Pennington et al. [23], and *FastText* by Bojanowski et al. [24], the NLP research has been revolutionized with the ability to represent text using high-dimensional semantic vector representations [25–27]. More recently, there has been a growing trend in employing transformer-based pre-trained models, including deep bidirectional transformer (BERT) [28], robust optimized BERT (RoBERTa) [29], distilled BERT (DistilBERT) [30], and XLNet [31], for text representation in NLP tasks.

Shaobo et al. [2] introduced a deep patent classification framework that utilized convolutional neural networks (CNNs). They started by representing the text of patents, which was extracted from the title and abstract of the USPTO-2 patent collection, using a skip-gram-based word-embedding model [2]. They then used the resulting high-dimensional semantic representations to train CNN model. Similarly, Lee et al. [3] also employed a CNN-based neural network model, however, they fine-tuned a pre-trained BERT model for text representations. A DNN-based framework employing Bi-LSTM-CRF and Bi-GRU-HAN models has been introduced to extract semantic information from patents' texts [7].

A multi-level classification framework [9] has been proposed utilizing fine-tuned transformer-based pre-trained models, such as BERT, XLNet, RoBERTa, and ELECTRA [32]. Their findings revealed that XLNet outperformed the baseline models in terms of classification accuracy. In another study, Roudsari et al. [20] addressed multi-level (sub-group level) patent classification tasks by fine-tuning a DistilBERT model for representing patent texts. Jiang et al. [6] presented a multi-modal technical document classification technique called *TechDoc*, which incorporated NLP techniques, such as word-embedding, for extracting textual features and descriptive images to capture information for technical documents. They modelled the classification task using CNNs, RNNs, and Graph neural networks (GNNs). Additionally, Kang et al. [33] employed a multi-modal embedding approach for searching patent documents.

A patent classification method called *Patent2vec* has been introduced, which leverages multi-view patent graph analysis to capture low-dimensional representations of patent texts [8]. Pujari et al. [34] proposed a transformer-based multi-task model (TMM) for hierarchical patent classification, and their experimental results showed higher precision and recall compared to existing non-neural and neural methods. They also proposed a method to evaluate neural multi-field document representations for patent text classification. Similarly, Aroyehun et al. [35] introduced a hierarchical transfer and multi-task learning approach for patent classification, following a similar methodology. Roudsari et al. [36] compared different word-embedding methods for patent classification performance. Li et al. [37] proposed a contrastive learning framework called *CoPatE* for patent embedding, aimed at capturing high-level semantics for very large-scale patents to be classified. An automated ensemble learning-based framework for single-level patent classification is introduced by Kamateri et al. [38].

However, to the best of our knowledge, none of the existing patent classification methods are explainable. Given the complexity of the multi-level classification task, it is crucial for users and patent experts to understand the reasoning behind the AI-enabled method's predictions, as it classifies patents into one of more than 67,000 classes (including sub-group classes). Therefore, the aim of this paper is to generate explanations that highlight relevant words, helping users understand the rationale behind the model's predictions. Taking inspiration from the effectiveness and interpretability of layer-wise relevance propagation (LRP) in other short-text classification tasks [39–41], we have adopted LRP [12] as the method for explaining the complex neural networks-based patent classification model.

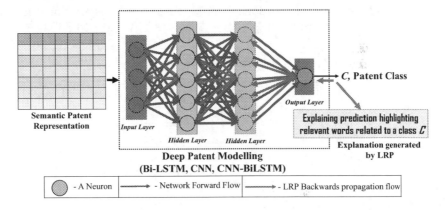

Fig. 1. A conceptual overview diagram of our explainable patent classification framework.

3   Explainable Patent Classification

Our proposed explainable patent classification framework consists of two major components, i) training DNN-based classification model using the semantic representation of patent text, and ii) explanation generation component leveraging layer-wise relevance propagation (LRP). The conceptual diagram with major components is depicted in Fig. 1. Our method first represents preprocessed patent texts semantically by high-dimensional vector leveraging pre-trained word embedding models. Then, the semantic representations for patent text are fed to train multiple DNN-based classification models including Bi-LSTM, CNN, and CNN-BiLSTM. For a particular deep patent classification model, our introduced LRP algorithm computes the relevance score towards a certain class for a given patent by redistributing the relevance score with backward propagation from the output layer to the input layer. Eventually, we get the score for patent terms that highlight the relevancy related to the predicted class of a given input patent.

3.1 Training Deep Neural Models

Before training any specific DNN-based patent classification model, we employ *FastText* word-embedding model to represent each word of patent text with a high-dimensional feature vector and the element of each vector carries semantic and contextual information of that word. *FastText* is a character n-gram-based embedding technique. Unlike, *Glove* and *Word2Vec*, it can provide a word vector for out-of-vocabulary (OOV) words. Patents' text contains less used scientific terms and some words that are higly context specific. For example, patent in the field of chemistry has a lot of reagents and chemical names, even for some new patents the reagents' names might be completely new, proposed by the inventors. Considering this intuition, we chose *FastText* embedding instead of *Glove* and *word2vec*. We make a sequence of embedding of the words for each patent and then fed it into the deep-learning model. Our trained different neural network models includes bidirectional LSTM (Bi-LSTM), convolutional neural networks (CNN), CNN-BiLSTM, a combination of CNN and Bi-LSTM.

3.2 Explaining Predictions with LRP

Let c denotes the predicted class for the input patent p. The LRP algorithm applies the layer-wise conservation principle to calculate the relevance score for features. The computation starts from the output layer and then redistributes the relevance weight, eventually back-propagating it to the input layers [39, 40]. In other words, the relevance score is computed at each layer of the DNN model. Following a specific rule, the relevance score is attributed from lower-layer neurons to higher-layer neurons, and each immediate-layer neuron is assigned a relevance score up to the input layers, based on this rule.

The flow of propagation for computing the relevance is depicted by the red arrow that goes from the output towards the input layers in Fig. 2. The figure conceptually reflects how the semantic representation of patent text leads to a particular class in DNN models and back-propagates the relevance score from the output layer to the input layer for explanations highlighting relevant terms aligned with the predicted class.

The prediction score, $f_c(p)$ by our deep patent classification model, which is a scalar value corresponding to the patent class c. Using LRP, our aim is to identify the relevance score for each dimension d of a given patent vector p for the target patent class c. Our objective is to compute the relevance score of each input feature (i.e., words) that illustrates how positively (or negatively) contributes to classifying the patent as class c (or another class).

Let z_j be the neuron of the upper layer and the computation of the neuron is calculated as

$$z_j = \sum_i z_i \cdot w_{ij} + b_j, \tag{1}$$

where w_{ij} be the weight matrix and b_j denotes the bias [40]. Given that the relevance score for upper-layer neurons z_j is R_j and we move towards lower-layer neurons to distribute that relevance. In the final layer, there is only one

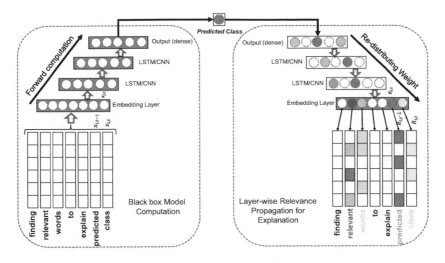

Fig. 2. A conceptual overview diagram illustrating the working flow of layer-wise relevance propagation (LRP) (Figure created based on [39]).

neuron (i.e., the prediction score) and in that case, R_j is the prediction score by the function $f_c(p)$. The redistribution of the relevance to the lower layers is done by following two major steps. We need to compute relevance messages to go from upper-layer to lower-layer neurons [40].

Let i be the immediate lower layer and its neurons are denoted by z_i. Computationally, the relevance massages $R_{i \leftarrow j}$ can be computed as followings [40].

$$R_{i \leftarrow j} = \frac{z_i \cdot w_{ij} + \frac{\epsilon \cdot sign(z_j) + \delta \cdot b_j}{N}}{z_j + \epsilon \cdot sign(z_j)} \cdot R_j.$$ (2)

The total number of neurons in the layer i is denoted as N and ϵ is the stabilizer, a small positive real number (i.e., 0.001). By summing up all the relevance scores of the neuron in z_i in layer i, we can obtain the relevance in layer i, $R_i = \sum_i R_{i \leftarrow j}$. δ can be either 0 or 1 (we use $\delta = 1$) [40,41]. With the relevance messages, we can calculate the amount of relevance that circulates from one layer's neuron to the next layer's neuron. However, the computation for relevance distribution in the fully connected layers is computed as $R_{j \rightarrow k} = \frac{z_{jk}}{\sum_j z_{jk}} R_k$ [39]. The value of the relevance score for each relevant term lies in [0,1]. The higher the score represents higher the relevancy of the terms towards the predicted class.

4   Experiments

This section presents the details about the datasets, experiment results, and discussion of generated explanation with LRP.

4.1 Dataset

AI-Growth-Lab Patent Dataset: We conducted experiments on a dataset containing 1.5 million patent claims annotated with patent class[1]. According to the CPC patent system, the classification is hierarchical with multiple levels including section, class, subclass, and group. For example, there are 667 labels in the subclass level [42]. However, for a better understanding of the generated explanations and the reasons behind a prediction for a given patent, we modeled the patent classification task with 9 general classes including *Human necessities, Performing operations; transporting, Chemistry; metallurgy, Textiles; paper, Fixed constructions, Mechanical engineering; lighting; heating; weapons; blasting engines or pumps, Physics, Electricity* and *General.*

BigPatent Dataset: BigPatent[2] dataset is prepared by processing 1.3 million patent texts [43]. However, the classification dataset contains in total of 35k patent texts with 9 above-mentioned classes as labels. They provided the dataset by splitting it into training, validation, and testing set, the number of samples are 25K, 5K, and 5K, respectively. There are two different texts for each patent, one is a raw text from patent claims and another version is the human-generated abstract summarized from the patent claims.

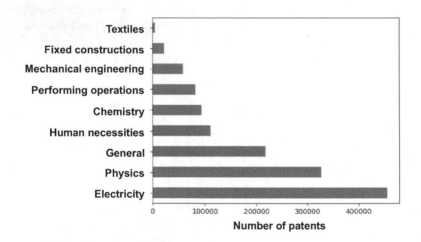

Fig. 3. The distribution of the patents for different class on AI-growth-Lab data

However, the number of samples per patent class is varied widely for both datasets, which means both are imbalanced dataset. The horizontal bar chart in Fig. 3 and 4 show the level of imbalance for both datasets. This imbalance distribution of samples per class poses an additional challenge in this multi-level classification task.

---

[1] Dataset: https://huggingface.co/AI-Growth-Lab [42].

[2] Dataset: https://huggingface.co/datasets/ccdv/patent-classification/tree/main.

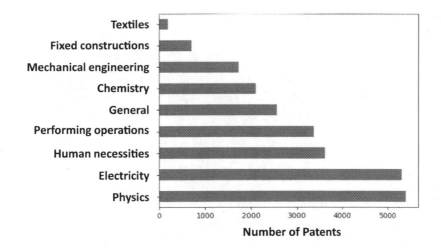

Fig. 4. The distribution of the patents for different class on BigPatent data

4.2 Experimental Setup

We conducted experiments using three different DNN models, namely Bi-LSTM, CNN, and CNN-BiLSTM, utilizing the *FastText* pre-trained word-embedding model for text representation in the embedding layers. The Bi-LSTM model consists of a layer of Bi-LSTM with 64 units after embedding layer, followed by another Bi-LSTM layer with 32 units, and then two fully-connected layers with 64 and 9 units, respectively. We applied the rectified linear units (ReLU) activation function in the hidden dense layer, and the softmax activation function in the output layer. For the CNN model, after the embedding layer, we have a 1-dimensional convolutional layer followed by a global average pooling layer, and finally, the output layer is a fully-connected layer with 9 units. The CNN-BiLSTM model has a convolutional layer followed by a global average pooling layer, and then the Bi-LSTM part is similar to the above-mentioned Bi-LSTM model. The activation functions in the fully connected hidden and output layers are ReLU and softmax, respectively. We implemented our methods using *scikit-learn* and *Keras*, and represented the patent text using the *FastText* pre-trained word-embedding model[3]. For implementing LRP for the Bi-LSTM network, we followed the method described in [40][4]. For the BigPatent dataset, the training, testing, and validation sets are already split. For the AI-Growth-Lab data, the ratio for the training and testing set is 80% and 20%, respectively.

---

[3] https://fasttext.cc/docs/en/crawl-vectors.html.
[4] https://github.com/ArrasL/LRP_for_LSTM.

Table 1. The performance of different deep patent classification models on two datasets in terms of precision, recall and f1-score. The best result is in **bold**.

Dataset	Method	Precision	Recall	F1-Score
AI-Growth-Lab	**Bi-LSTM**	**0.69**	**0.70**	**0.69**
	CNN	0.62	0.63	0.62
	CNN-BiLSTM	**0.69**	0.68	**0.69**
BigPatent	**Bi-LSTM**	**0.79**	**0.78**	**0.78**
	CNN	0.75	0.76	0.76
	CNN-BiLSTM	0.77	0.76	0.76

4.3   Performance Analysis

The performance of the proposed classification models was evaluated using three evaluation metrics, including Precision, Recall, and F1-Score, on two datasets, as shown in Table 1. The results demonstrate consistent performance across most of the deep classification models. Among them, the Bi-LSTM model exhibited better performance in terms of all evaluation metrics on both datasets. However, the performance of the other two models, CNN and CNN-BiLSTM, was also consistent and effective, though slightly lower than the Bi-LSTM model. Specifically, for the first dataset, CNN-BiLSTM performed equally well in terms of Precision (0.69) and F1-Score (0.69), while the performance of the CNN-based model was comparatively lower for the AI-Growth-Lab dataset, with a Precision of 62%, which was 7% lower than the best-performing Bi-LSTM model. However, for the BigPatent dataset, the CNN model exhibited considerably better performance, with a Precision of 75%, which was only 4% lower than the Bi-LSTM model. The performance difference between the models for the other two metrics was even lower, at 2%.

Table 2. Class-wise performance of Bi-LSTM model on BigPatent Dataset

Patent Class	label	Precision	Recall	F1-score
Human necessities	1	0.79	0.91	0.85
Performing_operations	2	0.74	0.66	0.70
Chemistry	3	0.75	0.88	0.81
Textiles	4	0.71	0.74	0.73
Fixed_constructions	5	0.65	0.70	0.67
Mechanical_engineering	6	0.60	0.84	0.70
Physics	7	0.75	0.82	0.78
Electricity	8	0.78	0.86	0.82
General	9	0.71	0.46	0.41

The performance of all DNN-based classifiers on the BigPatent dataset is significantly superior compared to the first dataset. This may be attributed to the fact that the BigPatent dataset includes finely-grained abstracts of patents which are generated by human assessors, taking into consideration the patent texts. As a result, the semantic representation of the fine-tuned text in the Big-Patent dataset is enriched compared to the raw patent claims in other dataset. We present the performance of Bi-LSTM model by showcasing the class-wise performance on the BigPatent dataset. Table 2 displays the performance across nine different patent classes. The Bi-LSTM model demonstrates favorable and consistent performance across most patent classes, with the exception of the *general* category. It is hypothesized that the patents in the *"general"* category may contain more commonly used terms compared to patents in other area-specific categories. Consequently, the captured semantic information may not be sufficient, potentially resulting in lower performance in terms of recall and F1-Score for the *"general"* class compared to other classes.

Table 3. Performance comparison with related works

Method	Precision	Recall	F1-Score
Out Method	0.79	**0.78**	**0.78**
Roudsari et al. [9] (Bi-LSTM)	0.7825	0.6421	0.68.42
Roudsari et al. [9] (CNN-BiLSTM)	0.7930	0.6513	0.6938
Shaobo et al. [2] (DeepPatent)	**0.7977**	0.6552	0.6979

We compared the performance of our models with similar models (Table 3) that used *FastText* embedding for patent text representation. Compared to existing works by Roudsari et al. [9] and Shaobo et al. [2], the performance of our trained models is effective. Roudsari et al. also trained similar models with semantic text representation with a pre-trained *FastText* word-embedding model. They also develop similar DNN models including Bi-LSTM and CNN-BiLSTM. Shaobo et al. [2] introduced CNN-based deep patent modelling employing *FastText* word-embedding model. The performance of our methods on Big-Patent data is higher than their models for all evaluation metrics except Precision. The comparison shows the effectiveness of our methods in classifying patents.

4.4   Generated Explanation for Prediction

We attempted to unbox the black-box nature of the deep patent classification model by adopting a layer-wise relevance propagation technique to compute the relevance score for each term by back-propagating the prediction score from the output layer to input layers. To represent the explanation per predicted class for a given patent text, we highlighted the related words that contributed to

1 a paper coating composition for enhancing the stiffness of p aper or paperboard comprising an alkali soluble polymer prep ared by polymerization of at least one monomer a and at least one monomer b wherein monomer a is selected from the gro up consisting of acrylic acid alkyl esters methacrylic acid alkyl esters styrene methyl styrene acrylonitrile vinyl acetate and 2 hydroxy alkyl acrylate and monomer b is selected from the gr oup consisting of acrylic acid methacrylic acid itaconic acid an d meth acrylamide wherein the paper coating composition co mprises 10 to 100 weight of the alkali soluble polymer and 90 to 0 weight of a further water soluble polymer and wherein th e further water soluble polymer is starch cellulosic ether carbo xy methyl cellulose

Fig. 5. An example explanation for a patent classified as *Chemistry* patents highlighting relevant words. The higher the intensity of the color, the better the relevancy of the words contributing to the prediction. (Color figure online)

1 a process for creating a paper pulp composition comprising the steps of combining raw paper calcium carbonate and starc h to create a dry mix adding polyvinyl alcohol and water to th e dry mix to create a slurry mixing the slurry in a mixer to crea te a substantially uniform pulp and curing the pulp until dry a dding a sanitizer to the slurry prior to mixing wherein the sanit izer is bleach

Fig. 6. An example explanation for a patent classified as *Chemistry* patents highlighting relevant words. The higher the intensity of the color, the better the relevancy of the words contributing to the prediction.

the classifier's prediction. As an example explanation, a patent is classified as *Chemistry*, and the related words that contributed to the prediction are highlighted in red color in Fig. 5. The figure shows the explanation highlighting relevant words for the patent that classified as *chemistry*. The intensity of the color represents the contributions of a particular word. The higher the intensity of the color (red), the better the relevancy the word is. We can see that from the figure, the most relevant words include, *alkali, alkyl, monomer, acid, acrylate, acrylonitrile, acetate, polymer, ether.* We can observed that the highlighted words are completely related to terms used in organic chemistry and the explanation makes sense why this patent has been classified as a chemical patent. The next relevant list of words is *soluble, water, stiffness, enhanching, etc..* These words are directly related to chemistry except *stiffness* and *enhancing.* Since *enhancing* the *stiffness* of the paper or paperboard is the objective of this patent, these words are selected as relevant. Figure 6 shows explanation for another *Chemistry* patent. We can also see that the relevant words are highlighted including *pulp, alcohol, sanitizer, calcium, carbonate, etc.,* are directly related to the chemistry field. To understand the impact of particular words, we vidualize the words in the form of word cloud in Fig. 7. The larger the word, the higher the relevancy of the word to the certain class.

Fig. 7. An example explanation for a patent classified as *Chemistry* patent highlighting relevant words in word cloud. The larger the font of the word, the better the relevancy of the words contributing to the prediction.

For another example patent in the field of *Electricity*, Fig. 8 illustrates the explanations highlighting relevant words that contributed to the classifier to decide that the patent is from *electricity* field. The most relevant words, in this case, include *power, channel, modem, device, bonded, bandwidth, data, etc.* We can see that all identified related words are used in *electricity* literature. The word *device* is used for common use in some other fields also, but this word also can be used to mention any electrical instrument in electricity-related explanation. Similar to the Fig. 7, we present the word cloud for explanation in Fig. 9. However, there are some words selected as relevant for both examples which are not relevant to the specific fields but can be used in literature for any field. One plausible reason is that those also might carry considerable importance in describing the any scientific object (i.e., explaining chemical reaction) and capture good contextual and semantic information in *FastText* embedding.

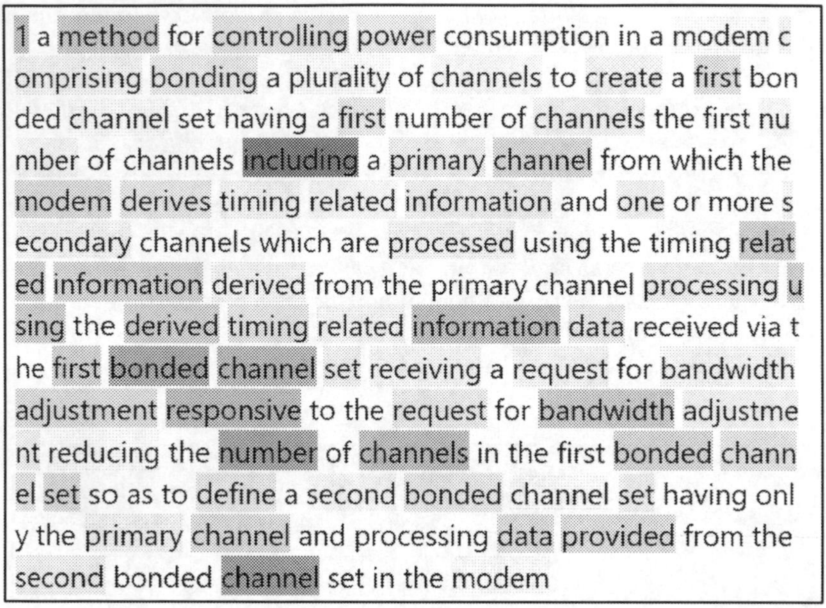

1 a method for controlling power consumption in a modem c
omprising bonding a plurality of channels to create a first bon
ded channel set having a first number of channels the first nu
mber of channels including a primary channel from which the
modem derives timing related information and one or more s
econdary channels which are processed using the timing relat
ed information derived from the primary channel processing u
sing the derived timing related information data received via t
he first bonded channel set receiving a request for bandwidth
adjustment responsive to the request for bandwidth adjustme
nt reducing the number of channels in the first bonded chann
el set so as to define a second bonded channel set having onl
y the primary channel and processing data provided from the
second bonded channel set in the modem

Fig. 8. An example explanation for a patent classified as *Electricity* patents highlighting relevant words. The higher the intensity of the color, the better the relevancy of the words contributing to the prediction.

method
provided
power
processing
request
bonding
derived
including
adjustment
controlling
timing
information
primary
responsive
data
secondary
define
derives
create

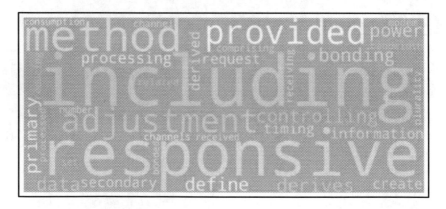

Fig. 9. An example explanation for a patent classified as *Electricity* patent highlighting relevant words in word cloud. The larger the font of the word, the better the relevancy of the words contributing to the prediction.

4.5 Limitations

Our model can explain the prediction for multi-label classification. Since the patents are classified in different levels and the patent classification system has a huge set of classes to classify in different levels, it should be explainable for multi-level classification also. This will be more challenging to explain the prediction for different subgroups-level classes. Another limitation is that our utilized pre-trained word-embedding model is not trained on the patent corpus. The local word-embedding model trained with patent corpus might capture better contextual and semantic information for scientific terms and jargon. Hence, the performance might be better than the current approach.

5   Conclusion and Future Direction

This paper aimed at explaining the predictions from DNN-based patent classification models with layer-wise relevance propagation technique to identify the relevance of different words in the patent texts for a certain predicted class. Layer-wise relevance propagation technique can capture context-specific explanatory and relevant words to explain the predictions behind certain predicted classes. The experimental results demonstrated the effectiveness of classifying patent documents with promising performance compared to existing works. We observed that the explanations generated by the LRP technique make it easier to understand why a certain patent is classified as a specific patent class. Most of the captured words have high relevancy with the patent domain, even though a few words marked as related are not that relevant (which, however, should also provide useful information to human expert in assessing the predictions). Even though our approach would still need to be evaluation with users, we can observe that the explanations are helpful to understand the question why a certain patent was classified into a specific class, and to assess the results of deep-learning-based complex artificial intelligence-enabled models.

Since patents have a lot of scientific and uncommon words and phrases (i.e., jargon) that are not often used in other texts, we plan to train a local word-embedding model with patent texts to have better representation in our future work. It would be interesting to apply a transformer-based approach for the same purpose. The explanations for sub-group level prediction and capturing the sub-group context will be even more explanatory. However, the generated explanations will need to be evaluated by human experts in the patent industry. Therefore, we plan to have a user-centric evaluation for the generated explanations and elicit more human-centric requirements to be addressed in the future for better adoption real-word applications.

Acknowledgment. This project has received funding from the European Union's Horizon 2020 research and innovation programme under the Marie Skłodowska-Curie grant agreement No 955422.

References

1. Kucer, M., Oyen, D., Castorena, J., Wu, J.: Deeppatent: large scale patent drawing recognition and retrieval. In: Proceedings of the IEEE/CVF Winter Conference on Applications of Computer Vision, pp. 2309–2318 (2022)

2. Li, S., Jie, H., Cui, Y., Jianjun, H.: Deeppatent: patent classification with convolutional neural networks and word embedding. Scientometrics **117**, 721–744 (2018)
3. Lee, J.-S., Hsiang, J.: Patent classification by fine-tuning Bert language model. World Patent Inf. **61**, 101965 (2020)
4. D'hondt, E., Verberne, S., Koster, C., Boves, L.: Text representations for patent classification. Comput. Linguist. **39**(3), 755–775 (2013)
5. Luo, M., Shi, X., Ji, Q., Shang, M., He, X., Tao, W.: A deep self-learning classification framework for incomplete medical patents with multi-label. In: Liu, Y., Wang, L., Zhao, L., Yu, Z. (eds.) ICNC-FSKD 2019. AISC, vol. 1075, pp. 566–573. Springer, Cham (2020). https://doi.org/10.1007/978-3-030-32591-6_61
6. Jiang, S., Hu, J., Magee, C.L., Luo, J.: Deep learning for technical document classification. IEEE Trans. Eng. Manag. (2022)
7. Chen, L., Shuo, X., Zhu, L., Zhang, J., Lei, X., Yang, G.: A deep learning based method for extracting semantic information from patent documents. Scientometrics **125**, 289–312 (2020)
8. Fang, L., Zhang, L., Han, W., Tong, X., Zhou, D., Chen, E.: Patent2vec: multi-view representation learning on patent-graphs for patent classification. World Wide Web **24**(5), 1791–1812 (2021)
9. Haghighian Roudsari, A., Afshar, J., Lee, W., Lee, S.: Patentnet: multi-label classification of patent documents using deep learning based language understanding. Scientometrics, pp. 1–25 (2022)
10. Shrikumar, A., Greenside, P., Kundaje, A.: Learning important features through propagating activation differences. In: International Conference on Machine Learning, pp. 3145–3153. PMLR (2017)
11. Lundberg, S.M., Lee, S.-I.: A unified approach to interpreting model predictions. Adv. Neural Inf. Process. Syst. **30**, 4765–4774 (2017)
12. Bach, S., Binder, A., Montavon, G., Klauschen, F., Müller, K.-R., Samek, W.: On pixel-wise explanations for non-linear classifier decisions by layerd-wise relevance propagation. PLoS ONE **10**(7), e0130140 (2015)
13. Kute, D.V., Pradhan, B., Shukla, N., Alamri, A.: Deep learning and explainable artificial intelligence techniques applied for detecting money laundering-a critical review. IEEE Access **9**, 82300–82317 (2021)
14. Shajalal, M., Boden, A., Stevens, G.: Explainable product backorder prediction exploiting CNN: introducing explainable models in businesses. Electron. Mark. **32**, 2107–2122 (2022)
15. Yang, G., Ye, Q., Xia, J.: Unbox the black-box for the medical explainable AI via multi-modal and multi-centre data fusion: a mini-review, two showcases and beyond. Inf. Fusion **77**, 29–52 (2022)
16. Adadi, A., Berrada, M.: Explainable AI for healthcare: from black box to interpretable models. In: Bhateja, V., Satapathy, S.C., Satori, H. (eds.) Embedded Systems and Artificial Intelligence. AISC, vol. 1076, pp. 327–337. Springer, Singapore (2020). https://doi.org/10.1007/978-981-15-0947-6_31
17. Ribeiro, M.T., Singh, S., Guestrin, C.: Why should i trust you? Explaining the predictions of any classifier. In: Proceedings of the 22nd ACM SIGKDD International Conference on Knowledge Discovery and Data Mining, pp. 1135–1144 (2016)
18. Binder, A., Montavon, G., Lapuschkin, S., Müller, K.-R., Samek, W.: Layer-wise relevance propagation for neural networks with local renormalization layers. In: Villa, A.E.P., Masulli, P., Pons Rivero, A.J. (eds.) ICANN 2016. LNCS, vol. 9887, pp. 63–71. Springer, Cham (2016). https://doi.org/10.1007/978-3-319-44781-0_8

19. Shalaby, M., Stutzki, J., Schubert, M., Günnemann, S.: An LSTM approach to patent classification based on fixed hierarchy vectors. In: Proceedings of the 2018 SIAM International Conference on Data Mining, pp. 495–503. SIAM (2018)
20. Roudsari, A.H., Afshar, J., Lee, C.C., Lee, W.: Multi-label patent classification using attention-aware deep learning model. In: 2020 IEEE International Conference on Big Data and Smart Computing (BigComp), pp. 558–559. IEEE (2020)
21. Le, Q., Mikolov, T.: Distributed representations of sentences and documents. In: International Conference on Machine Learning, pp. 1188–1196. PMLR (2014)
22. Mikolov, T., Sutskever, I., Chen, K., Corrado, G.S., Dean, J.: Distributed representations of words and phrases and their compositionality. Adv. Neural Inf. Process. Syst. **26**, 3111–3119 (2013)
23. Pennington, J., Socher, R., Manning, C.D.: Glove: global vectors for word representation. In: Proceedings of the 2014 Conference on Empirical Methods in Natural Language Processing (EMNLP), pp. 1532–1543 (2014)
24. Bojanowski, P., Grave, E., Joulin, A., Mikolov, T.: Enriching word vectors with subword information. Trans. Assoc. Comput. Linguist. **5**, 135–146 (2017)
25. Shajalal, M., Aono, M.: Sentence-level semantic textual similarity using word-level semantics. In: 2018 10th International Conference on Electrical and Computer Engineering (ICECE), pp. 113–116. IEEE (2018)
26. Shajalal, Md., Aono, M.: Semantic textual similarity between sentences using bilingual word semantics. Prog. Artif. Intell. **8**, 263–272 (2019)
27. Shajalal, Md., Aono, M.: Coverage-based query subtopic diversification leveraging semantic relevance. Knowl. Inf. Syst. **62**, 2873–2891 (2020)
28. Devlin, J., Chang, M.-W., Lee, K., Toutanova, K.: Bert: pre-training of deep bidirectional transformers for language understanding. arXiv preprint arXiv:1810.04805 (2018)
29. Liu, Y., et al.: Roberta: a robustly optimized Bert pretraining approach. arXiv preprint arXiv:1907.11692 (2019)
30. Sanh, V., Debut, L., Chaumond, J., Wolf, T.: DistilBERT, a distilled version of BERT: smaller, faster, cheaper and lighter. arXiv preprint arXiv:1910.01108 (2019)
31. Yang, Z., Dai, Z., Yang, Y., Carbonell, J., Salakhutdinov, R.R., Le, Q.V.: XLNet: generalized autoregressive pretraining for language understanding. Adv. Neural Inf. Process. Syst. **32**, 5753–5763 (2019)
32. Clark, K., Luong, M.T., Le, Q.V., Manning, C.D.: Electra: pre-training text encoders as discriminators rather than generators. arXiv preprint arXiv:2003.10555 (2020)
33. Kang, M., Lee, S., Lee, W.: Prior art search using multi-modal embedding of patent documents. In: 2020 IEEE International Conference on Big Data and Smart Computing (BigComp), pp. 548–550. IEEE (2020)
34. Pujari, S.C., Friedrich, A., Strötgen, J.: A multi-task approach to neural multi-label hierarchical patent classification using transformers. In: Hiemstra, D., Moens, M.-F., Mothe, J., Perego, R., Potthast, M., Sebastiani, F. (eds.) ECIR 2021. LNCS, vol. 12656, pp. 513–528. Springer, Cham (2021). https://doi.org/10.1007/978-3-030-72113-8_34
35. Aroyehun, S.T., Angel, J., Majumder, N., Gelbukh, A., Hussain, A.: Leveraging label hierarchy using transfer and multi-task learning: a case study on patent classification. Neurocomputing **464**, 421–431 (2021)
36. Roudsari, A.H., Afshar, J., Lee, S., Lee, W.: Comparison and analysis of embedding methods for patent documents. In: 2021 IEEE International Conference on Big Data and Smart Computing (BigComp), pp. 152–155. IEEE (2021)

37. Li, H., Li, S., Jiang, Y., Zhao, G.: CoPatE: a novel contrastive learning framework for patent embeddings. In: Proceedings of the 31st ACM International Conference on Information & Knowledge Management, pp. 1104–1113 (2022)
38. Kamateri, E., Stamatis, V., Diamantaras, K., Salampasis, M.: Automated single-label patent classification using ensemble classifiers. In: 2022 14th International Conference on Machine Learning and Computing (ICMLC), pp. 324–330 (2022)
39. Arras, L., Horn, F., Montavon, G., Muller, K.R., Samek, W.: What is relevant in a text document?: an interpretable machine learning approach. PloS one **12**(8), e0181142 (2017)
40. Arras, L., Montavon, G., Müller, K.R., Samek, W.: Explaining recurrent neural network predictions in sentiment analysis. arXiv preprint arXiv:1706.07206 (2017)
41. Karim, M.R., et al.: Deephateexplainer: explainable hate speech detection in under-resourced Bengali language. In: 2021 IEEE 8th International Conference on Data Science and Advanced Analytics (DSAA), pp. 1–10. IEEE (2021)
42. Bekamiri, H., Hain, D.S., Jurowetzki, R.: Patentsberta: a deep NLP based hybrid model for patent distance and classification using augmented SBERT. arXiv preprint arXiv:2103.11933 (2021)
43. Sharma, E., Li, C., Wang, L.: BIGPATENT: a large-scale dataset for abstractive and coherent summarization. arXiv preprint arXiv:1906.03741 (2019)

HOLMES: HOLonym-MEronym Based Semantic Inspection for Convolutional Image Classifiers

Francesco Dibitonto[1,2]([✉]) [iD], Fabio Garcea[1] [iD], André Panisson[3] [iD],
Alan Perotti[3] [iD], and Lia Morra[1] [iD]

[1] Department of Control and Computer Engineering, Politecnico di Torino, Torino,
Italy
francesco.dibitonto.work@gmail.com
[2] EVS Embedded Vision Systems, Verona, Italy
[3] CENTAI Institute, Turin, Italy

Abstract. Convolutional Neural Networks (CNNs) are nowadays the model of choice in Computer Vision, thanks to their ability to automatize the feature extraction process in visual tasks. However, the knowledge acquired during training is fully sub-symbolic, and hence difficult to understand and explain to end users. In this paper, we propose a new technique called HOLMES (HOLonym-MEronym based Semantic inspection) that decomposes a label into a set of related concepts, and provides component-level explanations for an image classification model. Specifically, HOLMES leverages ontologies, web scraping and transfer learning to automatically construct *meronym* (parts)-based detectors for a given *holonym* (class). Then, it produces heatmaps at the meronym level and finally, by probing the holonym CNN with occluded images, it highlights the importance of each part on the classification output. Compared to state-of-the-art saliency methods, HOLMES takes a step further and provides information about both *where* and *what* the holonym CNN is looking at. It achieves so without relying on densely annotated datasets and without forcing concepts to be associated to single computational units. Extensive experimental evaluation on different categories of objects (animals, tools and vehicles) shows the feasibility of our approach. On average, HOLMES explanations include at least two meronyms, and the ablation of a single meronym roughly halves the holonym model confidence. The resulting heatmaps were quantitatively evaluated using the deletion/insertion/preservation curves. All metrics were comparable to those achieved by GradCAM, while offering the advantage of further decomposing the heatmap in human-understandable concepts. In addition, results were largely above chance level, thus highlighting both the relevance of meronyms to object classification, as well as HOLMES ability to capture it. The code is available at https://github.com/FrancesC0de/HOLMES.

Keywords: deep learning · machine learning · XAI · explainability · convolutional neural networks · computer vision

L. Longo (Ed.): xAI 2023, CCIS 1902, pp. 475–498, 2023.
https://doi.org/10.1007/978-3-031-44067-0_25

1   Introduction

In recent years, the application of Machine Learning (ML) models has impacted the most disparate fields of application. In particular, Deep Learning (DL) models called Convolutional Neural Networks (CNNs) have become the de-facto standard approach to tackle Computer Vision (CV) problems, spanning from autonomous driving to image-based medical diagnosis, from satellite observation to advertisement-driven social media analysis [28].

Unfortunately, DL models are black-boxes, as their fully sub-symbolic internal knowledge representation makes it impossible for developers and users to understand the rationale behind the model decision process. This widely recognized limitation has multiple negative implications: (*i*) difficulty of adoption from domain experts [14], (*ii*) GDPR non-compliance [12], (*iii*) inability to detect learned spurious correlations [34], and (*iv*) risk of deploying biased models [22].

Due due this plethora of issues, the field of eXplainable Artificial Intelligence (XAI) has flourished in an attempt to make these black-box models more understandable from human developers and users [13].

In the specific case of CV tasks and CNN models, most XAI approaches are based on saliency and produce heatmaps [29], quantifying explanations in the form of *this image depicts a cat because of the highlighted region*. On the one hand, this approach can be sufficient to spot wrong correlations when the heatmap focuses on the wrong portion of the image, such as the background. On the other hand, a reasonably-placed heatmap is not a sufficient guarantee that the DL model is in fact implementing the desired task, and we argue that these shallow explanations are not enough for a human user to fully trust the algorithmic decision, nor for a developer to sufficiently debug a model in order to assess its learning progress. These approaches provide context-less label-level heatmaps: ironically, they pair deep models with shallow explanations. Conversely, when asked to justify an image-classification task, humans typically rely on the holonym-meronym (whole-part) relationship and produce part-based explanations, e.g. *this image depicts a cat (holonym), because there are pointy ears up there and a tail there, etc. (meronyms)*.

There is evidence that CNNs are capable of learning human-interpretable concepts that, although not explicitly labelled in the training set, are useful to detect classes for which labels are provided; for instance, scenes classification networks learn to detect objects present in scenes, and individual units may even emerge as objects or texture detectors [3]. At the same time, CNNs were shown to take shortcuts, relying on contextual or unwanted features for their final classification [8]; other works found CNNs being over-reliant on texture, rather than shape, for their final classification [9]. In this work, we tackle the important issue of how, and to what extent, post-hoc explanations can be linked to underlying, human-interpretable concepts implicitly learned by a network, with minimal effort in terms of annotation and supervision.

Our Research Question is therefore the following: *can we decompose the given label (holonym) into a set of related concepts*

(meronyms), and provide component-level explanations for an image classification DL model?

In this paper we propose HOLMES (HOLonym-MEronym based Semantic inspection), a novel XAI technique that can provide explanations at a low-granularity level.

Given an input image of a given class, its parts (meronyms) are extracted from a Knowledge Base through the holonym-meronym (whole-part) relationship. Images depicting each part are either extracted from a densely annotated dataset or collected through Web scraping, and then used to train a meronym model through transfer learning. The resulting model is therefore a part dectector for the component of the image. The application of XAI techniques on the meronym model can thus produce part-based explanations. HOLMES can therefore highlight the occurrence and locations in the image of both labelled objects and their parts. We evaluated our approach through insertion/deletion/preservation metrics, showing how the parts highlighted by our approach are crucial for the predictions.

The rest of the paper is organized as follows. In Sect. 2 we connect the proposed technique with other existing approaches in the XAI literature. In Sect. 3 we go through the core concepts behind HOLMES. In Sects. 4 and 5, we report experimental validation of the HOLMES pipeline. Finally, in Sects. 6 and 7 we discuss advantages and limitations of the proposed approach, as well as future studies we plan to conduct to enhance HOLMES capabilities.

2 Related Work

2.1 Feature Extraction and Transfer Learning

Deep Convolutional Neural Networks (CNNs) have been the de-facto standard models for computer vision in the last years [28]. These models typically encompass a number of convolutional layers, which act as feature extractors, followed by dense layers used for classification. The major drawback of these models is that, due to the large amount of parameters, training from scratch requires a vast amount of data and computational resources [33]. A common technique exploited to circumvent this problem is *transfer learning* [36], in which a model developed for a task is reused as the starting point for a model on a second task. The typical approach for CV tasks is to select a CNN that was pre-trained on the standard dataset of Imagenet [7], and reset and re-train the last dense layers on the new task. The underlying intuition of this approach is that CNNs learn a hierarchy of features in convolutional layers at different depths, starting from Gabor filters in the first layers to complex shapes in the last ones [36].

2.2 Interpretable and Explainable Machine Learning

The eXplainable Artificial Intelligence (XAI) research field tackles the problem of making modern ML models more human-understandable. XAI approaches typically belong to one of two paradigms, namely, interpretability and post-hoc explainability [1, 13]. Interpretable ML models are designed and trained in order to be, to some degree, passively transparent - that is, so that comprehensible information about the inner logic of the model is available without the application of other algorithms. Instead, explainability typically is performed *a posteriori* - it is a process that takes place after the ML model has been trained, and possibly even deployed. Explainability techniques apply external algorithms to the ML model in order to extract human-understandable information about the decision process that was produced by the training process.

Explainability methods can be further classified according to two orthogonal binary attributes: local/global and model agnostic/aware. Local methods provide an explanation for a single data point, while global methods aim to explain the behavior of the model as a whole, e.g., providing a joint explanation for all data points in the dataset. Model-agnostic methods can explain indifferently any type of black-box model, regardless of their typology or architecture, accessing input and outputs only. For instance, they could be applied even if the source code of the ML model is obfuscated or can be only accessed through APIs, provided that those can be invoked at will. Conversely, model-aware (also called model-specific) models exploit (and require access to) internal details of the black-box, such as gradients, and are therefore developed for specific kinds of ML models.

2.3   XAI for Computer Vision

Arguably the two most famous XAI approaches are LIME [24] and SHAP [17], both being local and model-agnostic. An important counterpoint in the field is the concept of global and model-specific approaches, as exemplified by TCAV [15]. This methodology allows for global interpretability, focusing on understanding high-level concepts used by the model across a broad set of inputs. However, for the specific task of computer vision, most approaches are model-aware and based on saliency.

When explaining image classification models, saliency methods compute pixel-level relevance scores for the model final output. These scores can be visualized as heat-maps, overlaid on the classified images, in order to be visually inspected by humans. One of these approaches is the Gradient-weighted Class Activation Mapping (Grad-CAM) [29], a model-aware, local, post-hoc XAI technique. Grad-CAM uses the gradient information flowing into the last convolutional layer of the CNN to assign importance values to each neuron for a particular decision of interest, such as a target concept like *dog*. By visualizing the positive influences on the class of interest (e.g., *dog*) through a global heatmap, Grad-CAM provides insight into which regions of the input image are 'seen' as most important for the final decision of the model. By overlaying this heatmap onto the input image, Grad-CAM facilitates a deeper understanding of the correlation between specific image features and the final decision.

Saliency maps methods such as Grad-CAM ask *where* a network looks when it makes a decision; the network dissection approach takes a step further and asks *what* a network is looking for. In [3], the authors find that a trained network contains units that correspond to high-level visual concepts that were not explicitly labeled in the training data. For example, when trained to classify or generate natural scene images, both types of networks learn individual units that match the visual concept of a *tree* even though the network was never taught the tree concept during training. The authors investigate this phenomenon by first identifying which individual components strongly correlate with given concepts (taken from a labelled segmentation dataset), and then turn off each component in order to measure its impact on the overall classification task. Following this line of investigation, [40] seeks to distill the information present in the whole activation feature vector of a neural network's penultimate layer. It achieves this by dissecting this vector into interpretable components, each shedding light on different aspects of the final prediction. Our work differs from the network dissection literature in the following ways: (i) we allow for representations of concepts that are scattered across neurons, without forcing them to be represented by a single computational unit; (ii) we do not require additional, domain-specific ground truth sources, relying instead on web scraping and general purpose-ontologies and (iii) we do not focus on the specific scene recognition task, embracing instead the part-of relationships of labels in the more general image classification task.

2.4 Ontologies and Image Recognition

Ontologies, and structured representation of knowledge in general, are typically ignored in most DL for image processing papers [28]. However, there are notable exceptions where efforts have been made to merge sub-symbolic ML models together with ontologies.

In [10], the authors leverage the fact that ImageNet labels are WordNet nodes in order to introduce quantitative and ontology-based techniques and metrics to enrich and compare different explanations and XAI algorithms. For instance, the concept of semantic distance between actual and predicted labels for an image classification task allows to differentiate a labrador VS husky misclassification as milder with respect to a labrador VS airplane case.

In [25], the authors introduced a hybrid learning system designed to learn both symbolic and deep representations, together with an explainability metric to assess the level of alignment of machine and human expert explanations. The ultimate objective is to fuse DL representations with expert domain knowledge during the learning process so it serves as a sound basis for explainability.

Among the global methods for explainability, TREPAN [6] is able to distill decision trees from a trained neural network. By pairing an ontology to the feature space, the authors use the ontological depth of features as a heuristic to guide the selection of splitting nodes in the construction of the decision tree, preferring to split over more general concepts.

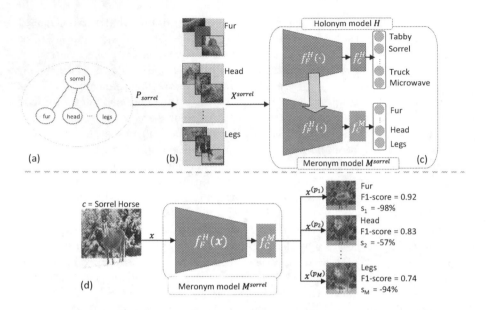

Fig. 1. HOLMES pipeline. Given an input image of class c, its parts (meronyms) are extracted from a Knowledge Base (a). Images depicting each part are either extracted from a densely annotated dataset or collected through Web scraping (b), and then used to train a meronym model by exploiting, through transfer learning, the implicit knowledge embedded in the original holonym model (c). The meronym model then produces part-based explanations, highlighting the most relevant parts for the class prediction (d).

3   Methodology

The proposed method, Holonym-Meronym based Semantic inspection (HOLMES), is a post-hoc approach that aims to explain the classification given by a CNN image classifier to an image in terms of its parts. It is indeed a model-dependent method, specifically tailored for CNNs. Hence, HOLMES takes as input the image whose class has been predicted, recovers its meronyms, and provides an explanation in terms of its parts.

Problem Formulation

Let us define the image classifier as a function $\mathcal{H} : \mathbf{x} \in \mathbb{R}^{h \times w \times ch} \mapsto c \in \mathcal{C}$, where $\mathbf{x}$ is an input image with dimensions $h \times w \times ch$ and $\mathcal{C}$ is the set of image classes. Lets assume that $\mathcal{H}$ is a CNN that can be expressed as a combination of two functions, a feature extractor $f_F^{\mathcal{H}} : \mathbf{x} \mapsto \mathbf{f}$ and a feed forward classifier $f_C^{\mathcal{H}} : \mathbf{f} \mapsto c$, where $\mathbf{f}$ is a feature vector. Let us define a holonym-meronym relationship mapping HolMe : $c \in \mathcal{C} \mapsto \{p_1, ..., p_n\}$ meaning that a whole object of class c, i.e. a holonym, is made of its parts, or meronyms $P_c = \{p_1, ..., p_n\}$. The goal of HOLMES is to explain the classification $\mathcal{H}(\mathbf{x}) = c$ through the meronyms

P_c, by highlighting which of the meronyms are important for the classification result. The explanation takes the form of a function $\xi : \mathbf{x} \mapsto \{(\mathbf{x}^{(p_i)}, s_i),\ p_i \in P_c\}$, where $\mathbf{x}^{(p_i)}$ is a saliency map that highlights the meronym p_i in the original image $\mathbf{x}$, and s_i is an explanation score associated to $\mathbf{x}^{(p_i)}$.

HOLMES solves this problem by training a new meronyms classifier $\mathcal{M}^c :$ $\mathbf{x} \mapsto p_i \in P_c$ as a combination of the same feature extractor $f_F^{\mathcal{H}}$ that is part of the image classifier $\mathcal{H}$ and a new feed forward classifier $f_{P_c}^{\mathcal{M}} : \mathbf{f} \mapsto p_i \in P_c$. The meronyms classifier is then used to determine which parts p_i are present in the input image $\mathbf{x}$ and to create saliency maps that correspond to these parts. Finally, each saliency map $\mathbf{x}^{(p_i)}$ is used to create a mask on $\mathbf{x}$, which is then classified by $\mathcal{H}$, and the drop of the classifier confidence in the class c is used to determine the importance of the selected parts.

The HOLMES pipeline comprises the following steps:

A) **Meronyms Extraction**: given an image $\mathbf{x}$ and its predicted class c, this first step consists of retrieving the list of the object parts P_c (Fig. 1(a)).
B) **Meronyms Image Data Collection**: once the object parts list P_c is available, a distinct dataset for each part shall be created in this second step (Fig. 1(b)).
C) **Meronyms model Training**: in this third step, the auxiliary meronyms models $\mathcal{M}^c$ are trained to recognize the object parts P_c by exploiting the knowledge (about the parts) embedded in the original CNN $\mathcal{H}$ (Fig. 1(c)).
D) **Explanations**: in this last step, a set of part-based explanations is produced, highlighting those parts which are most relevant for the class prediction (Fig. 1(d)).

3.1   Meronyms Extraction

The first step of the pipeline consists of constructing the holonym-meronym relationship mapping HolMe : $c \in \mathcal{C} \mapsto P_c$ by retrieving the visible parts P_c associated to the holonym concept c. Hence, HOLMES relies on external Knowledge Bases (KBs) which include part-of relationships, i.e. containing class concepts (e.g., camel, horse, etc.) and their respective list of parts (e.g., head, legs, etc.), along with information about their visibility. Thus, for obtaining the parts of an holonym concept, HOLMES queries one selected knowledge base for the desired holonym concept and results its associated visible meronyms. Concepts that are not present in the chosen reference KB are mapped to the respective WordNet [19] ontology concepts, and the *hypernym/hyponym relationship* is exploited: the WordNet semantical hierarchy is climbed back up to the first hypernym (i.e., a broader class, like *bird* for *seagull*) which occurs in the reference KB, and its associated (more generic) parts are then assigned to the initial holonym concept.

The meronyms extracted in the previous step are then divided in two categories: *hyper-meronyms* and *hypo-meronyms*. Given a generic list of meronyms, $P = \{p_1, p_2, \ldots, p_n\}$, hypo-meronyms are parts whose visual space is completely within any other part in P. The other parts whose visual space is not completely within any other part in P are the hyper-meronyms. For instance, for the holonym concept *cat*, the hyper-meronyms would be *head, legs, feet, tail*, given that none of them is visually contained in any other part, but rather, can only contain hypo-meronyms (e.g., *mouth, whiskers*, etc.).

For the final list of meronyms, only the hyper-meronyms are retained while hypo-meronyms are discarded. The final list of parts is thus defined as $P_c = \{p_1, p_2, \ldots, p_n\}$.

3.2 Meronyms Image Data Collection

Once the part set P_c for the target class c is available, the next step is to create a dataset $X^c = \{(\mathbf{x}_0, y_0), \ldots, (\mathbf{x}_n, y_n)\}$ where $\mathbf{x}_0, \ldots, \mathbf{x}_n$ are images corresponding to parts $y_0, \ldots, y_n \in P_c$. HOLMES can rely on a pre-existing labelled dataset, or it can exploit web image scraping to incrementally build a dataset for each meronym. In this scenario, HOLMES queries different web search engines for each part, by prefixing the holoynm first (e.g. *sorrel fur, sorrel head*, etc.) and downloads the associated images from each of those engines.

Due to the limited reliability of search engine results (discussed in Sect. 4), some obtained images could be still extraneous to the desired part concept. Moreover, duplicates could be present in the scraped parts' datasets. For these reasons, HOLMES integrates two additional sub-steps:

1. **deduplication**: duplicates are detected by means of the pHash [26] hash-based deduplication method, then they are removed from each meronym dataset.
2. **outlier removal**: meronyms images are mapped to a feature vector representation (e.g. using the output of the feature extractor or the activations of one of the feedforward layers of the classifier). The feature vectors are then fed to an outlier detection algorithm. The detected outliers are then removed from the meronym dataset.

3.3 Meronyms Model Training

The training phase is the core of the HOLMES method. In this step the concept parts are visually learned, so that they can later be provided as explanations. This is achieved by training an auxiliary CNN model $\mathcal{M}^c$, trained and evaluated on the collected meronym dataset X^c (training and evaluation are performed in disjoint sets).

Let us recall that the goal of HOLMES is to explain the target holonym CNN $\mathcal{H}(\mathbf{x}) = \hat{y}$, where $\mathbf{x}$ is an holonym image of class c and $\hat{y}$ its predicted class. Let us also recall that the CNN can be expressed as a combination of two functions $\mathcal{H}(\mathbf{x}) = f_C^{\mathcal{H}}(f_F^{\mathcal{H}}(\mathbf{x}))$, where $f_F^{\mathcal{H}}(\cdot)$ is a feature extractor, and $f_C^{\mathcal{H}}(\cdot)$ is a feedforward classifier. Previous works already demonstrated that the units contained in the last convolutional layers of a CNN tend to embed objects, and more specifically, objects parts as well [3,11], and HOLMES leverages on this fact to learn the parts by defining $\mathcal{M}^c(\mathbf{x}) = f_{P_c}^{\mathcal{M}}(f_F^{\mathcal{H}}(\mathbf{x}))$, where the feature extraction $f_F^{\mathcal{H}}(\cdot)$ is shared among the holonym $\mathcal{H}$ and meronym $\mathcal{M}^c$ models, whereas a feedforward classifier $f_{P_c}^{\mathcal{M}}(\cdot)$ is trained anew for each class c and each part list P_c.

The idea is to learn the parts concepts by using the same features learned by the original reference CNN model $\mathcal{H}$, such that the base knowledge for learning both the concept parts and the concepts themselves would be the same: effectively, HOLMES relies on transfer learning [36] for learning objects parts. Under the reasonable assumption that characteristic object parts, and consequently their associated features, are useful for the classification of the whole object itself, the same units which activate in the presence of the parts will also activate in presence of the object. For instance, a unit activating in the presence of a wheel, will also be likely to activate in the presence of a wheeled vehicle like a car. Hence, training $\mathcal{M}$ by keeping the feature extractor $f_F^{\mathcal{H}}$ intact will later allow us to understand if the knowledge about the parts was already available and embedded in the original model $\mathcal{H}$. Specifically, the feature maps obtained in the presence of the individual parts will be useful to create a visual explanation for the (holonym) predictions of the original model.

A held-out test set is used to calculate the per-part calibrated F1-score [31] to determine the degree to which each part was learned and distinguished by the others. The F1-score is calibrated to be invariant to the class prior, enabling the comparison of models trained on different numbers of meronyms.

3.4   Explanations

At the end of the previous step a trained meronyms CNN model $\mathcal{M}^c$ is obtained. For any input holonym image $\mathbf{x}$, this model outputs a set of prediction scores $Y_p = \{y_{p_1}, \ldots, y_{p_n}\}$, where n is the the number of parts the model was trained on, and $y_{p_1}, \ldots, y_{p_n}$ are the scores produced for each different part. Hence, by feeding the network with an holonym sample (such as a car image), a score about each of its parts (e.g., wheel, bumper, etc.) will be produced. Intuitively, the output scores reflect *how much* of each part the network sees in the input holonym image. Exploiting the fact that the network can 'see' the part concepts within an holonym image sample, we can look *where* the network exactly sees the parts, i.e., in which portion of the input image.

Specifically, the visualization of each part in the holonym image is obtained trough the state-of-the-art saliency method Grad-CAM [29]. After obtaining a saliency map $\mathbf{x}^{(p_i)}$ related to each part that the network can recognize, each saliency map $x^{(p_i)}$ is thresholded into a binary segmentation mask $m^{(p_i)} \equiv (x^{(p_i)} \geq T^{(p_i)})$, where $T^{(p_i)}$ is set to the qth percentile of the corresponding saliency map pixel distribution. We later feed the same input holonym image into the original CNN model, and verify whether each part is fundamental for the original network prediction, by ablating one part from the image at a time based on the meronyms masks $m^{(p_i)}$. By observing the score drop for the original predicted holonym class label (calculated in percentage, with respect to the original holonym score), we can determine how much the removed meronym was important in order to predict that class label: the more consistent the drop, the more significant the visual presence in the image of the part would be for the original model.

At this point, the input image $\mathbf{x}$ is associated to a set of saliency maps $\mathbf{x}^{(p_i)}$ for each part $p_i \in P_c$, and each saliency map is associated to a score drop $s_i \in S = \{s_1, s_2, ..., s_n\}$. Additionally, the per-part calibrated F1-score previously computed is used to measure the reliability of the part identification. We assume that a meronyms model which had difficulties to learn and distinguish a part, would have consequently achieved a low F1-score for that part. Hence, the parts whose holonym score drop s_i exceeds a threshold T_s and whose meronyms model are above a F1-score threshold T_{F1} are provided as part-based explanations for the original model prediction, as it would mean that those parts are both correctly detected by the meronym model and deemed relevant for the classification of the holonym.

4   Experimental Settings

HOLMES can generate part-based explanations for any model that can be expressed as a feature extractor and a feed forward classifier. In our experiments, we explain the outputs of a VGG16 [33] image classifier pre-trained on the ImageNet [7] dataset. In this section, we describe the application of the HOLMES pipeline in two different experimental settings to explain the outputs of the VGG16 model. In the first experiment, we exploit bounding boxes for objects and their parts from the PASCAL-Part dataset to explain and validate the results. In the second one, we first build a part-based mapping for many ImageNet classes, then we use scraping to build a dataset for training the meronyms models, and finally we generate part-based explanations and evaluate the results with insertion, deletion and preservation curves. Examples of HOLMES explanation on both datasets are provided in Fig. 2.

4.1   PASCAL-Part Dataset

The PASCAL-Part [5] dataset contains additional annotations over the PASCAL VOC 2010 dataset, i.e., bounding boxes for objects and their parts, that can be used as the holonym-meronym relationship mapping (HolMe). We held out a set of 50 images for each of the selected holonyms and their corresponding cropped meronym images that are used exclusively to evaluate the HOLMES explainability and part localization performance. The other images were used in the meronym models $\mathcal{M}^c$ training.

Meronyms Extraction Settings: The twenty classes in the Pascal VOC 2010 dataset can be divided in four macro-classes: (1) person, (2) animals (bird, cat, cow, dog, horse, sheep), (3) vehicles (aeroplane, bicycle, boat, bus, car, motorbike, train) and (4) indoor objects (bottle, chair, dining table, potted plant, sofa, tvmonitor). Two of the classes (person and potted plant) have no corresponding class in the ImageNet 1000 classes and thus are discarded. Other five classes

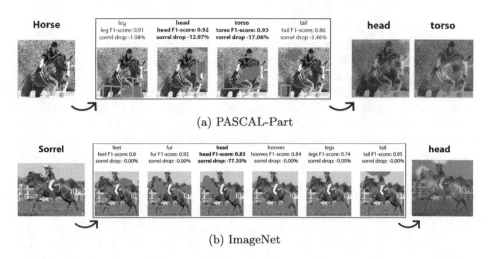

(a) PASCAL-Part

(b) ImageNet

Fig. 2. HOLMES Explanation example for the *horse* class – PASCAL-Part (a) and *sorrel* class – ImageNet (b). For each part, the corresponding ablation mask (grey), the per-part calibrated F1-score and the holonym score drop are shown. For PASCAL-Part, the ablation masks are compared against the ground truth bounding boxes (green). The final heatmap(s) show the part-based explanations. Two and one part are included in the explanations for examples (a) and (b), respectively, as they exceed both the holonym score drop threshold T_s (0.1) and the calibrated F1-score threshold T_{F1} (0.7).

were discarded because they do not have part-based annotations (boat, chair, dining table, sofa, and tvmonitor). For each of the 13 remaining classes, the respective meronyms P_c were extracted from the PASCAL-Part parts list. For the six animal classes we performed hyper-meronym selection as in [38], and for the remaining classes we selected the hyper-meronyms by majority voting. The final HolMe mapping is thus:

- $P_{bird} = P_{cat} = P_{dog} = P_{horse} = \{\text{head, torso, leg, tail}\}$
- $P_{cow} = \{\text{head, torso, leg, horn}\}$
- $P_{sheep} = \{\text{head, torso, leg}\}$
- $P_{aeroplane} = \{\text{stern, wheel, artifact wing, body, engine}\}$
- $P_{bicycle} = \{\text{saddle, wheel, handlebar}\}$
- $P_{motorbike} = \{\text{saddle, wheel, handlebar, headlight}\}$
- $P_{car} = P_{bus} = \{\text{window, wheel, headlight, mirror, door, bodywork, license plate}\}$
- $P_{train} = \{\text{coach, locomotive, headlight}\}$
- $P_{bottle} = \{\text{body, cap}\}$

Meronyms Image Extraction Settings: Once the holonym-meronym relationship mapping is defined, we extract the images to train the meronyms models. For each holonym image, we retrieved the bounding box coordinates associated with their parts P_c, and cropped the holonym image accordingly to produce a set of meronym images.

To obtain images compatible with the square VGG16 input, while preserving the aspect ratio and shape of each part, before cropping we extended the bounding box in the x or y direction to obtain a square crop, with the constraint of not overlapping other bounding boxes in the same image. Then, if a 1:1 aspect ratio was not completely reached, we applied padding to get a final square crop.

Moreover, the number of crops extracted for each meronym might be very different, e.g., for a *horse* meronym, there are more *leg* parts with respect to just one *head*. To avoid high class unbalance, we used data augmentation to balance the number of samples in each meronyms class. Specifically, we applied both random rotation and random shear, and one among the gaussian blur, emboss, and gaussian noise transformations to each cropped image. Finally, for each holonym class, the extracted meronyms samples were split into training/validation/test folds with ratios of 0.81/0.09/0.1.

Training and Explanations Settings: For each holonym, we built a separate meronym model $\mathcal{M}^c$ and we retrained a feed forward classifier $f_{P_c}^{\mathcal{M}}(\cdot)$ with the same structure of the original VGG16 classifier using Cross Entropy Loss. Common data augmentation techniques were employed: horizontal flipping, rotation, cropping, color jittering, and random gray scale. Each meronym model was trained for 100 epochs, with a batch size of 64 and learning rate of 0.001 (determined experimentally). Early stopping policy with patience set to 5 was used to avoid overfitting.

Regarding the explanations, the activations of the last convolutional layer of VGG16 were used to produce the Grad-CAM meronyms heatmaps, which are then binarized using a threshold $T^{(p_i)}$. We found $T^{(p_i)} = 83^{th}$ percentile by performing a grid search upon the [75, 90] percentile values and by finding the best trade-off between different causal metrics performance (described in the Evaluation section) on the whole PASCAL-Part training set, comprising all training holonym image samples. The masked pixels were ablated by replacing with the gray RGB value (as the ImageNet mean pixel is gray) for retaining the natural image statistics [27]. Finally, the T_s and T_{F1} thresholds were set to 10 and 0.7, respectively.

Evaluation Settings: The whole HOLMES pipeline was run and tested upon each validation image sample associated to each selected class. The meronyms localization performance was measured by computing the per-pixel AUC score of the HOLMES meronym heatmap versus the same meronym ground truth. To calculate this metric, each pixel was assigned the corresponding heatmap value as score: true positive pixels were those belonging to the actual part (i.e., falling within the bounding box), while the remaining pixels were labeled as false positives. The performance is compared to the per-pixel AUC score of the Grad-CAM holonym heatmap as baseline. Moreover, the faithfulness of HOLMES explanations was assessed by means of common causal metrics based on the deletion/insertion/preservation curves [16,23].

As mentioned before, HOLMES produces a set of part-based explanations, which are obtained by computing a set of saliency maps $\mathbf{X}^{(P_c)} = \{\mathbf{x}^{(p_i)}, \ p_i \in P_c\}$, each associated a specific part p_i. However, to assess the global quality of such explanations, all part-based saliency maps need to be merged into a unique heatmap, comprising all parts. Given the set of saliency maps $\mathbf{X}^{(P_c)}$, and the corresponding score drops $S = \{s_1, s_2, ..., s_n\}$ associated with the ablation of each part, the HOLMES global heatmap is obtained through a weighted linear combination of the part-based saliency maps. First, normalized score drops $Z = \{z_1, ..., z_n\}$ are calculated by dividing each score drop by the L1-Norm of S. Then, the global heatmap is obtained by summing each weighted heatmap element-wise: $G = \sum_{i \in n\mathbf{x}^{(p_i)}} z_i$. This weighting scheme emphasizes parts whose ablation causes a significant holonym class score drop.

After obtaining the global heatmap G for an input image in this way, it is possible to use causal metrics such as the areas under the insertion [23], the deletion [23] and the preservation curves [16] to assess the overall quality of the part-based explanations, whose information is combined into G. These metrics were computed for all held out PASCAL-Part validation images. Notably, distinct from simply replicating Grad-CAM results, our global heatmap stresses the pivotal role of part-based explanations, serving as an integral instrument to appraise the global effectiveness of the part-based explanations.

4.2   ImageNet

HOLMES can be applied in scenarios where part-level annotated datasets are not available. In this case, we leverage ontologies and image scraping to construct the required meronym datasets. In particular, we exploit the connection between Imagenet [7] labels and WordNet [19] nodes in order to retrieve a list of parts of the object-label, relying on the holonym-meronym (whole-part) relationship.

Meronyms Extraction Settings: Across the ImageNet 1000 class concepts, 81 of them were selected and treated as holonym classes. The selected holonym classes belong to two main categories:

1. Medium- or large-size animals
2. Medium- or large-size man-made objects

The size constraint is necessary to obtain acceptable training sets. In fact, the smaller the holonym (e.g., bugs in the animals category), the more troublesome it becomes to retrieve images of distinct parts by querying web search engines. Specifically, when querying for such parts, the engines tend to return images of the whole holonym concept instead (e.g., the whole butterfly when querying for a butterfly head). This would consequently result in meronyms datasets very similar among each other and with a strong visual overlap, thus greatly hindering the associated meronym model performance.

Therefore, for each of the 81 classes, the respective meronyms were extracted from the Visual Attributes for Concepts (VISA) [32] dataset. Hyper-meronyms were further extracted by manual filtering: the meronyms obtained from the ontology were manually categorized into hyper-meronyms and their respective hypo-meronyms. In this way, for each occurrence of a hyper-meronym, the associated hypo-meronyms were automatically filtered out.

Meronyms Image Scraping Settings: The Google and Bing web search engines were selected and queried for downloading the images. The number of downloads per part over all the engines was forcibly limited, since the pertinence of the images with respect to the desired part concept naturally decreases as more images are downloaded (e.g., after too many downloads for *sorrel head*, an engine would for instance start returning images depicting plants and flowers); a good rule-of-thumb is to limit the download to the first 100 items [18,20]. Finally, in order to further increase the dataset size for each part, the *Visually similar images* function of Google was exploited: for each downloaded image, the most visually similar ones are searched in this way and then added to the parts' samples. The download limit, i.e., the number of images to be downloaded for each part by each engine, was set to 40 for Google and 60 for Bing, since Bing showed to be slightly more reliable. The visually similar images download limit was instead set to 5. Duplicates and near-duplicates [21] are detected by means of the pHash [26] hash-based deduplication method. For outlier removal, meronyms images are mapped to a feature vector using the activations of the penultimate FC layer of VGG16 [33], which are then given as input to the PCA outlier detection algorithm [30], with the outlier contamination rate hyper-parameter set to 0.15. The scraped data was split into training/validation/test folds with proportions of 0.81, 0.09 and 0.1 respectively.

Training and Explanations Settings: The training and explanation steps are carried out with the same settings as detailed for the PASCAL-Part dataset (Sect. 4.1).

Evaluation Settings: The global heatmap is evaluated using the insertion, deletion, and preservation curves as detailed for the PASCAL-Part dataset (Sect. 4.1).

5   Results

The HOLMES pipeline was quantitatively and qualitatively evaluated in all its steps. Experimental validation aimed at determining i) to what extent HOLMES is able to correctly identify and locate meronyms?, ii) to what extent the classification score can be attributed to individual meronyms and iii) how good are the explanations generated by HOLMES?

RQ1: How well can HOLMES classify and locate meronyms?

As introduced in Sect. 4.1, the PASCAL-Part ontology contains 13 classes with an average of ≈ 4 visible parts per class. Following the procedure described in the experimental setting, on average ~ 750 sample per meronym were collected (~ 1400 after data augmentation), for a total of 74,772 training samples. For ImageNet, 81 classes were selected, with an average of ≈ 7 visible parts per image. Thus, web scraping was performed for a total of 559 meronyms, yielding on average ~ 450, of which 18% were detected as duplicates and 11% as outliers, and hence, eliminated. The final average number of images per part is ~ 320.

First, we assess HOLMES ability to *classify different meronyms* by reporting the distribution of the calibrated F1-scores of the $\mathcal{M}^c$ models, trained upon each training set X_c for each of the selected classes, is reported in Fig. 3 for both

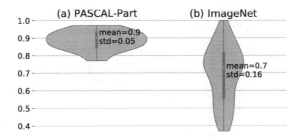

Fig. 3. Distribution (violin plot) of the average per-part calibrated F1-score.

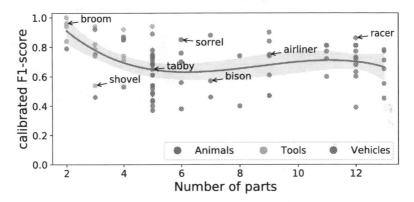

Fig. 4. Average per-part calibrated score as a function of the number of parts per holonym class (colored dots represent a holonym, blue line is the mean average per-part F1-score). (Color figure online)

PASCAL-Part and ImageNet dataset. The average F1-score was good in both cases, but higher on PASCAL-Part (0.9 ± 0.05 vs. 0.7 ± 0.16). This difference can be attributed, at least partially, to the higher precision of the PASCAL-Part reference standard, for which bounding boxes are available.

On the other hand, it can be observed from Fig. 4 how the performance degrades with the number of parts per class. This is especially evident for the ImageNet dataset, since the ontology is richer with more classes and more parts per classes. As the number of parts increases, the likelihood of visual overlap between images belonging to different parts also increases, negatively impacting the performance of the trained $\mathcal{M}^c$ model. Additionally, different class categories tend to be associated with a lower/higher number of meronyms: for instance, tools tend to have between one and four parts, animals between three and eight, and vehicles more than eight. Thus, we cannot exclude that the category may also play a role either by influencing the quality of the scraping, or the differentiation of the meronyms themselves.

The HOLMES meronyms localization performance was measured by computing the per-pixel AUC score of each HOLMES meronym heatmap against their PASCAL-Part ground truth bounding boxes. As a baseline, we could assume

Table 1. The HOLMES meronyms localization performance is measured by computing the average per-pixel AUC score of each HOLMES meronym heatmap (top row) against the holonym heatmap extracted the Grad-CAM (bottom row).

Method	horse	cat	bird	cow	dog	sheep	aeroplane	bicycle	bottle	bus	car	motorbike	train	Avg
HOLMES	0.77	0.74	0.8	0.77	0.74	0.75	0.74		0.76	0.67	0.75	0.68	0.74	0.71	**0.74**
Grad-CAM	0.68	0.68	0.71	0.66	0.71	0.62	0.76		0.63	0.6	0.65	0.62	0.66	0.62	0.66

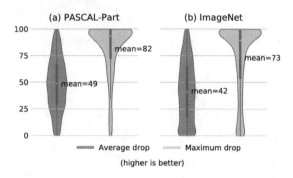

Fig. 5. Distribution (violin plots) of the average score drop and maximum score drop (in percentages) per image on the PASCAL-Part (a) and ImageNet (b) validation sets. The score drop is calculated for each image and meronym by ablating the corresponding mask; then, the average and maximum score drop are computed over all meronyms appearing in an image.

that either the meronym could be randomly assigned to any region of the image (in this case, AUC = 0.5), or we could focus on the actual holonym as extracted by the Grad-CAM algorithm and assume that the meronym is inside the region of the Grad-CAM holonym heatmap. This second choice offers a baseline that is harder to beat, but as reported in Table 1, the HOLMES meronyms explanations consistently localize the parts better and more precisely, compared to the whole Grad-CAM heatmaps which instead localize the entire object.

RQ2: To what extent the classification score can be attributed to individual meronyms?

Having established the ability to classify meronyms, the next step is to evaluate their impact on the holonym classifier $\mathcal{H}$, as exemplified in Fig. 2.

The distribution of the *per-meronym score drop*, i.e., the score drop observed for the holonym when the corresponding meronym is ablated, is reported in Fig. 5. The average score drop is 49% for PASCAL-Part and 42% for ImageNet, respectively, meaning that on average, the ablation of a single meronym roughly halves the holonym model confidence. When considering only the most significant part (i.e., the one associated with the highest score drop for each test image), the score drop increases to 82% on PASCAL-Part. Hence, in this dataset, individual meronyms have a substantial impact on the classifier output and, in most cases, the classification can almost be fully explained or attributed to a single meronym. On the other side, on ImageNet the mean maximum drop is lower (73%). In

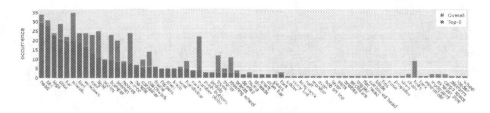

Fig. 6. Top-5 meronyms distribution. For each class, the top-5 meronyms are computed (i.e., the meronyms with the highest score drops on average). For each meronym, the total number of associated holonyms (blue) is compared with their frequency in the Top-5 meronym list (red). Meronyms are listed in descending order of frequency. (Color figure online)

fact, the mean ($\pm$ standard deviation) number of meronyms included in each explanation was 2.28 ± 2.46. Examples of explanations with one, two, three or more meronyms are provided in the Supplementary Material.

Conversely, when grouping images according to their holonym labels, the mean average drop and mean maximum drop were 50% and 80% for PASCAL-Part, and 46% and 73% for ImageNet, respectively. While the score distribution in Fig. 5 characterizes HOLMES behavior at the instance (image) level, the mean values provide insight into the general properties of the holonym classes. For instance, the mean maximum score drop on PASCAL-Part shows a bimodal distribution, with animal classes having a higher mean maximum drop than vehicles and man-made objects (78.5% vs. 62.1%). This entails that, on average, explanations for image belonging to animal classes are highly focused, with only one meronym almost explaining the entire holonym concept, whereas for other classes explanations require the combination of two or more meronyms. On ImageNet, we did not find a large difference between animals (70%), tools (73%), and vehicles (74%); however, we observed a wider variation between classes, with mean maximum drop ranging from 23% (zebra) to 95% (persian cat).

Different holonym classes may have an overlapping set of meronyms: this is especially evident for the richer ImageNet ontology. For instance, most of the animal classes have a head and a tail (although each class will be associated with its own training dataset and its own classifier $\mathbf{M}^c$). From this observation, we sought to understand if certain parts induced a consistent and substantial holonym score drop (Fig. 6). For instance, for classes belonging to the animal category, the meronyms head, tail, and legs frequently cause a consistent drop when ablated from the image. Similarly, for vehicles, the door, wheels and window meronyms have the highest impact on the holonym class prediction.

RQ3: How good are the explanations generated by HOLMES?

Finally, the overall quality of the generated explanations was evaluated. For the purpose of evaluating against Grad-CAM, which is not designed to provide part-based explanations, part-level heatmaps are linearly combined in a global heatmap, as detailed in Fig. 7. The AUC values under the insertion, deletion, and preservation curves are summarized in Table 2.

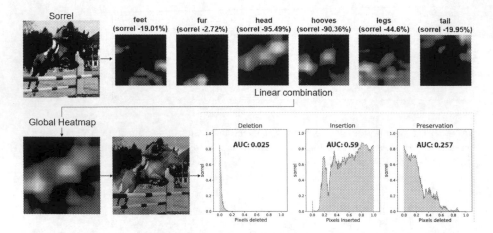

Fig. 7. HOLMES Global Explanation. Starting from an input image, the per-part heatmaps and the respective holonym score drops are obtained. Then, by a linear combination of the heatmaps, the global heatmap is obtained, and its quality is measured by means of the insertion/deletion/preservation metrics.

Table 2. Deletion/Insertion/Preservation AUCs for HOLMES and Grad-CAM.

Dataset	Method	Deletion ↓	Insertion ↑	Preservation ↑
PASCAL-	HOLMES	0.050±0.053	0.487±0.269	0.392±0.255
Part	GradCAM	0.052±0.060	0.505±0.277	0.381±0.264
ImageNet	HOLMES	0.112±0.113	0.660±0.252	0.538±0.257
	GradCAM	0.111±0.107	0.684±0.242	0.539±0.261

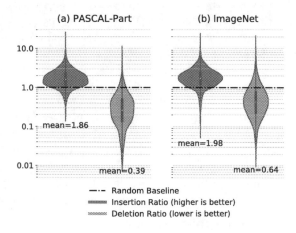

Fig. 8. Insertion/Deletion Ratio distribution (violin plot) for the PASCAL-Part (a) and ImageNet (b) datasets. The average insertion ratio (left) and the average deletion ratio (right) are calculated with respect to the random baseline (dotted black line).

On PASCAL-Part, the HOLMES insertion AUC is, on average, 0.96 times the GradCAM insertion AUC, while the average deletion AUC is 0.95 and the average preservation AUC is 1.03 times the respective GradCAM score. Analogously, on ImageNet, the average insertion, deletion, and preservation AUCs are 0.96, 1.01, and 0.99 times the corresponding GradCAM scores.

Additionally, we compared HOLMES against a random baseline obtained by dividing the images in super-pixels, which are then erased in random order. The random baseline is designed to account for the object scale: in fact, a good heatmap for a small object will yield a lower deletion AUC than an equally good heatmap for a larger object. As shown in Fig. 8, HOLMES metrics are substantially higher than the random baseline, with average insertion AUC 0.58 lower and average insertion AUC 1.77 higher than the baseline.

6 Discussion

Unlike previous methods [3], HOLMES does not require a densely annotated dataset with pixel-level annotations. Instead, it can be trained using weak annotations either in the form of bounding boxes, such as those available in the PASCAL-Part dataset [5], or relying on the potentiality of web scraping, which drastically reduces the annotation effort, whilst forgoing the limiting closed-world assumption intrinsic to traditional labelled datasets. The effectiveness of web scraping for object recognition has been established in previous works [18,35], which HOLMES capitalizes on and extends, using deduplication and outlier removal to reduce noise and increase variety in the training dataset. At the same time, retrieving high quality images for meronyms, as opposed to holonyms, introduces additional challenges which may impact dataset quality and, thus, the meronym models. Qualitatively, we observed that the pertinence of the retrieved images is generally good, but may decrease depending on the popularity of the meronym as a search term. Another specific challenge is the visual overlap, as it is difficult to find images that precisely isolate one and only one meronym.

Overall, quantitative evaluation on PASCAL-Part allowed us to conclude that the meronym models are capable of detecting object parts and locating their position within the image. This is achieved by exploiting, without any retraining or fine-tuning, the features learned by the holonym model, thus further supporting the conclusion that knowledge about object parts is implicitly embedded in deep neural networks [2,3,39].

Partly due to the imperfect background, the ablated mask does not always provide a perfect segmentation of the part itself, as shown in Fig. 2. In some cases, the ablated masks for different parts could be very similar, especially for meronyms that are physically next to each other. An example is provided by the meronyms *legs* and *hooves* for the holonym *sorrel*, as shown again in Fig. 2. Less frequently, it may occur that the ablated part may include a portion of the background; for instance, in the case of legs, some terrain or grass may be included. This may have an impact on the score drop observed when the corresponding part is deleted, and the resulting metrics.

The average F1-score for most holonyms ranges roughly between 0.6 and 1.0 for ImageNet, and between 0.8 and 1.0 for PASCAL-Part, spanning different categories of objects (animals, tools and vehicles), and up to 14 visible parts per class. The F1-score depends on the quality of the ground truth, but also on the number of meronyms that compose each object. Increasing the quality of scraping, and thus the meronym model, could allow HOLMES to recognize and include in the provided explanations an even larger pool of meronyms. In addition, HOLMES provides intrinsic safeguards against this type of noise, as only meronyms with sufficient F1-score are included in the explanations, and the user can readily inspect the heatmaps associated to each individual meronym.

Quantitative causal metrics based on the deletioninsertionpreservation curves confirm that the part-based explanations provided by HOLMES are effective in identifying those parts that are most relevant to the final classification, achieving results comparable to the state-of-the-art GradCAM method, and substantially above chance level. However, unlike GradCAM, HOLMES provides an articulated set of heatmaps, associated to human-interpretable concepts, and allows exploration of the impact of individual meronyms on the holonym classification, at both instance and class level.

HOLMES was evaluated on two distinct datasets, PASCAL-Part and ImageNet. Since both pipelines evaluate the same classifier, we attribute absolute differences in the insertion/deletion/preservation curves to the dataset themselves (e.g., how the images were sourced), and possibly to the domain shift between ImageNet and PASCAL-Part (given that the holonym classifier $\mathcal{H}$ was trained on ImageNet). However, the relative performance with respect to both baselines shows similar behavior, despite wide differences in how the meronym datasets X^c were sourced. HOLMES performs slightly better on PASCAL-Part, especially in terms of the deletion and preservation curves. Also, explanations on PASCAL-Part appear to be concentrated, on average, on fewer parts than ImageNet. Beyond the meronym datasets X^c, other factors could account for these differences: on the one hand, PASCAL-Part includes fewer and more distinct classes than ImageNet, thus potentially it includes images that are 'easier' to classify. On the other hand, the KB derived from PASCAL-Part annotations is simpler, with fewer meronyms (≈ 4 vs. ≈ 7 parts per class), and less visual overlap. Overall, HOLMES shows to be robust to the choice of experimental settings, and performs well even when exploiting more cost-effective annotations sourced through general purpose KBs and web scraping.

7   Conclusions and Future Work

In this paper we introduced HOLMES, an eXplainable Artificial Intelligence technique able to enrich image classification tasks with part-level explanations. Our approach allows to take a further step with respect to the standard label-level heatmaps which represent the state of the art in XAI for image classification. It proves valuable in integrating image classification models into decision support systems, as it provides more detailed explanations. These explanations can help both the model developer, aiding in debugging the classifier before deployment, and also the end user, assisting in assessing the level of trust in the classifier's predictions for previously unseen data.

Furthermore, HOLMES sheds light on how holonyms are learned and stored within a CNN during and after the training phase. Other recent research works proposed relevant contributions, such as [3,4], but with additional requirements (focus on scene recognition, need for a segmented ground truth) and without the connection of a DL model with a symbolic knowledge base such as an ontology.

We adopt a strategy that avoids confining concepts to a single computational unit. We contend that this approach aligns better with the robust learning capabilities of DL models while also facilitating greater expressive power in the symbolic domain. As shown in [2], models with equivalent discriminative abilities can exhibit varying degrees of interpretability, influenced by factors such as the architecture, regularization, and learning task.

Given the novelty of our proposed pipeline, there is room for exploration concerning alternatives for many components. First, a more refined scraping method could be employed to both increase the training sample size and its quality, for instance using more complex semantic expansion techniques, by using more robust outlier detection algorithms such as Robust and Kernel PCA, or by incorporating novel data purification techniques to obtain cleaner data [37].

Second, it could be useful to study the effects of using the activations of units belonging to different convolutional layers, or even sets of such layers, for producing HOLMES explanations; units belonging to different convolutional layers could better match some specific (part) concepts, and, accordingly, by means of their activations, a better explanation could be hence generated for those concepts. Also, more model architectures can be tested to see how this method results change according to the model which is used. For instance, shallower (e.g., VGG13) or deeper (e.g., VGG19) model architectures, or even different types of networks (e.g., Deep Residual Networks) could be inspected.

Third, alternative perturbation techniques can be tried for removing the relevant pixels of the parts; it was observed that substituting pixels with just constant values introduces contiguous shapes in the image, thus biasing, if even minimally, the prediction towards certain types of objects having a similar shape. Moreover, other types of semantic relationship can be studied for both retrieving the desired (visible) parts of a specific concept (either alternative or complementary to the proposed holonym-meronym relationship), and for mapping different concepts between different knowledge bases (in alternative to the proposed hypernym-hyponym relationship).

Finally, it emerges from the final results that the method performs better when considering for an object a small number of parts, preferably spaced enough to minimize visual overlap. Hence, a new strategy for selecting and filtering the meronyms of an object can be also studied.

References

1. Arrieta, A.B., et al.: Explainable artificial intelligence (XAI): concepts, taxonomies, opportunities and challenges toward responsible AI. Inf. Fusion **58**, 82–115 (2020)
2. Bau, D., Zhou, B., Khosla, A., Oliva, A., Torralba, A.: Network dissection: quantifying interpretability of deep visual representations. In: Computer Vision and Pattern Recognition (2017)
3. Bau, D., Zhu, J.Y., Strobelt, H., Lapedriza, A., Zhou, B., Torralba, A.: Understanding the role of individual units in a deep neural network. Proc. Natl. Acad. Sci. **117**(48), 30071–30078 (2020)
4. Chen, C., Li, O., Barnett, A., Su, J., Rudin, C.: This looks like that: deep learning for interpretable image recognition. Adv. Neural Inf. Process. Syst. **32**, 8930–8941 (2019)
5. Chen, X., Mottaghi, R., Liu, X., Fidler, S., Urtasun, R., Yuille, A.L.: Detect what you can: detecting and representing objects using holistic models and body parts. In: 2014 IEEE Conference on Computer Vision and Pattern Recognition, pp. 1979–1986 (2014)
6. Confalonieri, R., et al.: An ontology-based approach to explaining artificial neural networks. CoRR abs/1906.08362 (2019)
7. Deng, J., Dong, W., Socher, R., Li, L.J., Li, K., Fei-Fei, L.: ImageNet: a large-scale hierarchical image database. In: 2009 IEEE Conference on Computer Vision and Pattern Recognition, pp. 248–255 (2009)
8. Geirhos, R., et al.: Shortcut learning in deep neural networks. Nat. Mach. Intell. **2**(11), 665–673 (2020)
9. Geirhos, R., Rubisch, P., Michaelis, C., Bethge, M., Wichmann, F.A., Brendel, W.: Imagenet-trained CNNs are biased towards texture; increasing shape bias improves accuracy and robustness. In: International Conference on Learning Representations (2019)
10. Ghidini, V., Perotti, A., Schifanella, R.: Quantitative and ontology-based comparison of explanations for image classification. In: Nicosia, G., Pardalos, P., Umeton, R., Giuffrida, G., Sciacca, V. (eds.) LOD 2019. LNCS, vol. 11943, pp. 58–70. Springer, Cham (2019). https://doi.org/10.1007/978-3-030-37599-7_6
11. Gonzalez-Garcia, A., Modolo, D., Ferrari, V.: Do semantic parts emerge in convolutional neural networks? Int. J. Comput. Vis. **126**, 476–494 (2018)
12. Goodman, B., Flaxman, S.: European Union regulations on algorithmic decision making and a "Right to Explanation". AI Mag. **38**, 50–57 (2016)
13. Guidotti, R., Monreale, A., Ruggieri, S., Turini, F., Giannotti, F., Pedreschi, D.: A survey of methods for explaining black box models. ACM Comput. Surv. **51**(5), 1–42 (2018)
14. Jiang, H., Kim, B., Guan, M., Gupta, M.: To trust or not to trust a classifier. Adv. Neural Inf. Process. Syst. **31**, 5541–5552 (2018)
15. Kim, B., Wattenberg, M., Gilmer, J., Cai, C., Wexler, J., Viegas, F., et al.: Interpretability beyond feature attribution: quantitative testing with concept activation vectors (TCAV). In: International Conference on Machine Learning, pp. 2668–2677. PMLR (2018)
16. Lim, D., Lee, H., Kim, S.: Building reliable explanations of unreliable neural networks: locally smoothing perspective of model interpretation. In: 2021 IEEE/CVF Conference on Computer Vision and Pattern Recognition, pp. 6464–6473 (2021)
17. Lundberg, S.M., Lee, S.I.: A unified approach to interpreting model predictions. Adv. Neural Inf. Process. Syst. **30**, 4765–4774 (2017)

18. Massouh, N., Babiloni, F., Tommasi, T., Young, J., Hawes, N., Caputo, B.: Learning deep visual object models from noisy web data: how to make it work. In: 2017 IEEE/RSJ International Conference on Intelligent Robots and Systems, pp. 5564–5571 (2017)
19. Miller, G.: WordNet: a lexical database for English. Commun. ACM **38**(11), 39–41 (1995)
20. Molinari, D., Pasquale, G., Natale, L., Caputo, B.: Automatic creation of large scale object databases from web resources: a case study in robot vision. In: International Conference on Image Analysis and Processing (2019)
21. Morra, L., Lamberti, F.: Benchmarking unsupervised near-duplicate image detection. Expert Syst. Appl. **135**, 313–326 (2019)
22. Obermeyer, Z., Powers, B., Vogeli, C., Mullainathan, S.: Dissecting racial bias in an algorithm used to manage the health of populations. Science **366**(6464), 447–453 (2019)
23. Petsiuk, V., Das, A., Saenko, K.: Rise: randomized input sampling for explanation of black-box models. In: British Machine Vision Conference (2018)
24. Ribeiro, M.T., Singh, S., Guestrin, C.: Why should i trust you? Explaining the predictions of any classifier. In: Proceedings of the 22nd ACM SIGKDD International Conference on Knowledge Discovery and Data Mining, pp. 1135–1144 (2016)
25. Rodríguez, N.D., et al.: Explainable neural-symbolic learning (X-NeSyL) methodology to fuse deep learning representations with expert knowledge graphs: the MonuMAI cultural heritage use case. Inf. Fusion **79**, 58–83 (2022)
26. Samanta, P., Jain, S.: Analysis of perceptual hashing algorithms in image manipulation detection. Procedia Comput. Sci. **185**, 203–212 (2021). https://doi.org/10.1016/j.procs.2021.05.021
27. Samek, W., Binder, A., Montavon, G., Lapuschkin, S., Müller, K.R.: Evaluating the visualization of what a deep neural network has learned. IEEE Trans. Neural Netw. Learn. Syst. **28**(11), 2660–2673 (2017)
28. Sarraf, A., Azhdari, M., Sarraf, S.: A comprehensive review of deep learning architectures for computer vision applications. Am. Sci. Res. J. Eng. Technol. Sci. **77**, 1–29 (2021)
29. Selvaraju, R.R., Cogswell, M., Das, A., Vedantam, R., Parikh, D., Batra, D.: Grad-CAM: visual explanations from deep networks via gradient-based localization. Int. J. Comput. Vis. **128**(2), 336–359 (2019)
30. Shyu, M.L., Chen, S.C., Sarinnapakorn, K., Chang, L.: A novel anomaly detection scheme based on principal component classifier. In: Proceedings of International Conference on Data Mining, January 2003
31. Siblini, W., Fréry, J., He-Guelton, L., Oblé, F., Wang, Y.-Q.: Master your metrics with calibration. In: Berthold, M.R., Feelders, A., Krempl, G. (eds.) IDA 2020. LNCS, vol. 12080, pp. 457–469. Springer, Cham (2020). https://doi.org/10.1007/978-3-030-44584-3_36
32. Silberer, C., Ferrari, V., Lapata, M.: Visually grounded meaning representations. IEEE Trans. Pattern Anal. Mach. Intell. **39**(11), 2284–2297 (2017)
33. Simonyan, K., Zisserman, A.: Very deep convolutional networks for large-scale image recognition. In: International Conference on Learning Representations (2015)
34. Steging, C., Schomaker, L., Verheij, B.: The XAI paradox: systems that perform well for the wrong reasons. In: Proceedings of the 31st Benelux Conference on A.I. and the 28th Belgian Dutch Conference on Machine Learning (2019)
35. Yao, Y., et al.: Exploiting web images for multi-output classification: from category to subcategories. IEEE Trans. Neural Netw. Learn. Syst. **31**(7), 2348–2360 (2020)

36. Yosinski, J., Clune, J., Bengio, Y., Lipson, H.: How transferable are features in deep neural networks? Adv. Neural Inf. Process. Syst. **27**, 3320–3328 (2014)
37. Zhang, C., Wang, Q., Xie, G., Wu, Q., Shen, F., Tang, Z.: Robust learning from noisy web images via data purification for fine-grained recognition. IEEE Trans. Multimed. **24**, 1198–1209 (2021)
38. Zhang, Q., Wu, Y.N., Zhu, S.C.: Interpretable convolutional neural networks. In: 2018 IEEE/CVF Conference on Computer Vision and Pattern Recognition, pp. 8827–8836 (2018)
39. Zhou, B., Khosla, A., Lapedriza, À., Oliva, A., Torralba, A.: Object detectors emerge in deep scene CNNs. In: International Conference on Learning Representations abs/1412.6856 (2015)
40. Zhou, B., Sun, Y., Bau, D., Torralba, A.: Interpretable basis decomposition for visual explanation. In: Ferrari, V., Hebert, M., Sminchisescu, C., Weiss, Y. (eds.) ECCV 2018. LNCS, vol. 11212, pp. 122–138. Springer, Cham (2018). https://doi.org/10.1007/978-3-030-01237-3_8

Evaluating the Stability of Semantic Concept Representations in CNNs for Robust Explainability

Georgii Mikriukov[1,2]✉ , Gesina Schwalbe[1] , Christian Hellert[1] ,
and Korinna Bade[2]

[1] Continental AG, Hanover, Germany
{georgii.mikriukov,gesina.schwalbe,
christian.hellert}@continental-corporation.com
[2] Hochschule Anhalt, Bernburg, Germany
{georgii.mikriukov,korinna.bade}@hs-anhalt.de

Abstract. Analysis of how semantic concepts are represented within Convolutional Neural Networks (CNNs) is a widely used approach in Explainable Artificial Intelligence (XAI) for interpreting CNNs. A motivation is the need for transparency in safety-critical AI-based systems, as mandated in various domains like automated driving. However, to use the concept representations for safety-relevant purposes, like inspection or error retrieval, these must be of high quality and, in particular, stable. This paper focuses on two stability goals when working with concept representations in computer vision CNNs: stability of concept retrieval and of concept attribution. The guiding use-case is a post-hoc explainability framework for object detection (OD) CNNs, towards which existing concept analysis (CA) methods are successfully adapted. To address concept retrieval stability, we propose a novel metric that considers both concept separation and consistency, and is agnostic to layer and concept representation dimensionality. We then investigate impacts of concept abstraction level, number of concept training samples, CNN size, and concept representation dimensionality on stability. For concept attribution stability we explore the effect of gradient instability on gradient-based explainability methods. The results on various CNNs for classification and object detection yield the main findings that (1) the stability of concept retrieval can be enhanced through dimensionality reduction via data aggregation, and (2) in shallow layers where gradient instability is more pronounced, gradient smoothing techniques are advised. Finally, our approach provides valuable insights into selecting the appropriate layer and concept representation dimensionality, paving the way towards CA in safety-critical XAI applications.

Keywords: Concept Analysis · Semantic Concepts · Concept Stability

ⓒ The Author(s) 2023
L. Longo (Ed.): xAI 2023, CCIS 1902, pp. 499–524, 2023.
https://doi.org/10.1007/978-3-031-44067-0_26

1   Introduction

Advancements in deep learning in the last decade have led to the ubiquitous use of deep neural networks (DNNs), in particular CNNs, in computer vision (CV) applications like object detection. While they exhibit state-of-the-art performance in many fields, their decision-making logic stays opaque and unclear due to their black-box nature [4,44]. This fact raises concerns about their safety and fairness, which are desirable in fields like automated driving or medicine. These demands are formalized in industrial standards or legal regulations. For example, the ISO26262 [1] automotive functional safety standard recommends manual inspectability, and the General Data Protection Regulation [13] as well as the upcoming European Union Artificial Intelligence Act [43] both demand algorithm transparency. The aforementioned concerns are subject of XAI.

XAI is a subfield of AI that focuses on revealing the inner workings of black-box models in a way that humans can understand [5,27,37]. One approach involves associating semantic concepts from natural language with internal representations in the DNN's latent space [37]. In computer vision, a semantic concept refers to an attribute that can describe an image or image region in natural language (e.g., "pedestrian head", "green") [10,23]. These concepts can be associated with vectors in the CNN's latent space, also known as concept activation vectors (CAVs) [23]. Post-hoc CA involves acquiring and processing CAVs from trained CNNs [2,23,30], which can be used to quantify how concepts attribute to CNN outputs and apply it to verification of safety [35] or fairness [23]. However, in literature two paradigms of post-hoc CA have so far been considered separately, even though they need to be combined to fully compare CNN learned concepts against prior human knowledge. These paradigms are: supervised CA, which investigates pre-defined concept representations [10,23,35], and unsupervised CA, which retrieves learned concepts [11,49] and avoids expensive labeling costs. Furthermore, current XAI approaches are primarily designed and evaluated for small classification and regression tasks [2,35], whereas more complex object detectors as used in automated driving require scalable XAI methods that can explain specific detections instead of just a single classification output.

Besides adaptation to object detection use-cases, high-stakes applications like safety-critical perception have high demands regarding the quality and reliability of verification tooling [19, Chap. 11]. A particular problem is stability: One should obtain similar concept representations given the same CNN, provided concept definitions, and probing data. Instable representations that vary strongly with factors like CA initialization weights [31] or imperceptible changes of the input [40] must be identified and only very cautiously used. Stability issues may arise both in the retrieval of the concept representations, as well as in their usage. Retrieval instability was already identified as an issue in the base work [23], and may lead to concept representations of different quality or even different semantic meaning for the same concept. Instability in usage may especially occur when determining local concept-to-output attribution. In particular, the baseline approach proposed by Kim et al. [23] uses sensitivity, which is known to be brittle with respect to slight changes in the input [40,41].

This work tackles the aforementioned problems of OD-ready supervised and unsupervised CA, and measurement and improvement of stability in CA retrieval and attribution. Concretely, to solve these problems, we propose an XAI framework based on supervised and unsupervised CA methods for ODs. The unsupervised method is used to automatically mine concept samples, which are jointly used for supervised concept analysis with manually labeled concepts. Furthermore, stability metrics are suggested and tested. The respective main contributions of our work are:

- Proposal of two metrics and methodology for testing of *concept retrieval stability* and *concept attribution stability* in CA;
- Experimental study of *stability influence factors* in six diverse CNN models with different backbones with the main findings that *CAV dimensionality reduction may improve stability*, and that *gradient smoothing may be beneficial* for concept attribution stability in shallow layers;
- Adaptation of supervised and unsupervised concept-based analysis methods for *CA on common ODs*;
- Introduction of a post-hoc, label-efficient, concept-based *explainability framework* for classifiers and ODs allowing for concept stability estimation (Fig. 1).

In the following, we will first take a look at related work on concept analysis in Sect. 2. Our approaches for combining supervised and unsupervised CA, for CA in OD, and for stability measurement are then detailed in Sect. 3. Our experimental setup can be found in Sect. 4 with results detailed in Sect. 5.

2 Related Work

This section presents an overview of relevant supervised and unsupervised CA methods. Comprehensive XAI and CA surveys can be found in [4, 36, 44].

2.1 Supervised Concept Analysis

There are two primary paradigms in supervised CA methods: scalar-concept representation [6, 25, 34] and vector-concept representation [3, 10, 23]. Scalar concept representations refer to disentangled deep neural network (DNN) layer representations with a one-to-one correspondence between neurons and distinct semantic concepts. A prominent example and base work are Concept Bottleneck Models [25] (CBM). These introduce an interpretable bottleneck layer to DNNs by assigning each neuron to a specific concept, i.e., scalar-concepts. An extension CBM-AUC [34], enhances the model's capability by automatically learning unsupervised concepts (AUC) that describe the residual variance of the feature space. In contrast to the previous examples, Concept Whitening [6] is a post-hoc approach towards scalar-concepts. It transforms a feature space of a layer and reduces redundancy between neurons, making it more likely for each neuron to correspond to a single concept. IIN [9] is another post-hoc approach that trains an invertible neural network to map a layer output to a disentangled version, using pairwise labels. However, standard CNNs are typically highly entangled [22]. Hence, such scalar-concept approaches have to enforce the disentangled structure during training or utilize potentially non-faithful proxies [29]. Furthermore, they are limited to explaining a single layer.

Vector-concepts, on the other hand, associate a concept with a vector in the latent space. The base work in this direction still disregarded the distributed nature of CNN representations: The Network Dissection approach [3] aims to associate each convolutional filter in a CNN with a semantic concept. Its successor Net2Vec [10] corrects this issue by associating a concept with a linear combination of filters, resulting in a concept being globally represented by a vector in the feature space, the concept activation vector (CAV) [23]. A sibling state-of-the-art method for associating concepts with latent space vectors is TCAV [23], which also uses a linear model attached to a CNN layer to distinguish between neurons (in contrast to filters as in Net2Vec) relevant to a given concept and the rest. TCAV also proposes a gradient-based approach that allows for the evaluation of how sensitive a single prediction or complete class is to a concept. The concept sensitivity (attribution) for a model prediction is calculated by taking the dot product between the concept activation vector and the gradient vector backpropagated for the desired prediction. These vector-concept baselines for classification (TCAV) and segmentation (Net2Vec) of concepts have been extended heavily over the years, amongst others towards regression concepts [14,15], multi-class concepts [21], and locally linear [46,47] and non-linear [21] CAV retrieval. However, the core idea remained untouched.

While the TCAV paper already identifies stability as a potential issue, they reside to significance tests for large series of experiments leaving a thorough analysis of stability (both for concept retrieval and concept attribution) open, as well as investigation of improvement measures. Successor works tried to stabilize the concept attribution measurement. For example, Pfau et al. [30] do not use the gradient directly, but the average change of the output when perturbing the intermediate output towards the CAV direction in latent space in different degrees. This gradient stabilization approach follows the idea of Integrated Gradients [41], but no other approaches like Smoothed Gradients [40] have been tried. Other approaches also suggest improved metrics for global concept attribution [15]. However, to our knowledge, stability remained unexplored so far.

We address this gap by utilizing TCAV as a baseline global concept vector representation for the stability estimation. Moreover, as gradient-based method, it be adapted to estimate concept attributions in other model types, such as ODs (see Sect. 3.2). It is important to note that our stability assessment method is not limited to TCAV and can potentially be applied to evaluate the stability of other global concept representations.

2.2 Unsupervised Concept Analysis

Unsupervised methods for analyzing concepts are also referred to as concept mining [36]. These methods do not rely on pre-defined concept labels, but the acquired concepts are not always meaningful and require manual revision. There are two main approaches to concept mining: clustering and dimensionality reduction. Clustering methods, such as ACE [12] and VRX [11] group latent space representations of image patches (superpixels), obtained through segmentation algorithms. The resulting clusters are treated as separate concepts and can be used for supervised concept analysis. Invertible Concept Extraction (ICE) [49] is a dimensionality reduction method based on non-negative matrix factorization. It mines non-negative concept activation vectors (NCAVs) corresponding to the most common patterns from sample activations in intermediate layers of a CNN. The resulting NCAVs are used to map sample activations to concept saliency maps, which show concept-related regions in the input space.

To reduce the need in concept labeling, we opted to use ICE for unsupervised concept mining due to (1) its superior performance regarding interpretability and completeness of mined concepts compared to clustering [49], and (2) its simpler and more straightforward pipeline with less hyperparameters. Unlike ACE, it does not rely on segmentation and clustering results as an intermediate step, which makes it easier to apply.

2.3   Concept Analysis in Object Detection

There are only a few existing works that apply concept analysis methods to object detection, due to scalability issues. In [35] the authors adapt Net2Vec for scalability to OD activation map sizes, which is later used to verify compliance of the CNN behavior with fuzzy logical constraints [38]. Other TCAV-based works apply lossy average pooling to allow large CAV sizes [7,14], but do not test OD CNNs. However, these methods are fully supervised and require expensive concept segmentation maps for training, resulting in scalability issues regarding concept label needs. In order to reduce the need for concept labels, we propose adapting and using a jointly supervised and unsupervised classification approach for object detection, and investigate the impact of CAV size on stability. This also closes the gap that, to our knowledge, no unsupervised CA method has been applied to OD-sized CNNs so far.

3   Proposed Method

The overall goal targeted here is a CA framework that allows stable, label-efficient retrieval and usage of interpretable concepts for explainability of both classification and OD backbones. To address this, we introduce a framework that combines unsupervised CA (for semi-automated enrichment of the available concept pool) with supervised CA (for retrieval of CAVs and CNN evaluation) together with an assessment strategy for its stability properties. An overview of the framework is given in the following in Sect. 3.1, with details on how we adapted CA for OD in Sect. 3.2. Section 3.3 then presents our proposal of CAV stability metrics. Lastly, one of the potential influence factors on stability, namely CAV dimensionality and parameter reduction techniques, is presented in Sect. 3.4.

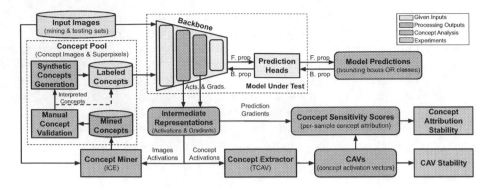

Fig. 1. The framework for estimation of CAV stability and concept attribution stability. The proposed solution utilizes unsupervised ICE to aid concept discovery and labeling, while supervised TCAV is used for the generation of concept representations.

3.1 Stability Evaluation Framework

The framework depicted in Fig. 1 aims to efficiently combine supervised and unsupervised CA methods for use in explainability or evaluation purposes, like our CA stability evaluation. To achieve this it (1) builds an extensible *Concept Pool* containing human-validated *Mined Concepts* extracted from trained *Model Under Test*, and (optionally) existing manually *Labeled Concepts*; and it (2) uses these concepts to obtain *CAVs* and, e.g., conduct *CAV Stability* and *Concept Attribution Stability* tests on object detection and classification models.

Concept Pool Creation/Extension. In some CV domains, it can be challenging to find publicly available datasets with high-quality concept labels. In order to streamline the manual annotation process and speed up concept labeling, we utilize unsupervised concept mining. The left side of Fig. 1 depicts the process of creating the *Concept Pool* (or extending it, if we already have an initial set of *Labeled Concepts*) by employing the *Concept Miner*. A concept in the concept pool is represented by a set of images or image patches showing the concept. To extract additional *Mined Concepts*, the *Concept Miner* identifies image patches that cause common patterns in the CNN *Image Activations*. The activations are extracted from the layer of interest of the *Backbone* of the *Model Under Test* for *Input Images* from the mining set. In our work, we utilize ICE [49] as the *Concept Miner* to obtain the image patches. The workflow of ICE is as follows: (1) it first mines NCAVs; then, for each NCAV and each sample from a test set (2) it applies NCAV inference, i.e., obtains a (non-binary) heatmap of where the NCAV activates in the image, and (3) masks the input image with the binarized heatmap. For details see Sect. 2.2 and [49]. The sets of mined image patches, alias concepts, next undergo *Manual Concept Validation*: A human annotator assigns a label to each *Mined Concepts*. These *Interpreted Concepts*, if meaningful, can either directly be added to the set of *Labeled Concepts* or be utilized in *Synthetic Concept Generation* to obtain more complex synthetic concept samples (see Sect. 4.4 and Fig. 3 for more details and visual examples). It should be noted that the *Concept Pool*, once established, is model-agnostic and can be reused for other models, and that the ICE concept mining approach can be exchanged by any other suitable unsupervised CA method that produces concept heatmaps during inference.

Concept Stability Analysis. Now that the *Concept Pool* is established, we can perform supervised CA to obtain *CAVs* for the concepts in the pool. The CAV training is done on the *Concept Activations*, i.e., CNN activations of concept images from the *Labeled Concepts* in the *Concept Pool*. Given *CAVs*, we can then calculate per-sample concept attribution using, e.g., backpropagation-based sensitivity methods [23]. The resulting *CAVs* and *Concept Sensitivity Scores* can then be used for local and global explanation purposes. To ensure their quality, this work investigates stability (*CAV Stability* and *Concept Attribution Stability*) of these for OD use-cases, as detailed in Sect. 3.3.

For supervised CA we use the base TCAV [23] approach: A binary linear classifier is trained to predict presence of a concept from the intermediate neuron activations in the selected CNN layer. The classifier weights serve as CAV, namely the vector that points into the direction of the concept in the latent space. The CAVs are trained in a one-against-all manner on the labeled concept examples from the *Concept Pool*. For concept attribution, we adopt the sensitivity score calculation from [23]: for a sample is the partial derivative of the CNN output in the direction of the concept, which is calculated as the dot product between the CAV and the gradient vector in the CAV layer. In this paper, we are interested in the stability of this retrieval process for obtaining CAVs and respective concept attributions.

3.2   Concept Analysis in Object Detectors

The post-hoc concept stability assessment framework described above, in particular the used TCAV and ICE methods, is out-of-the-box suitable for use with classification models. However, object detection networks pose additional challenges: besides larger sizes, they have different prediction heads and employ suppressive post-processing of the output.

Multiple Predictions. Unlike classification models that produce a single set of predictions per sample, object detectors may produce multiple predictions, requiring adaptions to TCAV and ICE.

For ICE the concept weights and importance estimation component require adjustments. The pipeline assesses the effect of small modifications to each concept on the final class prediction. For classification, this estimation is performed on a per-sample basis. For object detection, we switch that calculation to the per-bounding box approach.

The TCAV process of calculating CAVs remains unchanged. However, TCAV employs gradients backpropagated from the corresponding class neuron and concept CAV to assess the concept sensitivity of the desired output class. In object detectors, concept sensitivity can be computed for each prediction, or bounding box, by starting the backpropagation from the desired class neuron of the bounding box.

It is important to note that some object detection architectures predict an objectness score for each bounding box, which can serve as an alternative starting neuron for the backpropagation [24]. Nonetheless, we only use class neurons for this purpose in our experiments.

Suppressive Post-processing. Another challenge in object detection is explanation of False Negatives (FNs), which refer to the absence of detection for a desired object. Users may be especially interested in explanations regarding FN areas, e.g., for debugging purposes. While the raw OD CNN bounding box predictions usually cover all image areas, post-processing may filter out bounding boxes due to low prediction certainty or suppress them during Non-Maximum Suppression (NMS). To still evaluate concept sensitivity for FNs, we compare the list of raw unprocessed bounding boxes with the desired object bounding boxes specified by the user. We then use Intersection over Union (IoU) to select the best raw bounding boxes that match the desired ones, and these selected bounding boxes (i.e., their output neurons) are used for further evaluation.

3.3   Evaluation of Concept Stability

Concept Retrieval Stability. We are interested in concepts that are both *consistent* and *separable* in the latent space. However, these two traits have not been considered jointly in previous work. Thus, we define the generalized concept stability $\mathcal{S}_{L_k}$ metric for a concept C in layer L_k applicable to a test set X as

$$\mathcal{S}_{L_k}^C(X) := \mathtt{separability}_{L_k}^C(X) \times \mathtt{consistency}_{L_k}^C, \tag{1}$$

where, $\mathtt{separability}_{L_k}^C(X)$ represents how well tested concepts are separated from each other in the feature space, $\mathtt{consistency}_{L_k}^C$ denotes how similar are representations for the same concept when obtained with different initialization conditions.

Separability. The binary classification performance of each CAV reflects how effectively the concept is separated from other concepts, when evaluated in a concept-vs-other manner rather than a concept-vs-random approach. In the concept-vs-other scenario, the non-concept-class consists of all other concepts, whereas it is a single randomly selected other concept in the concept-vs-random scenario [23]. We choose the separability from Eq. 1 for a single concept C on the test set X as:

$$\mathtt{separability}_{L_k}^C(X) := f1_{L_k}^C(X) := \tfrac{1}{N}\sum_{i=1}^{N} f1(CAV_{L_k,i}^C; X) \in [0,1] \tag{2}$$

where $f1_{L_k}^C$ is the mean of relative F1-scores $f1(-;X)$ on X for $CAV_{L_k,i}^C$ of C in layer L_k for N runs i with different initialization conditions for CAV training.

Consistency. In TCAV, during the CAVs training, a limited amount of concept samples may lead to model underfitting, and significant inconsistency between

CAVs obtained for different training samples and initialization conditions [23]. Since cosine similarity was shown to be a suitable similarity measure for CAVs [10,23] we set the consistency measure to the mean cosine similarity between the CAVs in layer L_k of N runs:

$$\text{consistency}_{L_k}^C := \cos_{L_k}^C := \frac{2}{N(N-1)} \sum_{i=1}^{N} \sum_{j=1}^{i-1} \cos(\text{CAV}_{L_k,i}^C, \text{CAV}_{L_k,j}^C), \quad (3)$$

where $\cos(-,-)$ is cosine similarity, here between CAVs of the same concept C and layer L_k obtained during different runs i, j.

Concept Attribution Stability. Small changes in the input space may significantly change the output and, thus, the gradient values. TCAV requires gradients to calculate the concept sensitivity (attribution) of given prediction. Hence, gradient instability may have an impact on the explanations, and, in the worst case, change it from positive to negative attribution or vice versa.

We want to check, if such instability of gradient values influences concept detection. For this, we compare the vanilla gradient approach against a stabilized version using the state-of-the-art gradient stabilization approach Smooth-Grad [40]. It diminishes or negates the gradient instability in neural networks by averaging vanilla gradients obtained for multiple copies of the original sample augmented with a minor random noise. For comparison purposes, first the vanilla gradient is propagated backward with respect to the detected object's class neuron. This neuron is remembered and used then for the gradient backpropagation for noisy copies of SmoothGrad. TCAV concept attributions can naturally be generalized to Smoothgrad, defining them as:

$$\text{attr}_C^*(x) := \text{CAV}_C \circ \nabla^* f_{L_k \rightarrow}(f_{\rightarrow L_k}(x)), \quad (4)$$

where attr_C^* is the attribution of concept C in layer L_k for vanilla gradient ($* = \text{grad}$) or SmoothGrad ($* = \text{SG}$) for a single prediction for sample x, $\text{CAV}_C = \text{CAV}_{L_k,.}^C$, and $f_{\rightarrow L_k}$ is the CNN part up to L_k, $f_{L_k \rightarrow}$ the mapping from L_k representations to the score of the selected prediction and class.

Acc. As one approach, for each tested layer we build a confusion matrix for multiple test samples and bounding boxes therein, where $y_{\text{true}} = \text{sign}(\text{attr}_i^{\text{grad}})$ and $y_{\text{predicted}} = \text{sign}(\text{attr}_i^{\text{SG}})$ are predictions to compare the sign of concept attribution for SmoothGrad and vanilla gradient. On this, accuracy (Acc) is used to show the fraction of cases where SmoothGrad and vanilla gradient concept attributions have the same sign, i.e., where gradient instability has no impact.

CAD. As a second approach, to qualitatively evaluate the difference between the concept attribution of SmoothGrad and the vanilla gradient in the tested layer, we introduce the Concept Attribution Deviation (CAD) metric. It shows the average absolute attribution value change for all used concepts C and N runs, and, thus, describes the impact of gradient instability on concept attribution in a layer:

$$\mathrm{CAD}(x) := \frac{\sum_C \sum_i^N \left| \mathrm{attr}_{C,i}^{\mathrm{grad}}(x) - \mathrm{attr}_{C,i}^{\mathrm{SG}}(x) \right|}{\sum_C \sum_i^N \left| \mathrm{attr}_{C,i}^{\mathrm{grad}}(x) \right|}. \tag{5}$$

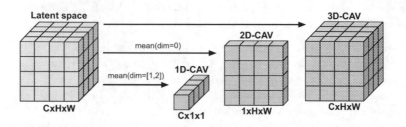

Fig. 2. Concept activation vectors (CAVs) of different dimensions.

3.4 CAV Dimensionality

The stability can be greatly affected by the number of CAV parameters, which is especially important in object detectors with large intermediate representations. Moreover, the larger CAV size leads to increased memory and computation requirements. The original TCAV paper proposes using 3D-CAV-vectors [23]. However, alternative translation invariant 1D- [10,49] and channel invariant 2D-CAV-representations, which have less parameters, are possible. If 3D-CAV's dimensions of OD's arbitrary intermediate layer are $C \times H \times W$, then dimensions of 1D- and 2D-CAV are $C \times 1 \times 1$ and $1 \times H \times W$ respectively, where C, H and, W denote *channel, height* and, *width* dimensions respectively (see Fig. 2).

The 1D-CAV provides during inference one presence score per channel, and possesses the property of translation invariance. This implies that only the presence or absence of a concept in the input space matters, rather than its size or location. In contrast, the 2D-CAV concentrates solely on the location of the concept, providing one presence score for each activation map pixel location. This can also be advantageous in certain circumstances (e.g., for the concepts "sky" or "ground"). The 3D-CAV provides during inference a single concept presence score for the complete image, depending both on location, size, and filter distribution of the concept. Meanwhile, it comes with the disadvantage of larger size and higher computational requirements.

Original 3D-CAVs do not require special handling of the latent space. But for evaluation of 1D- and 2D-CAVs, we preprocess incoming latent space vectors to match the CAV dimensionality by taking the mean along width and height, or channel dimensions respectively, as already successfully applied in previous work [7,14]. In other words, for the calculation of CAV with reduced dimensions, we aggregate activation functions and gradients along certain dimensions. CAV dimension size is a hyperparameter, which may impact CAV memory consumption, CAV stability, the overall performance of concept separation, CAV training speed, and following operations with CAVs (e.g., evaluation of the concept attribution). Thus, we also propose using our stability metrics for the selection of the optimal CAV dimension size.

4   Experimental Setup

We use the proposed framework to conduct the following experiments for OD and classification models: 1) evaluation of concept representation stability via the selection of representation dimensionality; 2) inspection of the impact of gradient instability in CNNs on concept attribution. The process of concept analysis in classifiers can be carried out using the default approaches proposed in the original papers [23,49], and it does not require any special handling.

In the following subsections, we describe selected experimental datasets and concept data preparation, models, model layers, and hyperparameter choices. Experiment results and interpretation are described later in Sect. 5.

4.1   Datasets

Object Detection. For unsupervised concept mining in object detectors and experiments with ODs, we use the validation set of MS COCO 2017 [26] dataset, containing 5000 real world images with 2D object bounding box annotations, including many outdoor and urban street scenarios. We mine concepts from bounding boxes of *person* class with the area of at least 20000 pixels, so the mined concept images have reasonable size and can be visually analyzed by a human. The resulting subset includes more than 2679 bounding boxes of people in different poses and locations extracted from 1685 images.

Classification. For concept stability experiments with classification model, we use BRODEN [3] and CycleGAN Zebras [50] datasets. BRODEN contains more than 60,000 images image and pixel-wise annotations for almost 1200 concepts of 6 categories. CycleGAN Zebras contains almost 1500 images of zebras suitable for supervised concept analysis.

4.2   Models

To evaluate the stability of semantic representations in the CNNs of different architectures and generations, we selected three object detectors and three classification models with various backbones.

Object Detection Models:

- one-stage YOLOv5s[1] [20] (residual DarkNet [16,32] backbone);
- two-stage FasterRCNN[2] [33] (inverted residual MobileNetV3 [17] backbone);

---

[1] https://github.com/ultralytics/yolov5.
[2] https://pytorch.org/vision/stable/models/faster_rcnn.

– one-stage SSD[3] [28] (VGG [39] backbone).

All evaluated object detection models are pre-trained on MS COCO [26] dataset. The models are further referred to as YOLO5, RCNN, and SSD.

Classification Models:

– residual ResNet50[4] [16];
– compressed SqueezeNet1.1[5] [18]
– inverted residual EfficientNet-B0[6] [42]

Classification models are pre-trained on ImageNet1k [8] dataset. The models are further referred to as ResNet, SqueezeNet, and EfficientNet.

Table 1. Shorthands l_i of selected classification CNN intermediate layers for Concept Analysis (l=layer, b=block, f=features, squeeze=s).

Classifier	layers						
	l_1	l_2	l_3	l_4	l_5	l_6	l_7
ResNet	l1.1.c3	l2.0.c3	l2.2.c3	l3.1.c3	l3.4.c3	l4.0.c3	l4.2.c3
SqueezeNet	f.3.s	f.4.s	f.6.s	f.7.s	f.9.s	f.10.s	f.11.s
EfficientNet	f.1.0.b.2.0	f.2.0.b.3.0	f.3.0.b.3.0	f.4.0.b.3.0	f.5.0.b.3.0	f.6.0.b.3.0	f.7.0.b.3.0

Table 2. Shorthands l_i of selected OD CNN intermediate layers for Concept Analysis (b=block, f=features, e=extra, c=conv).

OD	layers									
	l_1	l_2	l_3	l_4	l_5	l_6	l_7	l_8	l_9	l_{10}
YOLO5	3.c	4.cv3.c	5.c	6.cv3.c	7.c	8.cv3.c	10.c	14.c	17.cv3.c	18.c
RCNN	3.b.2.0	4.b.3.0	5.b.3.0	6.b.3.0	7.b.2.0	8.b.2.0	10.b.2.0	11.b.3.0	13.b.3.0	15.b.3.0
SSD	f.5	f.10	f.14	f.17	f.21	e.0.0	e.1.0	e.2.0	e.3.0	e.4.0

4.3   Layer Selection for Concept Analysis

To identify any influence of the layer depth on extracted concept stability, we must analyze the latent space of DNNs across multiple layers. To accomplish

---

[3] https://pytorch.org/vision/stable/models/ssd.
[4] https://pytorch.org/vision/stable/models/resnet.
[5] https://pytorch.org/vision/stable/models/squeezenet.
[6] https://pytorch.org/vision/stable/models/efficientnet.

| (a) Concept: "legs" | (b) Concept: "head" | (c) Concept: "torso" |

Fig. 3. Examples of synthetic concept samples generated using concept superpixels obtained from MS COCO.

this, we extract intermediate representations and concepts from ten intermediate convolutional layers of ODs and seven intermediate convolutional layers of classifiers. These layers are uniformly distributed throughout the backbones of CNNs. The names of the selected layers for each network are listed in Table 1 and Table 2, where each layer is identified by a symbolic name in the format of l_x, where x denotes the relative depth of the layer in the backbone (i.e., layers from l_1 to l_7 for classifiers and from l_1 to l_{10} for ODs).

In experiments, we use semantic concepts of medium-level (e.g., composite shapes) or high-level (e.g., human body parts) abstraction (Sect. 4.4). Shallow layers are ignored, as they mostly recognize concepts of low-level abstraction (e.g., color, texture), whilst deeper layers recognize complex objects and their parts [45,48].

4.4   Synthetic Concept Generation and Concept Selection

Object Detection. To conduct concept analysis experiments with object detectors, we generate synthetic concept samples using concept information extracted from MS COCO (see Fig. 1 and Sect. 3.1). We used ICE [49] to mine concept-related superpixels (image patches) from MS COCO bounding boxes of the *person* class that have an area of at least 20,000 pixels. Then, we visually inspected 30 mined concepts (10 for each following YOLO5 layer: 8.cv3.c, 9.cv1.c, and 10.c; see caption of Table 2 for notations) and selected 3 concepts semantically corresponding to labels "legs", "head", and "torso". Interestingly, we found that several concepts (e.g., "head", "legs") were present in more than one layer. We only picked one of the concepts of the same type based on the subjective quality. For each selected concept, we save 100 concept-related superpixels using a concept mask binarization threshold of 0.5.

Examples of the MS COCO synthetic concepts can be seen in Fig. 3. To generate a synthetic concept sample of a size of 640×480 pixels, 1 to 5 concept-related superpixels are selected and placed on a background of random noise drawn from a uniform distribution (alternatively, images of natural environments can be used as a background). Additionally, random scaling is applied to the superpixels before placement with a random factor between 0.9 and 1.1.

Classification. We use labeled concepts "stripes", "zigzags", and "dots" from BRODEN dataset to analyze the stability of concept representation and attribution in classification models on the examples of zebra images from the CycleGAN dataset.

4.5 Experiment-Specific Settings

Experiment 1: CAV Stability and Dimensionality. We conduct CAV-stability experiments for 1D-, 2D-, and 3D-CAVs (see Sect. 3.4) with YOLO5, RCNN, SSD, ResNet, SqueezeNet, and EfficientNet models to measure the potential concept retrieval stability in different networks and setups. For stability measurement, the number N of CAV retrieval runs with different initialization parameters is set to 15, which is similar to the ensemble size in [31], as we observed it is a good trade-off regarding computational speed. In each run, we utilize 100 samples per concept, dividing them into 80 for concept extraction and 20 for validation (estimation of $f1$).

To further examine the influence of the number of concept training samples on CAV stability, we also test three additional setups with 20, 40, and 60 training concept samples. The test has been conducted for all six networks.

Experiment 2: Gradient Stability in Concept Detection. For gradient stability experiments, ResNet and YOLO5 are selected as models with the best CAV stability from Experiment 2. Moreover, we validate setups with 1D- and 3D-CAVs to see how gradient instability affects concept attribution in CAVs of different dimensionality. For the computation of SmoothGrad, we use the hyperparameter values recommended in [40]: the number of noisy copies N is set to 50, and the amount of applied Gaussian noise is set to 10%.

5 Experimental Results

Table 3. Stability of generated CAVs of different dimensions for YOLO5.

CAV		l_1	l_2	l_3	l_4	l_5	l_6	l_7	l_8	l_9	l_{10}
cos	1D	**0.977**	**0.980**	**0.972**	**0.971**	**0.956**	**0.955**	**0.859**	**0.927**	**0.923**	**0.929**
	2D	0.522	0.342	0.483	0.526	0.729	0.590	0.670	0.670	0.715	0.666
	3D	0.346	0.378	0.467	0.553	0.577	0.617	0.664	0.707	0.652	0.602
$f1$	1D	**0.749**	**0.763**	**0.854**	**0.904**	**0.930**	**0.958**	**0.956**	**0.924**	**0.909**	**0.906**
	2D	0.427	0.404	0.400	0.458	0.499	0.488	0.547	0.571	0.558	0.523
	3D	0.576	0.592	0.663	0.723	0.858	0.872	0.941	0.884	0.876	0.852
S_{L_k}	1D	**0.732**	**0.748**	**0.830**	**0.878**	**0.889**	**0.915**	**0.821**	**0.857**	**0.839**	**0.841**
	2D	0.223	0.138	0.193	0.241	0.364	0.288	0.366	0.383	0.399	0.349
	3D	0.199	0.224	0.310	0.400	0.495	0.538	0.625	0.626	0.571	0.513

Table 4. Stability of generated CAVs of different dimensions for RCNN.

CAV		l_1	l_2	l_3	l_4	l_5	l_6	l_7	l_8	l_9	l_{10}
cos	1D	**0.965**	**0.977**	**0.979**	**0.976**	**0.970**	**0.973**	**0.980**	**0.946**	**0.933**	**0.893**
	2D	0.243	0.565	0.539	0.349	0.480	0.612	0.672	0.514	0.684	0.832
	3D	0.271	0.649	0.436	0.393	0.626	0.650	0.605	0.577	0.638	0.688
$f1$	1D	0.528	**0.588**	**0.730**	0.550	**0.762**	**0.809**	**0.724**	**0.888**	**0.946**	**0.944**
	2D	0.530	0.582	0.533	0.420	0.486	0.506	0.448	0.543	0.521	0.659
	3D	**0.536**	0.552	0.586	**0.563**	0.680	0.741	0.637	0.753	0.873	0.941
S_{L_k}	1D	**0.509**	**0.574**	**0.715**	**0.537**	**0.739**	**0.787**	**0.710**	**0.840**	**0.882**	**0.843**
	2D	0.129	0.329	0.287	0.147	0.233	0.309	0.301	0.279	0.357	0.548
	3D	0.145	0.358	0.255	0.221	0.426	0.482	0.385	0.435	0.557	0.647

Table 5. Stability of generated CAVs of different dimensions for SSD.

CAV		l_1	l_2	l_3	l_4	l_5	l_6	l_7	l_8	l_9	l_{10}
cos	1D	**0.972**	**0.965**	**0.961**	**0.947**	**0.954**	**0.945**	**0.916**	**0.917**	**0.927**	**0.933**
	2D	0.549	0.574	0.670	0.672	0.694	0.730	0.801	0.809	0.868	0.923
	3D	0.244	0.370	0.504	0.547	0.549	0.580	0.777	0.789	0.789	0.844
$f1$	1D	**0.666**	**0.758**	**0.909**	**0.888**	**0.949**	**0.962**	**0.897**	0.846	**0.874**	**0.858**
	2D	0.413	0.418	0.440	0.406	0.429	0.421	0.492	0.523	0.652	0.614
	3D	0.556	0.596	0.636	0.738	0.831	0.891	0.870	**0.880**	0.856	0.843
S_{L_k}	1D	**0.647**	**0.731**	**0.873**	**0.841**	**0.905**	**0.909**	**0.821**	**0.776**	**0.810**	**0.801**
	2D	0.227	0.240	0.295	0.273	0.298	0.307	0.394	0.423	0.566	0.567
	3D	0.136	0.221	0.320	0.404	0.456	0.517	0.676	0.694	0.675	0.712

Table 6. Stability of generated CAVs of different dimensions for ResNet.

CAV		l_1	l_2	l_3	l_4	l_5	l_6	l_7
cos	1D	**0.969**	**0.955**	**0.959**	**0.919**	0.953	0.882	0.869
	2D	0.861	0.918	0.839	0.906	**0.972**	**0.945**	**0.976**
	3D	0.726	0.684	0.672	0.749	0.705	0.624	0.648
$f1$	1D	0.668	0.856	0.847	0.910	0.944	0.983	0.960
	2D	0.402	0.369	0.406	0.588	0.598	0.356	0.423
	3D	**0.716**	**0.867**	**0.871**	**0.920**	**0.956**	**0.988**	**0.967**
S_{L_k}	1D	**0.647**	**0.817**	**0.812**	**0.836**	**0.900**	**0.868**	**0.834**
	2D	0.346	0.339	0.340	0.533	0.581	0.336	0.413
	3D	0.520	0.593	0.585	0.689	0.673	0.616	0.626

Table 7. Stability of generated CAVs of different dimensions for SqueezeNet.

CAV		l_1	l_2	l_3	l_4	l_5	l_6	l_7
cos	1D	**0.935**	**0.959**	**0.935**	**0.922**	**0.918**	**0.924**	**0.905**
	2D	0.806	0.839	0.799	0.862	0.847	0.860	0.809
	3D	0.773	0.750	0.779	0.758	0.795	0.807	0.760
$f1$	1D	0.547	0.654	0.863	**0.883**	**0.920**	**0.948**	**0.968**
	2D	0.381	0.364	0.377	0.409	0.453	0.551	0.506
	3D	**0.620**	**0.668**	**0.863**	0.877	0.911	0.932	0.961
S_{L_k}	1D	**0.511**	**0.627**	**0.807**	**0.815**	**0.845**	**0.876**	**0.876**
	2D	0.307	0.306	0.301	0.352	0.384	0.474	0.409
	3D	0.479	0.501	0.673	0.665	0.724	0.752	0.731

Table 8. Stability of generated CAVs of different dimensions for EfficientNet.

CAV		l_1	l_2	l_3	l_4	l_5	l_6	l_7
cos	1D	**0.924**	**0.929**	**0.936**	**0.933**	**0.892**	**0.898**	0.767
	2D	0.773	0.751	0.711	0.772	0.754	0.769	**0.884**
	3D	0.787	0.744	0.770	0.835	0.668	0.843	0.638
$f1$	1D	**0.377**	0.628	0.810	**0.922**	0.954	**0.986**	0.978
	2D	0.337	0.506	0.483	0.526	0.540	0.561	0.580
	3D	0.370	**0.688**	**0.836**	**0.922**	**0.960**	0.968	**0.979**
S_{L_k}	1D	**0.348**	**0.583**	**0.758**	**0.860**	**0.851**	**0.885**	**0.750**
	2D	0.260	0.380	0.344	0.406	0.407	0.431	0.513
	3D	0.291	0.512	0.643	0.770	0.641	0.816	0.625

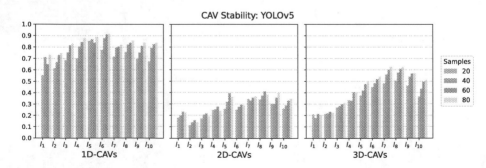

Fig. 4. Impact of number of concept samples on CAVs stability for YOLO5

5.1 CAV Stability and Dimensionality

The CAV stability results for 1D-, 2D- and 3D-CAVs in different layers of
YOLO5, RCNN, SSD, ResNet, SqueezeNet, and EfficientNet networks are presented in Tables 3 to 8. In addition, Figs. 4 to 9 visualize the impact of number
of training concept samples on the overall stability of 1D-, 2D- and 3D-CAVs.

CAV Dimensionality Impact. 3D-CAVs are obtained without intermediate
representation aggregation, and they demonstrate good concept separation ($f1$)
that can sometimes even outperform that of 1D-CAVs. This is typical for classifiers, where, for instance, in all layers of ResNet (Table 6) $f1$ of 3D-CAVs is the
highest. However, they for all models exhibit mediocre CAV consistency (cos),
possibly due to the larger number of parameters and a relatively small number
of training concept samples. Overall, 3D-CAVs are less stable than 1D-CAVs,
but still can be used for CA.

In contrast, 2D-CAVs exhibit relatively high consistency (e.g., in Table 6,
layers l_5, l_6, and l_7 have the top cos values for 2D-CAVs), but they have the
worst concept separation ($f1$), as observed in all tables. As a result, the overall 2D-CAV stability in all models is the worst. In 2D-CAVs, no distinction is
made between different channels in the latent space due to 3D-to-2D aggregation. The noticeable reduction of concept separation ($f1$) in 2D-CAVs reinforces
the assumption made in other works (e.g., [3,10]) that concept information is
encoded in different convolutional filters or their linear combinations.

1D-CAVs achieve the best overall CAV-stability due to their (mostly) best
consistency (cos) and good concept separation ($f1$). Moreover, 1D-CAVs have
the advantage of fast computation speed since they have fewer parameters. These
unique features of 1D-CAVs make them highly stable even in shallow layers,
where other CAVs may experience low stability. For example, in Table 3, the
stability of 1D-CAVs in layer l_1 $S_{L_k} = 0.732$ is substantially higher than that of
2D- and 3D-CAVs, which are only 0.223 and 0.199, respectively.

Based on our empirical findings, we recommend using 1D-CAV as the default
representation for most applications due to its superior overall stability. However, for safety-critical applications, we advise using our stability assessment
methodology prior to CA.

Concept Abstraction Level Impact. In OD models, experiments are conducted with concepts of medium-to-high levels of abstraction (complex shapes
and human body parts), which are usually detected in middle and deep layers of
the network [45]. Thus, it is expected that there will be worse concept separation
($f1$) in shallow layers, and this has indeed been observed across all dimension
sizes of CAVs (as shown in Tables 3–8).

However, this observation is not always valid for 2D-CAVs, as results have
shown that concept separation drops in some deeper layers. For instance, in
Table 4 l_4 and l_7 have $f1$ values 0.420 and 0.448, while for l_1 it is 0.530. Also,
Table 4 shows that the increase of $f1$ for 2D-CAVs is not as high as it is for
1D- and 3D-CAVs. The range of $f1$ for 2D-CAVs is between 0.420 to 0.659,
whereas for 3D-CAVs, it is between 0.536 to 0.941. These findings further support

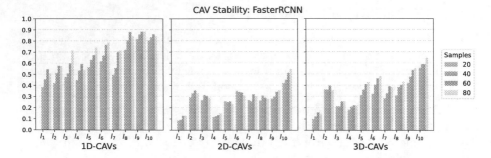

Fig. 5. Impact of number of concept samples on CAVs stability for RCNN

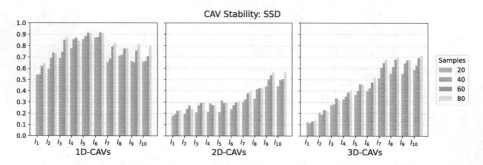

Fig. 6. Impact of number of concept samples on CAVs stability for SSD

the hypothesis that concept information is encoded in linear combinations of convolutional filters [3, 10].

Impact of Number of CAV Training Samples. Figures 4 to 9 demonstrate that increasing the number of training concept images has a positive impact on the stability of CAV. However, labeling concepts is a time-consuming and expensive process. Therefore, we recommend using at least 40 to 60 concept-related samples for training each CAV. In most cases, the stability obtained with 80 samples is only marginally better than that obtained with 40 (see Fig. 8) or 60 samples (see Fig. 4 and Fig. 6).

CNN Architecture Impact. From Tables 3 to 8 we see that top CAV stability (S_{L_k}) values achieved by ODs and classifiers for CAVs trained on the same concept datasets are very similar. However, due to architectural differences, the top stability values are achieved at different relative layer depths. For example, the top stabilities for 1D-CAVs in YOLO5, RCNN, and SSD object detectors are achieved in layers l_6, l_9, and l_6, respectively, with corresponding values of 0.915, 0.882, and 0.909 (see Tables 3, 4, and 5). Similarly, the top stability values for 1D-CAVs for ResNet, SqueezeNet, and EfficientNet classifiers are achieved in layers l_5, l_7, and l_6, respectively, with corresponding values of 0.900, 0.876, and 0.885 (Table 6, 7, and 8). The same tables show that the layers with top stability values may vary for different sizes of CAV dimensions even within the

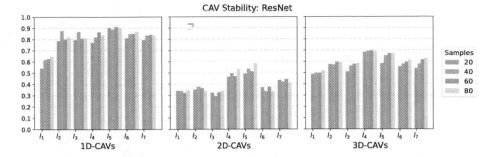

Fig. 7. Impact of number of concept samples on CAVs stability for ResNet

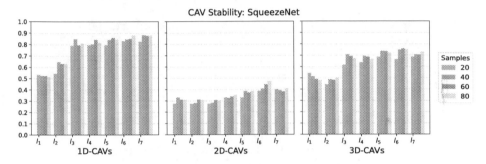

Fig. 8. Impact of number of concept samples on CAVs stability for SqueezeNet

same model (e.g., in Table 3, the YOLO5 top stabilities for 1D-, 2D-, and 3D-CAV are obtained in layers l_6, l_9, and l_8, respectively).

The CAV stability differences among inspected architectures can also be observed in Figs. 4 to 9. For example, in the case of 1D-CAV of ResNet (Fig. 7) and 1D- and 3D-CAVs of SqueezeNet (Fig. 8), we observe that the stability value quickly reaches its optimal values in the first one or two layers and remains similar in deeper layers. In other cases, such as 3D-CAV of SSD (Fig. 6) or all CAV dimensions of RCNN (Fig. 5), stability gradually increases with the relative depth of the layer. Finally, the stabilities of 1D- and 3D-CAVs of YOLO5 (Fig. 4) or 1D- and 3D-CAVs of EfficientNet (Fig. 9) grow until an optimal layer in the middle and slowly shrink after it.

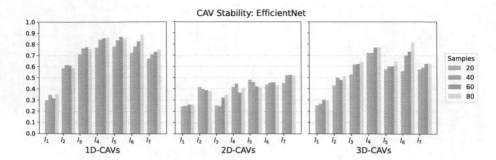

Fig. 9. Impact of number of concept samples on CAVs stability for EfficientNet

Table 9. Gradient stability in layers of ResNet for 1D-CAV.

Measure	l_1	l_2	l_3	l_4	l_5	l_6	l_7
TP	669	748	731	709	728	677	500
TN	718	697	704	727	724	791	1000
FP	52	26	33	30	26	19	0
FN	61	29	32	34	22	13	0
Acc	0.92	0.96	0.96	0.96	0.97	0.98	1.00
CAD, %	20.7	13.6	14.1	14.4	10.5	6.0	0.6

Table 10. Gradient stability in layers of ResNet for 3D-CAV.

Measure	l_1	l_2	l_3	l_4	l_5	l_6	l_7
TP	667	709	693	716	886	789	500
TN	687	721	721	709	561	688	1000
FP	80	41	43	41	26	13	0
FN	66	29	43	34	27	10	0
Acc	0.90	0.95	0.94	0.95	0.96	0.98	1.00
CAD, %	31.3	17.5	19.5	18.0	12.8	5.8	0.7

Table 11. Gradient stability in layers of YOLO5 for 1D-CAV.

Measure	l_1	l_2	l_3	l_4	l_5	l_6	l_7	l_8	l_9	l_{10}
TP	973	997	979	1012	998	989	998	1046	1065	771
TN	1014	994	1009	990	989	1038	1069	1042	1024	1331
FP	73	66	61	58	80	53	36	23	22	21
FN	76	79	87	76	69	56	33	25	25	13
Acc	0.93	0.93	0.93	0.94	0.93	0.95	0.97	0.98	0.98	0.98
CAD, %	24.1	27.4	26.4	28.0	27.9	22.5	17.6	13.8	10.9	14.5

Table 12. Gradient stability in layers of YOLO5 for 3D-CAV.

Measure	l_1	l_2	l_3	l_4	l_5	l_6	l_7	l_8	l_9	l_{10}
TP	959	1010	985	985	973	1001	1054	1032	1039	785
TN	1025	1012	1002	1007	980	990	1015	1057	1047	1321
FP	75	58	74	74	87	80	28	22	29	11
FN	77	56	75	70	96	65	39	25	21	19
Acc	0.93	0.95	0.93	0.93	0.91	0.93	0.97	0.98	0.98	0.99
CAD, %	27.2	29.6	28.5	29.7	30.6	29.2	15.7	14.3	11.5	14.1

5.2 Gradient Stability in Concept Detection

Based on the experimental results, it can be concluded that the negative impact of gradient instability on concept analysis using TCAV is minimal. The results presented in Tables 9 and 10 are based on 1500 concept attribution predictions (see Eq. 4) for 500 images and 3 concepts per image, for each tested layer of ResNet with 1D- and 3D-CAVs, respectively. Similarly, Tables 11 and 12 are built for each tested layer of YOLO5 with 1D- and 3D-CAVs, respectively, using 2136 concept attribution predictions for 712 bounding boxes and 3 concepts per bounding box.

SmoothGrad Impact. In the Tables 9 to 12, the relative depth of CNN backbone layers is increasing from left to right, while gradient backpropagation depth from outputs to CAV layer is increasing in right to left order. As expected, the gradient is becoming more unstable with backpropagation depth [40], resulting in higher CAD values in shallow layers compared to deeper layers. The higher number of concept attribution sign flips is observed in shallow layers (see Sect. 3.3), where accuracy (Acc) values in those layers are low. These observations confirm the negative correlation between CAD and Acc, where CAD increases as Acc decreases. This suggests that gradient smoothing techniques, such as Smooth-Grad, can have a higher impact on concept attribution values in shallow layers, where the gradient instability is higher.

Despite the negative correlation between CAD and Acc values, the overall accuracy values remain above 0.9 for all layers in the provided tables. The lowest accuracy value for ResNet of Acc $= 0.90$ is observed in Table 10 for l_1. For YOLO5 the lowest Acc $= 0.91$ is obtrained in l_5 (Table 12). This indicates that the sign of concept attribution is only changed for a minority of predictions across all tested networks and configurations. However, it is worth noting that CAD values can be high in shallow layers, for instance, CAD $= 31.3\%$ at layer l_1 of Table 10, resulting in a higher rate of concept attribution sign flipping compared to deeper layers.

The use of SmoothGrad comes at a higher computational cost compared to vanilla gradient. It is more than N times (number of noisy copies) computationally expensive, and mostly impacts concept attribution in shallow and middle layers of networks. Therefore, it is advisable to use SmoothGrad when conducting concept analysis in shallow layers of networks with large backbones such as ResNet101 or ResNet152.

CAV Dimensionality Impact. The use of 1D-CAV representations generally results in lower CAD values than 3D-CAVs, typically with a difference of 2–3%. This behavior can be attributed to the higher stability of 1D-CAVs, which is in turn caused by the lower number of parameters. The observation is consistent across all layers of ResNet and the majority of YOLO5 layers, as shown in Tables 9 to 12. However, the dimensionality of CAV does not affect the behavior of gradient instability in other regards: CAD remains higher and Acc lower in shallow layers regardless of the CAV dimensionality.

6   Conclusion and Outlook

This study proposes a framework and metrics for evaluating the layer-wise stability of global vector representations in object detection and classification CNN models for explainability purposes. We introduced two stability metrics: concept retrieval stability and concept attribution stability. Also, we proposed adaptation methodologies for unsupervised CA and supervised gradient-based CA methods for combined, labeling-efficient application in object detection models.

Our concept retrieval stability metric jointly evaluates the consistency and separation in the feature space of concept semantic concept representations obtained across multiple runs with different initialization parameters. We used the TCAV method as an example to examine factors that affect stability and found that aggregated 1D-CAV representations offer the best performance. Furthermore, we determined that a minimum of 60 training samples per concept is necessary to ensure high stability in most cases.

The second metric, concept attribution stability, assesses the impact of gradient smoothing techniques on the stability of concept attribution. Our observations suggest that 1D-CAVs are more resistant to gradient instability, particularly in deep layers, and we recommend using gradient smoothing in shallow layers of deep network backbones.

Our work provides valuable quantitative insights into the robustness of concept representation, which can inform the selection of network layers and concept representations for CA in safety-critical applications. For future work, it will be interesting to apply the proposed approaches and metrics to alternative global concept vector representations and perform comparative analysis.

Acknowledgments. The research leading to these results is funded by the German Federal Ministry for Economic Affairs and Climate Action within the project "KI Wissen - Entwicklung von Methoden für die Einbindung von Wissen in maschinelles Lernen". The authors would like to thank the consortium for the successful cooperation.

References

1. 32, I.S.: ISO 26262-1:2018(En): Road Vehicles – Functional Safety – Part 1: Vocabulary (2018). https://www.iso.org/standard/68383.html
2. Abid, A., Yuksekgonul, M., Zou, J.: Meaningfully debugging model mistakes using conceptual counterfactual explanations. In: Proceedings of the 39th International Conference on Machine Learning, pp. 66–88. PMLR, June 2022
3. Bau, D., Zhou, B., Khosla, A., Oliva, A., Torralba, A.: Network dissection: quantifying interpretability of deep visual representations. In: Proceedings of the IEEE Conference Computer Vision and Pattern Recognition, pp. 6541–6549 (2017)
4. Bodria, F., Giannotti, F., Guidotti, R., Naretto, F., Pedreschi, D., Rinzivillo, S.: Benchmarking and survey of explanation methods for black box models. arXiv preprint arXiv:2102.13076 (2021)
5. Carvalho, D.V., Pereira, E.M., Cardoso, J.S.: Machine learning interpretability: a survey on methods and metrics. Electronics 8(8), 832 (2019). https://doi.org/10.3390/electronics8080832
6. Chen, Z., Bei, Y., Rudin, C.: Concept whitening for interpretable image recognition. Nat. Mach. Intell. 2(12), 772–782 (2020)
7. Chyung, C., Tsang, M., Liu, Y.: Extracting interpretable concept-based decision trees from CNNs. In: Proceedings of the 2019 ICML Workshop Human in the Loop Learning, vol. 1906.04664, June 2019. CoRR
8. Deng, J., Dong, W., Socher, R., Li, L.J., Li, K., Fei-Fei, L.: Imagenet: a large-scale hierarchical image database. In: 2009 IEEE Conference on Computer Vision and Pattern Recognition, pp. 248–255. IEEE (2009)
9. Esser, P., Rombach, R., Ommer, B.: A disentangling invertible interpretation network for explaining latent representations. In: Proceedings of the 2020 IEEE Conference on Computer Vision and Pattern Recognition, pp. 9220–9229. IEEE, June 2020. https://doi.org/10.1109/CVPR42600.2020.00924
10. Fong, R., Vedaldi, A.: Net2Vec: quantifying and explaining how concepts are encoded by filters in deep neural networks. In: Proceedings of the IEEE Conference on Computer Vision and Pattern Recognition, pp. 8730–8738 (2018)
11. Ge, Y., et al.: A peek into the reasoning of neural networks: interpreting with structural visual concepts. In: Proceedings of the IEEE/CVF Conference on Computer Vision and Pattern Recognition, pp. 2195–2204 (2021)
12. Ghorbani, A., Wexler, J., Zou, J.Y., Kim, B.: Towards automatic concept-based explanations. Adv. Neural Inf. Process. Syst. 32 (2019)
13. Goodman, B., Flaxman, S.: European union regulations on algorithmic decision-making and a right to explanation. AI Mag. 38(3), 50–57 (2017). https://doi.org/10.1609/aimag.v38i3.2741
14. Graziani, M., Andrearczyk, V., Marchand-Maillet, S., Müller, H.: Concept attribution: explaining CNN decisions to physicians. Comput. Biol. Med. 123, 103865 (2020). https://doi.org/10.1016/j.compbiomed.2020.103865
15. Graziani, M., Andrearczyk, V., Müller, H.: Regression concept vectors for bidirectional explanations in histopathology. In: Stoyanov, D., et al. (eds.) MLCN/DLF/IMIMIC -2018. LNCS, vol. 11038, pp. 124–132. Springer, Cham (2018). https://doi.org/10.1007/978-3-030-02628-8_14
16. He, K., Zhang, X., Ren, S., Sun, J.: Deep residual learning for image recognition. In: Proceedings of the IEEE Conference on Computer Vision and Pattern Recognition, pp. 770–778 (2016)

17. Howard, A., et al.: Searching for MobileNetV3. In: Proceedings of the IEEE/CVF International Conference on Computer Vision, pp. 1314–1324 (2019)

18. Iandola, F.N., Han, S., Moskewicz, M.W., Ashraf, K., Dally, W.J., Keutzer, K.: Squeezenet: alexnet-level accuracy with 50x fewer parameters and <0.5 mb model size. arXiv preprint arXiv:1602.07360 (2016)

19. ISO/TC 22/SC 32: ISO 26262-8:2018(En): Road Vehicles — Functional Safety — Part 8: Supporting Processes, ISO 26262:2018(En), vol. 8. International Organization for Standardization, second edn., December 2018

20. Jocher, G.: YOLOv5 in PyTorch, ONNX, CoreML, TFLite, October 2020. https://github.com/ultralytics/yolov5, https://doi.org/10.5281/zenodo.4154370

21. Kazhdan, D., Dimanov, B., Jamnik, M., Liò, P., Weller, A.: Now you see me (CME): concept-based model extraction. In: Proceedings of the 29th ACM International Conference Information and Knowledge Management Workshops. CEUR Workshop Proceedings, vol. 2699. CEUR-WS.org (2020)

22. Kazhdan, D., Dimanov, B., Terre, H.A., Jamnik, M., Liò, P., Weller, A.: Is disentanglement all you need? Comparing concept-based & disentanglement approaches. CoRR abs/2104.06917 (2021)

23. Kim, B., Wattenberg, M., Gilmer, J., Cai, C., Wexler, J., Viegas, F., et al.: Interpretability beyond feature attribution: quantitative testing with concept activation vectors (TCAV). In: International Conference on Machine Learning, pp. 2668–2677. PMLR (2018)

24. Kirchknopf, A., Slijepcevic, D., Wunderlich, I., Breiter, M., Traxler, J., Zeppelzauer, M.: Explaining yolo: leveraging grad-cam to explain object detections. arXiv preprint arXiv:2211.12108 (2022)

25. Koh, P.W., et al.: Concept bottleneck models. In: International Conference on Machine Learning, pp. 5338–5348. PMLR (2020)

26. Lin, T.-Y., et al.: Microsoft COCO: common objects in context. In: Fleet, D., Pajdla, T., Schiele, B., Tuytelaars, T. (eds.) ECCV 2014. LNCS, vol. 8693, pp. 740–755. Springer, Cham (2014). https://doi.org/10.1007/978-3-319-10602-1_48

27. Linardatos, P., Papastefanopoulos, V., Kotsiantis, S.: Explainable AI: a review of machine learning interpretability methods. Entropy 23(1), 18 (2021). https://doi.org/10.3390/e23010018

28. Liu, W., et al.: SSD: single shot multibox detector. In: Leibe, B., Matas, J., Sebe, N., Welling, M. (eds.) ECCV 2016. LNCS, vol. 9905, pp. 21–37. Springer, Cham (2016). https://doi.org/10.1007/978-3-319-46448-0_2

29. Margeloiu, A., Ashman, M., Bhatt, U., Chen, Y., Jamnik, M., Weller, A.: Do concept bottleneck models learn as intended? arXiv preprint arXiv:2105.04289 (2021)

30. Pfau, J., Young, A.T., Wei, J., Wei, M.L., Keiser, M.J.: Robust semantic interpretability: revisiting concept activation vectors. In: Proceedings of the 2021 ICML Workshop Human Interpretability in Machine Learning, April 2021. CoRR

31. Rabold, J., Schwalbe, G., Schmid, U.: Expressive explanations of DNNs by combining concept analysis with ILP. In: Schmid, U., Klügl, F., Wolter, D. (eds.) KI 2020. LNCS (LNAI), vol. 12325, pp. 148–162. Springer, Cham (2020). https://doi.org/10.1007/978-3-030-58285-2_11

32. Redmon, J., Farhadi, A.: YOLOv3: an incremental improvement. arXiv preprint arXiv:1804.02767 (2018)

33. Ren, S., He, K., Girshick, R., Sun, J.: Faster R-CNN: towards real-time object detection with region proposal networks. Adv. Neural Inf. Process. Syst. 28 (2015)

34. Sawada, Y., Nakamura, K.: Concept bottleneck model with additional unsupervised concepts. IEEE Access 10, 41758–41765 (2022)

35. Schwalbe, G.: Verification of size invariance in DNN activations using concept embeddings. In: Maglogiannis, I., Macintyre, J., Iliadis, L. (eds.) AIAI 2021. IAICT, vol. 627, pp. 374–386. Springer, Cham (2021). https://doi.org/10.1007/978-3-030-79150-6_30

36. Schwalbe, G.: Concept embedding analysis: a review, March 2022. arXiv:2203.13909 [cs, stat]

37. Schwalbe, G., Finzel, B.: A comprehensive taxonomy for explainable artificial intelligence: a systematic survey of surveys on methods and concepts. Data Min. Knowl. Discov. (2023). https://doi.org/10.1007/s10618-022-00867-8

38. Schwalbe, G., Wirth, C., Schmid, U.: Concept embeddings for fuzzy logic verification of deep neural networks in perception tasks. arXiv preprint arXiv:2201.00572 (2022)

39. Simonyan, K., Zisserman, A.: Very deep convolutional networks for large-scale image recognition. arXiv preprint arXiv:1409.1556 (2014)

40. Smilkov, D., Thorat, N., Kim, B., Viégas, F., Wattenberg, M.: Smoothgrad: removing noise by adding noise. arXiv preprint arXiv:1706.03825 (2017)

41. Sundararajan, M., Taly, A., Yan, Q.: Axiomatic attribution for deep networks. In: Proceedings of the 34th International Conference on Machine Learning. Proceedings of Machine Learning Research, vol. 70, pp. 3319–3328. PMLR (2017)

42. Tan, M., Le, Q.: Efficientnet: rethinking model scaling for convolutional neural networks. In: International Conference on Machine Learning, pp. 6105–6114. PMLR (2019)

43. Veale, M., Borgesius, F.Z.: Demystifying the draft EU artificial intelligence act-analysing the good, the bad, and the unclear elements of the proposed approach. Comput. Law Rev. Int. **22**(4), 97–112 (2021)

44. Vilone, G., Longo, L.: Classification of explainable artificial intelligence methods through their output formats. Mach. Learn. Knowl. Extr. **3**(3), 615–661 (2021)

45. Wang, D., Cui, X., Wang, Z.J.: Chain: concept-harmonized hierarchical inference interpretation of deep convolutional neural networks. arXiv preprint arXiv:2002.01660 (2020)

46. Wu, W., et al.: Towards global explanations of convolutional neural networks with concept attribution. In: Proceedings of the 2020 IEEE/CVF Conference on Computer Vision and Pattern Recognition, pp. 8649–8658 (2020). https://doi.org/10.1109/CVPR42600.2020.00868

47. Zhang, Q., Wang, W., Zhu, S.C.: Examining CNN representations with respect to dataset bias. In: Proceedings of the 32nd AAAI Conference on Artificial Intelligence, pp. 4464–4473. AAAI Press (2018)

48. Zhang, Q., Wu, Y.N., Zhu, S.C.: Interpretable convolutional neural networks. In: Proceedings of the IEEE Conference on Computer Vision and Pattern Recognition, pp. 8827–8836 (2018)

49. Zhang, R., Madumal, P., Miller, T., Ehinger, K.A., Rubinstein, B.I.: Invertible concept-based explanations for CNN models with non-negative concept activation vectors. In: Proceedings of the AAAI Conference on Artificial Intelligence, pp. 11682–11690 (2021)

50. Zhu, J.Y., Park, T., Isola, P., Efros, A.A.: Unpaired image-to-image translation using cycle-consistent adversarial networks. In: Proceedings of the IEEE International Conference on Computer Vision, pp. 2223–2232 (2017)

Beyond One-Hot-Encoding: Injecting Semantics to Drive Image Classifiers

Alan Perotti[1]([✉]) [iD], Simone Bertolotto[1] [iD], Eliana Pastor[2] [iD], and André Panisson[1] [iD]

[1] CENTAI Institute, Turin, Italy
{alan.perotti,simone.bertolotto,andre.panisson}@centai.eu
[2] Politecnico di Torino, Turin, Italy
eliana.pastor@polito.it

Abstract. Images are loaded with semantic information that pertains to real-world ontologies: dog breeds share mammalian similarities, food pictures are often depicted in domestic environments, and so on. However, when training machine learning models for image classification, the relative similarities amongst object classes are commonly paired with one-hot-encoded labels. According to this logic, if an image is labelled as *spoon*, then *tea-spoon* and *shark* are equally wrong in terms of training loss. To overcome this limitation, we explore the integration of additional goals that reflect ontological and semantic knowledge, improving model interpretability and trustworthiness. We suggest a generic approach that allows to derive an additional loss term starting from any kind of semantic information about the classification label. First, we show how to apply our approach to ontologies and word embeddings, and discuss how the resulting information can drive a supervised learning process. Second, we use our semantically enriched loss to train image classifiers, and analyse the trade-offs between accuracy, mistake severity, and learned internal representations. Finally, we discuss how this approach can be further exploited in terms of explainability and adversarial robustness.

Keywords: Computer Vision · eXplainable Artificial Intelligence · Ontologies · Word Embeddings

1 Introduction

Deep Learning (DL) models have become the go-to method for addressing numerous Computer Vision (CV) tasks, such as image classification. Unlike traditional approaches that require manual feature extraction, DL streamlines the development of end-to-end pipelines that seamlessly integrate images as inputs to the learning process, thereby automating feature extraction and enhancing overall efficiency. This automation enables the training of DL models over extensive image datasets, which subsequently leads to enhanced model accuracy. However, the "black-box" nature of DL models presents challenges, as Machine Learning (ML) practitioners often struggle to understand the chain of transformations

L. Longo (Ed.): xAI 2023, CCIS 1902, pp. 525–548, 2023.
https://doi.org/10.1007/978-3-031-44067-0_27

that a DL model adopts to map an image into the final prediction. This lack of transparency is considered to be hampering the adoption of DL models in real-world scenarios, due to a plethora of reasons: lack of trust from domain experts, impossibility of thorough debugging from practitioners, lack of compliance to legal requirements regarding explainability, and potential systemic bias in the trained model [18]. The research field of eXplainable Artificial Intelligence (XAI) tackles this problem by trying to provide more insights about the inner decision process of ML models [11]. However, most XAI techniques for CV are post-hoc: they are applied on trained ML models, and typically try to correlated portions of the image to the resulting label by means of input perturbation or maskings [30,32,34]. A few other approaches try to modify the training procedure itself, hoping to gain more control over the model's internals, while at the same time maintaining competitive classification performances.

With this in mind, we remark how the standard DL pipeline for image classification trains the model to learn a mapping from images to labels. As inputs, images are loaded with semantic information that pertains to real-world ontologies: dog breeds share mammalian similarities, food pictures are often depicted in domestic environments, and so on. As outputs, labels are typically one-hot-encoded (OHE), implementing a rigid binary logic of 'one is class correct, all other classes are wrong'. There is therefore no semantics attached to these labels, as all dimensions of these OHE vectors are orthogonal. As a defective byproduct of this common ML framing, if an image is labelled as *spoon*, then *tea-spoon* and *shark* are equally wrong predictions, and would be equally penalised in terms of training loss during a training phase. However, labels can often be linked them to external sources of knowledge representation, ranging from structured knowledge bases such as ontologies [12] to embedding vectors [37] produced by language models. Our Research Question (RQ) is therefore the following:

> **RQ: How can we inject semantic information into a standard image classification learning process?**

In order to answer this question, in this paper we introduce a general approach that allows to inject any kind of auxiliary semantic vectors to OHE labels, and produce enriched vectors that we call *Semantically-Augmented Labels* (S-AL). S-AL can be used as ground truth with standard loss functions and neural architectures in ML tasks such as image classification. We can thus formulate additional Research Sub-Questions:

> – **RsQ1: How does S-AL perform ML-wise, both in terms of quantity and quality of errors?**
> – **RsQ2: What is the impact of S-AL concerning the learned internal representation of concepts?**
> – **RsQ3: What is the impact of S-AL on XAI?**

We answer all these questions empirically: first, we show how to encode both hierarchical information extracted from an ontology, and embedding vectors produced by a language model. Then we train several ML models using S-AL as targets, together with baseline models for benchmarking. We then analyse these models in terms of ML performance, structure of the feature space, and XAI heatmaps. We show how S-AL allows to maintain competitive classification accuracy while allowing for less semantically severe mistakes, and we show how the injection of semantic information improves both the space of learned features and the relative similarities of produced image explanations.

The remainder of the paper is structured as follows: Sect. 2 describes related and relevant research work, while Sect. 3 introduces our approach S-AL. Section 4 describes how we operationalise the answer to the sub-research questions RsQ1, RsQ2, and RsQ3, and in Sect. 5 we show and discuss our experimental results. Section 6 draws the final considerations and directions for future work.

2   Related Work

Neural Networks for Image Classification

Neural networks have proven to be effective in solving complex image classification tasks. Convolutional Neural Networks (CNNs) are the most widely used type of neural network for image classification. CNNs consist of multiple layers of convolutional and pooling operations that extract features from the input image. The extracted features are then fed into fully connected layers, which output the final classification probabilities. One of the most influential works in this field was the AlexNet architecture proposed in 2012 [17]. The architecture used five convolutional layers and three fully connected layers to achieve state-of-the-art performance on the ImageNet [8] dataset. Since then, many improvements have been made to the CNN architecture, such as the VGGNet [33] - however, the main structure of convolutional layers for feature extraction followed by dense layers for feature-to-label classification became a standard. A notable further development was the introduction of residual connections, starting from ResNet [15]. More recently, attention-based neural networks have been proposed for image classification. These models use attention mechanisms to selectively focus on important image regions, improving performance. SENet [16] is an example of this approach, achieving state-of-the-art performance on the ImageNet by using attention modules to selectively amplify important features. Overall, neural networks have shown great success in image classification tasks, and their performance continues to improve with new advancements in architecture and training techniques. However, the image classification training process commonly involves one-hot encoding for class labels and cross-entropy as a loss function. The problem of hierarchical classification was initially explored in the literature (see survey [31]), but never incorporated into standard training pipelines.

Semantic Auxiliary Information Sources

Including semantic information has proved beneficial in multiple contexts, such as model interpretability [10], image summarization [23], and image classification [4] itself. However, in standard image classification tasks, labels are OHE and convey any contextual information regarding their semantic value: *breakfast,* *lunch* and *mountain* are three equally-independent dimensions of a OHE ground truth vector. Clearly, structured representations of knowledge could provide auxiliary information concerning relations between (the concepts represented by) labels. The most common pairing of image classification dataset with external semantic information is Imagenet-Wordnet. ImageNet, as mentioned above, is a common benchmark for image classifiers; WordNet [12] is a large lexical database of English. Nouns, verbs, adjectives, and adverbs are grouped into sets of cognitive synonyms (synsets), each expressing a distinct concept. Synsets are interlinked by means of conceptual-semantic and lexical relations. The already-available link between the two is that all ImageNet are also nodes (synsets) within the WordNet graph. We remark that exploiting structured representation of knowledge like WordNet is surely an interesting research direction. Still, it excludes a plethora of other unstructured semantic information sources, such as word embeddings [37]. A word embedding is a learned latent representation for text that allows words with similar meaning to have a similar representation and is commonly used for Natural Language Processing downstream tasks [5]. Typically, the representation is a real-valued vector that encodes the meaning of the word in such a way that words that are closer in the vector space are expected to be similar in meaning. We remark that for word embeddings there is no underlying data structure connecting different terms: instead, reasoning task can exploit the pairwise similarity between embeddings.

Injecting Semantics in Image Classification Tasks

In recent times, some research work has again proposed to integrate image classification with auxiliary information regarding the semantic context of labels. The most common procedure is to exploit structured representations of knowledge, such as ontologies, and extract from them a hierarchy of labels. The existing approaches differ on how they incorporate class hierarchies in the training process: the literature distinguishes them among label embedding, hierarchical loss, and hierarchical architecture-based methods.

Label-embedding approaches encode hierarchies directly into the class label representation using soft embedding vectors rather than one-hot encoding. Some works directly use the taxonomic hierarchy tree of class to derive soft labels, also known as hierarchical embedding [1–4,13,19,39]. Barz and Denzler [2] derive a measure of semantic similarity between classes using the lowest common ancestor (LCA) height in a given hierarchy tree. The loss function combines two terms: a standard cross-entropy loss for the image classification target and a linear loss to enforce similarity between the image representations and the class semantic embedding. Bertinetto et al. [4] also adopt the LCA to derive soft labels which encode the semantic information and use standard cross-entropy loss. Using tax-

onomic hierarchy trees to encode hierarchies allows the direct use of prior semantic knowledge without needing external models or training procedures. On the
other hand, it limits its application to problems for which a taxonomic hierarchy
tree is available. Other works proposed in the context of zero-shot classification
avoid the use of taxonomies by exploiting text embeddings [1,13,39]. For example, DeViSE [13] derives class embedding using a pre-trained word2vec model
on Wikipedia; these works were originally proposed in the context of zero-shot
classification. Few works explore both hierarchical and text embeddings. For
example, Liu et al. [19] combine the hyperbolic embedding learned with Word-
Net hierarchy with the word ones using the Glove model but for the context of
zero-shot recognition.

Hierarchical loss methods integrate hierarchical semantic information by modifying the training loss function [4,7,14,36,38] belong to this category. Bertinetto
et al. [4] propose a hierarchical cross-entropy (HXE) which is the weighted sum
of the cross-entropies of the conditional probabilities derived by conditioning
the predictions for a particular class on the parent-class probabilities. Garg et
al., in Hierarchy Aware Features (HAF) [14], propose a multi-term loss function
to optimize fine label prediction while capturing hierarchical information. The
approach leverages multiple classifiers, one at each level of the taxonomic tree
hierarchy, with a shared feature space. In our work, we include semantic information directly via soft labels and also generalize for non-hierarchical semantic
information.

Hierarchical architecture-based methods integrate the class hierarchy directly
into the model architecture at the structural level. Approaches as [6,22,27] fall
into this category. Hierarchical architecture-based methods are suitable for only
hierarchy-based semantic information. We propose to encode class relations from
generic semantic information, from hierarchy trees to word embeddings.

Our work proposes a label-embedding strategy that encodes semantics into class
similarity embedding from general semantic information, be it taxonomic tree
hierarchies or word embeddings. Moreover, differently than existing approaches,
we explicitly address the assessment of the semantic-aware representation in the
derived models.

eXplainable and Interpretable Artificial Intelligence

Explainable Artificial Intelligence (XAI) refers to the ability of an AI system to
explain its decisions and reasoning in a way that humans can easily understand.
The need for XAI arises from the fact that many AI systems, particularly deep
learning models, operate as black boxes, making it difficult for humans to understand how they arrive at their decisions [11]. There are two main approaches
to achieving XAI: ex-post explainability and the design of intrinsically interpretable architectures. Ex-post explainability involves analyzing the outputs of
a trained AI model and deriving explanations from them ([24,28,30,32,34], inter
alia). This approach is commonly used with standard black-box models that lack
inherent interpretability, such as deep neural networks. In contrast, interpretable
architectures aim to be intrinsically (more) transparent from the outset. These

models typically use simpler algorithms (such as decision trees or rule-based systems) as building blocks, or provide prototype-based explanations [29].

In the specific case of explainability for image classification, it is worth mentioning that one of the driving domains is medical diagnosis [35]. From the algorithmic standpoint, most approaches belong to the ex-post category, and therefore extract explanation from already-trained, standard image classifiers. One popular technique is *Saliency Mapping* [32], a method for computing the spatial support of a given class in a given image (image-specific class saliency map) using a single back-propagation pass through a classification convolutional model. Other approaches are gradient-based attributions, such as *Integrated Gradients* [34] and *Input X Gradient* [30]: these algorithms assign an importance score to each input feature by approximating the integral of gradients of the model's output with respect to the inputs along the path (straight line) from given baselines/references to inputs. The common outputs of these systems are heatmaps - graphical representations of the importance of different regions in an image for the classification decision made by the neural network. Heatmaps are typically overlaid on the original image, in order to better inspect the highlighted areas. Explaining image classifiers through heatmaps has notably received criticism [29], as heatmaps explaining different classes often correspond to very similar heatmaps. For instance, in the famous example reported in Fig. 1, Rudin et al. [29] showed how the heatmaps for *Siberian Husky* and *Transverse Flute* were very similar.

Fig. 1. Same model, same image, different classes, similar heatmaps [29].

3   Semantically-Augmented Labels

In this Section, we formally define our approach S-AL. We combine OHE ground truth vectors with auxiliary information, thus creating semantically augmented labels. Such labels can then be used in supervised image classification tasks in place of standard OHE vectors, so that no custom training loss or model architecture is necessary.

3.1   Semantic-Augmented Labels

Consider an image classification dataset, with X images and Y labels, and assume that $\bar{y}$ indicates the OHE ground-truth label spanning over C different classes (e.g. 10 in MNIST [9], 1000 in ImageNet [8]). Suppose we want to train a ML model in order to learn a mapping from X to Y. Then, if for an image $x \in X$ the model predicts the vector $\hat{y}$, the loss function is Cross-Entropy $(\bar{y}, \hat{y}) = -\sum_{i \in C} \bar{y}(i) \odot \log(\hat{y}(i))$.

Now, let $e_j \in \mathbb{R}^D$ be a D-dimensional real vector containing auxiliary information for class $j \in C$. Let $EM \in \mathbb{R}^{C \times D}$ be the embedding matrix stacking e_j, $\forall j \in C$. We then compute the Gram matrix of the set of vectors e_j, i.e. $EM \cdot EM^T$, and call it the *auxiliary information matrix*; furthermore, $\forall j \in C$, we call $EM \cdot EM^T[j] = \tilde{y}$ the auxiliary label for class j. Every $\tilde{y}$ vector has C elements and represents the similarities of the auxiliary information of the given class with all other auxiliary vectors.

In a first formulation, one can then define an enriched loss function as

$$-\left[\beta \sum_{i \in C} \bar{y}(i) \odot \log(\hat{y}(i)) + (1 - \beta) \sum_{i \in C} \tilde{y}(i) \odot \log(\hat{y}(i)) \right] \tag{1}$$

where the parameter β governs the balance between standard cross-entropy (leftmost addendum) and the novel regularisation term pertaining to the auxiliary information (rightmost addendum).

However, the OHE labels $\bar{y}$ and the auxiliary labels $\tilde{y}$ can be combined into augmented labels $\overset{+}{y}$ as follows:

$$\overset{+}{y} \equiv \beta \bar{y} + (1 - \beta) \tilde{y} \tag{2}$$

We can then merge Eq. 1 with Eq. 2, thus producing the loss function:

$$-\sum_{i \in C} \overset{+}{y}(i) \odot \log(\hat{y}(i)) \tag{3}$$

which corresponds to Cross-Entropy$(\overset{+}{y}, \hat{y})$. Therefore, we can enrich OHE ground truth vectors $\bar{y}$ with custom auxiliary information vectors $\tilde{y}$, producing semantically-augmented label vectors $\overset{+}{y}$ that can be plugged as ground truth vectors for in a standard cross-entropy loss function, and exploit them, for instance, for an image classification training/learning process.

Algorithm 1. Generation of Semantically-Augmented Labels

Require: class number C, auxiliary vectors $e_1, ..., e_C$
1: OHE matrix $\leftarrow$ identity matrix $C \times C$
2: Embedding matrix EM $\leftarrow$ Stack($[e_1, ..., e_C]$)
3: Auxiliary matrix AM $\leftarrow EM \cdot EM^T$
4: Augmented matrix S-AL $\leftarrow \beta$OHE $+ (1 - \beta)$AM
5: **return** S-AL

Our approach is summarised in Algorithm 1. In a nutshell, we can collect auxiliary information about the labels, stack them in an embedding matrix EM (line 2), then compute the Gram matrix of EM (line 3) and use its vectors as auxiliary labels for each class. We then compute a weighted sum of OHE labels with the auxiliary matrix AM and obtain semantically-augmented labels $\overset{+}{y} \in \mathbf{R}^{C \times C}$ (line 4) that can be used downstream as ground truth in standard cross-entropy loss. We stress that our approach is general, as it exploits the pairwise similarities of auxiliary labels, regardless of whether they belong to an ontology or not. In order to exemplify our approach and drive the experimental section, in the next Subsections we will discuss how to generate S-AL for two selected sources of auxiliary information: label hierarchies and word embeddings.

3.2   Exploiting Taxonomies

An ontology is a description of classes, properties, and relationships in a domain of knowledge. If the labels of the image classification task can be organised in an ontology, their relative position in the data structure can provide additional information about the relative similarity of the semantic concepts - e.g., one would expect the path from *spoon* to *tea-spoon* to be considerably shorter than the path from *spoon* to *shark*. A classical example of this link from the neural domain to the symbolic one is the aforementioned ImageNet-Wordnet link: every ImageNet label is a node in the Wordnet ontology. In principle, this allows to exploit semantic information when training or explaining ImageNet-based image classification ML models; however, this resourceful connection has seldom been exploited. In this paper, we focus on CIFAR100[1], a common image classification benchmarking dataset with the additional feature that its labels are connected in a taxonomy, outlined in Fig. 2.

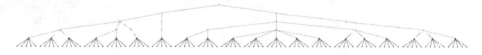

Fig. 2. Supporting taxonomy for the CIFAR100 labels.

CIFAR100 includes 100 classes, represented by the leaves of the tree. The authors of the dataset further group the 100 labels into 20 five-sized macro-classes, also called *coarse labels* or *superclasses*. For instance, the labels *maple, oak, palm, pine, willow* are clustered together in the macro-class *trees*. This original two-layered taxonomy corresponds to the two lowest layers of Fig. 2. The taxonomy was further extended with additional layers, corresponding to even larger groupings of labels. The resulting taxonomy encompasses 100 level-0 labels, 20 level-1

---

[1] http://www.cs.toronto.edu/$\sim$kriz/cifar.html.

labels, 8 level-2 and 4 level-3 labels, and 2 level-4 labels, with the single level-5 label corresponding to the *root* node of the taxonomy. Throughout the paper, we will often refer to hierarchical *depths* or *levels*.

In order to extract auxiliary information vectors from this taxonomy, we first extract the leave-to-root path of each class, and then stack the OHE of every step in the path. For instance, a class with path 23-45-5 will be encoded as the concatenation of three OHE vectors, with hot elements in position 23, 45 and 5 respectively. For CIFAR100, the resulting embedding matrix EM is depicted in Fig. 3.

Fig. 3. Taxonomy-derived embedding matrix EM for the CIFAR100 labels.

This matrix has 100 rows, encoding all classes in C. Since the hierarchy has 5 levels, we obtain an embedding dimension D of 500, due to the stacking of 5 100-units OHE vectors. One can observe that the leftmost part of EM corresponds to the identity matrix of the single classes, whereas the rightmost part has only hot elements in the first two columns, since the level-4 labels can only be 0 or 1. As a minor implementation detail, we remark that the zero-padding will have no influence when computing the Gram matrix of EM in order to obtain the semantically-augmented labels.

For CIFAR100, the auxiliary labels $EM \cdot EM^T$ are computed from the embedding matrix EM depicted in Fig. 3. By combining the auxiliary labels with the OHE labels, the resulting S-AL matrix is depicted in Fig. 4a.

Re-arranging the CIFAR100 classes for semantic similarity (Fig. 4b), one can visually inspect the S-AL. We observe how these labels capture similarities at various hierarchical depths, represented by coloured blocks of different size. The diagonal represent self-similarities, while the small regular five-by-five blocks along the diagonal represent the similarities within macro-groups of labels (corresponding to the coarse labels in CIFAR100, such as the *tree* case mentioned above). Larger blocks correspond to higher levels in the taxonomy. The S-AL depicted in Fig. 4a will be used as ground truth to train image classifiers in the experimental part of the paper. We remark that the re-arrangement is for visualisation purposes, and that the matching between class index and S-AL is never modified.

For further visual inspection, in Fig. 5 we report a t-SNE [21] embedding of the hierarchy-augmented labels for CIFAR100. t-SNE (*t-distributed Stochastic*

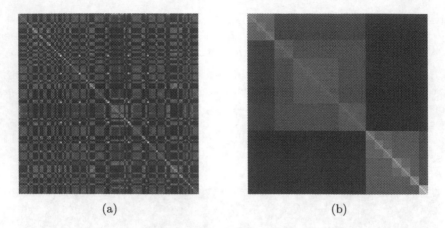

(a)   (b)

Fig. 4. Taxonomy-derived S-AL matrix for the CIFAR100 labels. The original class order (a) can be taxonomically sorted (b) for visual inspection.

Neighbour Embedding) is an unsupervised dimensionality reduction technique for embedding high-dimensional data in a low-dimensional space of two dimensions.

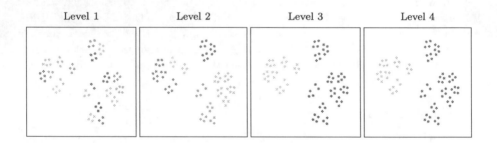

Fig. 5. t-SNE compression of the S-AL for CIFAR100 classes.

The color-coding is applied afterwards and corresponds to labels at different hierarchical depths, going from level-1 (original 100 CIFAR100 coarse labels) to level-4 (two macro-groups below the root in Fig. 2). At level-0 all data points would be coloured with 100 independent colours, whereas level-5 would be monochromatic, so we omit these two panels. Instead, we depict the color-coding for all other depths in the taxonomy, showing how S-AL display similarities at every aggregation level. The intuition that will drive our experiments is that these augmented labels can be a better ground truth, with respect to simple/standard OHE vectors, for image classification tasks.

3.3   Exploiting Word Embeddings

It is not always the case that labels belong to an ontology or can be arranged in a hierarchical taxonomy. Our approach allows to exploit any auxiliary information about a label, provided that it can be expressed as a vector. We argue that Word Embeddings represent the perfect candidate for this: it is straightforward to obtain vector representations for labels, and the Euclidean distance (or cosine similarity) between two word vectors provides an effective method for measuring the linguistic or semantic similarity of the corresponding words.

Fig. 6. GloVe-derived embedding matrix *EM* for the CIFAR100 labels.

In this paper we exploit GloVe [25] (*Global Vectors for Word Representation*) to obtain the vector representations of all 100 classes of CIFAR100. The resulting augmented labels are depicted in Fig. 6. One can observe how these vectors are denser, compared to the ones extracted from the ontology and displayed in Fig. 3. However, we follow the same procedure outlined in Algorithm 1, thus obtaining a S-AL matrix that we will later use as image classification ground truth for the experimental phase. We remark that in this case we are not tapping into CIFAR00's provided taxonomy - instead, we are interested in exploring the contextual relationship between labels (emerging from GloVe embeddings) when paired with the visual similarities that occurs in CIFAR100 images. The GloVe-derived S-AL for CIFAR100 are depicted in Fig. 7a. In Fig. 7b, we show a different class arrangement, defined through a hierarchical clustering procedure. We remark again that this is merely for visualisation purposes, and has no impact on the downstream training task.

As for the taxonomical case, we ran our S-AL through t-SNE in order to visually inspect whether they preserve some structure at different hierarchical depths. We remark that, in this case, the hierarchical structure is not part of the augmented labels, which are computed from OHE labels and GloVe embeddings; instead, we use hierarchical levels to visualise and inspect the obtained S-AL.

It is not surprising that the t-SNE embedding of GloVe augmented labels in Fig. 8 is less clustered when compared to the hierarchical labels in Fig. 5, but

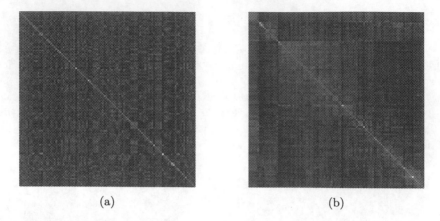

(a)   (b)

Fig. 7. GloVe-derived S-AL matrix for the CIFAR100 labels.

Level 1   Level 2   Level 3   Level 4

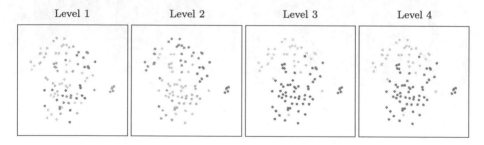

Fig. 8. t-SNE visualisation of the GloVe-augmented labels

at the same time one can appreciate the structure emerging at levels 3 and 4. These augmented labels derive from word embeddings, so their relative similarities might follow a different logic with respect to the hierarchical ones: for instance, in panel 3 there is a lonesome light blue dot in the lower half, surrounded by red ones. That dot is *sea*, and amongst the surrounding red dots we have *aquarium_fish, crab, crocodile, dolphin, flatfish, otter, shark, trout, turtle, whale*. These marine (or at least aquatic) animals are taxonomically very different from *sea*, and this is captured by the different colour-coding, but they clearly share semantic similarities with *sea* and the proximity of these points in the (t-SNE reduced) S-AL space shows how the semantic information extracted from GloVe embeddings carries this information.

4   Experimental Settings

In this section we describe the experimental settings that we adopted to train models and evaluate the impact of injecting knowledge in the image classification process through S-AL.

4.1 Data and Models

As mentioned in the previous Section, we focus on CIFAR100, an image classification dataset commonly used as benchmark. We exploited the CIFAR100 taxonomy and GloVe embeddings of the labels to generate S-AL; furthermore, we refer to the taxonomy in Fig. 2 when discussing depths/levels.

The set of image classifiers we trained for our experimental phase is the following:

- **XENT:** we trained a Wide ResNet model with standard cross-entropy, to be used as a reference point for fine-grained image classification accuracy, and as a baseline for all other evaluations.

- **HAF** refers to the Hierarchy Aware Features (HAF) model as described in Garg et al. [14]. We used the available code and re-trained the model for comparison with S-AL when dealing with taxonomically-enriched labels. However, we remark that HAF is explicitly trained on the hierarchy, and therefore cannot be used for comparison in the GloVe-based set of experiments.

- **SOFT*** refers to the soft-label approach of Bertinetto et al. [4]. As we did for HAF, we adopted already used values for the hyperparameters, in order to reproduce the original results. For SOFT*, we trained two parametrised versions, SOFT4 and SOFT30. Also SOFT* is limited to be used for the taxonomical case only.

- **HT-AL*** is a family of models trained with our S-AL approach, where the auxiliary information is obtained from the hierarchical taxonomy (HT), as discussed in Subsect. 3.2. For every model HT-ALx, x indicates the value of β used to compute the S-AL.

- **WE-AL***, analogously, is a family of models trained with our S-AL approach, where the auxiliary information is obtained from a word embedding (WE), as discussed in Subsect. 3.3.

The synopsis of these models is summarised in Table 1.

Table 1. Overview of models of the experimental phase

Model(s)	Label	Notes
XENT	OHE	Baseline
SOFT4	Hierarchy	Cannot encode embeddings
SOFT30	Hierarchy	Cannot encode embeddings
HAF	Hierarchy	Cannot encode embeddings
HT-ALβ	Hierarchy-augmented	Our approach
WE-ALβ	GloVe-augmented	Our approach

We briefly report how, while we kept all architecture models as similar as possible, including the number of training epochs, we observed how HAF required more training time with respect to all other models (with a factor spanning from ×3 to ×4). We conjecture that this is due to the higher complexity of the architecture (multiple classification heads) and the fact that the training loss is composed by four independent terms.

4.2   Image Classification

The very first metric to be taken into account is, obviously, classification accuracy - that is, the percentage of (out-of-sample) datapoints that a model is able to correctly classify. We extend this metric by evaluating it at every ontological depth: for instance, since *maple* and *oak* (level-0 labels) are both *trees* (level-1 label), a *maple* image which is classified as *oak* will be considered a level-0 error, but a level-1 correct classification.

Second, we measure the average mistake severity, a performance measure introduced by Bertinetto et al. [4]. The mistake severity takes into account misclassified images, and measures the *lowest common ancestor* (LCA) distance between true and predicted labels; the average LCA across all misclassifications is then reported. This error metric ignores the *quantity* of mistakes made by the model, trying to characterise their *quality* instead. Clearly, this entails that if model A classifies all images correctly but one, and in that single case the semantic distance is high (e.g. *maple - rocket*), and model B misclassifies all images but always predicting ontologically similar classes (e.g. *maple - oak*), the mistake severity will rank B as the best method of the two. Therefore, we argue that mistake severity, albeit informative, should also be paired with other metrics, such as explainability.

4.3   Representation Learning

We are interested in investigating whether S-AL impacts the inner knowledge representation learned by a ML model. To do so, we use all models as feature extractors and analyse the feature space on which the out-of-sample images are projected. Intuitively, standard OHE-supervised training forces the ML model to project all images of one class to a compact point cloud, but there is nothing enforcing that point clouds of similar classes should be close to each other. Our hope is that, by injecting semantic information, the compactness of single point clouds is preserved, but the feature space is reorganised in such a way that semantically similar classes are geometrically close. To measure this, for each taxonomy level x we assign each feature vector to its corresponding level-x label - e.g., for level-1 we label *trees* each feature vector corresponding to images of maples, oaks, etc. We then run several clustering evaluation metrics on the resulting partition system to inspect the compactness of the emerged clusters.

4.4   Explainability

Finally, we test the impact of our approach on the produced explanations. We conduct our experiments in order to inspect whether S-AL, by injecting auxiliary information in the image classification process, manages to mitigate the husky-flute effect mentioned in Sect. 2. Ideally, the similarity of two heatmaps should be proportional to the ontological proximity of the two classes they explain.

We exploiting three standard explainers (*Integrated Gradients*, *Input-X Gradient*, and *Saliency*), all available within the Captum library[2]. We then produce explanations (heatmaps) for every image in the CIFAR100 test set, for every ML model listed above, and every output neuron, corresponding to a class. We are interested in comparing the true class, and true class heatmap, with all other classes. For instance, referring again to the famous example in Fig. 1, we are interested in comparing the classes of *husky* and *flute*, and the heatmaps produced for *husky* and for *flute*. For brevity, we will refer to the true class heatmap as *true_heatmap* and to any currently explained class heatmap as *expl_heatmap*.

We rely on the CIFAR100 ontology to define the semantic pairwise distance between classes. We observe that there is no consensus regarding metrics for heatmap comparison or benchmarking, and we therefore implemented several custom functions:

- **Mean Absolute Difference:** average absolute value of the per-pixel difference between *true_heatmap* and *expl_heatmap*.

- **Deletion Curve Distance:** using the *true_heatmap* to rank pixels, spanning from the highest-scoring to the lowest-scoring locations, we progressively remove elements from both *true_heatmap* and *expl_heatmap*. At each step we compute the sum of the two remaining heatmaps, and compare the two resulting curves. This metric is inspired by the Deletion Curve [26].

- **Spearman Distance:** we compute the Spearman-ranking correlation between the two heatmaps, normalising it in the 0–1 range.

- **Progressive Binarisation:** we extract a set of progressive thresholds from the *true_heatmap* and use them to binarise both heatmaps. We then check the intersection of the resulting pairs of masks at each step.

5   Experimental Results

5.1   Image Classification

Our first goal is to verify how S-AL models perform in terms of image classification error quantity and quality: we report our results in Table 2. Each row

---

[2] https://captum.ai/.

Table 2. Accuracy and mistake severity for all trained ML models.

	Error@1	Error@5	MS	HD@1	HD@5	HD@20
XENT	22.462	6.234	2.364	0.531	2.242	3.178
SOFT-4	32.580	16.480	2.206	0.719	1.235	2.223
SOFT-30	26.650	8.940	2.331	0.621	1.375	2.798
HAF	22.420	6.414	2.251	0.505	1.422	2.640
HT-AL ($\beta = 0.30$)	23.390	7.690	2.237	0.523	1.233	2.195
HT-AL ($\beta = 0.35$)	22.820	7.510	2.252	0.514	1.236	2.195
HT-AL ($\beta = 0.40$)	22.718	7.398	2.218	0.504	1.233	2.192
HT-AL ($\beta = 0.45$)	22.760	7.060	2.219	0.505	1.242	2.194
HT-AL ($\beta = 0.50$)	22.710	7.240	2.262	0.514	1.256	2.199
WE-AL ($\beta = 0.30$)	23.230	7.640	2.303	0.535	1.836	2.808
WE-AL ($\beta = 0.35$)	23.270	7.240	2.312	0.538	1.841	2.817
WE-AL ($\beta = 0.40$)	23.260	7.040	2.311	0.538	1.851	2.822
WE-AL ($\beta = 0.45$)	22.870	6.920	2.320	0.530	1.849	2.815
WE-AL ($\beta = 0.50$)	22.760	6.820	2.291	0.521	1.864	2.823
WE-AL ($\beta = 0.55$)	22.380	6.820	2.332	0.522	1.879	2.824
WE-AL ($\beta = 0.60$)	22.490	6.490	2.349	0.528	1.887	2.833
WE-AL ($\beta = 0.65$)	22.450	6.290	2.325	0.522	1.907	2.834
WE-AL ($\beta = 0.70$)	22.206	6.314	2.307	0.512	1.914	2.843
WE-AL ($\beta = 0.75$)	22.270	6.420	2.302	0.513	1.931	2.853

indicates a model; the columns indicate the top-1 and top-5 classification error percentage (*Error@1, Error@5*), the average hierarchical distance between true and predicted labels for misclassifications, also called *mistake severity* (*MS*), and the average hierarchical distance when taking into account the top-k predictions (*HD@1, HD@5, HD@20*). We remark that *MS* takes only into account misclassified data points, while *HD@k* includes all cases. We thus successfully reproduced [4,14] the results of XENT, HAF and SOFT*. We observe that SOFT4 and SOFT30 do not produce competitive results in terms of accuracy, and we therefore exclude them for further experiments. HAF, on the other hand, yields competitive scores and will be kept. Regarding our models, reasonable choices for β seem to be 0.4 for HT-AL and 0.7 for WE-AL: from now on we will therefore conduct experiments with HT-AL ($\beta = 0.4$) and WE-AL ($\beta = 0.7$), which we will simply indicate as HT-AL and WE-AL.

We therefore select XENT, HAF, HT-AL and WE-AL. For these models we run multiple experiments with different seeds in order to obtain error bars. We report the results in the first row of Table 3, corresponding to level-0. Furthermore, for the selected models we report error and MS at different hierarchical depths. The results of Table 3 can be also visualised as scatterplots, and we do so in Fig. 9.

Table 3. Error and MS, at all hierarchical depths, for our selected models.

Level		XENT	HAF	HT-AL	WE-AL
0	Error@1	22.462 ± 0.283	22.420 ± 0.203	22.718 ± 0.267	22.206 ± 0.430
	Error@5	6.234 ± 0.118	6.414 ± 0.230	7.398 ± 0.148	6.314 ± 0.080
	MS	2.364 ± 0.025	2.251 ± 0.018	2.218 ± 0.021	2.307 ± 0.022
1	Error@1	14.002 ± 0.170	13.470 ± 0.188	13.554 ± 0.153	13.598 ± 0.396
	Error@5	3.058 ± 0.086	3.966 ± 0.187	5.218 ± 0.114	3.556 ± 0.151
	MS	2.188 ± 0.027	2.082 ± 0.029	2.042 ± 0.023	2.134 ± 0.027
2	Error@1	9.182 ± 0.184	8.372 ± 0.107	8.312 ± 0.128	8.652 ± 0.283
	Error@5	1.322 ± 0.032	2.256 ± 0.143	3.672 ± 0.064	1.770 ± 0.154
	MS	1.812 ± 0.026	1.741 ± 0.030	1.698 ± 0.020	1.782 ± 0.013
3	Error@1	4.488 ± 0.108	3.780 ± 0.129	3.552 ± 0.119	4.088 ± 0.167
	Error@5	0.396 ± 0.030	0.976 ± 0.093	2.238 ± 0.093	0.790 ± 0.095
	MS	1.661 ± 0.020	1.641 ± 0.034	1.635 ± 0.018	1.656 ± 0.012
4	Error@1	2.966 ± 0.131	2.424 ± 0.177	2.254 ± 0.094	2.682 ± 0.144
	Error@5	0.196 ± 0.021	0.626 ± 0.087	1.660 ± 0.091	0.404 ± 0.066
	MS	1.000 ± 0.000	1.000 ± 0.000	1.000 ± 0.000	1.000 ± 0.000

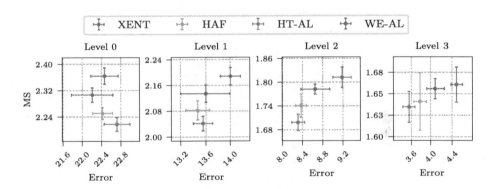

Fig. 9. Error and MS, ad different hierarchical depths, for the selected models.

In accordance with the previous Sections, each panel represents a specific depth, or level, in the CIFAR100 hierarchy. We omit the panel of level-5, since it corresponds to the hierarchy root, and level-4, since at that level there are only two sub-groups, and therefore the mistake severity has constant value of 1. Concerning accuracy (*error*, x-axis), we observe how all alternative models (HT-AL, WE-AL and HAF) perform comparably to XENT at level-0 (fine labels, standard classification), but outperform it for all other levels. Concerning MS, the model ranking is the same at all depths: HT-AL performs best, followed by HAF, then WE-AL, and finally XENT. We remark that HT-AL and HAF were trained on labels derived from CIFAR100, while WE-AL was not. We observe how HAF's MS error bar widens as the levels progress. In general, these experiments confirm our expectation that the injection of auxiliary knowledge can mitigate the hierarchical distance of misclassifications of a ML model at all hierarchical levels while maintaining competitive accuracy results.

5.2   Representation Learning

Besides confirming that S-AL produces models which are competitive in terms of classification accuracy, we are also interested in peeking into the internal representation of knowledge that they have learned. In order to do so, we use our selected trained models XENT, HAF, HT-AL and WE-AL as feature extractors, mapping all images of the test set of CIFAR100 into a 512-dimensional latent feature space. As a first experiment, we use t-SNE again to reduce the dimensionality of the feature space, so that it can be visually inspected. We color-code all data points according to their label at different hierarchical levels, and report the resulting scatterplot in Fig. 10. As a second step of analysis, we compute the pairwise cosine similarities between feature vectors, and report it in Fig. 11. We observe how XENT shows no emerging structure besides the diagonal, HAF displays similarity blocks at different depths. Also HT-AL displays similarity blocks, but with strong visual importance to level-4 (two macro-blocks); finally, WE-AL shows shows a visually weaker structure.

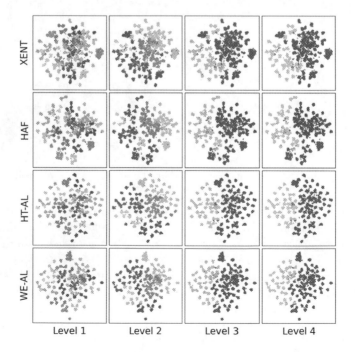

Fig. 10. t-SNE compression of the feature vectors extracted from the CIFAR100 test set. Colour-coded afterwards according to level-k labels.

Fig. 11. Visual inspection of the feature spaces for the selected models. From left to right: XENT, HAF, HT-AL, and WE-AL.

However, besides intuitive visual inspections, we are interested in quantitatively characterising the feature space of each model. In order to do so, for each model and hierarchy level k, we partition the feature vectors into clusters according to their level-k labels, and run cluster validation metrics to assess the compactness of the emerging point clouds. We report the results in Table 4. The selected cluster evaluation metrics are the Silhouette score, (a standard choice), the Calinski-Harabasz score, and S-Dbw, the best metric according to a comparative review by Liu et al. [20] Our results show that our models systematically outperform XENT at every hierarchical level in terms of cluster validation metrics. Furthermore, HT-AL provides better S-Dbw scores than HAF. This confirms our expectation: S-AL allows for a structured internal representation learning, so that ontologically-similar labels are projected into contiguous areas of the feature space.

Table 4. Clustering evaluation for all feature spaces.

Level	Metric	XENT	HAF	HT-AL	WE-AL
0	Silhouette (↑)	0.211 ± 0.002	0.232 ± 0.002	0.280 ± 0.003	0.299 ± 0.004
	Calinski-Harabasz (↑)	162.5 ± 1.3	271.4 ± 3.1	298.3 ± 3.2	181.3 ± 2.2
	S-Dbw (↓)	0.613 ± 0.001	0.512 ± 0.002	0.493 ± 0.002	0.588 ± 0.002
1	Silhouette (↑)	0.083 ± 0.001	0.163 ± 0.002	0.110 ± 0.000	0.100 ± 0.001
	Calinski-Harabasz (↑)	178.1 ± 1.7	552.8 ± 4.4	583.9 ± 3.7	185.4 ± 0.9
	S-Dbw (↓)	0.863 ± 0.001	0.698 ± 0.001	0.688 ± 0.001	0.859 ± 0.001
2	Silhouette (↑)	0.052 ± 0.001	0.156 ± 0.001	0.098 ± 0.001	0.059 ± 0.001
	Calinski-Harabasz (↑)	221.0 ± 2.0	841.8 ± 3.9	1200.1 ± 7.4	250.9 ± 1.6
	S-Dbw (↓)	0.918 ± 0.001	0.763 ± 0.001	0.717 ± 0.001	0.906 ± 0.001
3	Silhouette (↑)	0.043 ± 0.001	0.146 ± 0.001	0.121 ± 0.002	0.050 ± 0.002
	Calinski-Harabasz (↑)	253.9 ± 4.2	1040.1 ± 5.4	2239.8 ± 11.3	327.6 ± 4.5
	S-Dbw (↓)	0.933 ± 0.002	0.802 ± 0.002	0.736 ± 0.003	0.922 ± 0.001
4	Silhouette (↑)	0.037 ± 0.001	0.136 ± 0.002	0.311 ± 0.002	0.050 ± 0.001
	Calinski-Harabasz (↑)	302.6 ± 8.9	1519.2 ± 19.1	5111.6 ± 38.5	467.4 ± 6.9
	S-Dbw (↓)	0.989 ± 0.001	0.917 ± 0.000	0.799 ± 0.000	0.975 ± 0.001

5.3   Explainability

Finally, we inspect the heatmaps produced by XAI algorithms, looking for correlations between ontological label proximity and generated heatmap similarity. We generate 48 million distance measures (10000 images in the CIFAR100 test set × 100 possible classes × 4 selected models × 3 XAI algorithms × 4 distance metrics), and partition them according to the original two-levels CIFAR100 taxonomy or the more relevant five-levels one, thus approaching the 100M data points. For space constraints, below we only show a selected subset of results. For Fig. 12, we focused on the *Progressive Binarisation* metric, and we partitioned on the original two-levels CIFAR100 taxonomy - which is why the x-axis has violins for the semantic distances of 0, 1, and 2. Every row of panels corresponds to an explainer (respectively, *Integrated Gradients*, *Input X Gradients* and *Saliency*), and every column corresponds to a selected model: XENT, HAF, HT-AL, WE-AL. For all panels, a violin plot at position k represents the aggregation of heatmap distances that involved labels at ontological distance k. For the *husky-flute* example image, the *husky* label has distance 0 (true label), the *dog* label has distance 1 (similar label), and the *flute* label has distance 2 (faraway concept). Thus, the *husky-heatmap/dog-heatmap* distance would end up in the 2-distance violin (regardless of model, metric, and explainer). We note that all distance-0 violins correspond to trivial same-heatmap comparisons, and therefore correspond to 0. Our goal is to have higher/wider violins for distance-2, with respect to distance-1. We observe that XENT has a non-null baseline, and this is likely due to the visual similarity of images belonging to similar classes.

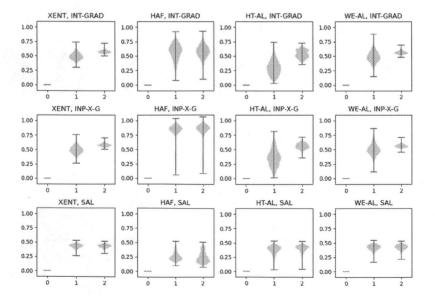

Fig. 12. Relation between ontological label distance and produced heatmaps

HAF produces almost identical violins for distance 1 and distance 2 in all panels. Conversely, S-AL models produce pairs of distinguishable violins - especially for the HT-AL model: this shows that the auxiliary information injected in the augmented labels positively conditioned the model's training. Finally, we note how *Saliency* systematically fails to detect any ontology-driven distance.

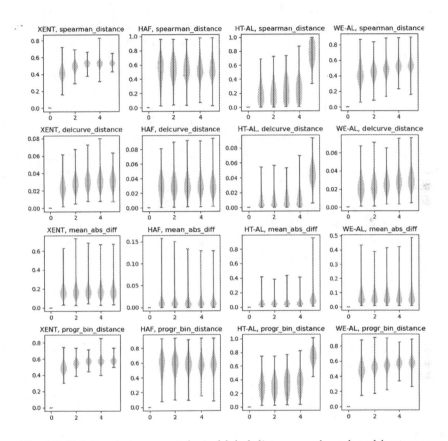

Fig. 13. Relation between ontological label distance and produced heatmaps

For Fig. 13, we used the full 5-levels CIFAR100 ontology, all models (one per column), all distance metrics (one per row), and we focused on the *Integrated Gradients* explainer. As for the previous case, we observe how XENT has a nontrivial baseline, HAF does not capture the taxonomical hierarchy information, while HT-AL does. Curiously, the heatmaps corresponding to distance-5 labels seem remarkably more different than the others, while only minor differences appear from distance-1 to distance-4 labels. This seems to correlate with the two blocks visible in Fig. 11, second panel.

6   Conclusions and Future Work

In this paper, we introduced **Semantically-Augmented Labels**, a general approach to combine OHE labels with arbitrary auxiliary semantic information so that the resulting augmented ground truth can be used for image classification training procedures, without the need for custom loss functions or model architectures. Starting from the benchmark dataset of CIFAR100, we showed how to apply our approach to ontological information (**HT-AL**) and GloVe-derived word embedding vectors (**WE-AL**). We conducted experiments and analysed the impact and implications of our approach in terms of machine learning performance, organisation of the learned feature space, and characterisation of the produced explanation heatmaps. We showed how our approach allows to train ML models whose accuracy is competitive with respect to a classically trained baseline; at the same time, our models showed interesting results in terms of generalisation to super-classes (level > 1 error rates), organisation of the feature space (cluster quality) and differentiation between explanations (heatmap distances).

We hope this approach can provide a useful middle ground in the debate between post-hoc explainability and the design of custom interpretable models. With the former, we share the goal of exploiting as much as possible existing standard architectures and loss functions, since (i) they have proved to work very well and (ii) this allows to tap into a plethora of boilerplate code and existing repositories. On the other hand, we share with the latter the intuition that intervening in the learning phase, rather than after it, allows for more room for action.

Concerning directions for future work, the first natural evolution is to tackle bigger datasets, such ad iNaturalist or ImageNet. While both image datasets are paired with hierarchical taxonomies of labels, we are interested in exploring the impact of injecting different types of embedding-based semantic information.

Another line of research we are already exploring is whether S-AL models can display increased robustness to adversarial attacks. Intuitively, it is often speculated that adversarial attacks exploit anomalies in the decision boundary of an image classifier. The injection of auxiliary semantic information could allow for more control of the learned feature space, thus making it more adherent to human intuition - for instance, projecting *turtle* and *rifle* images on non-neighbouring areas. This might make the decision boundary smoother and less prone to human-counterintuitive mistakes.

Acknowledgments. This work has been partially supported by the "National Centre for HPC, Big Data and Quantum Computing" - Spoke 1 funded by NextGenerationEU.

References

1. Akata, Z., Reed, S., Walter, D., Lee, H., Schiele, B.: Evaluation of output embeddings for fine-grained image classification. In: Proceedings of the IEEE Conference on Computer Vision and Pattern Recognition (2015)

2. Barz, B., Denzler, J.: Hierarchy-based image embeddings for semantic image retrieval. In: 2019 IEEE Winter Conference on Applications of Computer Vision (WACV), pp. 638–647. IEEE (2019)
3. Bengio, S., Weston, J., Grangier, D.: Label embedding trees for large multi-class tasks. In: Advances in Neural Information Processing Systems, vol. 23 (2010)
4. Bertinetto, L., Mueller, R., Tertikas, K., Samangooei, S., Lord, N.A.: Making better mistakes: leveraging class hierarchies with deep networks. In: Proceedings of the IEEE/CVF Conference on Computer Vision and Pattern Recognition (2020)
5. Camacho-Collados, J., Pilehvar, M.T.: Embeddings in natural language processing. In: Proceedings of the 28th International Conference on Computational Linguistics: Tutorial Abstracts, Barcelona, Spain (Online) (2020)
6. Chang, D., Pang, K., Zheng, Y., Ma, Z., Song, Y.Z., Guo, J.: Your "flamingo" is my "bird": fine-grained, or not. In: Proceedings of the IEEE/CVF Conference on Computer Vision and Pattern Recognition, pp. 11476–11485 (2021)
7. Deng, J., Berg, A.C., Li, K., Fei-Fei, L.: What does classifying more than 10,000 image categories tell us? In: Daniilidis, K., Maragos, P., Paragios, N. (eds.) ECCV 2010, Part V. LNCS, vol. 6315, pp. 71–84. Springer, Heidelberg (2010). https://doi.org/10.1007/978-3-642-15555-0_6
8. Deng, J., Dong, W., Socher, R., Li, L.J., Li, K., Fei-Fei, L.: ImageNet: a large-scale hierarchical image database. In: 2009 IEEE Conference on Computer Vision and Pattern Recognition, pp. 248–255 (2009)
9. Deng, L.: The MNIST database of handwritten digit images for machine learning research. IEEE Signal Process. Mag. **29**(6), 141–142 (2012)
10. Dong, Y., Su, H., Zhu, J., Zhang, B.: Improving interpretability of deep neural networks with semantic information. In: IEEE CVPR (2017)
11. Došilović, F.K., Brčić, M., Hlupić, N.: Explainable artificial intelligence: a survey. In: 2018 41st International Convention on Information and Communication Technology, Electronics and Microelectronics (MIPRO), pp. 0210–0215 (2018)
12. Fellbaum, C.: WordNet: An Electronic Lexical Database. Bradford Books (1998)
13. Frome, A., et al.: DeViSE: a deep visual-semantic embedding model. In: Advances in Neural Information Processing Systems, vol. 26 (2013)
14. Garg, A., Sani, D., Anand, S.: Learning hierarchy aware features for reducing mistake severity. In: Avidan, S., Brostow, G., Cissé, M., Farinella, G.M., Hassner, T. (eds.) ECCV 2022. LNCS, vol. 13684, pp. 252–267. Springer, Cham (2022). https://doi.org/10.1007/978-3-031-20053-3_15
15. He, K., Zhang, X., Ren, S., Sun, J.: Deep residual learning for image recognition. In: Proceedings of the IEEE Conference on Computer Vision and Pattern Recognition (2016)
16. Hu, J., Shen, L., Sun, G.: Squeeze-and-excitation networks. In: Proceedings of the IEEE Conference on Computer Vision and Pattern Recognition (2018)
17. Krizhevsky, A., Sutskever, I., Hinton, G.E.: ImageNet classification with deep convolutional neural networks. In: Advances in Neural Information Processing Systems, pp. 1097–1105 (2012)
18. Lipton, Z.C.: The mythos of model interpretability: in machine learning, the concept of interpretability is both important and slippery. Queue **16**(3), 31–57 (2018)
19. Liu, S., Chen, J., Pan, L., Ngo, C.W., Chua, T.S., Jiang, Y.G.: Hyperbolic visual embedding learning for zero-shot recognition. In: Proceedings of the IEEE/CVF Conference on Computer Vision and Pattern Recognition, pp. 9273–9281 (2020)
20. Liu, Y., Li, Z., Xiong, H., Gao, X., Wu, J.: Understanding of internal clustering validation measures. In: IEEE International Conference on Data Mining (2010)

21. van der Maaten, L., Hinton, G.: Visualizing data using t-SNE. J. Mach. Learn. Res. **9**, 2579–2605 (2008)
22. Morin, F., Bengio, Y.: Hierarchical probabilistic neural network language model. In: International Workshop on Artificial Intelligence and Statistics. PMLR (2005)
23. Pasini, A., Giobergia, F., Pastor, E., Baralis, E.: Semantic image collection summarization with frequent subgraph mining. IEEE Access **10**, 131747–131764 (2022)
24. Pastor, E., Baralis, E.: Explaining black box models by means of local rules. In: Proceedings of the 34th ACM/SIGAPP Symposium on Applied Computing, SAC 2019, pp. 510–517. Association for Computing Machinery (2019)
25. Pennington, J., Socher, R., Manning, C.D.: GloVe: global vectors for word representation. In: EMNLP, vol. 14, pp. 1532–1543 (2014)
26. Petsiuk, V., Das, A., Saenko, K.: RISE: randomized input sampling for explanation of black-box models (2018)
27. Redmon, J., Farhadi, A.: YOLO9000: better, faster, stronger. In: Proceedings of the IEEE Conference on Computer Vision and Pattern Recognition, pp. 7263–7271 (2017)
28. Ribeiro, M.T., Singh, S., Guestrin, C.: "Why should I trust you?": explaining the predictions of any classifier. In: ACM SIGKDD 2016, KDD 2016 (2016)
29. Rudin, C.: Stop explaining black box machine learning models for high stakes decisions and use interpretable models instead. Nat. Mach. Intell. **1**(5), 206–215 (2019)
30. Shrikumar, A., Greenside, P., Kundaje, A.: Learning important features through propagating activation differences. In: Precup, D., Teh, Y.W. (eds.) Proceedings of the 34th International Conference on Machine Learning, vol. 70. PMLR (2017)
31. Silla, C.N., Freitas, A.A.: A survey of hierarchical classification across different application domains. Data Min. Knowl. Disc. **22**, 31–72 (2011)
32. Simonyan, K., Vedaldi, A., Zisserman, A.: Deep inside convolutional networks: visualising image classification models and saliency maps. In: Workshop at International Conference on Learning Representations (2014)
33. Simonyan, K., Zisserman, A.: Very deep convolutional networks for large-scale image recognition. arXiv preprint arXiv:1409.1556 (2014)
34. Sundararajan, M., Taly, A., Yan, Q.: Axiomatic attribution for deep networks. In: International Conference on Machine Learning (2017)
35. van der Velden, B.H., Kuijf, H.J., Gilhuijs, K.G., Viergever, M.A.: Explainable artificial intelligence (XAI) in deep learning-based medical image analysis. Med. Image Anal. **79**, 102470 (2022)
36. Verma, N., Mahajan, D., Sellamanickam, S., Nair, V.: Learning hierarchical similarity metrics. In: IEEE Conference on Computer Vision and Pattern Recognition (2012)
37. Wang, S., Zhou, W., Jiang, C.: A survey of word embeddings based on deep learning. Computing **102**, 717–740 (2019)
38. Wu, H., Merler, M., Uceda-Sosa, R., Smith, J.R.: Learning to make better mistakes: semantics-aware visual food recognition. In: Proceedings of the 24th ACM International Conference on Multimedia, pp. 172–176 (2016)
39. Xian, Y., Akata, Z., Sharma, G., Nguyen, Q., Hein, M., Schiele, B.: Latent embeddings for zero-shot classification. In: Proceedings of the IEEE Conference on Computer Vision and Pattern Recognition, pp. 69–77 (2016)

Finding Spurious Correlations
with Function-Semantic Contrast Analysis

Kirill Bykov[1,2,4(✉)] ⓘD, Laura Kopf[2,3] ⓘD, and Marina M.-C. Höhne[2,3,4,5] ⓘD

[1] Department of Electrical Engineering and Computer Science, Technische Universität Berlin, 10587 Berlin, Germany
[2] Understandable Machine Intelligence Lab, Leibniz Institute for Agricultural Engineering and Bioeconomy, 14469 Potsdam, Germany
`{kbykov,lkopf,mhoehne}@atb-potsdam.de`
[3] Department of Computer Science, University of Potsdam, 14476 Potsdam, Germany
[4] BIFOLD – Berlin Institute for the Foundations of Learning and Data, 10587 Berlin, Germany
[5] UiT the Arctic University of Norway, 9037 Tromsø, Norway

Abstract. In the field of Computer Vision (CV), the degree to which two objects, e.g. two classes, share a common conceptual meaning, known as semantic similarity, is closely linked to the visual resemblance of their physical appearances in the data: entities with higher semantic similarity, typically exhibit greater visual resemblance than entities with lower semantic similarity. Deep Neural Networks (DNNs) employed for classification exploit this visual similarity, incorporating it into the network's representations (e.g., neurons), resulting in the functional similarity between the learned representations of visually akin classes, often manifesting in correlated activation patterns. However, such functional similarities can also emerge from spurious correlations — undesired auxiliary features that are shared between classes, such as backgrounds or specific artifacts. In this work, we present the *Function-Semantic Contrast Analysis* (FSCA) method, which identifies potential unintended correlations between network representations by examining the contrast between the functional distance of representations and the knowledge-based semantic distance between the concepts these representations were trained to recognize. While natural discrepancy is expected, our results indicate that these differences often originate from harmful spurious correlations in the data. We validate our approach by examining the presence of spurious correlations in widely-used CV architectures, demonstrating that FSCA offers a scalable solution for discovering previously undiscovered biases, that reduces the need for human supervision and is applicable across various Image Classification problems.

Keywords: Explainable AI · Shortcut identification · Representation Analysis · Clever-Hans effect · Black-box model auditing

---

The original version of this chapter was previously published non-open access. A Correction to this chapter is available at https://doi.org/10.1007/978-3-031-44067-0_33

L. Longo (Ed.): xAI 2023, CCIS 1902, pp. 549–572, 2023.
https://doi.org/10.1007/978-3-031-44067-0_28

1   Introduction

In recent years, Deep Learning has exhibited remarkable progress in addressing the diverse challenges in the field of Computer Vision (CV) [21], such as image classification [24,79], object detection [77,80], and semantic segmentation [39,50]. This success can be largely attributed to the powerful hierarchical representations learned by DNNs, which are capable of capturing intricate patterns and features within visual data [7]. However, a prevailing concern remains the inherent obscurity of the learned representations within these models. As a consequence, DNNs are often referred to as "black-box" systems, since their internal mechanisms are not readily interpretable or comprehensible to human observers.

While being powerful in capturing intricate patterns within the data, DNNs are susceptible to learning spurious correlations—coincidental relationships, often driven by an unobserved confounding factor, which may lead the model to identify and rely on such misleading patterns [31,68]. Model dependence on such artifactual features could lead to poor generalization performance of the model on different datasets and pose a substantial risk in the case of safety-critical areas. As such, the identification and subsequent mitigation of these spurious correlations within models are crucial for the development of robust and trustworthy Computer Vision systems.

In this work, we propose a new method called *Function-Semantic Contrast Analysis* (FSCA)[1], which aims to identify spurious correlations between the neural representations (i.e. neurons) given that target concepts of each representation are known. The proposed approach is based on the idea of analyzing the contrast between two distinct metrics: the functional distance, which measures the relationships between representations based on the correlations in activation patterns, and the knowledge-based semantic distance between concepts, these representations were trained to encode. Hypothesizing that spurious correlations frequently arise between semantically distant classes due to the influence of an unobserved factor, FSCA analyzes the contrast between these two distance measures, ultimately identifying potentially spurious pairs with high disagreement between metrics. FSCA offers a scalable approach that considerably reduces dependence on human supervision, thereby providing a robust means for the comprehensive evaluation of "black-box" models.

2   Related Works

To address the problem of the opacity of Deep Neural Networks given their widespread popularity across various domains, the field of *Explainable AI* (XAI) has emerged [27,36,49,61,62]. The primary goal of XAI is to provide insights into the decision-making processes of complex AI systems, allowing humans to comprehend, trust, and effectively manage these systems [67]. One important class of explainability approaches, known as *post-hoc* explainability methods, seeks to

---

[1] The code for FSCA can be accessed via the following GitHub link: https://github.com/lapalap/FSCA.

explain the decision-making processes of trained models without interfering in their training procedure [38,70]. These methods can be broadly classified into two types based on the scope of their analysis: *local* explanation methods, which focus on explaining model decisions for specific inputs, and *global* explanation methods, which aim to interpret general decision-making strategies, allowing for audits and investigations of models across diverse populations and shedding light on the roles of various model components.

Local explanation methods often provide explanations to the decision-making process on a given data point in the form of attribution maps, distributing relevance scores among features of the input, emphasizing the most critical attributes for the prediction. Various methods, such as Layer-wise Relevance Propagation (LRP) [3], GradCAM [64], LIME [58], Integrated Gradients [73], and SHAP [45] have been introduced, and have proven to be effective in explaining the decision-making process in Computer Vision models [15,75], including Bayesian Neural Networks [13,19]. To tackle the interpretability issue of attribution maps, several enhancing techniques were introduced, such as SmoothGrad [71], NoiseGrad [18], and Augmented GradCam [51]. Significant focus has been devoted to examining and assessing the effectiveness of local explanation techniques [30,33,34]. However, the primary limitation of local explanation methods lies in their ineffectiveness in probing the unknown behaviors of the models. While they prove beneficial for examining existing, known hypotheses, they are ineffective when it comes to uncovering unknown hypotheses, including the identification of unknown spurious correlations and shortcuts [1].

Conversely, *global* explanation methods aim to interpret the general decision-making strategies employed by the models by shedding light on the roles of specific components such as neurons, channels, or output logits, which are often referred to as representations. Such approaches enable a more general insight into the decision-making strategies of the models, thus facilitating the discovery of unknown and unexpected behavior within these models. Methods such as Network Dissection [4,5], Compositional Explanations of Neurons [52], and MILAN [35] have been developed to explain the functionality of these latent representations by associating them with human-comprehensible concepts. Activation Maximization Methods [25], on the other hand, aim to explain the concept behind the model's representations by identifying the inputs that maximally activate a particular neuron or layer in the network and hence, visualize the features that have been learned by the specific representation. These activation maximization images, also referred to as signals, embody the features that the representations have learned to detect and they could be either sampled from an existing dataset [11,17] or generated artificially through an optimization procedure [53–55].

2.1   Spurious Correlations in Computer Vision Models

While excelling at various Computer Vision tasks by being able to learn complex and intricate representations of the data, Deep Neural Networks are susceptible to learning spurious correlations from data. Such correlations represent apparently related variables that, upon closer inspection, reveal a connection rooted in mere coincidence or an underlying, often obscured, factor [31,68]. This phenomenon, commonly referred to as "Shortcut learning" or "Clever-Hans effect" [2,42,76], often manifesting in a strong contrast between desired and actual learning strategy within the model. In the following discussion, we provide a general overview of these correlations, which have been identified across a range of CV tasks.

Co-occurring Objects. In the field of image classification, as well as in other CV subdomains, images often contain not only the primary object of interest but also secondary objects in the background. Deep Neural Networks (DNNs) trained on such data can establish associations between the primary objects and frequently occurring secondary objects. Examples of such learned correlations could be fingers and band-aids [69], trains on tracks, or bees and flowers [40]. [66] observed that classifiers heavily depend on the context in which objects are situated, performing poorly in less common contexts, e.g., the absence of a typical co-occurring object. In experiments using the MS COCO dataset [44] it was discovered that classifiers for specific classes, like "Keyboard", "Mouse", and "Skateboard", are highly sensitive to contextual objects and exhibit poor performance when encountered outside their usual context, such as for instance, keyboards often go unrecognized without a nearby monitor [66].

Object Backgrounds. A prevalent type of spurious correlation arises between background features and target labels [78]. For example, a classifier may rely on a snowy background to identify huskies in images, instead of focusing on the target feature "Husky" [58]. Such correlations could stem from selection bias in training datasets, as demonstrated by the Waterbirds dataset [60], where the target label ("Waterbird" or "Landbird") is spuriously correlated with background features (water or land) in most training images [29]. Another example involves classifying cows and camels [6], where the target label ("Cow" or "Camel") is spuriously correlated with background features (green fields or desert) in most images. [69] identified numerous instances of background spurious features in ImageNet.

Biases and Stereotypes. Racial and gender biases stand as notable examples of undesired behavior, leading to adverse real-world consequences, particularly for marginalized groups. These biases can materialize in various ways, such as underdiagnosis in chest radiographs among underrepresented populations [65], or racially discriminatory facial recognition systems that disproportionately misidentify darker-skinned females [16]. Researchers have found instances of racial, religious, and Americentric biases embedded in the representations of the CLIP model [57]. Generative models like Stable Diffusion [59] also exhibit biases that perpetuate harmful racial, ethnic, gendered, and class stereotypes [8]. Other harmful spurious correlations have been found, such as associations between skin tone and sports or gender and professions [72,82].

Artifacts. Spurious correlations often arise from the presence of artifacts in images across various classes. These artifacts are secondary objects that hold no semantic connection with the primary class, and their coincidental association is unnatural and irregular. For instance, in the ImageNet dataset, Chinese watermarks have been found to influence numerous classes, such as "carton", "monitor", "broom", "apron" and "safe" [20], resulting in up to 26.7% drop in performance when watermarks are added to every class in the validation dataset [43]. This phenomenon has also been observed in the PASCAL VOC 2007 dataset [26], where a photographer's watermark frequently appears in images from the "horse" class [42]. Consequently, the trained model inadvertently learns this association, affecting its overall performance. Additionally, spurious correlations caused by artifacts have been noted in medical applications, such as skin lesion detectors, where artifacts like rulers and human-made ink markings or stains are present [10]. Similarly, hospital-specific metal tokens in chest X-ray scans [28,81] and radiologist input artifacts in brain tumor MRI classification [76] have been found to impact the accuracy of these applications.

2.2   Finding and Suppressing Spurious Correlations

The primary challenge in identifying spurious correlations stems from the lack of a concrete definition or criteria that differentiate them from "permissible" correlations. This ambiguity is reflected in the majority of methods' reliance on extensive human oversight. *Spectral Relevance Analysis* (SpRAy) was designed to aid in the identification of spurious correlations by clustering local attribution maps for future manual inspection [2,42]. However, the dependence on local explanations restricts the range of spurious correlations identified to basic, spatially static artifacts. This limitation necessitates a significant amount of human supervision and tailoring of the method's various hyperparameters to suit the specific problem at hand, which subsequently constrains the detection of unknown, unexpected correlations. The *Data-Agnostic Representation Analysis* (DORA) method approaches the problem of spurious correlations from a different angle, by analyzing relationships between internal representations [17]. The authors introduced the functional *Extreme-Activation* distance measure between representations, demonstrating that representations encoding undesired spurious concepts are often observed to be outliers in this distance metric.

A subsequent challenge is to revise or update the model after identifying spurious correlations. The *Class Artifact Compensation* framework was introduced, enabling the suppression of undesired behavior through either a fine-tuning process or a post-hoc approach by injecting additional layers [2]. An alternative method involves augmenting the training dataset after uncovering an artifact, so that the artifact is shared among all data points, rendering it an unusable feature for recognition by the model [43]. To suppress spurious behavior in transfer learning, a straightforward method was proposed to first identify representations that have learned spurious concepts, and then, during the fine-tuning phase, exclude these representations from the fine-tuning process [20].

2.3   Visual-Semantic Relationship in Computer Vision

In the field of Computer Vision, both visual and semantic similarities play cru-cial roles in the comprehension and interpretation of images and their underlying concepts. Visual similarity refers to the resemblance between two images based on their appearances, whereas semantic similarity denotes the extent of relat-edness between the meanings or concepts associated with the images. A widely accepted definition of semantic similarity takes into account the taxonomical or hierarchical relationships between the concepts [32]. There is a general obser-vation that semantic and visual similarities tend to be positively correlated, as an increase in semantic similarity between categories is typically accompanied by a rise in visual similarity [14,23]. DNNs trained on Computer Vision tasks demonstrate the ability to indirectly learn class hierarchies [9].

3   FSCA: Function-Semantic Contrast Analysis

In this work, we propose a novel method called *Function-Semantic Contrast Analysis* (FSCA). This method allows to identify pairs of output representations that may possess spurious associations. FSCA capitalizes on the functional distance between representations, which can be calculated using the activa-tions of representations on the given dataset, and the knowledge-based semantic distance between concepts, obtained from taxonomies or other knowledge databases. By examining the contrast between the two distance met-rics, our primary focus lies in revealing pairs of representations that exhibit a high degree of functional similarity but whose underly-ing concepts are semantically very different, i.e., which are located in the first quadrant of Fig. 1. While disagreements between func-tional and semantic distances are often nat-ural, as some concepts may share visual sim-ilarity while remaining semantically distinct [14], we observe that such behavior frequently results from undesired correlations present in the training data.

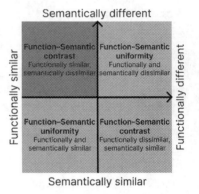

Fig. 1. Various cases of function-semantic relationship. This figure illustrates four primary scenarios of potential relationships between functional and semantic distances. In our analysis, we mainly focus on instances where representations exhibit high functional similar-ity, while the concepts they were trained to detect differ semanti-cally, illustrated in the first quad-rant of the figure.

3.1   Method

Let us consider a neural network layer $\mathcal{F} = \{f_1, ..., f_k\}$, consisting of k distinct functions, $f_i(x) : \mathbb{D} \to \mathbb{R}, \forall i \in 1, ..., k$, referred to as *neural representations*, that are mappings from the data domain $\mathbb{D}$ to the activation of the i-th neuron in the layer. We further assume that the concepts associated with each representation are known, and define a set of concepts $\mathcal{C} = \{c_1, ..., c_k\}$, where c_i denotes the concept underlying the representation $f_i(x)$, $\forall i \in 1, ..., k$. Thus, we can define the set $\mathcal{P} = \{(f_1, c_1), ..., (f_k, c_k)\} \subset \mathcal{F} \times \mathcal{C}$, as a collection of representation-concept pairs.

We consider that two distance metrics, $d_{\mathcal{F}}$ and $d_{\mathcal{C}}$, that are defined on the respective sets $\mathcal{F}$ and $\mathcal{C}$: $d_{\mathcal{F}} : \mathcal{F} \times \mathcal{F} \to \mathbb{R}$, $d_{\mathcal{C}} : \mathcal{C} \times \mathcal{C} \to \mathbb{R}$, where $d_{\mathcal{F}}$ is measuring the functional distance between learned representations in the networks, and $d_{\mathcal{C}}$ measures the semantic distance between the concepts these representations are trained to encode. Accordingly, we define two $k \times k$ distance matrices, F and C, as follows:

$$F = \begin{bmatrix} d_{\mathcal{F}}(f_1, f_1) \ldots d_{\mathcal{F}}(f_1, f_k) \\ \vdots \quad \ddots \quad \vdots \\ d_{\mathcal{F}}(f_k, f_1) \ldots d_{\mathcal{F}}(f_k, f_k) \end{bmatrix}, \quad C = \begin{bmatrix} d_{\mathcal{C}}(c_1, c_1) \ldots d_{\mathcal{C}}(c_1, c_k) \\ \vdots \quad \ddots \quad \vdots \\ d_{\mathcal{C}}(c_k, c_1) \ldots d_{\mathcal{C}}(c_k, c_k) \end{bmatrix}. \quad (1)$$

Given two neural representations $f_i, f_j \in \mathcal{F}$ with corresponding concepts $c_i, c_j \in C$, one can assess the contrast between functional and semantic distance by comparing the values between $d_{\mathcal{F}}(f_i, f_j)$ and $d_{\mathcal{C}}(c_i, c_j)$. However, such an approach might not be optimal since functional and semantic distance measures can possess distinct scales. To overcome this challenge, we suggest a non-parametric approach, where the ranks of distances within their corresponding distributions are analyzed instead.

In the following, a collection of unique distances are collected from the upper triangular portion of the distance matrices, including the main diagonal and all elements above it:

$$F_\Delta = \{d_{\mathcal{F}}(f_i, f_j) \mid \forall i \in \{1, ..., k\}, \forall j \in \{i, ..., k\}\}, \quad (2)$$
$$C_\Delta = \{d_{\mathcal{C}}(c_i, c_j) \mid \forall i \in \{1, ..., k\}, \forall j \in \{i, ..., k\}\}. \quad (3)$$

We define matrices F^*, C^* as

$$F^* = \begin{bmatrix} d_{\mathcal{F}}^*(f_1, f_1) \ldots d_{\mathcal{F}}^*(f_1, f_k) \\ \vdots \quad \ddots \quad \vdots \\ d_{\mathcal{F}}^*(f_k, f_1) \ldots d_{\mathcal{F}}^*(f_k, f_k) \end{bmatrix}, \quad C^* = \begin{bmatrix} d_{\mathcal{C}}^*(c_1, c_1) \ldots d_{\mathcal{C}}^*(c_1, c_k) \\ \vdots \quad \ddots \quad \vdots \\ d_{\mathcal{C}}^*(c_k, c_1) \ldots d_{\mathcal{C}}^*(c_k, c_k) \end{bmatrix}, \quad (4)$$

where $\forall i, j \in \{1, ..., k\}$

$$d_{\mathcal{F}}^*(f_i, f_j) = \mathrm{cdf}_{F_\Delta}^{-1}(d_{\mathcal{F}}(f_i, f_j)), \quad d_{\mathcal{C}}^*(c_i, c_j) = \mathrm{cdf}_{C_\Delta}^{-1}(d_{\mathcal{C}}(c_i, c_j)), \quad (5)$$

and cdf^{-1} correspond to the inverse of the cumulative distribution function (percentile).

Finally, for every pair of neural representations we define the *function-semantic contrast score* based on the difference between the percentile of the functional distance, and the percentile from the semantic distance between corresponding concepts.

Definition 1. *Given* $\mathcal{P} = \{(f_1, c_1), \ldots, (f_k, c_k)\} \subset \mathcal{F} \times \mathcal{C}$, *as a collection of representation-concept pairs, corresponding to the outputs of a DNN and two metrics* $d_{\mathcal{F}}, d_{\mathcal{C}}$ *defined on* $\mathcal{F}, \mathcal{C}$, *respectively. Furthermore, let* F_{Δ}, C_{Δ} *be a collection of unique distances among neural representations and concepts, respectively. For* $p_i, p_j \in \mathcal{P}$ *we define contrast score as*

$$\text{fsc}\,(p_i, p_j) = \text{cdf}_{C_{\Delta}}^{-1}\,(d_{\mathcal{C}}(c_i, c_j)) - \text{cdf}_{F_{\Delta}}^{-1}\,(d_{\mathcal{F}}(f_i, f_j))\,. \tag{6}$$

Contrast scores range from -1 to 1, with high contrast scores indicating cases where representations display significant functional similarity, while the underlying concepts are semantically distinct. This particular type of function-semantic relationship is our primary focus and is illustrated in Fig. 1.

In practice, to detect spurious correlations within the output representations, each pair of representations is assigned a contrast score, and pairs are sorted in descending order. Pairs with the highest contrast scores highlight the discrepancy between the model's perception and the human-defined semantic distance. Subsequently, each pair can be manually investigated by a human to determine the causal reason for such contrast.

3.2   Selecting a Distance Metric Between Representations

A crucial aspect of our proposed method's performance lies in the choice of an appropriate distance metric for the comparison of the output representations, which must reflect the similarity in activation patterns between pairs of representations within the network. Consider the dataset $\mathcal{D} = \{x_1, \ldots, x_N\} \subset \mathbb{D}$, consisting of N independent and identically distributed data points from the data distribution. For a layer $\mathcal{F}$ with k representations, we define vector $A_i = (f_i(x_1), \ldots, f_i(x_N)) \subset \mathbb{R}^N, \forall i \in \{1, \ldots, k\}$, which contains the activations of the i-th representation across the dataset. We assume that all vectors $A_i, \forall i \in \{1, \ldots, k\}$ are standardized, with a sample mean of 0 and a standard deviation of 1.

Our approach permits flexibility in choosing the distance metric between representations. In this work, we utilize the *Extreme-Activation* (EA) distance metric, derived from the analysis of natural data [17]. Drawing inspiration from the study of Activation-Maximization signals (AMS), which are data points that maximally activate a given representation, the EA distance quantifies the extent to which two representations are activated by each other's AMS. This provides insights into how the representations are influenced by the features present in the AMS.

To calculate the pair-wise Extreme-Activation distance, the dataset $\mathcal{D}$ is partitioned into n disjoint blocks, $D = \bigcup_{i=1}^n D_t, D_t = \{x_{td+1}, \ldots, x_{(t+1)d+1}\}, \forall t \in \{0, \ldots, n-1\}$, each of length d. Subsequently, for each representation $f_i \in \mathcal{F}, \forall i \in \{1, \ldots, k\}$, we define a set of natural Activation-Maximization signals (n-AMS) as $S_i = \{s_1^i, \ldots, s_n^i\}$, where

$$s_t^i = \arg\max_{x \in D_t} f_i\,(x)\,, \forall t \in \{0, \ldots, n-1\}. \tag{7}$$

For every two representations $f_i, f_j \in \mathcal{F}$, we define their pair-wise representation activation vectors (RAVs) r_{ij}, r_{ji} as:

$$r_{ij} = \begin{pmatrix} \frac{1}{n} \sum_{t=1}^{n} f_i \left(s_t^i \right) \\ \frac{1}{n} \sum_{t=1}^{n} f_j \left(s_t^i \right) \end{pmatrix}, \quad r_{ji} = \begin{pmatrix} \frac{1}{n} \sum_{t=1}^{n} f_i \left(s_t^j \right) \\ \frac{1}{n} \sum_{t=1}^{n} f_j \left(s_t^j \right) \end{pmatrix}. \tag{8}$$

Subsequently, we define the pair-wise Extreme-Activation distance between two representations as the cosine of the angle between their corresponding RAVs.

Definition 2 (Extreme-Activation distance). *Let f_i, f_j be two neural representations, and r_{ij}, r_{ji} be their pair-wise RAVs. We define a pair-wise Extreme-Activation distance as*

$$d_{\mathcal{F}} \left(f_i, f_j \right) = \frac{1}{\sqrt{2}} \sqrt{1 - \cos \left(r_{ij}, r_{ji} \right)}, \tag{9}$$

where $\cos(A, B)$ is the cosine of the angle between vectors A, B.

Extreme-Activation distance quantifies the activation of n-AMS between two representations, offering a valuable metric for examining the relationships among intricate non-linear functions [17]. In contrast to other metrics, such as Pearson correlation, the EA distance utilizes a small subset of n-AMS for each representation, enabling a straightforward visual inspection of Activation-Maximization signals. This metric, grounded in the measure of how two representations are co-activated on their most activating signals, allows practitioners to easily discern the shared visual features between two sets of n-AMS.

Figure 2 demonstrates the EA distance between two representations, corresponding to the "Snow leopard" and "Crossword puzzle" classes, derived from an ImageNet [22] pre-trained DenseNet161 network [37]. This figure enables an effortless assessment of the functional similarity between the two representations. We can observe that the RAVs are not perpendicular, implying a functional dependence between the representations. Moreover, a visual inspection of the n-AMS for both representations reveals a similar black-and-white texture pattern that both representations have learned to detect.

EA distance measure varies between 0 and 1. Low values correspond to small angles between RAVs, indicating that both representations are highly activated on each other's AMS. Perpendicular RAVs, which represent cases where the representations are indifferent to each other's AMS, yield a distance equal to $\frac{1}{\sqrt{2}} \approx 0.7071$. Higher EA distance signifies situations where the n-AMS of the representations negatively affect one another, meaning the AMS of one representation deactivates the other.

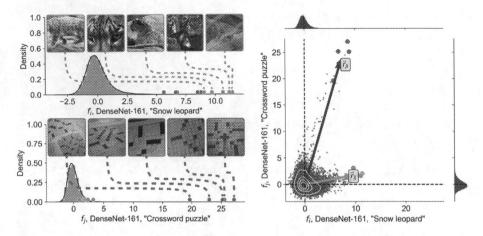

Fig. 2. Interpreting the Extreme-Activation Distance. Given two output representations from the DenseNet161 network, f_i and f_j, corresponding to the "Snow leopard" and "Crossword puzzle" classes respectively, two sets of n-AMS signals were sampled (orange and blue, respectively). The left figures display the distribution of activations for both representations across the ImageNet-2012 validation dataset, with the positions of the n-AMS indicated. The right figure presents the pair-wise RAVs, alongside activation of all data points (gray) and representations-specific n-AMS (blue, orange). The EA distance measures the cosine of the angle between RAVs vectors. (Color figure online)

3.3　Selecting a Distance Metric Between Concepts

The choice of functional and semantic distances between representations and concepts, respectively, is critical. Semantic distance should encapsulate human-defined relationships, particularly ensuring that these distances do not rely on spurious or undesired correlations. Function-Semantic Contrast Analysis (FSCA) can utilize any concept metric, including expert-defined knowledge-based distance measures. For example, semantic distances can be derived from the Word-Net database [48], which groups English words into synsets connected by semantic relationships.

In this work, we employ the *Wu-Palmer* (WUP) distance metric defined on the WordNet taxonomy database. The WUP distance is based on the depth of the least common subsumer (LCS), which is the most specific synset that is an ancestor of both input synsets [56]. The WUP distance computes relatedness by considering the depth of the LCS and the depths of the input synsets in the hierarchy.

Definition 3. *Let $c_i, c_j \in \mathcal{C}$, be two concepts, and let w_i, w_j be the corresponding synsets from the WordNet taxonomy database. The Wu-Palmer distance is defined as:*

$$d_{\mathcal{C}}(c_i, c_j) = 1 - 2\frac{l(r, lcs(w_i, w_j))}{l(r, w_i) + l(r, w_j)},$$

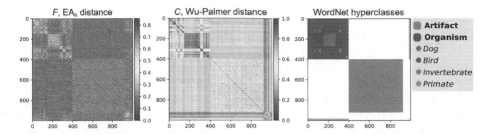

Fig. 3. Illustration of functional and semantic distance matrices. From left to right: EA distance between DenseNet161 output representations, Wu-Palmer distance between 1000 ImageNet classes, and a visualization of the location of several highly interesting hyperclasses within the distance matrices.

where lcs(x, y) is the Least Common Subsumer [56] of two synsets x and y, r is the taxonomy root, and l(x, y) is the length of the shortest path between WordNet synsets x, y.

The WUP distance takes into account the specificity of the common ancestor, rendering it more robust to the structure of the WordNet hierarchy in comparison to other semantic distance metrics such as *Shortest-Path* distance or *Leacock-Chodorow* [17,63]. Moreover, the Wu-Palmer distance offers a more fine-grained measure of relatedness. Figure 3 demonstrates the Wu-Palmer distance between 1000 ImageNet classes that share natural connections to WordNet synsets. The structure of the semantic distance matrix (center) aligns with the location of the primary groups of classes within the dataset, as illustrated in the figure to the right.

4   Experiments

This section provides a detailed examination of various implemented experiments. These include an evaluation of the performance of the FSCA method in light of the given ground truth. Furthermore, we explore the practical application of FSCA to the widely-employed DenseNet-161 model. Finally, we conduct a broad assessment of ImageNet-trained models, focusing on the relationship between performance and the functional similarities between representations.

4.1   Evaluation Given the Ground Truth

To evaluate the effectiveness and suitability of the proposed methodology, we investigated its capability to identify instances of representation pairs previously acknowledged to exhibit spurious correlations. This analysis utilized two ImageNet-trained models, specifically GoogLeNet [74] and DenseNet-161 [37], both previously reported to possess a significant proportion of output representations susceptible to watermark text detection [20].

Consider $\mathcal{P}_G, \mathcal{P}_D$ as collections of representation-concept pairs for 1000 output representations - essentially, the pre-softmax output logit representations from the two networks. For each of these models, employing a technique akin to that described in [20], we identified subsets $\mathcal{Z}_G \subset \mathcal{P}_G, \mathcal{Z}_D \subset \mathcal{P}_D$ of representation-concept pairs with high discriminatory capability (AUROC > 0.9) towards watermarked images, implying that such representations exhibit spurious correlations towards watermarked images and generally assign higher activations to the images, where the watermark is present. For GoogLeNet there were found $|\mathcal{Z}_G| = 21$ output representations, such as "carton", "broom", "apron" and others, while for DenseNet-161 there were found $|\mathcal{Z}_D| = 22$ high-discriminatory representations. We applied FSCA to both sets $\mathcal{P}_G$ and $\mathcal{P}_D$ using the functional Extreme-Activation distance, computed over $n = 10$ n-AMS with parameter $d = 5000$. For the semantic distance between concepts, we chose the Wu-Palmer distance, considering the inherent link between ImageNet concepts and the WordNet taxonomy. After calculating Function-Semantic Contrast (FSC) scores for each pair of representations, we compared these scores between two groups: those pairs known to be susceptible to spurious correlations and the rest. More specifically, we defined two sets:

$$\mathrm{FSC}_G^- = \{\mathrm{fsc}(p_i, p_j) \mid \forall p_i, p_j \in \mathcal{P}_G, i > j, p_j \in \mathcal{P}_G \setminus \mathcal{Z}_G\}, \tag{10}$$

$$\mathrm{FSC}_G^+ = \{\mathrm{fsc}(p_i, p_j) \mid \forall p_i, p_j \in \mathcal{Z}_G, i > j\}, \tag{11}$$

where FSC_G^- denotes the set of FSC scores for representation-concept pairs from GoogLeNet, in which at least one representation was not identified as being susceptible to Chinese watermark detection. Conversely, FSC_G^+ represents the FSC scores for the representation-concept pairs where both representations were recognized to be susceptible to spurious correlations. We similarly defined sets FSC_D^- and FSC_D^+ for the DenseNet-161 model. GoogLeNet and DenseNet-161, 210 and 231 pairs of representations were respectively flagged as exhibiting spurious correlation, among a total of 499500 pairs.

Figure 4 visually presents the differences between the FSC$^-$ and FSC$^+$ distributions for both models. For each model, the FSC scores for "watermark" pairs, defined as pairs of representations where both classes were identified as susceptible to watermark detection, are consistently higher than those for other representation pairs. This observation was further corroborated by the Mann-Whitney U test [46] under a standard significance level (0.05).

If we constrain the FSCA analysis solely to representation pairs exhibiting substantial functional similarity, specifically those falling within the top 2.5% ($d_{\mathcal{F}}^* \leq 0.025$), the results for GoogLeNet indicate 8 spurious pairs (out of 210) among the top 1000 pairs with the highest FSC, 38 within the top 5000, and 52 within the top 10000. Implementing the same methodology with DenseNet-161 yields no spurious pairs (out of 231) within the top 1000, 32 pairs within the top 5000, and 42 within the top 10000. This infers that by focusing exclusively on representation pairs with high functional similarity, we can recover 25% (52 pairs out of 210) and 18% (42 pairs out of 231) of pairs displaying known spurious correlations, merely by scrutinizing 2% (10000 pairs) of the total representation pairs. Our results suggest that FSCA tends to allocate high FSC scores to pairs of representations known to be susceptible to spurious correlations, thereby lending further credibility to the proposed methodology. However, it's important to note a limitation in this experiment: while we have a knowledge of spurious correlations due to the reliance on Chinese watermarks, we cannot ascertain potential correlations among other pairs.

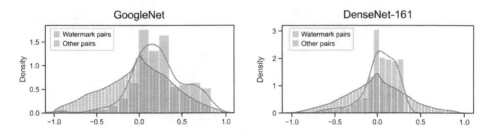

Fig. 4. The contrast between the distribution of FSC scores among pairs of representations known to be susceptible to spurious correlations (Chinese watermarks, orange), and all other pairs (blue). The figure demonstrates that FSCA typically assigns higher FSC scores to pairs recognized as having spurious correlations. (Color figure online)

4.2   Identifying Spurious Correlations in ImageNet Trained DenseNet-161

To demonstrate the potential utility and relevance of our proposed approach, we investigated in detail the results of the FSCA of the widely-used ImageNet-trained DenseNet-161 model. Hyperparameters for the analysis were kept the same as in the previous experiment, namely, we employed functional Extreme-Activation distance metric with $n = 10$, allowing us to analyze the co-activation of representations based on the 10 Activation-Maximization images, providing a straightforward method for interpreting the shared features that the representations are trained to recognize. Due to the impracticality of examining all pairs, our analysis focused solely on pairs with high functional similarity based on Extreme-Activation, specifically those within the top 1% of the smallest distances, and in total 1000 with the highest contrast scores were analyzed. We report several significant categories of correlations observed between the logit class representations of the DenseNet-161 model, found by the FSCA method.

Shared Visual Features. Since semantic distance offers a metric for evaluating the conceptual differences between entities, it is natural for some concepts, despite being semantically distinct, to share visual features with one another. Such relationships between representations could be considered natural to the image classification model.

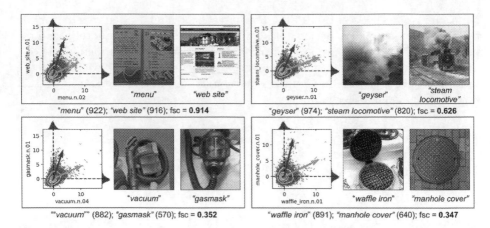

Fig. 5. Illustration of several representation pairs sharing natural visual features. The figure shows four different pairs of representations, with each subfigure depicting the geometry of pairwise RAVs and two n-AMS per representation. The observed functional similarities are attributed to the natural visual similarity between classes and are not considered spurious, as the representations detect features characteristic of each other.

Some of the most intriguing relationships we observed include the functional similarity between representations corresponding to the classes "geyser", "steam locomotive", "volcano", and "cannon", owing to the shared visual feature of smoke fumes. Representations for the classes "menu", "website", "envelope", "book jacket", and "packet" exhibit a high degree of functional relationship due to the shared textual feature, which could be considered a natural characteristic for such classes. Furthermore, representations for crossword "puzzle" and "snow leopard" share similar behavior in detecting black and white grid patterns (illustrated in Fig. 2), "waffle iron" and "manhole cover" representations display a high degree of similarity due to their ability to detect specific grid patterns, and "mailbox" and "birdhouse" logits demonstrate a strong degree of co-activation of each other's n-AMS, resulting from the visual similarity of the objects. Several of the described relationships are illustrated in Fig. 5, by the pair-wise RAVs between their representations together with their n-AMS.

Co-occurring and Mislabeled Objects. This category refers to objects that frequently co-occur, allowing the network to learn associations between two objects, due to the constraints of the classification problem to assign one class per image. Examples of such relationships can be found in the representations of "cup", "espresso maker", "coffeepot", and "teapot", all reported to frequently co-occur in each other's image backgrounds as secondary objects. Intriguing examples include the high similarity of "plate" and "dungeness crab" representations, as the n-AMS for the crab representation illustrates an already prepared crab on a plate, "cardoon" (flower) and "bee" representations, and "hay" and "harvester". Additionally, we detected that functional similarity can be caused by misattribution of labels, such as between "tiger" and "tiger cat", where we were able to determine that the latter class also contains images of tigers, even though the class description states that it is a specific breed of cats exhibiting textural patterns of black stripes, similar to tigers.

Object Backgrounds. FSCA analysis of the functionally most similar representations yielded several groups of representations, that exhibit functional similarity due to the shared background only. Such a conclusion could be derived from the fact that representations are significantly co-activated with each other's n-AMS, while the only shared feature among them is the background.

– **Snow** We can consider the snow background among the most interesting examples of such spurious correlations. This feature is shared between representations such as "snowmobile", "ski", and "shovel".
– **Mountain** The commonality of the mountain background is observed across representations including "alp", "marmot", "mountain bike", and "mountain tent", with the latter two possessing descriptive references to the background within their respective names.
– **Underwater** The underwater background is shared between representations such as "snorkel", "coral reef", "scuba diver", and "stingray", which collectively share a bluish shade and describe natural marine environments.
– **Savannah** The shared background of the savannah, characterized by golden or green grasslands, is observed across representations of animal species such as "zebra", "impala", "gazelle", "prairie chicken", and "bustard".
– **Water** The water background encompasses the view of the water surface, as well as the presence of animals or objects above the water, including "pier", "speedboat", "seashore", and "killer whale".

Artifacts. Among the reported pairs of representations yielded by FSCA, we were able to detect representations "safe", "scale", "apron", "backpack", "carton", and "swab" that exhibited high functional similarities caused by the presence of Chinese watermarks in their n-AMS. This result is consistent with previous works that reported these classes as having a strong ability to differentiate between watermarked and non-watermarked images [20].

By employing FSCA we were able to identify the new unknown spurious correlation, manifesting in the dependence of several classes on the presence of young children in the image. A high functional similarity was reported between the "diaper" class, naturally containing a lot of young children in the images, and several other representations, including the "rocking chair" representation. Inspection of the training dataset revealed a significant amount of images of children (without diapers) sitting in a "rocking chair". Since the ImageNet dataset does not have a specific class dedicated to children, this represents a latent factor that corresponds to the functional similarity of such classes.

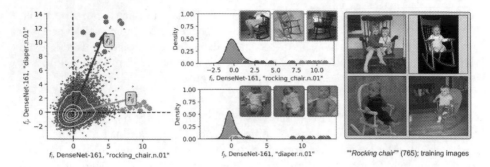

Fig. 6. Discovery of previously unknown spurious correlation between "diaper" and "rocking chair". The high FSCA contrast score (0.35), indicates a high discrepancy between function and semantic distances. Investigation of the training dataset revealed that such behavior could be explained by the dependency of both representations on the presence of a child in the image.

Figure 6 illustrates the Extreme-Activation distance, alongside with the n-AMS for the representations "diaper" and "rocking chair", and several examples from the ImageNet-2012 training dataset from the class "rocking chair". This spurious correlation was unexpected and could be considered artifactual for this class. The fact that "rocking chair" employs the presence of children as additional evidence for prediction is demonstrated in Fig. 7, where the model's prediction shifts towards the "rocking chair" class after adding an image of a child on top of the image of the chair. Furthermore, FSCA reported the following representations to have high functional similarity with the "diaper" representation: "crib", "bassinet"[2], "cradle", "hamper", "band-aid", "bib"[3], and "bath towel".

"dining table" (532)	**0.36**	*"rocking chair"* (765)	**0.90**
"folding chair" (559)	**0.27**	*"folding chair"* (559)	**0.04**
"pedestal" (708)	**0.08**	*"dining table"* (532)	**0.02**

Fig. 7. Differences in the model's predictions before and after adding an image of a child to the image.

Another intriguing and previously unknown spurious correlation that we identified involves the dependence of several classes on images of fishermen. This correlation was observed between the "reel" class and several fish classes, namely "coho" and "barracouta". Figure 8 furnishes evidence that the relationship between the "reel" and "coho" representations is primarily based on the presence of fishermen, often paired with a specific water background. This is further underscored by the model's prediction given an image of a fisherman - the model confidently assigns a fish label to the image, despite the absence of any fish in the picture. Although this correlation bears similarity to the previously

---

[2] A basket (usually hooded) used as a baby's bed.

[3] Top part of an apron; covering the chest.

reported correlation between the "tench" and the presence of human fingers [12], our findings show that representations like "coho" and "barracouta" display a broader dependency on the existence of a fisherman within the image. This is evidenced even in instances where human fingers are not visible in the image, as exemplified by the right-hand image in Fig. 8.

Fig. 8. Illustration of the spurious correlation between "reel" and "coho" representations, which appears to emerge due to the common latent feature of the presence of fishermen in the images. Our investigation revealed that a significant portion of the training dataset consists of images featuring fishermen. This relationship consequently leads to the possibility of the network misclassifying images of fishermen as the "fish" category.

Summary. Our examination of the top 1000 pairs of representations, as ranked by function-semantic contrast scores, suggests that around half of the detected correlations might be explained as "unintended" correlations. These correlations can be linked to the frequent co-occurrence of objects (32%), dependencies on shared backgrounds (12.3%), or a shared unnatural factor (2.6%), as visualized in Fig. 9. Nevertheless, we recognize that such categorization might oversimplify the actual interconnections between representations. It is uncommon for a single specific factor to account for the functional similarities observed between neural representations.

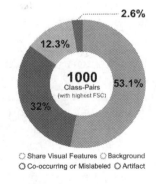

Fig. 9. Chart represents the distribution of identified causes for the correlations among the top 1000 pairs of representations, having the highest reported function-semantic contrast (FSC) scores.

4.3 Better Models Tend to Have Fewer Associations

The analysis of the DenseNet-161 models surfaced a variety of correlations, including those that might be deemed natural as well as those potentially regarded as undesired or even harmful. Subsequently, we were motivated to examine whether higher-performing models exhibited fewer correlations among their output representations. For this investigation, we gathered 78 different ImageNet classification models from the `Torchvision` library [47], with the weight parameters set to "`IMAGENET1K_V1`". For each model, we computed the pairwise Extreme-Activation distance between output representations using the ImageNet-2012 validation dataset, leveraging parameters analogous to those in our preceding experiment. This process yielded 78 distance matrices $F_i \in \mathbb{R}^{1000 \times 1000}, i \in [1, 78]$. To quantify the degree of correlation between output representations within models, we calculated the Frobenius norm of the difference between the Extreme-Activation distance matrix F_i and a matrix Q for each of the 78 models:

$$Q = \frac{1}{\sqrt{2}} \left(\mathbb{1} - \mathbb{I} \right), \tag{12}$$

where $\mathbb{1}$ is a $k \times k$ matrix with all elements equal to 1, $\mathbb{I}$ is the identity matrix, and $k = 1000$. Matrix Q is the distance matrix between representations in the ideal scenario of total disentanglement. Hence, the norm of the difference between F_i and Q serves as an indicator of the interconnectivity of the representations.

Figure 10 illustrates the correlation between the extent to which the models' representations are correlated (top graph, y-axis) and their Top-5 performance on ImageNet (top graph, x-axis). Our observations indicate that models delivering superior performance achieve a lower norm, suggesting that enhanced performance aligns with better disentanglement and reduced correlation among output layer representations. The bottom graph in the same figure provides a visual representation of this, displaying distance matrices calculated across various networks.

5   Discussion and Conclusion

In the present work, we introduce a new technique, Function-Semantic Contrast Analysis (FSCA), designed to uncover spurious correlations between representations, when target concepts are known. FSCA reduces human supervision by systematically scoring and ranking representation pairs based on the function-semantic contrast. We have demonstrated the feasibility of our approach by uncovering several potentially unrecognized class correlations as well as rediscovering known correlations.

The primary limitation of our method relates to its reliance on a semantic metric that, despite broadly reflecting visual similarity between objects, isn't entirely accurate in assessing visual similarity between two concepts. We aim to research alternative semantic metrics, including expert-defined ones, that take visual similarity into account in our future work. Another challenge is the undefined nature of spurious correlations, necessitating human oversight to discern whether a correlation is harmful. Nevertheless, our study found that analyzing 1000 representation pairs from the DenseNet-161 model only required around 3

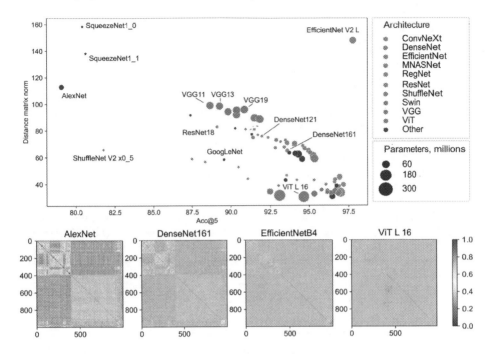

Fig. 10. Better performing models achieve higher disentanglement of representations. The top figure illustrates the relationship between ImageNet top-5 validation accuracy (x-axis) across the 78 models from the `Torchvision` library, along with the Frobenius norm of the difference between the EA distance measure and Q (y-axis).

human hours, uncovering previously undetected artifacts, and hence, the demand for human supervision is significantly reduced by FSCA.

While we have demonstrated the applicability of FSCA on ImageNet-trained networks, this approach is scalable in terms of its application to other image classification problems. Since WordNet encompasses a broad range of synsets, it is often quite simple to connect classes and concepts, as shown in the example of CIFAR-100 [17,41]. Moreover, semantic distance can be measured using other knowledge-based datasets or by relying on expert assessments.

As Deep Learning approaches are becoming more popular in various disciplines, it becomes increasingly imperative to audit these models for potential biases, ensuring the cultivation of fair and responsible machine learning frameworks. Our presented FSCA method offers a scalable solution for practitioners seeking to explain the often opaque and enigmatic behavior of these learning machines. By doing so, we contribute to a more transparent and ethically-grounded understanding of complex deep learning systems, promoting responsible and trustworthy AI applications across various domains.

Acknowledgements. This work was partly funded by the German Ministry for Education and Research through the project Explaining 4.0 (ref. 01IS200551).

References

1. Adebayo, J., Muelly, M., Abelson, H., Kim, B.: Post hoc explanations may be ineffective for detecting unknown spurious correlation. In: International Conference on Learning Representations (2022)
2. Anders, C.J., Weber, L., Neumann, D., Samek, W., Müller, K.R., Lapuschkin, S.: Finding and removing clever hans: using explanation methods to debug and improve deep model. Inf. Fusion **77**, 261–295 (2022)
3. Bach, S., Binder, A., Montovon, G., Klauschen, F., Müller, K.R., Samek, W.: On pixel-wise explanations for non-linear classifier decisions by layer-wise relevance propagation. PLoS ONE **10**(7), e0130140 (2015)
4. Bau, D., Zhou, B., Khosla, A., Oliva, A., Torralba, A.: Network dissection: quantifying interpretability of deep visual representations. In: Proceedings of the IEEE Conference on Computer Vision and Pattern Recognition, pp. 6541–6549 (2017)
5. Bau, D., et al.: GAN dissection: visualizing and understanding generative adversarial networks. arXiv preprint arXiv:1811.10597 (2018)
6. Beery, S., Van Horn, G., Perona, P.: Recognition in terra incognita. In: Proceedings of the European Conference on Computer Vision (ECCV), pp. 456–473 (2018)
7. Bengio, Y., Courville, A., Vincent, P.: Representation learning: a review and new perspectives. IEEE Trans. Pattern Anal. Mach. Intell. **35**(8), 1798–1828 (2013)
8. Bianchi, F., et al.: Easily accessible text-to-image generation amplifies demographic stereotypes at large scale (2022)
9. Bilal, A., Jourabloo, A., Ye, M., Liu, X., Ren, L.: Do convolutional neural networks learn class hierarchy? IEEE Trans. Visual Comput. Graphics **24**(1), 152–162 (2017)
10. Bissoto, A., Valle, E., Avila, S.: Debiasing skin lesion datasets and models? Not so fast. In: Proceedings of the IEEE/CVF Conference on Computer Vision and Pattern Recognition Workshops, pp. 740–741 (2020)
11. Borowski, J., et al.: Natural images are more informative for interpreting CNN activations than state-of-the-art synthetic feature visualizations. In: NeurIPS 2020 Workshop SVRHM (2020)
12. Brendel, W., Bethge, M.: Approximating CNNs with bag-of-local-features models works surprisingly well on ImageNet (2019)
13. Brown, K.E., Talbert, D.A.: Using explainable AI to measure feature contribution to uncertainty. In: The International FLAIRS Conference Proceedings, vol. 35 (2022)
14. Brust, C.-A., Denzler, J.: Not just a matter of semantics: the relationship between visual and semantic similarity. In: Fink, G.A., Frintrop, S., Jiang, X. (eds.) DAGM GCPR 2019. LNCS, vol. 11824, pp. 414–427. Springer, Cham (2019). https://doi.org/10.1007/978-3-030-33676-9_29
15. Buhrmester, V., Münch, D., Arens, M.: Analysis of explainers of black box deep neural networks for computer vision: a survey. Mach. Learn. Knowl. Extract. **3**(4), 966–989 (2021)
16. Buolamwini, J., Gebru, T.: Gender shades: intersectional accuracy disparities in commercial gender classification. In: Proceedings of the 1st Conference on Fairness, Accountability and Transparency, pp. 77–91. PMLR (2018)
17. Bykov, K., Deb, M., Grinwald, D., Müller, K.R., Höhne, M.M.C.: DORA: exploring outlier representations in deep neural networks. arXiv preprint arXiv:2206.04530 (2022)
18. Bykov, K., Hedström, A., Nakajima, S., Höhne, M.M.C.: NoiseGrad-enhancing explanations by introducing stochasticity to model weights. In: Proceedings of the AAAI Conference on Artificial Intelligence, vol. 36, pp. 6132–6140 (2022)

19. Bykov, K., et al.: Explaining Bayesian neural networks. arXiv preprint arXiv:2108.10346 (2021)
20. Bykov, K., Müller, K.R., Höhne, M.M.C.: Mark my words: dangers of watermarked images in ImageNet (2023)
21. Chai, J., Zeng, H., Li, A., Ngai, E.W.: Deep learning in computer vision: a critical review of emerging techniques and application scenarios. Mach. Learn. Appl. **6**, 100134 (2021)
22. Deng, J., Dong, W., Socher, R., Li, L.J., Li, K., Fei-Fei, L.: ImageNet: a large-scale hierarchical image database. In: 2009 IEEE Conference on Computer Vision and Pattern Recognition, pp. 248–255. IEEE (2009)
23. Deselaers, T., Ferrari, V.: Visual and semantic similarity in Imagenet. In: CVPR 2011, pp. 1777–1784. IEEE (2011)
24. Dosovitskiy, A., et al.: An image is worth 16×16 words: transformers for image recognition at scale. In: ICLR (2021)
25. Erhan, D., Bengio, Y., Courville, A., Vincent, P.: Visualizing higher-layer features of a deep network. Technical report, Univeristé de Montréal (2009)
26. Everingham, M., Van Gool, L., Williams, C.K.I., Winn, J., Zisserman, A.: The PASCAL visual object classes challenge 2007 (VOC2007) results. http://www.pascal-network.org/challenges/VOC/voc2007/workshop/index.html
27. Gade, K., Geyik, S.C., Kenthapadi, K., Mithal, V., Taly, A.: Explainable AI in industry. In: Proceedings of the 25th ACM SIGKDD International Conference on Knowledge Discovery & Data Mining, KDD 2019, pp. 3203–3204. Association for Computing Machinery, New York (2019)
28. Gautam, S., Höhne, M.M.C., Hansen, S., Jenssen, R., Kampffmeyer, M.: Demonstrating the risk of imbalanced datasets in chest X-ray image-based diagnostics by prototypical relevance propagation. In: 2022 IEEE 19th International Symposium on Biomedical Imaging (ISBI), pp. 1–5. IEEE (2022)
29. Ghosal, S.S., Ming, Y., Li, Y.: Are vision transformers robust to spurious correlations? (2022)
30. Guidotti, R.: Evaluating local explanation methods on ground truth. Artif. Intell. **291**, 103428 (2021)
31. Haig, B.D.: What Is a spurious correlation? Underst. Stat.: Stat. Issues Psycho. Educ. Soc. Sci. **2**(2), 125–132 (2003)
32. Harispe, S., Ranwez, S., Janaqi, S., Montmain, J.: Semantic similarity from natural language and ontology analysis. Synthesis Lect. Hum. Lang. Technol. **8**(1), 1–254 (2015)
33. Hedström, A., Bommer, P., Wickstrøm, K.K., Samek, W., Lapuschkin, S., Höhne, M.M.C.: The meta-evaluation problem in explainable AI: identifying reliable estimators with MetaQuantus. arXiv preprint arXiv:2302.07265 (2023)
34. Hedström, A., et al.: Quantus: an explainable AI toolkit for responsible evaluation of neural network explanations and beyond. arXiv preprint arXiv:2202.06861 (2022)
35. Hernandez, E., Schwettmann, S., Bau, D., Bagashvili, T., Torralba, A., Andreas, J.: Natural language descriptions of deep visual features. In: International Conference on Learning Representations (2021)
36. Holzinger, A., Saranti, A., Molnar, C., Biecek, P., Samek, W.: Explainable AI methods - a brief overview. In: Holzinger, A., Goebel, R., Fong, R., Moon, T., Müller, K.R., Samek, W. (eds.) xxAI 2020. LNCS, vol. 13200, pp. 13–38. Springer, Cham (2022). https://doi.org/10.1007/978-3-031-04083-2_2

37. Huang, G., Liu, Z., Van Der Maaten, L., Weinberger, K.Q.: Densely connected convolutional networks. In: Proceedings of the IEEE Conference on Computer Vision and Pattern Recognition, pp. 4700–4708 (2017)
38. Kenny, E.M., Ford, C., Quinn, M., Keane, M.T.: Explaining black-box classifiers using post-hoc explanations-by-example: the effect of explanations and error-rates in XAI user studies. Artif. Intell. **294**, 103459 (2021)
39. Kirillov, A., et al.: Segment anything. arXiv preprint arXiv:2304.02643 (2023)
40. Kolesnikov, A., Lampert, C.H.: Improving weakly-supervised object localization by micro-annotation (2016)
41. Krizhevsky, A., Hinton, G., et al.: Learning multiple layers of features from tiny images. University of Toronto (2009)
42. Lapuschkin, S., Wäldchen, S., Binder, A., Montavon, G., Samek, W., Müller, K.R.: Unmasking Clever Hans predictors and assessing what machines really learn. Nat. Commun. **10**(1), 1096 (2019)
43. Li, Z., et al.: A Whac-a-mole dilemma: shortcuts come in multiples where mitigating one amplifies others. In: Proceedings of the IEEE/CVF Conference on Computer Vision and Pattern Recognition (CVPR), pp. 20071–20082 (2023)
44. Lin, T.-Y., et al.: Microsoft COCO: common objects in context. In: Fleet, D., Pajdla, T., Schiele, B., Tuytelaars, T. (eds.) ECCV 2014. LNCS, vol. 8693, pp. 740–755. Springer, Cham (2014). https://doi.org/10.1007/978-3-319-10602-1_48
45. Lundberg, S.M., Lee, S.I.: A unified approach to interpreting model predictions. In: Advances in Neural Information Processing Systems, vol. 30 (2017)
46. Mann, H.B., Whitney, D.R.: On a test of whether one of two random variables is stochastically larger than the other. Ann. Math. Stat. 50–60 (1947)
47. Marcel, S., Rodriguez, Y.: Torchvision the machine-vision package of torch. In: Proceedings of the 18th ACM International Conference on Multimedia, pp. 1485–1488 (2010)
48. Miller, G.A.: WordNet: a lexical database for English. Commun. ACM **38**(11), 39–41 (1995)
49. Minh, D., Wang, H.X., Li, Y.F., Nguyen, T.N.: Explainable artificial intelligence: a comprehensive review. Artif. Intell. Rev. 1–66 (2022)
50. Mo, Y., Wu, Y., Yang, X., Liu, F., Liao, Y.: Review the state-of-the-art technologies of semantic segmentation based on deep learning. Neurocomputing **493**, 626–646 (2022)
51. Morbidelli, P., Carrera, D., Rossi, B., Fragneto, P., Boracchi, G.: Augmented Grad-CAM: heat-maps super resolution through augmentation. In: ICASSP 2020–2020 IEEE International Conference on Acoustics, Speech and Signal Processing (ICASSP), pp. 4067–4071. IEEE (2020)
52. Mu, J., Andreas, J.: Compositional explanations of neurons. In: Advances in Neural Information Processing Systems, vol. 33, pp. 17153–17163 (2020)
53. Nguyen, A., Yosinski, J., Clune, J.: Understanding neural networks via feature visualization: a survey. In: Samek, W., Montavon, G., Vedaldi, A., Hansen, L.K., Müller, K.-R. (eds.) Explainable AI: Interpreting, Explaining and Visualizing Deep Learning. LNCS (LNAI), vol. 11700, pp. 55–76. Springer, Cham (2019). https://doi.org/10.1007/978-3-030-28954-6_4
54. Nguyen, A.M., Yosinski, J., Clune, J.: Innovation engines: automated creativity and improved stochastic optimization via deep learning. In: Proceedings of the 2015 Annual Conference on Genetic and Evolutionary Computation, pp. 959–966 (2015)
55. Olah, C., Mordvintsev, A., Schubert, L.: Feature visualization. Distill **2**(11), e7 (2017)

56. Pedersen, T., Patwardhan, S., Michelizzi, J., et al.: WordNet::similarity-measuring the relatedness of concepts. In: AAAI, vol. 4, pp. 25–29 (2004)
57. Radford, A., et al.: Learning transferable visual models from natural language supervision. In: Proceedings of the 38th International Conference on Machine Learning, pp. 8748–8763. PMLR (2021)
58. Ribeiro, M.T., Singh, S., Guestrin, C.: "Why should i trust you?": explaining the predictions of any classifier. In: Proceedings of the 22nd ACM SIGKDD International Conference on Knowledge Discovery and Data Mining, pp. 1135–1144 (2016)
59. Rombach, R., Blattmann, A., Lorenz, D., Esser, P., Ommer, B.: High-resolution image synthesis with latent diffusion models. In: Proceedings of the IEEE/CVF Conference on Computer Vision and Pattern Recognition, pp. 10684–10695 (2022)
60. Sagawa, S., Koh, P.W., Hashimoto, T.B., Liang, P.: Distributionally robust neural networks for group shifts: on the importance of regularization for worst-case generalization (2020)
61. Samek, W., Montavon, G., Lapuschkin, S., Anders, C.J., Müller, K.R.: Explaining deep neural networks and beyond: a review of methods and applications. Proc. IEEE **109**(3), 247–278 (2021)
62. Samek, W., Montavon, G., Vedaldi, A., Hansen, L.K., Müller, K.R.: Explainable AI: Interpreting, Explaining and Visualizing Deep Learning, vol. 11700. Springer, Cham (2019). https://doi.org/10.1007/978-3-030-28954-6
63. Scriver, A.: Semantic distance in WordNet: a simplified and improved measure of semantic relatedness. Master's thesis, University of Waterloo (2006)
64. Selvaraju, R.R., Cogswell, M., Das, A., Vedantam, R., Parikh, D., Batra, D.: Grad-CAM: visual explanations from deep networks via gradient-based localization. Int. J. Comput. Vision **128**(2), 336–359 (2019)
65. Seyyed-Kalantari, L., Zhang, H., McDermott, M.B.A., Chen, I.Y., Ghassemi, M.: Underdiagnosis bias of artificial intelligence algorithms applied to chest radiographs in under-served patient populations. Nat. Med. **27**(12), 2176–2182 (2021)
66. Shetty, R., Schiele, B., Fritz, M.: Not using the car to see the sidewalk - quantifying and controlling the effects of context in classification and segmentation. In: Proceedings of the IEEE/CVF Conference on Computer Vision and Pattern Recognition, pp. 8218–8226 (2019)
67. Shin, D.: The effects of explainability and causability on perception, trust, and acceptance: implications for explainable AI. Int. J. Hum Comput Stud. **146**, 102551 (2021)
68. Simon, H.A.: Spurious correlation: a causal interpretation. J. Am. Stat. Assoc. **49**(267), 467–479 (1954)
69. Singla, S., Feizi, S.: Salient ImageNet: how to discover spurious features in deep learning? In: International Conference on Learning Representations (2022)
70. Slack, D., Hilgard, A., Singh, S., Lakkaraju, H.: Reliable post hoc explanations: modeling uncertainty in explainability. In: Advances in Neural Information Processing Systems, vol. 34, pp. 9391–9404 (2021)
71. Smilkov, D., Thorat, N., Kim, B., Viégas, F., Wattenberg, M.: SmoothGrad: removing noise by adding noise. arXiv preprint arXiv:1706.03825 (2017)
72. Stock, P., Cisse, M.: ConvNets and ImageNet beyond accuracy: understanding mistakes and uncovering biases. In: Proceedings of the European Conference on Computer Vision (ECCV), pp. 498–512 (2018)
73. Sundararajan, M., Taly, A., Yan, Q.: Axiomatic attribution for deep networks. In: International Conference on Machine Learning, pp. 3319–3328. PMLR (2017)
74. Szegedy, C., et al.: Going deeper with convolutions. In: Proceedings of the IEEE Conference on Computer Vision and Pattern Recognition, pp. 1–9 (2015)

75. Tjoa, E., Guan, C.: A survey on explainable artificial intelligence (XAI): toward medical XAI. IEEE Trans. Neural Netw. Learn. Syst. **32**(11), 4793–4813 (2020)
76. Wallis, D., Buvat, I.: Clever Hans effect found in a widely used brain tumour MRI dataset. Med. Image Anal. **77**, 102368 (2022)
77. Wu, X., Sahoo, D., Hoi, S.C.: Recent advances in deep learning for object detection. Neurocomputing **396**, 39–64 (2020)
78. Xiao, K., Engstrom, L., Ilyas, A., Madry, A.: Noise or signal: the role of image backgrounds in object recognition (2020)
79. Yu, J., Wang, Z., Vasudevan, V., Yeung, L., Seyedhosseini, M., Wu, Y.: CoCa: contrastive captioners are image-text foundation models. arXiv preprint arXiv:2205.01917 (2022)
80. Zaidi, S.S.A., Ansari, M.S., Aslam, A., Kanwal, N., Asghar, M., Lee, B.: A survey of modern deep learning based object detection models. Digit. Signal Process. 103514 (2022)
81. Zech, J.R., Badgeley, M.A., Liu, M., Costa, A.B., Titano, J.J., Oermann, E.K.: Variable generalization performance of a deep learning model to detect pneumonia in chest radiographs: a cross-sectional study. PLoS Med. **15**(11), e1002683 (2018)
82. Zhao, J., Wang, T., Yatskar, M., Ordonez, V., Chang, K.W.: Men also like shopping: reducing gender bias amplification using corpus-level constraints. In: Proceedings of the 2017 Conference on Empirical Methods in Natural Language Processing, pp. 2979–2989. Association for Computational Linguistics, Copenhagen (2017)

Explaining Search Result Stances
to Opinionated People

Zhangyi Wu[1]([✉]) [ID], Tim Draws[2] [ID], Federico Cau[1] [ID], Francesco Barile[1] [ID],
Alisa Rieger[2] [ID], and Nava Tintarev[1] [ID]

[1] Maastricht University, Maastricht, Netherlands
`zhangyi.wu@student.maastrichtuniversity.nl`,
{`federico.cau,f.barile,n.tintarev`}`@maastrichtuniversity.nl`
[2] Delft University of Technology, Delft, Netherlands
{`t.a.draws,a.rieger`}`@tudelft.nl`

Abstract. People use web search engines to find information before
forming opinions, which can lead to practical decisions with different
levels of impact. The cognitive effort of search can leave opinionated
users vulnerable to cognitive biases, e.g., the *confirmation bias*. In this
paper, we investigate whether stance labels and their explanations can
help users consume more diverse search results. We automatically classify and label search results on three topics (i.e., *intellectual property
rights*, *school uniforms*, and *atheism*) as *against*, *neutral*, and *in favor*,
and generate explanations for these labels. In a user study (N=203), we
then investigate whether search result stance bias (balanced vs biased)
and the level of explanation (plain text, label only, label and explanation) influence the diversity of search results clicked. We find that stance
labels and explanations lead to a more diverse search result consumption. However, we do not find evidence for systematic opinion change
among users in this context. We believe these results can help designers
of search engines to make more informed design decisions.

Keywords: Explainable Search · Confirmation Bias · User Study

1 Introduction

Web search that can lead to consequential decision-making frequently concerns *debated topics*, topics that different people and groups disagree on, such
as *whether to vaccinate a child* or *whether nuclear energy should be used as
a power source*. Prior research has shown that the interplay between search
engine biases and users' cognitive biases can lead to noteworthy behavioral patterns. For instance, when search result stance biases interact with cognitive user
biases, information seekers may experience the *search engine manipulation effect*
(SEME): the tendency to adopt the stance expressed by the majority of (highly-ranked) search results [3,9,15,33]. However, these results have only been studied
and found for users who are undecided, not for users who already have strong
opinions, who we refer to as *opinionated* users.

© The Author(s), under exclusive license to Springer Nature Switzerland AG 2023
L. Longo (Ed.): xAI 2023, CCIS 1902, pp. 573–596, 2023.
https://doi.org/10.1007/978-3-031-44067-0_29

High cognitive demand during complex web searches can increase the risk of cognitive biases [6]. One such bias is the *confirmation bias*, which involves a preference for information that aligns with preexisting beliefs while disregarding contradictory information during the search process [6,31]. Interventions to mitigate confirmation bias during web search have aimed at decreasing engagement with attitude-confirming and increasing engagement with attitude-opposing information [38], i.e., reducing interaction with search results that confirm a user's attitude and increasing interaction with search results that challenge a user's attitude. Interventions to reduce interaction with particular items have also been investigated in the context of misinformation. One effective method for reducing interaction with misleading content involves *labels* to flag certain items [10,23,29].

The core issue with confirmation bias during web search, similar to the related issues of misinformation and SEME, is that users consume biased content. This motivated us to investigate interventions to increase the diversity of consumption and specifically whether labels indicating stance, and their explanations, are likewise successful for confirmation bias mitigation during search on debated topics. Therefore the goal of these interventions is to promote unbiased web search and mitigate the effects of users' confirmation bias and underlying (stance) biases in a *search engine result page* (SERP). Consequently, this paper aims to address the following question: ***Do automatically generated stance labels and explanations of the labels for search results increase the diversity of viewpoints users engage with, even if search results are biased?***

To address this question, we test three hypotheses. Previous work has found that undecided users are likely to change their opinion when exposed to biased search results, since they select more search results reflecting a certain opinion [3,14,15,33]. However, in this study we restrict participants to opinionated users, having *strong* existing opinions on a topic, and investigate whether ***H1a):*** *Users who are exposed to viewpoint-biased search results interact with <u>less diverse results</u> than users who are exposed to balanced search results.*

Second, informative labels have been shown to mitigate confirmation bias in search results [38]. Therefore, in this study, we investigate whether simple stance labels (*against, neutral,* and *in favor*), and stance labels with explanations (importance of keywords) are effective for mitigating confirmation bias. This leads to ***H1b):*** *Users who are exposed to search results with (1) stance labels or (2) stance labels with explanations for each search result interact with more diverse content than users who are exposed to regular search results.*

Third, if the labels are effective in reducing confirmation bias, we would expect an interaction effect between the bias in search results and explanation level (plain, label, label plus explanation): ***H1c)*** *Users who are exposed to search results with (1) stance labels or (2) stance labels with explanations are less susceptible to the effect of viewpoint biases in search results on clicking diversity.*

We investigate these hypotheses in a pre-registered between-subjects user study ($N=203$) simulating an open search task.[1] Our results show that both

---

stance labels and explanations, led to a more diverse search result consumption compared to plain (unlabeled) search result pages. However, we did not find evidence that the explanations influenced opinion change. We believe these results can help designers of search engines to make more informed design decisions.

2   Related Work

Explainable Artificial Intelligence (XAI) aims to help people understand the decisions and predictions AI systems make. In this paper, we investigate specifically how XAI can support users in searching for disputed topics. Search for debated topics is highly subjective: when users search the web to seek advice or form opinions on these kinds of topics, not just search result *relevance* but also the stance of content is influential [3,14,15,33,38]. To mitigate undesired effects such as biased opinion change, earlier work has measured and increased the fairness [18,50,53] and viewpoint diversity in search results [13,34,47].

On the user interface side, it could be fruitful to label and explain the stance represented on a search engine results page (or SERP). These labels are related to the task known as *stance detection*, which is predominantly applied in a *target-specific* fashion. That is, detecting not just a sentiment, but how it is referred to in relation to a specific topic or claim (often referred to as the *target*, e.g., "people should wear school uniforms") [2]. Stance detection is a multi-class classification task (i.e., typically classifying documents into *against*, *neutral*, and *in favor*, so predictive performances are most commonly reported in terms of macro F1 scores [24]. Furthermore, web search interventions targeting the mitigation of undesired effects, such as SEME, require *cross-target* stance detection models to quickly respond to the large variety of debated topics users may search for. Here, stance detection models are applied to data sets where each document may be relevant to one of many potential topics [2,24]. Constructing models that classify documents into stances related to *any* topic in such a way may lead to weaker predictive accuracy compared to target-specific methods, but makes stance detection more generalizable and scalable. Cross-target ternary stance detection by previous work (e.g., on news articles or tweets) have ranged roughly from macro F1 scores of .450 to .750 [1,4,5,21,36,49].

Also comparable are the cross-topic stance detection models evaluated using the *Emergent* data set (and its follow-up version, the *2017 Fake News Challenge* data set) which have achieved macro F1 scores of up to .756 [20,39,41]. While the main contribution of this paper is not to improve on the state of the art for stance detection, the stance detection method (DistilBERT) used here is comparable to this state of the art (macro F1 of 0.72). DistilBERT is much smaller than other pre-trained models, and handles small datasets well [42,44,46].

What XAI methods are suitable for explaining stance detection to users? Stance detection can be seen as a text classification task. For text classification, explanations containing *input features* have been found to be highly adaptable and often meaningful to humans [12,28].

The way in which explanations can be visualized depends on the data type, purpose, and audience. Many current methods indicate input features as feature importance using a saliency map [37,45]. When the features are readable texts, saliency information is shown by highlighting the most significant input at word or token level [22]. There have been some instances where researchers used text-based saliency maps to demonstrate their findings [19]. To the best of our knowledge, no previous work has explored whether highlighting salient words in search results would mitigate people's clicking bias. One of the most closely related works found that feature-based explanations could help users simulate model predictions for search results [12]. Another similar study involves a verbal saliency map using a model-agnostic explainer and a human evaluation of explanation representations of news topic classifier and sentiment analysis [17]. Their finding is that the saliency map makes explanations more understandable and less cognitively challenging for humans than heatmap visualization. However, our work differs from theirs in several ways: we study explanations in the context of search engines, and we have conducted a full-fledged user study while they only performed a pilot study.

Contribution to Knowledge for XAI. Previous XAI literature has contributed to explaining information retrieval systems, focusing on the interpretability of document-retrieval mechanisms [25,26,52]. For example, the authors of [52] propose a listwise explanation generator, which provides an explanation that covers all the documents contained in the page (e.g., by describing which query aspects were covered by each document). These explanations were not evaluated by people. Another paper studied how well explanations of individual search results helped people anticipate model predictions [12], but did not consider cognitive or stance bias. In contrast to previous work, this paper examines how explanations affect users, considering the potential mitigation of their cognitive biases on search engine manipulation effects (SEME). In doing so, we see a need to address both potential (stance) bias within a search result page, and the bias of users consuming these results. To the best of our knowledge, this is also the first work to conduct empirical experiments on users' *behavior* in response to explanations in the context of information retrieval.

3   Methodology

This section describes the materials we used for organizing the user study (e.g., data set, stance detection model, explanation generation, and search interface).

3.1   Data Preparation

To train, test, and explain the stance detection model, we considered a public data set containing search results related to three debated topics (i.e., *atheism, intellectual property rights*, and *school uniforms*) [13].[2] [13] motivate the selection

---

[2] The data set is available at https://osf.io/yghr2.

Table 1. Topic and stance distribution in the used data.

Topic	N	Stance Distribution
		Against – Neutral – In Favor
Intellectual property rights	378	10.5% – 17.7% – 71.7%
School uniforms	395	21.5% – 36.7% – 41.8%
Atheism	352	19.8% – 46.3% – 33.8%
Total	1125	17.3% – 33.3% – 49.3%

of these three topics because they offer valid arguments for both supporting and opposing viewpoints. Additionally, they argue that opinions on these topics have diverse impacts, ranging from concerning mainly the user (atheism) to businesses (intellectual property rights) and society (school uniforms). These data include URLs, titles, snippets, and stance labels for a total of 1475 search results, which had been retrieved via API or web crawling from two popular web search engines.

Stance labels had been assigned (by experts) on seven-point Likert scales (i.e., including three degrees of opposing or supporting a topic), which we mapped into the three categories *against*, *neutral*, and *in favor* (i.e., which is what most current stance detection methods handle). Using the provided URLs, we crawled the full web page text bodies (stripped of any HTML tags) for all search results. We here dropped 347 search results from the data as their text bodies could not be retrieved (e.g., because of 404 errors), leaving 1125 search results accompanied by their respective text bodies. Finally, we processed the retrieved contents by truncating each document's middle section, retaining only its head and tail, then concatenating each search result's title, snippet, and the head section and tail section, while ensuring that the result is exactly 510 tokens long. We removed all other information from the data aside from the documents' stance labels. Table 1 shows the stance distribution per topic in our final data set.

3.2 Stance Detection Model

After pre-processing (tokenization), we developed the model for classifying search results into against, neutral, and in favor. The dataset was split into training (75%) and validation/test (25%) sets. We fine-tuned the model for different hyperparameters. After every epoch the validation set were evaluated to monitor its learning progress. Once the model's evaluation loss stops to decrease for 5 epochs the training is terminated and is evaluated based on the unseen test set, and the result is considered the general performance that we report. The best-performing model and learned parameters were used as the predictor for identifying labels and generating explanations.

Tokenization. Before training the stance classification model, we needed further preprocessing of the raw search results. Specifically, we had to *tokenize* each word before feeding the search results into the model. The tokenization

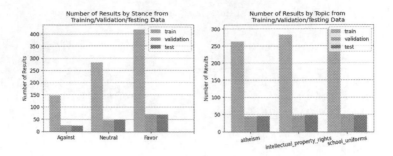

Fig. 1. Distributions of Attributes Across the Training, Validation and Test Set

process performs tasks such as handling subwords, adding special tokens to pad a sequence of words to a `max length`, or indicating the beginning or end of a sequence. In our work, we instantiated the DistilBERT tokenizer using the Auto-Tokenizer class provided by the `transformers` [48]. We set the `length` of the tokenizer to a size of 512.

Training Details. Similar to previous work performing search result stance classification [12], we built one cross-topic model using our entire data set. First, we split the dataset in a stratified manner, which preserves the percentage of the topic and labels in each subset. Figure 1 shows the final split across the training, validation, and test sets on both topics and labels. Then, we classified search results into stance categories (i.e., *in favor*, *against*, or *neutral*), using a pre-trained version of the uncased DistilBERT base model [40] from HuggingFace. Specifically, we fine-tuned DistilBERT using 75% (843) of the documents in our data and split the remaining 25% (282) equally for validation and testing. Due to the relatively small size of our dataset, we tried to avoid over-fitting by using neural network dropout and stopping training when evaluation loss stops improving for 5 epochs [43,51]. We trained using the same dataset split and experimented with learning rates ranging from $5e$–6 to $1e$–4. Regarding the remain hyper-parameters, the models were optimized using the Adam optimizer with a learning rate of $1e-5$, the batch size was set to 8 and we set the dropout rate of both attention layers and fully connected layers to 0.4.

Metric. In our stance detection task, we have three labels to be classified, and their distribution is uneven. To take performance on all stances into account, we considered the macro F1 score, defined as the average of the F1 scores for each of the three stances:

$$macro_{F1} = (F1(stance = favor) + F1(stance = neutral) + F1(stance = against))/3 \quad (1)$$

Model Performance. We obtained a stance detection model by fine-tuning the DistilBERT model for our downstream classification task. The fine-tuning process was completed through HuggingFace's `Trainer` interface. The progress of each run was tracked using Weights & Biases.[3] We observed that the learning rate of $1e$–5 gave the best performance with a macro F1 score of 0.72.[4]

3.3   Creating Explanations

Instance Selection. For the user study, we selected search results correctly predicted by the model, picking them mainly from the test set and some from the validation set. As mentioned before, the train, validation, and test sets were split in a stratified way, which preserves the frequencies of our target classes. To assemble search results for our study, we randomly drew 21 *correctly predicted* search results per topic from our test and validation data (i.e., seven against, seven neutral toward, and seven in favor of the topic). The SERPs later displayed 10 results per page.

LIME Parameter Tuning. After we fine-tuned and evaluated the model on the search result corpus, we used LIME (Local Interpretable Model-Agnostic Explanations) to explain the model's predictions [37].[5] For text data, LIME outputs a list of features (tokens) from the input sentence, ranked by their importance w.r.t. a model's specific prediction. We generated the explanations by setting the neighborhood size to learn the linear model to 5000, kernel_width to 50,[6] and showing the top 20 important tokens (or less based on the text length) belonging to the model's predicted class.

3.4   Search Engine

Architecture. We implemented our web-based search interface using the SearchX platform as a basis [35]. The web application has both a front-end and a back-end. The front-end is built on NodeJS using React and Flux frameworks and manages users' data by sending logs to the back-end, which mainly handles the retrieval of search results from the database and stores the logs from the front-end.

---

[3] https://wandb.ai.

[4] Due to a minor error in evaluation, a slightly higher macro F1 score was reported in the pre-registration. However, this erroneous score did not influence the training process or affect our user study.

[5] https://github.com/marcotcr/lime.

[6] We tried multiple kernel sizes (10, 25, 50, and 75) and chose a value of 50 since we got a slight increase in the R2 scores for each LIME local prediction on the test set of about 3–4% on average compared to the other sizes.

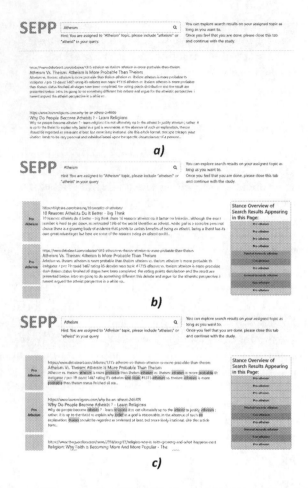

Fig. 2. Different conditions for the SERP display. *a)* Text-only Search Result Page. *b)* Predicted stance labels. *c)* Predicted stance labels and Explanations.

Interface. We designed the search interface as follows. As soon as users open the homepage of the study, saw a search bar positioned at the top of the page, where they may enter their queries. The search engine showed results only when the input query included one or more keywords referring to the user's assigned topic (among atheism, intellectual property rights, and school uniforms). Otherwise, showed a message informing users that no results were found for their query. We provided users with the topic and the specific keyword to include in the query with a sentence below the search bar. For the *Atheism* topic, the keywords are "atheist" or "atheism", for the *intellectual property right* topic, the keywords are "property right", "intellectual right" or "intellectual property right", while for the *school uniform* topic, keywords are "uniform" or "school uniform".

After the users inserted a query including the above mentioned keywords, the interface displayed a list of matched results. This set of search results had a different arrangement based on the random condition a user was assigned to. We set up three SERP display conditions (see Sect. 4.2): 1) text-only SERP, 2) SERP with labels; and 3) SERP with labels and explanations. The text-only SERP showed ten search results without any extra information. Each search result had two parts: a clickable title redirecting the user to the corresponding webpage and a snippet showing some of its content. Figure 2 a) shows the layout of this type of interface. The SERP with labels introduces two new features: the labels indicating the original content's stance and an overview of all the search results labels on the right side of the webpage. As shown in Fig. 2 b), we assigned a different color representing each viewpoint. We also added extra information to each label, indicating whether the document is *against, neutral, or in favor* of the topic. The third type of SERP interface makes use of a mono-chromatic saliency map (see Fig. 2 c), highlighting the top 20 words that best contribute to the prediction in the search result snippet. Due to the space limitation of the interface, not all the feature would appear in the snippet. The color of the saliency map aligns with the color of the label. We use the same color for all 20 feature words regardless of their significance to make it less complicated for users to understand.

Table 2. Templates for the first SERP (i.e., the top 10-ranked search results) in each SERP ranking bias condition.

Rank	Biased Opp. (T1)	Biased Supp. (T2)	Balanced (T3)
1	Against	Favor	Neutral
2	Against	Favor	Neutral
3	Against	Favor	Neutral
4	Against	Favor	Neutral
5	Favor	Against	Against
6	Neutral	Neutral	Neutral
7	Against	Favor	Favor
8	Favor	Against	Against
9	Neutral	Neutral	Neutral
10	Against	Favor	Favor

Biased Versus Balanced Results. We ranked search results depending on the ranking bias condition randomly assigned to each user. Specifically, we created *biased* and *balanced* top 10 search result ranking templates, according to which we would later display search results to users. Biased search results were biased either in the *against* or *in favor* direction and thus contain only results of one of these two stance classes in the top four ranking spots (the remaining six results were balanced across stance classes). Users who were assigned to the *biased* condition would see search results biased in the opposite direction compared to their pre-search opinion (e.g., if they were in favor of school uniforms, they would see results biased against school uniforms). Users who were assigned to the balanced condition would see a similar search result page, but with neutral search results in the top four spots. Neutral results either do not contain any arguments on the debated topic or equally many arguments in both directions.[7] Table 2 shows an overview of the ranking templates.

4   User Study Setup

4.1   Research Ethics and Pre-registration

We deployed the web application on servers owned by the Faculty of Maastricht University (UM server) and secured the connection through HTTPS protocol with SSL certificates. The study was reviewed and accepted by our review board. The data collected from users, ranging from demographical information to user's clicking behaviours, are all stored anonymously in the server. Prior to the launch of the user study, the research question, hypotheses, methodology, measurements, etc. were pre-registered on the Open Science Framework. Only minor changes were made, including balancing the number of participants in the different conditions, change the way we measure users' attitude change, and correcting a computation error in the macro F1 score.

4.2   Variables

In our study, each subject could look at search results (i.e., 10 search results per page) accompanied by different features. We analyzed the participants' attitudes and interaction behavior (with a focus on the proportion of clicks on attitude-confirming search results).

Independent variables.

- *Topic* (between-subjects, categorical). Participants were assigned to one topic (i.e., atheism, intellectual property rights, or school uniforms) for which they have a strong pre-search attitude (i.e., strongly opposing or strongly supporting). If a participant had no strong attitude on any topic, they ended the study. If a participant had multiple strong attitudes, they were assigned to the topic that has the fewest participants at that point in the study (i.e., to move toward a balanced topic distribution).

---

[7] We chose this setup to make the conditions as comparable as possible, e.g., rather than displaying results in alternating fashion in the balanced condition.

- *SERP ranking bias* (between-subjects, categorical). There were two types of ranking conditions: biased and balanced. For each of these two conditions, we preset a ranking template (see Table 2). Participants would see a search result page with ten items which were ranked in accordance with the template. If a user was assigned to the biased condition, they would see opposing-biased search results if their pre-search attitude was *in favor* (i.e., 3) and supporting-biased search results if their pre-search attitude was *against* (i.e., −3).
- *SERP display* (between-subjects, categorical). Each participant saw search results accompanied by one of these features: (1) plain text results without stance labels, (2) results with predicted stance labels (Fig. 2 b), or (3) results with predicted stance labels and highlighted explanations (Fig. 2 c).

Dependent Variable.

- *Shannon Index* (numerical). The Shannon Index was applied to measure the diversity of users' clicks. Let N be the total number of clicks made in one session, n_0, n_1, n_2 be the number of clicks of "against", "neutral" and "favor" items respectively. The formula for computing clicking diversity is: $-\sum_{i=0}^{2} \frac{n_i}{N} \ln(\frac{n_i}{N})$. The convention for no occurrence of a class is to ignore it as $\ln(0)$ is undefined [27]. For instance, the Shannon Index for $(0, 1, 3)$ is $0 + 0.34 + 0.21 = 0.55$. The minimum value of the Shannon Index is 0, which indicates that there is no diversity and only one viewpoint was clicked on. When each class is equal the Shannon entropy has the highest value (for three classes, this would be $3 * (-\frac{1}{3}) \ln(\frac{1}{3}) = 1.1$).

Descriptive and Exploratory Measurements. We used these variables to describe our sample and for exploratory analyses, but we did not conduct any conclusive hypothesis tests on them.

- *Demographics* (categorical). We asked participants to state their gender, age group, and level of education from multiple choices. Each of these items includes a "prefer not to say" option.
- *Clicks on Neutral Items* (numerical). In a balanced SERP, the majority of items were neutral. We were specifically interested in whether participants' engagement with search results with a neutral stance is affected by the SERP display condition.
- *Clicking Diversity* (numerical). We logged the clicking behavior of participants during the survey and computed the ratio of pre-search attitude-confirming vs. attitude-opposing search results among the results a user has clicked on. Clicks on neutral search results were not regarded for this variable.
- *Attitude Change* (numerical). In line with previous research [14,15,38], we asked participants to select their attitudes on debated topics before and after the experiments using a seven-point Likert scale ranging from "strongly opposing" to "strongly supporting". The difference between their two answers is then assessed in the analysis.
- *Textual feedback* (free text). We asked participants to provide feedback on the explanations and the task.

Procedure. Participants completed the study in three steps as described below. The survey was conducted on Qualtrics[8], while the interaction with search results occurred on our own server.

Step 1. After agreeing to an informed consent, participants were asked to report their gender, age group, and level of education. Participants were first asked to imagine the following scenario:

> *You and your friend were having a dinner together. Your friend is very passionate about a debated topic and couldn't help sharing his views and ideas with you. After the dinner, you decide to further inform yourself on the topic by conducting a web search.*

Furthermore, participants were asked to state their attitudes concerning each debated topic (see Sect. 3.1; including one attention check for which we specifically instruct participants on what option to select from a Likert scale).

Step 2. We introduced participants to the task and subsequently assigned them to one of the three debated topics (i.e., *atheism*, *intellectual property rights*, and *school uniforms*) depending on their pre-search attitudes and randomly assigned them to one SERP ranking bias condition and one SERP display condition (see Sect. 4.2). Participants were then asked to click on a link leading them to our search platform (i.e., SEPP; see Sect. 3.4). Here, participants could enter as many queries as they want, as long as those queries include their assigned topic term (e.g., `school uniforms pros and cons` for the topic *school uniforms*). Regardless of what or how many queries participants enter, they always received search results from the same pool of 21 available search results relevant to their assigned topic (i.e., seven against, seven neutral, and seven in favor; see Sect. 3.1). With every query that participants entered, they received those search results ranked according to the ranking template associated to their assigned SERP ranking bias condition (see Sect. 3.4) for the first SERP and randomly drawn search results (following the template) for consequent searches.[9] Depending on the SERP display condition participants were assigned to, they could see either plain search results, search results accompanied by stance labels, or search results accompanied by stance labels with additional explanations. Participants were made aware that the search results they were seeing might be biased and that there were limited results. After entering a query, participants were free to explore search results as long as they wish and click on links that lead to the presented web pages, or enter new queries. Users were instructed to return to the Qualtrics survey when they were done searching.

Step 3. Finally, in the questionnaire, we asked participants to report their post-search attitude (towards their assigned topic). Further, we asked them to provide textual feedback on the explanations and the task. We also included another

---

[8] https://www.qualtrics.com/.

[9] Whenever a user enters a new query, the first SERP (i.e., displaying the top 10 results) will always show search results according to the template, whereas pages 2 and 3 will show the 21 search results relevant to the topic in random order.

attention check to filter out low-quality data in this post-interaction question-naire. The attention checks consisted of one straightforward question with sug-gested response options. We excluded the data of participants who failed one or more of the attention checks from data analysis.

Recruitment Methods. In this study, we used Prolific[10] and Qualtrics[11] to manage the participants and design survey workflow, respectively. The workflow of our study, including the informed consent, screening questions, and link to the survey, were all completed on Qualtrics. In the recruitment platform Prolific, we only selected participants with a minimum age of 18 (in compliance with research ethics), and fluent in English, as our dataset only contains English results.

Sample Details. We anticipated to observe medium effects for *SERP display* and *SERP ranking bias* on *clicking diversity* (Cohen's $f = 0.25$). Thus, we determined in an a priori power analysis for a between-subjects ANOVA (see Sect. 4.2) a required sample size of 205 participants, assuming a significance threshold of $\alpha = \frac{0.05}{3} = 0.017$ (testing three hypotheses), a desired power of $(1-\beta)$ $= 0.8$ and considering that we tested, depending on the hypothesis, six groups (i.e., three SERP display conditions: *without stance labels, with stance labels, with stance labels and explanation*; and 2 SERP ranking bias conditions: *biased towards the attitude-opposing viewpoint, balanced*) using the software *G*Power* [16]. We aimed for a balanced distribution across topics and conditions.

Participants were required to be older than 18 and with a high proficiency of English (i.e., as reported by *Prolific*). Participants could only participate in our study once. As mentioned above, we excluded participants from data analysis if they did not pass one or more attention checks. We also excluded participants from data analysis if they did not access our search platform at all or if they did not click on any links during their search.

Statistical Analyses. To test our three hypotheses, we conducted Analysis of Variance (ANOVA), looking at the main and interaction effects of the three independent variables (1) the topic, (2) *SERP display* (without stance labels, with stance labels, with stance labels and explanation) and (3) *SERP ranking bias* (biased towards the attitude-opposing viewpoint, balanced) on the *shannon index* (H1a, H1b, H1c). Aiming at a type 1 error probability of $\alpha = 0.05$ and applying Bonferroni correction to correct for multiple testing, we set the signif-icance threshold to $\frac{0.05}{3} = 0.017$. We added *topic* as an additional independent variable to this analysis to control for its potential role as a confounding factor.

In addition to the analyses described above, we conducted posthoc tests (i.e., to analyze pairwise differences) to determine the exact differences and effect size, Bayesian hypothesis tests (i.e., to quantify evidence in favor of null hypotheses), and exploratory analyses (i.e., to note any unforeseen trends in the data) to better understand our results.

---

[10] https://prolific.co.
[11] https://www.qualtrics.com/.

5   Results

The overarching objective of this research is to investigate the effect of extra visual elements such as stance labels and text explanations on users' interaction behaviours, especially in terms of clicking diversity. In this section, we present the final results of the study with 203 participants and address our research question and hypotheses.

Descriptive Statistics. Prior to analyzing the primary statistics, it is necessary to first examine the demographic data. In general, young people made up most of our participants (see Fig. 3). The educational level data reveal that the majority of participants have completed at least some level of higher education, with a smaller percentage have completed advanced degrees.

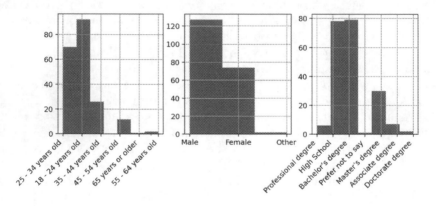

Fig. 3. Demographic information of participants: Bar chart showing the distribution of users' age, gender, and education level.

Participants were roughly equally distributed across the three topics: 70 *atheism*, 66 *intellectual property rights*, and 67 *school uniforms*. Regarding factors such as bias and interface types that were randomized by Qualtrics workflow, their distributions are also balanced, with 102 participants accessed the biased SERPs and 101 accessed balanced SERPs, and 72 users view text-only SERP display, 64 viewed labelled interface and 67 viewed interface with saliency maps. In the pre-survey attitude test, 130 people were granted the access to our survey by expressing rather negative (against) viewpoints towards a specific topic, while only 73 people expressed a positive stance.

Figure 4 shows the diversity of users' clicks as measured by the Shannon index across conditions. For balanced SERPs, the mean Shannon diversity index starts from 0.63 when there are explanation, then it slightly reduces to 0.55 in labelled interface, and drastically drop to 0.24 for the text SERP. For unbalanced SERPs, the trend is similar, from 0.64 to roughly 0.52, but the reduction is less drastic. In

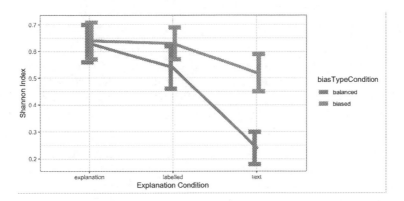

Fig. 4. Shannon Index across SERP Display conditions, split by ranking bias conditions. Error bars represent confidence intervals.

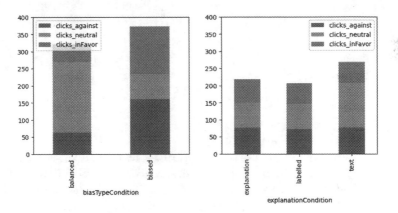

Fig. 5. Number of clicks on items of each stance made by users under different conditions. Left: different bias type, Right: different interface

short, those who interacted with balanced pages overall scored somewhat lower in Shannon diversity.

Figure 5 shows the stacked histogram representing users' click history under different conditions. In the left subplot, we see that *neutral* items attracted more clicks than *favor* and *against* combined in the balanced setting. In the biased setting, however, the number neutral clicks starts to shrink and user start to visit polarized contents more. It is notable that users clicked more *neutral* items in the text-only SERP display. The other two types of interface seem to generate very similar amounts of clicks for each stance.

5.1   Hypothesis Tests

We ran an ANOVA test to examine the relationship between the variable *Shannon index* and other predictor variables, including *explanation condition, bias type* and *assigned topic*. Table 3 contains the results of the ANOVA test, including the F-statistic, p-value, and degrees of freedom for each variable and interaction. We also included the assigned topic in the test to control for topic as a potential confounding factor.

Table 3. ANOVA results for the Shannon index and independent variables including the explanation level, bias type, the interaction between explanation and bias type, and the topic the user holds strong opinion towards. Under our reduced significance threshold, only the *Explanation* effect is significant.

Variable	Df	Sum Sq	Mean Sq	F	p
SERP Ranking Bias	1	0.81	0.8146	4.911	.027
SERP Display	2	2.54	1.2712	7.664	<.001
Topic	2	0.03	0.0158	0.095	.909
SERP RB:SERP Display	2	0.65	0.3256	1.963	.143
Residuals	195	32.34	0.1659		

H1a: Users who are exposed to viewpoint-biased search results interact with less diverse results than users who are exposed to balanced search results. To test this hypothesis, we examine the Shannon diversity of clicks made by users who viewed viewpoint-biased search engine result pages (SERPs) to those who did not. Figure 4 suggests that users who were exposed to more balanced search results clicked on somewhat less diverse content. However, in the ANOVA summary (Table 3), we see that the influence of bias type ($F = 4.911, df = 1, p = .027$, Cohen's $f = 0.16$) is not statistically significant, given the significance threshold of .017. We thus do not find any conclusive evidence for a difference in the diversity of clicked results between bias conditions.

H1b: Users who are exposed to search results with (1) stance labels or (2) stance labels with explanations for each search result interact with more diverse content than users who are exposed to regular search results. Regarding H1b, compare users' clicks in different SERP displays. The results of the ANOVA shows a significant effect of explanation condition on clicking diversity ($F = 7.664, df = 2, p < .001$, Cohen's $f = 0.28$). This suggests that there is a difference in the diversity of content interacted between users who were exposed to (1) plain search results, (2) search results with stance labels, or (3) search results with stance labels and also explanations. We conducted a pairwise Tukey test to determine whether there are significant differences between SERP display levels (text, label, explanation). We found significant differences between `text-label` and `text-explanation` (with adjusted p-values of .0008 and .012, respectively), suggesting that both stance labels and stance labels with explanations led to more diverse clicks compared to the regular SERPs. The p-value of `labelled-explanation` group is .723, indicating that there may be no difference in Shannon diversity between the *labelled* and *explanation* group.

H1c: Users who are exposed to search results with (1) stance labels or (2) stance labels with explanations are less susceptible to the effect of viewpoint biases in search results on clicking diversity. This hypothesis concerns the interaction effect between SERP display and bias types on the Shannon index. Our ANOVA (Table 3) did not reveal any evidence for such an interaction effect ($F = 1.963, df = 2, p = .143$, Cohen's $f = 0.02$). In other words, when users are looking at different types of SERP displays but are exposed to the same level of viewpoint bias, our results do not contain evidence that users will click more diverse items because explanations and labels are visible.

5.2 Exploratory Analysis

To further understand our results, we also conducted exploratory analysis. Note that these analyses were not preregistered.

Clicks on Neutral Items. To better understand why the search results were more diverse in the labeled and explanation conditions, we looked closer at the distribution across the three viewpoints. In Fig. 5, we can already see a larger number of neutral results for the text-only condition. Furthermore, in every SERP display, users who were exposed to a balanced page clicked on more neutral items on average. This may be due to their tendency to click on highly-ranked neutral items while being unaware of the stance.

We conducted an exploratory ANOVA to investigate the effects of biases and interfaces on the number of clicks on neutral items. Table 4 lists the test results.

Table 4. Results of the ANOVA analysis on for number of neutral clicks.

Variable	Df	Sum Sq	Mean Sq	F	p
SERP Ranking Bias	1	84.3	84.30	44.308	<.001
SERP Display	2	23.1	11.54	6.067	.003
SERP RB:SERP Display	2	15.6	7.79	4.096	.018
Residuals	197	374.8	1.90		

We can observe that both explanation condition and bias condition had main effects on click diversity. Also their interaction is significant. This means that users may click on more neutral results in the balanced condition, and especially so when SERPs do not contain any stance labels or explanations.

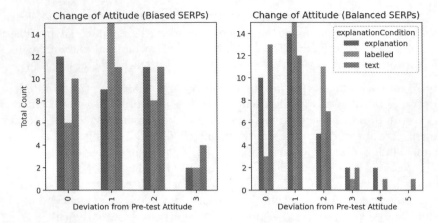

Fig. 6. Histogram visualizing the difference between pre- and post-survey attitudes. Each group of bins indicates the number of people in a bias type setting who changed their viewpoints towards their assigned topic by a certain number of points. The X-axis indicates the normalized difference of attitude between the pre- and post-survey answers measured by a 7-point Likert Scale.

Table 5. Absolute values of attitude change per condition.

Bias Type	SERP display	Attitude Change (Mean)	Attitude Change (Median)	Skewness
Balanced	Text-only	1.14	1.00	1.31
	Labelled	1.30	1.00	0.15
	Explanation	1.15	1.00	1.10
Biased	Text-only	1.25	1.00	0.20
	Labelled	1.19	1.00	0.35
	Explanation	1.09	1.00	0.25

Attitude Change. Previous research showed that mildly opinionated users' attitude change can differ across levels of ranking bias [3,8,14,15,33]. However, this effect has, to the best of our knowledge, not yet been shown for strongly opinionated users such as in our study. We intended to measure the attitude change by subtracting the post-search viewpoint t_1 from the pre-search viewpoint t_0, and thus the difference would range from -6 to 6. We summarize users' attitude change in Fig. 6 and Table 5.

From Fig. 6, we observe that only a few participants developed large attitude changes (absolute value > 3) after the survey. In Table 5, the mean absolute attitude change ranges from 1.0 to 1.3. The median statistics appear to be very stable; under all conditions, 1 is always the central value. We performed an exploratory ANOVA on the absolute *attitude change* variable (Table 6) but do not find any convincing evidence for an effect of any independent variables on attitude change in our scenario, i.e., apart from a potential role of the topic ($F = 4.132, df = 2, p = .017$) that would need to be further investigated.

Table 6. ANOVA Results: absolute value of users' attitude change

Variable	Df	Sum Sq	Mean Sq	F	p
SERP Ranking Bias	1	0.01	0.013	0.014	.907
SERP Display	2	0.56	0.282	0.296	.744
Topic	2	7.88	3.938	4.132	.017
SERP RB:SERP Display	2	0.55	0.277	0.290	.748
Residuals	195	185.88	0.953		

5.3 Qualitative Feedback

After excluding feedback with fewer than four characters like "no", "nope" etc., there are 59 substantial comments. Positive feedback indicated that participants perceived the search results to be diverse: *"I thought the search engine was quite varied as it provided different types of sources"*. Other participants perceived the viewpoint labels to be accurate: *"The search engine was very useful, and the classification of the information was accurate."* At least some participants were able to perceive the bias in the search result pages: *"the results against atheism were promoted to the top results of the search, it was not an impartial search result"*. While we aimed to mimic a real search engine, some participants may have realized that the results were reshuffled: *"It appears the results of the search were similar or the same in each new search. I'm not sure the words used to determine the stance of the page were appropriate."*

6   Discussion and Limitations

We found a significant effect of *SERP display* on clicking diversity. That is, participants who were exposed to viewpoint labels or viewpoints labels with explanations consumed more diverse results than plain text search. While both non-text SERP displays affect users' click diversity over text-only SERP displays, we cannot observe any additional effect from the SERP display with labels and explanations over the label-only SERP display. Our results suggest that this difference can be explained by a predominance of clicks on the neutral stance in the text-only condition. This, alongside the qualitative comments, suggests that participants trusted and used the labels and explanations to inform themselves diversely. Contrary to our expectations, we did not find evidence for a difference between *biased and balanced search results*, in terms of click diversity. Furthermore, exploratory analyses revealed that users exposed to balanced SERPs clicked on more neutral items.

We further found no exploratory evidence that intervention types (bias of search results; explanation level) affect participants' viewpoints. This later result is not necessarily surprising, given that the participants in this study held strong opinions on the topic. We also would not expect a change because the task given to participants was formulated as low-stakes and open-ended (inform yourself about the topic after speaking to an opinionated friend).

Limitations and Future work. Our study has at least two important limitations. First, each search result in the data set we considered only had one overall viewpoint label, and this was limited to *against, neutral,* and *in favor.* This allowed for scalability but does not reflect the full nuances of online search results. For example, an essay or blog post could express highly diverse perspectives but still receive a positive stance label if that is its overall conclusion. Secondly, our study carefully aimed to balance a controlled environment with maintaining ecological validity. Despite this, it is possible that participants recognized that this was not a true search engine when issuing new queries. Similarly, the selection of templates allowed for some structured reshuffling of results. However, this also meant that strong opinions (contrary to the active user) were always at the top of biased search results. For the balanced condition there were also more neutral results. This likely contributed to the higher diversity of search results selected in the biased condition. In addition, ranking fairness metrics could have been used for the ranked lists, which could have led to slightly different results. Further work is required to disentangle the relationship between position bias and confirmation bias, and to replicate the study with different templates.

7   Conclusion

In this paper, we studied the impact of stance labels and explanations of these labels for search on disputed topics. We found that stance labels and explanations led to a more diverse search result consumption. However, we cannot conclude that explanations have an extra effect in addition to labels on user's click diversity. Whether consuming diverse or more neutral results is preferable is in itself a debated topic. Backfire effects, where users become even more invested in their pre-existing beliefs, are possible when users consume strongly opposing views [32]. Greater diversity can further induce wrong perceptions of present evidence: for example, portraying climate change deniers and believers equally can give the impression that climate change is an open issue and thus may be worse than indeed weighing the evidence on both sides [11]. How much stance diversity is ideal can thus depend on individual user traits [30] and may lie somewhere between the extremes [7]. While these are domains and a context where confirmation biases are expected to be large, similar cognitive biases are likely to occur in other decision-making tasks where XAI is used. Further work is needed to catalogue different scenarios of opinion formation in different domains where confirmation bias may be present.

Acknowledgments. This project has received funding from the European Union's Horizon 2020 research and innovation programme under the Marie Skłodowska-Curie grant agreement No 860621.

References

1. Aldayel, A., Magdy, W.: Your stance is exposed! Analysing possible factors for stance detection on social media. In: Proceedings of the ACM on Human-Computer Interaction, vol. 3(CSCW), pp. 1–20 (2019)
2. Aldayel, A., Magdy, W.: Stance detection on social media: state of the art and trends. Inf. Process. Manage. **58**(4), 102597 (2021). https://doi.org/10.1016/j.ipm.2021.102597
3. Allam, A., Schulz, P.J., Nakamoto, K.: The impact of search engine selection and sorting criteria on vaccination beliefs and attitudes: two experiments manipulating Google output. J. Med. Internet Res. **16**(4), e100 (2014). https://doi.org/10.2196/jmir.2642. http://www.jmir.org/2014/4/e100/
4. Allaway, E., McKeown, K.: Zero-shot stance detection: a dataset and model using generalized topic representations. In: Proceedings of the 2020 Conference on Empirical Methods in Natural Language Processing (EMNLP), pp. 8913–8931. Association for Computational Linguistics, Online (2020). https://doi.org/10.18653/v1/2020.emnlp-main.717. https://aclanthology.org/2020.emnlp-main.717
5. Augenstein, I., Rocktäschel, T., Vlachos, A., Bontcheva, K.: Stance detection with bidirectional conditional encoding. In: Proceedings of the 2016 Conference on Empirical Methods in Natural Language Processing, pp. 876–885. Association for Computing Machinery, New York, NY, USA (2016)
6. Azzopardi, L.: Cognitive biases in search: a review and reflection of cognitive biases in information retrieval (2021)
7. Bail, C.A., et al.: Exposure to opposing views on social media can increase political polarization. Proc. Natl. Acad. Sci. **115**(37), 9216–9221 (2018)
8. Bink, M., Schwarz, S., Draws, T., Elsweiler, D.: Investigating the influence of featured snippets on user attitudes. In: ACM SIGIR Conference on Human Information Interaction and Retrieval. CHIIR 2023, ACM, New York, NY, USA (2023). https://doi.org/10.1145/3576840.3578323
9. Bink, M., Zimmerman, S., Elsweiler, D.: Featured snippets and their influence on users' credibility judgements. In: ACM SIGIR Conference on Human Information Interaction and Retrieval, pp. 113–122. ACM, Regensburg Germany (2022). https://doi.org/10.1145/3498366.3505766
10. Chen, S., Xiao, L., Kumar, A.: Spread of misinformation on social media: what contributes to it and how to combat it. Comput. Hum. Behav. **141**, 107643 (2023). https://doi.org/10.1016/j.chb.2022.107643
11. Cushion, S., Thomas, R.: From quantitative precision to qualitative judgements: professional perspectives about the impartiality of television news during the 2015 UK general election. Journalism **20**(3), 392–409 (2019)
12. Draws, T., et al.: Explainable cross-topic stance detection for search results. In: CHIIR (2023)
13. Draws, T., et al.: Viewpoint diversity in search results. In: Kamps, J., et al. (eds.) ECIR 2023. LNCS, vol. 13980, pp. 279–297. Springer, Cham (2023). https://doi.org/10.1007/978-3-031-28244-7_18
14. Draws, T., Tintarev, N., Gadiraju, U., Bozzon, A., Timmermans, B.: This is not what we ordered: exploring why biased search result rankings affect user attitudes on debated topics. In: Proceedings of the 44th International ACM SIGIR Conference on Research and Development in Information Retrieval, pp. 295–305. SIGIR 2021, Association for Computing Machinery, New York, NY, USA (2021). https://doi.org/10.1145/3404835.3462851. https://dl.acm.org/doi/10.1145/3404835.3462851

15. Epstein, R., Robertson, R.E.: The search engine manipulation effect (SEME) and its possible impact on the outcomes of elections. Proc. Natl. Acad. Sci. **112**(33), E4512–E4521 (2015). https://doi.org/10.1073/pnas.1419828112. http://www.pnas.org/lookup/doi/10.1073/pnas.1419828112
16. Faul, F., Erdfelder, E., Buchner, A., Lang, A.G.: Statistical power analyses using g* power 3.1: tests for correlation and regression analyses. Behav. Res. Meth. **41**(4), 1149–1160 (2009)
17. Feldhus, N., Hennig, L., Nasert, M.D., Ebert, C., Schwarzenberg, R., Möller, S.: Constructing natural language explanations via saliency map verbalization. arXiv preprint arXiv:2210.07222 (2022)
18. Gezici, G., Lipani, A., Saygin, Y., Yilmaz, E.: Evaluation metrics for measuring bias in search engine results. Inf. Retrieval J. **24**(2), 85–113 (2021). https://doi.org/10.1007/s10791-020-09386-w
19. Gohel, P., Singh, P., Mohanty, M.: Explainable AI: current status and future directions. arXiv preprint arXiv:2107.07045 (2021)
20. Hanselowski, A., et al.: A retrospective analysis of the fake news challenge stance-detection task. In: Proceedings of the 27th International Conference on Computational Linguistics, pp. 1859–1874. Association for Computational Linguistics, Santa Fe, New Mexico, USA (2018). https://aclanthology.org/C18-1158
21. Hardalov, M., Arora, A., Nakov, P., Augenstein, I.: Few-shot cross-lingual stance detection with sentiment-based pre-training. In: Proceedings of the AAAI Conference on Artificial Intelligence, vol. 36, pp. 10729–10737. AAAI (2022)
22. Jin, W., Carpendale, S., Hamarneh, G., Gromala, D.: Bridging AI developers and end users: an end-user-centred explainable AI taxonomy and visual vocabularies. In: Proceedings of the IEEE Visualization, Vancouver, BC, Canada, pp. 20–25 (2019)
23. Kaiser, B., Wei, J., Lucherini, E., Lee, K., Matias, J.N., Mayer, J.: Adapting security warnings to counter online disinformation. In: 30th USENIX Security Symposium (USENIX Security 2021), pp. 1163–1180 (2021)
24. Küçük, D., Can, F.: Stance detection: a survey. ACM Comput. Surv. **53**(1), 1–37 (2021). https://doi.org/10.1145/3369026
25. Leonhardt, J., Rudra, K., Anand, A.: Extractive explanations for interpretable text ranking. ACM Trans. Inf. Syst. **41**(4), 1–31 (2023). https://doi.org/10.1145/3576924
26. Lyu, L., Anand, A.: Listwise explanations for ranking models using multiple explainers. In: Kamps, J., et al. (eds.) ECIR 2023. LNCS, vol. 13980, pp. 653–668. Springer, Heidelberg (2023). https://doi.org/10.1007/978-3-031-28244-7_41
27. MacKay, D.J.: Information Theory, Inference and Learning Algorithms. Cambridge University Press, Cambridge (2003)
28. Madsen, A., Reddy, S., Chandar, S.: Post-hoc interpretability for neural NLP: a survey. ACM Comput. Surv. **55**(8), 1–42 (2022)
29. Mena, P.: Cleaning up social media: the effect of warning labels on likelihood of sharing false news on Facebook. Policy Internet **12**, 165–183 (2020). https://doi.org/10.1002/poi3.214
30. Munson, S.A., Resnick, P.: Presenting diverse political opinions: how and how much. In: Proceedings of the SIGCHI Conference on Human Factors in Computing Systems, pp. 1457–1466 (2010)
31. Nickerson, R.S.: Confirmation bias: a ubiquitous phenomenon in many guises. Rev. Gen. Psychol. **2**, 175–220 (1998)
32. Nyhan, B., Reifler, J.: When corrections fail: the persistence of political misperceptions. Polit. Behav. **32**(2), 303–330 (2010)

33. Pogacar, F.A., Ghenai, A., Smucker, M.D., Clarke, C.L.: The positive and negative influence of search results on people's decisions about the efficacy of medical treatments. In: Proceedings of the ACM SIGIR International Conference on Theory of Information Retrieval, pp. 209–216. ACM, Amsterdam The Netherlands (2017). https://doi.org/10.1145/3121050.3121074

34. Puschmann, C.: Beyond the bubble: assessing the diversity of political search results. Digit. Journal. **7**(6), 824–843 (2019). https://doi.org/10.1080/21670811.2018.1539626

35. Putra, S.R., Moraes, F., Hauff, C.: SearchX: empowering collaborative search research. In: The 41st International ACM SIGIR Conference on Research & Development in Information Retrieval, pp. 1265–1268 (2018)

36. Reuver, M., Verberne, S., Morante, R., Fokkens, A.: Is stance detection topic-independent and cross-topic generalizable? - a reproduction study. In: Proceedings of the 8th Workshop on Argument Mining, pp. 46–56. Association for Computational Linguistics, Punta Cana, Dominican Republic (2021). https://doi.org/10.18653/v1/2021.argmining-1.5

37. Ribeiro, M.T., Singh, S., Guestrin, C.:"Why should i trust you?": explaining the predictions of any classifier. In: Proceedings of the 22nd ACM SIGKDD International Conference on Knowledge Discovery and Data Mining (2016)

38. Rieger, A., Draws, T., Tintarev, N., Theune, M.: This item might reinforce your opinion: obfuscation and labeling of search results to mitigate confirmation bias. In: Proceedings of the 32nd ACM Conference on Hypertext and Social Media, pp. 189–199. HT 2021, Association for Computing Machinery, New York, NY, USA (2021). https://doi.org/10.1145/3465336.3475101

39. Roy, A., Fafalios, P., Ekbal, A., Zhu, X., Dietze, S.: Exploiting stance hierarchies for cost-sensitive stance detection of web documents. J. Intell. Inf. Syst. **58**(1), 1–19 (2022). https://doi.org/10.1007/s10844-021-00642-z

40. Sanh, V., Debut, L., Chaumond, J., Wolf, T.: DistilBERT, a distilled version of BERT: smaller, faster, cheaper and lighter. ArXiv abs/1910.01108 (2019)

41. Sepúlveda-Torres, R., Vicente, M., Saquete, E., Lloret, E., Palomar, M.: Exploring summarization to enhance headline stance detection. In: Métais, E., Meziane, F., Horacek, H., Kapetanios, E. (eds.) NLDB 2021. LNCS, vol. 12801, pp. 243–254. Springer, Cham (2021). https://doi.org/10.1007/978-3-030-80599-9_22

42. Silalahi, S., Ahmad, T., Studiawan, H.: Named entity recognition for drone forensic using BERT and distilBERT. In: 2022 International Conference on Data Science and Its Applications (ICoDSA), pp. 53–58. IEEE (2022)

43. Srivastava, N., Hinton, G., Krizhevsky, A., Sutskever, I., Salakhutdinov, R.: Dropout: a simple way to prevent neural networks from overfitting. J. Mach. Learn. Res. **15**(1), 1929–1958 (2014)

44. Staliūnaitė, I., Iacobacci, I.: Compositional and lexical semantics in RoBERTa, BERT and distilBERT: a case study on COQA. arXiv preprint arXiv:2009.08257 (2020)

45. Sundararajan, M., Taly, A., Yan, Q.: Axiomatic attribution for deep networks. In: International Conference on Machine Learning (2017)

46. Tong, J., Wang, Z., Rui, X: A multimodel-based deep learning framework for short text multiclass classification with the imbalanced and extremely small data set. Comput. Intell. Neurosci. **2022** (2022)

47. White, R.: Beliefs and biases in web search. In: Proceedings of the 36th International ACM SIGIR Conference on Research and Development in Information Retrieval, pp. 3–12. ACM, Dublin Ireland (2013). https://doi.org/10.1145/2484028.2484053

48. Wolf, T., et al.: Transformers: state-of-the-art natural language processing. In: Proceedings of the 2020 Conference on Empirical Methods in Natural Language Processing: System Demonstrations, pp. 38–45. Association for Computational Linguistics (2020). https://www.aclweb.org/anthology/2020.emnlp-demos.6

49. Xu, C., Paris, C., Nepal, S., Sparks, R.: Cross-target stance classification with self-attention networks. In: Proceedings of the 56th Annual Meeting of the Association for Computational Linguistics (vol. 2: Short Papers), pp. 778–783. Association for Computational Linguistics, Melbourne, Australia (2018). https://doi.org/10.18653/v1/P18-2123. https://aclanthology.org/P18-2123

50. Yang, K., Stoyanovich, J.: Measuring fairness in ranked outputs. In: Proceedings of the 29th International Conference on Scientific and Statistical Database Management, pp. 1–6. ACM, Chicago IL USA (2017). https://doi.org/10.1145/3085504.3085526

51. Ying, X.: An overview of overfitting and its solutions. In: Journal of Physics: Conference Series, vol. 1168, p. 022022. IOP Publishing (2019)

52. Yu, P., Rahimi, R., Allan, J.: Towards explainable search results: a listwise explanation generator. In: Proceedings of the 45th International ACM SIGIR Conference on Research and Development in Information Retrieval, pp. 669–680. SIGIR 2022, Association for Computing Machinery, New York, NY, USA (2022). https://doi.org/10.1145/3477495.3532067

53. Zehlike, M., Yang, K., Stoyanovich, J.: Fairness in ranking: a survey. arXiv:2103.14000 [cs] (2021). http://arxiv.org/abs/2103.14000

A Co-design Study for Multi-stakeholder Job Recommender System Explanations

Roan Schellingerhout[✉] [ID], Francesco Barile [ID], and Nava Tintarev [ID]

Department of Advanced Computing Sciences, Maastricht University,
Maastricht, The Netherlands
{roan.schellingerhout,f.barile,n.tintarev}@maastrichtuniversity.nl

Abstract. Recent legislation proposals have significantly increased the demand for eXplainable Artificial Intelligence (XAI) in many businesses, especially in so-called 'high-risk' domains, such as recruitment. Within recruitment, AI has become commonplace, mainly in the form of job recommender systems (JRSs), which try to match candidates to vacancies, and vice versa. However, common XAI techniques often fall short in this domain due to the different levels and types of expertise of the individuals involved, making explanations difficult to generalize. To determine the explanation preferences of the different stakeholder types - candidates, recruiters, and companies - we created and validated a semi-structured interview guide. Using grounded theory, we structurally analyzed the results of these interviews and found that different stakeholder types indeed have strongly differing explanation preferences. *Candidates* indicated a preference for brief, textual explanations that allow them to quickly judge potential matches. On the other hand, *hiring managers* preferred visual graph-based explanations that provide a more technical and comprehensive overview at a glance. *Recruiters* found more exhaustive textual explanations preferable, as those provided them with more talking points to convince both parties of the match. Based on these findings, we describe guidelines on how to design an explanation interface that fulfills the requirements of all three stakeholder types. Furthermore, we provide the validated interview guide, which can assist future research in determining the explanation preferences of different stakeholder types.

Keywords: Explainable AI · Job Recommender Systems · User Studies · Grounded Theory

1 Introduction

Within the emerging field of explainable artificial intelligence (XAI), a substantial amount of research has attempted to make the inner workings of AI models more transparent [11,18]. While such information can assist developers in understanding their model (e.g., by allowing the detection of bugs and biases, understanding feature importance), it is often complicated and requires considerable a priori knowledge of AI to interpret. However, the use of AI has become

© The Author(s), under exclusive license to Springer Nature Switzerland AG 2023
L. Longo (Ed.): xAI 2023, CCIS 1902, pp. 597–620, 2023.
https://doi.org/10.1007/978-3-031-44067-0_30

commonplace in user-controlled environments, such as the recommender systems used by different commercial platforms (e.g., YouTube, TikTok, Amazon). In such environments, explanations cannot assume AI knowledge, as the majority of explainees are lay users. Moreover, different types of users interact with such systems - the stakeholders. These stakeholders consist of every individual or group who affects, or is affected by, the delivery of recommendations to users [1]. Stakeholders can be strongly diverse, coming from different backgrounds and having distinct expertise. As such, the way in which an explanation is conveyed to each stakeholder individually should be fine-tuned to their specific needs.

One field where such fine-tuned explanations are especially crucial is recruitment. Recruitment is inherently a multi-stakeholder domain, as users (candidates) need to be linked to vacancies (provided by companies) by recruiters. These three main stakeholders all rely on the same recommendations but can require widely different explanations. For example, telling a candidate that a vacancy is relevant for them as it comes with a high salary can be an acceptable explanation. However, the same explanation will be useless for the company, as that salary will be provided to every other potential candidate. Furthermore, a candidate and a recruiter might only look at a handful of recommendations per session, while a company could receive hundreds of applicants for a single vacancy. Therefore, the explanation requirements of each stakeholder are unique and require a tailored design.

This paper attempts to determine the explanation preferences of the stakeholders of a job recommender system: job seekers, companies, and recruiters. This is done through the execution of a co-design study, which allows stakeholder representatives to manually indicate how they prefer an explanation to be presented to them. Therefore, this research aims to answer the following research question:

RQ: *What are the explanation preferences of recruiters, candidates, and company representatives for job recommender systems?*

Our results show interesting differences in the preferences of the different stakeholders. Regarding the preferred types of explanations, *candidates* preferred brief written explanations, as their main interest is to be able to quickly judge the potential matches proposed by the system. On the contrary, company's *hiring managers* preferred visual, graph-based explanations, as these allow a comprehensive overview at a glance. Finally, *recruiters* preferred more exhaustive textual explanations, as those provided them with more talking points to convince both parties of the match. These results allow us to provide design guidelines for an interface that fulfills the requirements of all three stakeholder types. Furthermore, the co-design study allowed us to validate and improve the used interview guide.

2   Related Work

Within the field of explainable AI, there is no single agreed-upon method to provide explanations [2]. Different use cases require different approaches, each with their own strengths and weaknesses.

One of the most common methods of providing explanations is through text [5,24]. Textual explanations consist of brief sections of text that explain the rationale of the XAI model. Such texts often contain information on the impact different features had on the prediction and how those features interacted with each other. There are multiple ways to generate such texts, e.g., through the use of large language models (LLMs) [19] or predefined templates [36].

Another popular approach is the use of feature attribution maps: visualizations that show the importance of different features to the prediction [23]. Such maps can take different forms, depending on the specific task and data involved. When using tabular data, bar charts are often used to show the contribution of each different feature type to the prediction. When using multi-dimensional data, such as images or time series, are used, heatmaps can provide an overview of the importance of the different dimensions interacting with each other [9].

A further explanation type that has been gaining popularity recently, is the knowledge graph-based explanation [31]. These explanations depend on the connections within a knowledge graph to explain the rationale behind a prediction. This is usually done by highlighting important nodes and edges within the graph, which provide 'paths' from the subject to the recommended item, accompanied by their importance to the model's prediction [35].

2.1   Challenges in Multi-stakeholder Explainability

In multi-stakeholder environments, explanations need to meet additional requirements [1]. An explanation that is sufficient for a developer, is not necessarily understandable for a user or provider, and vice versa [30]. There are multiple strategies to deal with this discrepancy, each with its own strengths and weaknesses. The most obvious solution is to create individual explanations for the different stakeholders [37]. Although this leads to the most fine-tuned explanations, it introduces an additional layer of complexity to the system as a whole. Another approach would be to simply use a single explanation, but to present it differently based on the stakeholders' level of expertise [1]. Unfortunately, it can be difficult to incorporate the different stakeholder perspectives simultaneously - some facts could be confidential or sensitive for a specific stakeholder, making it challenging to incorporate them in the explanation, even when they are relevant. Similarly, a highly specific overview of how the model came to the prediction might be useful for a developer, but will be too confusing for a lay user or provider.

2.2   Explainability in Job Recommender Systems

Explaining reciprocal recommendations, such as job recommendations, tends to be more difficult than standard recommendations, as the preferences of both parties need to be considered. Kleinerman et al. [13] looked at explainability for recommender systems in online dating and found that explanations that consider both parties outperform one-sided explanations in high-cost scenarios (such as recruitment). In particular, explanations based on specific feature values are useful, although only a few features should be included to prevent information overload. In high-cost scenarios, explanations should not stay limited to personal preferences (e.g. 'you should apply for this job because you want a company that has X attributes'), but should also incorporate an explanation of why the other party is likely to agree (e.g. 'they are likely to accept you, because they are looking for a candidate with Y skills').

In job recommender systems (JRSs) specifically, explainability has largely gone unexplored. While some previous work has incorporated some degree of explainability within their JRSs, the explanations are often limited and seem to have been included as an afterthought [14,32,37]. Even when explainability has been included, authors usually fail to consider all stakeholders, tailoring the explanations to developers only. Furthermore, explanations are often solely evaluated anecdotally, leaving their quality up for debate [21]. One could argue that reciprocal, easy-to-understand explainability should be at the core of the models' design in a high-risk, high-impact domain such as recruitment. Where previous research mainly falls short, is in the understandability of their explanations: while their models can technically explain some part of their predictions, the explanations tend to be unintuitive and/or limited, either staying too vague [14,32] or being hard to understand [37]. In previous work, we found that, when dealing with users with limited AI knowledge, such as recruiters, job seekers, and most company representatives, having clear, straightforward explanations is crucial [28,30]. To accomplish this, structured requirements engineering needs to be conducted in order to determine the preferences of all stakeholders, after which explainable JRSs will need to be designed with those requirements as a starting point.

2.3   Determining Stakeholder Preferences

In order to determine the explanation preferences of different stakeholders, their requirements, struggles, and level of expertise need to be documented. To accomplish this, multiple approaches exist; for example, whenever the preferences of a stakeholder are already largely known (e.g., through previous research) questionnaires can be used in combination with different alterations of some explanation type [30]. The results of these questionnaires could then be used to 'fine-tune' the already-known explanation type to better fit the exact stakeholders. However, within job recommendation, stakeholder preferences (beyond candidates) are mostly unknown [27]. Therefore, it is better to determine the stakeholder preferences from the ground up, allowing them to assist in shaping the explanations themselves. Thus, (semi-structured) interviews are highly useful, as they give stakeholders the freedom to indicate their exact preferences and requirements regarding explanations [16].

2.4   Contributions

Explainability within multi-stakeholder environments has largely gone unexplored. Research that has touched upon this topic, has often stuck to offline methods of evaluation, which fall short in high-impact domains, such as recruitment and healthcare. Therefore, this paper aims to lay the foundation for future research on explainable multi-stakeholder recommendation. We do so firstly by providing a validated interview guide that can be used to extract the explanation preferences of different stakeholder types. Furthermore, we extend the current literature on explainable job recommender systems by not just focusing on a single stakeholder, but providing guidelines on how explanations should be designed for all stakeholders involved.

3   Methodology

In order to discover the preferences of different stakeholders, semi-structured interviews were conducted using example explanations [10]. During these semi-structured interviews, the participants were asked to answer substantive questions based on the provided explanations, as well as questions to indicate what aspects of different explanations they prefer. These substantive questions were used to gauge their understanding of the explanations. This is important, as previous research found that preference and understanding do not necessarily go hand in hand [30]. In our study, we are interested in particular in highlighting the specific explanation preferences of the specific stakeholders. Hence, we decompose our main research question into the following three sub-questions:

SQ1: What type of explanation is most suited for the different stakeholders?
SQ2: What aspects of explanations make them more suited for each stakeholder?
SQ3: In what way can different explanation types be combined to make them useful for each stakeholder?

3.1   Hypotheses

In this study, we consider three different explanation types (see Sect. 3.4): (i) graph-based explanations; (ii) Textual explanations; and (iii) Feature attribution explanations. While the graph-based explanations will most likely be best suited for individuals with a fair amount of prior AI knowledge, the general lay users will probably gravitate towards the textual explanations, as those are both expressive and fairly easy to process [26]. Considering the graph-based explanations contain the most information, but are expected to be the hardest to read, and the opposite holds for the feature attributions, the textual explanations are likely to strike a good balance between the two. These considerations lead us to formulate two hypotheses related to the **SQ1**:

- **H1a**: *The graph-based explanation will be best suited for individuals with prior AI knowledge.*

- **H1b**: *The textual explanations will be best suited for individuals without prior AI knowledge.*

Furthermore, we considered that feature attribution maps are usually the easiest and fastest way to get an overview of the model's rationale, but at the same time, they have a fairly limited extent [30]. The textual explanation will be more complex and take more time to process, but will provide a more comprehensive explanation in return. Lastly, the graph-based explanations will take the longest to process and might be difficult to interpret by themselves, but will contain the most complete explanation as a result. We then expect differences among the stakeholders, and formulate the following hypothesis related to the **SQ2**:

- **H2**: *The different stakeholders (candidates, companies, and recruiters) will have different preferences related to the explanation types.*

Finally, we considered that explanations consisting of a single type may be either too limited in their content, or too difficult to interpret. This problem can be addressed by incorporating aspects from different types into a single explanation type [30]. For example, textual explanations can help in assisting the stakeholders in how to read the graph-based explanation. Furthermore, the feature attribution map can be useful when the stakeholder prefers to get a good (albeit limited) overview at a glance [28]. We further hypothesize then that also regarding the preferences in terms of combining basic explanations into hybrid strategies, the stakeholders will have differences. Hence, we formulated the following hypothesis related to the **SQ3**:

- **H3**: *The different stakeholders (candidates, companies, and recruiters) will have different preferences on how to combine explanation types to obtain a hybrid explanation.*

3.2   Semi-structured Interview Guide

A comprehensive guide was created to conduct the semi-structured interviews (Appendix B). However, this guide is susceptible to possible biases, ambiguities, incorrect assumptions about prior knowledge, etc. Thus, during the interviews, we dedicated time specifically to determining the quality of the questions in order to update, and eventually validate them. The questions in the interview guide were based upon previous works [6,7,13,25], but required validation for a multi-stakeholder scenario. In addition to validating the interview guide, the interviews also allowed the stakeholders to co-design the explanation representations to fit their needs. The interviews were conducted with a small sample of the different stakeholders ($n = 2$ for each stakeholder type) to verify the adequacy of the explanations and the guide for each group individually. Considering the fact that each participant was interviewed three times (once for each explanation type), we collected a large amount of data per participant. Due to the richness of this data, the relatively small sample size still allowed us to perform an in-depth analysis for each stakeholder type. Previous works also indicates that a small sample can be sufficient in qualitative analysis, as long as the data itself is of high enough quality [8,20]. Note that the user study was approved by the ethical committee of our institution.[1]

3.3   Data and Model

The explanations used for the interviews were generated using a job recommendation dataset provided by Zhaopin.[2] This dataset contains information on 4.78 million vacancies, 4.5 thousand candidates, and 700 thousand recorded interactions between the two. For candidates, the dataset stores information such as their degree(s), location, current and desired industry, skill set, and experience. For vacancies, features such as the job description, job title, salary, (sub-)type, required education, location, and starting date were recorded. The interactions between candidates and vacancies consist of four stages: no interaction, browsed, delivered, and satisfied. Considering the data in the dataset was exclusively in Mandarin Chinese, all unstructured data was automatically translated to English using deep-translator.[3]

These three different tables were combined together into a single knowledge graph, wherein candidates, vacancies, and categorical features formed the set of nodes. The edges consisted of relations between these nodes, such as candidates interacting with vacancies or vacancies being of a specific (sub-)type. This single, large knowledge graph was then converted to individual sub-graphs between candidates and vacancies that had interacted (positives), and between those who had not interacted (negatives) using the k random walks algorithm [17]. Each of these sub-graphs therefore could be given a score from 0 (no interaction), to 3 (satisfied), which allowed us to treat the task as a ranking problem based on sub-graph prediction.

The explainable model was based on the graph attention network (GAT) [33], implemented using PyTorch geometric.[4] Considering performance was not the goal of this research, we opted for a straightforward architecture consisting of a single GATv2Conv-layer, followed by two separate GATv2Conv-layers - one for the company-side prediction and explanation, and one for the candidate-side prediction and explanation. Both these layers were followed by their own respective fully-connected layer, which provided the company- and candidate-side prediction score. The harmonic mean of these two scores was then considered the final 'matching score'. Optimization was done using the Adam optimizer [12] (learning rate $= 1*10^{-3}$) with LambdaRank loss based on normalized Discounted

---

[1] Ethical Review Committee Inner City faculties (Maastricht University).

[2] https://tianchi.aliyun.com/dataset/31623/.

[3] https://pypi.org/project/deep-translator/.

[4] https://www.pyg.org/.

Cumulative Gain @ 10 (nDCG@10) [4]. Hyperparameter tuning was done using grid search going over different configurations of hyperparameters [15]. Since our aim was not to get state-of-the-art performance, the number of different configurations tested was fairly limited. Even so, the optimal configuration led to an nDCG@10 of 0.2638 (Appendix A).

Considering the goal of our research was not to evaluate the explanation quality of the specific model, but rather to investigate stakeholder preferences in general, the examples used during the interviews were manually selected based on the following criteria: graph size, perceived sensibility, and accessibility of the industry for evaluation. By sticking to seemingly sensible explanations that did not require knowledge of the specific industry at hand, we aimed to make the stakeholders' evaluation dependent solely on the representation of the explanation, rather than the quality of the model's explanations in general.

3.4   Explanation Types

The explanation types that were examined in this study were the following:

Graph: a visualization of paths in a knowledge graph. In our case, this consists of (a sub-set of) the paths within the candidate-vacancy sub-graph, weighted by the importance ascribed to them by the model (Fig. 1);

Textual: a short text that explains which features contributed to the recommendation in what way. The textual explanations are generated using a large language model (LLM) (in this case, ChatGPT February 13 version [22]), which is given the full graph explanation as input, and tasked to summarize it in an easy-to-read way (Fig. 2);

Feature attribution: a visualization (such as a bar chart) that shows which features were most important to the model when creating the explanation (Fig. 3). This bar chart is also based on the paths within the knowledge graph - the sizes of the bars are calculated using the sum of incoming edge weights, similar to PageRank [3].

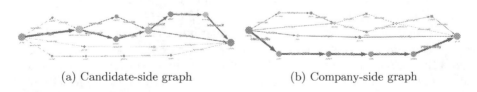

(a) Candidate-side graph   (b) Company-side graph

Fig. 1. An example of knowledge graph paths being used as an explanation for a recommendation.

The XAI model has analyzed various connections between jobs and users to determine if a particular user (user 4119) would be a good fit for a specific job (job 147542). The model looked at the relationships between different jobs and users, as well as the importance of these relationships, to make its prediction.

In this case, the model found that user 4119 has a strong connection to the role of Administrative Commissioner, and this connection is considered to be very important for explaining why user 4119 would be a good match for job 147542. Additionally, the model found that job 147542 has a connection to the role of secretary, which is also considered important. The model also found that the Administrative Commissioner role has a connection to the assistant role, which in turn has a connection to the secretary role and job 147542.

In summary, the XAI model determined that user 4119 would be a good fit for job 147542 based on the strong connection between user 4119 and the Administrative Commissioner role, as well as the connections between the Administrative Commissioner role, the assistant role, the secretary role, and job 147542.

Fig. 2. An example of a textual explanation used as an explanation for a recommendation

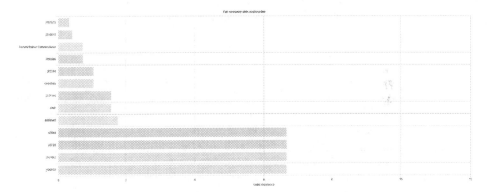

Fig. 3. An example of a feature attribution map used as an explanation for a recommendation.

3.5 Analysis

The answers provided by the participants were analyzed using grounded theory (GT) [34] using *Atlas.ti*[5]. This process was done separately for each stakeholder type, in order to create distinct results for each type. We started by assigning manually-generated codes to individual statements made by the participants

---

[5] https://atlasti.com/.

(open coding). These codes were then grouped together into distinct categories using axial coding to provide a higher-level overview of the complaints and preferences of each stakeholder type. Lastly, selective coding was conducted to combine each stakeholder type's categories into a single theory. The higher-level categories, as well as the theories, were then used to improve the prototypical explanation.

3.6   Participant Demographics

The participants were recruited through personal connections in collaboration with Randstad Groep Nederland[6], the largest recruitment agency in the Netherlands. The sample consisted of 4 women and 2 men, of various ages ($\mu = 39.2, SD = 11.3, l = 23, h = 53$), with various backgrounds (tech, finance, healthcare, marketing, etc.). The participants had largely different levels of expertise w.r.t. AI, ranging from no knowledge whatsoever to a Bachelor's degree in a related field. Each interview took approximately one hour, and candidates were paid €11,50 for their time.

4   Results

Based on the answers given by the different stakeholder representatives, the interview guide has been updated, and the preliminary preferences of each stakeholder type have been determined. The full transcripts of each interview are available on GitHub.

4.1   Interview Guide

The interview guide (Table 2) has been validated based on responses from the participants. While the interview guide was largely proven to be adequate for determining the explanation preferences of different stakeholders, some changes have been made based on the feedback we received.

Firstly, we added an additional question to the section on **usefulness**: '*how could you see yourself using the explanation in your daily work/task?*' Even when some of the participants could see that an explanation was sensible, or could be helpful in making a decision, they mentioned that they would personally stick to using another approach (e.g., a different type of explanation, or doing things manually). Although this is likely to come up using the current interview guide already, we decided to also explicitly ask the question - after all, the goal of creating an explainable model is that users end up actually using the explanations to assist them in their decision-making.

We additionally added a new question to the **correct interpretation** section of the guide: "*how would you put the model's explanation into your own words?*"

---

[6] https://www.randstad.nl/.

While the participants often managed to quickly identify the most/least important features and components of the explanation, that did not necessarily indicate they properly understood the entire rationale. For example, some participants correctly identified the importance of the different job types to the explanation, but they could not properly connect all the dots, causing them to be unable to view the explanation as a single whole. By explicitly asking them to define the explanation in their own words, it becomes clear whether they adequately understand the entire explanation, or are still grasping at straws.

Lastly, we changed one of the questions in the section on **transparency**: "can you think of anything that would further improve your understanding?" has been changed to "what information is missing that could allow you to get a better understanding of the model's recommendation?". The previous phrasing of the question was too general, making it difficult for participants to answer it on the spot. By directly asking them for information that is missing, it should be easier for them to come up with an answer, albeit a more indirect one.

The updated, validated interview guide can be seen in Table 1.

4.2 Stakeholder Preferences

Each of the transcripts has been analyzed, and the analyses have been grouped based on stakeholder type. An overview of the generated codes, categories, theories, and relevant quotes can be found in Appendix C.

4.2.1 Candidates. In line with our hypothesis, the textual explanation was well-received by the candidates. Although the candidates did receive the explanations favorably, they indicated some issues that should be addressed. For one, the specific language used in the explanation made it more difficult for the candidates to parse it correctly. Candidates also sometimes wound up losing track of the essence of the explanation, specifically when multiple trains of thought were addressed in a single paragraph, or whenever points were reiterated multiple times (*"it's a bit more clear, but I don't know... I still can't follow it completely. I find it very hard to read"*, P2, Q1.1). However, the candidates still managed to correctly identify the main arguments on which the recommendation was based. They did indicate that they would prefer to be able to evaluate the text at a glance, i.e., by putting crucial information clearly at the top of the text (*"Information like the city, and what the salary is, or things of the sorts, are currently not included"*, P1, Q4.2). They did not fully trust the model, but found it to be a nice 'brain-storming partner', which could support them in their decision (*"if I had any doubts, the explanation would take those away"*, P2, Q3.2), and provide them with some interesting vacancies to explore on their own. Furthermore, the explanation contained the full ID of candidates and vacancies relevant to the recommendation. Considering the candidates have no access to the actual database, these IDs turned out to be of little value, and actually overwhelmed the candidates. Additionally, while multiple different vacancies were mentioned in the explanation, these were not directly accessible to the candidates - something they considered to be unintuitive.

Table 1. The validated, updated interview guide.

Evaluation Objective	Objective Description	Questions	Probing questions
1. Correct interpretation	To assess whether or not the stakeholder can correctly interpret the explanation	1.1 What information/features do you think were most important for this prediction? 1.2 What was the least important? 1.3 How would you put the model's explanation into your own words?	1.1.1 What did you look at to come to that conclusion?
2. Transparency	To determine the explanation's effect on understanding the model's inner workings	2.1 Does the explanation help you comprehend why the system gave the recommendation?	2.1.1 What components help you specifically? 2.1.2 What information is missing that could allow you to get a better understanding of the model's recommendation
3. Usefulness	To evaluate how useful the explanations are considered to be	3.1 Does the explanation make sense to you? 3.2 Does the explanation help you make a decision? 3.3 How could you see yourself using the explanation in your daily work/task?	3.1.1 What do you consider sensible (e.g., focus on specific features)? 3.1.2 What do you consider insensible? 3.2.1 Would you prefer a model with explanations over one without?
4. Trust	To gauge the explanation's impact on the model's trustworthiness	4.1 Do you think the prediction made by the model is reliable? 4.2 If this recommendation was made for you, would you trust the model to have made the right decision?	4.2.1 Anything specific that makes you say that (e.g., something makes no sense, or is very similar to how you look at things)?
5. Preference	To figure out the personal preference of the stakeholder	5.1 What would you like to see added to the current explanation? 5.2 What would you consider to be redundant within this explanation?	5.1.1 Any specific information that is missing? 5.1.2 Any functionality that could be useful? 5.2.1 Anything that should be removed? 5.2.2 Or be made less prevalent?

The graph-based explanation turned out to be difficult to use for the candidates without receiving some additional help on how to interpret it. Especially the full, unsimplified version of the graph, in which all of the different paths were visible, turned out to be too overwhelming and complex to be useful (after being corrected on their interpretation: *"Now I get that the thin lines were kind of like side tracks that weren't successful"*, P2, Q2.1). However, with some additional guidance on how it was structured, and by considering the simplified view of the graph, the candidates eventually correctly understood its content. Still, the amount of information contained within the graph was more confusing than helpful - for example, the types and values of the edges were constantly visible, meaning there was a lot of text present at all times. Considering the candidates did not necessarily understand the meaning of the edge types and values, they did not get any benefit from them. While the graph was indicated to give them a better understanding of the model's actual rationale, it also made them question the adequacy of the recommendation to an extent. Because vacancies different from the one being recommended were included in the graph as well, sometimes at locations seemingly 'closer' to the candidate, they were unsure why *those* vacancies were not recommended to them (*"It feels quite strange, that the path passes through different relevant vacancies, but we just ignore those"*, P1, Q1.1). Therefore, providing candidates with information on why alternative vacancies were not recommended could be helpful.

The current implementation of the feature attribution chart turned out to be close to useless for providing an explanation to the candidates. Since it ascribed importance to different vacancies and candidates (i.e., similar vacancies and candidates, which were included to allow for collaborative filtering [29]), which they were not familiar with, it did not contribute to their understanding of the model's prediction. However, they did indicate how feature attribution could be made useful: for the bar chart to relate to their individual skills, so the candidates could understand which of their own skills were considered most important for the recommendation at a glance (*"That it shows what is important for the match, for example, that your experience with Excel matters, but that your ability to be a truck driver wasn't important"*, P1, Q1.1). This would allow them to quickly verify and scrutinize recommendations. For example, if they saw a specific skill they possess was attributed a lot of importance by the model, even though they would not enjoy performing it as their job. Thus, the feature attribution chart should stick only to the personal, actionable features of the candidates. To still include previous vacancies fulfilled by the candidate, they could alternatively be grouped by job type, so that they could be represented as a single bar relating to their experience in that field (*"the function types make sense to me, but the individual vacancies and candidates do not"*, P1, Q3.1).

4.2.2   Recruiters. As was hypothesized, the recruiters found the textual explanations to be informative and useful. Although they found the texts to indicate some redundancy, as well as some tricky language, they considered them to be rather useful regardless. They immediately understood the main message of the text, but found that some information was reiterated too often (*"It keeps beating around the bush with the same words"*, P3, Q2.1). The recruiters explicitly stated that they would not blindly trust the model, even when accompanied by a sensible explanation - they would always want to be able to manually verify its recommendation by reading the CV and vacancy text (*"Very little is told about the candidate, and the vacancy, but I just have to trust that ... it would be nice to check if it's actually right"*, P3, Q2.1). However, as long as they considered that the explanation made sense, they would *"move that CV and vacancy to the top of their list"*. Furthermore, being able to quickly rule out specific candidates or vacancies was something they considered highly important. As a result, they strongly preferred to have the most crucial information, such as commuting time, and whether some minimum requirements were met, to be at the top of the explanation. The recruiters internally disagreed on how long the text should be (*"it doesn't need to be brief. It's nice to have things to talk about"*,

P3, Q5.2; *"Three paragraphs of three sentences would be fine"* P4, Q5.1). One argument for having a longer text, was that it would provide the recruiter with more subject matter to discuss when trying to convince a candidate or company of the match's aptitude. On the other hand, having a shorter text that only focuses on the main arguments provided by the model would make it quicker for recruiters to compare different recommendations, after which they could come up with further arguments for the best one themselves.

Although the recruiters managed to correctly interpret the graph, they found it to add little value for the most part (*"I understand it, but it means little to me"*, P4, Q1.1). While they indicated that it could be useful in some specific scenarios, such as texts with a high level of complexity, or when having to support their final decision to a supervisor, they generally did not consider it to add any benefit compared to the textual explanation. Despite the fact that they developed a better understanding of the models' actual rationale, they doubted that they would use it much in their day-to-day tasks (*"If I would have to use this for every vacancy, or every candidate, it would become a problem"*, P4, Q1.1). In the scenarios where they would consider it to be beneficial, they gravitated strongly toward the simplified version of the graph, considering the connections deemed unimportant by the model to be counterproductive in understanding the explanation. Only when a candidate or company would ask specifically about whether a specific skill, or past job, was taken into account, would they make use of the full version of the graph.

Similarly to the candidates, the feature attribution chart in its current form did not assist the recruiters in correctly understanding the explanation. Again, though, did they indicate that a different type of bar chart could be useful in some scenarios. One use case for a bar chart the recruiters considered useful, was for it to be a central 'hub' of sorts, where all possible vacancies for a candidate (and vice versa) were displayed, sorted by their matching score (*"No, I would personally go for something like a top 10, for example"*, P3, Q2.1). This would allow the recruiters to quickly determine which potential matches are feasible enough to explore further. However, as an actual method of explaining the prediction, they indicated that the text, sometimes combined with the graph, would already be sufficient, causing the feature attribution chart to be largely irrelevant.

4.2.3 Company Representatives. As opposed to the candidates and recruiters, the company representatives were less positive about the textual explanation. Considering the company-side explanation contained a higher level of abstraction, it took the company representatives multiple iterations before they properly understood the explanation (*"Now that I read it again, I see that it goes from person A, to B, to C."*, P5, Q3.2). They also found it difficult to take the explanation at face value, being wary of terms such as 'relevant experience' - rather opting to manually verify whether the mentioned experience was actually relevant for the vacancy (*"But judging how relevant the experience is for this vacancy, isn't possible based on this explanation"*, P5, Q1.2). Although a more detailed explanation could alleviate some of this hesitance, it would also lead to an even more complex explanation, possibly worsening the understandability further.

On the other hand, the company representatives were considerably more positive about the graph explanation. Specifically, the simplified view of the graph allowed them to grasp the prediction at a glance. Where the textual explanation required some puzzling before the relations between different candidates, vacancies, and job types became clear, the company representatives quickly managed to detect the relevant relations in the graph (*"This adds everything I need ... For me it's simply a matter of checking why the model made its decision - that being the line at the bottom, and that would be all"*, P6, Q2.1). As a result, the graph explanation also improved their trust in the model; one recruiter even mentioned that, given a high-enough performance of the model, they would simply use the simplified graph as a sanity check, fully trusting the model if the explanation seemed somewhat reasonable (*"If the model does what it says it does, I would simply trust it"*, P6, Q3.2).

The feature attribution map was again received poorly. The company representatives indicated that it did not help them get a better understanding of the model's reasoning compared to the graph (*"It's usable, but it doesn't clarify why we ended up with the recommended candidate"*, P5, Q2.1). However, the company representatives did consider the feature attribution chart to be useful in a different scenario - to verify the model paid no attention to irrelevant details. With some tweaks, such as changing vacancy IDs into actual titles, the bar chart would allow company representatives to make sure the model did not pay attention to something that the company determined to be irrelevant to the position. Furthermore, an aggregated version of the feature attribution chart, which displays which types of features were considered most by the model, could help the company representatives parse the textual explanation more easily, allowing them to direct most of their attention to the more important information (*"This is what I was looking for while reading the text. I tried to determine these values in my head, but I kept getting distracted"*, P5, Q2.1).

5   Discussion

We discuss our results in relation to the three sub-research questions, for each type of stakeholder: which type of explanation is most suited, what makes these explanations most suitable, and can different explanation types be meaningfully combined. We discuss each research question in turn.

5.1   SQ1: What Type of Explanation is Most Suited for the Different Stakeholders?

When analyzing the results regarding preferences for the different stakeholders, we notice that *candidates* prefer short, clearly structured, straightforward texts, which allow them to quickly browse and judge the vacancies. These texts should include what they consider the most important information: features like travel distance, salary, and minimum requirements. This information should be central and easy to identify, preferably in bullets. *Recruiters* also prefer texts, but disagree on the amount of text that is required. Thus, a short text, that centrally mentions potential 'deal-breakers' and gives the main few arguments to motivate why a match was made should be the default. However, recruiters also prefer to have access to a more exhaustive text, which can provide them with more material that could be used to convince both parties (candidate and company) to agree with the match. On the contrary, *company representatives* prefer graph-based explanations, as those assist them in quickly getting an overview of even more complex explanations at a glance. Such a representation also allows them to quickly scan different information, while reading would require more time and effort. These results are somewhat in line with our hypotheses H1a and H1b, but not entirely. While one of the candidates did have a lot of knowledge of AI, she still preferred the textual explanation. On the other hand, both company representatives did not have a strong background in AI, but preferred the graph-based explanations. We argue that it is not the AI knowledge per se that makes the graph preferable, but the amount of experience with, and affinity towards, reading graphs and charts.

5.2 SQ2: What Aspects of Explanations Make Them More Suited for Each Stakeholder?

We also looked more specifically at the motivation for why certain stakeholders prefer certain explanations. For *candidates*, the textual explanations were largely preferred due to their simplicity, and because they felt more 'personal'. In particular, they preferred texts using simple language, that is clearly structured and not longer than a few short paragraphs. *Recruiters* also preferred the textual explanations, due to their simplicity compared to the graph- and feature-based explanations. In particular, they struggled to interpret the visualizations and felt quite overwhelmed due to their 'math-heavy' nature. Furthermore, the text directly assists them in their day-to-day tasks, as they can almost use some of the paragraphs verbatim to try and convince companies and candidates of the adequacy of a match. Finally, for *company representatives*, the graph-based explanations were preferred, largely due to their ability to make more complex, high-level connections, within the data visible at a glance. Within the textual explanations, it became difficult for them to figure out the full line of reasoning of the model, due to there being a lot of 'steps' from the vacancy to the candidate, which made it hard to process. The bar chart also made the text more accessible, but the graph-based explanation was considered a better option.

5.3 SQ3: In What Way Can Different Explanation Types Be Combined to Make Them Useful for Each Stakeholder?

Finally, we evaluated the stakeholders' preferences in terms of hybrid explanations, indicating how to combine different explanations together. Our results highlight how the feature-based explanation was poorly received by all stake-holders; however, they also indicated it to have potential, in case it is used to support one of the other explanation types. The unanimous aversion to the feature-based explanation was likely due to their failure to find a niche, either being too general to be useful in the simplified version, or too specific (and thus overwhelming) in the full version. For both *candidates and recruiters*, the textual explanations should be the center of the explanation, by default in its simplified form. The user should then have the possibility to access additional informa-tion, using a toggle to get a more descriptive version of the text. Considering the difficulty of conveying relative importance levels within a text, the feature attribution map can be linked (i.e., through matching color coding) to clarify the text. The graph-based explanation can then be used as an optional addition, in case the text itself is not clear enough, or if the user wants even more evidence for a specific suggestion.

On the contrary, *company representatives* prefer the simplified graph to be central, supported by a textual explanation. Within the graph, most details (e.g., exact values) should be made optional, so that it is not overwhelming: they mainly want to be able to quickly parse the most critical paths in the graph, and only look at details when necessary. Additionally, a bar chart indicating how important different feature types were, could be used to complement the text, in order to help them focus their attention on the paragraphs touching on those feature types.

5.4 Limitations and Future Work

A key limitation to acknowledge is the relatively small sample size we used. Considering we only interviewed two individuals from each stakeholder type, it is possible that some of our results are based on their personal biases, which may not be representative of the entire population. We attempted to minimize these biases through careful selection of participants, making sure to include individuals from different backgrounds, both in terms of their expertise and per-sonal characteristics. This limited sample did allow us to focus on the quality of the data we collected; due to the limited number of participants, it was feasible to interview them for longer periods of time. Considering the large amount of data gathered through the interviews, we believe that this limitation does not deteriorate the quality of the findings. Furthermore, the aim of this paper was to lay the groundwork for future research on explainable job recommender sys-tems through the creation of a reusable interview guide, as well as determining general stakeholder preferences and differences. I.e., our aim was not to conclu-sively determine the exact, ultimate preferences of the stakeholders, but rather to allow for future research to have a solid foundation for more specific research. Regardless, future research should aim to make use of the validated interview guide with a larger sample. By making use of the guidelines we provided on how to represent automatically-generated explanations, it should be possible to design a single, hybrid explanation, that can be evaluated more quickly. As a result, interviews will take less time, making it more practical to use a larger sample size.

Furthermore, we acknowledge room to improve the model we used to generate explanations, and that it may therefore not have generated the most sensible explanations. To counteract this behavior, we manually selected explanations that seemed suitable for the interviews. Future work could therefore use the provided interview guide to evaluate and compare explanations generated using a number of different techniques (e.g., attention mechanisms, saliency, post hoc methods). Different model architectures could also be compared in order to determine which architectures generate better explanations (either for a specific evaluation objective, or as a whole).

Lastly, another venue for future research could be to evaluate the textual explanations generated through different means. Although the explanations generated by ChatGPT were sufficient for our study, comparing them to differently-generated explanations (e.g., by different LLMs, people with varying levels of expertise) could lead to interesting insights.

5.5   Conclusion

In this paper, we aimed to develop and validate an interview guide for determining the explanation preferences of different stakeholder types. Additionally, we aimed to establish guidelines for creating XAI-generated explanations for different stakeholders within the field of job recommendation. The interview guide was largely proven to be adequate for determining the preferences of different stakeholders; a few minor changes were made to it in order to attain more concrete responses from the participants. Through the use of the interview guide, we found that candidates prefer explanations to take the shape of a short, clearly-structured text, that centrally contains the most crucial information. Recruiters, on the other hand, also preferred textual explanations, but were less strict on it having to be brief - indicating that longer texts could be useful in some scenarios. Company representatives indicated a preference towards graph-based explanations, as those allowed them to get a comprehensive overview of even more complex explanations.

Appendix

A   Hyperparameter Tuning

The optimal hyperparameter configuration we found, is the following:

- hidden_dimensions = 10
- output_dimensions = 100
- number_of_layers = 2
- attention_heads = 5
- dp_rate = 0.01
- learning_rate = 0.001
- epochs = 1

An overview of all configurations we tested, can be found on GitHub

B Preliminary Interview Guide

Table 2. The preliminary interview guide.

Evaluation Objective	Objective Description	Questions	Probing questions
1. Correct interpretation	To assess whether or not the stakeholder can correctly interpret the explanation	1.1 What information/features do you think were most important for this prediction? 1.2 What was the least important?	1.1.1 What did you look at to come to that conclusion?
2. Transparency	To determine the explanation's effect on understanding the model's inner workings	2.1 Does the explanation help you comprehend why the system gave the recommendation?	2.1.1 What components help you specifically? 2.1.2 Can you think of anything that would further improve your understanding?
3. Usefulness	To evaluate how useful the explanations are considered to be	3.1 Does the explanation make sense to you? 3.2 Does the explanation help you make a decision?	3.1.1 What do you consider sensible (e.g., focus on specific features)? 3.1.2 What do you consider insensible? 3.2.1 Would you prefer a model with explanations over one without?
4. Trust	To gauge the explanation's impact on the model's trustworthiness	4.1 Do you think the prediction made by the model is reliable? 4.2 If this recommendation was made for you, would you trust the model to have made the right decision?	4.2.1 Anything specific that makes you say that (e.g., something makes no sense, or is very similar to how you look at things)?
5. Preference	To figure out the personal preference of the stakeholder	5.1 What would you like to see added to the current explanation? 5.2 What would you consider to be redundant within this explanation?	5.1.1 Any specific information that is missing? 5.1.2 Any functionality that could be useful? 5.2.1 Anything that should be removed? 5.2.2 Or be made less prevalent?

C   Grounded Theory Results

C.1   Candidates

Table 3. The quotes, open codes, and categories discovered by using grounded theory for the candidates' responses.

Quotes	Open codes	Category
"You should separate the recommended and supporting vacancies"	Different instances of the same group should be easily distinguishable	Don't mix different types of information
"I find it very difficult that the vacancies, candidates, and vacancy types or on the same axis … I don't understand it anymore"	Having different feature types in the same bar chart is confusing	
"if this was important for me as a candidate, I would want to know"	The bar chart should refer only to personal information	
"It could be that the system is missing some information about you … like that you want to work from home … which would allow you to cross it off the list immediately"	Make 'deal-breakers' extremely clear	An explanation should very quickly allow for verification and scrutiny
"A candidate would not want to spend all of their time dissecting a graph"	Having to extract information carefully is a bother	
"I would definitely want to look at the vacancy"	Manual follow-up should be easy	
"And that those small lines, for us, as people looking for a vacancy, are not very useful"	Only include supporting arguments	Make all non-crucial information optional
"Yes, because this is some pretty difficult use of language … and those values are not clear to me at all to be honest"	Specific values lead to overwhelm	
"Now it's saying the same thing for the third time in a row already"	Only repeat information when summarizing	

Theory (Based on Table 3): Candidates want to be able to determine whether or not a vacancy is relevant at a glance. To do so, the explanation needs to be brief and straight to the point. Once the candidate has found a potentially interesting vacancy, they should be able to explore the explanation in more detail. Considering their difficulty in parsing both the graph and feature attribution explanation, the textual explanation should always be central, with the other two merely functioning as further support.

C.2   Recruiters

Table 4. The quotes, open codes, and categories discovered by using grounded theory for the recruiters' responses.

Quotes	Open codes	Category
"It's nice when there's more text to talk about on the phone, as long as it's not the same thing over and over again"	A lot of text can help in having enough subject matter while talking to clients	The explanation should be useable as evidence while justifying a match to a client
"if you want to back up your decision during a meeting, where they expect reports and whatnot, it would be very nice"	The graph can provide a more 'objective' explanation	
"if the first paragraph is about their skills, the second about their experience, and the third about their interests, a longer text would still be nice"	Each paragraph of the text should address a different aspect	
"I don't think this is required to actually start calling; it's more of a convenience when you want to understand the reasoning"	Knowing the general rationale is enough to take action already	The exact details of the prediction are irrelevant most of the time
"There's a few things that are crucial when making a match ... and if those are not in order, I don't even need to see the prediction"	Possible points of contention should already have been considered	
"I don't want to know anything I don't need to know ... there's no use in that"	The simple version of explanations is usually sufficient	
"you simply get told that this is the correct match ... and if you can look at the vacancy, you can check if it's correct"	Recruiters should be able to easily verify the model's claims	Recruiters should always feel like they have the final say
"I would never blindly set up a meeting; I would always want to speak to the candidate beforehand of course"	Recruiters first want to discuss the match with both sides before accepting it	

Theory (Based on Table 4**):** Recruiters prefer the model to act mainly as a supportive tool. This means that the strongest arguments the model puts forward should be front and center. This allows them to use the explanations when defending their decision, be it to their supervisor or a client. They will always want to manually verify the claims made by the model, but due to the explanation, they are likely to consider predicted matches before all else. The exact details of how the model came to its prediction will oftentimes be irrelevant, but are nice to have accessible in case additional evidence should be provided.

C.3 Company Representatives

Table 5. The quotes, open codes, and categories discovered by using grounded theory for the company representatives' responses.

Quotes	Open codes	Category
"this is what I had, after reading the text four times, this path is generally what I had understood"	The textual explanation can require multiple iterations to become clear	Complex relations should still be easy to grasp
"at one point you understand how it works ... and then you won't even look at the text anymore, the graph will be all you need"	The graph is quick and easy to use once it's understood	
"the complex graph should be banned"	The general idea of the explanation should be clear at a glance	
"that's why I would rather pick that one, over the recommended one, because that one seems closer to the vacancy."	Alternative candidates should also receive explanations	Exploring alternatives should be integrated in the system
"it could be a close call, you know? So then you can make your own assessment, and verify if the model got it right"	Having an overview of all possible candidates is useful to verify and scrutinize	
"if we want someone for 0.8 FTE, but their motivation letter says 0.6 FTE, it already becomes a no-go"	Human factors, such as candidates' motivation letters, are hard to integrate into a prediction	
"if the model has been designed in such a manner that I know it has checked everything, there's no need for me to manually check everything as well"	Given high enough performance, the explanation merely becomes a sanity check	Explanations are mainly useful for surprising results
"you already have an expectation of what the outcome will be. You're only going to start interrogating the model once the prediction doesn't match your expectation"	Detail only matters when the recommendation is unintuitive	

Theory (Based on Table 5**):** Company representatives want the explanations to assist them as quickly as possible. Due to their generally higher level of experience in reading charts and graphs, the graph explanations actually help the most with this. However, even though the graph can give them an explanation at a glance, they still want to be able to explore further, in case the graph comes across as surprising or unintuitive. In such a scenario, they either want to study the explanation in more detail, e.g., through additionally reading the textual explanation, or they want to manually look into alternative candidates. The feature attribution map could easily be converted into a 'hub' for them, where they can get an overview of alternative candidates for a vacancy.

References

1. Abdollahpouri, H., et al.: Multistakeholder recommendation: survey and research directions. User Model. User-Adap. Inter. **30**, 127–158 (2020)
2. Arya, V., et al.: One explanation does not fit all: a toolkit and taxonomy of AI explainability techniques. arXiv preprint arXiv:1909.03012 (2019)
3. Bianchini, M., Gori, M., Scarselli, F.: Inside pagerank. ACM Trans. Internet Technol. (TOIT) **5**(1), 92–128 (2005)
4. Burges, C., Ragno, R., Le, Q.: Learning to rank with nonsmooth cost functions. In: Advances in Neural Information Processing Systems, vol. 19 (2006)
5. Cambria, E., Malandri, L., Mercorio, F., Mezzanzanica, M., Nobani, N.: A survey on XAI and natural language explanations. Inf. Process. Manag. **60**(1), 103111 (2023)
6. Chen, L., Pu, P.: Trust building in recommender agents. In: Proceedings of the Workshop on Web Personalization, Recommender Systems and Intelligent User Interfaces at the 2nd International Conference on E-Business and Telecommunication Networks, pp. 135–145 (2005)
7. Cramer, H., et al.: The effects of transparency on trust in and acceptance of a content-based art recommender. User Model. User-Adap. Inter. **18**(5), 455–496 (2008)
8. Dworkin, S.L.: Sample size policy for qualitative studies using in-depth interviews (2012)
9. Fauvel, K., Lin, T., Masson, V., Fromont, É., Termier, A.: XCM: an explainable convolutional neural network for multivariate time series classification. Mathematics **9**(23), 3137 (2021)
10. Garcia-Gathright, J., Hosey, C., Thomas, B.S., Carterette, B., Diaz, F.: Mixed methods for evaluating user satisfaction. In: Proceedings of the 12th ACM Conference on Recommender Systems, pp. 541–542 (2018)
11. Hagras, H.: Toward human-understandable, explainable AI. Computer **51**(9), 28–36 (2018)
12. Kingma, D.P., Ba, J.: Adam: a method for stochastic optimization. arXiv preprint arXiv:1412.6980 (2014)
13. Kleinerman, A., Rosenfeld, A., Kraus, S.: Providing explanations for recommendations in reciprocal environments. In: Proceedings of the 12th ACM Conference on Recommender Systems, pp. 22–30 (2018)
14. Le, R., Zhang, T., Hu, W., Zhao, D., Song, Y., Yan, R.: Towards effective and interpretable person-job fitting. In: International Conference on Information and Knowledge Management, Proceedings, pp. 1883–1892 (2019). https://doi.org/10.1145/3357384.3357949
15. Liashchynskyi, P., Liashchynskyi, P.: Grid search, random search, genetic algorithm: a big comparison for nas. arXiv preprint arXiv:1912.06059 (2019)
16. Longhurst, R.: Semi-structured interviews and focus groups. Key Methods Geogr. **3**(2), 143–156 (2003)
17. Lovász, L.: Random walks on graphs. Comb. Paul Erdos Eighty **2**(1–46), 4 (1993)
18. Mei, A., Saxon, M., Chang, S., Lipton, Z.C., Wang, W.Y.: Users are the north star for AI transparency. arXiv preprint arXiv:2303.05500 (2023)
19. Menon, S., Vondrick, C.: Visual classification via description from large language models. arXiv preprint arXiv:2210.07183 (2022)
20. Morse, J.M.: Determining sample size (2000)

21. Nauta, M., et al.: From anecdotal evidence to quantitative evaluation methods: a systematic review on evaluating explainable AI. arXiv preprint arXiv:2201.08164 (2022)
22. OpenAI: ChatGPT: optimizing language models for dialogue (2022). https://openai.com/blog/chatgpt/
23. Palacio, S., Lucieri, A., Munir, M., Ahmed, S., Hees, J., Dengel, A.: XAI handbook: towards a unified framework for explainable AI. In: Proceedings of the IEEE/CVF International Conference on Computer Vision, pp. 3766–3775 (2021)
24. Poli, J.P., Ouerdane, W., Pierrard, R.: Generation of textual explanations in XAI: the case of semantic annotation. In: 2021 IEEE International Conference on Fuzzy Systems (FUZZ-IEEE), pp. 1–6. IEEE (2021)
25. Pu, P., Chen, L., Hu, R.: A user-centric evaluation framework for recommender systems. In: Proceedings of the Fifth ACM Conference on Recommender Systems, pp. 157–164 (2011)
26. Purificato, E., Manikandan, B.A., Karanam, P.V., Pattadkal, M.V., De Luca, E.W.: Evaluating explainable interfaces for a knowledge graph-based recommender system. In: IntRS@ RecSys, pp. 73–88 (2021)
27. de Ruijt, C., Bhulai, S.: Job recommender systems: a review. arXiv preprint arXiv:2111.13576 (2021)
28. Schellingerhout, R., Medentsiy, V., Marx, M.: Explainable career path predictions using neural models (2022)
29. Su, X., Khoshgoftaar, T.M.: A survey of collaborative filtering techniques. Adv. Artif. Intell. **2009** (2009)
30. Szymanski, M., Millecamp, M., Verbert, K.: Visual, textual or hybrid: the effect of user expertise on different explanations. In: 26th International Conference on Intelligent User Interfaces, pp. 109–119 (2021)
31. Tiddi, I., Schlobach, S.: Knowledge graphs as tools for explainable machine learning: a survey. Artif. Intell. **302**, 103627 (2022)
32. Upadhyay, C., Abu-Rasheed, H., Weber, C., Fathi, M.: Explainable job-posting recommendations using knowledge graphs and named entity recognition. In: Conference Proceedings - IEEE International Conference on Systems, Man and Cybernetics, pp. 3291–3296 (2021). https://doi.org/10.1109/SMC52423.2021.9658757
33. Veličković, P., Cucurull, G., Casanova, A., Romero, A., Lio, P., Bengio, Y.: Graph attention networks. arXiv preprint arXiv:1710.10903 (2017)
34. Walker, D., Myrick, F.: Grounded theory: an exploration of process and procedure. Qual. Health Res. **16**(4), 547–559 (2006)
35. Wang, X., He, X., Cao, Y., Liu, M., Chua, T.S.: KGAT: knowledge graph attention network for recommendation. In: Proceedings of the 25th ACM SIGKDD International Conference on Knowledge Discovery & Data Mining, pp. 950–958 (2019)
36. Wrede, C., Winands, M.H., Wilbik, A.: Linguistic summaries as explanation mechanism for classification problems. In: The 34rd Benelux Conference on Artificial Intelligence and the 31th Belgian Dutch Conference on Machine Learning (2022)
37. Yıldırım, E., Azad, P., Öğüdücü, ŞG.: biDeepFM: a multi-objective deep factorization machine for reciprocal recommendation. Eng. Sci. Technol. Int. J. **24**(6), 1467–1477 (2021)

Explaining Socio-Demographic and Behavioral Patterns of Vaccination Against the Swine Flu (H1N1) Pandemic

Clara Punzi[1,2,3]($\boxtimes$) (ID), Aleksandra Maslennikova[2,3] (ID), Gizem Gezici[1,2] (ID),
Roberto Pellungrini[1,2], and Fosca Giannotti[1,2]

[1] Scuola Normale Superiore, Pisa, Italy
clara.punzi@sns.it
[2] KDD Lab, ISTI-CNR, Pisa, Italy
[3] Department of Computer Science, University of Pisa, Pisa, Italy

Abstract. Pandemic vaccination campaigns must account for vaccine skepticism as an obstacle to overcome. Using machine learning to identify behavioral and psychological patterns in public survey datasets can provide valuable insights and inform vaccination campaigns based on empirical evidence. However, we argue that the adoption of local and global explanation methodologies can provide additional support to health practitioners by suggesting personalized communication strategies and revealing potential demographic, social, or structural barriers to vaccination requiring systemic changes. In this paper, we first implement a chain classification model for the adoption of the vaccine during the H1N1 influenza outbreak taking seasonal vaccination information into account, and then compare it with a binary classifier for vaccination to better understand the overall patterns in the data. Following that, we derive and compare global explanations using post-hoc methodologies and interpretable-by-design models. Our findings indicate that socio-demographic factors play a distinct role in the H1N1 vaccination as compared to the general vaccination. Nevertheless, medical recommendation and health insurance remain significant factors for both vaccinations. Then, we concentrated on the subpopulation of individuals who did not receive an H1N1 vaccination despite being at risk of developing severe symptoms. In an effort to assist practitioners in providing effective recommendations to patients, we present rules and counterfactuals for the selected instances based on local explanations. Finally, we raise concerns regarding gender and racial disparities in healthcare access by analysing the interaction effects of sensitive attributes on the model's output.

Keywords: Explainable AI · Chain classification · Vaccine hesitancy · Vaccination Patterns · Protected Groups

1 Introduction

In recent years, the Covid-19 outbreak has considerably raised global awareness about pandemics. While the long-term effects of the strategies employed

The original version of this chapter was previously published non-open access. A Correction to this chapter is available at https://doi.org/10.1007/978-3-031-44067-0_33

to defeat Covid-19 have yet to be determined, studies about other pandemics, such as the 2009 pandemic caused by the A(H1N1)pdm09[1] virus (abbreviated as H1N1 or "swine flu" which is responsible for between 150.000 and 575.000 deaths globally in 2009[2]), revealed that vaccination is a crucial tool whose effectiveness extends beyond single-person immunisation by protecting entire communities through a phenomenon known as "herd immunity" [13,29]. Therefore, national governments must allocate the necessary resources and prepare the population, beginning with informational and awareness-raising campaigns, so that the highest possible vaccination rates can always be achieved. Notably, understanding local contexts and health-related behaviors is essential to the success of a vaccination campaign [18,41]. Vaccine-related concerns in particular pose a major threat to adequate coverage [26]. Indeed, *vaccine hesitancy*, which the World Health Organization (WHO) defines as "the delay in acceptance or refusal of vaccination despite the availability of vaccination services" [28], is listed as one of the top 10 threats to global health[3].

Within the broader context of *vaccine hesitancy*, we simulate a real case scenario of H1N1 flu vaccine prediction and further examine the factors that examine *vaccine hesitancy* with Explainable AI (XAI) techniques. We foresee that explanations corresponding to the outcomes of the predictions will lead to insightful observations. Health officers and practitioners could elicit pivotal communication strategies to adopt based on the objectives of the vaccination campaign (e.g., by refuting or supporting specific opinions or behaviors). Moreover, explanations can reveal demographic or social barriers to immunisation that health officers primarily responsible for planning should address in order to implement the required systemic changes (such as the elimination of administration fees). Additionally, within the EU, i.e., if the proposed model is implemented in the EU, or its decisions affect EU citizens, explicability is required by law for high-risk AI applications such as the ones pertaining to health[4]. In the scope of this work, distinct explainable methods enable us to investigate the most influential features in the overall decision-making process of the presented AI-based models as well as case-specific justifications, i.e., *local* explanations. We also provide *counterfactual* explanations for *what-if* inquiries, as research shows that, in everyday life, individuals often rely on counterfactuals, i.e., what the model would predict if the input were marginally tweaked [8]. Specifically, we devote a substantial component of our analysis to the subsample of individuals that are not-vaccinated (H1N1) despite being at risk for developing severe symptoms. We also conduct an in-depth analysis of the correlation and impact of sensitive attributes, such as ethnicity and gender, on *vaccine hesitancy*.

---

[1] https://web.archive.org/web/20120505042135/http://www.who.int/influenza/gisrs_laboratory/terminology_ah1n1pdm09/en/.

[2] https://www.drivendata.org/competitions/66/flu-shot-learning/page/210/.

[3] https://www.who.int/news-room/spotlight/ten-threats-to-global-health-in-2019.

[4] https://gdpr.eu/tag/gdpr/.

To the best of our knowledge, this is the first work that presents an Explainable AI-based Clinical Decision Support System (CDSS)[5] that uses a comprehensive, carefully curated national survey benchmark dataset regarding the 2009 H1N1 flu pandemic, jointly prepared by the United States (US) National Center for Health Statistics (NCHS) and Centers for Disease Control and Prevention (CDC). Our proposed Explainable CDSS predicts whether a certain individual will receive the H1N1 vaccine based on the given behavioral and socio-demographic features, including one related to the uptake of the seasonal vaccine. Additionally, we implement a baseline model consisting of a binary classifier that only predicts whether a particular individual will get vaccinated or not regardless of the type of vaccine (i.e., seasonal or H1N1) to disclose general vaccination patterns in the US. The most similar work to ours is a recent preprint that presents an AI-based CDSS for COVID-19 *vaccine hesitancy* [2]. Yet, in [2], researchers do not use a comprehensive benchmark dataset that has been prepared by an official agency, but rather they employ a small survey dataset that they collected using Qualtrics (a web-based survey tool), which includes only 2000 instances in total. In addition to this, the authors present a more coarse-grained study in which the XAI methods are only utilised to find the most significant factors that impact a person's decision in the overall dataset and among different ethnic groups without using local explanations or counterfactuals.

Our main contributions can be summarised as follows:

1. We propose an AI-based CDSS to predict *vaccine hesitancy* in the US using a comprehensive benchmark dataset collected during the 2009 H1N1 flu pandemic by the US National Center for Health Statistics.
2. We leverage various XAI techniques to identify the most critical behavioral, socio-demographic, and external factors that have the greatest influence on *vaccine hesitancy*, primarily in the critical situation of the H1N1 flu outbreak, with the aim of providing evidence-based recommendations that could aid health officials and practitioners in developing effective vaccination campaigns.
3. Our findings demonstrate that doctor recommendations are essential for alleviating *vaccine hesitancy*, hence, we incorporate both *local* and *global* explanations to assist healthcare providers by providing sample tailored recommendations, particularly for the patients deemed at high risk of the H1N1 flu. These explanations can be used to select the optimal communication strategy based on a given patient, and if this patient is a non-vaccinated high-risk individual, then we further generate *counterfactuals* that can be exploited to persuade the patient.
4. As anticipated, our results from a real-world scenario also reveal *social injustice* issues in accessing healthcare services and report that the lack of health insurance is one of the most significant factors in *vaccine hesitancy*, which is typically associated with *sensitive attributes* such as belonging to particular gender and ethnic groups.

---

[5] CDSS: An application that analyzes data to help healthcare providers make decisions and improve patient care.

The remainder of the paper is structured as follows. In Sect. 2 we first provide some related work, then in Sect. 3 we describe the technical details of our *vaccine hesitancy* prediction framework, which is composed of the classification models and the XAI methods we used. In Sect. 4 we detail the experimental setup, present the results and further discuss them. Finally, in Sect. 5 we mention the limitations with several potential future work directions and conclude the paper.

2   Background and Related Work

In recent times, XAI has drawn significant attention [1, 19–21, 27, 35–37, 39, 40] primarily due to the growing concern surrounding the lack of transparency in AI applications. Humans seem to be programmed to investigate the causes behind the action; hence, they are reluctant to adopt techniques that are not explicitly interpretable, tractable, and trustworthy [24], particularly in light of the growing demand for ethical AI [5]. Studies demonstrate that providing explanations can increase understanding, which can help improve trust in automated systems [1]. Thus, XAI methods provide justifications that enable users to comprehend the reason behind a system output in a specific context. These methods can be divided into post-hoc, i.e. explanations obtained by external methods, such as SHAP (*SHapley Additive exPlanations*) [27], LIME (*Local Interpretable Model-Agnostic Explanations*) [35]), and LORE (*LOcal Rule-based Explanations*) [19], and explainable-by-design (transparent) methods, i.e. built to be explainable, such as linear models, k-nearest neighbours, and decision trees. The post-hoc XAI methods can be classified as *model-specific* or *model-agnostic* based on the underlying model to be explained and if an explainer does not consider the black box internals and learning process, it is a *model-agnostic* approach. In addition to the aforementioned post-hoc methods, ANCHOR [36] which is a successor of LIME and outputs easy-to-understand if-then rules is a *model-agnostic* explainer, as well. Moreover, the state-of-the-art XAI methods can also be differentiated as *global*, or *local*. The global approaches explain the whole decision logic of a black box model, whereas the local approaches focus on a specific instance. Based on this categorisation, SHAP is a global explainer, whereas LIME, LORE, and ANCHOR are local explainers. INTGRAD [40], DEEPLIFT [39], and GRAD-CAM [37] are saliency mapping-based methods for neural networks that are model-specific, and local explainers.

XAI in Healthcare. AI-based CDSSs are computer systems developed to assist in the delivery of healthcare and can be helpful as a *second set of eyes* for clinicians [3]. The trust issue is particularly obvious in CDSS where health professionals have to interpret the output of AI systems to decide on a specific patient's case. Therefore, it is vital that XAI applications to AI-based CDSS increase trust by allowing healthcare officials to investigate the reasons behind its suggestions. Cai et al. reveal that clinicians expressed a desire for preliminary information regarding fundamental, universal characteristics of a model, such as its inherent strengths and limitations, subjective perspective, and overarching design objective, rather than solely comprehending the localized, context-dependent rationale behind each model decision. There have been many attempts to leverage XAI in healthcare [9–11,17,33,38]. In [9], scholars investigate the expectation of pathologists from the AI-based CDSS assistant. This qualitative lab study reveal that the medical experts have a desire for preliminary information regarding fundamental, universal characteristics of a model, such as its inherent strengths and limitations, subjective perspective, and overarching design objective, rather than solely comprehending the localized, context-dependent rationale behind each model decision. In [17], researchers analyse an AI-based imaging CDSS designed to assist health practitioners in detecting COVID cases in the scope of examining the explanation needs of different stakeholders. In [10], scholars propose an AI-based CDSS that predicts COVID-19 diagnosis using clinical, demographic, and blood variables and employs XAI to extract the most essential markers. In [33], authors present the results of a user study on the impact of advices from a CDSS on healthcare practitioners' judgment. For detailed surveys, please refer to [11]. Finally, in [38], the authors propose instead a classification model on a social media dataset that first distinguish misleading from non-misleading tweets pertaining to COVID-19 vaccination, then extract the principal topics of discussion in terms of *vaccine hesitancy* and finally apply SHAP to identify important features in model prediction.

Classification Models in Tabular Data. The state-of-the-art approaches for prediction tasks on tabular data suggest the employment of ensemble tree-based models. In general, boosting methods build models sequentially using the entire dataset, with each model reducing the error of the previous one. Differently from other gradient-boosting ensemble algorithms, such as XGBoost [14] and Light-GBM [25], CatBoost (proposed by Yandex) [15] employs balanced trees that not only allow for quicker computations and evaluation but also prevent overfitting. For such a reason, together with the peculiar structure of our dataset, we decided to firstly rely on this model. Notably, Catboost includes a built-in function for feature selection that removes features recursively based on the weights of a trained model. Feature scores provide an estimate of how much the average prediction changes when a feature's value is altered[6]. Consequently, despite being classified as a black box, CatBoost retains some global interpretability. As a second classification model, we use TabNet (proposed by Google) [4], a deep neural network devised specifically for tabular data and classified as an explainable-by-design model. TabNet's architecture combines two important advantages of state-of-the-art classification approaches: the explainability of tree-based algorithms and the high performance of neural networks. In addition to global interpretability, Tabnet implements local interpretability for instance-wise feature selection, unlike CatBoost.

---

[6] https://catboost.ai/en/docs/concepts/fstr.

3   The Explainable AI-Based CDSS of Vaccine Hesitancy

3.1   Dataset

We used the dataset from the *National 2009 H1N1 Flu Survey (NHFS)*, a questionnaire conducted in the US during the 2009 H1N1 flu outbreak[7] to monitor vaccination coverage and produce timely estimates of vaccination coverage rates[8]. The survey contains questions about influenza-related behaviours, opinions regarding vaccine safety and effectiveness as well as disease history etc. (the full NHFS questionnaire can be found on the CDC website[9]). The dataset contains 26.707 instances, 36 categorical features (the first being the ID of each anonymized individual), all of which are binary, ordinal, or nominal, and two additional binary variables that can be used as targets, namely, the seasonal and H1N1 flu vaccination status. As anticipated, the features include demographic data (e.g. sex, race, geographic location), health-related behaviors (e.g., washing hands, wearing a face mask), and opinions about flu and vaccine risks. Note that a competition has been launched on this benchmark dataset[10] hence, for a complete description of the dataset, please refer to the competition website.

Preprocessing. All features in the dataset are conceptually categorical, but most of them are reported as numerical rankings or binary variables, so we only applied transformation on the remaining 12 categorical features (4 ordinal, 3 binary, and 5 multinominal). We used manual ordinal encoding for the ordinal and binary, and one-hot encoding for the multinominal ones. Also, since the dataset contains missing values in most columns, we applied iterative imputation: a strategy that models each feature with NaNs as a function of other features in a round-robin fashion. We initialized it as the most frequent value of the given variable and we set the Random Forest Classifier as the base model for the iteration step. To avoid the imputation of missing values from other synthetic data, we substituted the imputed values only at the end of the process. Lastly, in the baseline model that does not consider vaccination type, to better interpret the explanations, we merged vaccine-specific features by computing the average of corresponding H1N1 and seasonal vaccine feature scores (for instance, instead of having two separate features representing opinions about seasonal and H1N1 vaccine effectiveness, we used their average as a proxy for overall opinion about vaccine effectiveness).

3.2   Classification Models

We implemented two binary classification models for predicting the uptake of the H1N1 vaccine and the vaccine in general (regardless of the vaccine type,

---

[7] https://www.cdc.gov/flu/pandemic-resources/2009-h1n1-pandemic.html.

[8] https://www.drivendata.org/competitions/66/flu-shot-learning/page/213/.

[9] https://ftp.cdc.gov/pub/Health_Statistics/NCHS/Dataset_Documentation/NIS/nhfs/nhfspuf_DUG.PDF.

[10] https://www.drivendata.org/competitions/66/flu-shot-learning/page/210/;.

seasonal or H1N1), with the latter serving as a baseline model. In both cases, we used two state-of-the-art machine learning algorithms for classification on categorical tabular data, namely, CatBoost [34] and TabNet [4]. For the main task of predicting the uptake of the H1N1 vaccine, we decided to rely on a multi-label classifier chain since we discovered, during the data exploration phase, a positive correlation between the two target variables of seasonal and H1N1 vaccination (moderate Pearson coefficient: $\rho = 0.38$). We performed an exhaustive grid search with cross-validation on the training dataset to determine the best hyperparameters, which were then used to train the classifiers. Furthermore, given the significant imbalance in the distribution of the dataset with respect to the joint combination of the seasonal and H1N1 vaccines, we compared the performance of the selected models on augmented training datasets derived through various upsampling strategies. These techniques included a naive random over-sampling approach, where new instances of the underrepresented class were generated by picking samples at random with replacement, as well as the Synthetic Minority Oversampling Technique (SMOTE, [12]) and the Adaptive Synthetic sampling method (ADASYN, [22]). Nevertheless, none of these methods led to a significant improvement in the F1 score (see Table 1), hence we opted to maintain the initial dataset for subsequent analyses. It should be noted that, in contrast to the H1N1 model, the baseline classification model did not exhibit an imbalanced class distribution. The best performance for both the baseline and H1N1 model was achieved by CatBoost classifier.

Table 1. Model performances.

Model	Upsampling	AUC (weighted)	F1-score (weighted)	AUC (macro)	F1-score (macro)
CatBoost Classifier Chain	-	0.75	**0.87**	0.77	**0.77**
	Random oversampling	**0.79**	0.83	**0.79**	0.75
	SMOTE	0.77	0.84	0.77	0.76
	ADASYN	0.77	0.84	0.77	0.76
TabNet Classifier Chain	-	0.73	**0.82**	0.73	**0.73**
	Random oversampling	0.75	0.80	0.75	0.72
	SMOTE	0.71	0.81	0.71	0.72
	ADASYN	**0.76**	0.80	**0.76**	0.73
CatBoost Baseline	-	0.77	0.77	0.77	0.77
TabNet Baseline	-	0.75	0.75	0.75	0.75

3.3 XAI Methods

We initially obtained the global feature importance scores from TabNet [4] and CatBoost's [15] built-in functions, and compared them to SHAP-based feature rankings. This choice is based on the fact that SHAP [27] offers a wide range of analysis tools and its feature rankings have demonstrated greater stability compared to the built-in functions of tree-based ensemble models [42]. Then, we inspected the interaction effects between features; in particular, we examined the impact of *sensitive* attributes, such as ethnicity and gender, on the model prediction. After that, we *locally* explained specific test set instances: we computed local feature importance scores with SHAP [27] and LIME [35] and extracted *counterfactuals* from LORE [19][11] The instances were chosen from the subpopulations of high-risk individuals declared by the US H1N1 recommendations[12], for further discussion please see Sect. 4.2.

The goodness, usefulness, and satisfaction of an explanation should be considered when assessing the validity and convenience of an explanation technique [6]. In the scope of this study, we conducted both quantitative and qualitative assessments. On the one hand, we ensured that our explainers had a high degree of fidelity, i.e., that they could accurately approximate the prediction of the black box model [30]. On the other hand, we discussed the actual usefulness of the explanations from the perspective of the end-user, i.e., a health official or practitioner.

4 Results and Discussion

4.1 H1N1 Vaccine Hesitancy Model vs Baseline

In this part, we compare the global explanations of the baseline and H1N1 vaccine hesitancy models. First of all, we retrieved feature importance rankings using CatBoost, which is a black-box model that enables a certain degree of global interpretability, and TabNet, which is an explainable-by-design method. Figure 1a displays the feature importance rankings of the baseline model. Both models significantly rely on whether a doctor recommended a vaccination, personal opinion regarding vaccine efficacy, and age. Notably, the CatBoost model prioritises personal judgment about the risks of getting sick without vaccination and the availability of health insurance, while TabNet disregards these features entirely. In the H1N1 model (See Fig. 1b), the feature importance ranking of CatBoost differed considerably from TabNet. Both models significantly rely on the doctor's recommendation and opinion on vaccine efficacy, but age was not a determining factor. The features of opinions about the risk of getting sick and health insurance were only considered by CatBoost in the baseline model,

---

[11] We did not use the recent version of LORE [20] which is more stable and generates actionable features as claimed by the authors since we could not execute the code in their github repo.

[12] https://www.cdc.gov/h1n1flu/vaccination/acip.htm.

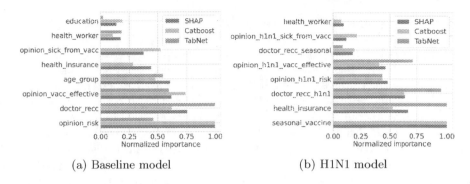

(a) Baseline model   (b) H1N1 model

Fig. 1. Comparison of different feature importance rankings, sorted according to SHAP rankings.

while both models deem them significant for the H1N1 prediction. Interestingly, TabNet ignores the most crucial feature of CatBoost which is the seasonal vaccination status.

In addition, we computed post-hoc explanations by applying SHAP [27] to the model with the best classification performance, namely CatBoost [15]. It is noteworthy that SHAP achieved a significantly *high fidelity* score of 0.92, which is indicative of its capacity to accurately mimic the underlying black-box model. Using Tree SHAP as the algorithm to compute Shapley values, we discovered, as expected, that SHAP feature rankings were comparable to those provided by CatBoost for both the baseline and H1N1 models. In the following sections, we will refer primarily to SHAP when discussing about global explanations.

4.2   Vaccine Hesitancy in High-Risk Individuals

Due to the H1N1 vaccine's limited availability during the campaign's initial phase, health officials advised people at the highest risk for viral effects or those caring for them to receive the vaccine first. These target subpopulations were (1) adults who live with or care for children under 6 months, (2) healthcare workers, (3) adults aged 25 to 64 with certain chronic health conditions, (4) people aged 6 months to 24 years, and (5) pregnant women. In our work, however, we note that the target group (5) could not be analyzed since the dataset did not contain the related information, and condition (4) was slightly modified to (4') 18-to-34-year-old, as this is the lowest age group reported in the dataset.

We used XAI techniques to understand why some high-risk individuals **do not** vaccinate in order to lay the basis for effective doctor recommendations. Indeed, the findings discussed in Sect. 4.1 indicate that doctor recommendations are crucial for promoting vaccination not only among the general population but also, and most importantly, among individuals at high risk of being severely affected by a pandemic influenza outbreak. In the following, we show how local explanations generated by SHAP [27], LIME [35], and LORE [19] can be leveraged by physicians to design effective, patient-specific communication strategies for recommending vaccination. As a first example, consider the subject with the identifier $id = 24210$, a white woman who satisfies criteria (3) and (4'). In this instance, our model accurately predicted that she had declined the H1N1 vaccination against the doctor's recommendation. As depicted in Figs. 2a and 2b, the feature importance scores computed by SHAP and LIME concur that her belief that the vaccine was not very effective and her refusal to receive the seasonal vaccine had a substantial negative impact on the vaccination outcome. Based on LORE's counterfactual (*fidelity* $= 0.99$), we found that the doctor's recommendation was ineffective because she or he failed to raise the subject's opinion about the vaccine's efficacy and the swine flu's threat. Furthermore, LORE identified having health insurance and living in a particular geographical region as conditions for a positive vaccination outcome. Unfortunately, the actionability of these features is debatable, revealing the existence of social disparities in vaccination.

As a second example, we consider the subject with $id = 23241$, a black woman who meets criteria (1), (3), and (4'). Similar to the previous subject, the model accurately predicted that she had declined the H1N1 vaccination, but this time we know she did not receive a doctor's recommendation. SHAP and LIME (*fidelity* $= 1$) evaluate this fact to be extremely negative in terms of feature importance, along with other factors such as not having received the seasonal vaccine, having a very low opinion of the risk of becoming sick with H1N1 flu without vaccination, and not having health insurance. In addition, LIME scored unfavorably for its lack of employment in specific industries and professions. LORE (*fidelity* $= 0.99$) provided a coherent decision rule and a few counterfactual explanations that, first and foremost, required a doctor's recommendation and that, additionally, indicate that an effective recommendation would be one capable of increasing the subject's opinion regarding the effectiveness of the H1N1 vaccine, allowing her to obtain health insurance, and convincing her to also receive the seasonal vaccine. Interestingly, some counterfactuals also included conditions indicating non-belonging to the "black" or "other or multiple" ethnic group, as well as geographically-based criteria, which however are subject to the same limitations as those previously noted regarding the actionability of certain counterfactual.

4.3   Social Injustice in Healthcare

The US healthcare system has been widely acknowledged and recorded to exhibit structural inequalities that are often linked to particular ethnic and gender categories [16,23]. The same holds true specifically in the campaigns for H1N1 [7], COVID-19 [31], and seasonal vaccine [32]. Therefore, socio-demographic factors like gender and ethnicity, as well as social injustice in healthcare access, should be taken into account when interpreting studies about vaccine hesitancy, as the refusal to be vaccinated may be due to structural barriers, such as a lack of health insurance in a country where public health is not guaranteed. Indeed, our results confirm that health insurance coverage is one of the most important predictive factors, especially in the H1N1 model, as shown in Sect. 4.1, and the counterfactual explanations in Sect. 4.2 consistently identified health insurance

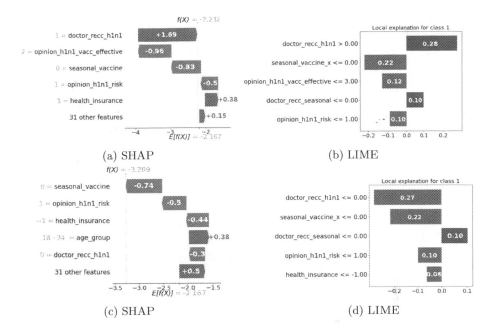

(a) SHAP   (b) LIME

(c) SHAP   (d) LIME

Fig. 2. Local explanations for $id = 24210$ (top row, true class $= 0$, predicted class $= 0$), and $id = 23241$ (bottom row, true class $= 0$, predicted class $= 0$).

as a key driver in promoting vaccination in the subpopulation at high-risk with respect to H1N1.

The impact of *health insurance, ethnicity*, and *sex* on the model's predictions is illustrated in the dependence scatter plots in Fig. 3. In these three plots, points are displayed based on their coordinates (x, y) as feature value (x) and Shapley value (y), where each point refers to an observation. For instance, Fig. 2a displays that the perceived threat posed by H1N1 has the greatest interactive effect with health insurance in predicting vaccine uptake, while in Fig. 2b and Fig. 2c, for the sensitive attributes: ethnicity and gender, health insurance is the most interactive feature. In Fig. 2b, ethnicity does not significantly impact the model's decision among the *white* subpopulation, since the corresponding data points are not dispersed, whereas other three subpopulations exhibit a greater degree of variation which might point to racial disparities in access to vaccination campaigns. In terms of gender, the plot in Fig. 2c reveals that men are more likely to be vaccinated irrespective of their health insurance, as most Shapley values are positive. This observed bias of the H1N1 classifier towards men conveys that there may have been real-world factors that favored men's access to the vaccine. Interestingly, women with health insurance are less likely to be vaccinated, whereas men are more likely. The aforementioned trend in the decision rules of SHAP [27], LIME [35], and LORE [19] is corroborated by the plot in Fig. 2a, as only a minimal fraction of points without health insurance (or with no information provided) are associated with positive Shapley values. For repro-

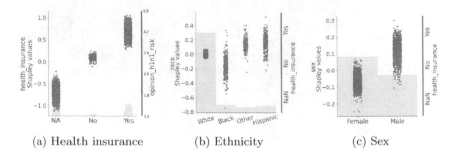

(a) Health insurance   (b) Ethnicity   (c) Sex

Fig. 3. Dependence scatter plots for the H1N1 model – the x-axis denotes the feature values, the y-axis refers to Shapley values, coloring is based on the values of the feature in the secondary y-axis (most interactive feature chosen by SHAP).

ducibility purposes, our code is publicly available at https://github.com/gizem-gg/H1N1-VaccineHesitancy-CDSS.

5   Conclusion and Future Work

In this work, we proposed an AI-based Explainable CDSS for predicting and assessing hesitancy towards the swine flu vaccination uptake. XAI methodologies assist us in identifying doctor recommendation, health insurance, seasonal vaccine adoption, and personal opinion regarding vaccine efficacy as the most influential factors in H1N1 vaccination. On the basis of counterfactual explanations, we provided physicians with suggestions for effectively conveying to their patients the need to receive the H1N1 vaccine, with a focus on those at high risk for severe symptoms. In particular, we discovered that communication strategies that can improve the subject's opinion of the effectiveness of the H1N1 vaccine and the threat posed by the swine flu are more likely to function as catalysts for change. Moreover, our analysis highlights the crucial role of health insurance, which reflects actual disparities in healthcare access in the US, and illustrates how vaccination campaigns can be hampered not only by vaccine reluctance but also by economic constraints. Likewise, it has been found that membership in marginalized groups based on gender, ethnicity, or geography can result in individuals with a higher risk profile opting out of vaccination. A major limitation of our analysis is the large number of missing values regarding health insurance, which is one of the most important features for our model. Second, our algorithm of choice for counterfactual explanation is based on a genetic algorithm for neighborhood generation. It could be interesting to compare different algorithms for neighborhood generation. Moreover, the choice of the attribute to consider in counterfactual generation should be guided by the principle of actionability, to focus on feature that healthcare professional can act upon. As future work, we plan to address these limitations and evaluate the efficacy of the proposed Explainable AI-based CDSS framework by conducting a comprehensive user case study with health officials and physicians.

Acknowledgements. We sincerely thank Dr. Andrea Beretta (CNR-ISTI) for his invaluable guidance and insightful discussions.

This work has been supported by the European Union under ERC-2018-ADG GA 834756 (XAI), by HumanE-AI-Net GA 952026, and by the Partnership Extended PE00000013 - "FAIR - Future Artificial Intelligence Research" - Spoke 1 "Human-centered AI".

It has been realised also thanks to computational (data and algorithms) resources of "SoBigData++: European Integrated Infrastructure for Social Mining and Big Data Analytics" (http://www.sobigdata.eu), G.A.No.871042 and by NextGenerationEU - National Recovery and Resilience Plan Resilienza, PNRR) - Project: "SoBigData.it - Strengthening the Italian RI for Social Mining and Big Data Analytics" - Prot. IR000001 3 - Notice n. 3264 of 12/28/2021.

References

1. Adadi, A., Berrada, M.: Peeking inside the black-box: a survey on explainable artificial intelligence (XAI). IEEE Access **6**, 52138–52160 (2018)
2. Alharbi, R., Chan-Olmsted, S., Chen, H., Thai, M.T.: Cultural-aware machine learning based analysis of covid-19 vaccine hesitancy. arXiv preprint arXiv:2304.06953 (2023)
3. Antoniadi, A.M., et al.: Current challenges and future opportunities for XAI in machine learning-based clinical decision support systems: a systematic review. Appl. Sci. **11**(11), 5088 (2021)
4. Arik, S.O., Pfister, T.: TabNet: attentive interpretable tabular learning. In: Proceedings of the AAAI Conference on Artificial Intelligence, vol. 35, no. 8 (2021)
5. Birhane, A.: Algorithmic injustice: a relational ethics approach. Patterns **2**(2), 100205 (2021)
6. Bodria, F., Giannotti, F., Guidotti, R., Naretto, F., Pedreschi, D., Rinzivillo, S.: Benchmarking and survey of explanation methods for black box models. CoRR abs/2102.13076 (2021)
7. Burger, A.E., Reither, E.N., Mamelund, S.-E., Lim, S.: Black-white disparities in 2009 H1N1 vaccination among adults in the United States: a cautionary tale for the COVID-19 pandemic. Vaccine **39**(6), 943–951 (2021)
8. Byrne, R.M.: The Rational Imagination: How People Create Alternatives to Reality. MIT Press, Cambridge (2007)
9. Cai, C.J., Winter, S., Steiner, D., Wilcox, L., Terry, M.: "Hello AI": uncovering the onboarding needs of medical practitioners for human-AI collaborative decision-making. Proc. ACM Hum.-Comput. Interact. **3**(CSCW), 1–24 (2019)
10. Chadaga, K., Prabhu, S., Bhat, V., Sampathila, N., Umakanth, S., Chadaga, R.: A decision support system for diagnosis of covid-19 from non-covid-19 influenza-like illness using explainable artificial intelligence. Bioengineering **10**(4), 439 (2023)
11. Chaddad, A., Peng, J., Xu, J., Bouridane, A.: Survey of explainable AI techniques in healthcare. Sensors **23**(2), 634 (2023)
12. Chawla, N.V., Bowyer, K.W., Hall, L.O., Kegelmeyer, W.P.: Smote: synthetic minority over-sampling technique. J. Artif. Int. Res. **16**(1), 321–357 (2002)
13. Chen, D.S.: Hepatitis b vaccination: the key towards elimination and eradication of hepatitis B. J. Hepatol. **50**(4), 805–816 (2009)
14. Chen, T., et al.: Xgboost: extreme gradient boosting. R Package Version 0.4-2, vol. 1, no. 4, pp. 1–4 (2015)

15. Dorogush, A.V., Ershov, V., Gulin, A.: Catboost: gradient boosting with categorical features support. arXiv preprint arXiv:1810.11363 (2018)

16. Garfield, R., Majerol, M., Damico, A., Foutz, J.: The uninsured: a primer. Key facts about health insurance and the uninsured in America. The Henry James Kaiser Family Foundation, Menlo Park (2016)

17. Gerlings, J., Jensen, M.S., Shollo, A.: Explainable AI, but explainable to whom? An exploratory case study of XAI in healthcare. In: Handbook of Artificial Intelligence in Healthcare: Vol 2: Practicalities and Prospects (2022)

18. Glanz, K., Bishop, D.B.: The role of behavioral science theory in development and implementation of public health interventions. Annu. Rev. Public Health **31**(1), 399–418 (2010)

19. Guidotti, R., Monreale, A., Giannotti, F., Pedreschi, D., Ruggieri, S., Turini, F.: Factual and counterfactual explanations for black box decision making. IEEE Intell. Syst. **34**(6), 14–23 (2019)

20. Guidotti, R., et al.: Stable and actionable explanations of black-box models through factual and counterfactual rules. Data Min. Knowl. Discov. 1–38 (2022)

21. Guidotti, R., Monreale, A., Ruggieri, S., Turini, F., Giannotti, F., Pedreschi, D.: A survey of methods for explaining black box models. ACM Comput. Surv. **51**(5), 1–42 (2018)

22. He, H., Bai, Y., Garcia, E.A., Li, S.: Adasyn: adaptive synthetic sampling approach for imbalanced learning. In: 2008 IEEE International Joint Conference on Neural Networks (IEEE World Congress on Computational Intelligence), pp. 1322–1328 (2008). https://doi.org/10.1109/IJCNN.2008.4633969

23. Hoffman, C., Paradise, J.: Health insurance and access to health care in the united states. Ann. N. Y. Acad. Sci. **1136**(1), 149–160 (2008)

24. Holzinger, A., Biemann, C., Pattichis, C.S., Kell, D.B.: What do we need to build explainable AI systems for the medical domain? arXiv preprint arXiv:1712.09923 (2017)

25. Ke, G., et al.: Lightgbm: a highly efficient gradient boosting decision tree. In: Advances in Neural Information Processing Systems, vol. 30 (2017)

26. Li, L., Wood, C.E., Kostkova, P.: Vaccine hesitancy and behavior change theory-based social media interventions: a systematic review. Transl. Behav. Med. **12**(2), 243–272 (2021)

27. Lundberg, S.M., Lee, S.I.: A unified approach to interpreting model predictions. In: Advances in Neural Information Processing Systems, vol. 30 (2017)

28. MacDonald, N.E.: Vaccine hesitancy: definition, scope and determinants. Vaccine **33**(34), 4161–4164 (2015)

29. Macedo, C.G.D.: Director's letter: the defeat of polio. Bull. Pan Am. Health Organ. (PAHO) **27**(1), 1993 (1993)

30. Molnar, C.: Interpretable Machine Learning. A Guide for Making Black Box Models Explainable, chap. Properties of Explanations (2022)

31. Njoku, A., Joseph, M., Felix, R.: Changing the narrative: structural barriers and racial and ethnic inequities in COVID-19 vaccination. Int. J. Environ. Res. Public Health **18**(18), 9904 (2021)

32. Okoli, G.N., Abou-Setta, A.M., Neilson, C.J., Chit, A., Thommes, E., Mahmud, S.M.: Determinants of seasonal influenza vaccine uptake among the elderly in the united states: a systematic review and meta-analysis. Gerontol. Geriatr. Med. **5**, 233372141987034 (2019)

33. Panigutti, C., Beretta, A., Giannotti, F., Pedreschi, D.: Understanding the impact of explanations on advice-taking: a user study for AI-based clinical decision sup-

port systems. In: Proceedings of the 2022 CHI Conference on Human Factors in Computing Systems, pp. 1–9 (2022)

34. Prokhorenkova, L., Gusev, G., Vorobev, A., Dorogush, A.V., Gulin, A.: Catboost: unbiased boosting with categorical features. In: Proceedings of the 32nd International Conference on Neural Information Processing Systems, NIPS 2018, pp. 6639–6649. Curran Associates Inc., Red Hook (2018)

35. Ribeiro, M.T., Singh, S., Guestrin, C.: "Why should i trust you?" explaining the predictions of any classifier. In: Proceedings of the 22nd ACM SIGKDD International Conference on Knowledge Discovery and Data Mining (2016)

36. Ribeiro, M.T., Singh, S., Guestrin, C.: Anchors: high-precision model-agnostic explanations. In: Proceedings of the AAAI Conference on Artificial Intelligence, vol. 32 (2018)

37. Selvaraju, R.R., Cogswell, M., Das, A., Vedantam, R., Parikh, D., Batra, D.: Grad-cam: Visual explanations from deep networks via gradient-based localization. In: Proceedings of the IEEE International Conference on Computer Vision, pp. 618–626 (2017)

38. Sharma, S., Sharma, R., Datta, A.: (Mis) leading the COVID-19 vaccination discourse on twitter: an exploratory study of infodemic around the pandemic. IEEE Trans. Comput. Soc. Syst. (2022)

39. Shrikumar, A., Greenside, P., Kundaje, A.: Learning important features through propagating activation differences. In: International Conference on Machine Learning, pp. 3145–3153. PMLR (2017)

40. Sundararajan, M., Taly, A., Yan, Q.: Axiomatic attribution for deep networks. In: International Conference on Machine Learning, pp. 3319–3328. PMLR (2017)

41. Weston, D., Ip, A., Amlôt, R.: Examining the application of behaviour change theories in the context of infectious disease outbreaks and emergency response: a review of reviews. BMC Public Health **20**(1) (2020)

42. Zacharias, J., von Zahn, M., Chen, J., Hinz, O.: Designing a feature selection method based on explainable artificial intelligence. Electron. Mark. **32**(4), 2159–2184 (2022)

Semantic Meaningfulness: Evaluating Counterfactual Approaches for Real-World Plausibility and Feasibility

Jacqueline Höllig[1]([✉])[iD], Aniek F. Markus[2][iD], Jef de Slegte[3][iD], and Prachi Bagave[4][iD]

[1] FZI Forschungszentrum Informatik, Karlsruhe, Germany
hoellig@fzi.de
[2] Department of Medical Informatics, Erasmus University Medical Center, Rotterdam, The Netherlands
[3] Data Analytics Lab, Vrije Universiteit Brussel, Brussel, Belgium
[4] Delft University of Technology, Delft, The Netherlands

Abstract. Counterfactual explanations are rising in popularity when aiming to increase the explainability of machine learning models. This type of explanation is straightforward to understand and provides actionable feedback (i.e., how to change the model decision). One of the main challenges that remains is generating meaningful counterfactuals that are coherent with real-world relations. Multiple approaches incorporating real-world relations have been proposed in the past, e.g. by utilizing data distributions or structural causal models. However, evaluating whether the explanations from different counterfactual approaches fulfill known causal relationships is still an open issue. To fill this gap, this work proposes two metrics - Semantic Meaningful Output (SMO) and Semantic Meaningful Relations (SMR) - to measure the ability of counterfactual generation approaches to depict real-world relations. In addition, we provide multiple datasets with known structural causal models and leverage them to benchmark the semantic meaningfulness of new and existing counterfactual approaches. Finally, we evaluate the semantic meaningfulness of nine well-established counterfactual explanation approaches and conclude that none of the non-causal approaches were able to create semantically meaningful counterfactuals consistently.

Keywords: Explainable AI · Machine Learning · Counterfactual Explanations · Evaluating Explanations · Interpretability · Structural Equation Models · Causal Graphs

J. Höllig and A. F. Markus—Authors contributed equally to this work.

This work was carried out with the support of the German Federal Ministry of Education and Research (BMBF) within the project "MetaLearn" (Grant 02P20A013) and received funding from the Innovative Medicines Initiative 2 Joint Undertaking (JU) under grant agreement No 806968. The JU receives support from the European Union's Horizon 2020 research and innovation programme and EFPIA. This work is also partially supported by the SPATIAL project funded by European Union's Horizon 2020 research and innovation programme under grant agreement No. 101021808.

L. Longo (Ed.): xAI 2023, CCIS 1902, pp. 636–659, 2023.
https://doi.org/10.1007/978-3-031-44067-0_32

1   Introduction

With the performance increase of machine learning (ML) models (especially deep learning), their application in real-world settings is growing. Algorithms learn from large amounts of data to discover patterns, often with the ultimate goal of supporting decision-making. However, the resulting models are often considered black boxes due to their vast number of parameters. Providing explanations for these black boxes has become crucial for applications with significant social impact (e.g., pre-trial bail [8], credit risk assessment [18], health care [17,25]). As a result, there is increasing social and legal pressure on letting individuals that are significantly affected by models, understand why an ML model obtained a certain prediction (e.g., 'right to explanation' in the EU General Data Protection Regulation (GDPR) [9,41]).

For example, consider an ML model supporting decisions on personal loan applications. If the application is rejected, an affected person might want to know why their loan application was not approved. A counterfactual explanation can be used to provide such an explanation as a "what-if"- scenario: e.g., "if the income had been 5.000 higher, the loan would have been accepted". Counterfactual explanations describe the closest change to the original input features that would change the outcome [42]. This type of explanation is valuable because the explanations are contrastive [26] and provide guidance on recovering from unfavorable predictions. Algorithmic recourse is a closely related term that is often used to refer to the required actions to change the outcome, with an intention to 'act' rather than 'understand' [15]. In line with Verma et al. [40], we use the term counterfactual explanations and algorithmic recourse interchangeably.

Various algorithms have been proposed to generate counterfactual explanations. In the simplest form, counterfactuals can be generated for a classifier g by minimizing a distance d between an original data point x and a possible counterfactual instance x^{cf} resulting in a class change from y to y^{cf}. The following optimization problem can be derived: $\min_{x} d(x, x^{cf})$ subject to $g(x) \neq g(x^{cf})$ [42]. However, this optimization problem often leads to unrealistic and infeasible counterfactuals. Therefore, later work has extended the formulation to satisfy additional desiderata (e.g., sparsity, data manifold adherence, causality) [40].

One of the biggest challenges that remain is generating meaningful counterfactuals that are coherent with real-world relations. First, counterfactual explanations should satisfy causal relations (e.g., additional years of education are accompanied by an increase in age). Second, counterfactual explanations should lead to changes in the real world when acted upon (i.e. changes translate to a causal effect). Causal models are a way of describing real-world relations. Despite Wachter et al. [42] already advocating for the usefulness of counterfactuals generated from causal models, only a few works (e.g., [13,15,24]) are based on causal assumptions. One of the reasons is that structural causal models (SCM) - including the causal graph and structural equations - are hard to obtain. While it is often possible to draw a causal graph based on expert knowledge, assumptions about the form of structural equations are generally not testable and may not hold in practice [31]. Therefore, most counterfactual explanation approaches bypass SCM and direct their effort to provide realistic counterfactuals with surrogate models (e.g., [3,7,22,29,39]), constraints (e.g., [32,38]) or using the inherently learned information in the classifier (e.g., [23,37,45]). Quantifying to what extent causal relations and effects are satisfied is especially hard for those noncausal approaches due to a lack of ground truth. Hence, causal capabilities are often approximated by evaluating user constraints or data distributions (e.g., [19,29]). However, this type of evaluation only states if a counterfactual is following a certain distribution or meets some predefined constraint. No evidence is given whether the changes follow a causal chain.

Various works from social sciences (e.g. [4,26]) emphasized the importance of causality for good explanations. To evaluate whether the explanations from different counterfactual approaches indeed fulfill known causal relationships, we introduce the notion of semantic meaningfulness for counterfactual generation approaches. The semantic meaningfulness of a counterfactual generation algorithm describes the fraction of generated counterfactuals that are coherent with real-world relations. We propose two measures: the fraction of counterfactual explanations that lead to the same outcome in the real world ('*Semantic Meaningful Output*') and the fraction of known causal relationships fulfilled by the counterfactual explanation ('*Semantic Meaningful Relations*'). We evade the issue of missing SCMs by providing different datasets with causal graphs that can be used to benchmark new and existing approaches. The main contributions of this paper are as follows:

1. We define semantic meaningfulness for counterfactual generation approaches and propose two metrics to evaluate different levels of semantic meaningfulness.
2. We provide six datasets with known SCMs that can be leveraged to benchmark the semantic meaningfulness of new and existing counterfactual approaches.
3. We evaluate the semantic meaningfulness of nine well-established counterfactual explanation approaches for three ML models.

2   Related Work

Following the literature on counterfactuals, the proposed explanations should be sparse (i.e., entails limited features [12,40]), realistic (i.e. is near the training data [40] - also called data manifold adherence), actionable (i.e., contains mutable features [40]), feasible (i.e., adhering to real-world relations [24]) and plausible (i.e., perceived as sensible by human users [36]) to be useful in practice. Depending on the author, *feasibility* is described as counterfactuals that are proximate and connected to regions of high data density (e.g., [29,32]) or as satisfying causal relations between features (e.g., [24]). We follow the definition of Mahajan et al. [24], who view feasibility as a causal concept that cannot be addressed with statistical constraints alone. Closely related to the notion of feasibility is *plausibility*. Depending on the operationalization of the concept, some consider explanations plausible that are close to the test instances, using the "right" features, or faithful to the distribution or training data [12]. We define plausibility following Keane et al. [16] emphasizing the importance of the psychological aspect of explanations by describing plausibility as the degree to which explanations make sense to human users. The main difference with other desiderata is the emphasis on the relevance of the explanations to human users. To ensure relevance for the end-user we consider an explanation as plausible if the explanations lead to the same outcome in the real world.

The body of work addressing counterfactual generation largely falls into four categories: adding specific distances or user constraints to the original data [1, 11, 27, 35, 38, 42], learning the underlying data structure [6, 22, 32], using feature extraction effects of a specific ML model [23, 37, 45], and using (fully or partially defined) SCMs [14, 24]. For an overview of counterfactual explanation methods, we refer the reader to Verma et al. [40] and Karimi et al. [12]. Most approaches that aim to generate feasible counterfactuals, rely on learning the underlying data structure. However, feasibility is a causal concept and cannot be achieved by statistical constraints alone [24].

While some benchmarking frameworks for evaluating Explainable Artificial Intelligence methods [2, 10] and especially counterfactual explanations [28] have been proposed, the evaluation of the causality of explanations is still an open issue. Evaluating counterfactual approaches is mostly done by quantifying the desirable properties of a counterfactual explanation (e.g., [28]). For example, *validity* measures whether a counterfactual explanation was able to flip the classifier's decision [7, 13, 23, 24, 28]. *Proximity* is the user-specified distance (e.g., mean absolute error) between the original instance and the counterfactual [13, 23, 24, 28]. *Sparsity* quantifies the number of changes made to the input [13, 28] and *diversity* is a measure for the similarity of the different counterfactual explanations when multiple explanations are generated [40]. Sometimes *constraint feasibility* is also measured by checking user-given constraints [24, 28]. However, evaluating feasibility - especially for non-causal models - is neglected [24]. Laugel et al. [19] suggest two measures that are applicable to most counterfactual approaches to quantify feasibility proximity (i.e. whether a counterfactual is a local outlier) and concreteness (i.e. whether a counterfactual is connected to other correctly classified observations from the same class). However, their measures are data-driven and therefore not able to test coherence with real-world relations. Other feasibility metrics are only applicable to specific counterfactual generation approaches (e.g., confidence lower bound for probabilistic recourse [13], interpretability score [24, 39], causal-edge score in case the true SCM is known [24]). There exists no agnostic metric that is applicable to all counterfactual generation approaches to evaluate the fulfillment of real-world relations. Hence, a thorough evaluation investigating whether explanations from different counterfactual approaches (especially non-causal approaches) fulfill known causal relationships, is still missing.

3   Semantic Meaningfulness

Consider a classifier g that predicts some instances $X = \{x_0, \ldots, x_n\}$ as class $Y = \{y_0, \ldots, y_n\}$. A counterfactual approach h generates, based on the observable input instances X and classifier g, explanations via counter-examples $X^{cf} = \{x_0^{cf}, \ldots, x_n^{cf}\}$ for each $x \in X$. Each counterfactual explanation x^{cf} consists of features $x^{cf} = \{v_1^{cf}, \ldots, v_m^{cf}\}$ and shows why a classifier g predicted class y for a data point x instead of counterfactual class y^{cf}. Depending on the used approach h, the generated counterfactuals may or may not be coherent with real-world relations. To benchmark a counterfactual approach h for its capabilities to depict real-world relations, we introduce the notion of semantic meaningfulness. Semantic meaningfulness is calculated as the fraction of counterfactual changes $\Delta x = x - x^{cf}$ that 1) lead to the same outcome in the real world (*plausibility*) and that 2) fulfill the known causal relationships (*feasibility*).

We assume that one can capture real-world relations in the form of SCMs. We rely on the work of Pearl [30] and define a causal model as a triple (U, V, F) of sets where U is a set of latent background variables, V is a set of observed variables $V = \{v_1, \ldots, v_n\}$, and F is a set of functions $\{f_1, \ldots, f_n\}$ showing the relations between V. We assume observable relations $f_i = f_i(PA_i, U_i)$ with a deterministic function f_i depending on $v_i \subseteq V$ parents in the graph (denoted by PA_i) and a stochastic unexplainable (exogenous) variable $U_i \subseteq U$ for $i = \{1, \ldots, n\}$. To intervene on variable V_i in the SCM, one substitutes the equation $V_i = f_i(PA_i, U_i)$ with some constant $V_i = v$ for some v.

Given a counterfactual approach h, a number of generated explanations $X^{cf} = \{x_1^{cf}, \ldots, x_n^{cf}\}$ and a (fully or partially defined) SCM (U, V, F), we postulate the following metrics:

Theorem 1 (Semantic Meaningful Output).   *The counterfactual explanation approach has Semantic Meaningful Output, if intervening on the SCM (U, V, F) with $X^{cf} = \{x_1^{cf}, \ldots, x_n^{cf}\}$ yields the results $Y^{cf} = \{y_1^{cf}, \ldots, y_n^{cf}\}$ obtained by the classifier g.*

Quantifying Semantic Meaningful Output (SMO) presented in Theorem 1 leads to the fraction of plausible counterfactual explanations, i.e. that lead to the same outcome in the real world (captured in the SCM).

$$SMO \overset{\text{def}}{=} \frac{1}{|X^{cf}|} \sum_{e \in X^{cf}} \mathbb{1}_{g(e)=SCM(e)} \tag{1}$$

Theorem 1 only indicates if the counterfactual approach generates plausible outcomes in the real world. Therefore, we propose a second metric to measure the fulfillment of known causal relationships. Although the output of an approach might be semantically meaningful, the changes Δx made to obtain the counterfactual do not necessarily fulfill real-world relations. Therefore, we also introduce Semantic Meaningful Relations (SMR) in Theorem 2, quantifying the fraction of causal relationships fulfilled.

Theorem 2 (Semantic Meaningful Relations). *A counterfactual explanation approach has Semantic Meaningful Relations, if intervening on the SCM* (U, V, F) *with* $X^{cf} = \{x_1^{cf}, ..., x_n^{cf}\}$ *yields for the features* v^{cf} *of all counterfactual explanations* $v_i \neq v_i^{cf}$ *to fulfill* $f_i(PA_i, U_i)$ *after intervention on the parents of a feature with* $PA_i = v_{PA_i}^{cf}$ *for each counterfactual explanation* $\forall n$.

Quantifying Theorem 2, leads to the fraction of fulfilled causal relations for an explanation x^{cf}.

$$SMR \overset{\text{def}}{=} \frac{1}{|X^{cf}|} \sum_{e \in X^{cf}} (\frac{1}{|e|} \sum_{i \in e} \mathbb{1}_{e_i = f_i(e_{PA_i}, U_i)}) \tag{2}$$

While Eq. (1) can only be calculated with fully defined SCMs, Eq. (2) allows making statements about relationship coherence for partially defined SCMs and thereby estimation of semantic meaningfulness.

3.1 Illustration of Metrics

Building on the personal loan application example in Sect. 1, we give a set of examples to illustrate the proposed semantic meaningfulness metrics, using a simplified version of the German Credit dataset inspired by Karimi et al. [15]. Consider an individual (input instance x) with {Age: 40, Education: Bachelor, Income: 30.000, Savings: 2.000} for which the black-box model g recommends the loan not to be approved {Risk: High}. The objective of counterfactual generation algorithms h is to provide an instance x^{cf} for which the credit is approved according to ML model g (validity). The proposed counterfactual explanation might look similar, e.g., $x^{cf} = \{$ Age: 45, Education: Bachelor, Income: 35.000, Savings: 5.000 $\}$. Assuming this explanation is valid ($y \neq y^{cf}$), it might or might not satisfy semantic meaningful output (plausibility) and relations (feasibility). Figure 1 shows the possible scenarios of (dis)alignment with real-world relations (represented by the SCM).

First, the proposed counterfactual x^{cf} may satisfy both semantic meaningful output and relations (Fig. 1a). For instance, we expect income to increase with age and education to saturate after a certain age. Since the counterfactual instance fulfills these expectations (i.e. age is increased as well as savings and income, but education is unchanged), we consider it feasible. Furthermore, suppose the counterfactual x^{cf} (that flipped the outcome of the classifier), also leads to a change in the outcome in the SCM (i.e. risk changes to low when the explanation is acted upon), then we consider it plausible. Second, the causal relations may be satisfied, but may not lead to the expected change in outcome according to the SCM. Figure 1b visualizes this case; income increases with age and savings with income (both as expected). However, as opposed to before, the proposed counterfactual does not lead to a change in outcome in the SCM.

Consider now another counterfactual explanation, e.g., $x^{cf'} = \{$ Income: 40.000 $\}$. This counterfactual explanation $x^{cf'}$ might not cohere with causal relations, even though it might be valid. Income is the only changing input, which does not align with the expectation that savings will increase due to this change when income has passed a certain minimum threshold. Furthermore, we expect an increase in income to be related to other factors, such as a change in age and/or education. If this is not reflected in the proposed counterfactual (as in Fig. 1c), the semantic meaningful relations are not satisfied. However, it can still happen that the counterfactual explanation $x^{cf'}$ does lead to a change in the outcome in the SCM and therefore has semantic meaningful output due to an erroneous classification by g. Finally, it can be that both semantic meaningful output and relations are violated (Fig. 1d).

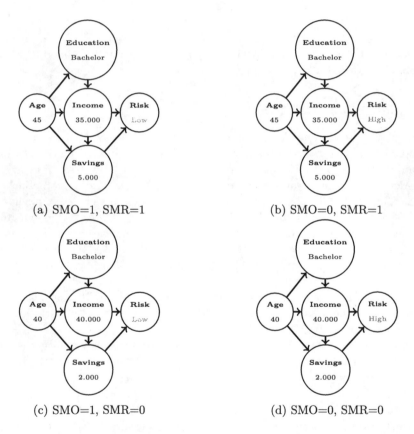

Fig. 1. Example of Semantic Meaningful Output (SMO) and Relation (SMR) metrics based on simplified Credit data. Blue: the values changed in the proposed counterfactual explanation. Green: denotes SMO = 1, which means that the SCM and ML model predict the same outcome. Red: indicates SMO = 0, which means the predictions of the SCM and ML model are different. (Color figure online)

3.2   Relation to Prior Work

In this section, we reflect on other related concepts, notations, and metrics proposed in the literature and clarify the relation to our work.

- **Karimi et al.** [13] propose a probabilistic approach to counterfactual generation based on fully or partially defined SCMs that takes uncertainty into account. In their evaluation, they introduce the notion of validity, which is, in their case, defined as the percentage of individuals for which the recommended action results in a favorable prediction under the true (oracle) SCM. This notion is closely related to our notion of SMO. In contrast to Karimi et al. [13], SMO expects a full counterfactual explanation as input (i.e. intervention on all endogenous variables) instead of a minimal action. Further, they do not consider the fraction of fulfilled relations (like SMR). We argue that checking if parent-child relationships are still fulfilled for generating meaningful counterfactuals is essential. A counterfactual output might be meaningful under a given SCM without fulfilling any given causal relationships.
- **Mahjan et al.** [24] propose the causal-edge score, which is the ratio of the log-likelihood of a counterfactual with respect to the likelihood of the original data given a causal-edge distribution. This is related to our metric SMR, but their proposed constraint feasibility measure only calculates the faction of counterfactuals that satisfy a given user-level constraint and not how well an approach is able to capture semantic meaningful relations.
- **Afrabandpey et al.** [1] propose the notion of global (domain expert constraints) and local feasibility (end-user constraints) closely related to the constraint feasibility proposed by Mahjan et al. [24]. Both notions are highly dependent on human input and can, therefore, not capture semantic meaningful relations fully. However, their assumption that a domain expert can give feedback on the causal relationship between at least some features can be exploited to calculate SMR at least partly.
- **Karimi et al.** [11] formulate plausibility constraints with logic formulas to account for semantics such as immutable features. In contrast to our notion of plausibility (adhering to a realistic counterfactual), their notion of plausibility is restricted to consistency with training data (e.g., same data type and range) and the detainment of immutable features. As argued in Sect. 2, the reliance on training data is often insufficient.
- Finally, the **validity metric** is closely related to the SMO metric proposed in this work. In fact, where validity quantifies whether a counterfactual explanation can flip the classifier's decision, SMO quantifies whether a counterfactual explanation can flip the outcome of the SCM (which we assume represents the user's mental model of the world).

4   Benchmark Datasets

To show the operationalizability of the metrics, we selected six datasets with known SCMs that we can use to measure semantic meaningfulness. The datasets have different complexities; the synthetic datasets contain only 3 variables (with varying relations), whereas the semi-synthetic datasets have a larger number of endogenous variables (8, 7 and 11) with a wider range of values. We use the following datasets for benchmarking (for causal graphs, see Appendix A):

Synthetic Datasets. As a first example, we base ourselves on the synthetic toy dataset consisting of 3 variables used by Karimi et al. [13]. We consider all three variants proposed to test the semantic capabilities of the counterfactual approaches on different types of relationships.

a) Linear SCM

$$
\begin{aligned}
&X_1 := U_1 && U_1 \sim MoG(0.5\mathcal{N}(-2, 1.5) + 0.5\mathcal{N}(1, 1) \\
&X2 := -X_1 + U_2 && U_2 \sim \mathcal{N}(0, 1) \\
&X3 := 0.05X_1 + 0.025X_1 + U_3 && U_3 \sim \mathcal{N}(0, 1) \\
&Y := Bernoulli((1 + e^{-2.5(X_1+X_2+X_3)})^{-1})
\end{aligned}
$$

b) Non-linear SCM

$$
\begin{aligned}
&X_1 := U_1 && U_1 \sim MoG(0.5\mathcal{N}(-2, 1.5) + 0.5\mathcal{N}(1, 1)) \\
&X2 := -1 + \frac{3}{1+e^{-2X_1}} + U_2 && U_2 \sim \mathcal{N}(0, 1) \\
&X3 := 0.05X_1 + 0.025X_1 + U_3 && U_3 \sim \mathcal{N}(0, 1) \\
&Y := Bernoulli((1 + e^{-2.5(X_1+X_2+X_3)})^{-1})
\end{aligned}
$$

c) Non-additive SCM

$$
\begin{aligned}
&X_1 := U_1 && U_1 \sim MoG(0.5\mathcal{N}(-2, 1.5) + 0.5\mathcal{N}(1, 1)) \\
&X2 := 0.25\,\mathrm{sgn}(U_2)X_1^2 + (1 + U_2^2) && U_2 \sim \mathcal{N}(0, 0.25) \\
&X3 := -1 + 0.1\,\mathrm{sgn}(U_3)(X_1^2 + X_2^2) + U_3 && U_3 \sim \mathcal{N}(0, 1) \\
&Y := Bernoulli((1 + e^{-2.5(X_1+X_2+X_3)})^{-1})
\end{aligned}
$$

Nutrition Dataset. For the next example, the aim is to predict survival based on demographic and laboratory measurements from the National Health and Nutrition Examination Survey [5]. We created an SCM for this first semi-synthetic dataset with the help of ShapleyFlow [43] and approximated the distribution with the help of the original dataset.

Age	$X_1 := U_1$	$U_1 \sim \mathcal{N}(25, 1)$
Sex	$X_2 := U_2$	$U_2 \sim \mathcal{N}(0, 1)$
Blood Pressure	$X_3 := 0.02X_1 + U_3$	$U_3 \sim \mathcal{N}(0, 1)$
SBP.	$X_4 := 0.12X_3 + U_4$	$U_4 \sim \mathcal{N}(80, 1)$
Pulse Pressure	$X_5 := 0.02X_4 + U_5$	$U_5 \sim \mathcal{N}(10, 1)$
Inflamation	$X_6 := U_6$	$U_6 \sim \mathcal{N}(0, 1))$
Poverty Index	$X_7 := U_7$	$U_7 \sim \mathcal{N}(0, 1)$
Sedimation RAE	$X_8 := 0.03X_7 + U_8$	$U_8 \sim \mathcal{N}(0, 1)$
Risk	$y := (-0.21X_2 - 0.59X_1 + 0.03X_8 - 0.04X_7 + 0.02X_5 + 0.1X_4) > -6$	

Credit Dataset. The second semi-synthetic dataset is a modification of the German Credit data and also extracted from the work of Karimi et al. [13]. The dataset contains information on personal loan applications, e.g., demographics and financial attributes, with the goal to distinguish people with good (i.e. approve loan) or bad (i.e. decline loan) credit risks.

Gender	$X_1 := U_1$	$U_1 \sim Bernoulli(0.5)$
Age	$X_2 := -35 + U_2$	$U_2 \sim Gamma(10, 3.5)$
Education	$X_3 := -0.5 + (1 + e^{-(-1+0.5X_1+(1+e^{-0.1X_2})+U3)})-1$	$U_4 \sim \mathcal{N}(0, 0.25)$
Loan Amount	$X_4 := 1 + 0.01(X_2 - 5)(5 - X_2) + X_1 + U_4$	$U_4 \sim \mathcal{N}(0, 4)$
Loan Duration	$X_5 := -1 + 0.01X_2 + 2X_1 + X_4$	$U_5 \sim \mathcal{N}(0, 9)$
Income	$X_6 := -4 + 0.1(X_2 + 35) + 2X_1 + X_1X_3 + U_6$	$U_6 \sim \mathcal{N}(0, 4))$
Savings	$X_7 := -4 + 1.5 \cdot 1_{X_6>0}X_6 + U_7$	$U_7 \sim \mathcal{N}(0, 25)$
Output	$Y := Bernoulli((1 + e^{-0.3(-X_4-X_5+X_6+X_7+X_6X_7)-1})$	

Economic Dataset. As last example, we consider a dataset with information on economic growth [44]. Xu et al. [44] modeled the relationship between economic growth and (factors related to) electricity consumption for China using data from the National Bureau of Statistics of China[1]. We adopted the SCM from Xu et al. [44] and approximate the distribution from the data. We further transformed the original regression problem into a classification problem by dividing the outcome (i.e. economic growth) into two classes, by setting a threshold equal to the mean.

Energy Source Struct.	$X_1 := U_1$	$U_1 \sim \mathcal{N}(0, 1)$
Informatization Level	$X_2 := 0.836X_4 + 0.464X_3 + U_2$	$U_2 \sim \mathcal{N}(0, 11)$
Ecological Awareness	$X_3 := 0.889X_4 + U_4$	$U_4 \sim \mathcal{N}(17, 90)$
Electricity Cons.	$X_4 := U_4$	$U_4 \sim \mathcal{N}(0, 100000)$
Electricity Investment	$X_5 := 0.898X_4 + U_5$	$U_5 \sim \mathcal{N}(0, 99999)$
Investment Other	$X_6 := 0.783X_5 + U_6$	$U_6 \sim \mathcal{N}(0, 15))$
Employment	$X_7 := 0.789X_4 + U_7$	$U_7 \sim \mathcal{N}(0, 70)$
Secondary Industry	$X_8 := 0.566X_4 + 0.561X_2 + U_8$	$U_8 \sim \mathcal{N}(0, 2000)$
Teritary Industry	$X_9 := 0.537X_4 + 0.712X_2 + U_9$	$U_9 \sim \mathcal{N}(0, 2000)$
Prop. non-agriculture	$X_{10} := 0.731X_8 + 0.612X_9 + 0.662X_6 + 0.605X_2 + U_{10}$	$U_{10} \sim \mathcal{N}(0, 100)$
Labor Productivity	$X_{11} := 0.918X_4 + U_{11}$	$U_{11} \sim \mathcal{N}(0, 500000)$
Output	$Y := (0.538X_6 + 0.426X_7 + 0.826X_{11} + 0.293X_2 +$ $0.527X_{10} + 0.169X_4 + 0.411X_1) > 500.000$	

5   Empirical Evaluation

With the help of the proposed metrics, we evaluate the capabilities of nine well-established counterfactual explanation approaches for three ML models trained on three synthetic and three semi-synthetic datasets. We used the CARLA Recourse library [28] for the implementation of the counterfactual approaches and classifiers. The implementation of our metrics follows the CARLA implementation structure and can, therefore, easily be used in combination with the CARLA Benchmarking Tool. The code for our experiments can be found on GitHub[2].

---

[1] http://www.stats.gov.cn/english/Statisticaldata/AnnualData/.
[2] https://github.com/JHoelli/Semantic-Meaningfulness.

Figure 2 shows a visualization of our experimental flow. First, we generate data based on the SCM to ensure data compliance. This is important to avoid any noise influencing the generation of counterfactuals. Next, we draw 10.000 samples and divide those samples into a 75/25 train/test split. We train our classifier with the training data as described in Sect. 5.1. Throughout the experiments, the (generated) datasets and trained classifiers remain the same. For each combination of dataset, classifier, and counterfactual approach described in Sect. 5.2, we try to generate 250 counterfactual explanations. We evaluate the semantic meaningfulness of the resulting explanations with our proposed metrics and analyze the results in Sect. 5.3.

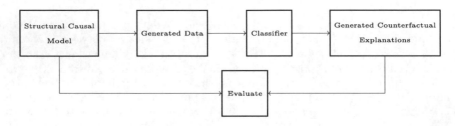

Fig. 2. Flow of data in experiments.

5.1   Machine Learning Models

For each dataset, we train a Linear Model, a Random Forest (RF) with 5 estimators and a max depth of 5, and a Multilayer Perceptron (MLP) with three hidden layers of size 18, 9 and 3. The MLP is trained for ten epochs with a batch size of 16 and a learning rate of 0.001. The performance of the classifiers are measured with the Area under the Curve (AUC) and can be found in Table 1. Note, that the classifiers achieve high or almost perfect (Linear, MLP) discrimination between classes for the three simple, synthetic datasets (i.e. Linear, Non-linear, and Non-additive SCM).

Table 1. Classifier performance as measured by AUC on each dataset.

	Nutrition	Credit	Economic	Linear SCM	Non-linear SCM	Non-additive SCM
Linear	0.88	0.76	0.83	1.0	1.0	1.0
Random Forest	0.85	0.82	0.81	0.81	0.97	0.73
MLP	0.9	0.69	0.82	1.0	1.0	0.99

5.2   Counterfactual Approaches

We compare 9 counterfactual generation approaches that we categorized in causal-based (1x), constraint-based (4x), surrogate-based (2x) and model-specific (2x) approaches, based on the taxonomy presented by Verma et al. [40]. In this section, we give a short description of each method. All methods were applied to the Linear and MLP models except for the model-specific approaches, which were (only) applied to the RF models.

Causal-Based:

– Causal Recourse (CR) [15] aims to find the minimal cost set of actions that results in a counterfactual instance favorable to the classifier g. A^* specifies the actions to be performed for a minimal causal recourse. Thereby, x^{SCF} is not a structural counterfactual obtained by intervening the SCM, but the minimal action needed to obtain x^{SCF}. As this method incorporates causal relations, we use this as a sanity check for our proposed metrics.

Constraint-Based:

– Wachter et al. (W-CF) [42] find a counterfactual explanation with the smallest change (distance/cost) relative to the original datapoint that is classified differently. This method assumes independent features. As hyperparameters, the default parameters proposed by [28] are used.
– Growing Spheres (GS) [20] is a method that generates samples around the original datapoint by growing hyperspheres until the desired class label is found.

Surrogate-Based:

– Counterfactual Latent Uncertainty Explanations (CLUE) [3] uses a generative model (variational autoencoder with arbitrary conditioning) that takes the classifiers uncertainty into account and generates counterfactual explanations that are likely to occur under a data distribution. As hyperparameters, the default parameters proposed by [3] are used.
– Counterfactual Conditional Heterogeneous Autoencoder (CCHVAE) [29] generates faithful counterfactuals by ensuring that the produced counterfactuals are proximate (i.e., not local outliers) and connected to regions with substantial data density (i.e., close to correctly classified observation. The counterfactual search is thereby included into a data density approximator, in this case a Variational Autoencoder (VAE). Counterfactuals are sampled from the latent space of the VAE.
– Counterfactual Recourse Using Distangled Subspaces (CRUDS) [7] creates counterfactuals by using a conditional subspace VAE with the goal to satisfy underlying structure of the data. Default parameter from the CARLA Recourse library are used.

- Actionable Recourse (AR) [38] is based on integer programming and only applicable to linear models (e.g., logistic regression models, linear support vector machines). For non-linear models, coefficients are approximated with LIME [34]. As we do not only apply AR for linear models, but also need to approximate coefficients with LIME for MLP, we categorize AR as a surrogate-based approach.

Model-Specific:

- Flexible Optimizable Counterfactual Explanations for Tree Ensembles (FOCUS) [23] is an approach for finding counterfactuals for non-differentiable models, e.g., tree ensembles. The method uses a probabilistic approximation of the original tree ensemble.
- Feature Tweaking (FT) [37] exploits the internals of a tree-based ensemble classifier by tweaking the feature-based representation of a true negative instance such that the modified instances result in a positive classification when re-inputted to the classifier.

5.3   Results

We present results evaluating nine counterfactual explanation approaches using the proposed SMO and SMR metrics across six datasets. In particular, we investigate the semantic meaningfulness of different counterfactual approaches (Sect. 5.3), the influence of the classifier (performance) on the semantic meaningfulness of the counterfactual approaches (Sect. 5.3), and the relationship between the two semantic meaningfulness metrics (Sect. 5.3).

Existing (Non-causal) Counterfactual Approaches Vary in Semantic Meaningfulness. Figure 3 shows the results evaluating the semantic meaningfulness of different counterfactual approaches. As a sanity check, we first applied a causal-based approach. Due to the large increase in computation time for an increasing number of endogenous variables and relations, only results for the synthetic datasets could be obtained (see Fig. 3a–c). Using CR on these datasets, SMO has a median of 1 and a mean slightly below 1, indicating that our proposed metric aligns with the SCM and works as intended. Erroneous classifications of the ML classifier can explain why the mean is slightly less than 1 for SMO. SMR is equal to 1 for both the Linear and Non-linear SCM, showing causal relations are satisfied. For the Non-additive SCM, on average, only 2 out of 3 possible relationships could be fulfilled. This is because the counterfactuals returned by CR are not supposed to fulfill all constraints of the graph, but rather include a minimal change that would conclude in the desired result by iterating through the graph (i.e., CR returns a minimal action set). Overall, the nearly perfect values for SMO and SMR found for the causal method, indicate that our proposed method works as intended.

We further find that the constraint-based approach W-CF scores very low on SMR, indicating that this method (assuming independence between features) is

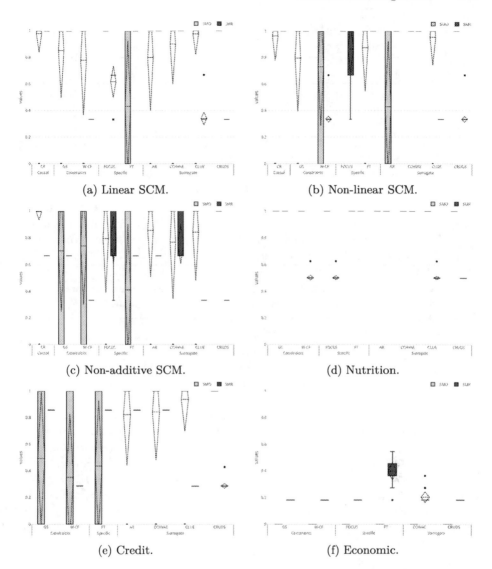

(a) Linear SCM.

(b) Non-linear SCM.

(c) Non-additive SCM.

(d) Nutrition.

(e) Credit.

(f) Economic.

Fig. 3. Semantic Meaningful Output (SMO) and Relation (SMR) metrics averaged over ML models. The bars show the median and the interquartile distance. The dotted lines show the mean and the standard deviation. When only one horizontal line is shown for a given counterfactual approach, it means the mean, standard deviation, and median are the same for SMO and/or SMR.

non-compliant with known causal relations. Combined with the slightly higher SMO, the method generates counterfactuals that are likely to have a realistic output but with a combination of features that is unlikely to be observed in the real world. GS offers a higher SMR compared to W-CF. The better performance compared to W-CF might result from the optimization function that includes a sparsity constraint (a penalization on feature changes) and their optimization heuristic.

Next, we observe that the surrogate-based approaches CCHVAE, CLUE, and CRUDS score relatively high on SMO. However, the performance on SMR varies; whereas CLUE and CRUDS score very low across all datasets, CCHVAE scores reasonably well. This occurs despite all VAE-based approaches being trained with the same parameter settings. A reason for the worse performance of CRUDS and CLUE might be the optimization function based on the decoded latent (similar to the W-CF function with additional restrictions), which can result in counterfactuals changing the outcome but not fulfilling the causal relations. Meanwhile, the nearest neighbor style search in the latent space provided by CCHVAE, leads to possibly further distance counterfactuals by sampling in the latent space for distance to a higher likelihood of obtaining learned constraints. For AR the linear coefficients were approximated by applying LIME [34]. The quality of these linear models can largely differ, leading to higher variability and worse average values for SMO and SMR compared to deep learning based VAEs. Note, that for the Economic dataset CLUE and AR are missing; CLUE was not able to find valid counterfactuals and the integer programming problem size of AR is too large to be calculated with the open source version of CPLEX.

Finally, for the model-specific approaches (FT and FOCUS) we observe a high SMR, but a lower SMO. These approaches could only be applied to Forest Classifiers, but the high SMR shows it could capture the causal relations from the underlying forest well.

From the model-agnostic and non-causal counterfactual approaches, we conclude surrogate-based approaches perform slightly better than constraint-based approaches. This is expected as these approaches consider the data manifold. From the constraint-based approaches, only CCHVAE and CRUDS were applicable to all datasets. CCHVAE performed consistently best on SMR across all datasets, while it still had a similar SMO compared to other approaches (e.g., CRUDS). Surprisingly, model-specific approaches also captured causal relations well and even outperformed CCHVAE on the Non-additive SCM and Economic datasets. The weak performance of all approaches on SMR for the Economic dataset can be explained by the small number of exogenous variables (#2) in combination with a high number of endogenous variables (#9)[3]. Overall, the results show the performance of the counterfactual approaches differs between datasets and diverges for the most complex dataset (Fig. 3f) compared to the simpler datasets (Fig. 3a–e).

---

[3] While 1 of 3 relations are always fulfilled for the synthetic dataset, this is only the case for 2 out of 11 are in the Economic dataset. This leads to a significantly lower minimum performance (and can explain the worse results).

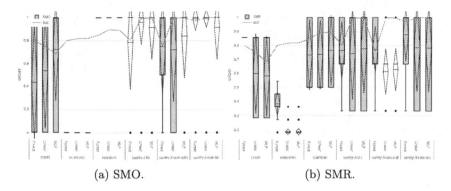

(a) SMO.   (b) SMR.

Fig. 4. Semantic Meaningful Output (SMO) and Relation (SMR) metrics performance averaged over counterfactual approaches. The red line denotes the classifier performance in terms of AUC. (Color figure online)

The Importance of a Good Classifier for Meaningful Counterfactual Explanations. Next, we investigate between-classifier differences. Figure 4 shows the results for different datasets and ML models, averaged over counterfactual approaches. The classifier performance is visualized with the red line.

In Fig. 4a, we see that the performance of SMO is not directly related to the quality of the classifiers. For instance, MLP has the highest SMO on the Credit dataset, even though it achieves the lowest AUC. However, SMO is at least indirectly related to performance via data complexity. The SMO and classifier performance are both highest for the simple synthetic datasets. In Fig. 4b, we observe better classifier performance roughly corresponds to better SMR - except for Non-additive SCM. For this dataset, both the Linear and MLP model show a promising classifier performance, even though the counterfactual approach based SMR results in a worse score than for Random Forest. It can be concluded that Linear and MLP based counterfactual approaches have issues creating semantic meaningful counterfactuals for non-additive relations. The model-specific approaches evade this issue, using the features extracted by the classifier models.

Although the results indicate that the counterfactual explanations generated on classifiers with higher AUC were more coherent with causal relations (independent of the counterfactual generation approach), we conclude good classifier performance is necessary but not sufficient.

Semantic Meaningful Output and Relations Measures Are both Needed. Finally, we evaluate the connection between SMO and SMR. Figure 5 shows the connection between SMO, SMR, and the notion of validity (i.e. a counterfactual that changes the class predicted by the ML model from y to y^{cf}). We found that, out of the total 23,750 counterfactuals we tried to generate, 71% were valid. From those valid counterfactuals, 71% achieved a semantic meaningful output (SMO = 1), and only 42% of those also fulfilled complete semantic meaningful relations (SMR = 1). This means that 58% of the counterfactual explanations had semantic meaningful output, without satisfying semantic meaningful relations (SMR<1). As semantic meaningful output can be caused by an erroneous classification of the desired class by the ML model or achieved with unrealistic feature combinations, evaluating feature combinations for causal relations is important. This underscores the need for the combined use of the two metrics. On the other hand, 7% of the counterfactuals with perfect semantic relationships (SMR = 1) did not satisfy semantic meaningful output, which could be caused by imperfect classifications of the ML classifier.

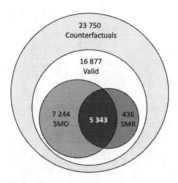

Fig. 5. Venn Diagram visualizing overlap between Semantic Meaningful Output (SMO), Semantic Meaningful Relations (SMR), and Validity metrics for counterfactuals. Note that this plot only includes perfect semantic relationships (SMR = 1).

6   Practical Implications

In this section, we highlight how the proposed metrics and benchmark datasets are useful for different target audiences:

- Developers of counterfactual approaches can use the metrics to quantify the causal capabilities of their methods on the provided set of benchmark datasets, enabling direct comparisons of existing and new approaches in a transparent, replicable, and unified way. The datasets (and SCMs) with varying levels of complexity allow developers to understand limitations and identify directions for improvement.
- Practitioners and users of counterfactual explanations can use the metrics with the benchmark datasets to get insight into the causal capabilities of different approaches. When used in combination with other potentially important metrics (e.g., sparsity [12] and actionability [40]), this can be used to guide the choice between different explanation approaches by examining several metrics (and potential arising trade-offs) for datasets (and SCMs) with varying levels of complexity. For example, for classification model debugging,

explanations via edge cases might be interesting (acceptance of poorer causal capabilities for lower sparsity and proximity) to understand the classifier's inner workings. However, if counterfactual explanations are intended for the use in consequential decision making (i.e., to provide an explanation to individuals affected by models), counterfactual approaches replicating the real world are preferred (acceptance of higher sparsity and proximity for better causal capabilities).

7   Conclusion

In this work, we proposed two metrics in combination with (semi-)synthetic datasets to measure the ability of counterfactual generation approaches to depict real-world relations. This allows for benchmarking new and existing counterfactual approaches based on Semantic Meaningful Output (i.e., the fraction of explanations that lead to the same outcome in the real world) and Relations (i.e., the fraction of fulfilled causal relationships). A priori benchmarking of methods is important as SCMs are often (fully or partially) missing for problems of interest, making it impossible to apply causal-based counterfactual explanation approaches (e.g., [15]) and/or evaluate explanations for a given problem. This work overcomes the - typically existing - lack of ground truth when measuring to what extent causal relations and effects are satisfied for (non-causal) counterfactual generation approaches.

Based on the six (semi-)synthetic datasets evaluated in this work, we conclude that nine well-established counterfactual approaches differ in semantic meaningfulness, with drastically decreasing overall performance for more complex datasets. We found surrogate approaches work well for simple datasets, but could perform better on datasets with a larger number of variables (e.g., Economic dataset). Further, we show that the ML model must sufficiently capture causal relations for the counterfactuals to align with the SCM. Although this might seem straightforward, there is little work considering classifier performance when evaluating counterfactual desiderata (e.g., realisticness or feasibility). Finally, the proposed metrics can only capture the notion of semantic meaningfulness when used in combination; observing semantic meaningful output (i.e., plausible explanations) for a counterfactual generation approach does not necessarily imply semantic meaningful relations (i.e., feasible explanations), and vice versa.

Note that our notion of semantic meaningfulness only evaluates if a counterfactual is causally consistent. Whether a counterfactual is actionable (i.e., a user can change the output of the model by doing an action), is not part of this work. Usually, actionability is considered when generating counterfactual explanations by setting features as mutable or immutable (e.g., [40]). Furthermore, evaluating semantic meaningfulness on any real-world dataset is still an open issue due to the complexity of obtaining a fully specified SCM.

We only evaluated the counterfactual approaches on a small set of models (Linear, Random Forest, Multilayer Perceptron) that were trained on relatively simple (semi-)synthetic datasets. Even though the proposed metrics and benchmarks work independently of the model and the counterfactual approach chosen, not all counterfactual approaches could be applied to all models and datasets. First, we could not apply the causal-based approaches to the three semi-synthetic datasets (due to the large computation power needed), which could have given a better insight into the relative performance of these methods in relation to non-causal approaches. Second, only the model-specific approaches were usable for Random Forest, as the remaining counterfactual approaches (currently) only work for gradient-based models in the CARLA Recourse library.

In future work, it would be interesting to analyze more classifiers (e.g., Convolutional Neural Networks) with varying performance, more complex SCMs (e.g., containing more than 10 endogenous variables and more complex relations), and extend the notion of semantic meaningfulness to different data types (e.g., images [33], time series [21]) to expand the applicability of our approach. Our study showed that capturing causal relations while generating counterfactuals is still an open problem. For one, counterfactual generation approaches based on causal relations lack real-world applicability. Moreover, none of the non-causal approaches were able to create semantic meaningful counterfactuals consistently, resulting in unreliable explanations not necessarily coherent with known causal relationships. Although there might not be a direct relationship between the performance of SMO/SMR on the benchmark datasets and the dataset of interest, the metrics can be used to develop an understanding of the limitations of explanation generating methods, which is crucial for adequate application and interpretation of counterfactual explanation methods. Quantifying semantic capabilities is just the first step to developing counterfactual approaches with better causal capabilities.

Acknowledgements. We would like to thank the organizers of the eXplainable AI Summer School (XAISS) 2022 in Delft and Martin Pawelczyk, who inspired us to do this research.

A   Causal Graphs

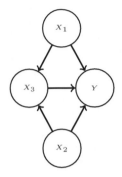

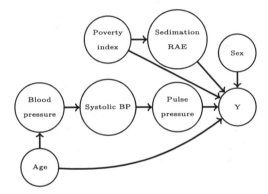

Fig. 6. Synthetic datasets.

Fig. 7. Nutrition dataset.

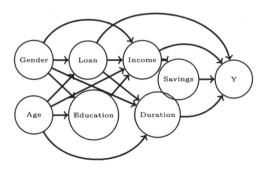

Fig. 8. Credit dataset.

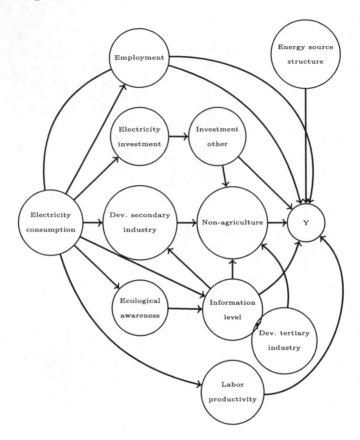

Fig. 9. Economic dataset.

References

1. Afrabandpey, H., Spranger, M.: Feasible and desirable counterfactual generation by preserving human defined constraints. arXiv preprint arXiv:2210.05993 (2022)
2. Agarwal, C., et al.: Openxai: towards a transparent evaluation of model explanations. arXiv preprint arXiv:2206.11104 (2022)
3. Antoran, J., Bhatt, U., Adel, T., Weller, A., Hernández-Lobato, J.M.: Getting a CLUE: a method for explaining uncertainty estimates. In: International Conference on Learning Representations (2021)
4. Byrne, R.M.: Counterfactuals in explainable artificial intelligence (XAI): evidence from human reasoning. In: IJCAI, pp. 6276–6282 (2019)
5. Cox, C., et al.: Plan and operation of the nhanes i epidemiologic followup study, 1992. Vital and health statistics. Ser. 1, Programs and collection procedures, vol. 35, pp. 1–231 (1997)
6. Dhurandhar, A., et al.: Explanations based on the missing: towards contrastive explanations with pertinent negatives. In: Advances in Neural Information Processing Systems, vol. 31 (2018)

7. Downs, M., Chu, J.L., Yacoby, Y., Doshi-Velez, F., Pan, W.: Cruds: counterfactual recourse using disentangled subspaces. In: ICML WHI 2020, pp. 1–23 (2020)
8. Dressel, J., Farid, H.: The accuracy, fairness, and limits of predicting recidivism. Sci. Adv. **4**(1) (2018)
9. European Commission: 2018 reform of EU data protection rules (2018). http://data.europa.eu/eli/reg/2016/679/oj
10. Hedström, A., et al.: Quantus: an explainable AI toolkit for responsible evaluation of neural network explanations and beyond. J. Mach. Learn. Res. **24**(34), 1–11 (2023)
11. Karimi, A.H., Barthe, G., Balle, B., Valera, I.: Model-agnostic counterfactual explanations for consequential decisions. In: International Conference on Artificial Intelligence and Statistics, pp. 895–905. PMLR (2020)
12. Karimi, A.H., Barthe, G., Schölkopf, B., Valera, I.: A survey of algorithmic recourse: contrastive explanations and consequential recommendations. ACM Comput. Surv. **55**(5), 1–29 (2022)
13. Karimi, A.H., von Kügelgen, J., Schölkopf, B., Valera, I.: Algorithmic recourse under imperfect causal knowledge: a probabilistic approach (2020)
14. Karimi, A.H., von Kügelgen, J., Schölkopf, B., Valera, I.: Towards causal algorithmic recourse. In: Holzinger, A., Goebel, R., Fong, R., Moon, T., Müller, K.R., Samek, W. (eds.) xxAI 2020. LNCS, vol. 13200, pp. 139–166. Springer, Cham (2022). https://doi.org/10.1007/978-3-031-04083-2_8
15. Karimi, A.H., Schölkopf, B., Valera, I.: Algorithmic recourse: from counterfactual explanations to interventions. In: Proceedings of the 2021 ACM Conference on Fairness, Accountability, and Transparency, FAccT 2021, pp. 353–362. Association for Computing Machinery, New York (2021). https://doi.org/10.1145/3442188.3445899
16. Keane, M.T., Kenny, E.M., Delaney, E., Smyth, B.: If only we had better counterfactual explanations: five key deficits to rectify in the evaluation of counterfactual XAI techniques. arXiv preprint arXiv:2103.01035 (2021)
17. Kelly, C.J., Karthikesalingam, A., Suleyman, M., Corrado, G., King, D.: Key challenges for delivering clinical impact with artificial intelligence. BMC Med. **17**, 1–9 (2019)
18. Khandani, A.E., Kim, A.J., Lo, A.W.: Consumer credit-risk models via machine-learning algorithms. J. Bank. Financ. **34**(11), 2767–2787 (2010)
19. Laugel, T., Lesot, M.J., Marsala, C., Detyniecki, M.: Issues with post-hoc counterfactual explanations: a discussion. arXiv preprint arXiv:1906.04774 (2019)
20. Laugel, T., Lesot, M.J., Marsala, C., Renard, X., Detyniecki, M.: Inverse classification for comparison-based interpretability in machine learning. arXiv preprint arXiv:1712.08443 (2017)
21. Lawrence, A.R., Kaiser, M., Sampaio, R., Sipos, M.: Data generating process to evaluate causal discovery techniques for time series data. CoRR (2021)
22. Liu, S., Kailkhura, B., Loveland, D., Han, Y.: Generative counterfactual introspection for explainable deep learning. In: 2019 IEEE Global Conference on Signal and Information Processing (GlobalSIP), pp. 1–5 (2019). https://doi.org/10.1109/GlobalSIP45357.2019.8969491
23. Lucic, A., Oosterhuis, H., Haned, H., de Rijke, M.: Focus: flexible optimizable counterfactual explanations for tree ensembles. In: Proceedings of the AAAI Conference on Artificial Intelligence, vol. 36, pp. 5313–5322 (2022)
24. Mahajan, D., Tan, C., Sharma, A.: Preserving causal constraints in counterfactual explanations for machine learning classifiers. arXiv preprint arXiv:1912.03277 (2019)

25. Markus, A.F., Kors, J.A., Rijnbeek, P.R.: The role of explainability in creating trustworthy artificial intelligence for health care: a comprehensive survey of the terminology, design choices, and evaluation strategies. J. Biomed. Inform. **113**, 103655 (2021). https://doi.org/10.1016/j.jbi.2020.103655
26. Miller, T.: Explanation in artificial intelligence: insights from the social sciences. Artif. Intell. **267**, 1–38 (2019)
27. Mothilal, R.K., Sharma, A., Tan, C.: Explaining machine learning classifiers through diverse counterfactual explanations. In: Proceedings of the 2020 Conference on Fairness, Accountability, and Transparency, FAT* 2020, pp. 607–617. Association for Computing Machinery, New York (2020). https://doi.org/10.1145/3351095.3372850
28. Pawelczyk, M., Bielawski, S., Heuvel, J.V.D., Richter, T., Kasneci, G.: Carla: a python library to benchmark algorithmic recourse and counterfactual explanation algorithms. arXiv preprint arXiv:2108.00783 (2021)
29. Pawelczyk, M., Broelemann, K., Kasneci, G.: Learning model-agnostic counterfactual explanations for tabular data. In: Proceedings of The Web Conference 2020, WWW 2020, pp. 3126–3132. Association for Computing Machinery, New York (2020). https://doi.org/10.1145/3366423.3380087
30. Pearl, J., et al.: Models, Reasoning and Inference, vol. 19, no. 2. Cambridge University Press, Cambridge (2000)
31. Peters, J., Janzing, D., Schölkopf, B.: Elements of Causal Inference: Foundations and Learning Algorithms. The MIT Press, Cambridge (2017)
32. Poyiadzi, R., Sokol, K., Santos-Rodriguez, R., De Bie, T., Flach, P.: Face: feasible and actionable counterfactual explanations. In: Proceedings of the AAAI/ACM Conference on AI, Ethics, and Society, AIES 2020, pp. 344–350. Association for Computing Machinery, New York (2020). https://doi.org/10.1145/3375627.3375850
33. Reddy, A.G., Balasubramanian, V.N.: Candle: an image dataset for causal analysis in disentangled representations. In: Proceedings of the AAAI Conference on Artificial Intelligence (2022)
34. Ribeiro, M.T., Singh, S., Guestrin, C.: Model-agnostic interpretability of machine learning. arXiv preprint arXiv:1606.05386 (2016)
35. Sharma, S., Henderson, J., Ghosh, J.: Certifai: a common framework to provide explanations and analyse the fairness and robustness of black-box models. In: Proceedings of the AAAI/ACM Conference on AI, Ethics, and Society, AIES 2020, pp. 166–172. Association for Computing Machinery, New York (2020). https://doi.org/10.1145/3375627.3375812
36. Smyth, B., Keane, M.T.: A few good counterfactuals: generating interpretable, plausible and diverse counterfactual explanations. In: Keane, M.T., Wiratunga, N. (eds.) ICCBR 2022. LNCS, vol. 13405, pp. 18–32. Springer, Cham (2022). https://doi.org/10.1007/978-3-031-14923-8_2
37. Tolomei, G., Silvestri, F., Haines, A., Lalmas, M.: Interpretable predictions of tree-based ensembles via actionable feature tweaking. In: Proceedings of the 23rd ACM SIGKDD International Conference on Knowledge Discovery and Data Mining, KDD 2017, pp. 465–474. Association for Computing Machinery, New York (2017). https://doi.org/10.1145/3097983.3098039
38. Ustun, B., Spangher, A., Liu, Y.: Actionable recourse in linear classification. In: Proceedings of the Conference on Fairness, Accountability, and Transparency, FAT* 2019, pp. 10–19. Association for Computing Machinery, New York (2019). https://doi.org/10.1145/3287560.3287566

39. Van Looveren, A., Klaise, J.: Interpretable counterfactual explanations guided by prototypes. In: Oliver, N., Pérez-Cruz, F., Kramer, S., Read, J., Lozano, J.A. (eds.) ECML PKDD 2021. LNCS (LNAI), vol. 12976, pp. 650–665. Springer, Cham (2021). https://doi.org/10.1007/978-3-030-86520-7_40

40. Verma, S., Dickerson, J., Hines, K.: Counterfactual explanations for machine learning: a review. arXiv preprint arXiv:2010.10596 (2022)

41. Voigt, P., Von dem Bussche, A.: The EU General Data Protection Regulation (GDPR). A Practical Guide, 1st edn. Springer, Cham (2017). https://doi.org/10.1007/978-3-319-57959-7

42. Wachter, S., Mittelstadt, B., Russell, C.: Counterfactual explanations without opening the black box: automated decisions and the GDPR. Harv. J. Law Technol. **31**, 841 (2018)

43. Wang, J., Wiens, J., Lundberg, S.: Shapley flow: a graph-based approach to interpreting model predictions. In: Banerjee, A., Fukumizu, K. (eds.) Proceedings of the 24th International Conference on Artificial Intelligence and Statistics. Proceedings of Machine Learning Research, vol. 130, pp. 721–729. PMLR (2021). https://proceedings.mlr.press/v130/wang21b.html

44. Xu, G., Yang, H., Schwarz, P.: A strengthened relationship between electricity and economic growth in china: an empirical study with a structural equation model. Energy **241**, 122905 (2022). https://doi.org/10.1016/j.energy.2021.122905

45. Zhao, W., Oyama, S., Kurihara, M.: Generating natural counterfactual visual explanations. In: Bessiere, C. (ed.) Proceedings of the Twenty-Ninth International Joint Conference on Artificial Intelligence, IJCAI 2020, pp. 5204–5205. International Joint Conferences on Artificial Intelligence Organization (2020). https://doi.org/10.24963/ijcai.2020/742. Doctoral Consortium

Correction to: Explainable Artificial Intelligence

Luca Longo (iD)

Correction to:
Chapters 28 and 31 in: L. Longo (Ed.): *Explainable Artificial Intelligence*, CCIS 1902, https://doi.org/10.1007/978-3-031-44067-0

The chapters Finding Spurious Correlations with Function-Semantic Contrast Analysis, written by Kirill Bykov, Laura Kopf, Marina M.-C. Höhne, and [ExplainingSocio-Demographic and Behavioral Patterns of Vaccination Againstthe Swine Flu (H1N1) Pandemic|https://link.springer.com/chapter/10.1007/978-3-031-44067-0_31], written by Clara Punzi, Aleksandra Maslennikova, Gizem Gezici, Roberto Pellungrini, Fosca Giannotti, were originally published electronically on the publisher's internet portal without open access. With the authors' decision to opt for Open Choice the copyright of the chapter changed on November 9th, 2023 (K. Bykov et al.) and on October 31st, 2023 (C. Punzi et al.) to © The Author(s) 2023, and the chapter is forthwith distributed under a Creative Commons Attribution 4.0 International License.

The updated version of these chapters can be found at
https://doi.org/10.1007/978-3-031-44067-0_28
https://doi.org/10.1007/978-3-031-44067-0_31

© The Author(s) 2024
L. Longo (Ed.): xAI 2023, CCIS 1902, p. C1, 2024.
https://doi.org/10.1007/978-3-031-44067-0_33

Author Index

L. Longo (Ed.): xAI 2023, CCIS 1902, pp. 661–664, 2023.
https://doi.org/10.1007/978-3-031-44067-0

Printed in the United States
by Baker & Taylor Publisher Services